BERLITZ®

·B·L·U·E·P·R·I·N·T·

EUROPE A-Z

Editorial coordination: Anna-Lena Bergkvist
Layout: Doris Haldemann
We would like to thank the Berlitz team of local correspondents in each of the different countries. We wish also to extend our thanks in particular to Ken Bernstein, Don Allan and Alice Taucher.
City and area maps: Falk-Verlag, Hamburg
Europe Road Atlas: Hallwag AG, Bern.

Contents

Maps

Illustrations—captions and credits

Cover pictures: Greece (J. Bétant), Venice (D. Michellod), Hungary (C. Huber); **pp. 2–3:** Rhine cruise, Boppard, Germany (M. Jacot); **p. 8:** Chairlift, Tyrol, Austria (J. Donatsch); **p. 16:** Château de Chambord, France (C. Huber); **pp. 18–19:** Cycling, Denmark (E. Mandelmann); **p. 21:** Poseidon's temple, Soúnion, Greece (D. Vittet); **p. 24:** Count Kerry, Ireland (E. Jaquier); **p. 25:** Fontainebleau, France (M. Jacot); **p. 28:** Portofino, Italy (J.-C. Vieillefond); **p. 29:** Alpenhorn player, Switzerland (D. Vittet); **pp. 34–35:** TGV, France (G. Bosshard); **p. 40:** *Gabrielle d'Estrées et sa Sœur,* anonymous, 16th century, Louvre, Paris, France (E. Mandelmann); **p. 52:** Viennese musician (J.-C. Vieillefond); **p. 53:** Zillertal, Austria (J. Donatsch); **pp. 78–79:** Ghent, Belgium (C. Huber), **p. 111:** Charles Bridge, Prague, Czechoslovakia (Čedok/K. Vlček); **p. 117:** Slapy Lake, Czechoslovakia (Čedok/B. Landisch); **p. 127:** Dragør, Denmark (Danish Tourist Board/P. Eider); Countryside near Copenhagen (E. Mandelmann). **p. 132:** Copenhagen, Denmark (E. Mandelmann); **p. 148:** Kuopio, Finland (P. Solbjerghøj); **p. 153:** Aalto's Finlandia Hall, Helsinki, Finland (P. Solbjerghøj); **pp. 164–5:** Brittany, France (C. Huber, M. Jacot); **p. 173:** French Riviera (M. Jacot); **p. 178:**

Saint-Tropez, France (M. Jacot); **p. 185:** Louvre Pyramide, Paris (C. Huber); **p. 187:** Palais des Papes, Avignon, France (M. Jacot); **p. 193:** Casino, Monaco (M. Jacot); **p. 209:** Bernkastel-Kues, Germany (M. Jacot); **p. 212:** Pretzels galore, Munich, Germany (E. Jaquier); **p. 215:** Schloss Charlottenburg, Berlin, Germany (C. Huber); **p. 224:** Bavaria, Germany (E. Jaquier); **p. 235:** Siesta time, Athens, Greece (D. Vittet); **p. 240:** Death mask/Minoan fresco, National Archaeological Museum, Athens, Greece (D. Vittet); **pp. 242–3:** Santoríni, Greece (D. Vittet); **p. 257:** View from Royal Palace, Budapest, Hungary (E. Jaquier); **p. 261:** Eszterházy Palace, Fertőd, Hungary (E. Jaquier); **p. 284:** Sheep farmer, Ireland (E. Jaquier); **p. 299:** Sicily, Italy (Kurt Ammann); **p. 307:** Adriatic, Italy (C. Huber); **p. 309:** Giotto's *Kiss of Judas,* Scrovegni Chapel, Padua, Italy (C. Huber); **p. 315:** Cathedral, Florence, Italy (J. Mohr); **p. 324:** Vittoriosa, Malta (K. Welsh); **p. 329:** Carnival, Malta (National Tourist Organization, Malta); **p. 343:** Amsterdam canalfront, Netherlands (S. Langereis); **p. 350:** Reclaimed polder land in East Flevoland, Netherlands (KLM); **pp. 366–7:** Lyse Fjord near Stavanger, Norway (W. Imber); **p. 379:** Royal Castle, Warsaw, Poland (Len Sirman Press/C. Bowman); **p. 389:** Algarve, Portugal (J. Donatsch); **p. 398:** Donkeys and windmill, Portugal (D. Gignoux); **p. 403:** Fish and fowl (D. Gignoux); **p. 429:** Frigiliana, Costa del Sol, Spain (K. Welsh); **p. 433:** Bullfighter, Spain (K. Welsh); **p. 440:** Costa Blanca, Spain (D. Henderson); **p. 443:** Benidorm, Spain (D. Henderson); **pp. 460–1:** Around Stockholm, Sweden (J.-C. Vieillefond); **p. 481:** Stein am Rhein, Switzerland (D. Vittet); **p. 488:** Valais region, Switzerland (C. Huber); **pp. 492–3:** Swiss landscapes (C. Huber); **p. 495:** Folk art, Switzerland (D. Vittet); **pp. 508–9:** Cotswold village, U.K. (E. Mandelmann); **p. 519:** Tongue, Scotland (R. Giles); **p. 525:** Sudeley Castle, U.K. (E. Mandelmann); **p. 529:** Hunting, U.K. (E. Mandelmann); **p. 539:** Kremlin, Moscow, U.S.S.R. (Novosti); **p. 548:** Cathedral, Zagorsk, U.S.S.R. (Magnum/R. Rowan); **p. 559:** Lake Bled, Yugoslavia (H.R. Uthoff); **p. 562:** Orthodox church, Macedonia, Yugoslavia (C. Huber).

Although we make every effort to ensure the accuracy of all the information in this book, changes occur incessantly, particularly since Eastern Europe opened up. We cannot therefore take responsibility for facts, addresses and circumstances in general that are constantly subject to alteration.

This guide also exists in pocket format as Berlitz Pocket Guide Europe.

Europe—an overview

Europe is booming, Europe is blooming. As its frontier barriers fall to form a vital economic union, Europe is humming with the excitement of momentous change. Part of the new open-house spirit is a rush in each country to look its best for the neighbors and show off its special attractions. The rejuvenated "Old World" has never been more alluring or easier to visit.

A trip through Europe was once an essential part of a classical education for the wealthy. The "Grand Tour" often took half a year, cost no object. Today, exposure to the European heritage is just as "broadening", but now it's affordable and more fun. Wherever you go you'll share the pleasure with visitors from all over the world, especially Europeans themselves rediscovering their richly varied continent.

We are all a bit European. Europe is the fountainhead of many ideas and attitudes that are common denominators of global civilization. Whether implanted by colonization, trade, instant communications or supersonic travel, the seeds have been spread and borne fruit literally everywhere. That's why coming to Europe is returning to the source.

Europe is where so much of what we take for granted began; parliaments and penicillin, Gothic church architecture and golf, the automobile and ice cream. Nevertheless, for all its underlying familiarity, it's no place like home. There's only one Venice. The Parthenon has many imitators, but no equals. For that matter, so has the Parisian *croissant*. One bite proves it's everything you hoped it would be. And so is the little sidewalk café that serves it under a striped awning overlooking the Seine, with Notre Dame rising out of a fringe of trees in the background.

You'll experience this same thrill of recognition beside the Colosseum in Rome, or steaming between the mountain walls of a Norwegian fjord, or throwing darts in an English pub. These are the originals. The turreted castles of Bavaria surpass the images you remember from your first book of fairy tales. Hearing a favorite Mozart mass sung in a Salzburg church reveals heavenly new dimensions. Whether it's your first trip or your fifth, you'll wake up each day eager for the show to begin again.

Geographically, Europe stretches from the Atlantic Ocean to the Ural Mountains and from the Mediterranean to the Arctic Circle. Ethnically, Europeans and their languages all came at different periods of a distant past from an area of Central Asia between India and the Caucasus. Historically, when the descendants of these tribes weren't fighting each other they were out conquering and colonizing the rest of

the world. But they found time to produce Plato and Pasteur, Einstein and Newton, Beethoven and the Beatles, and they have influenced the world far out of proportion to their continent's size—7 percent of the planet's land and 15 percent of its population.

In 1990 the winds of freedom blew down the Berlin Wall and much else with it. The Iron Curtain between East and West crumbled into dust. The two Germanys reunited. Prague, Budapest and Warsaw flung open their doors to Western tourists and businessmen. The 12 countries of the European Economic Community, from Portugal to Greece, adopted a common passport and headed for a single currency. Even Britain's insularity seemed doomed by the "chunnel" soon to link England and France under the English Channel. European commissions dealing with everything from farm prices to the environment marked a uniting Europe's emergence as a superpower, more than the sum of its parts, but with each part distinctly itself.

Far from becoming homogenized, each country celebrates its delightful individuality. Borders may blur, but even neighbors like Germany and France will always remain as different as beer and wine. In fact, the drive toward political and economic unification in Europe has been counterbalanced by a strong revival of regional traditions. The Scots buckle on their kilts and toss the caber at Scottish games, Basques run before the bulls in the streets of Pamplona, Catalan, Welsh, and Breton are among the regional languages making a comeback. Simply driving a few miles in Europe can transport you to a totally different culture.

Just a few weeks' European holiday can encompass the dreams of a lifetime. How about a smörgåsbord in Stockholm, Shakespeare at Stratford, shopping in Paris, a cruise down the castled Rhine, hiking through wildflowers in the Alps, immersion in the Renaissance art of Florence and total relaxation on a Greek island beach? Yet it's often the smallest things that linger longest in the memory: wandering troubadours, school children in uniform, a flower-decked village street, a fleamarket haggle… or eating the native cheese on the spot where it's made. Just think of all the sights you've always dreamed of seeing and let a travel agent do the rest.

Nowadays it is easy to take in destinations that once were behind the Iron Curtain—medieval Prague and Cracow, the great museums of Dresden and Leipzig, Budapest on the Danube, midsummer White Nights in Leningrad.

Tourism is one of Europe's oldest and best-organized industries. Innkeepers really want your business; service is a profession taught at university-level hotel schools. English has become the lingua franca for travelers from Lisbon to Helsinki (and is sometimes easier to understand on the Continent than in Cockney London). All sorts of special deals are available on European railroads. And distances are not great. Dublin and Vienna may be worlds apart in atmosphere, but closer by air than New York and New Orleans. No, you won't need special shots, or, in most cases, visas.

You can choose organized excursions or "do" Europe at your own pace. No elaborate preparations are necessary to join the pageant of Western culture. Just climb the hill from your Athens taverna to the theater where Sophocles and Aristophanes broke into show business. Or stroll into the Barcelona courtyard where Ferdinand and Isabella welcomed Columbus back from the new world.

The ever new *old* world is ready to welcome you!

Europe in a nutshell

The typical first-timer's trip to Europe sticks to the easy-to-reach, truly essential sights: London for pageantry and the least troubling language problem; Paris for its culture, elegance and romance; with a sidetrip to a nearby "Olde Worlde" city like Brussels or Amsterdam. The virtue of this itinerary is a maximum of contrasts with a minimum of mileage.

The same could be done by concentrating on another region, for instance Germany, Austria, Switzerland and Italy, offering mountains and the sea, northern efficiency and Latin *dolce farniente,* and several thousand years of history. You could also visit Scandinavia in a limited time; in spite of its relatively unified culture, history and heritage, the region is rich in diversity: mountains and flatlands, kingdoms and a republic, seafarers and artisans.

The myriad permutations depend on factors as unconnected as the season, the availability of flights or package tours, and your own budget and special interests. You can combine skiing with historical monuments, folklore and hearty cooking in half a dozen east and west European countries. Archaeology and a suntan go together naturally on many a Mediterranean island. Lovers of escapist countryside, sea air and quaint old villages might choose Ireland or Norway, but enthusiasts of nightlife and gourmet excesses should look elsewhere.

Some visitors all but disregard the celebrated attractions to devote themselves to individual interests or obsessions. If searching for your European roots, the village of your ancestors will be more fascinating than any capital city. If mountain climbing is your mania, you're likely to bypass the historic charms of Lucerne and hasten to the Matterhorn. Or you may resist the mainstream tourist temptations in order to track

13

down a favorite artist, writer or composer—Norway for Munch, Denmark for Hans Christian Andersen, Poland for Chopin.

Because of Europe's compactness, and sheer volume of its sights and activities, it's easy to combine narrow and broad interests. France's famed beaches are only a few hours' drive from some of its finest modern art museums, for instance, and the best shopping may be around the corner from a cathedral bulging with masterpieces. London is less than an hour's flight from Paris.

With thorough advance planning, providing you don't try to cover the whole continent in one frantic flurry, you'll be able to encompass a generous helping of Europe's greatness.

To start you thinking, here is a terse, necessarily oversimplified survey of the strong points of the countries of Europe. Except for the mini-states, the attractions are divided between the capital or dominant city and the hinterland.

Andorra. Shopping, beautiful mountain scenery.

Austria. *Vienna:* imperial elegance, music, art, nostalgia.
Provinces: castles, appealing towns and villages, skiing and hiking.

Belgium. *Brussels:* international atmosphere, history, food.
Provinces: medieval towns, folklore, art.

Bulgaria. *Sofia:* spacious modern city on ancient site. *Provinces:* Black Sea resorts, historic monasteries.

Czechoslovakia: *Prague:* Baroque palaces, all-round charm. *Provinces:* romantic castles, spas, caves.

Denmark. *Copenhagen:* urban charm, relaxed regal rituals, parks, beers. *Provinces:* ancient monuments, tidy scenery, folklore.

Finland. *Helsinki:* neo-Classical and modern architecture, harbor life, shopping. *Provinces:* forests, lakes, Russian influences, saunas.

France. *Paris:* boulevards, parks, history, art, fashion, shopping. *Provinces:* cathedrals, châteaus, cuisine, wines, winter and summer resorts.

Germany. *Berlin and principal cities:* sophisticated city life, fine art galleries, beers and wines, high-quality shopping, classical and avant-garde culture. *Provinces:* historic walled towns, half-timbered houses, fairy-tale castles, impressive monasteries, spas, scenic river cruises.

Greece. *Athens:* classical cultural monuments, outdoor living.
Provinces: beaches, archaeological sites, typical villages.

Hungary. *Budapest:* Danube romance, joie de vivre. *Provinces:* Turkish relics, vineyards, puszta cowboys.

Iceland. *Reykjavik:* museums, harbor. *Provinces:* volcanic scenery, glaciers, geysers.

Ireland. *Dublin:* Georgian architecture, literary associations, pubs. *Provinces:* poignant scenery, prehistoric relics, amiable villages, fishing.

Italy. *Rome:* historical and artistic monuments, Vatican, relaxed lifestyle, chic shopping. *Provinces:* precious cities, bewitching villages, food, wine, sea sports.

Liechtenstein. Mountain scenery, medieval castles, postage stamps.

Luxembourg. Forests, hilltop setting of capital, medieval villages.

Malta. Ancient monuments, medieval fortifications, unique culture, beaches.

Monaco. Sea views, princely glamor, gambling.

Netherlands. *Amsterdam:* canals, architecture, museums, naughty night-life. *Provinces:* windmills, tulips, art museums, handicrafts.

Norway. *Oslo:* Viking ships, harbor life, medieval fort. *Provinces:* fjords, fishing villages, arctic landscape, folk art.

Poland. *Warsaw:* rebuilt medieval atmosphere, parks. *Provinces:* historic churches, castles, unspoiled mountains.

Portugal. *Lisbon:* Moorish ramparts, Golden Age monuments, elegant avenues. *Provinces:* historic churches, endless beaches, handicrafts, wines.

Romania. *Bucharest:* vast modern urban plan, parks. *Provinces:* folklore, quaint towns, monasteries, beaches.

Spain. *Madrid:* Prado Museum, Royal Palace, bullfights, cafés. *Provinces:* castles, windmills, walled cities, beaches, folklore, wines.

Sweden. *Stockholm:* medieval and futuristic city planning, waterfront, tasteful shopping. *Provinces:* fishing ports, forests, lakes, smörgåsbord.

Switzerland. *Zurich:* medieval churches, lakeside life, stylish shopping. *Provinces:* Alpine spectacle, skiing, sophisticated resorts, winsome villages.

15

United Kingdom. *London:* royal buildings and ceremonial, historic churches, museums, theater, shopping. *Provinces:* cathedrals, castles, venerable universities, lakes and lochs, stately homes.

U.S.S.R. *Moscow:* imperial palaces, cathedrals, boulevards. *Provinces:* onion-domed churches, elegant palaces.

Yugoslavia. *Belgrade:* ancient fortress-park, big-city bustle. *Provinces:* Venetian relics in Adriatic ports, islands, resorts, mountain scenery.

When to go

The extreme contrasts in Europe's climate are reflected in its scenery, from Arctic tundra to Mediterranean palm trees. The continent can be divided into four climatic regions. Maritime climate affects the Atlantic coastal zones, including important areas of the U.K., France and Norway, whereas eastern France and central areas of Europe come under the combined influences of maritime and continental weather. Continental climate—the coldest, snowiest winters—covers Finland and northern Sweden, and Mediterranean climate, the subtropical combination of hot summers and mild but wet winters, extends all along Europe's southern tier.

When thinking when to go, take into account whether you're heading north or south, but remember in winter, even in the south, you cannot be absolutely guaranteed of warm weather, and you should always come prepared for a spell of something less than a heat wave.

Month by month

January and February: Mild in the Algarve, Costa del Sol and the Greek islands; skiing in the Alps.

March: Early springtime on Mediterranean isles; Alpine ski season until early April (prices, crowds and snow diminish after Easter).

April: Paris in the springtime; cloudless mild days in Madrid; Venice, after hibernation, revives.

May: Best of all worlds in northern Europe—long, sunny days in Scotland, Ireland, Scandinavia.

June: Midnight sun's joy in northern Russia and Scandinavia; flawless weather in the Aegean islands.

July: Tourist throngs arrive, prices climb. But climate remains fine almost everywhere except sweltering Athens and Madrid.

August: Parisians abandon Paris to the foreigners; suntan weather nearly everywhere, though beaches are packed.

September: Crowds thin out while weather almost everywhere remains idyllic.

October: Indian summer's delights linger in southern Europe.

November and December: Shirtsleeves persist on Costa del Sol, Crete and Sicily, ski season in the Alps begins in late November.

How to get there

By far the most convenient, rapid and economical way of getting to Europe is by air. However, if you don't want to pay hundreds of dollars' more for your ticket than the passenger across the aisle, allow plenty of time and patience for planning your trip. Read the newspaper ads, telephone the airline companies and national tourist offices, and scout around for a knowledgeable, dependable travel agent. To cope with fickle fares, you have to stay a step ahead.

The "normal" economy fare, allowing free stops along the way and valid on all airlines, is considerably higher than an excursion fare on the same scheduled flight. The airlines offer these bargain rates to travelers willing to forego flexibility, plan ahead and pay in advance. Under the plan called APEX (Advance Purchase Excursion), a round-trip ticket must be bought and paid for early, typically 30 days before the flight. The reservations out and back, cheaper on certain days of the week, are

unalterable. If you want to curtail or extend your vacation you'll have to pay the difference between APEX and a full-fare economy ticket. Excursion fares cost even less in "off-seasons" (generally anytime outside the summer and holiday rushes).

Standby fare, available on certain runs, is a cheap, last-minute, one-way ticket sold on a first-come, first-served basis when seats are available. For spontaneous travelers who can survive possible delays or disappointments, this is a gratifying way to save money while flying the big airlines.

Charter flights offer economy but a rigid timetable. Some airlines devote themselves exclusively to charter business, but many seats on scheduled flights of the major companies are also sold on a charter basis, through agents specializing in group excursions and package tours. The package might include air and land transportation, hotels and meals. As with other bargain tickets, these deals must normally be paid for at least 30 days in advance and there is a penalty for cancellation.

If you are really terrified of flying, you could always get to Europe by sea. The only major passenger ship still plying the North Atlantic on a regular basis is the Cunard flagship, the *Queen Elizabeth 2*. Since the liner is often assigned cruises in the Caribbean or round-the-world voyages, Atlantic crossings are not the weekly events of yore. However, the schedules are published far in advance. Other luxurious liners occasionally cruise from North America to Europe or back, at the beginning or end of a season, changing over from, for instance, the winter Caribbean market to the summer Scandinavian cruises. There are occasional sailings from Australia and New Zealand to Europe, and a more frequent line service from South Africa.

Planning your trip

Every country with a tourist industry maintains tourist offices abroad in capital or major cities dedicated to spreading the word. The national tourist office (it can go under a variety of names) is often a rich source of facts and ideas. If you're near enough to drop in for a visit you should browse among the maps and brochures and ask questions. Write or phone for information—they often have clear, instructive booklets. But it's important to specify your interests as far as possible; don't just ask for all there is about a country. And they don't act as travel agents.

These you will also find eager to help you. For all the computers they now mobilize, travel agents are still only human. Their idea of a perfect vacation may not coincide with yours; the hotel they recommend may have changed owners; or the weather may be nobody's fault. Still, having a travel agent you can rely on is a great comfort. And it's virtually always free!

Assuming you have found the perfect travel agent—all-knowing, cooperative and patient—do your part by starting to plan early. Read up on the places you want to go to. Tell the agent how much time you have and when, how much money you are willing to spend, and what you are hoping for. Confide the little personal pluses and minuses that can make a big difference in planning: your interest in folklore or stamp collecting, an aversion to oily food or noisy hotels.

Since travel agencies support themselves from the commissions paid by airlines, hotels, excursion companies and the like, there is an understandable enthusiasm for five-star hotels and first-class tickets. But once you have made clear your requirements, a good travel agent will take pride in finding the latest cut-price deal, if that's more your style. He can be a big help in choosing a hotel and making the

20

reservations for you. (You'll be billed for any international telex or telephone charges incurred.) Be sure to take with you the confirmed reservation documents in case of confusion on arrival; during big conventions or peak tourist seasons, some hotels have been known to overbook.

The variety of accommodations in Europe is part of the adventure. If you're accustomed to luxury you won't have to compromise, and the service may reach new heights. Middle-range hotels in Europe include some old institutions full of atmosphere as well as utilitarian modern establishments. The economy end of the scale offers a chance to come closer to the real life of the country in family-run small hotels and home-style boardinghouses, where you may have to walk down the hall to find the toilet and bath. Most European governments classify hotels from five-star luxury down to one-star simplicity, which helps to disclose what you're getting into. But the ratings are based on the facilities available, not the service or charm.

Note that the hotel industry tends to penalize the single traveler, charging a surcharge for one person occupying a double room; and single rooms are sometimes less easy to come by. If you're vacationing alone you may receive a warmer welcome in a small hotel or *pension* and save a lot in the bargain.

You may choose to sleep in a castle. This is a thoroughly feasible idea, especially in the U.K., France, Germany, Portugal and Spain. The settings, clearly, are glorious and in most cases, modern conveniences have been installed.

Providing you're staying in one spot for several weeks, consider renting a furnished villa or apartment...if you don't mind a bit of cooking while on vacation.

Once you reach Europe, you will be impressed by the profusion of tourist information offices operated by the individual countries and cities. They are often found at the airport, at train stations, and in general in central city locations, pointed out by signs (often the international "i" sign). At a minimum, a tourist office usually offers maps, what-to-see leaflets, and lists of hotels and restaurants. If you're taking your chances and traveling without reservations, this office may help you find a hotel room—even if it usually doesn't recommend a particular restaurant. However, it's only prudent to arrive fairly early in the day. Many tourist offices also have foreign exchange desks and sell sightseeing tours and theater tickets. Even if you arrive with your plans decided down to the last excursion, it's worthwhile visiting the tourist office in case some new attraction has opened or, as seems to occur with depressing frequency, the museums have changed their hours.

Preparation for the trip

In this section we cover some practical general points that will help your trip go smoothly. More detailed information is given in the chapters concerning individual countries.

Camping
The highly developed network of campsites in Europe includes quite luxurious installations with swimming pools, restaurants and shops. But at the height of the tourist season you'll have to plan ahead; the sites at famous beauty spots tend to be chronically full. Most countries publish lists of their principal campsites with details of amenities, capacity and tariffs. You can obtain these directories from the national tourist offices before leaving home or on arrival. You'll need an International Camping Carnet, issued by your national camping association, or from one of the European camping federations when you're on the spot. Note that off-site camping is forbidden in several countries, and not advisable in some others.

Children
Your amiable and (perhaps) docile children can take only small doses of boredom, inconvenience and strain. To ease the rigors of travel for them, plan and pack well. Keep handy a supply of games, books, toys and diversions, as well as airsick remedies and equipment for cuts, bruises, insect bites or whatever else may strike.

There's no accounting for juvenile taste, so the great works of art and culture may well take second place to boat rides, zoos or beaches. Keep the outings short and varied, and remember that merely seeing how other children live is a sound educational experience.

Crime
Pickpockets and snatch-and-grab artists work the tourist beat in many countries, and muggings are becoming quite frequent. Take reasonable precautions wherever you travel: carry no more cash than you need, keep valuables in the hotel's safety deposit box, don't leave your property visible in a car, keep a close eye on your luggage at airports and stations, change money in banks.

Duty-free shopping
Airports and airlines encourage travelers to carry Scotch to Scotland and perfumes to Paris because duty-free shopping brings them important profits. From airport to airport the range of prices is remarkably

wide, but as a general rule it's notably cheaper to buy such things as alcohol, tobacco and luxury imports at the airport or on the aircraft than in town. Although prices on the plane may be slightly below the tariffs on the ground, the variety of goods on sale in flight obviously is restricted.

Emergencies
Telephone numbers for use in emergencies are listed under "Emergencies" in the country-by-country chapters of this book. You will be able to find the addresses and telephone numbers of consulates in the telephone directory. Consulates are often overburdened, so don't be upset if the staff doesn't rush to battle stations for your missing traveler's checks or dispute with a shop owner. But the consulate can recommend English-speaking doctors and lawyers if needed and, in a real emergency, offer assistance—and sympathy.

Handicapped
Knowledgeable travel agents keep track of tours designed for the needs of the handicapped. What distinguishes them from other package tours is the attention paid to avoiding obstacles that could magnify the

difficulties of the disabled. In the hotels chosen, wheelchairs have free run, and there are no special hazards for the sightless. The travel arrangements aim at easing the pressure, with time to relax between flights and sights.

Handicapped passengers traveling on their own always receive sympathetic attention from the airlines. But it's important to advise them in advance what facilities may be required—wheelchair at the airport, special loading onto the plane, or any other individual service.

Health hints

Only hypochondriacs will set out for Europe with foreboding and bulging kits of pills. Even in the most benign of settings, though, the occasional illness can strike—a cold, a headache or a stomach upset. So it doesn't hurt to take along some familiar remedies. If you do buy medicines abroad, read the directions carefully; the strength of nonprescription drugs may differ from what you're accustomed to—even for aspirins.

Although no vaccinations are required for European countries in normal circumstances, unless you're arriving via an infected area, ask your doctor whether he recommends any shots.

Check your medical insurance. Even Britons, entitled to free medical care in European Community countries under reciprocal agreements, are advised to take out medical insurance for a completely worry-free trip to the Continent.

Hours
Banking and post-office hours, listed under each country in this book, attract the interest of the average tourist only when they become a problem: is there time to cash a traveler's check or send a telegram? In general, business hours are businesslike in Europe, except in some southern countries which honor the tradition of the siesta; there, the lunch break can last two or more hours, extending the working and shopping day into the evening. Mealtimes are straightforward except in Spain, Italy and Greece, where dinner may start very late (9 p.m. is perfectly common).

Insurance
At airports around the world machines selling flight insurance are commonplace. They issue policies that would enrich your beneficiaries in the event of a plane crash. Although these vending-machine policies ease the last-minute worries and superstitions of many travelers, they are no bargains.

If you have a regular insurance agent, ask whether you should take any special steps before a trip. Your belongings may already be covered, and your normal health insurance could well suffice in case of illness or accident abroad.

Travel agents routinely sell flight cancellation insurance, a worthwhile hedge if you're on a charter flight, package tour or APEX flight. Should illness force you to abandon the trip before or during your vacation, your losses would be covered—including, for example, the full-price replacement ticket you'd need to buy to get home early.

Languages
The language spoken by the people around you is close to their hearts. Try to learn a few words, an achievement much appreciated everywhere. At the very least, learn what language *not* to attempt. You'll make no friends trying out your high-school German in Geneva (where the native language is French). English is always understood at airline offices, travel agencies, big hotels and other institutions dealing with foreigners. The man or woman in the street in the cities of northern Europe is more likely to know English than in southern Europe, while small-town folk everywhere tend to be less experienced in foreign languages.

Mail

If you don't know where you'll be staying you can have mail sent to you *poste restante* (general delivery). You'll need your passport as identification to pick up mail at the *poste restante* window of the post office.

Money

Even the most experienced travelers suffer confusion in a new country with a bewildering exchange rate and unfamiliar coins and bills. You may feel more at ease if you change a small amount of money into the foreign currency before you get there; you'll need the currency of the country to pay for taxi, bus or rail tickets and tipping porters. Some exchange firms sell expensive but useful "tip packs". You can familiarize yourself with the currency on the way, and arrive without rushing off to find a bank.

Study the exchange rate in the newspaper or on the chart in the bank window before you dip into international finance. Be sure to estimate how much foreign currency you ought to receive for your traveler's check—at least roughly. That way careless or larcenous clerks can't get away with egregious errors, like moving a decimal point.

Traveler's checks are the safest way to transport money, providing you follow instructions on signing and co-signing them, keeping a record of serial numbers and the dates and places of encashment.

Credit cards are widely accepted in European hotels, restaurants and stores catering to tourists—but not always the type of card you carry. Look for the symbols of the cards they recognize, as posted in the window or doorway. Note that the exchange rate eventually charged to you may not be as favorable as the rate you would have obtained had you paid in cash.

The exchange rate is a recurrent problem when converting your traveler's checks or cash into foreign funds. In most countries you'll do better at a bank; and you'll also lose a percentage if you shop or pay bills in your own currency rather than the local money.

If your bank issues Eurocheques, you have an instant source of funds almost everywhere in Europe. If not, it's still a good idea to take along some of your personal checks from your hometown bank. With proper identification they would probably be accepted when paying bills, at least in an emergency.

Packing

Travel light, for you never know when you'll have to be your own porter. If it turns out you've packed too little you can buy what you lack almost anywhere in Europe. But do remember to include a thoroughly

27

comfortable pair of walking shoes, an extra pair of spectacles in case of loss or breakage, and any prescription drugs you're supposed to take. Also recommended: a sweater, even for southern zones on cool summer nights, a raincoat, a small bar of soap, and an international converter plug for your electric shaver or hairdryer. Remember to pack items of immediate need in your hand luggage—documents, medicines and toiletries for the trip (airlines allow you one bag per passenger, small enough to fit under the seat).

When choosing your clothing, favor conservative colors and styles for the cities. Clever travelers often pack only clothes of matching colors, giving maximum utility to each item in a minimum wardrobe. (Details of clothing requirements are given in the country-by-country chapters.)

Mark your luggage clearly: the identification tag is not infallible; it might be ripped off in transit. So be sure your name and address can also be found *inside* the suitcase, should it go astray. To make your baggage easier to recognize on the carousel when you reach your destination, tie a

bright ribbon around the handle or decorate the sides with a strip or two of colored tape. Remember that it is easier to carry two light suitcases rather than one heavy one.

Make a last-minute check before departure: passport, air ticket, hotel and travel documents, traveler's checks, credit cards, driver's license... and your address book, so you can send postcards to friends.

Passports and visas

You must have a passport to cross the frontiers of Europe. Your passport is also the indispensable proof of identity, required at every turn: checking into a hotel, cashing a traveler's check, claiming mail at a general delivery window ... and returning home. Your travel agent will tell you where and how to apply for a passport; allow as much time as possible. And because no document can substitute for a passport, be sure to protect it always. If ever it does get lost or stolen, inform the

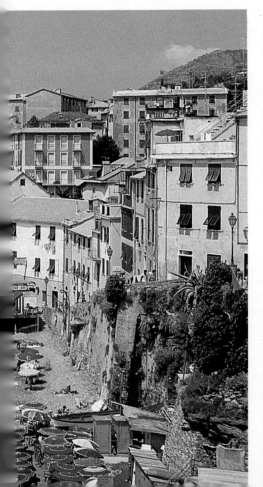

consulate and police immediately; replacements sometimes take some time.

A visa is a foreign government's stamp of approval in your passport indicating that you may enter. To obtain a visa you must normally apply to a consulate of that country before your trip, although *some* countries issue visas at the border or airport on arrival. Citizens of the United States and Canada do not require visas to enter the western European countries; the eastern countries are slowly easing the red tape. In view of the ever-changing situation, it's imperative to check before a trip.

Telephones

Generally, you can direct-dial locally, nationally and overseas from any telephone, even on the street—if you have a pocketful of coins. Calls at night and on weekends are often cheaper. But phoning overseas from your hotel room can be appallingly expensive, for surcharges of several hundred percent are often levied. Budget-conscious travelers use, wherever possible, a public telephone office or any suitable automatic phone.

Touring Europe

By car

Europe's well-developed system of expressways makes short work of intercity drives, allowing more time for exploring the back roads of tranquil beauty and history. The best part of touring by car is flexibility—the delight of following a whim, free from the tyranny of timetables.

But it's not all joy. Gasoline is expensive, some countries charge tolls on expressways (see country-by-country chapters), and cars can become a nuisance in big cities with their congested, narrow streets and chronic parking problems.

Renting a car in Europe. Some airlines and travel agencies offer a fly-drive formula combining a special air fare with an attractive car rental arrangement at the destination. Or you can reserve a rental car for yourself before you leave home, to be picked up on arrival at the airport or railroad station or delivered to your hotel. If you can't plan ahead, or if you prefer to make your arrangements on the spot, you have the choice of big international rental companies or the more competitive local firms. In the event of a breakdown, the big enterprise may be in a better position to give you a speedy replacement. Whatever the case, be sure to check the car carefully before you take it away, particularly noting safety aspects like the tires, brakes and lights.

What renting a car will cost you depends on several factors: basic rates (daily, weekly or special), mileage charges, tax and insurance. A substantial deposit may be demanded; alternatively, holders of major credit cards can sign a blank voucher—though this might become a disadvantage if the final charges come into dispute. The minimum age for renting a car is usually 21, and in some cases as high as 25. And you'll need a valid driver's license. If you give advance notice, you can often rent a car in one country and return it in another.

On the road in Europe. The highway network of Western Europe is up to the highest world standards. The expressways are well designed and maintained. In certain countries (such as France, Spain or Italy) you have to pay a toll in exchange for the speed and convenience of expressways. The older, parallel roads are usually dependable and, except at vacation times, free-flowing. The back roads in remote parts of Western Europe, and some trunk roads of Eastern Europe, are less convenient. They can prove narrow and difficult to navigate; you may suddenly encounter sheep, donkey-carts, children, or old people un-accustomed to traffic. Or another vehicle, convinced it has the road to itself. Mountain passes require concentration and driving skill.

Driving in European cities is often less efficient and rapid, and more stressful and harassing, than the public transportation facilities available. Many towns have banned cars entirely from historic central districts, enhancing the pleasure of sightseers and sidewalk café patrons but further aggravating the plight of motorists, desperately looking for somewhere to park. Almost everywhere, parking meters are as much a part of the cityscape as traffic lights, and the search for a vacant spot can fray tempers. For longer-term parking, underground facilities have been greatly expanded. In tow-away zones careless parking is potentially very expensive in money and time. Some cities have zones in which parked cars must display time discs showing when they arrived; if the permitted period has expired, a ticket may be issued. The discs are widely available, free, usually from auto clubs, local banks and filling stations, among other sources.

Gasoline is measured by the liter (slightly more than a quart). Filling stations can be far apart in sparsely settled areas—for instance, remote parts of Scandinavia—so wilderness tourists should replenish the tank at every opportunity.

Breakdowns. Free emergency telephones are installed along many expressways. Members of automobile associations receive reciprocal privileges from auto clubs in other countries, often including free breakdown service. You can also pull off the road and raise the car's hood to attract the attention of a passing police patrol: they give emergency assistance to any car in need.

Regulations. Your home driver's license is recognized anywhere in Western Europe. But if you intend to drive in Greece (which uses a different alphabet) or Spain, you should definitely have an international driving licence. These multilingual documents are quickly available from your motoring association. Along with your license you must have a document proving you are insured for liability in case of an accident. Car rental firms include these forms with the registration and contract papers.

Only three countries in Europe drive on the left: the United Kingdom, Ireland and Malta. It takes special care to overcome the feeling of being on the "wrong side" of the road, with the most danger and confusion at crossroads and traffic circles and when first taking the wheel after a break. In all other European countries the rule is: drive on the right, pass on the left, and, in most places, yield to traffic coming from the right.

Almost all countries require you to wear seat belts in the front seat and several of them banish children to the back seat. Speed limits vary significantly from country to country. For instance, the expressway maximum in France is 81 miles per hour (130 kilometers per hour) but in Denmark it's a sedate 62 mph (100 kph). If you're caught, the police almost everywhere are authorized to fine you on the spot. But—small consolation—they give receipts...

Drunken driving is a grave offense, but the definition is hard to pin down. Whatever the law, keep in mind that European beers may be stronger than the brands you are accustomed to, and a little wine can go a long way.

By train

Intercity travel by train is fast, convenient and comfortable in most of Europe, with the added advantages of economy, the scenery, and the chance to meet local people. Second-class facilities, especially on long-distance trains, are at least adequate, while first-class is often sumptuous, with air-conditioning, sound-proofing, panoramic windows and armchair luxury.

The fastest trains are France's TGVs (*Train à grande vitesse*), which cruise as fast as 186 miles an hour (about 300 kph) linking Paris with provincial centers and neighboring Switzerland. Some 200 cities are served by the EuroCity network. Ordinary express trains with first- and second-class seats also make good time. Local and regional trains, though, can be as slow as they are colorful.

Visitors residing outside Europe and North Africa can take advantage of the *Eurailpass,* for sale at travel agencies and railroad offices. The pass is also sold in Europe at Eurail Aid offices and major railroad stations. It is valid on the rail network of 17 European countries but not in Britain, which has its own, comparable *Britrail Pass.* Included in the Eurail bargain are trains, buses and ferries run by the railroads, and discounts on some international ferry crossings, certain lake and river ships and cable cars. The *Eurail Youthpass* is a similar deal for passengers between 12 and 26 years of age. Children aged four to 11 pay half price; those under four travel free. The *Inter-Rail Card* is a flat-rate pass valid for one month's travel for passengers up to age 26. The *Rail-Europ-S Card* entitles senior citizens to purchase train tickets at reduced prices. And most national railways sell tourist passes on the spot, good for a specific time period in either first or second class, or circular tickets for a fixed itinerary. One of the national or international passes could bring a significant saving for any visitor planning more than a few train journeys. It's also a relief to be able to hop aboard any train you like—except long-haul express trains such as TGVs, which require seat reservations—without having to stand in line to buy a ticket. Note that large cities usually have more than one principal station (London has seven), so make sure you leave from the right one: best confirm the details of departures, arrivals and transfers.

Railroad timetables look like puzzles until you learn some of the formulas and symbols. And you'll have to be alert to time changes as you cross frontiers, especially in the confusion of daylight saving time. Timetables and announcements follow the 24-hour clock, a further complication for the uninitiated. If a train leaves at midnight, it's listed as 00:00. A train arriving at midnight is given as 24:00. Information clerks in the stations are accustomed to dealing with foreigners.

To gain time and save on hotel bills, some travelers schedule overnight train trips. First-class sleepers offer considerable luxury, and even, in rare cases, showers. An alternative is a *couchette* in a sleeping compartment with four berths in first class and six in second class. Sleeping-car attendants collect tickets and passports and keep them until the next morning to save the inconvenience of border formalities during the night. In any case, frontiers in Western Europe are almost non-existent obstacles for train passengers. Officials normally board the trains and check passports and customs details en route. Border complications in Eastern Europe are becoming less oppressive, too.

Food is generally available on all but local trains, if only a trolley pushed up and down the aisle, stocked with sandwiches, cakes, bottled drinks, and coffee and tea from vacuum flasks. On inter-city express

33

trains there are either self-service buffet-and-bar cars or fully fledged dining cars. The quality of the food varies drastically from one country to another.

Bus tours
At any leading tourist attraction, from a Norwegian fjord to the Strait of Gibraltar, the roads are aswarm with luxurious, air-conditioned chartered buses. The license plates may be French or Dutch but the sightseers behind the big tinted windows could well be Americans or Australians on package tours. Big and small travel agencies in many

distant countries organize bus tours in cooperation with European operators, who meet the incoming flights. Touring by bus relieves the traveler of some concerns and, assuming the itinerary is right, the fellow-travelers congenial and the driver and guide competent, this can be an agreeable, economical way to see the scenic and cultural highspots. Arrangements for bus tours—a weekend or a month—can be made on the spot once you're in Europe, but it's generally advisable to make arrangements before leaving home for the longer, more popular routes. Some short itineraries (one or two days) are run so often, mostly in summer, that you may be able to join a tour at very short notice.

By bus

Inter-city buses criss-cross Europe, challenging the trains on certain routes but generally complementing them, and at competitive fares. The well-organized bus system is run by the national railway companies themselves. There are inclusive tours as well as transportation-only tickets permitting you to choose your own route and accommodations day by day. Regularly scheduled buses go to areas the railroads miss, and in mountain regions they expertly negotiate roads most drivers would rather not tackle.

Cruises

As modern mass air travel has become prosaic, the romance of the cruise liner has been revived and enhanced. The accent now is on the unhurried sea voyage featuring shore excursions by day and pampering and entertainment while rolling up the mileage aboard ship at night. Combining air and sea elements, the traveler can cover the long distances by plane and save the ship for scenic waters. For instance, you can fly to Lisbon and join a cruise to Gibraltar, Sicily, Dubrovnik, Piraeus and the nearby Greek islands, picking up your homeward flight somewhere along the way. Or you can unwind during the cruise from a British port to, say, Scandinavia. The top-of-the-line ships offer every facility from saunas and swimming pools to *haute cuisine* and nightclub acts. Smaller ships charging lower fares sail the same seas more austerely. Among the advantages of cruising are the convenience of a "floating hotel" which eliminates daily packing and unpacking, the possibilities for meeting people, and the enforced relaxation. But serious travelers who want to take in all the sights may find the time ashore too brief.

Europe has its memorable freshwater cruises, as well. Tourists dawdle down the Rhine sampling wine from the vineyards along the banks, or sail down the Danube from Vienna to Budapest. The rivers and canals of the U.K., Ireland, France or the Netherlands may be experienced at greatest leisure aboard boats or barges, either crewed or on a sail-it-yourself arrangement.

Ferries

Something of the excitement of a cruise ship may be experienced on the big ferries, such as those plying the North Sea, the Baltic and the Mediterranean. On the longer runs there's time to enjoy duty-free drinks and a leisurely dinner before retiring to a stateroom for a night's sleep. Small ferries, on which the local farmers take their goats to market, offer the kind of adventure you'll long remember.

City transportation

Intensive networks of public transportation ease the problems of getting around Europe's cities. Local tourist offices, which usually provide free maps of subway, bus and trolley lines, may sell all-inclusive tickets valid for one day or longer. Otherwise, in many cities tickets are dispensed from coin machines at bus and streetcar stops. Although the intricacies of routes and ticketing are unpredictable, don't be intimidated, for instructions may even be occasionally printed in English, and passers-by generously offer advice.

In some cities taxis cruise for customers but elsewhere they wait at stands or accept telephone reservations—sometimes all three methods apply. Meters regulate the price in most cities but extra charges are common. One certainty links all taxi services: a cab is hard to find in the rain or at rush hour.

Biking

It's not going to be everyone's choice, but cycling is a healthy way of getting close to Europe and its people. It doesn't have to be an exhausting grind. If you plan reasonable daily stages you'll have time enough to enjoy the countryside and arrive in good spirits. And if it becomes too hilly or rainy you can put your bike on a train and head for another part of the Continent. If you're planning to take your own bicycle to Europe, be sure to check with the airline well in advance to learn whether it can be carried overseas free as a normal piece of baggage. Another option: the national railways of several countries (e.g. France) rent bikes at rail stations; you can turn in the bike at the other end of the country if you wish, at no extra charge.

Hiking

Some of Europe's most inspiring sights can only be seen after braving a strenuous hiking trail. But don't undertake mountain-climbing adventures unless you have enough experience, the proper equipment, and a guide. Most places where there are mountains of touristic interest provide simple huts for overnight stays. For less taxing hikes as well as serious treks it's wise to decide your route beforehand and let someone know your plans. Be sure to carry extra covering for protection from sun, rain or cold.

Hitchhiking

For young people with extra-tight budgets and plenty of time, traveling by thumb is an attractive option. The dangers, of course, are well known. Girls hitchhiking in pairs are considerably safer than singles, and mixed couples fare reasonably well. Hitching on expressways is universally outlawed, though in some countries, it's worthwhile trying accesses to expressways. Experts recommend traveling with little luggage, displaying an easy-to-read destination sign, picking a spot on the edge of town where the driver can easily pull over in safety... and lots of luck.

Enjoying Europe

Sightseeing
In Venice, of course, you'll do it by boat. You can see the sights of other European cities, as well, from their canals, rivers, lakes or harbors: Amsterdam, London, Oslo, Paris, Stockholm, Copenhagen, Moscow and Zurich, for instance. The excitement of a boating expedition and the waterline perspective add to the pleasure and understanding and often help you get an overall grasp of the city. But bus tours remain the most efficient, if expensive, way to get your bearings.

Before you set forth, check in at the local tourist office, usually found at the rail station or in the center of the historic part of town. Pick up the free maps and brochures for an idea of the top attractions and where they are. Then sign up for a city tour for overall orientation. By the end of the day you'll recognize the landmarks, have a feeling for directions and distances, and know what you want to see in more detail.

Excursions, unfortunately, can be imperfect... or worse. Customers sometimes complain about extended interruptions to the sightseeing schedule—visits to handicraft factories, shops and restaurants. But there is always a demand for stops, if only for the rest room facilities. In some places, though, tour guides enter into dubious arrangements with shopkeepers who pay kickbacks when busloads of tourists are funneled in. Beware of such shopping "opportunities"; you are under no obligation to buy anything, even if you've been given a free lecture and drink.

Even the best guided tours necessarily glide past important museums and monuments, sometimes only to avoid the trouble of parking and unleashing a throng of tourists. On your own you can spend as much time as you want at each location, alternating between the sacred and the profane, the cathedrals and the cafés, the museums and the shops. In many cities the bulk of historic attractions are within walking distance of one another; streets and zones reserved for pedestrians make sightseeing even more appealing.

But no country's character is solely symbolized by its capital. The true heart often beats outside, in specific landscapes and local villages, within reach of even the most hasty traveler. From Dublin it's an easy outing to the Curragh, the great prairie of horse racing and breeding, and the ruins of ancient monasteries. The whole town of Toledo, a daytrip from Madrid, is a jewel of Spanish civilization, largely unchanged since El Greco painted it. A short jaunt from Helsinki takes in the house where Jean Sibelius lived... and on the way you'll delight in the scenery he pictured in music. You can take an organized excursion, drive yourself or experiment with the local buses or trains. Whichever way you choose, you'll get more out of the trip if you do your homework: read the pamphlets and guidebooks, and if at all possible, dig into the more profound sources: James Joyce to understand Dublin, Conan Doyle for London, Balzac for Paris, Dostoyevski for Leningrad.

Shopping

For most tourists, the shopping urge is as irrepressible as the fascination of travel itself. Foreign fields can yield new ideas, old masters and quality unavailable at home.

The most basic goal of the shopper is a souvenir, a reminder of the trip. Nothing says it must be tawdry. For the price of a kitsch corkscrew spoofing the most famous statue in Brussels you could probably buy a lasting keepsake of handmade lace. In more remote areas you can still buy handicrafts direct from the artisan, for enduring memories of people as well as places.

At its best, shopping itself can be a happy memory of your trip, whether or not you buy anything. What could be more revealing than to experience the dignified understatement of a smart Bond Street shop, or, a couple of miles away, the hubbub of an uninhibited street market?

Because of currency fluctuations and inflation, it's hard to predict where the really advantageous shopping will be found. Country-by-country chapters detail the possibilities, from Austria's antiques to the United Kingdom's knitwear.

Serious and, indeed, professional shoppers come to Europe for the auctions of art works and antiques. Even if you're not in a position to buy, the sheer excitement of the bidding is something to savor. Among the great names of auction houses: Sotheby's and Christies in London, the Dorotheum in Vienna and Paris's Hôtel Drouot.

At the other end of the scale, Europe's flea markets buzz with insight into the local character. If you do find something you want—an old book, a promising painting or a tarnished candlestick—be prepared to haggle fiercely over the price. Buyers who know the merchandise and the language (and flea-market slang) stand a better chance to come away with a good bargain than obvious tourist novices. But polite if cheery

39

haggling, a bit of persistence and psychology can get you a long way.

In many European countries a huge sales tax or Value Added Tax (VAT) is added, usually invisibly, to the cost of everything you might buy. Most visitors from overseas can avoid paying this sales tax, typically 15 percent of the price tag, but it takes some paperwork. One way is to have the shop ship your merchandise home for you. Or you may pay the VAT, fill out a form, and apply for a refund when you go through customs on the way out of the taxing country.

Always save receipts for everything you buy; keep them handy, all in a bunch, to show at customs on your return.

Cultural Europe

Even if you were totally allergic to it, you could hardly sidestep culture in Europe. It's in the very streets and squares themselves. And the cities are chock-a-block with museums, universities and opera houses. Even the small towns and villages harbor wonders of art or architecture, or play host to some avant-garde music festival. You can follow Western culture back to its origins in the excavations of Italy and Greece, and beyond, to its primitive precursors—mural paintings in caves in France and Spain.

Package tours organized overseas or on the spot in Europe, conducted by authorities on art or archaeology, cater to specialized interests—like Minoan culture, Orthodox monasteries or Renaissance palaces. For travelers with more general goals, almost every town or region can come up with many layers of culture from Stone Age relics to modern art.

The Ancient Greeks originated art galleries and museums more than two thousand years ago. Some museums, with humble and inadequately lit displays, seem to have changed little over a century or more. But many of Europe's finest museums have introduced modern techniques to add to comfort as well as understanding.

Even medium-sized museums can overwhelm the eyes and mind, not to mention the feet. Don't try to take in every single picture or exhibit. Before plunging in, invest in a map, brochure or catalogue explaining the collection, then decide which highlights you want to see. Even with a plan of attack, an hour can feel like a long time in a museum, so take frequent breaks—a minute or two seated before a wall-sized painting, or a longer respite in the museum's coffee shop.

In your pursuit of culture, don't ignore the illuminating footnotes all around you. The controversial Beaubourg museum in Paris introduces modern art to 8 million visitors a year, but the building's revolutionary architecture is as stimulating as its contents. And in the plaza outside, sample the nonstop carnival of fire-eaters, jugglers and mimes. Europe's great cathedrals attract tour buses for their sublime architecture, paintings and statues. Don't overlook, however, the human side of things, faces that seem to emerge from the paintings themselves, voices and cries of centuries past, and the bustle of the vendors outside.

Lovers of music and drama will find thrilling performances on stages everywhere in Europe. In the theatrical arena the U.K. clearly takes precedence, with institutions like the National Theatre and the Royal Shakespeare Company setting the pace, and dozens of commercial and avant-garde companies rounding out the scene. But where great actors perform you don't have to know the language. Nobody could be

41

unmoved by Goethe at Berlin's Schiller-Theater, or Molière at the Comédie Française in Paris.

Opera soars above language barriers, especially in hallowed houses like La Scala in Milan, Vienna's Staatsoper, or Moscow's Bolshoi. Unless a superstar tops the bill, last-minute tickets are often available. Nor should tickets be a problem for the topflight symphony orchestras.

Europe's music festivals, mostly in summer, are major events around which many music lovers arrange their vacations. Some big cities put on annual music festivals, but a special atmosphere pervades the festivities at charming sites like Bayreuth, Gstaad, Salzburg or Spoleto. In addition, many a colorful village that foreigners have never heard of puts on its own version of a festival of music, drama or art. If you come across one, stay and enrich your travel experience.

Leaving Europe

In packing for your journey home, keep handy all the documents you'll need on the trip, including shopping receipts for possible customs perusal, as well as items you shouldn't have to hunt for on your return, such as your car or house keys. If you anticipate a drastic change in climate, be sure that appropriate clothes are easy to find, preferably in your hand-baggage.

If you have acquired so many purchases that your baggage has now become oversized or overweight, consider mailing the excess home (if time is not crucial) or shipping it by airfreight.

Our chart below lists the quotas for the main duty-free items that customs men of all countries look for when travelers come home.

	Cigarettes	Cigars	Tobacco	Liquor	Wine
Australia	250	or 250 g.	or 250 g.	1 l.	or 1 l.
Canada	200	and 50	and 900 g.	1.1 l.	or 1.1 l.
Eire	200	or 50	or 250 g.	1 l.	and 2 l.
New Zealand	200	or 50	or 250 g.	1.1 l	and 4.5 l
S. Africa	400	and 50	and 250 g.	1 l.	and 2 l.
U.K.	200	or 50	or 250 g.	1 l.	and 2 l.
U.S.A.	200	and 100	and *	1 l.	or 1 l.

* A reasonable quantity.

AUSTRIA

Along the Blue Danube, the elegant legacy
of Maximilian and Mozart still flourishes.

The imperial history of Austria has molded its mood and gracious pace. The Habsburg empire, launched by Maximilian I in 1493, spread its influence from Vienna to Venice, and held sway in faraway Burgundy and Holland. Through maneuver and marriage the dynasty became Europe's most powerful force, but in the 19th century Napoleon, and then revolution, diminished the domain to the Balkans, and finally, after World War I, the Austro-Hungarian empire fizzled completely. All that remained were snow-heaped mountains, enchanted forests and sunsoaked vineyards...and picture-book villages and the eternal elegance of Vienna.

Austria hoards an emperor's ransom of art. Where Mozart, Haydn and Schubert composed their thoughts, the cultural life still thrives. You'll never witness a more perfect "Magic Flute" or Viennese operetta, and here you can see the original Vienna Boys' Choir, or dance an oldtime waltz in the park. The "Beautiful Blue Danube", which inspired Strauss and others, has lost its tint but still serves as Austria's international waterway; cool, shimmering lakes and natural hot springs provide counterpoint.

Some of Europe's best skiing is just up the mountain from Austria's cultural treasures, making it a country of perfect compromise for outdoor and indoor types. You can ride a horse through invigorating forest paths, or come inside to watch the prodigies of the Spanish Riding School, the equine equivalent of topflight ballet.

This is a land of *Gemütlichkeit,* the air of snug comfort you find in a village inn or a city café. Sipping coffee or the local wine is taken seriously, as is the merciless regime of Wienerschnitzel, goulash and Sachertorte. Traditions linger charmingly. Out in the country, Austrians still wear dirndl skirts, or lederhosen with a feather in the cap. And if the gentlemen kiss the ladies' hands, and address the men with eloquent formality, it's only natural in a small republic with a legacy of imperial grandeur. Ancient castles aren't the only heritage of Austria's monumental past.

44

Facts and figures

Population:	7.6 million
Area:	32,374 sq. miles (83,850 sq. km.)
Capital:	Vienna (*Wien*, 1.5 million)
Other cities:	Graz (245,000) Linz (200,000) Salzburg (140,000) Innsbruck (120,000) Klagenfurt (90,000)
Language:	German
Religion:	Catholic (84%), Protestant (6%)
Time zone:	GMT + 1, EST + 6; DST (Apr.–Sep.)
Currency:	*Schilling* (abbr. *S*) = 100 *Groschen* (abbr. *g.*) Coins: 10, 50 Groschen; 1, 5, 10, 20 S Bills: 20, 50, 100, 500, 1,000 S
Electricity:	220 volt, 50 cycle, AC

Planning your trip

Visa requirements. See pp. 29–30.

Vaccination requirements. None (see also p. 25).

Currency restrictions. Import and export of foreign currencies is unrestricted. Any amount of Austrian Schillings may be imported, but only up to 50,000 S may be taken out of the country. Banks must report transactions of 100,000 shillings or more, in line with laws aimed at preventing money-laundering.

Climate. The weather in Austria tends to be extreme—hot in the summer and cold in the winter, with moderate rain- and snowfall. Temperatures decrease and precipitation increases with altitude.

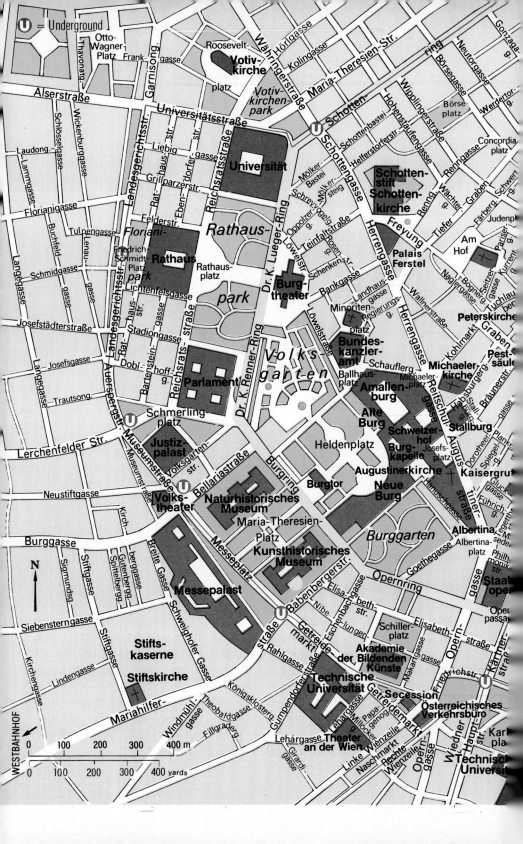

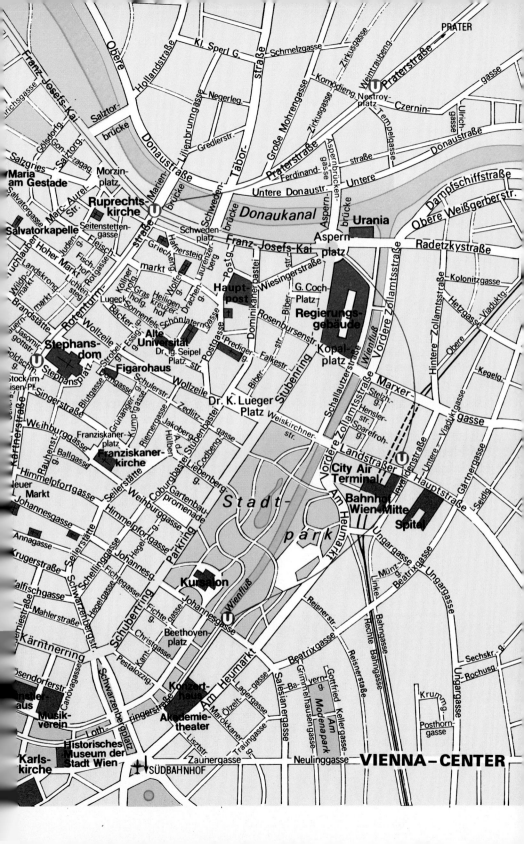

Some average daily temperatures:

Vienna		J	F	M	A	M	J	J	A	S	O	N	D
average daily	°F	34	38	47	58	67	73	76	75	68	56	45	37
maximum*	°C	1	3	8	15	19	23	25	24	20	14	7	3
average daily	°F	25	28	30	42	50	56	60	59	53	44	37	30
minimum*	°C	-4	-3	-1	6	10	14	15	15	11	7	3	-1

Innsbruck													
average daily	°F	34	40	51	60	68	74	77	75	69	58	46	36
maximum*	°C	1	4	11	16	20	24	25	24	21	15	8	2
average daily	°F	20	24	0	39	46	52	55	54	49	40	0	24
minimum*	°C	-7	-5	0	4	8	11	13	12	10	5	0	-4

* Minimum temperatures are measured just before sunrise, maximum temperatures
  in the afternoon.

Clothing. In summer take light clothing, with a warm sweater or jacket
for chilly evenings, especially up in the mountains. Rainwear is
advisable all year round. Stout walking shoes are essential for Alpine
rambles and a pair of sunglasses may come in handy. In winter, you will
need an overcoat and appropriate footwear against the cold and wet.
The Austrians like to dress up for the theater, concert and opera. A dark
suit or cocktail dress is nearly always appropriate. On special occasions,
such as Vienna Festival and premieres, a tuxedo or evening dress is often
worn.

Duty-free allowances

	Cigarettes		Cigars		Tobacco	Liquor		Wine
1)	400	or	100	or	500 g.	1 l.	and	2 l.
2)	200	or	50	or	250 g.	1 l.	and	2 l.
Perfume: approx. 50 g. *Toilet water:* approx. 300 g. *Gifts:* up to a value of 400 S duty-free								
1) residents of countries outside Europe 2) residents of Europe								

Hotels and accommodations

Hotels. A booklet listing all hotels according to class, rates and facilities is issued annually by the Austria Information Center. Other accommodation possibilities are inns *(Gasthof)* and boardinghouses *(Pension)*. The personal atmosphere of boardinghouses makes them popular for a longer stay. It is advisable to make reservations well in advance, particularly during the summer season (May–Sep.) and for the Christmas and Easter holidays. The famous old luxury hotels around the Opera in Vienna are often full.

In Vienna, the tourist information offices at the airport, main rail stations, at the west and south expressway exits and in Opernpassage (the underground passage at the Opera) can make room arrangements for you.

Visiting the Tyrol, it's possible to stay at a Tyrolean farmhouse *(Bauernhof)*, and for the high-altitude tourists, dormitory-style accommodations in mountain huts *(Schutzhütte)* may be just the thing. The Tyrolean Tourist Office distributes lists of hotels, vacation apartments and farmhouses, but cannot make reservations; instead contact the accommodation desk at Innsbruck railroad station; tel. (05222) 237 66.

Youth hostels. There is a large, modern hostel near the Danube as you enter Vienna from the north with two and four beds to a room. You can obtain a map and information there about the other 100 hostels in Austria. Austrian Youth Hostels Association, Gonzagagasse 22 (Schottenring), 1010 Vienna; tel. 533 53 53.

Camping. There are many campsites in Austria—at lakeside, in meadows or mountain areas, or near towns. Five major campsites are located inside the city limits of Vienna. Some offer caravans for rent. Brochures are available from Österreichischer Camping Club, Johannesgasse 20, 1010 Vienna.

Austrian tourist offices abroad

Australia	A.N.T.O., 19th floor, 1 York Street, Sydney, 2000, NSW; tel. (02) 27 85 81
Canada	A.N.T.O., 2 Bloor Street East, Suite 3330, Toronto, Ontario M4W 1A8; tel. (416) 967 3381
Eire	A.N.T.O., Merridon Hall, Strand Road, Sandymount, Dublin 4; tel. (01) 83 04 88
South Africa	A.N.T.O., The Galaxy, 2193 Park Tower, Johannesburg; tel. (011) 482 1480

U.K.	A.N.T.O., 30 St. George Street, London W1R OAL; tel. (071) 629 0461
U.S.A.	A.N.T.O., 500 Fifth Avenue, Suite 2009-2022, New York, NY 10110; tel. (212) 944-6880
	A.N.T.O., 11601 Wilshire Boulevard, Suite 2480, Los Angeles, CA 90025, tel. (213) 477-3332
	A.N.T.O., 4800 San Felipe Street, Suite 500, Houston, TX 77056; tel. (713) 850-9999

On the spot

Banks and currency exchange. Banking hours are generally 8 a.m. to 12:30 p.m. and 1:30 to 3 p.m., Monday through Friday, with late closing at 5:30 p.m. on Thursdays. Outside banking hours, you may also change money at travel agencies and hotels, but the rate won't be as good. There are exchange bureaus in Innsbruck and Vienna at the main railroad stations, in Vienna also at the tourist office in Opernpassage, at Stephansplatz and at the airport. Money-changing machines (CHANGE) are to be found in Kärntnerstrasse, at the side of the Opera, and near the cathedral, Stephansdom, in Vienna.

Credit cards and traveler's checks. Both are welcome in most large restaurants, hotels and shops, although some of the older Viennese hotels may still not accept them. The rates when cashing a traveler's check are best in banks or exchange offices. Eurocheques may be cashed at all post offices.

Mail and telecommunications. Post offices are usually open between 8 a.m. and 6 p.m., with one or two hours for lunch. In Vienna, the main post office (Fleischmarkt 19) and branches at the main railroad stations offer 24-hour-a-day service for registered, air and express mail. In Innsbruck and other cities the main post office or a counter stay open round the clock. Stamps can also be bought from tobacco shops. Mailboxes are yellow or blue.

Telegrams can be sent from telegraph offices, and night letters *(Brieftelegramm)* are transmitted like telegrams and delivered with the mail of the day. There is a public telex in the main telegraph office in Vienna (Börseplatz 1).

Public telephones can be recognized by a sign showing a black telephone receiver in a yellow circle and the word *Fernsprecher*. Instructions are usually posted in several languages. The Austrian telephone network is largely automatic and you can dial direct to many Western European countries, even from some phone booths. Note that on certain old-style telephones, you have to press a red button for connection the moment your party answers. For surcharges and low rates, see also p. 30.

Some useful telephone numbers:

Directory information (Austria)	16
Operator for foreign area codes for direct dialing	08
Operator (international)	09
Fire	122
Ambulance	144
Police (emergency)	133

Newspapers. Leading Austrian dailies are *Kurier, Kronen-Zeitung* and *Die Presse*. Most major European newspapers and the *International Herald Tribune* are sold at airports, hotels and large city newsstands.

Tourist information

Vienna	Kinderspitalgasse 5; tel. (01) 42 42 25 (phone service seven days a week). Offices also in the Opernpassage (pedestrian underpass near the Opera), in the West-bahnhof and Südbahnhof railroad stations and at the airport
Salzburg	Sigmund-Haffner-Gasse 16; tel. (0662) 8042/2232
Innsbruck	Tyrolean Tourist Office; Bozner Platz 6; tel. (0512) 5320
Graz	Herrengasse 16 (Landhaus); tel. (0316) 70 52 41
Linz	Altstadt 17; tel. (0732) 2393

Legal holidays

Jan. 1	New Year's Day	**Movable dates:**
Jan. 6	Epiphany	Good Friday
May 1	Labor Day	Easter Monday
Aug. 15	Assumption	Ascension Day
Oct. 26	National Day	Whit Monday
Nov. 1	All Saints' Day	Corpus Christi
Dec. 8	Immaculate Conception	
Dec. 25	Christmas Day	
Dec. 26	St. Stephen's Day	

Transportation

Air. Vienna has direct connections with most European cities. Some international flights go to Salzburg. Domestic flights operate between Vienna, Graz, Innsbruck, Linz, Klagenfurt and Salzburg.

Major airport. Vienna: Schwechat (11 miles/18 km. from city center). Duty-free shop. An airport bus runs between the city air terminal and the airport every 20 or 30 minutes. **Linz:** Hörsching (10 miles/15 km. from city center). Duty-free shop. Bus service to the main railroad station.

Rail. Trains are usually punctual and comfortable. Dining and sleeping cars are attached on longer runs, and express trains connect all major cities. There's the *Rabbit Card,* which entitles the holder to four days of unlimited rail travel during a period of ten days. At less than half the price, the regional "Netzkarte" offers the same conditions but is limited to one of the 18 regions of Austria. There is also a *Rabbit Card Junior* for those under 26. For *Eurailpass,* see p. 33.

Postal buses. Outlying places not on the rail system are all served by the postal bus system. Buses are fast, punctual and quite comfortable. Buy tickets at the bus station or on the bus itself. If you intend to use the system extensively, inquire about weekly tickets for unlimited travel in certain regions.

Boats, waterways. Boats on the Danube River operate daily from June 1 to late September between Vienna and Krems, Melk, Linz and Passau. Steamers are equipped with restaurant. Schedules and fares are available at most tourist offices or at the Austrian Danube Steamship Company.

Local public transportation. Most cities have streetcars and buses. Vienna also has a subway system *(U-bahn)* with at present four operating lines. This is clearly the quickest way of getting around Vienna beyond the city center. The same tickets are valid for all forms of public transportation in the city. You can buy booklets of five tickets at a reduced rate. Validate tickets aboard buses or streetcars or at the entrance to the subway. Also available are 1-, 3- and 8-day tickets for unlimited travel anywhere in Vienna.

Taxis. Cabs can be hailed in the street, ordered by telephone or found at a taxi stand. They are metered. It's possible to reserve one in advance.

Car rental. Both international and local firms operate. Some companies have desks at Vienna's Schwechat airport. You can find the addresses of leading firms in the yellow pages of the telephone directory under "Autovermietung". See also pp. 30–31.

Driving in Austria. Drive on the right, pass on the left. Make sure that your car carries a red reflector warning triangle for use in case of breakdown and a first-aid kit. Seat belts must be worn, and children under 12 should sit in the back seat. Streetcars have priority and may not be passed on the right when they are slowing down to stop. On mountain roads, yield right of way to the motorists ascending. Speed limits are 81 mph (130 kph) or 62 mph (100 kph) on expressways, 62 mph or 50 mph (80 kph) on other roads, and 31 mph (50 kph) in towns. Secondary roads are winding and narrow. Gradients of between 6 and 15 percent are common in the Alps. A number of roads and tunnels charge tolls, notably the Brenner and Tauern expressways, the Grossglockner Alpine road and the Arlberg tunnel. Blood alcohol limit is 80 mg./100 ml. and drunken driving is considered a serious offense. For breakdown assistance, phone 120 (ÖAMTC–Austrian Automobile, Motorcycling and Touring Association) or 123 (ARBÖ–Austrian Automobile, Motorcycling and Cycling Association). Gasoline available is normal (87–92 octane), super (96–99 octane), lead-free (91 octane) and diesel. To park in "blue zones" in Vienna you'll need parking permits from 8 a.m. to 6 p.m., with a 90 minutes limit. Permits are sold in banks and tobacco shops.

Some distances: Vienna–Graz 125 miles (200 km.), Salzburg 180 miles (300 km.), Innsbruck 290 miles (470 km.).

Bicycle rental. You can generally rent a bicycle for the day or by the hour at railroad stations and in major resorts. In some localities there are special trails for cyclists.

Rest rooms. Public facilities are usually found in railroad stations and near main squares, often in the pedestrian underpasses. You may have to pay a set fee for soap and towels. Have a couple of Schillings handy in case the door has a slot. Ladies are *Damen* and gentlemen are *Herren*.

Emergencies. All emergency numbers are listed at the front of the telephone directory.

Ambulance	144	Fire	122
Police	133		

Police. The police are divided into *Polizei* in the towns, and the *Gendarmerie* in the countryside. If you are fined for any reason the police have the right to ask you to pay on the spot.

Crime and theft. Compared to most parts of the world, Austria's crime and theft rate is quite low, but one should, nevertheless, take the usual precautions and not leave anything valuable in the car or hotel room.

Medical care and health. The standard of medical treatment is generally high. Pharmacies *(Apotheke)* are open Monday through Friday and Saturday morning during normal business hours. For night and Sunday service, all pharmacies display the address of the nearest shop remaining on duty. For insurance, see pp. 25–26.

The Viennese tap water is not only safe to drink but also tastes good, as it comes directly from the Styrian Alps.

Embassies and consulates. Most consulates and all embassies are in Vienna. Consult the listings in the telephone directory under "Botschaften" for embassies and "Konsulate" for consulates.

Social customs. The Austrians are a very friendly and hospitable people. Among themselves they have developed an elaborate system of courtesy. Shaking hands is usual on meeting and taking leave of a person. A good spot to get to know and talk with Viennese people without any formality is at the Heurigen taverns where you can join total strangers at the long tables for a glass of wine. The Tyrol is relaxed, casual, friendly, and village inns are ideal places for making new friends. You'll see lots of local people out on the hiking trails and on ski runs, especially at weekends and during holidays. Wish them "Grüss Gott" and you'll probably fall into conversation.

Enjoying Austria

Food and drink. A cup of coffee and a piece of cake—it may not sound like much, but in Austria it opens up a world of possibilities, particularly in Vienna. The question is not just milk or cream, but whether to order *einen kleinen Mokka,* small, strong and black, *einen Braunen,* very Viennese, with a dash of milk, *einen Kapuziner,* topped with whipped cream. Then there is the question of cake. You can have any kind *mit Schlag,* with cream, but you must decide among the famous *Sachertorte* (chocolate and jam), walnut, hazelnut, cherry or apple. The variations are endless and the decisions difficult.

Breakfast is likely to be quite light; the difference from a continental breakfast is the selection of cold meats—ham, salami—and cheese served with the rolls.

Austrian specialties are soups, like *Leberknödelsuppe* (liver dumpling soup) or *Gulaschsuppe* (goulash soup). Main dishes include *Wiener-schnitzel* (breaded veal cutlets) and *Wienerbackhendl* (boned breaded

55

fried chicken) or *Tafelspitz* (boiled beef with chive or horseradish sauce). For a spicier dish try a Hungarian goulash full of beef chunks stewed with onions, garlic, paprika and heart of celery, with lots of spice, or maybe *cevapcici,* peppery meatballs from Serbia.

If you're looking for some very traditional Austrian food, then leave a lot of room for a *Tiroler Mus* (a semolina soup enriched with butter), *Tiroler Gröstl,* a hearty dish of beef or pork sautéed with diced potatoes, chives and other herbs, or *Zillertaler Krapfen,* a sort of ravioli filled with grated potatoes, chives and sour cream.

Knödel come in all shapes and flavors, either sweet or savory; stuffed with bacon or liver, plain or with a sweetened cream cheese, or it could hide a hot apricot in the center *(Marillenknödel).* Another hot favorite is *Salzburger Nockerl* (a sweet soufflé omelette). Other desserts served warm: *Apfelstrudel* (apple, raisin and cinnamon in thin pastry) and *Palatschinken* (thin pancakes filled with for example nuts).

Austrians like to drink wine or beer with their meals. The beer is of the pilsner type, served cold and quite strong. The wine is usually white, medium dry. The best-known of Austrian white wines is the Gumpolds-kirchner. The Danube Valley produces wine with a light natural sparkle: Kremser, Dürnsteiner and Langenloiser. Austrian red wines can be a bit flat, so try some from the South Tyrol (Italy). It is worth ordering your white wine *herb* (dry) as they are often sweetened to what producers imagine to be popular taste. *Schnaps* is widely enjoyed, whether before the meal to stimulate the palate, or to round off the meal. It's distilled from fruit and often flavored with herbs. Otherwise try the fruit in the form of some excellent juices.

Lunch is served from noon to 2:30 p.m. and dinner 6 to 9 p.m.

Entertainment. Vienna is the home of the world-famous State Opera and the Vienna Boys' Choir. The major music season runs from September to June, climaxing with the Vienna Festival in May and June with concerts and theater performances by artists from all over the world. The two famous orchestras, the Wiener Philharmoniker and the Wiener Symphoniker, perform throughout the winter season. Otherwise, the most typical entertainment in Vienna remains the violin music of the Balkan restaurants and the Schrammelmusik of the Heurigen wine-gardens. During the summer months, concerts take place in old palaces and gardens. Salzburg hums with music lovers during its annual Mozart festival in July and August. Elsewhere there are the usual discos, nightclubs, cabarets and casinos. Most foreign movies are dubbed into German, but some movie theaters show them in the original version with subtitles.

Annual events and festivals. *New Year's Day:* Strauss Concert by the Wiener Philharmoniker in Vienna. *January–February:* World Cup ski racing at Innsbruck, Kitzbühel, Schladming and Bad Kleinkirchheim. Ski jumping at Bergisel (near Innsbruck). *February–March:* Carnival (Fasching) preceding Lent. *May:* May Day celebrations in Tyrol. Spring Festival at Neustift (classical and folk music). *May–June:* Vienna Festival (Wiener Festwochen). *Late June–late August:* Carinthian Summer Festival (classical music) at Ossiach and Villach. *July–August:* Salzburg Festival. *Late July–late August:* Bregenz Festival featuring opera, operetta and concerts. *November–December:* Christkindlmarkt (Salzburg—pre-Christmas cakes and candy market). *New Year's Eve:* Emperor's Ball in the Hofburg in Vienna.

Taxes, service charges and tipping. Since a service charge is included in hotel and restaurant bills, tipping is not obligatory. Tipping recommendations: taxi drivers, round off fare, porters 10 S per piece, hatcheck 5–10 S, hairdressers and barbers 10–15%.

Sports and recreation. There are good sports facilities all over the country, with hiking and mountain climbing as obvious favorites. During winter, ski slopes do a brisk trade for all standards of skier with excellent tuition. Tennis, ice skating and riding are available all year round. Top spectator sports are soccer and ice hockey. Also try to attend a trotting derby—there's even one for Viennese Fiaker drivers.

TV and radio. Programs are in German, but news in English is broadcast every day at 8:05 a.m. on Programme One, and American Forces broadcasts can be picked up quite easily. Blue Danube Radio gives information in English.

What to buy. Vienna is a good center for antiques, old coins and stamps. Other favorite buys are Augarten porcelain from the national workshops and *petit point* embroidery on handbags and cushions, loden coats, traditional clothes, hiking boots and dress shoes. Skiing and mountaineering equipment is of excellent quality. Gastronomically speaking, you might want to take home *Schnaps, Tiroler Speck* (cured spiced ham) and *Mozart Kugeln* (marzipan chocolates). As a visitor you can have the sales tax reimbursed (see p. 38).

In Vienna you will find the more elegant shops on the Kärntnerstrasse, Graben and Kohlmarkt.

Shops are open from 8 or 9 a.m. to 6 p.m., Monday through Friday with a break for lunch. On Saturday, most shops close at noon or 1 p.m.

Sightseeing

Vienna. St. Stephen's Cathedral *(Stephansdom)*★ dominating the Inner City; Romanesque western façade, Gothic tower and Baroque altars; intricately patterned roof; carved Gothic pulpit; elevator in the north tower to the cathedral's giant Pummerin bell and splendid view. Hofburg★, home of Austria's rulers since the 13th century, featuring Imperial Chapel *(Burgkapelle)* where the celebrated Vienna Boys' Choir *(Wiener Sängerknaben)* sings Mass Sunday mornings; Imperial Apartments with splendid Gobelin tapestries; Franz Josef's simple bedroom and the Empress Elizabeth's gymnasium; the dining room with its sumptuously laid table. The Treasury *(Schatzkammer)* with the crown jewels. National Library, called the *Prunksaal,* a great oval hall with frescoes and walnut bookcases, built by the famous Viennese architect Fischer von Erlach. The Spanish Riding School, a unique Viennese institution, in a majestic white setting of two galleries, supported on 46 columns, where the Lipizzaner horses perform to the music of gavotte, quadrille and waltz. Graben, fashionable shopping street with its Pillar of the Plague *(Pestsäule)*. Kärntnerstrasse, a traffic-free pedestrian zone with many of Vienna's smartest shops and open-air cafés. Stock-im-Eisen, first mentioned in 1533, where locksmiths arriving in Vienna used to drive a nail. Karlskirche★, by Fischer von Erlach, the most important of the city's Baroque churches, with a dome reminiscent of St. Peter's in Rome. Museum of Fine Arts *(Kunsthistorisches Museum)*★ encompassing a broad spectrum of Western European art, notably a magnificent collection of Pieter Brueghel the Elder, Cellini's gold-enamelled salt-cellar and an Egyptology section including mummified crocodiles. Albertina, the world-famous collection of nearly 40,000 original drawings housed at the south end of the Hofburg. Figarohaus, now museum devoted to Mozart, where the great composer wrote many of his works, notably *The Marriage of Figaro*. The Prater with the Giant Wheel *(Riesenrad)*, dominating the city with its familiar silhouette since 1897. The Opera *(Staatsoper)*, destroyed during the last war, rebuilt in romantic style. The Ring, a great boulevard, encircling the Inner City as a green belt, lined with official buildings, museums, theaters. Vienna's traditional coffee houses. Belvedere, widely regarded as Vienna's finest flowering of Baroque residential architecture, now housing art collections, linked by beautiful Baroque Gardens. Schönbrunn Palace★, the summer residence of the Habsburgs, a masterpiece in the Rococo style of the 18th century, elaborate woodwork in white and gold, crystal chandeliers, immense variety in decoration, the dazzling luxury of the ballrooms and dining

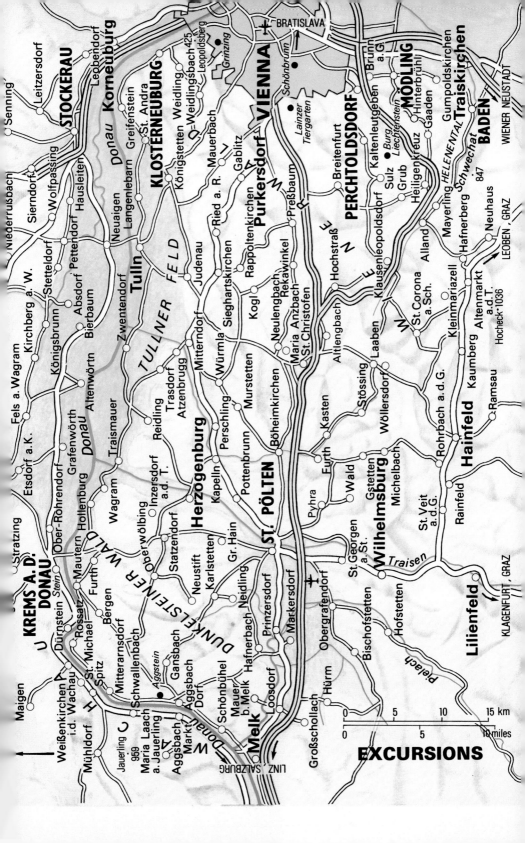

EXCURSIONS

rooms in contrast to another of Emperor Franz Josef's spartan bedrooms; the romantic gardens with the Gloriette, a neo-Classical colonnade on the crest of a hill with panoramic view. Grinzing, wine-growing village with Heurigen wine-gardens, where a pine branch signals that the new white wine can be tasted, to the sound of Schrammel music. Höhenstrasse up to Kahlenberg and Leopoldsberg, with breath-taking view of Vienna and countryside. Abbey of Klosterneuburg with the splendid Verdun Altar of 1181.

Lower Austria and Burgenland. The Wachau*, in the Danube Valley, picturesque landscape with vineyards, rustic villages and medieval castles. Krems, heart of the region's wine industry; Gothic residential architecture of the arcaded Gozzoburg at Hoher Markt, Krems's oldest square, and Renaissance Town Hall *(Rathaus)* with pentagonal bay window. Dürnstein, romantic medieval town, famous as the site of the imprisonment of Richard the Lion-Hearted; wrought-iron signs of the inns along the main street *(Hauptstrasse)*. Melk*, site of fortresslike Benedictine Abbey towering over the Danube; Abbey church with great octagonal dome; the interior decoration including gold ornaments, frescoes and marble. Vienna Woods *(Wienerwald)*, where princes went hunting and composers wrote masterpieces. Heiligenkreuz, Cistercian Abbey from 1135; 13th-century cloister with 300 red columns. Baden, Roman-era spa, where the gentry of Vienna wandered in the Kurpark to the strains of Johann Strauss's walzes. Rohrau, the birthplace of Joseph Haydn, with his beautifully restored thatched-roof house. The shallow Neusiedler See, teeming with wildfowl. Mörbisch, village on the Hungarian border with spotless whitewashed houses decorated with flowers and corn.

Upper Austria. Linz, capital of Upper Austria, a busy port on the Danube; Hauptplatz, the main square, with Trinity column; St. Martin's Church built by Charlemagne in the 8th century; Provincial Museum of Upper Austria. Baroque Abbey of St. Florian, where composer Anton Bruckner was organist; Altdorfer Gallery with paintings by Albrecht Altdorfer, master of the Danubian school, and Imperial Apartments. Steyr with Stadtplatz, the main square, in form of a street lined by fine houses with characteristically overhanging first floor.

Salzkammergut*, enchanting scenery of lakes, mountains, meadows and summer and winter resorts. St. Wolfgang, resort on Wolfgangsee with the legendary White Horse Inn; outstanding 15th-century Gothic altar by Michael Pacher in town church. Bad Ischl, summer residence of Emperor Franz Josef for 70 years; the Imperial villa *(Kaiservilla)* in magnificent garden and Biedermeier-style buildings. Hallstatt, small town clinging to the slope, giving its name to archaeology's Hallstatt Period (1000–500 B.C.); Dachstein Ice Caves and Krippenstein reached by a funicular. Lake Gosau* *(Gosausee),* with remarkable view of Dachstein from lakeside.

Styria. Graz*, university town and capital of Styria; 16th-century Renaissance Landhaus (provincial parliament) featuring courtyard with three tiers of arcades and old well; Arsenal *(Zeughaus)* containing about 29,000 weapons of all kinds. Nearby, Austrian Open Air Museum with old rural homes. The popular winter resort of Schladming.

Salzburg*. Mozart's town. Hohensalzburg, the archbishops' 12th-century castle high above the town; monumental ceramic stove in the Golden Room; Princes' rooms noted for intricate late-Gothic decoration. Getreidegasse, the great shopping street of Salzburg's old town; Renaissance and Baroque façades ornamented by wrought-iron guild signs. Mozart's birthplace at number 9, now an enchanting museum. The 17th-century Residenz, another palace of the powerful archbishops, where the young Mozart conducted many concerts. Mirabell Gardens adorned with statues; grand ceremonial staircase with lovely marble angels. Cathedral *(Dom)* in Italian Renaissance style with Baroque overtones flanked by two symmetrical towers.

Province of Salzburg. Badgastein, spa with radioactive hot springs. Zell am See*, charming lakeside summer and winter resort. Krimml Waterfalls dropping 1,250 feet (380 m.). Grossglockner Highway*, scenic tollway leading south from Zell am See to Heiligenblut with branch road to Franz-Josefs-Höhe and panoramic view of the Grossglockner, highest mountain in Austria (12,454 feet/3,797 m.).

Carinthia. Austria's vacationland. Klagenfurt, business and administrative center of Carinthia. Sophisticated Velden and Pörtschach, popular resorts at the Wörthersee.

The Tyrol*. Important tourist region. Innsbruck*, historic capital of the Tyrol since 1420; site of the 1964 and 1976 Winter Olympic Games; Maria-Theresienstrasse, the main shopping street, with magic panorama of the old town's 15th- and 16th-century houses set against the deep green forest; Triumphal Arch, erected 1765 to celebrate Habsburg wedding; Little Golden Roof *(Goldenes Dachl),* an ornate loggia covered by a roof of gilded copper shingles, symbol of Innsbruck's old

61

town; the bright yellow and white Hofburg, built by Maria Theresa; opulent Rococo decoration and furnishings, particularly in Giant's Hall *(Riesensaal);* Court church *(Hofkirche)* south of the palace featuring the monumental tomb of Maximilian, the emperor surrounded by 28 bronze statues of his ancestors; Museum of Popular Arts *(Tiroler Volkskunstmuseum)* with collection of peasant costumes and Tyrolean interiors and furniture.

Kitzbühel*, elegant, internationally known ski resort. Mayrhofen, resort village; old timbered houses with carved balconies decorated with flowers. Ladis, delightful village of 800-year-old houses; beautiful frescoes around the bay windows. Rattenberg, medieval houses painted in all colors with graceful gable windows, arched doorways. Stams Abbey, a highlight of the Tyrol's monastic Baroque architecture; lavishly decorated, grandiose interior. Seefeld, sophisticated ski resort. St. Anton am Arlberg, pioneer ski resort. Arlberg mountain region. Brenner expressway to the Adriatic region with impressive Europe Bridge.

The Vorarlberg. Bregenz, capital of the province of Vorarlberg and lake resort at Lake Constance; Vorarlberg Museum; cableway to Pfänder with panoramic view of the lake and Bregenz. Medieval fortified town of Feldkirch, with a charming arcaded square. Idyllic summer and winter resorts.

For some useful expressions in German, see p. 226.

BELGIUM
and LUXEMBOURG

Often a battlefield, the land of Flemings
and Walloons plays host to the Eurocrats.

By the standards of many venerable nations of Europe, Belgium is an upstart. A revolution in 1830 established Belgium as an independent kingdom, but freedom has yet to solve the country's cultural problem, a linguistic abyss severing north from south. The Flemings in the northern region, the majority, speak Flemish, while the Walloons in the south are French speaking; and Brussels, in the middle, is warily bilingual.

Belgium is one of Europe's most densely populated and highly industrialized countries. It is also one of the most fought-over. History provided a seemingly endless series of invaders from Caesar and the Vikings to Adolf Hitler, and an over-endowment of famous battlefields, from Waterloo to Ypres to Bastogne.

Belgium has contributed generously to Europe's cultural heritage, starting with the great Flemish artists like Rogier van der Weyden, Pieter Brueghel and Peter Paul Rubens. In the 20th century the country has served the arts in original ways: pace-setting ballet, the surrealism of René Magritte and the detective stories of Georges Simenon.

Gourmets agree that Belgium does wonders with food. The pâté, sausages and smoked ham are great delicacies, and the bracing North Sea coast provides a feast of seafood—all washed down by the exceptionally tasty beer. Experts pronounce Belgian *frites* the world's greatest French-fried potatoes.

The capital of Belgium, Brussels, is the capital of Europe, of the Common Market and NATO and other international bodies. Thanks to the Eurocrats, the cost of living rises faster than the skyscrapers hemming in the Gothic towers of the old town. The provincial centers have their own proud heritage: Bruges, with swans patrolling its canals, is as pretty a town as you'll find. Ghent's lovely old houses and formidable Gothic cathedral stand out. And in the great port and industrial center of Antwerp you can visit the house where Rubens lived, and discover that artists don't have to be poor to be great.

Facts and figures

Population:	10 million
Area:	11,778 sq. miles (30,515 sq. km.)
Capital:	Brussels (*Bruxelles/Brussel*, 150,000/ GUA 1 million)
Other major cities:	Antwerp (*Antwerpen/Anvers*, 490,000) Liège (*Luik*, 440,000) Ghent (*Gent/Gand*, 235,000) Bruges (*Brugge*, 120,000)
Language:	Flemish (60%), French (33%); Flemish is spoken in the north, French in the south, and German in a small area in the east. Brussels is officially bilingual.
Religion:	Catholic (90%)
Time zone:	GMT + 1, EST + 6; DST (Apr.–Sep.)
Currency:	Belgian *franc* (abbr. *BF* or *FB*) = 100 *centimes* Coins: 50 centimes (rare), 1, 5, 20, 50 BF Bills: 100, 500, 1,000, 5,000 BF
Electricity:	220 volt, 50 cycle, AC

Planning your trip

Visa requirements. See pp. 29–30.

Vaccination requirements. None (see also p. 25).

Currency restrictions. There are no limitations on the importing or exporting of either local or foreign currencies.

65

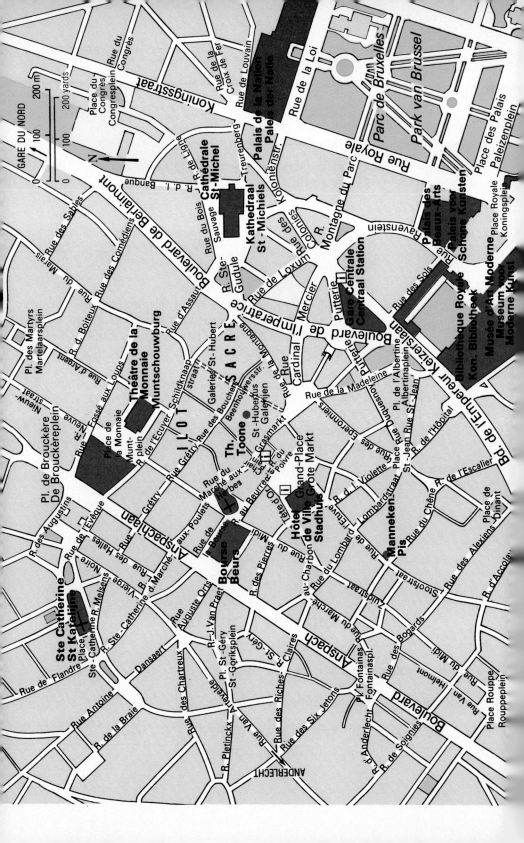

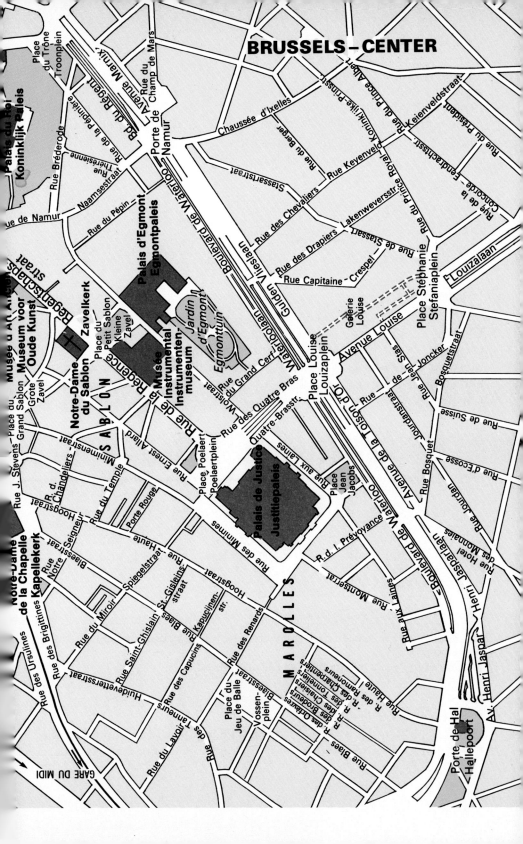

BRUSSELS – CENTER

Climate. From the coast inland to about Brussels, the climate is temperate maritime; in the Ardennes, conditions become more continental with colder winters and warmer summers. Rain can be expected at any time of the year. Snow usually doesn't affect traffic in large cities.

Some average daily temperatures:

Brussels		J	F	M	A	M	J	J	A	S	O	N	D
average daily maximum*	°F	40	44	51	58	65	72	73	72	69	60	48	42
	°C	4	7	10	14	18	22	23	22	21	15	9	9
average daily minimum*	°F	30	32	36	41	46	52	54	54	51	45	38	32
	°C	-1	0	2	5	8	11	12	12	11	7	3	0

* Minimum temperatures are measured just before sunrise, maximum temperatures in the afternoon.

Clothing. Don't forget to take along a sweater or jacket for summer evenings. Warm clothing is essential in winter, and you may need rainwear at any time of the year. In the evenings, at better restaurants and hotels, men are required to wear a jacket (not necessarily a tie).

Duty-free allowances

	Cigarettes		Cigars		Tobacco	Liquor		Wine
1)	200	or	50	or	250 g.	1 l.	and	2 l.
2)	300	or	75	or	400 g.	1½ l.	and	5 l.

Perfume: 1) 50 g.; 2) 75 g.
Toilet water: 1) ¼ l.; 2) ³/₈ l.
Gifts: 1) 2,000 F max. value; 2) 15,800 F max. value

1) goods bought outside EEC countries or duty-free goods bought in EEC countries
2) non-duty-free goods bought in EEC countries

Hotels and accommodations

Hotels. The Belgian National Tourist Office puts out an annual guide. There's no official grading system, but each city's tourist office issues a list of approved hotels, presented according to price and facilities. Room rates must be posted at the reception desk and in each room. Ask for the corporate rate. Advance reservations are recommended. You can make room reservations anywhere in Belgium through a free service offered by Belgique Tourisme Réservations, BTR, P.O. Box 41, 1000 Brussels 23; tel. (02) 230 50 29.

Apartments, bungalows and villas can be rented for a vacation period, particularly in Brussels, the Ardennes or along the coast. Write to the local tourist office for details.

Farmhouse arrangements are becoming popular again, particularly in coastal regions. Ask for the national tourist office's special brochure *Budget Holidays*.

Youth and student accommodations are available in town and in the country. Some addresses are featured in the *Budget Holidays* brochure, but for full details contact your national student travel organization or youth hostel association.

Camping. Belgium has more than 500 government-licensed campsites, graded in four categories. Most are located in the Ardennes and along the coast, but there are some sites in other parts of the country, a few within striking distance of the capital. Ask the Belgian National Tourist Office for its free camping brochure.

In some areas, particularly along the coast, camping is only permitted on recognized sites. Elsewhere, local farmers will often give you permission to pitch a tent on their land for the night.

Belgian tourist offices abroad

U.K.   38 Dover Street, London W1X 3RB;
tel. (071) 499 5379

U.S.A.   745 Fifth Avenue, New York, NY 10022;
tel. (212) 758-8130

On the spot

Banks and currency exchange. Banking hours are generally 9 a.m. to 3:30 or 4 p.m., Monday through Friday. Some banks are open Saturday morning. In Brussels and Antwerp, currency-exchange offices operate in the city center, at the airport and in railroad stations, usually until 9 or 10 p.m. every day of the week.

Credit cards and traveler's checks. Credit cards may be used in many hotels, restaurants, gas stations and stores. Signs are posted indicating which cards are accepted. Traveler's checks are also widely accepted. A standing, flat-rate minimum charge is made for any amount, so you lose money if you cash them in dribs and drabs. Don't forget to take your passport when you go to change money. Eurocheques are accepted by many businesses, including gas stations.

Mail and telecommunications. In Belgium, post offices are separate from telephone and telegraph offices. Look for the words *POSTES/POSTE-RIJEN* in shiny white letters on a red background. Hours are normally from 9 a.m. to 5 p.m. Smaller offices, particularly in the country, may take a lunchtime break or close earlier in the afternoon. In Brussels, the post office at 48 A, avenue de Fonsny (right by Gare du Midi) is open 24 hours a day, every day of the week. Stamps may also be bought from bookshops, newsstands, hotel lobbies and vending machines. Mailboxes are red.

Larger towns have at least one *Téléphone-Télégraphe/Telefoon-Tele-graaf* (TT) office. In Brussels TT offices can be found at 17, boulevard de l'Impératrice (near the Gare Centrale), at rue Henri Maus (next to the Bourse), at 1, avenue de Fonsny (at the Gare du Midi) and at the airport. Away from your hotel the TT office is the place to go to make intercontinental calls, or to send telegrams, telefaxes and telexes. Public telephones can be found at railroad stations, in post offices, department stores and in the street. Phone booths decorated with European national flags can be used to direct-dial to most Western European countries. Instructions are in English, Dutch, French, and German. Take plenty of 5- or 20-franc pieces or buy a "Telecard" (many booths operate with these electronic cards) from the post office. For surcharges and low rates, see p. 30.

Consult the yellow pages if you need a particular service. At the beginning of volume A, you find indexes in English, French, Dutch and German. Some useful telephone numbers:

Information (Brussels)   997
Information (rest of Belgium)   957

Operator (for Europe)	904
Operator (for other countries)	987
Ambulance/Fire brigade	100
Police, gendarmerie, emergency	101

Newspapers. Main dailies are *Le Soir* and *La Libre Belgique* (French) and *Het Laatste Nieuws* and *De Standaard* (Flemish). Foreign newspapers, including the *International Herald Tribune,* are on sale at major newsstands in city centers and at some hotels. The Brussels *Bulletin,* an English-language weekly, covers entertainment and other news of interest to tourists.

Tourist information. Most Belgian towns have a tourist office, usually close to the railroad station or central square. Signs to look for:

French	*Flemish*
Office du tourisme	Verkeersbureau
Syndicat d'initiative	Informatiebureau
Renseignements	Inlichtingen

Opening hours are usually 8:30 or 9 a.m. to noon, and 2 p.m. to 5 or 7 p.m.

Brussels	Grand-Place (Town Hall); tel. (02) 513 89 40
Antwerp	Gildekamerstraat 9; tel. (03) 232 01 03 / 232 22 84
Bruges	Vlamingstraat 55; tel. (050) 33 73 44
Ghent	Borluutstraat 9; tel. (091) 25 36 41 / 23 36 41

Legal holidays

Jan. 1	New Year's Day	**Movable dates:**
May 1	Labor Day	Easter Monday
July 21	National Day	Ascension Day
Aug. 15	Assumption	Whit Monday
Nov. 1	All Saints' Day	
Nov. 11	Armistice Day	
Dec. 25	Christmas Day	

Transportation

Air. Brussels has the only truly international airport in Belgium. A number of European flights go to Antwerp, Liège, Charleroi and Ostend. There are no domestic flights.

Major airport. Brussels National Airport at Zaventem (8 miles/12 km. from city center). Duty-free shop. There is a direct rail link to Gare du Nord or Gare Centrale in Brussels from about 6 a.m. to midnight. Buy your ticket at the station or at the tourist office in the baggage claim hall. Buses connect the airport with Liège, Ghent, Antwerp and Hasselt/Maastricht.

Rail. Belgium's rail network provides good coverage of the country, and international links are good. Some trains have dining cars. Trains are classed as I/C (Intercity), I/R (Inter-regional), P (Rush-hour service) and L (Local) in descending order of rapidity. The capital's five main rail stations are Gare du Nord for domestic and international trains and the airport shuttle, Gare Centrale for domestic trains and the airport shuttle, Gare du Midi for domestic and international trains, Gare de Schaerbeek for auto trains, and Gare du Quartier Léopold for domestic trains and some departures to Luxembourg.

Tourists will find the *B-Tourrail* good value. It entitles the holder to 5 days unrestricted travel within a period of 17 days anywhere in Belgium. Another flat-rate ticket, the *Benelux Tourrail* pass, must be bought in Belgium, the Netherlands or Luxembourg. All other tickets are easiest to get in Belgium. For *Eurailpass,* see p. 33.

Local public transportation. Most Belgian cities are served by buses, and Brussels, Antwerp and Ghent also operate streetcars and subway systems. For the subway, buy tickets at the station. In Brussels and Antwerp, buy bus and streetcar tickets on board. If you plan to use public transportation a great deal, special reduced tickets are available for either a number of trips or for a specified length of time. Ask for details at subway information offices.

Taxis. Cabs wait at taxi stands, outside stations, large hotels and other key points in the city. You can also order them by telephone. Taxis are metered and the price is all-inclusive for any number of passengers or amount of luggage; no supplement is charged for night trips. Rates increase once the taxi leaves the city limits. Traveling by taxi is expensive, but a tip is not expected.

Car rental. Addresses to international and local rental firms can be found in the yellow pages. The best-known companies have desks at Brussels airport. Chauffeur-driven cars are also available. Credit cards are the preferred means of payment. See also pp. 30–31.

Driving in Belgium. Drive on the right, pass on the left. The car must carry a red reflector warning triangle, a first-aid kit and a fire-

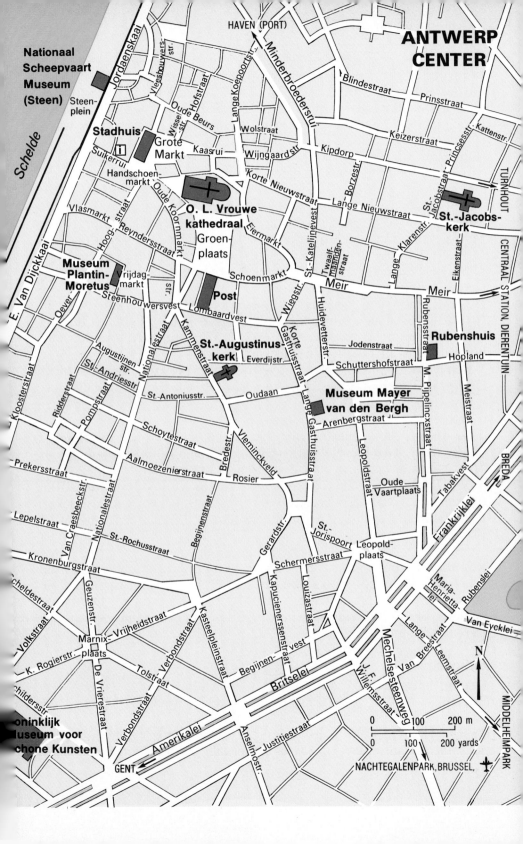

extinguisher. Seat belts are compulsory and children under 12 years are not allowed in the front seat. Blood alcohol limit is 80 mg./100 ml. Gasoline available is normal (90–94 octane), super (98–100 octane), lead-free and diesel. Speed limits are 75 mph (120 kph) on expressways, 37 mph (60 kph) in towns, and otherwise as signposted.

To park in a "blue zone", buy a special disc from a garage, bookshop or newsstand. Otherwise look for signs marked 1–15 and 16–31 and bisected by a red slash: these mean that parking is not permitted on that side of the road on the dates noted. The Roman figures I and II indicate alternate side of the street parking on odd and even days respectively. Many roads don't have marked traffic lanes, but are generally well surfaced. Expressways are fully lighted right across the country. Yield right of way to traffic coming from the right unless otherwise indicated. Streetcars have priority at all times. In case of a breakdown, use the emergency phones along expressways, or telephone (02) 736 59 59 (Royal Automobile Club de Belgique, Brussels), (02) 233 22 11 (Touring Club de Belgique, Brussels) or (03) 252 62 70 (Vlaamse Automobilistenbond in Antwerp) for further instructions.

Some distances: Brussels–Antwerp 29 miles (46 km.), Liège 43 miles (70 km.), Ostend 73 miles (118 km.).

Bicycle rental. Heavy city traffic and inadequate cycle paths in Brussels deter all but the keenest cyclist, but the suburban Forêt de Soignes offers many safe bicycle paths through scenic woods. Look under "Bicyclettes & cyclomoteurs"/"Fietsen & bromfietsen" in the yellow pages. Bicycles can also be rented at certain railroad stations. Rail travelers are given priority and reduced rates, so show your rail ticket. Best areas for cycling are in the provinces of Antwerp and West Flanders.

Rest rooms. Public rest rooms can be found in larger subway and rail stations, department stores and museums. If there's an attendant on duty, a tip is customary. Street facilities are best avoided. Doors are marked *WC, Toilettes/Toiletten, Dames* (ladies) and *Messieurs/Heren* (gentlemen).

Emergencies

Doctor emergency,		Ambulance	100
Brussels	648 80 00	Gendarmerie	101

Police. The "men in blue" come in two varieties: the municipal *police/politie* and the *gendarmerie/rijkswacht*. As a rule, the police are the ones you turn to for information or assistance—while the *gendarmerie* deal with large-scale operations such as crowd control and traffic supervision.

Crime and theft. Standard precautions are in order—deposit documents and valuables in the hotel safe, and leave the glove compartment in your car empty and open. Pickpockets are a fact of life by the Grand-Place, the Bourse and at Brussels' Sunday market near Gare du Midi, and it's best to avoid the red-light district near Gare du Nord after dark.

Medical care and health. Clinics and hospitals are plentiful. It's said that in case of emergency one is never more than a 20-minute ride away from a medical center in Belgium. Health care is of high standard but expensive. Many doctors speak English. Pharmacies are recognized by a green cross. A few pharmacies in every district stay open after hours. Weekly lists of those on duty are posted outside every pharmacy, and in the weekend newspapers. For insurance, see pp. 25–26.

Tap water is drinkable.

Embassies and consulates. These are grouped together under the heading "Ambassades, consulats"/"Ambassades, Consulaten" in the telephone directory.

Social customs. Belgians have great respect for social formalities and take some time to get onto a first-name basis. At social gatherings, it's usual to greet and say goodbye to each person individually with a handshake. In shops, restaurants, on the telephone or wherever, always start off with a polite word of greeting.

Enjoying Belgium

Food and drink. If you think that a vacation in Belgium means an unremitting diet of freshly caught mussels, steamed and served with a savory broth, French fries *(frites)* that have been fried once and then dipped again briefly into boiling oil to give a special crackly finish, and one or more of Belgium's four excellent traditional beers, well that's up to you. All three specialties are available in abundance and are excellent, but it doesn't stop there. Belgium boasts a wide range of eating places from taverns and cafés that serve a meat platter, some pâté, sausage or cheese with a salad and a glass of wine or beer, to elegant restaurants.

Wherever you go, portions are huge and second helpings usually follow as a matter of course.

The standard of cuisine is high whether it's a simple steak grilled over a wood fire or an unexpected but mouthwatering combination of rabbit with prunes. Belgium offers many specialties. Among the hors d'oeuvres is a beer soup *(soupe à la bière)* made with beer, chicken stock and onions, or pâté known as *potjesvlees* of veal, pork and rabbit. *Flamiche* is a savory cheese pie with leeks or onions, and *tomate aux crevettes* are tomatoes filled with shrimps and mayonnaise.

The best-known main dish is probably *waterzooi,* traditionally chicken but sometimes fish stewed with leeks in bouillon with cream and egg yolks. *Anguille au vert* is eel flavored with any number of green herbs, but most popularly sorrel, sage and parsley. Two splendid stews are the *carbonnade,* pieces of lean beef browned in a pan and then cooked with lots of onions and beer, and the Flemish *hochepot* which uses oxtail or pigs' feet, ears and snout. *Lapin à la flamande* is made of pieces of rabbit marinated in beer and vinegar and then braised in onions and prunes. Excellent game comes from the Ardennes.

Among the vegetables are *asperges de Malines,* locally grown asparagus dressed with melted butter and crumbled hard-boiled eggs, and, naturally, *choux de Bruxelles.* The Brussels sprouts are usually prepared with chestnuts and pieces of bacon, and then cooked lightly in goose fat.

Afterwards, try the strong *remoudou* cheese, or the *djotte de Nivelles,* or look for the two-layered pancake filled with cheese known as a *double.* The best-known dessert is waffles *(gaufres),* but why not try the *crêpes aux pommes* (apple pancakes), *beignets de Bruxelles* (a type of fritter), *tarte au riz* (rice tart), *manons* (chocolate filled with fresh cream) or the famous *speculoos* (spicy gingerbreads cut in the shape of kings, queens, bishops and knights).

There's a good choice of beer with your meal: Gueuze—slightly sour with a fine foaming head, Lambic—a younger beer with no head but a lot of strength, Faro—similar to Lambic but with much lower alcohol content, and more difficult to find nowadays, and Kriek—a reddish beer with the fruity taste of cherries that are added during the Lambic's fermentation. Around Antwerp you may find *trappiste* beer, a dark malt, and *pils,* a light beer. Belgium doesn't produce any notable wines, but restaurants pride themselves on providing a wide and sensitive selection of French and German wines. You won't find any liquor in bars, only in restaurants, but try the *péguet,* a slightly sweet gin produced around Brussels.

Lunch is served from 12 to 3 p.m., dinner 7 to 10 p.m.

Entertainment. Music plays an important part in Brussels' and Antwerp's cultural life. Opera is of an internationally high standard in both cities. Concerts and recitals are held all over the city during summer. A special Brussels attraction is the puppet theater which offers a program of *Macbeth, Faust* and *The Count of Monte Cristo* delivered in a mixture of classical French and Brussels patois. Brussels is also the place for nightclubs and discos. Movies are shown in their original version with French and Dutch subtitles.

Annual events and festivals. Many of Belgium's popular festivals find their roots in religious events. Mardi Gras is celebrated all over Belgium, with dancing and processions. At most of the seaside towns, masses are said in the summer to bless the sea. A charity ball known as the Ball of the Dead Rat and the Shrimp Ball in the fishermen's district are held in Ostend. Check with the local tourist office. *May:* Queen Elisabeth of Belgium Music Competition in Brussels. Holy Blood Procession at Bruges. *May/June:* Port Festival in Blankenberge. *July:* Brussels' largest festival—the Ommegang pageant.

Taxes, service charges and tipping. Sales tax (abbreviated BTW or TVA) and service charges are almost always included in hotel and restaurant bills. Anything extra for the waiter is optional. Airport porters have fixed rates, taxi rates are all-inclusive. Tipping recommendations: hotel porters or bellboys 30 BF per bag or errand, hatcheck 20 BF, barbers 20%, and movie/theater ushers 10 BF per person.

Sports and recreation. Cycling, whether at Tour de France speed or more gently on a tricycle made for two, is a popular Belgian pastime. A good ride is from Knokke-Heist along the sea-wall to the Dutch border and back. Sand-sailing and water sports like windsurfing and waterskiing are also popular. You can rent a boat for a quiet sail or go fishing (buy a permit at the post office for inland fishing). Hikers have marked trails that go all over the countryside, while horse riding is best in the Forest of Soignes. There are golf courses in Brussels, Ghent, Antwerp, Ostend and Knokke-Heist. For tennis, ask at the tourist office for the nearest courts.

TV and radio. Belgian cable television feeds in as many as 24 channels in Flemish and French, including programs from Britain (BBC 1 and BBC 2), France, Germany, Luxembourg and, frequently in English, the Netherlands, but not CNN yet.

You'll be able to listen to English-language stations on your hotel radio or any portable one. Broadcasts include the U.S. Armed Forces Network on 101.7 FM and the BBC World Service on 648 medium wave/AM. On the Dutch-language TV channels, foreign movies and interviews are generally shown in the original language with subtitles.

What to buy. Favorite buys include lace, machine-made or handmade; handwoven tapestries found in antique shops in the Sablon area; glassware and crystal from Liège, Charleroi and Malines on sale in Brussels' Avenue Louise and on the *grands boulevards;* pewter brought in from Halle, and leather, a Brussels specialty; wooden toys made in Spa and Verviers. Antwerp is the place for diamonds and wrought ironware. Edible souvenirs include *pralines* (filled chocolates), *babeluttes* (hard candies) and *speculoos* (gingerbread).

Stores are generally open from 9:15 or 9:30 a.m. to 6:30 p.m., Monday through Saturday. Most department stores stay open at midday, but smaller shops close for an hour or two.

Sightseeing

Brussels. Capital of Europe, headquarters of the Common Market and NATO. The Grand-Place*, one of Europe's finest medieval squares bounded by magnificent Renaissance-style houses formerly belonging to guilds and corporations; flower market and bird market on Sundays. Gothic Town Hall *(Hôtel de Ville)* on the square, tower topped with a copper statue of Saint Michael slaying the devil. Municipal Museum in King's House *(Maison du Roi)*, with some 14th- and 15th-century original stone sculptures from the Town Hall façade. Nearby Manneken-Pis, the city mascot, a 24-inch (0.6-m.) bronze statue of a boy watering a fountain, designed by Duquesnoy in 1619. North of Grand-Place, L'Ilot Sacré (The Sacred Isle), a largely traffic-free area where some of the restored houses contain restaurants, art galleries and craft shops. The Galeries St.-Hubert, glass-vaulted arcades of boutiques and

restaurants, an idea pioneered by Jean-Pierre Cluysenaar in 1846. The city opera house *(Théatre de la Monnaie)*, where the first rumbles of the 1830 revolution took place, leading to national independence. Gothic St. Michael's Cathedral* featuring five 16th-century stained-glass windows showing the town's Spanish, Burgundian and Austrian rulers; beautiful Chapelle du Saint-Sacrement. Le Sablon*, now elegant district with antique shops and restaurants. Grand Sablon Square, bordered by 17th- and 18th-century houses with restored façades, site of weekend antique market. Petit Sablon Square offering a peaceful garden with 19th-century bronze statues. Elegant porch and Baroque pulpit in Gothic Church of Notre-Dame du Sablon. Les Marolles, busy working-class neighborhood. Notre-Dame de la Chapelle, with mausoleum of the great artist Pieter Brueghel; and the house where he is supposed to have lived. Porte de Hal, remnants of city's 14th-century fortified ramparts. 18th-century Royal Palace, the office of the King, overlooking Brussels Park. Gigantic Palace of Justice, the biggest building erected in the 19th century, dominating the city. Fine Arts Museum divided in two: Museum of Ancient Art *(Musée d'Art Ancien)** up to mid-19th century with excellent collection of Brueghel and Rubens; and Museum of Modern Art with fine late 19th- and 20th-century collections. Royal Museum of Art and History*, vast collections from all over the world, from china to sedan chairs. The Instrument Museum with rare musical instruments. Brewery Museum tracing brewing through the years in a country where beer is the favorite drink. Avenue Louise, the city's most elegant shopping street. Bois de la Cambre, the citizens' favorite park and a lovely setting for a picnic, at the end of Avenue Louise. House of Erasmus in the borough of Anderlecht, where the great humanist once lived, now an attractive museum.

West Flanders. Sandy beaches, excellent sporting facilities. Oostduin-kerke with the last horseback fishermen of Europe. Blankenberge, resort for festivals, parades, jazz and cabaret. Knokke-Heist, one of Europe's most elegant resorts with casino. Delightful natural reserve of the Zwin close to the Dutch border. De Hann, known as the "green resort", with sandy, pine-scented woods. De Panne specializing in sand-yachting. Channel ports of Ostend and Zeebrugge.

Bruges*, the province's principal city; 13th-century belfry *(Belfort)* housing Europe's most famous carillon, with 47 bells and covered market *(Halle)** at the Markt; neo-Gothic Government Palace, seat of Provincial Council of West Flanders; Basilica of St. Basil and of the Holy Blood built in 12th century and Museum of the Holy Blood containing golden and silver reliquary; Town Hall *(Stadhuis)* begun in

1376; lovely Green Quay *(Groene Rei)* with its tree-lined gardens bordering the canal; Carolingian Church of St. Donation (ca. 900); fine lace collection in Storie House, home of portrait painter Jose Storie; Groeninge Museum* with rich collection of early Flemish paintings; Church of Our Lady *(Onze Lieve Vrouwekerk)*, famous for its white marble Madonna by Michelangelo; mausoleums of Mary of Burgundy and Charles the Bold; Beguinage *(Begijnhof)*, founded in 1245, today inhabited by Benedictine nuns; St. Savior's Cathedral *(St.-Salvator)*, oldest church in Bruges with remarkable stained-glass windows and beautifully carved 15th-century choir stalls; St. Walburga's Church with remarkable communion table and pulpit; Jerusalem Church, built according to the plans of the Holy Sepulchre in Jerusalem; Folklore Museum containing West Flanders folklore, popular art and costumes; St. Janshuismolen windmill (1770); Town gates with remnants of medieval fortifications; world's first stock exchange house *(ter Beurze)* (15th century); Memling Museum* installed in 800-year-old hospital of St. John, with collection of Memling paintings.

Series of signposted routes in countryside including Bachten-de-Kupe Route to medieval town of Lo and moated castle at Beauvoorde, Stijn Streuvels Route to historic city of Kortrijk in old flax region and Molenland Route, known for its windmills.

Ghent. Panoramic view of city from St. Michael's Bridge. Old Flemish Gothic and Renaissance guild houses on Graslei (Grass Quay)* and Koornlei (Corn Quay), contrasting with austere 12th-century warehouse. 15th-century Drapers' Hall *(Lakenhalle)*, center of Ghent's ancient prosperity. Town Hall *(Stadhuis)*, an attractive mix of Gothic and Renaissance. St. Bavon's Cathedral *(Sint-Baafskathedraal)* in buttermilk and gray stone and red brick, built 13th to 16th centuries; crypt with murals and church treasure. Joost Vydt Chapel, housing the polyptych by Jan Van Eyck, *The Adoration of the Mystic Lamb*. Moated Gravensteen Castle featuring dungeons and museum of instruments of torture. Dulle Griet (Angry Maggie), enormous iron cannon used in the 15th century to fire 750-pound (340-kg.) stone balls. Museum voor Volkskunde (Folklore Museum) based in a 14th-century children's home. Fine Arts Museum *(Museum voor Schone Kunsten)* and Museum van Oudheden in the Abbey of Bijloke with collection of old artefacts.

Antwerp. Europe's third largest port and important diamond market. Gothic cathedral* with octagonal dome and majestic steeple built during 14th and 15th centuries; houses clustering round the walls giving

81

impression of parish integrated with its church; Rubens masterpieces in the ten chapels; St. Anthony's chapel with a stained-glass window (1503) of Henry VII of England kneeling with his queen. Green Square *(Groenplaats)*, once a cemetery, now a lively square with open-air cafés, trees and statue of Rubens. Town Hall *(Stadhuis)*, a combination of Renaissance columns and Gothic lattice windows and gables. Grand-Place *(Grote Markt)* lined by guild houses, restored to original 16th-century splendor. Brabo fountain, giving the town its name: *hand werpen* (hand-throw). Rubens' House *(Rubenshuis)*★, containing Rubens' personal collection of ancient sculpture, Italian and Flemish art and some of Rubens' work. Rubens Chapel in St.-Jacobskerk, where the artist and his family are buried. Plantin-Moretus Museum★, the elegant Renaissance house of Christophe Plantin with a marvelous history of printing, books and handwriting; most precious exhibit Biblia Regia (Polyglot Bible) in eight volumes, printed between 1568 and 1572 in five languages; Gutenberg Bible from 1455 and a copy of Papal Index of forbidden books, from 1569. Royal Museum of Fine Arts *(Koninklijk Museum voor Schone Kunsten)*★ housing a first-class collection of Flemish art, with works by Rubens. National Maritime Museum *(Nationaal Scheepvaart Museum)* in a castle known as the Steen, informing about Antwerp's long relationship with the sea. Tours of the busy port★.

Wallonia. Tournai★ with Romanesque Notre Dame Cathedral from 12th and 13th centuries and Museum of Fine Arts displaying Flemish masters like Rubens. Town of Waterloo with Wellington Museum; south of the battlefield Ferme du Caillou, Napoleon's headquarters; Butte du Lion with monument honoring the place where Prince of Orange was wounded; fine view of the battlefield from the mound with cast-iron lion; La Belle Alliance, the farm where Blücher and Wellington met to congratulate each other. Liège, large river port and gateway to the Ardennes, featuring Fine Arts Museum and Museum of Folklore *(Musée de la Vie wallonne)*. The Ardennes★, lovely vacationland of rolling wooded hills, charming small towns with inviting inns, excellent campsites and tasty game; Bastogne where World War II Battle of the Bulge took place. Dinant in Meuse Valley, with collegiate church and citadel. Namur, dominated by rocky cliff with citadel; 18th-century cathedral and Archaeological Museum; luxury casino. The village of Binche, famous for its Shrove Tuesday carnival.

For some useful expressions in Dutch, see p. 352.
For some useful expressions in French, see p. 196.

Luxembourg

Although it is small and quaint, Luxembourg can't be confused with one of those Ruritanian ministates, postage-stamp-sized enclaves of folklore and philately. This country of considerable economic power is an increasingly cosmopolitan pivot of European politics and high finance. The blast furnaces and factories are hidden amid rustic charm, while the smokeless industries of banking and international affairs add sophistication to the spectacularly perched capital city.

Surrounded by France, Belgium and Germany, the Grand Duchy of Luxembourg has always been a highspot on the classic European invasion routes. In the 20th century Germany invaded Luxembourg in two world wars. While today's tourists inspect the capital's historic forts connected by miles of tunnels, the nation is defended by an army scarcely a couple of battalions strong.

Luxembourg contains hundreds of square miles of thick forest as well as mountains, grazing land and vineyards. The Mosel River valley produces some dry white wines that bring credit to Luxembourg and inspire tasting tours for connoisseurs.

With an overwhelmingly Catholic population, Luxembourg is inclined to picturesque religious processions, solemn or joyous. The polyglot people have a language for every occasion: they all speak French, German and the *Letzebuergisch* dialect of medieval German, and most can express themselves in English as well.

Luxembourg City, with its clifftop setting, is a base for tours of the countryside, where medieval villages have been faithfully restored after the passing of World War II. The capital itself is a model of the prosperity sought by the European Community, whose bureaucrats throng the city for meetings of the Council of Ministers and other international bodies. In at least one area of contemporary achievement Luxembourg can't compete with most of its EC partners: the nightlife is subdued.

Facts and figures

Population:	365,000
Area:	999 sq. miles (2,586 sq. km.)
Capital:	Luxembourg (80,000)
Language:	National language is "Letzebuergisch", a local dialect of German; French and German are official languages
Religion:	Catholic (95%)
Time zone:	GMT + 1, EST + 6; DST (Apr.–Sep.)
Currency:	Luxembourg *franc* (abbr. *F*) = 100 *centimes*. (The Belgian franc is also in wide circulation at parity.) Coins: 50 centimes (rare); F 1, 5, 20, 50 Bills: F 100, 500, 1,000, 5,000
Electricity:	220 volt, 50 cycle, AC

Planning your trip

Visa requirements. See pp. 29–30.

Vaccination requirements. None (see also p. 25).

Currency restrictions. None.

Climate. Luxembourg enjoys a mild continental climate with few extremes. Fog is common in autumn, and snowfall can be quite heavy in winter.

Some average daily temperatures:

Luxembourg		J	F	M	A	M	J	J	A	S	O	N	D
average daily maximum*	°F	37	40	49	57	65	70	73	71	66	56	44	39
	°C	3	4	10	14	18	21	23	22	19	13	7	4

* Minimum temperatures are measured just before sunrise, maximum temperatures in the afternoon.

average daily	°F	29	31	35	40	46	52	55	54	50	43	37	33
minimum*	°C	-1	-1	1	4	8	11	13	12	10	6	3	0

Clothing. Dress should be suitable for a generally temperate climate. Take along a sweater and a jacket in the summer and warm outer clothes in winter. A raincoat is advisable at all times of the year.

Duty-free allowances

	Cigarettes		Cigars		Tobacco	Liquor	Wine
1)	300	or	75	or	400 g.	1½ l. and	5 l.
2)	200	or	50	or	250 g.	1 l. and	2 l.

Perfume: 1) 75 g.; 2) 50 g.
Toilet water: 1) ³/₈ l.; 2) ¼ l.
Gifts: 1) F 15,800 max. value; 2) F 2,000

1) non-duty-free merchandise bought in EEC countries
2) merchandise bought outside EEC countries or duty-free merchandise bought in EEC countries

Hotels and accommodations

Hotels. Luxembourg city has only a limited number of hotels, so reservations should be made well in advance, particularly during the high season and for weekends. The booklet *Hotels, Auberges, Restaurants, Pensions* is available at the rail station, the airport and at tourist offices.

Camping. There are several campsites in Luxembourg. Ask for the camping guide issued by the tourist office.

Luxembourg tourist offices abroad

U.K. Luxembourg National Tourist Office, 36/37 Piccadilly, London W1V 9PA; tel. (071) 434 2800

U.S.A. 801 Second Ave., New York, NY 10017; tel. (212) 370-9850

On the spot

Banks and currency exchange. Banking hours are 8:30 a.m. to noon, 2 to 4:30 p.m., Monday through Friday. Foreign currency can also be changed at the railroad station and airport virtually day and night, seven days a week, otherwise at some of the larger hotels.

Credit cards and traveler's checks. Most credit cards and traveler's checks are widely accepted in the capital.

Mail and telecommunications. Post-office hours are 8 a.m. to noon, and 2 to 4:30 p.m. at city offices, and variable in country districts. The post office at the railroad station is open 24 hours a day, and the one at the airport from 7 a.m. to 10 p.m.

Direct dialing operates within Luxembourg and to many other countries. The two main post offices have public telex facilities. For surcharges and low rates, see p. 30.

Some useful telephone numbers:

Information		Operator	
(domestic)	017	(international)	0010
Information		Emergencies	012
(international)	016		

Newspapers. Main local dailies are *Républicain Lorrain* (French) and *Luxembourger Wort* (German). Most major European newspapers, including the Paris-edited *International Herald Tribune,* are available at large newsstands.

Tourist information

Luxembourg   City tourist office, Place d'Armes; tel. 22 809

Legal holidays

Jan. 1	New Year's Day	**Movable dates:**
May 1	Labor Day	First Monday of Lent
June 23	National Day	Easter Monday
Aug. 15	Assumption	Ascension
Nov. 1	All Saints' Day	Whit Monday
Nov. 2	All Souls' Day	
Dec. 25, 26	Christmas	

Transportation

Air. The Grand Duchy's only commercial airport, near the capital, is served by direct flights from a number of major European and North American cities.

Airport. Luxembourg: Findel (4 miles/7 km. from city center). Duty-free shop. Short- and long-term parking is available, and there is a regular bus service to and from the station (air terminal).

Rail. Access by train is quite easy from most points. The *Benelux Tourrail* ticket, valid for 16 days of unlimited travel within Luxembourg, Belgium and the Netherlands, can be bought at a local travel agency or railroad station. For *Eurailpass,* see p. 33.

Local public transportation. Both the capital and the Grand Duchy as a whole are served by an adequate bus network.

Taxis. Telephone numbers for various taxi services (at the airport, in the capital and in the country) are listed in the telephone directory.

Car rental. Among the international and local agencies represented in Luxembourg, some have desks at the airport. See also pp. 28–29.

Driving in Luxembourg. The car should carry a red reflector warning triangle to be used in case of emergency. Seat belts must be worn. Blood alcohol limit is 80 mg./100 ml. Gasoline available is normal (90–92 octane), lead-free (95 octane), super (98–99 octane) and diesel.

Drive on the right, pass on the left. Using the horn in the capital is forbidden. Speed limits are 31 or 37 mph (50 or 60 kph) in built-up areas, 75 mph (120 kph) on expressways, and 56 mph (90 kph) on other roads. Expressways to Brussels in Belgium and Trier in Germany are under construction. Unless indicated otherwise you must give way to traffic coming from the right. In case of a breakdown, call 31 10 31.

Emergencies. In an emergency (ambulance, police, fire) dial 012.

Police. Local police impose on-the-spot speeding fines.

Crime and theft. As everywhere crime is on the increase, but only normal commonsense precautions need be taken.

Medical care and health. Health services are very good but expensive. The capital has a hospital and an outpatient clinic. Many doctors in the capital speak English. One city pharmacy remains open at all times; see the daily newspapers for details. For insurance, see pp. 25–26.

Tap water is safe to drink.

Embassies and consulates. Look in the telephone directory under "Ambassades" or "Consulats".

Social customs. Luxembourgers are friendly and like to use their foreign-language skills. They're delighted when visitors use the local dialect for phrases of greeting and thanks. Despite the large number of foreigners that reside in or transit through their country, Luxembourgers jealously guard their separate identity and should by no means be considered as vaguely French, German or Belgian.

Enjoying Luxembourg

Food and drink. There is no shortage of good food in modestly priced restaurants, both in Luxembourg city and the country towns and villages. The rivers of the Grand Duchy supply fine crayfish, pike and trout, while other specialties include *treipen* (black pudding) and sausages, served with mashed potatoes and horseradish, and delicious Ardennes ham. *Frites* (the local version of French fried potatoes) are to be found everywhere and it's worth trying *rou tou tou*, an unusual vegetable dish made from potatoes and onions.

Dessert can either be one of the locally produced cheeses or a pastry such as the *tarte aux quetsches* which is made with small plums.

Beers are brewed without chemical additives, and the local white Mosel wines are very drinkable. There are some locally distilled liqueurs if you feel like something stronger.

Lunch is served from noon to 2 p.m., dinner 8 to 9:30 p.m.

Entertainment. There are a few nightclubs near the rail station. The discos and movie theaters are also located near the center of town. Movies are generally shown in their original language with subtitles. Plays (in French and German), ballets and operas are occasionally staged. In summer, daily concerts animate the Place d'Armes.

Annual events and festivals. Check with the local tourist office so you don't miss local festivals. *May:* Dancing Procession in Echternach. *June–July:* Classical Music Festival at Echternach. *July:* Theater and Music Festival at Wiltz. *September:* Grape and Wine Festival in Grevenmacher.

Taxes, service charges and tipping. Tax and service charges are generally included in hotel and restaurant bills. Tipping recommendations: round up payments to taxi drivers, hairdressers and waiters; porters at the airport F 20–25 per bag; at the theater, etc. a F 20 hatcheck charge may be obligatory.

Sports and recreation. There is a fine 18-hole golf course near the airport, while the River Mosel and Petite Suisse regions provide recreation in the form of hiking, camping and boating. Ice skating is popular in winter.

Soccer, handball and basketball are the most popular spectator sports.

TV and radio. TV programming is in French. German, Belgian and French telecasts can also be picked up. Radio broadcasts are in French or German. Radio Luxembourg puts out an English-language program, "Community Radio", between 2 and 5:30 p.m., and also broadcasts in English throughout the night.

What to buy. Among souvenirs worth taking home are the cast-iron miniature firebacks, called *tak*, which depict castles, arms and other subjects in the Grand Duchy. There is delicately decorated porcelain, crystal and earthenware pottery. Or you can take back some records of authentic Luxembourg songs, and a bottle of local wine or liqueur.

Shopping hours are 8 a.m. to noon and 2 to 6 p.m., Tuesday through Saturday, and 2 to 6 p.m. on Mondays.

Sightseeing

Luxembourg*. City divided into districts connected by 110 bridges and five viaducts. Ruins of Bock Fortress on promontory surrounded by Alzette River. The Fishmarket with many historic buildings at the crossroads of the Roman roads. Gate of Three Towers from the 11th century. Monumental Citadel of St. Esprit dominating the lands of the south. Across the river ancient shrine of the Chapel of St. Quirinus. Remarkable 13-mile (21-km.) network of underground passages, casemates, hewn from rock, linking 53 forts. Beautiful Corniche promenade following 17th-century ramparts around Old City, view of Rham plateau. Valuable collection of 17th- to 19th-century paintings in gallery of the Pescatore Foundation. State Museums in the Fishmarket housing various art, archaeological and natural history collections. Magnificent Grand Ducal Palace with strong Italian Renaissance influence. 17th-century Church of St. Michel with 10th-century foundations. Gothic Cathedral of Notre Dame built by the Jesuits, with monument at the tomb of Count John the Blind. National Library in former Jesuit college. Grand Duchess Charlotte bridge leading from Pfaffenthal quarter to European Centre on the Kirchberg plateau. Shopping in the lively Place d'Armes, Wednesday and Saturday markets in Place Guillaume.

Excursions. Crossroads in Ettelbruck named for Attila the Hun. Clervaux with 12th-century castle and photo-essay "The Family of Man". North to Vianden through beautiful, wild hills and valleys, with ruined castles. Treasures of medieval Vianden*, including splendid castle, now restored, and a small museum in the house where author Victor Hugo lived in exile. Through Ardennes, south to Diekirch, unspoiled and peaceful. Romantic rocky terrain of the Moellerdall, known as Petite Suisse "pocket Switzerland"*. Wide range of attractions (hang-gliding, swimming, boating, hiking) in Echternach with 15th-century Town Hall, Louis XIV pavilion, Benedictine Abbey and stately burghers' homes. Spa waters at Mondorf-les-Bains. Unique mining museum at Rumelange 295 feet (90 m.) underground.

For some useful expressions in French, see p. 196.
For some useful expressions in German, see p. 226.

BULGARIA

*In the Balkans, the cradle of Slavic
culture rocks to a bagpipe's wail.*

Land of antique gold and fragrant fields of roses, of rugged Balkan mountains and smooth Black Sea beaches, Bulgaria straddles a crossroads of conquest whose turbulent history goes back more than 2,500 years. Then it was Thrace, an important kingdom of Hellenic times. It became Bulgaria in the early 9th century when invading Bulgars from Central Asia, followed by Slavs, founded a nation that is one of Europe's oldest survivors.

The mountains cover two-thirds of the country, great for skiing in winter and for hiking, riding and camping in summer. They were a refuge for Bulgarian Christians during more than 500 years of Turkish occupation that began in the 1300s. In their cliffs and on remote ridges Bulgarians built fortress monasteries, notably at Rila, where the Slavonic language and Cyrillic alphabet were preserved.

In the valleys, river basins and along the Danube are picturesque villages where the upper storeys of timbered houses project over narrow cobbled streets. In the long Valley of the Roses, these flowers are the cash crop, grown as a major export: oil for perfume. Elsewhere you'll see fields of Turkish tobacco, vineyards that produce excellent red wine, and everywhere the little goats that are milked to make Bulgaria's delicious yoghurt.

Thracian tombs stand out as rounded hillocks in the plains. At Plovdiv, the second city after Sofia, the capital, golden treasures from the 4th century B.C. are on display, along with a Roman theater. The frescoes of the royal tomb at Kazanlak are also protected as a World Heritage site, as is the Byzantine church at Boaiana on the outskirts of Sofia. The gold-domed capital sits in a plain, surrounded by mountains that are snow-capped in winter.

The Black Sea beach resorts with their high-rise hotels represent one side of today's Bulgaria. As new political freedom sweeps the region, post-Communist Bulgaria is eagerly wooing visitors from the West.

Facts and figures

Population:	8.9 million
Area:	42,823 sq. miles (110,911 sq. km.)
Capital:	Sofia (1.2 million)
Other major cities:	Plovdiv (540,000) Varna (355,000) Bourgas (285,000) Russe (200,000) Stara Zagora (140,000) Pleven (130,000)
Language:	Bulgarian
Religion:	Predominantly Bulgarian Orthodox (96%)
Time zone:	GMT + 2, EST + 7; DST (Apr.–Sep.)
Currency:	*Lev* (plural *leva*) = 100 *stotinki* Coins: 1, 2, 5, 10, 20, 50 stotinki; 1, 2 leva Bills: 1, 2, 5, 10, 20 leva
Electricity:	220 volts, 50 cycles, AC

Planning your trip

Visa requirements. See pp. 29–30.

Vaccination requirements. None (see also p. 25).

Currency restrictions. No local currency may be taken into or out of the country. There is no restriction on the amount of foreign currency that may be imported, provided it is declared upon arrival. The same amount minus what has in the meantime been changed into leva may subsequently be exported.

Climate. Bulgaria's climate is in general temperate continental, with hot summers and cold winters, though much milder conditions prevail on the coast and in sheltered valleys. Winter in Sofia can be harsh, with temperatures well below freezing.

93

Some average daily temperatures:

Sofia		J	F	M	A	M	J	J	A	S	O	N	D
average daily maximum*	°F	35	39	50	60	69	76	81	79	70	63	48	38
	°C	2	4	10	16	21	24	27	26	22	17	9	4
average daily minimum*	°F	25	27	33	42	50	56	60	59	52	46	37	28
	°C	−4	−3	1	5	10	14	16	15	11	8	3	−2
Varna													
average daily maximum*	°F	42	43	51	60	71	79	86	85	78	69	55	45
	°C	6	6	11	16	22	26	30	29	26	21	13	7
average daily minimum*	°F	30	30	36	44	53	61	65	64	58	52	43	34
	°C	−1	−1	2	7	12	16	19	18	14	11	6	1

* Minimum temperatures are measured just before sunrise, maximum temperatures in the afternoon.

Clothing. Light clothing is adequate in summer. Warm clothes including a heavy overcoat and winter shoes are necessary in most parts of the country in winter.

Duty-free allowances

Cigarettes	Cigars	Tobacco	Liquor	Wine
200	or 250 g. of other tobacco products		1 l. and	2 l.

Perfume: 100 g.
Gifts: Up to a max. amount of 50 leva.

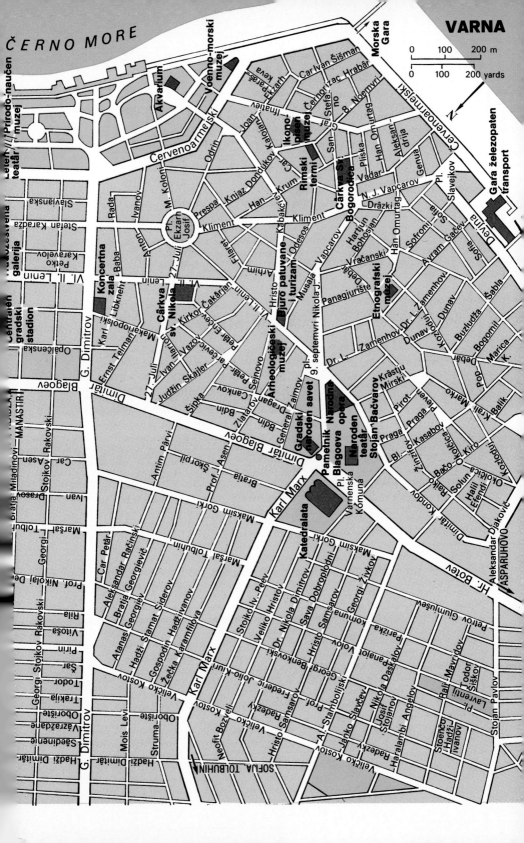

Hotels and accommodations

With hotel space at a premium, you are advised to make reservations well in advance, e.g. the time you apply for your visa. Otherwise, reservations may be made through the Bulgarian National Tourist Organization, 1, Boulevard Vitoša; tel. 4 33 31, telex 22583.

Bulgarian tourist offices abroad

U.K.   National Tourist Office, 18 Princes Street, London W1R 7RE; tel. (071) 449 6988/89

U.S.A.   Balkan Holidays, 161 East 86th Street, New York, NY 10028; tel. (212) 722-1110

On the spot

Banks and currency exchange. Banking hours are generally 8 a.m.– 12:30 p.m. and 1–3 p.m., Monday through Friday, and until 11 a.m. on Saturdays. Currency may only be changed at official exchange offices at the airport, banks, major hotels (Balkantourist hotels), national tourist offices and department stores. Outside banking hours, money can also be changed at a limited number of other points.

Credit cards and traveler's checks. Internationally recognized credit cards are accepted at major hotels, restaurants and currency-exchange offices. Traveler's checks are generally not accepted, except from guests at the Sheraton Hotel.

Mail and telecommunications. In Sofia, the main post office at 6, ul. Gourko has a telegram counter operating 24 hours a day. The telephone headquarters at 4, ul. Gourko are open round the clock. Major hotels will handle long-distance calls (expect some waiting time), cables and telex communications.

Some useful telephone numbers:

Inquiries	122
Operator (long-distance, domestic)	121
Operator (international)	0123
Information	144
Taxi	142

Newspapers: Principal daily newspapers are *Duma, Demokratsia, Svoboden Narod, Trud* and *Dialog.* Some of the Western dailies are on sale. *Sofia News* is published once a week in English, French, German, Spanish, Russian and Bulgarian and can be purchased at any newsstand.

Tourist information

Sofia: 1, Boulevard Vitoša, Sofia; tel. 4 33 31.

Legal holidays:

Jan. 1	New Year's Day	Sep. 9	Socialist Revolution Day
Mar. 3	Liberation from Ottoman rule	Dec. 25, 26	Christmas
May 1	Labor Day		
May 24	SS Cyril and Methodius; Alphabet, Education and Culture Day		

Transportation

Air. A limited number of flights link Sofia directly with a handful of West-European cities; same-day connections are available from most main centers. Frequent domestic services to Bourgas, Gorna Oriahovitza, Plovdiv, Russe, Silistra, Sofia, Varna and Vidin.

Major airport. Vrajdebna (7 miles/11 km. from city center). Dutyfree shops in both arrival and departure lounges. Special bus service every few minutes to town terminal.

Rail. Frequent daily services operate between major towns. Seating is comfortable; dining facilities are provided. Express trains require advance seat reservations (through Balkantourist agencies).

Local public transport. City transportation is highly organized. Tickets must be purchased in advance at any tobacco shop or newsstand.

Taxis. Taxis are available in the main cities, and can be rented by the day.

Car rental. Cars can be rented through major international agencies at Sofia airport and from Balkantourist agencies, but it is wise to make your reservations early, at the same time as you work out your other travel arrangements.

Driving in Bulgaria. A translation of your home license, or an international driver's license is required. Speed limits: 31 or 37 mph (50 or 60 kph) in towns, 75 mph (120 kph), on expressways and 50 mph (80 kph) on other roads. Use of seat belts is compulsory, and a red reflector warning triangle must be carried. Blood alcohol limit is a strictly enforced zero. Most roads are quite well maintained and clearly signposted. Service stations, located only at considerable intervals, are generally open 6 a.m.−9 p.m.; on main roads, some operate round the clock. Gasoline is bought with coupons from travel agencies at the border and at Balkantourist offices. Gasoline available is normal (86 octane), medium (93 octane), super (96 octane) and diesel. An expressway to link Sofia, Plovdiv, Bourgas, Varna and Sofia is under construction. Some stretches are already open to traffic.

Breakdown patrol vehicles on principal highways can undertake many repairs on the spot; tel. 146.

Some distances: Sofia−Plovdiv 96 miles (155 km.), Bourgas 250 miles (400 km.), Varna 310 miles (500 km.).

Crime and theft. Avoid any illegal currency transactions, which could lead to serious trouble. Normal precautions are in order to guard against petty theft.

Medical care and health. Medical services are well organized throughout the country. Free emergency attention is provided for all foreigners, and in non-vital cases treatment is reasonably priced at set fees. Though not many doctors are likely to speak your language, basic communication will be assured. Take along with you a supply of any pharmaceutical products you need on a regular basis. A clinic for foreigners is situated at 35, Boulevard P. Eftimij, Sofia; tel. 88 36 31.

Embassies and consulates. Hotels maintain lists of diplomatic representations.

Social customs. Remember that in this country a nod means "no" and a shake of the head means "yes".

98

Enjoying Bulgaria

Food and drink. All hotels serve both local and international dishes. Typical Bulgarian food can be found in *mehana* restaurants. Some popular national dishes are *tarator* (chilled cucumber-and-yoghurt soup), *ovneshko vareno* (boiled mutton), *moussaka* (potato and ground pork-and-veal casserole), *sarmi* (cabbage or grape leaves stuffed with rice and ground pork and veal). Grilled meats are also great favorites. Examples include *Kebap* (skewered and grilled meat served with a spicy sauce), *kebapcheta* (spiced, ground pork and veal), *kewfteta* (spiced, ground pork and veal with raw onions), *shishcheta* (spit-roasted pork), *parjola* (grilled pork tenderloin) and *meshana skara* (mixed grill).

Bulgarian wines can be surprisingly good. Try Misket (white) or Kaberné (red). The local plum brandy, *slivova,* aniseed-flavored *mastika* and vodka are quite strong. Besides local beer, Czech, German and Polish brands are available.

Lunch is served from noon to 2:30 p.m., dinner from 7 to 10 or 11 p.m.

Entertainment. Sofia has a dozen theaters, an opera house, musical hall and concert halls. A few nightclubs can be found. Most restaurants have dance bands. Some Western films are shown in their original language.

Taxes, service charges and tipping. Hotel and restaurant bills are all inclusive. While tipping is officially discouraged, gratuities are nevertheless welcomed; they should be given discreetly. Tipping recommendations: 1–2 levs for all services.

Sports and recreation. Tennis, swimming and bowling facilities exist in main centers and resorts, and skiing is popular in the Vitosha mountains, just a few miles outside Sofia.

Soccer, boxing, basketball, volleyball, wrestling and cycling are popular spectator sports.

TV and radio. Aside from the regular Bulgarian scheduling, in summer Varna radio and TV and (between 10:30 and 11:15 a.m.) Sofia TV broadcast short tourist-oriented programs in English, French, German and Russian.

What to buy. Good buys include embroidered dresses, tablecloths, icons, woodcarvings, wrought iron and copper, leather goods, rose essence, ceramics and costumed dolls. Special Corecom shops, located in tourist centers and major hotels, sell a wide range of merchandise (food, drink, cosmetics, dresses, photo supplies) for hard currency.

Shopping hours: generally 9 a.m.–1 p.m. and 2–7 p.m., Monday–Saturday.

Sightseeing

Sofia. Alexander Nevsky Cathedral*, sumptuous neo-Byzantine church completed in 20th century, with major collection of icons on display in the crypt. St. Sofia church, after which the city was named, built in 6th century. 4th-century Rotunda of St. George. 16th-century Bania-Bashi Mosque, recalling centuries of Turkish rule. Dimitrov Mausoleum with embalmed body of Bulgaria's Stalinist ruler. National History Museum, spotlighting golden treasures from ancient Thrace. Boyana church* with treasured 13th-century frescoes.

Historic towns. Plovdiv*, 8,000-year-old river city on the Thracian Plain: ancient amphitheater of Philippopolis (founded by Philip of Macedonia), Roman aqueduct and forum, Old Plovdiv protected zone of historic buildings; Archaeological Museum, featuring golden treasure from 4th century B.C. Veliko Tarnovo, with restored elements of medieval royal city and nearby monastery of the Transfiguration, founded in 14th century. Preslav, the Bulgarian capital in 10th century, including museum of art.

Monasteries. Rila*, fortress-like complex, one of the biggest Orthodox monasteries in the Balkans, distinguished by 14th-century tower, an immense iconostasis, vivid frescoes and a museum of church regalia and documents. Bansko*, a charming old town lying in foothills of Pirin Mountains, with Church of Holy Trinity (1835), incredibly ornate sculpted wooden interior. Frescoes of female saints. Icon museum. Bačkovo, 11th-century monastery near Plovdiv with celebrated 19th-century murals. Rojen, founded in the 14th-century, with stained-glass windows and unusual iconostasis and altar in church built in 1600. Ivanovo*, with church, chapels and monks' cells carved out of a

100

cliffside, and extraordinarily original frescoes from 13th and 14th centuries.

Black Sea coast. Varna★, Bulgaria's 3rd biggest city, a port founded in 6th century B.C.: miles of coastline devoted to lushly landscaped Maritime Park, remains of Roman baths from 2nd century, Archaeological Museum with regional antiquities and coin collection. Drouzhba, the "original" resort. Golden Sands (Zlatni Pyassatsi), with 4 kms of—predictably—golden sands. Albena, modern and "swinging" resort beside 6-km beach. Balchik★, romantic, white stone, old town that can be reached by boat from Varna. Burgas, more industrialised than Varna and without its charm, but some interesting buildings. Nesebar★, settled by ancient Thracians on a rocky peninsula, with 10 Paleochristian and medieval churches and historic houses. Sunny Beach (Slanchev Bryag), largest Bulgarian Black Sea resort. Sozopol, ancient fishing port still operating, its restful charm attracting artists and writers as well as retired sea captains. Primorski, small fishing village, at estuary of River Dyavolska, Ahtopol, near Turkish border, a small and charming ancient trading port with shipwrecks to be scoured, surrounded by orchards.

Some useful expressions in Bulgarian

good morning/afternoon	dobro outro/dobur den
good evening/night	dobur vecher/leka nosht
good-bye	dovizhdane
yes/no	da/ne
please/thank you	molya/blagodarya
excuse me	izvinyavaïte
you're welcome	molya
where/when/how	kude/koga/kak
how long/how far	kolko vreme/kolko daleche
yesterday/today/tomorrow	vchera/dnes/outre
day/week/month/year	den/sedmitza/mesetz/godina
left/right	lyavo/dyasno
up/down	gore/dolou
good/bad	dobre/losho
big/small	golyam/maluk
cheap/expensive	eftino/skupo
hot/cold	goreshto/stoudeno
old/new	star/nov
open/closed	otvoreno/zatvoreno
free (vacant)/occupied	svobodno/zaeto
early/late	rano/kusno
easy/difficult	lesno/troudno
Does anyone here speak English/French/German?	Govori li nyakoi angliiski/frenski/nemski?
What does this mean?	Kakvo znachi tova?
I don't understand.	Ne razbiram.
Please write it down.	Molya napishete go.
Do you take credit cards/traveller's cheques?	Vzemate li kreditni karti/travel chek?
Waiter!/Waitress!	Kelner!/Kelnerka!
Where are the toilets?	Kude e toaleta?
I'd like…	Az bih iskal…
How much is that?	Kolko strouva tova?
What time is it?	Kolko e chasut?
Help me please.	Pomognete mi, molya.
Just a minute.	Edin moment.

CZECHOSLOVAKIA

*New waves return a landlocked land of charm
and culture to the mainstream of Europe.*

Although it's only one-fourth the size of Spain, Czechoslovakia holds its own when it comes to castles: 2,500 of them at last count. Many are restored to their centuries-old majesty and mobilized to serve the tourist imperative. A city in itself, Prague Castle, looming over the rest of Prague, includes stirring symbols of church and state, from a thousand-year-old cathedral to the office of the country's president.

Straddling the Vltava River, Prague is at least as beautiful as any other European capital. The "city of a hundred spires" has been embellished by every architectural artifice from Gothic arcades to Art Nouveau sylphs. Every detail—every tower and turret, pillar and portal—excels. Even the bridge the Holy Roman Emperor built is a work of art. Prague is about three times the size of its cultural rival, the Danube port of Bratislava, the capital of Slovakia. Typical of the convoluted history of central Europe, Bratislava served as the capital of *Hungary* for a couple of hundred years. Czechoslovakia's national languages are Czech and Slovak, which, happily, are mutually comprehensible.

The country's industry, once at the technical vanguard of Europe, is now trying to catch up after four communist decades. Agriculture occupies a smaller place in the economy, but the crops contribute to the general good cheer: hops for the original Pilsner beer, grapes for some quite acceptable wines, and plums for the local firewater, *slivovice*. The cuisine leans to hearty, peasant-style dishes with dumplings to soak up the gravy, followed by plum-stuffed cheese dumplings for dessert.

The patron saint of Czechoslovakia is Good King Wenceslas (actually he was only a prince). The nation's most memorable fictional character, the Good Soldier Schweik, inspired generations of pacifists and strugglers against bureaucracy. In a manner of speaking, the two good men converged in 1989: Wenceslas Square was the focus of the battle of wits called the Velvet Revolution, which sent the communists packing and a dissident playwright to Prague Castle.

Facts and figures

Population:	15.6 million
Area:	49,373 sq. miles (127,869 sq. km.)
Capital:	Prague (*Praha,* 1.2 million)
Other major cities:	Bratislava (435,000) Brno (389,000) Ostrava (330,000) Košice (232,000) Pilsen (*Plzeň* , 175,000)
Languages:	Czech and Slovak
Religion:	Catholic (75%) with a significant Protestant minority
Time zone:	GMT + 1, EST + 6; DST (Apr.–Sep.)
Currency:	Czechoslovak crown (*koruna,* abbr. *Kčs*) = 100 *halers* Coins: 5, 10, 20, 50 halers, Kčs 1, 2, 5. Bills: Kčs 10, 20, 50, 100, 500, 1,000
Electricity:	220 volt, 50 cycle, AC

Planning your trip

Visa requirements. See pp. 29–30.

Vaccination requirements. None (see also p. 25).

Currency restrictions. Czechoslovak currency may not be brought into or taken out of the country. There is no limit on foreign currencies. Generally, foreign visitors are required to change the equivalent of 30 German marks (15 marks per child aged 6–15 years) per day at the basic exchange rate. For anything over this amount, the rate is doubled—in your favor. Holders of specified major credit cards or Čedok vouchers and official invitees are exempt from this requirement. Note that holders of a Čedok voucher can change money at a particularly advantageous rate at Čedok agencies, but these sums cannot be converted back afterwards.

Climate. Continental climate, quite hot summers, often very cold winters. Rain throughout the year. In winter, city streets are rapidly cleared of snow.

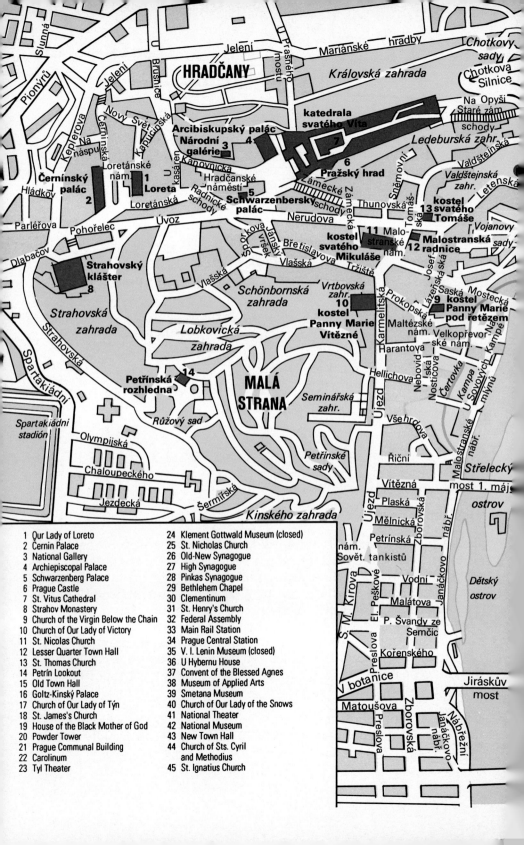

HRADČANY

Slunná
Pionýrů
Keplerova
Jelení
Brusnice
Nový Svět
Kapucínská
Na náspu
Černínská
U Prašného mostu

Mariánské hradby
Chotkovy sady
Chotkova Silnice
Královská zahrada
Na Opyši
Staré zám
schody
Ledeburská zahr.
Valdštejnská
Valdštejnská zahr.
Letenská

Arcibiskupský palác
Národní galérie **3** **4**
katedrala svatého Víta
7 **6**
Pražský hrad
Zámecké schody
Zámecká
Sněmovní
Thunovská
Tomáš

Loretánské nám. **1**
Loreta
Hradčanské náměstí
Kanovnická
Radnické schody
5
Schwarzenberský palác
Nerudova

Černínský palác
Hládkov
2
Loretánská
Úvoz
Parléřova
Pohořelec
Dlabačov

13 kostel svatého Tomáše
11 Malo-stranské nám.
kostel svatého Mikuláše
Malostranská radnice 12
Vojanovy sady
Josefská
Lázeňská
Saská
Mostecká

Strahovský klášter 8
Strahovská zahrada
Spork ova
Jánský vršek
Vlašská
Břetislavova
Vlašská
Schönbornská zahrada
Vrtbovská zahr.
10 kostel Panny Marie Vítězné
Tržiště
Prokopská
Karmelitská
Maltézské nám.
9 kostel Panny Marie pod řetězem
Velkopřevorské nám.
Čertovka
Kampa

Lobkovická zahrada
Harantova
Hellichova
Nebovid ská
Nosticova
U Sovových mlýnů
Malostranské nábř.

Petřínská rozhledna **14**
MALÁ STRANA
Semínářská zahr.
Újezd
Všehrdova

Spartakiádní
Spartakiádní stadión
Olympijská
Růžový sad
Petřínské sady
Říční
Vítězná
Střelecký
most 1. máj
ostrov

Chaloupeckého
Jezdecká
Šermířská
Kinského zahrada
Plaská
Mělnická
Petřínská
Dětský ostrov

nám. Sovět. tankistů
S. M. Kirova
Preslova
Kirova
El. Peškové
Vodní
Malátova
P. Švandy ze Semčic
Kořenského
V botanice
Matoušova
Preslova
Zborovská
Janáčkovo nábř.
Jiráskův most
Nábřeží Janáčkovo nábř.

1 Our Lady of Loreto
2 Černin Palace
3 National Gallery
4 Archiepiscopal Palace
5 Schwarzenberg Palace
6 Prague Castle
7 St. Vitus Cathedral
8 Strahov Monastery
9 Church of the Virgin Below the Chain
10 Church of Our Lady of Victory
11 St. Nicolas Church
12 Lesser Quarter Town Hall
13 St. Thomas Church
14 Petrín Lookout
15 Old Town Hall
16 Goltz-Kinský Palace
17 Church of Our Lady of Týn
18 St. James's Church
19 House of the Black Mother of God
20 Powder Tower
21 Prague Communal Building
22 Carolinum
23 Tyl Theater

24 Klement Gottwald Museum (closed)
25 St. Nicholas Church
26 Old-New Synagogue
27 High Synagogue
28 Pinkas Synagogue
29 Bethlehem Chapel
30 Clementinum
31 St. Henry's Church
32 Federal Assembly
33 Main Rail Station
34 Prague Central Station
35 V. I. Lenin Museum (closed)
36 U Hybernu House
37 Convent of the Blessed Agnes
38 Museum of Applied Arts
39 Smetana Museum
40 Church of Our Lady of the Snows
41 National Theater
42 National Museum
43 New Town Hall
44 Church of Sts. Cyril and Methodius
45 St. Ignatius Church

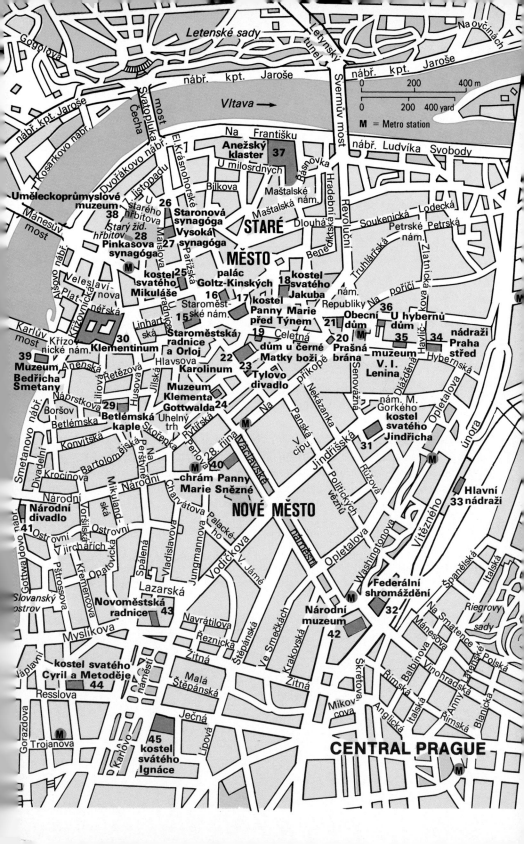

Letenské sady

Gogolova

nábř. kpt. Jaroše

Košárkovo nábř.

Mánesův most

nábř. kpt. Jaroše

Svatopluka Čecha most

Dvořákovo nábř.

17. listopadu

U starého hřbitova

E. Krásnohorské

Maiselova

Pařížská

nábř. kpt. Jaroše

Vltava →

Na Františku

Na Anežský klaster 37

U milosrdných

Bílkova

Maštalské nám.

Maštalská

Dlouhá

STARÉ

Letynský tunel

Svermův most

nábř. Ludvíka Svobody

0   200   400 m

0   200   400 yard

M = Metro station

Bašnovka

Hradební

Revoluční

Benediktská

Soukenická   Lodecká

Petrské   Petrská
nám.

Truhlářská

Zlatnická

Klimentská

Uměleckoprůmyslové muzeum 38

26 Staronová synagóga

Vysoká synagóga 27

Starý žid. hřbitov

Pinkasova synagóga 28

kostel svatého Mikuláše 25

Platnéřská

Veleslavínova

Aišovo nábř.

Žatecká

Linhartská

Anenská

Maiselova

Radniční

Karoliny Světlé

palác Goltz-Kinských

MĚSTO

Staroměstské nám.

16   17 kostel Panny Marie před Týnem

18 kostel svatého Jakuba

nám. Republiky

Na poříčí

36

Obecní dům

U hybernů dům

nádraží Praha střed

Havlíčkova

Klementinum 30

Karlův most

Křižovnické nám.

Mariánské nám.

15

Staroměstská radnice a Orloj

Hlavsova

22

19 dům u černé Matky boží

Celetná

21

20

Prašná brána

Na příkopě

muzeum V. I. Lenina

35   34

Hybernská

39 Muzeum Bedřicha Smetany

Retězová

Karolinum

23

Tylovo divadlo

Nekázanka

nám. M. Gorkého

Opletalova

Jilská

Husova

Muzeum Klementa Gottwalda 24

Rytířská

28. října

Na můstku

Panská

V cípu

kostel svatého Jindřicha 31

Boršov

Nápŕstkova

Anenská

29

Betlémská kaple

Uhelný trh

Skořepka

Perlová

Na Perštýně

Bartolomějská

Konviktská

Divadelní

Mikulandská

Národní

Spálená

Vladislavova

Jungmannova

Palackého

Václavské náměstí

Jindřišská

Růžová

Politických vězňů

Žitná

Hlavní 33 nádraží

Italská

Španělská

Smetanovo nábř.

Betlémská

Krocínova

Pštrossova

Křemencova

Voršilská

Ostrovní

NOVÉ MĚSTO

Vodičkova

V Jámé

Jindřišská

Opletalova

Washingtonova

Vítěžného

Federální shromáždění

Mánesova

Riegrovy sady

Národní divadlo 41

Gottwaldovo nábř.

Ostrovní

V jirchářích

Lazarská

Novoměstská radnice 43

Navrátilova

Řeznická

Štěpánská

Ve Smeckách

Krakovská

Národní muzeum 42

Škrétova

Slovanský ostrov

Slovanský ostrov

Myslíkova

Ječná

Štěpánská

Malá Štěpánská

Žitná

Žitná

Mikovcova

Anglická

Italská

Balbínova

Vinohradská

Římská

Ánny Letenské

Polská

Blanická

Římská

Václavská

Resslova

kostel svatého Cyril a Metoděje 44

Karlovo náměstí

Ječná

Lípová

Gorazdova

Trojanova

45 kostel svátého Ignáce

CENTRAL PRAGUE

Some average daily temperatures:

Prague

		J	F	M	A	M	J	J	A	S	O	N	D
average daily maximum*	°F	49	53	64	73	82	88	91	89	84	71	57	50
	°C	10	11	18	23	28	31	33	32	29	22	14	10
average daily minimum*	°F	7	10	18	29	36	44	49	47	38	29	24	14
	°C	−13	−12	−8	−2	2	7	9	8	4	−2	−5	−10

Brno

		J	F	M	A	M	J	J	A	S	O	N	D
average daily maximum*	°F	34	37	47	59	68	74	77	76	70	58	45	38
	°C	1	3	8	15	20	23	25	25	21	14	7	3
average daily minimum*	°F	24	24	30	39	47	53	57	55	49	40	35	30
	°C	−5	−5	−1	4	9	12	14	13	9	4	2	−1

* Minimum temperatures are measured just before sunrise, maximum temperatures in the afternoon.

Clothing. Light clothing, with something a bit warmer for occasional chilly days, is adequate in summer; a warm overcoat and heavy shoes are needed in winter. Rainwear will come in handy throughout the year. Comfortable low-heel shoes are a must for the sightseeing walks on cobblestones in Prague.

Duty-free allowances

Cigarettes	Cigars	Tobacco	Liquor	Wine
250	or	similar quantity of other tobacco products	1 l.	and	2 l.

Perfume:	reasonable quantity
Toilet water:	½ l.
Gifts:	Kčs 1,000 max. value

Upon arrival in Czechoslovakia, it's advisable to declare or present a list of all personal articles of value (portable dictating machine, typewriter, camera, calculator, etc.) to the customs official, who will confirm that these items have actually been imported for personal use.

Hotels and accommodations

Hotels. In view of the acute shortage of hotel rooms, reservations should always be made well in advance. Be sure you have a confirmation before your departure. Bills must be settled in hard currency. Hotels are officially classified according to the scope and standard of their services, from "A★ de luxe" at the top, through A★, B★ and B to a very modest "C". (Sometimes the scale is symbolized by stars—five for the most luxurious, one star for the most basic.) To earn the A★ de luxe rating a hotel must have superior rooms and elaborate facilities of the sort international businessmen expect. If you're aiming down a notch or two to A★ or B★, you won't be roughing it. And some hotels with fewer stars outdo the posh modern palaces in architectural charm and friendly service. But "C" class hotels truly have no frills.

If you arrive without a reservation, go to the main reservation center of Čedok, the country's biggest travel agency, at Panská 5, Prague 1, or to Pragotur, U Obecního domu 2, Prague 1. While the accommodations situation is slowly improving, the number of visitors to this beautiful city is, too. The secret is to visit out of season, if possible—the place looks just as magical in the cold!

Botels. For an efficient alternative to a conventional hotel you can stay in a converted river-boat, called a "botel". Prague has three of these floating hotels permanently moored along the Vltava. The amenities rate three stars.

Czechoslovak tourist offices abroad

U.K.   17–18, Old Bond Street, London W1X 3DA; tel: (071) 629 6058/9

U.S.A.   10 East 40th Street, New York, N.Y. 10016, tel. (212) 689-9720

On the spot

Banks and currency exchange. Banking hours are 8 a.m.–noon and 1–5 p.m., Monday–Friday.

Foreign currency and traveler's checks can be changed at Čedok (the state tourist office) branches, and hotel reception desks also have currency-exchange services open on Sundays and holidays. Foreign currency may also be changed at the bank against Tuzex coupons (available at Čedok offices and border crossing points) for purchases at Tuzex hard-currency shops. Goods bought with the coupons (valid for 12 months), are duty free. The problem is that these coupons cannot be changed back into the original currency. Therefore, it's better to use Western money, or charge cards, in the Tuzex shops.

Credit cards and traveler's checks. Several internationally recognized credit cards as well as major traveler's checks are widely accepted in tourist-oriented establishments.

Mail and telecommunications. Post offices handle mail, telegrams, telex and telephone services. Postage stamps are also available where post-cards are sold.

Telephone, telegraph and telex services are also available at major hotels. Long-distance calls are best placed from the post office or the hotel. Direct dialing exists to most European countries and many countries beyond.

The main post offices in Prague (Jindřišská, Prague 1) and Bratislava (Bratislava nám. SNP 39) are open 24 hours a day. Brno's central post office (Poštovská 3/5) offers round-the-clock service during spring and fall fairs.

Some useful numbers:

Fire	150	Ambulance with doctor	155
Information (domestic)	121	Police	158
Information		Time	112
(international)	0149	Wake-up service	125
		Weather	117

Newspapers. Principal Czechoslovakian dailies are *Rudé Právo, Pravda, Práce, Mladá Fronta, Svobodné Slovo* and *Lidová Demokracie.* Some foreign newspapers (e.g. *Le Monde* and the *Financial Times*) are available at hotels.

Tourist information

Prague   Čedok (state travel agency), Na Příkopě 18, Prague 1; tel. 22 08 25. For accommodations, ring 26 18 92

Bratislava   Čedok, Divadelni 3; tel. 2 39 22/2 33 03/2 31 66

Brno   Čedok, Štúrova 9b; tel. 5 20 81/5 51 95

Legal holidays

January 1	Nový rok	New Year's Day
May 1	Svátek práce	May Day
May 9	Vítězství nad fašismem	Victory over Fascism
July 5	Slovanští věrozvěsti sv. Cyril a Metoděj	Slavic Missionaries St. Cyril and St. Methodius
October 28	První československá republika	First Czechoslovak Republic
December 24	Štědrý den	Christmas Eve
Dec. 25–26	Svátek vánoční	Christmas/Boxing Day
Movable date: Velikonoční pondělí		Easter Monday

Transportation

Air. Prague is far and away the major gateway to Czechoslovakia, though a limited number of international flights operate to Brno and Bratislava. ČSA operates daily flights all year between Prague and a number of towns. Air-taxi service is available but reservations should be made a week in advance.

Major airports. Prague. Ruzyně (11 miles/17 km. from city center). Duty-free shop. Airport bus service, also city bus. **Bratislava.** Ivanka (7 miles/11 km. from city center). Duty-free shop. Airport and city bus service. **Brno.** Turany (4 miles/7 km. from city center), mainly domestic. Airport bus service.

Rail. An extensive rail network with first- and second-class service covers the country. Trains tend to be crowded, and it's advisable to reserve in advance. Sleeping accommodations can be booked through Čedok or at a railroad station. Long-distance expresses have dining cars. Trains are comfortable but not always punctual.

Long-distance buses. An extensive long-distance bus system covers the entire country with three or four runs daily between main towns.

112

Suburban services are well developed. Vehicles are comfortable and run on time. Tickets may be bought at the terminus or directly from the driver.

Local public transportation. All streetcars and buses have automatic ticket punchers which means tickets must be bought in advance, either at hotel desks or any tobacco shop, or from coin-operated machines in the subway, and at main streetcar stops in Prague. Prague has three subway lines.

Taxis. The best place to find a taxi is at a taxi stand, for example outside hotels, department stores and railroad stations, or have your hotel reception desk call a cab. They start the meter from the moment they are called. Taxis can be scarce after 9 p.m.

Car rental. Car-rental agencies have booths at airports and offices in the major cities. Insurance extras are added to the rental rates. Chauffeur-driven cars can be rented either through Pragocar or Čedok.

Driving in Czechoslovakia. Motorists must have a valid home and international driver's license. Roads, though often rather narrow, are well maintained and mostly asphalted. An expressway connects Prague, Brno and Bratislava. Speed limits are 68 mph (110 kph) on expressways and 56 mph (90 kph) on main roads outside towns. A 37 mph (60 kph) speed limit is in force in built-up areas. The alcohol limit is a strictly enforced zero; fines are high for drinking and driving or for speeding. At the border you must buy gasoline coupons. Gasoline cannot be sold at pumps for cash. Check the latest situation when you arrange your trip. Gasoline available is special (90 octane), super (96 octane), lead-free (less widely available) and diesel (with vouchers only).

Cars parked in a no-parking zone may be towed away. Use of seat belts is compulsory, and a red reflector warning triangle must be carried. Foreigners bringing their own cars to Czechoslovakia are advised to contact Autoturist Road Service which operates throughout the country and will provide a list of its patrol points; any service station can also direct you to the closest patrol point. Motorists renting a car will receive all information and emergency phone numbers from the car rental agency. Heavy commercial traffic on weekdays slows down motoring on the nation's principal arteries.

Some distances: Prague–Pilsen 56 miles (90 km.), Brno 125 miles (200 km.), Bratislava 205 miles (330 km.), Košice 425 miles (680 km.).

Rest rooms. Your best bet is to seek out the conveniences in a hotel or restaurant or Metro (subway) station in Prague. Toilets are often signposted in the English manner, "WC". Men's facilities may be marked "Muži" or "Páni", and women's "Ženy" or "Dámy" or by picture-signs.

Emergencies. In an emergency you can phone the following numbers 24 hours a day:

Police	158
Fire	150
Emergency first aid	155

Police. The police wear military-style olive-drab uniforms, but with white blouses in summer. Police patrol cars are yellow and white with the letters VB (for *Veřejná Bezpečnost,* public security) on either side. The police emergency telephone number is 158.

Crime and theft. Violent crime is still rare by the standards of Western Europe or the United States, but thefts do happen. Lock your car and put your valuables in the hotel safe. Be alert to the danger of pick-pockets in crowded places.

Don't become a criminal yourself: changing money on the black market is an offence in Czechoslovakia.

Medical care and health. Medical care is very good. A clinic for foreigners is located at Karlovo náměsti 32, Prague, where English and some other Western languages are spoken. First aid is generally given without charge. For more serious medical care, payment must be effected in foreign currency where no reciprocal agreements exist between Czechoslovakia and the traveler's country. Medical fees are moderate.

Drugs other than the simplest analgesics require a doctor's prescription. Every town has pharmacies with night service. Tap water is safe to drink.

Embassies and consulates. Embassies and consulates are listed in the telephone directory under "Zastupitelské úřady".

Social customs. Handshakes all around upon arrival and departure mark any meeting, business or private. Invitations to homes are not frequent, and on such occasions a gift of flowers or a bottle of good wine will be appreciated. A certain amount of Central-European charm still tends to mark social occasions.

114

Enjoying Czechoslovakia

Food and drink. Restaurants and most hotels offer international cuisine. Czechoslovak fare can be categorized as hearty, down-home cooking, often delicious and always filling; this is not the place to fret about your diet. Popular local dishes include *vepřová* (roast pork) or *husa* (goose) with *zelí* (sauerkraut). Most such dishes are served with *knedlíky* (dumplings). Snacks comprise *guláš* (goulash), *ledvinky* (fried kidneys) or *játra* (fried liver). Aside from conventional restaurants *(restaurace),* you can eat in *vinárny* ("wine restaurants") and *privnice* (pubs or taverns). *Kavárny* (cafés) serve snacks. For a spartan self-service cafeteria, try a *jídelna*. A tempting variety of inexpensive snacks can be bought at street stands. A *bramborák* is a potato pancake served on a piece of paper. An even less delicate form of "finger food" is *pečená klobása* (roast sausage), offered on a paper plate with a slice of bread and a squirt of mustard, but no fork.

Wines: imported Bulgarian, French or Hungarian are common along with domestic wines from Czech regions (Ludmila—both red and white), Moravia (Vavřinecké, Frankovka, Rulandské—red; Veltlinské zelené, Vlašský Ryzling, Burgundské—white) or Slovakia (Košický poklad, Nitrianská perla, Bratiskavské Hrozno—white; Kláštorné—red). Wine cellars serve from the cask. Czechoslovakia is noted for its fine beers, both light and dark. Pilsner Urquell, Budweiser and Staropramen—all light beers—are particularly good. Those who prefer a dark beer will enjoy Braník. Go for a drink at the beer halls of U Fleků or Sv. Tomáš, both former monasteries.

Mealtimes: lunch, noon–2:30 p.m.; dinner, 6:30–10 p.m.

Entertainment. From the frivolous to the highbrow, from discos to grand opera, all tastes are satisfied on the entertainment scene. Music reaches the highest standards in Czechoslovakia, and so does the theater; if language is a problem, try the multi-media *Laterna Magika* spectacle in Prague. Tickets tend to be surprisingly inexpensive. The Prague Spring Music Festival in May offers a wide program of classical music. In summer, concerts are held daily in Prague's parks. Movie theaters show some foreign films in the original version but most are dubbed. The main cities have nightclubs and discos.

Taxes, service charges and tipping. Service charges are generally included in hotel and restaurant bills. Tips are appreciated. Tipping recom-

115

mendations: waiters 10%; taxi drivers 10%; hotel porters Kčs 5 per piece; hairdressers Kčs 20. Hatcheck facilities usually charge 50 halers per article, which is generally rounded off to the next crown.

Sports and recreation. Skiing, skating, soccer, volleyball and tennis are popular, as are hunting, fishing, mountain hiking and climbing. Golf is played mainly near Prague and in Karlovy Vary (Karlsbad) and Mariánské Lázně (Marienbad).

Soccer is by far the most popular spectator sport but skiing, skating, volleyball and tennis competitions are held in season.

TV and radio. Radio and TV programs are in Czech and Slovak. In Bratislava and southern Moravia, Austrian television can be received. On the radio, tourist information is broadcast daily in summer in English, French and German.

What to buy. Crystalware, china, porcelain, costume jewelry, antiques and old books can be bought at Tuzex shops with vouchers or hard currency. In Prague, UVA, Slovakia and Úluv are good for handicrafts, Bijoux de Bohême for jewelry, České Sklo a Keramika for glass and ceramics, and Moser for crystalware. Department stores in large towns make good shopping.

Hours: Monday–Friday, 8:30 a.m.–6 p.m.; Saturdays until 2 p.m. Food shops open from 6 a.m. to 6 p.m., Saturdays 6–11 a.m.

On departure, there's a tight limit (500 Kčs) on the amount of purchases you can take out of Czechoslovakia, with the exception of items purchased with hard currency at Tuzex shops or by credit card. So keep your receipts. It is forbidden to export antiques, many foodstuffs, furs, shoes and children's clothing, unless you can prove they were acquired through Tuzex.

Sightseeing

Prague. Castle District: Hradčany Square with Baroque palaces and Military Museum; National Gallery and outstanding collection of old Bohemian art; Prague Castle*, a clifftop complex encompassing St. Vitus Cathedral, founded in the 10th century, and Royal Palace with majestic medieval halls; Loreta shrine*, cloisters and lavish treasury. Strahov Monastery* including two Baroque churches and National Literature Museum. Charles Bridge*, Prague's first Vltava River crossing, lined with sculptures. Old Town Square*, surrounded by charming historic buildings including Old Town Hall, begun in 14th century. Carolinum, home of Charles University, founded 1348. Old Jewish Cemetery with ancient gravestones; historic synagogues; Jewish Town Hall. Wenceslas Square*, throbbing hub of New Town; National Museum in neo-Renaissance palace. Neoclassical Smetana Theater, specializing in Czech operas. Main Rail Station, early 20th-century Art Nouveau production. Lavishly restored Neo-Renaissance National Theater. Park-like Charles Square, Prague's biggest square, laid out in 1348. Villa Amerika, housing Antonín Dvořák Museum. Bertramka, villa in wooded estate where Mozart polished *Don Giovanni.*

Excursions from Prague. Hluboká Castle*, ancient fortress converted into romantic castle. Karlovy Vary (formerly Karlsbad), famous spa town favored by distinguished 18th- and 19th-century figures. Karlštejn Castle*, hilltop bulwark built by Charles IV to protect crown jewels; Konopiště Castle, 13th-century fortress converted into hunting lodge by Archduke Franz Ferdinand. Kutná Hora, 13th-century silver-mining town with extravagant cathedral and Italian Court. Lidice, village martyred by German SS troops in World War II, with memorial garden and museum. Mariánské Lázně (Marienbad in German), mineral springs resort where great artists and writers "took the waters". Plzeň, industrial city, home of the original Pilsener lager beer, to which a local museum is devoted.

Moravia. Brno, large industrial city topped by almost invulnerable 13th-century Špilberk Castle, with infamous dungeons in which distinguished prisoners were held; restored Cathedral of SS. Peter & Paul with landmark twin spires and 14th-century statue of Madonna and Child; St. Thomas church with former monastery attached; neo-Gothic

118

St. James church. Slavkov (Austerlitz in German), site of fateful battle of 1805, with monument to the fallen. Pernštejn, giant 13th-century castle with collection of antiques and weapons. Moravian Karst region of caves and limestone formations. Lednice, with medieval castle in its own park including tropical greenhouse.

Slovakia. Bratislava*, on the Danube (spanned by bold modern suspension bridge), beneath huge, much-restored castle on clifftop; St. Martin's Cathedral, begun in 14th-century, site of coronation of Hungarian monarchs; Old Town Hall containing museum; former Primate's Palace with sweeping façade; Michael Gate and Baroque tower; neo-Renaissance Slovak National Theater, Franciscan Church (13th-century Gothic) with hexagonal tower. Pleštany, spa town noted for mineral water and mud baths. Trnava, historic town with well-preserved fortifications and Gothic cathedral. Tatra National Park, including highest mountains in the Carpathians. Slovak Paradise, protected landscape of ravines and waterfalls. Bardejov, town with well-restored 14th-century houses and fortifications. Košice, site of Stone Age settlement, with Gothic cathedral and restored medieval urban ensemble.

Some useful expressions in Czech

good morning/afternoon	dobré ráno/dobré odpoledne
good evening/night	dobrý večer/dobrou noc
good-bye	na shledanou
yes/no	ano/ne
please/thank you	prosím/děkuji
excuse me	promiňte
you're welcome	rádo se stalo
where/when/how	kde/kdy/jak
how long/how far	jak dlouho/jak daleko
yesterday/today/tomorrow	včera/dnes/zítra
day/week/month/year	den/týden/měsíc/rok
left/right	vlevo/vpravo
up/down	nahoře/dole
good/bad	dobrý/špatný
big/small	velký/malý
cheap/expensive	levný/drahý
hot/cold	horký/studený
old/new	starý/nový
open/closed	otevřeno/zavřeno
free (vacant)/occupied	volno/obsazeno
early/late	brzy/pozdě
easy/difficult	snadný/obtížný
Does anyone here speak English/French/German?	Mluví zde někdo anglicky/francouzsky/německy?
What does this mean?	Co to znamená?
I don't understand.	Nerozumím.
Please write it down.	Prosím, napište to.
Do you take credit cards/traveller's cheques?	Přijímáte úvěrové legitimace/cestovní šeky?
Waiter!/Waitress!	Pane vrchní!/Paní vrchní!
Where are the toilets?	Kde jsou toalety?
I'd like…	Rád bych…
How much is that?	Kolik to stojí?
What time is it?	Kolik je hodin?
Help me please.	Pomozte mi, prosím.
Just a minute.	Okamžik.

DENMARK

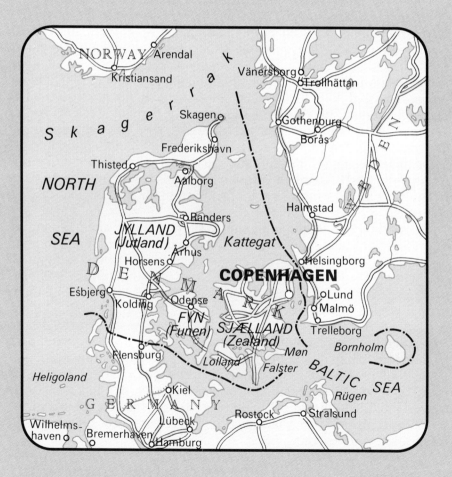

In Scandinavia's most crowded, coziest country, the old values still count.

As folksy as Hans Christian Andersen, Denmark is easygoing yet efficient. The whole cozy country lives up to the definition of "Danish design"—the functional allied to the tasteful. The most densely populated of the Scandinavian nations, Denmark makes the most of its tidy farms, exporting rich butter and cheese to go with the Danish pastry. Industry ticks over in the background, producing everything from chemicals to ships.

Outside Amalienborg Palace in Copenhagen, you can watch the sentries dressed like toy soldiers in tall black bearskin hats. The restrained pomp of Europe's oldest-running royal dynasty recalls Denmark's imperial past, when the white-crossed red flag ruled from Greenland and Iceland to the Virgin Islands.

Denmark occupies the Jutland peninsula and—a boon for the ferrymen—nearly 100 inhabited islands. No place is more than 30 miles from the sea, appropriately in the bastion of the ancient Viking conquerors.

Denmark revels in the long sunny summer days when life moves outdoors, but Scandinavian winters coldly compensate. Snow, though, doesn't necessarily mean skiing: the country's highest "mountain" reaches only 568 feet above sea level. Thanks to the flat terrain, cycling is a way of life, and a way of working off some of the excesses of all those open sandwiches and beer.

Nearly one-third of the nation's population lives in Copenhagen, a city built on a human scale. Traffic is banned from a historic central zone of shops and cafés. When the Danes, the least formal of the Scandinavians, want to unwind, they head for Copenhagen's Tivoli Gardens, 20 acres of food, flowers and fireworks, slot machines and symphony concerts. In the swinging 60's Copenhagen fired the first salvoes of the sexual revolution; the atmosphere is more subdued now but still uncensored, and anything goes.

Yet only a few miles beyond the city limits, in the most serene woods and farmland, values as old as the castles and cathedrals still reign.

122

Facts and figures

Population:	5.1 million
Area:	16,629 sq. miles (43,069 sq. km.)
Capital:	Copenhagen *(København,* 1.4 million)
Other cities:	Aarhus *(Århus,* 250,000)
	Odense (170,000)
	Aalborg (155,000)
	Esbjerg (80,000)
Language:	Danish
Religion:	Protestant (98%)
Time zone:	GMT + 1, EST + 6; DST (Apr.–Sep.)
Currency:	Danish *krone* (abbr. *kr.*) = 100 *øre*
	Coins: 25, 50 øre; kr. 1, 5, 10, 20
	Bills: kr. 50, 100, 500, 1,000
Electricity:	220 volt, 50 cycle, AC

Planning your trip

Visa requirements. See pp. 29–30.

Vaccination requirements. None (see also p. 25).

Currency restrictions. There is no limit on the amount of Danish or foreign currency that can be brought into or taken out of the country by non-residents. However, anything over kr. 50,000 can be exported only if it does not exceed the amount originally imported.

Climate. Some average daily temperatures:

Copenhagen		J	F	M	A	M	J	J	A	S	O	N	D
average daily	°F	36	36	41	51	61	67	71	70	64	54	45	40
maximum*	°C	2	2	5	11	16	19	22	21	18	12	7	4
average daily	°F	28	28	31	38	46	52	57	56	51	44	38	34
minimum*	°C	-2	-2	-1	3	8	11	14	14	11	7	3	1

* Minimum temperatures are measured just before sunrise, maximum temperatures in the afternoon.

123

The Danish coastal climate is temperate, usually damp and windy. Winter snow falls are rarely heavy, and city streets are usually clear (though often wet).

Clothing. A raincoat comes in handy between May and October. Even in the height of summer, nights can be chilly, so don't go out without a sweater or wrap. Casual clothes are appropriate for most occasions, though the better hotels and clubs require men to wear a tie in the evening.

Duty-free allowances

	Cigarettes		Cigars		Tobacco	Liquor	Wine
1)	400	or	100	or	500 g.	1 l. and	2 l.
2)	400	or	100	or	500 g.	1½ l. and	4 l.
3)	300	or	75	or	400 g.	1½ l. and	4 l.
4)	200	or	50	or	250 g.	1 l. and	2 l.

Perfume: 1), 4) 50 g.; 2), 3) 75 g.
Toilet water: 1), 4) ¼ l.; 2), 3) ³/₈ l.
Gifts: 1), 4) kr. 350 max. value; 2), 3) kr. 2,300 max. value

1) residents outside Europe, duty-free items bought in EEC countries or items obtained outside the EEC
2) residents outside Europe, non-duty-free items bought in EEC countries
3) residents of Europe, non-duty-free items bought in EEC countries
4) residents of Europe, duty-free items bought in EEC countries; and residents of Europe, goods bought outside EEC countries

Hotels and accommodations

Hotels. Denmark does not have an official rating system, but hotel information compiled at tourist offices gives an indication of various facilities. Combine this information with the prices quoted and you get a fair idea of quality.

"Mission hotels" are temperance hotels. Reasonably priced and popular with Danish family visitors, they sell beer and wine to guests. The old stagecoach inns *(kro)* offer a high standard of service and traditional Danish food.

Other types of accommodations include motels, housekeeping cottages, vacation houses, farmhouse apartments and vacation camps.

At peak vacation periods, Copenhagen can be bursting at the seams with visitors. If you haven't reserved ahead, the Accommodation

Bureau ("Kiosk P") at the Central Station can usually come up with a room. The bureau is open daily from 9 a.m. to midnight in summer.

Youth hostels. The Danish Tourist Board publishes a complete list of youth hostels around the country. There is no age limit, but membership cards are required (available on the spot). Bed linen can be rented at some hostels (sleeping bags may not be used).

Camping. Sites approved by the Camping Council range from one- to three-star categories and cover basics from drinking water to provision stores and duty camp-wardens. Unless you have an International Camping Carnet, you obtain a Camping Pass for foreigners, valid for the rest of the year, at the first site visited.

Danish tourist offices abroad

Australia	The Danish Tourist Board, 60 Market Street, P.O.Box 4531, Melbourne, Vic. 3001
Canada	The Danish Tourist Board, P.O.Box 115, Station "N", Toronto, Ont. M8V 3S4; tel. (416) 823-9620
U.K.	The Danish Tourist Board, Sceptre House, 169–173 Regent Street, London W1R 8PY; tel. (071) 734 2637/8
U.S.A.	Scandinavian Tourist Board, Denmark–Sweden, 8929 Wilshire Boulevard, Suite 300, Beverly Hills, CA 90211; tel. (213) 657-4808
	Scandinavian Tourist Board, Denmark–Sweden, 150 North Michigan Avenue, Suite 2110, Chicago, IL 60601; tel. (312) 726-1120
	Scandinavian National Tourist Offices, 655 Third Avenue, 18th floor, New York, NY 10017; tel. (212) 949-2333

On the spot

Banks and currency exchange. Copenhagen's banks open from 9:30 a.m. to 4 p.m., Monday through Friday (until 6 p.m. on Thursdays). In the provinces, hours vary.

In Copenhagen, exchange offices operate at the Central Station from 7 a.m. to 9 p.m. daily, at Handelsbank branch on Østergade (Strøget) from 9 a.m. to 5:30 p.m., Monday–Wednesday, to 6 p.m. Thursday and

125

Friday, and to 2 p.m. Saturday; and, from May 1 to mid-September, at the entrance to Tivoli (H.C. Andersens Boulevard 22) from noon to 11 p.m.

Credit cards and traveler's checks. Both are widely accepted.

Mail and telecommunications. The main post office in Tietgensgade (just behind Tivoli) is open from 9 a.m. to 7 p.m., Monday through Friday, and from 9 a.m. to 1 p.m. on Saturdays. The post office at the Central Station is open from 9 a.m. to 10 p.m., Monday through Friday, from 9 a.m. to 4 p.m. on Saturdays, and from 10 a.m. to 5 p.m. on Sundays and holidays. Newsstands and souvenir shops also sell stamps. Mailboxes are red.

Apart from the public telephone booths, some newspaper and tobacco stands also have public telephones. Unused coins are *not* returned, even if your number is busy, but you can call another number, or repeat the busy number, until the time you've paid for runs out. Rather than coins, some public phones accept cards (called "Telet"), available at newsstands and shops all over town. See also p. 30.

The main telegraph office at Købmagergade 37 handles phone calls, telegrams *(fonotelex)*, fax and telex from 9 a.m. to 10 p.m. every day. Telegrams can also be sent from post offices or by phone; the staff usually understands English.

For long-distance calls within Denmark, there are no area codes, just dial the 8-digit number of the person you want to call.

Some useful telephone numbers:

Information (domestic)	0033	Telegrams	0022
Information (international)	0039	Police, fire, ambulance	000
Operator assistance	0030		

Newspapers. Leading Copenhagen dailies are *Berlingske Tidende* and *Politiken.* Major British and continental newspapers and U.S. news weeklies are on sale at newsstands, shops and hotels throughout central Copenhagen, as is the *International Herald Tribune,* edited in Paris. A free English-language brochure, *Copenhagen This Week,* lists information for visitors.

Tourist information. All Danish cities and most small towns have a tourist information office, marked by a large letter "i" on a green background.

Copenhagen H.C. Andersens Boulevard 22 (at Tivoli entrance by the Town Hall); tel.. 33 11 13 25

Legal holidays

Jan. 1	New Year's Day	**Movable dates:**
June 5	Constitution Day	Maundy Thursday
	(afternoon)	Good Friday
Dec. 25	Christmas	Easter Monday
and 26		General Prayer Day
		(4th Friday after Easter)
		Ascension Day
		Whit Monday

Transportation

Air. A major European gateway, Copenhagen Airport is one of the busiest on the Continent. Connections to points within Europe are excellent. There is air service to nearly a dozen Danish cities and towns, none of which is more than a 30-minute flight from Copenhagen. Although Denmark is small, air travel is popular, especially to islands of the Danish archipelago. Domestic connections can sometimes be included in overseas tickets at no extra charge.

Major airport. Copenhagen Airport (6 miles/10 km. from city center). Duty-free shop. Airport buses run from the terminal building to the Central Station in Copenhagen, 30 minutes away. Hovercraft and bus and hydrofoil services operate to nearby Malmö, Sweden.

Rail. Modern express trains *(Lyntog)* equipped with buffet bars and public phones serve the Jutland route, as do ordinary inter-city trains. Most rail travel in Denmark requires taking a ferry, on which dining and/or cafeteria facilities are always provided. Seat reservations are advisable (obligatory on express trains). The *Nordic Tourist Ticket* is good for 21 days of unlimited rail travel in Denmark, Finland, Norway and Sweden. For *Eurailpass,* see p. 33.

Boats, waterways. Regular ferry services link most islands and the mainland. On summer weekends particularly, ferry space should be reserved in advance. Every year the Danish Tourist Board issues a brochure giving details of fares, schedules and telephone numbers for reservations. All boats have a dining room and/or cafeteria.

Local public transportation. All major cities have excellent bus transportation, and the Greater Copenhagen area has a rapid-transit train, *S-tog.* On the bus, buy your ticket from the driver; traveling by the rapid-transit train, be sure your ticket has a time stamp on it or stamp it at the entrance to the platform.

Copenhagen Card. Similar to a plastic credit card, this tourist discount card is valid for unlimited travel on buses and trains in metropolitan Copenhagen, and gives free access to many museums and sights and up to 50 percent discount on ferries connecting Zealand with Sweden and on hydrofoils between Copenhagen and Malmö. The card is valid for one, two or three days and is on sale at travel agencies and main railroad stations in Denmark and at certain Copenhagen hotels.

Taxis. Cabs display a "Taxi" or "Taxa" sign. You can hail a taxi on the street or order one by phone. Most drivers speak English.

Car rental. In addition to the major international companies, there are various local firms. Some have desks at Copenhagen Airport. They are listed in the yellow pages of the telephone directory under "Auto-udlejning". See also pp. 30–31.

Driving in Denmark. You should have a red reflector warning triangle and a parking disc which you can obtain free from police stations, garages, post offices and many banks. (Rented cars have one in the glove compartment.) Use of seat belts is compulsory. Police require blood tests from all drivers involved in accidents in which personal injury occurs. With more than 50 mg./100 ml. blood alcohol level, a driver faces a stiff fine, loss of license for a year and possible imprisonment.

Drive on the right, pass on the left. The Danes are generally well-disciplined drivers. Clear indication should always be given when changing lanes, whether on expressways or Copenhagen boulevards. Weaving from one lane to another is a punishable offense. Be alert for bike and moped riders to your right, often on their own raised pathways, but sometimes separated from you by a white line, which you may not cross. Bridges and expressways are toll-free. Speed limits are 62 mph (100 kph) on expressways, 50 mph (80 kph) on other roads and 31 mph (50 kph) in built-up areas. All vehicles must have low-beam headlights switched on at all times, even in broad daylight. Gasoline available is normal (92 octane), super (96 or 98 octane), lead-free and diesel.

For emergency assistance or towing service, call the Copenhagen office of Falck: 33 14 22 22. You'll be referred to another number if necessary.

Some distances: Copenhagen–Aarhus 62 miles (100 km.) plus ferry Kalundborg–Aarhus, ca. 3 hours; Esbjerg 105 miles (170 km.) plus ferry Korsør–Nyborg, ca. 1½ hours.

129

Bicycle rental. Why not join the Danes in their great national pastime—touring country lanes and woodlands by bike? Tourist offices will supply you with the names of rental companies. Many railroad stations also have bikes for rent. Consult the booklet *Cycling Holidays in Denmark*, available free from the Danish Cyclist Federation and the Danish Tourist Board.

Rest rooms. Rest rooms are indicated by a pictograph or the words *WC, Toiletter, Damer* (ladies)/*Herrer* (gentlemen) or *D/H*. There's no charge unless you see it clearly marked to the contrary.

Emergencies. The all-purpose emergency number is 000, and it's free—coins are not needed. Ask for police, fire or ambulance as required. Speak distinctly (English is understood).

Police. All officers are members of the national force. Danish policemen wear black uniforms. Most of them patrol in blue-and-white or white cars with the word "Politi" in large letters. Police are always courteous to foreigners. All officers speak English.

Crime and theft. Late at night, it can be dangerous in the area behind Copenhagen's Central Station. Avoid the Christiania area day and night. Otherwise take normal commonsense precautions.

Medical care and health. Medical services are excellent. In the event of serious illness, foreigners are treated or hospitalized without charge. Dial 0041 to call a doctor in an emergency. Medical and pharmaceutical supplies are readily available, but Danish law requires a doctor's prescription for almost all drugs stronger than aspirin. In Copenhagen, Steno Apotek (pharmacy) at Vesterbrogade 6 C opposite the Central Station (tel. 33 14 82 66) is open 24 hours a day. Most medical personnel speak at least passable English. For insurance, see pp. 25–26.

Tap water is safe to drink.

Embassies and consulates. Consult the red telephone directory under "Ambassader og konsulater".

Social customs. Danes are open-minded and uninhibited, but they do observe certain formalities. It's usual to shake hands when you meet someone or bid them farewell. If you're invited to lunch or dinner at a private home, bring flowers, chocolates, wine or liquor to the hostess. At the table, you shouldn't drink until the host has made a welcome toast. The man seated to the left of the hostess is expected to propose a toast of thanks during dessert.

130

Enjoying Denmark

Food and drink. Food is not—quite—an obsession, but it's taken seriously and the standard is high. Restaurants often serve a special dish of the day *(dagens ret)* and the "Dan-menu" (two courses at a fixed price). The *daglig kort* ("daily card") usually features dishes less expensive than those listed on the more formal menu *(spisekort)*. Out of town, an old coaching inn *(kro)* can provide a charming setting for a special meal.

Breakfast in a Danish hotel is a far cry from the spartan continental breakfast of croissant and coffee. Bread and rolls, meat, cheese, jam, pastries and possibly an egg are accompanied by a glass of milk or fruit juice followed by tea or coffee.

Cold food is Denmark's outstanding culinary specialty. *Smørrebrød* are thickly buttered slices of rye or white bread covered with one of a variety of delicacies like smoked eel *(røget ål)*, roast beef, liver paste *(leverpostej)*, or shrimps *(rejer)*. But don't confuse *smørrebrød* with the Swedish word *smörgåsbord,* the pan-Scandinavian buffet, known in Denmark as the *koldt bord* ("cold table"). Larger restaurants offer an endless array of dishes in their *koldt bord. En platte* is a cold dish (a miniature *koldt bord*) consisting of six to eight specialties.

For an appetizer, most Danes prefer fish, or perhaps, a selection of canapés. Herring is a great favorite, served pickled, marinated or fried, with a sherry, vinegar, curry or fennel dressing. The succulent red Greenland shrimps are keen competitors in the popularity stakes. Lobster is widely available (but not cheap), as is crab, salmon, cod and halibut. *Rødspætte filet med remoulade,* red-spotted plaice served deep fried with lemon and tartare sauce is a local favorite.

Danes eat a lot of steak, usually served with herb butter and French fries *(fransk bøf),* or with fried onions and potatoes *(engelsk bøf).* Danes have a way with the humble meatball *(frikadeller),* a finely ground mixture of pork and veal, often served with potato salad. They make delicious hash, too: *biksemad,* a combination of diced potatoes, onions and meat with a fried egg on top. If you like hamburgers, try the crumbling Danish version *(hakkebøf). Pariserbøf* is a slightly cooked, almost raw, hamburger topped with raw egg yolk, raw onion, capers, horseradish and other seasonings.

Favorite desserts include *æblekage,* stewed apples with vanilla, served with alternating layers of cookie crumbs, topped with whipped cream, and *bondepige med slør,* a mixture of rye-bread crumbs, apple sauce, sugar and whipped cream.

The national drink is beer. Denmark boasts 100 or more breweries,

131

including some renowned around the world. *Pilsner* (lager) is the most common type of beer, but you will also find stronger variants like *exportøl* and *elefantøl*. And then there is *akvavit,* the fiery local schnapps, served only with food. Scotch whiskey, vodka and gin are readily available but very expensive both in bars and retail shops. The local Cherry Heering makes a pleasant after-dinner drink. Good wine is expensive; the house wine *(husets vin)* is usually acceptable and more reasonably priced.

Lunch is served from noon to 2 p.m., dinner from 6 to 10 p.m.

Entertainment. From September to June, opera and ballet are featured at the Royal Theater, showcase for the Royal Danish Ballet. Try to see the company in a performance of one of Bournonville's classics. In the summer the concert hall in Tivoli Gardens is the scene for performances of classical music and dance. Copenhagen is a popular center for jazz. Movies are shown in their original language with Danish subtitles. Details of entertainment possibilities can be found in *Copenhagen This Week* and on the next-to-last page of local newspapers.

Annual events and festivals. Denmark has no great religious festivals or processions, but festivities are in the air all the time. A few specials, however: *April:* Numus Festival in Aarhus. *Mid-June–early July:* Viking Festival, plays, mead and barbecues at Frederikssund. *June 23:* St. John's Eve, celebration with bonfires all over the country. *June–July:* Copenhagen Summer Festival, involving rock concerts, chamber music, and so on. *Late June–early July:* Roskilde Festival, greatest pop festival in Northern Europe, with jazz and rock in a delightful setting.

Taxes, service charges and tipping. Sales tax and service charges are always included in the price at hotels and restaurants. There is no tipping in Denmark, though it's customary to leave the odd krone tip for rest-room attendants . Give a small tip to the taxi driver at the airport if he helps you with your luggage.

Sports and recreation. In or around the capital, the possibilities range from swimming, sailing and waterskiing to bike riding and golf, depending on the season.

The top spectator sport is soccer. Exciting if mainly amateur matches are played every weekend almost all the year round. Trotting at Klampenborg, horse and cycle races also draw large crowds.

TV and radio. While most programming is in Danish, foreign TV shows and movies are shown in the original language. On Denmark's Radio 3, news is broadcast in English at 8:15 a.m., Monday through Saturday.

133

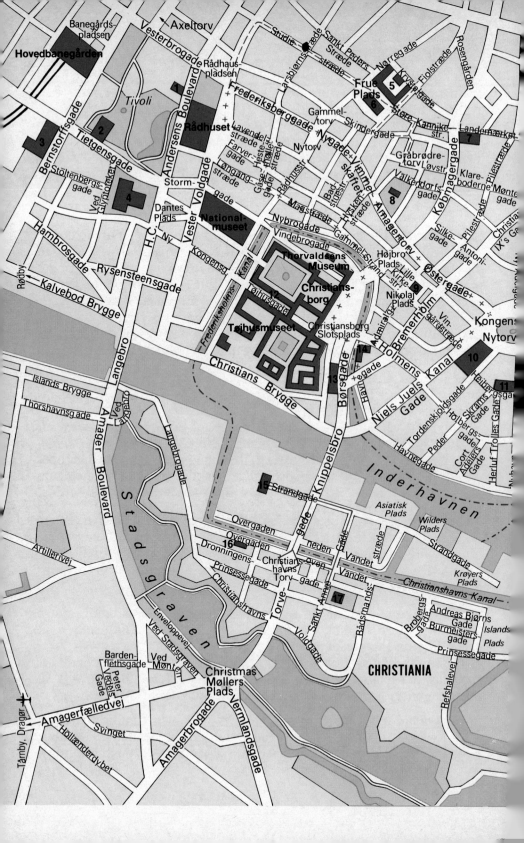

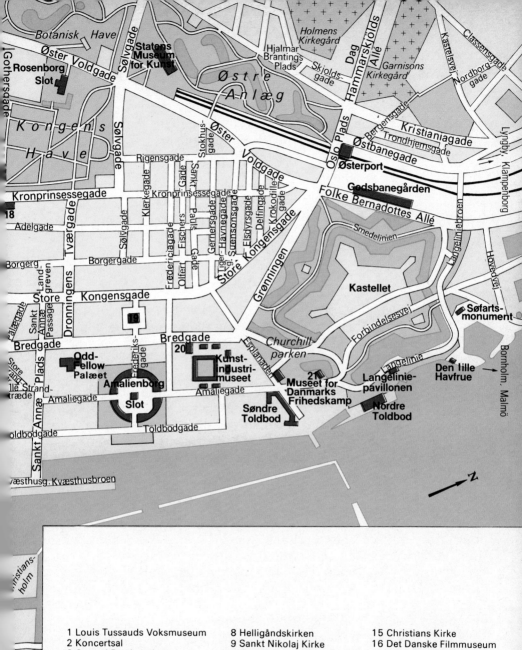

1 Louis Tussauds Voksmuseum
2 Koncertsal
3 Central Postbygningen
4 Ny Carlsberg Glyptotek
5 Universitetet
6 Domkirken
7 Rundetårn

8 Helligåndskirken
9 Sankt Nikolaj Kirke
10 Det Kongelige Teater
11 Charlottenborg
12 Teaterhistorisk Museum
13 Børsen
14 Holmens Kirke

15 Christians Kirke
16 Det Danske Filmmuseum
17 Vor Frelsers Kirke
18 Davids Samling
19 Marmorkirken
20 Sankt Ansgar Kirke
21 St. Alban's Church

COPENHAGEN

What to buy. Look for Danish-designed glassware, housewares, porcelain and silver jewelry, including pieces set with Danish amber. Flora Danica jewelry has a floral motif, with flowers and leaves dipped in silver and gold. Danish modern furniture is among the world's best. Other good buys include furs, knitwear, pipes and toys. In Copenhagen, the main shopping area is along the linked pedestrian-only streets of Strøget, Fiolstræde and Købmagergade. In some cases, sales tax is deducted (see p. 40).

Shopping hours. Generally 9 a.m. to 5:30 p.m., Monday–Thursday, until 7 or 8 p.m. on Fridays, 12 noon or 2 p.m. on Saturdays. Some stores close all day on Monday or Tuesday.

Sightseeing

Copenhagen. The Old Town, including: National Museum, displaying everything from prehistoric Danish rock carvings to Mongolian tents; the Thorvaldsen Museum, dedicated to the great Danish sculptor; the imposing Christiansborg Castle, containing the Parliament, Supreme Court and a complex of museums; the ornamented Stock Exchange *(Børsen)* with its characteristic spire; and Strøget, the city's charming pedestrian shopping zone between Rådhuspladsen and Kongens Nytorv. Nyhavn ("new harbor"), the one-time "sailors' street", with a mixture of taverns, discotheques, clubs, luxury apartments and good restaurants. Amalienborg Square, with four identical Rococo palaces, including Amalienborg Palace★, home of the royal family; changing of the guard daily at 11:30 a.m. when the Queen is in residence. The Little Mermaid *(Den lille Havfrue)*★ from Hans Christian Andersen's famous fairy tale. The Round Tower *(Rundetårn)* from 1642, an astronomical observatory with a 700-foot (215-m.) spiral causeway. Rosenborg Castle (1607), a museum spanning Danish royal history over the past 300 years. Christianshavn (Christian's Harbor), with a panoramic view from Our Savior's Church *(Vor Frelsers Kirke)*. Copenhagen City Museum and Kierkegaard Collection, a favorite with children, featuring a scale model of the city center in the mid-16th century. Ny Carlsberg Glyptotek Museum★, an important collection of Egyptian, Greek, Roman and Etruscan art. Royal Museum of Fine Arts *(Statens Museum for Kunst)*, featuring everything from the Dutch old masters to the modern Danes. Tivoli Gardens★ in the heart of the city, an amusement park in a garden setting with more than 20 snack bars and restaurants, shops, a concert hall, mouse circus, donkey rides, pantomime theater. Town Hall Square *(Rådhuspladsen)* and the red-brick Town Hall, center of modern Copenhagen. Grundtvig's Memorial Church, on Bispebjerg in north-

136

west Copenhagen, commemorating the man once called Denmark's greatest son.

Zealand (Sjælland). Dragør★, an 18th-century fishing village with cobbled alleys and a seafaring museum. Open-Air Folk Museum *(Frilandsmuseet)*★ at Sorgenfri, a 90-acre (36-ha.) site containing farmhouses, cottages and workshops from different parts of Denmark, furnished in authentic style. Louisiana Modern Art Museum★ at Humlebæk, with Henry Moore and Alexander Calder sculptures and Chagall murals; excellent temporary exhibitions. Helsingør/Elsinore, with green-roofed Kronborg Castle★, "Hamlet's castle", overlooking the Sound, with Sweden a quarter of an hour away. Renaissance Frederiksborg Castle★, fully restored after a fire in 1859. Roskilde★ with its 800-year-old cathedral *(Domkirken)*, containing the tombs of 37 monarchs of Denmark; Viking Ship Museum; Lejre's Ancient Town *(Oldtidsbyen)*, a research center where a group of people lives in Iron-Age style. Kalundborg and its famous 800-year-old Church of Our Lady. Fine Vallø Castle at the Bay of Køge.

Funen (Fyn). Odense★, birthplace of Hans Christian Andersen, with a museum dedicated to the world-famous fairy-tale writer; a market-gardening center with a charming Old Town; Railroad Museum; good shopping possibilities. Romantic Egeskov Castle (1554), a red-brick construction sporting round towers and green turrets. Svendborg, a picturesque sailor's town with a 13th-century church and attractive shopping area. Nyborg, a pleasant harbor town, site of Denmark's oldest castle (1170).

Jutland Peninsula (Jylland). Known for its beaches, particularly in the west; 500 offshore islands. Legoland★, a tourist attraction featuring miniature replicas of everything from Danish castles to the Mount Rushmore monument; famous doll collection; the world's most extravagant doll's house, Ticiana's Palace; amusement park. Two major towns: Aarhus, Denmark's second city, once a Viking settlement, today an important port; Den Gamle By, a reconstructed medieval town in a city park, including a botanical garden; Museum of Art, displaying 18th-century and contemporary Danish work; Moesgård Museum of Prehistory, home of the famous 1,600-year-old Grauballe Man. Aalborg, cultural and administrative center of North Jutland, once an important Viking market town; outstanding Modern Art Museum; Jens Bang's Stone House, a Renaissance mansion, the seat of the Guild of Christian IV; the beautiful Cathedral of St. Botolph; Viking settlement and burial grounds at Lindholm Høye. Ribe, with medieval half-timbered and red-brick houses; 800-year-old church.

137

Some useful expressions in Danish

good morning/afternoon	godmorgen/goddag
good evening/night	godaften/godnat
good-bye	farvel
yes/no	ja/nej
please/thank you	vær så venlig/tak
excuse me	undskyld
you're welcome	åh, jeg be'r
where/when/how	hvor/hvornår/hvordan
how long/how far	hvor længe/hvor langt
yesterday/today/tomorrow	i går/i dag/i morgen
day/week/month/year	dag/uge/måned/år
left/right	venstre/højre
up/down	op/ned
good/bad	god/dårlig
big/small	stor/lille
cheap/expensive	billig/dyr
hot/cold	varm/kold
old/new	gammel/ny
open/closed	åben/lukket
free (vacant)/occupied	fri/optaget
early/late	tidlig/sen
easy/difficult	let/svær
Does anyone here speak English/French/German?	Er der nogen her, der taler engelsk/fransk/tysk?
What does this mean?	Hvad betyder dette?
I don't understand.	Jeg forstår ikke.
Please write it down.	Vær venlig at skrive det.
Do you take credit cards/ traveler's checks?	Tager De kreditkort/ rejsechecks?
Waiter!/Waitress!	Tjener!/Frøken!
Where are the toilets?	Hvor er toilettet?
I'd like…	Jeg vil gerne have…
How much is that?	Hvor meget koster det?
What time is it?	Hvad er klokken?
Help me please.	Vær venlig at hjælpe mig.
Just a minute.	Et øjeblik.

FINLAND

Land of lakes and forests,
with a sauna to break the ice.

Getting to know the Finns may seem an insuperable challenge. Their language, a distant cousin of Hungarian, is a bewilderment of compound suffixes producing endless words always accented on the first syllable. And on casual acquaintance, the people seem coolly reserved. But there's nothing like sharing a sauna to break the ice. The Finns invented the devilish routine of basking in heat hot enough to boil an egg, flailing each other with birch twigs, and jumping in the nearest lake...to be repeated until relaxation is total.

For centuries Finland was squeezed between the ambitions of its neighbors, Sweden and Russia. Swedish is still an official, if minority, language, while the Russian legacy lives on in the onion-domed churches and crystal-clear vodka. Under the czar, Helsinki was transformed from a small port town into the capital of the Russian Grand Duchy of Finland (established in 1812). The neo-Classical buildings of the 19th century give the city a certain stately distinction, now more than matched by the startlingly innovative architecture of modern Finland.

Events have moved fast since independence in 1917: invasion by the Soviet army in 1939, defeat in the "winter war" and in World War II. But the plucky Finns salvaged freedom and democracy from the wreckage of war, and the country prospered as a bridge between east and west.

Finland is Europe's fifth largest country in area—and one of its least populous. With its trackless forests and 62,000 lakes, Finland is the supreme fresh-air country. Even in urban Helsinki there are hundreds of parks, while north of the lakelands and historic smaller towns sprawls Lapland, sparsely inhabited by 200,000 people and as many reindeer. Here nothing distracts from the grandeur of open land and sky and, in spring and autumn, the eerie, inspiring spectacle of the Northern Lights. In summer the midnight sun stimulates all of nature, human included.

140

Facts and figures

Population:	4.8 million
Area:	130,500 sq. miles (338,127 sq. km.)
Capital:	Helsinki (*Helsingfors,* 485,000/GUA 785,000)
Other cities:	Tampere (*Tammerfors,* 165,000/GUA 240,000) Turku (*Åbo,* 165,000/GUA 240,000) Espoo (*Esbo,* 160,000) Vantaa (*Vanda,* 145,000) Oulu (*Uleåborg,* 95,000)
Language:	Finnish (93%), Swedish (6%)
Religion:	Protestant (91.5%)
Time zone:	GMT + 2, EST + 7; DST (Apr.–Sep.)
Currency:	Finnish mark *(markka,* abbr. *mk)* = 100 *penni (p)* Coins: 5, 10, 20, 50 p; 1, 5, 10 mk. Bills: 10, 50, 100, 500, 1,000 mk.
Electricity:	220 volt, 50 cycle, AC

Planning your trip

Visa requirements. See pp. 29–30.

Vaccination requirements. None (see also p. 25).

Currency restrictions. There is no limit on the amount imported, whether in Finnish or foreign currency. Non-residents may take out up to the amount declared on entry.

Climate. Weather can be suprisingly hot during the summer, and very cold in winter (December to April). Most rain falls between September and December. Snow can cause traffic holdups in early winter and spring. The sun shines up to 20 hours in summer, while in December and January there are only about six hours of daylight. The midnight sun lights the north in June and July.

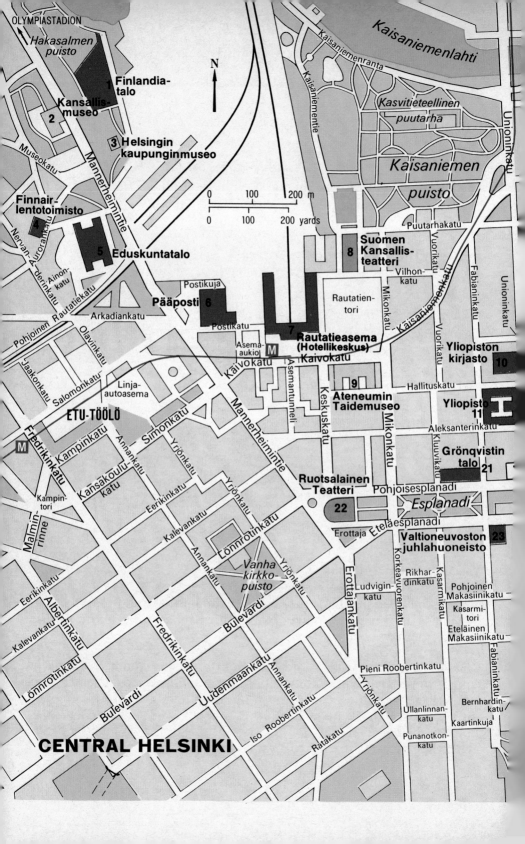

OLYMPIASTADION

Hakasalmen puisto

N

1 **Finlandia-talo**

Kansallis-museo

2

3 **Helsingin kaupunginmuseo**

Finnair-lentotoimisto

4

5 **Eduskuntatalo**

Museokatu

Mannerheimintie

Nervan- Auroran-katu

Ainon-katu

Postikuja

Pääposti 6

Arkadiankatu

Pohjoinen Rautatiekatu

Olavinkatu

Jaakonkatu

Salomonkatu

Postikatu

7 **Rautatieasema (Hotellikeskus)** Kaivokatu

Asema-aukio

M

Kaivokatu

Linja-autoasema

ETU-TÖÖLÖ

Fredrikinkatu

M

Kampinkatu

Simonkatu

Annankatu

Yrjönkatu

Kansakoulu-katu

Kampin-tori

Malmin-rinne

Eerikinkatu

Kalevankatu

Yrjönkatu

Annankatu

Eerikinkatu

Albertinkatu

Kalevankatu

Lönnrotinkatu

Vanha kirkko-puisto

Lönnrotinkatu

Fredrikinkatu

Bulevardi

Bulevardi

Uudenmaankatu

Annankatu

Iso Roobertinkatu

Ratakatu

CENTRAL HELSINKI

0   100   200 m

0   100   200 yards

Kaisaniemenlahti

Kaisaniemenranta

Kaisaniemen-tie

Kasvitieteellinen puutarha

Kaisaniemen puisto

Unioninkatu

Puutarhakatu

8 **Suomen Kansallis-teatteri**

Vilhon-katu

Rautatien-tori

Mikonkatu

Vuorikatu

Kaisaniemenkatu

Fabianinkatu

Vuorikatu

Unioninkatu

Yliopiston kirjasto

10

Hallituskatu

9 **Ateneumin Taidemuseo**

Keskuskatu

Mikonkatu

Kluuvikatu

Yliopisto

11

Aleksanterinkatu

Grönqvistin talo 21

Ruotsalainen Teatteri

22

Pohjoisesplanadi

Eteläesplanadi

Esplanadi

Erottaja

Valtioneuvoston juhlahuoneisto 23

Erottajankatu

Ludviginkatu

Korkeavuorenkatu

Rikhar-dinkatu

Kasarmikatu

Pohjoinen Makasiinikatu

Kasarmi-tori

Eteläinen Makasiinikatu

Fabianinkatu

Pieni Roobertinkatu

Yrjönkatu

Bernhardin-katu

Ullanlinnan-katu

Kaartinkuja

Punanotkon-katu

Asemantunneli

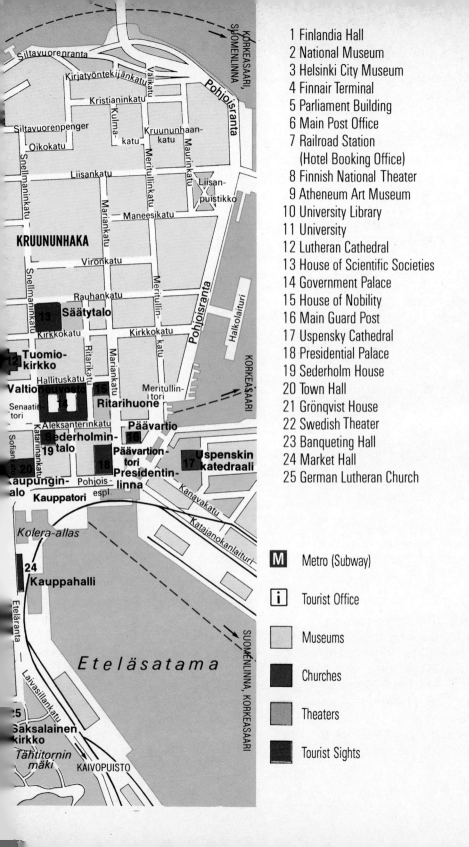

1 Finlandia Hall
2 National Museum
3 Helsinki City Museum
4 Finnair Terminal
5 Parliament Building
6 Main Post Office
7 Railroad Station
  (Hotel Booking Office)
8 Finnish National Theater
9 Atheneum Art Museum
10 University Library
11 University
12 Lutheran Cathedral
13 House of Scientific Societies
14 Government Palace
15 House of Nobility
16 Main Guard Post
17 Uspensky Cathedral
18 Presidential Palace
19 Sederholm House
20 Town Hall
21 Grönqvist House
22 Swedish Theater
23 Banqueting Hall
24 Market Hall
25 German Lutheran Church

M   Metro (Subway)

i   Tourist Office

  Museums

  Churches

  Theaters

  Tourist Sights

Some average daily temperatures:

Helsinki		J	F	M	A	M	J	J	A	S	O	N	D
average daily	°F	26	25	32	44	56	66	71	68	59	47	37	31
maximum*	°C	-3	-4	0	6	14	19	22	20	15	8	3	-1
average daily	°F	17	15	20	30	40	49	55	53	46	37	30	23
minimum*	°C	-9	-10	-7	-1	4	9	13	12	8	3	-1	-5

*Minimum temperatures are measured just before sunrise, maximum temperatures in the afternoon.

Clothing. In summer, light clothing is adequate with something warm for the evening. A raincoat is always advisable. For winter, take warm clothing, including a heavy overcoat, hat and fur-lined boots. In Helsinki and other big towns better restaurants often insist on jacket and tie for men.

Duty-free allowances

	Cigarettes		Cigars	Tobacco	Liquor		Wine
1)	400	or	500 g. of other tobacco products		1 l.	and	1 l.
2)	200	or	250 g. of other tobacco products		1 l.	and	1 l.

1) residents of countries outside Europe
2) residents of Europe

Hotels and accommodations

Hotels. Standards tend to be quite high as most hotels and motels are new. About one third of all Finnish hotel beds are in Helsinki; even so it's best to make reservations between May and September. Finnish Tourist Board offices in Finland and abroad offer a brochure called *Hotels, Motels, Hostels,* which lists all the facilities available. The Hotel Reservation Center at Asema-aukio 3, next to Helsinki railroad station, deals only with Helsinki and the immediate surrounding area.

To encourage visitors to come by car, the government sponsors a special discount program offering books of *Finn Cheques,* valid in some

150 hotels throughout the country. These checks can only be purchased outside the country. They are good from June 1 to August 31. Further information is available from Finnish Tourist Board offices and travel agencies for Scandinavia abroad. Most hotels have a sauna.

Summer hotels. These are usually student dormitories turned over to the public during June, July and August. They provide adequate accommodations in modern buildings at attractive rates.

Farmhouses. Some farm families take in guests on a full-board basis, with the chance to participate in the work of the farm if they wish. Ask at the tourist office for the brochure *Farm Holidays in Finland.*

Holiday cottages. From humble huts to luxury villas, around 6,000 vacation cottages are available nationwide. Ask for the brochure *Finnvacations.*

Holiday villages. These are self-contained bungalows in rustic settings. Some holiday villages are open all year round and make excellent winter vacation homes. Ask for the brochure *Holiday Villages in Finland.*

Youth hostels. Finland imposes no age limit, despite the name *(retkeilymaja)*. Hostels affiliated with the Finnish Youth Hostel Association (SRM) are marked by a triangular sign with the initial letters in white on a blue background. Visitors should have a membership card of their national youth hostel organization; non-members are admitted, but have to pay a surcharge.

Camping. There are some 350 campsites, 200 of which belong to the Finnish Travel Association. Sites are indicated by the international blue-and-white sign with a pictograph of a tent inside the letter "C", and graded by stars from one to three. The Finnish camping season starts around the end of May in the south and lasts into September. In northern Lapland, the season is only about two months long. An international or Finnish camping card is required—obtainable at the sites. The Tourist Board's brochure *Camping sites and youth hostels* gives details on sites and camping in Finland. You can also contact the Finnish Travel Association, Camping Department, at Mikonkatu 25, SF-00100 Helsinki 10.

Finnish tourist offices abroad

U.K.	Finnish Tourist Board UK Office, 66/68 Haymarket, London SW1Y 4RF; tel. (071) 839 4048
U.S.A.	Finnish Tourist Board NA Office, 655 Third Avenue, New York, NY 10017; tel. (212) 370-5540

On the spot

Banks and currency exchange. Banks are normally open between 9:15 a.m. and 4:15 p.m., Monday through Friday. Outside banking hours, money can be changed at hotels or currency-exchange offices. There are exchange offices at Helsinki railroad station (11 or 11:30 a.m.–6 p.m. daily), Olympic Harbor Helsinki (9 a.m.–noon, 3–6 p.m.), Katajanokka Harbor in Helsinki, Turku and Naantali harbors (open during the arrival and departure of ships), Helsinki airport (7 a.m.–11 p.m. daily).

Credit cards and traveler's checks. Major credit cards are accepted in most hotels and restaurants, service stations, department stores and shops. Internationally recognized traveler's checks are easily cashed, although you may need your passport for identification.

Mail and telecommunications. Post offices are identified by the words *Posti–Post,* and are generally open from 9 a.m. to 5 p.m., Monday through Friday. The main post office in Helsinki at Mannerheimintie 11 is open from 8 a.m. to 10 p.m. weekdays, 11 a.m. to 10 p.m. on Sundays. Mailboxes are yellow, with a black post-horn. You can also buy stamps at stationery shops, hotels and railroad stations and from yellow stamp machines. Telegrams *(sähke)* can be sent from the post office or from your hotel.

You can dial direct to most countries; see the telephone book for instructions. Phone booths everywhere can be used for long-distance calls. See also p. 30.

Some useful telephone numbers:

Information (Helsinki)	012	News in English	040
Information (other domestic)	020	Telegrams	021
Information (international)	92020	Police, fire and medical help (Helsinki)	000

Newspapers. The principal daily newspapers are *Helsingin Sanomat* and *Uusi Suomi* in Finnish, and *Hufvudstadsbladet* in Swedish. Newsstands in hotels and railroad stations carry most major European newspapers, including the *International Herald Tribune,* usually the day after publication. *Helsinki This Week* is distributed free at hotels.

Tourist information. Most Finnish cities and towns have their own tourist information office, almost always centrally located on the main

146

street or market square, and marked by a large letter "i" on a green background. Telephone 058 for recorded tourist information in English.

Helsinki   Pohjoisesplanadi 19; tel. (0) 169 37 57

Legal holidays

		Movable dates:
Jan. 1	New Year's Day	Epiphany
May 1	Labor Day	(Sat. nearest to Jan. 6)
Dec. 6	Independence Day	Good Friday
Dec. 24,	Christmas	Easter Monday
25, 26		Ascension
		(Sat. after Ascension Day)
		Whit Saturday
		Midsummer Day (Sat. nearest
		to June 24)
		All Saints' Day (Sat.
		nearest to Nov. 1)

Transportation

Air. Helsinki is Finland's only truly international airport, although flights go to Sweden from Maarianhamina, Turku and Vaasa. An efficient air system links about 20 domestic airports around the country. The *Finnair Holiday Ticket,* available only to non-residents of Scandinavia, offers unlimited travel within the country for 15 days, at a flat rate. "Midnight-sun-flights" leave Helsinki for Lapland daily from mid-May to mid-July.

Major airport. Helsinki: Vantaa (12 miles/19 km. from city center). Duty-free shop. There is a bus service every 10 to 30 minutes.

Rail. Trains are clean and comfortable, and operate between cities and towns everywhere except the far north. A reservation is necessary on express trains. There is a special *Finnrail Pass* for unlimited travel for periods of eight, 15, 22 days, or one month. Bring your passport when purchasing the ticket. There are also special group, family and tourist tickets available. *Nordic Tourist Ticket* permits 21 days of unlimited rail travel in Finland, Denmark, Norway and Sweden. For *Eurailpass,* see p. 33.

Long-distance buses. Both regular and express services go all over the country. Traveling by bus is a convenient and inexpensive way of seeing

Finland. There are reductions for families and groups. The *Lapland tourist ticket* is valid in both Finnish and Norwegian Lapland.

Boats, waterways. There are regular boat services to the Tourist Islands. Åland ferries leave from Turku and Naantali. Old-fashioned steamers ply many lakes in Finland's lake district, but only from May to September. In winter the sea and Finland's lakes are frozen. Icebreakers keep major ports in southern Finland open.

Local public transportation. Buses and streetcars serve Helsinki and other major centers. On vehicles marked with a black "E" on a yellow background, you pay the driver. Otherwise buses and streetcars have machines inside the vehicle for validating tickets bought beforehand. Books of multi-trip tickets for unlimited travel on buses and streetcars are available, as are 24-hour tourist tickets. There is also a limited subway system in Helsinki for which bus and streetcar tickets are valid.

Helsinki Card. The Helsinki Tourist Association issues Helsinki Cards covering entrance to museums, travel on city buses, on streetcars, subway and boats, hotel-rate discounts etc. The card is valid for periods of one, two or three days and can be purchased at the Helsinki City Tourist Office.

Taxis. Taxis have an orange border around the license plate and are marked *Taksi*. They display a yellow light when they are free. Cabs can be hailed on the street or found at a taxi stand. If you telephone for a cab, the meter goes on as soon as they receive the call, so a considerable amount can clock up before you get in. A service charge is included in the fare. All taxis have meters. There is a surcharge on weekends and at night.

Car rental. All major international firms are represented in Finland and there are lists of local companies at tourist information offices. Otherwise look under "Autovuokraamoja" or "Biluthyrning" in the yellow pages of the telephone directory. See also pp. 30–31

Driving in Finland. Drive on the right, pass on the left. Every car must have a red reflector warning triangle available for emergencies. Use of seat belts is compulsory. Keep low-beam headlights on, even in broad daylight. Winter tires are obligatory from December 1 to the end of February. Traffic is generally light on Finnish roads. Main roads are good throughout the country but many secondary roads are unsurfaced. The few expressways which exist are limited to some stretches around the major towns. Watch out for elk and reindeer wandering in the road, especially at dusk. If you collide with an elk or reindeer you must report it to the police. Speed limits are 31 mph (50 kph) in town, 37–75 mph (60–120 kph) on the open road as marked, 75 mph (120 kph) on expressways. Blood alcohol limit is 50 mg./100 ml. and drunken driving is punishable by a heavy fine and/or a jail sentence. Gasoline available is normal (92 octane), super (96 and 99 octane), lead-free and diesel. In case of breakdown, call (0) 6940 496 (Automobile and Touring Club service number) for further instructions.

Some distances: Helsinki–Lahti 56 miles (90 km.), Turku 100 miles (165 km.), Tampere 110 miles (175 km,), Vaasa 260 miles (415 km.).

Bicycle rental. Cycling is popular in Finland and bikes can often be rented at youth hostels, tourist offices, hotels, campsites and resort villages, as well as sports shops. There are several planned bicycle tours to choose from. Ask at the local tourist office for further details.

Emergencies. In Helsinki dial 000 free from any telephone to report police, fire and medical emergencies. In other towns emergency numbers are listed in the first pages of telephone directories.

Police. Finnish police wear dark blue uniforms, and in summer, gray shirts with dark blue shoulder straps replace jackets. Police cars have

149

"Poliisi" written on them in large white letters. Many police officers speak English, particularly those on duty in resort and tourist areas.

Crime and theft. Look after your purse or wallet in the underground shopping center at Helsinki Railway Station, otherwise, no special precautions are necessary.

Medical care and health. Quality of service and fees are both high; so make sure you are fully insured. Pharmacies *(apteekki)* in Finland are strictly for medication, much of which is on prescription. After hours, pharmacies post the address of the nearest emergency branch in the window or on the door. Most doctors speak English. For insurance, see pp. 25–26.

Tap water is safe to drink.

Embassies and consulates. Embassies are listed in the telephone book under their names in each respective language, e.g. (in English) American Embassy, British Embassy, Canadian Embassy, etc.

Social customs. Of people in the Northern countries perhaps the Finns are the most conservative when it comes to social customs. Finns are a hospitable people, and are quick to invite foreigners to join in the sauna ritual. If invited to a meal, don't touch your drink until the host has proposed a toast, and take some flowers for the hostess.

Enjoying Finland

Food and drink. The Finns are hearty eaters, starting with a solid breakfast and on to the never-ending cold buffet, *voileipäpöytä,* at which you are expected to fill your plate several times with the different types of fish, meat and salad.

Mealtimes are earlier than elsewhere in Europe, lunch starts at about 11 a.m., and dinner may well be eaten at about 5 p.m. at home, or 7 p.m. in a restaurant.

Breakfast usually starts with a glass of juice, followed by coffee or tea, with different types of bread and rolls, butter, jam, cheese, eggs and sausage.

For lunch or dinner you will find that fish and shellfish tend to dominate the menu. A popular starter is *silakka* (Baltic herring), which is available all year round and can be fried, baked, grilled or smoked, salted or marinated. It is often served with boiled potatoes and a small glass of vodka. A variation on this is *silakkalaatikko,* a Baltic herring and potato casserole.

A specialty from certain Finnish lakes is *muikku,* a white freshwater fish. You might like to try it in *kalakukko,* a rye bread with *muikku* and pork baked into it, served sliced with butter. The same fish also provides *muikunmäti,* or roe, served Russian style on toast or pancakes with chopped onions, pepper and fresh or sour cream. The Finns welcome the crayfish *(ravut)* season which occurs between the end of July and early September.

On the meat side is reindeer *(poro, poronliha)*. It can be served in many different ways: *poronkäristys* (in cream sauce), *savustettua poronlihaa* (cold smoked), or *poronkieli* (tongue), either smoked or with lemon sauce. Another regular item on the menu is game: *sorsa* (duck), *fasaani* (pheasant), *riekko* (white ptarmigan), *jänis* (hare), *karhu* (bear), and *hirvi, hirvipaisti* (elk).

Some very traditional specialties are *hernekeitto,* a thick pea soup with pieces of pork, usually served on Shrove Tuesday, and *karjalanpiirakka,* a thin shell of rye dough, containing rice or potatoes and eaten hot with chopped egg and butter.

The Finns have a good selection of cheeses including hard Emmental-type cheeses and soft brie-style cheeses. If you're near a cheese shop buy some *piimäjuusto* (buttermilk cheese), or *ilves* (baked loaf-shaped cheese).

Favorite desserts, available only during the summer months, are wild berries. Cakes are popular, but not after a meal; these are eaten between meals with coffee, the national drink, consumed countless times per day.

Strong alcoholic drinks are served only in licensed restaurants, but you will find No. I and No. III Beers in cafeterias. The latter is marginally stronger than the former. Restaurants serve No. IV Beer as well as wines and liquor. It's worth trying some of the domestic liqueurs such as Lakka, yellow cloudberry liqueur, Polar, red cranberry, Mesimarja, red Arctic bramble or Vaapukka, red raspberry. And the drink that accompanies almost every traditional dish is vodka, served straight or perhaps combined with juices or even liqueurs.

Entertainment. The theater is well and truly alive in Finland with more than 30 professional theaters, supported by the government, and several thousand amateur groups. Most plays are in Finnish, many are translated from foreign languages, but some are shown in English. Concerts are performed regularly in Finlandia Hall and the Rock Church in Helsinki, with Finland's own Sibelius featuring high on the list of composers. There is plenty of dancing, either in nightclubs, discos or late-night restaurants. Movies are shown in the original language.

Annual events and festivals. *February:* Finlandia Ski Race. *April 30:* nationwide welcome to spring (students' celebrations are especially lively) followed by May Day celebrations. *June:* Midsummer Eve celebrations, Kuopio Dance and Music Festival. *June–July:* Jyväskylä Arts Festival. *July:* Pori Jazz Festival, Nurmijärvi Outdoor Drama Festival, Kaustinen Folk Music Festival, Savonlinna Opera Festival. *August:* Turku Music Festival, Tampere Theater Summer. *August–September:* Helsinki Festival featuring music and drama.

Taxes, service charges and tipping. Tipping is not a widespread habit in Finland. The service charge is included at hotels and restaurants. Waiters and taxi drivers don't expect tips, but a few extra coins for good service is customary. Barbers and hairdressers are not tipped. Tipping recommendations: porters 5 mk per bag, hatcheck 3–5 mk per person.

Sports and recreation. Depending on the time of year, you can try swimming (indoor or outdoor), boating and sailing (lakes, sea), tennis, squash, hiking, cycling, skiing, fishing and hunting. During summer, Finns enjoy watching soccer and athletics, while popular winter spectator sports are cross-country skiing and ice hockey.

TV and radio. Programming is in Finnish and Swedish. All foreign movies are shown in the original language with subtitles.

What to buy. Glass and ceramics with original modern designs by Finnish craftsmen of worldwide reputation, kitchenware, textiles of cotton or linen fibers, handicrafts, sports and leisure wear in bright colors, boots, furs, children's wear, candles, wooden items, jewelry, knives.

Shops are usually open from 8:30 or 9 a.m. until 5 p.m. (department stores until 8 p.m.), Monday through Friday, until 2 or 4 p.m. on Saturdays. Helsinki Railway Station has an underground shopping center with closing hours as late as 10 p.m.

Sightseeing

Helsinki. Beautifully proportioned Senate Square *(Senaatintori)*★, designed by the architects Engel and Ehrenström, with many-domed neo-Classical Lutheran Cathedral *(Tuomiokirkko),* Government Palace, university and contrasting stone structure of Sederholm House. Overflowing vegetable stalls at Market Square *(Kauppatori)* and freshly caught fish sold from boats in Cholera Basin. Symbol of Helsinki—Havis Amanda fountain with sea nymph by Ville Vallgren. Attractive neo-Classical Town Hall facing market. Nearby dignified Presidential Palace with sentry on guard. Bridge over canal to Katajanokka peninsula dominated by enormous red-brick Uspensky Cathedral★. Kaivopuisto district of ornate wooden villas with astronomical observatory on hill, Spa Park. Cygnaeus Art Collection with paintings by national artists. Esplanadi, elegant shopping street with stunning window displays and handsome buildings. Convivial Kappeli café and restaurant once frequented by Sibelius. Statuary in Esplanadi park. Aleksanterinkatu "Christmas Street" with annual decorations. Art Deco style railroad station (1916), one of the masterpieces of world-famous Finnish architect Eliel Saarinen. Paintings by 20th-century artists in Amos Anderson Art Museum. Kaisaniemi park with Botanical

Gardens. Ateneum Art Gallery. Helsinki's longest street, Mannerheim-intie, named after Finland's hero, Marshal Mannerheim, with Parliament Building in gray granite. Nearby Rock Church *(Temppeliaukion kirkko)*★ carved out of the solid rock, superb example of modern Finnish architecture. National Museum★, with exhibits revealing Finland from prehistoric times to the present. Finlandia Hall★ in marble, congress center and concert hall, designed by the great Alvar Aalto. Hietaniemi Cemetery and grave of the Finnish unknown soldier. Sibelius Monument in a park laid out in honor of the composer.

Helsinki's Tourist Islands. Korkeasaari, site of what is said to be the world's northernmost zoo, marvelous beaches and harbor views. Suomenlinna (Sveaborg)★, once a key fortress island, old fortifications, museums, fine views of Helsinki. Seurasaari with Finland's oldest open-air museum, more than 80 buildings transplanted from all over the country; site of folk festivals.

Daytrips from Helsinki. Gallen-Kallela Museum on outskirts of Espoo, former home and studio of painter Akseli Gallen-Kallela. Espoo, model of modern urban design and fourth biggest city, with ecologically planned Tapiola Garden City, dramatic Auditorium of Institute of Technology, a modern glassed-in northern version of the Greek amphitheater by Aalto, and striking Dipoli Student Union building in stone, wood and concrete. Ainola, home and burial place of the composer Jean Sibelius in Järvenpää.

South Coast. Porvoo/Borgå, strategically placed historic town, Swedish stronghold and favorite of Finnish painters; wooden houses painted red, yellow and blue, riverside warehouses; Edelfelt-Vallgren Museum, outlines of careers of sculptor Ville Vallgren and painter Albert Edelfelt; wooden neo-Classical Runeberg House in the old town honoring national poet Johan Ludvig Runeberg. Haikko, nearby village, with beautiful stately home and views of Gulf of Finland. Hanko/Hangö, port and former naval base; fashionable spa, frequented by the 19th-century Russian aristocracy; 9 miles of sandy beaches; waterbus to Hauensuoli with trading emblems and coats of arms carved on the rocks by passing sailors since the 15th century. Turku/Åbo with ever-visible spire of medieval cathedral★, regarded by Finns as their national church; interesting tombs inside cathedral; two universities serving the Finnish-speaking majority and the minority of Swedish speakers; Sibelius Museum, memorabilia and photographs of composer; Orthodox Church with glowing Byzantine decoration inside; Luostarinmäki quarter★, original 17th-century buildings used as artisans' workshops;

Wäinö Aaltonen Museum, sculpture and painting, works by Finland's greatest contemporary sculptor. Turku castle containing Historical Museum. Ruissalo island connected to mainland at Turku by bridge. Naantali with sturdy church of St. Bridget above harbor; Town Museum with local artefacts; center for crafts, particularly textiles.

Åland Islands. Approximately 6,500 islands, some tiny and uninhabited, culturally Swedish with autonomy over internal affairs. Mariehamn/Maarianhamina, largest of Åland communities; Norra Esplanadgatan (North Esplanade) runs width of town with Åland Museum; Self-Government House at East Harbor; Åland Maritime Museum at West Harbor; Museum ship, *Pommern,* from 1903, preserved in original state. Open-air museum Jan Karlsgården with old farmhouses, barns, saunas. Medieval churches and colorful maypoles.

The Lake District. 62,000 lakes. Lappeenranta, gateway to the Soviet Union and Great Saimaa*, daytrips by boat to Vyborg just over the Soviet border through Saimaan canal; old Orthodox Church within the citadel. Savonlinna, popular lake resort on Lake Saimaa with storybook castle, Olavinlinna* (opera festival in the castle courtyard each July); Vääräsaari (Spa Island), site of Finland's first casino and spa; picturesque steamers. Country house Rauhalinna, amazing combination of styles. Beautiful excursion route to Kuopio (Heinävesi route). Orthodox monastery, fine collection of icons, in Byzantine style at Heinävesi. Kuopio, the seat of the Finnish Orthodox Church, with Art Nouveau Market Hall, interesting Orthodox Church Museum* displaying priceless works of religious art; Kuopio Museum of peasant arts and crafts; observation tower with magnificent views across Lake Kallavesi. Lahti, winter resort and site of Finlandia Ski Race. Hämeenlinna, Sibelius' birthplace, with 13th-century castle. Tampere, industrial textile town, Pyynikki, ridge stretching from city center with open-air theater; observation tower on Särkänniemi peninsula with view of Tammerkoski Rapids; planetarium, aquarium.

Lapland. Frontier province stretching from below Arctic Circle almost to Arctic Ocean with 200,000 inhabitants. Rovaniemi, rebuilt after being burned down in 1944; plans drawn up by Alvar Aalto, street plan in shape of reindeer antlers; Lappia House, congress center with Lapland Provincial Museum—7,800-year-old carving of moose; Lutheran church. Arctic Circle Cabin actually on Arctic Circle. Pohtimolampi with world's only reindeer driving school.

155

Some useful expressions in Finnish

good morning/afternoon	hyvää huomenta/päivää
good evening/night	hyvää iltaa/yötä
good-bye	hyvästi
yes/no	kyllä/ei
please/thank you	olkaa hyvä/kiitos
excuse me	anteeksi
you're welcome	ei kestä
where/when/how	missä/milloin/kuinka
how long/how far	miten kauan/miten kaukana
yesterday/today/tomorrow	eilen/tänään/huomenna
day/week/month/year	päivä/viikko/kuukausi/vuosi
left/right	vasen/oikea
up/down	ylös/alas
good/bad	hyvä/huono
big/small	suuri/pieni
cheap/expensive	halpa/kallis
hot/cold	kuuma/kylmä
old/new	vanha/uusi
open/closed	avoin/suljettu
free (vacant)/occupied	vapaa/varattu
early/late	aikainen/myöhäinen
easy/difficult	helppo/vaikea
Does anyone here speak English/French/German?	Puhuuko kukaan englantia/ranskaa/saksaa?
What does this mean?	Mitä tämä tarkoittaa?
I don't understand.	En ymmärrä.
Please write it down.	Olkaa hyvä ja kirjoittakaa se.
Do you take credit cards/traveler's checks?	Voinko maksaa luottokortilla/matkašekillä?
Waiter!/Waitress!	Tarjoilija!/Neiti!
Where are the toilets?	Missä on wc?
I'd like…	Haluaisin…
How much is that?	Mitä se maksaa?
What time is it?	Paljonko kello on?
Help me please.	Auttaisitteko minua.
Just a minute.	Odottakaa hetkinen.

FRANCE
and MONACO

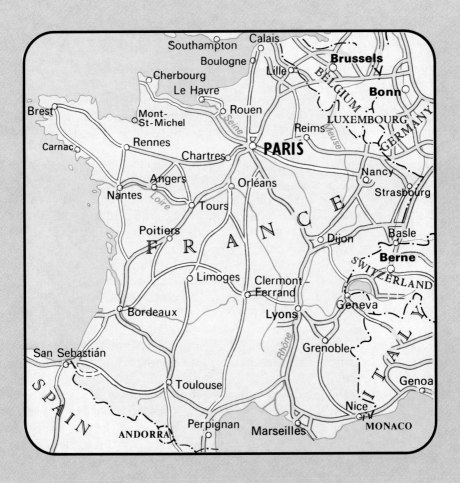

Grandeur, style and the good things of life from the Alps down to the seas.

Art lovers mount Montmartre, the frivolous flock to the Folies Bergère, the devout congregate in Lourdes, and sun-worshippers focus on the Riviera. From the bottomless trove of masterpieces in the Louvre to the topless beaches of Saint-Tropez, Western Europe's biggest country caters to all tastes in all seasons.

Style and sophistication give a special sparkle to everyday life in France: even the simplest clothes are worn with flair, and *la nouvelle cuisine* is a treat for the eye as well as the palate. Always keen on the good things in life, the French gave the world a certain idea of restaurants and bikinis, and, less predictably, invented the convenience of dry-cleaning, cars, buses and elevators. And France has always been fervently devoted to culture, whether the government was run by Charlemagne or Charles de Gaulle.

The artistic, intellectual, political and financial capital of France is Paris, with its own inimitable cityscape. The Seine and its bridges, the squares and boulevards, mansions and palaces, even the bars and bistros where the Impressionists lingered give the City of Light an unrivalled aura of romance. But for all its power and appeal, Paris has no monopoly on the grandeur of France. Each of the regions has its special greatness and charm, from the slopes of three-mile-high Mont-Blanc to the sweeping Atlantic; the invasion coast of Normandy, with its historic churches and castles; Brittany's ancient megaliths and Celtic folklore; the Romanesque architecture and the wine of Burgundy; the sensuous scenery of the Loire's château country; the Roman relics and scented fields of Provence...

In each region the local food merits serious attention, whether it's as traditional as *coq au vin* or as avant-garde as the latest lobster-and-mint concoction; it all adds up to what is widely considered the best eating in the world. And while you're studying the wines, save a glass for the cheese, of which the French have several hundred varieties... typical of a land of individualists who demand the best.

Facts and figures

Population:	55 million
Area:	212,919 sq.miles (547,026 sq.km.)
Capital:	Paris (2.2 million/GUA 8.7 million)
Other major cities:	Lyons (*Lyon,* 410,000/GUA 1.2 million) Marseilles (*Marseille,* 870,000/GUA 1,1 million) Lille (170,000/GUA 950,000) Bordeaux (210,000/GUA 640,000) Toulouse (345,000/GUA 540,000) Nice (335,000/GUA 450,000) Nantes (240,000/GUA 465,000) Strasbourg (250,000/GUA 375,000)
Language:	French
Religion:	Catholic (88%)
Time zone:	GMT + 1, EST + 6; DST (late Mar.–end Sep.)
Currency:	French *franc* (abbr. F or FF) = 100 *centimes* (ct.) Coins: 5, 10, 20, 50 centimes; 1, 2, 5, 10 F Bills: 20, 50, 100, 200, 500 F
Electricity:	Generally 220 volt, 50 cycle, AC, with 110 volt in some areas

Planning your trip

Visa requirements. See pp. 29–30.

Vaccination requirements. None (see also p. 25).

Currency restrictions. There's no limit on the importation or exportation of local or foreign currencies or traveler's checks, but amounts exceeding 50,000 French francs or equivalent must be declared on arrival.

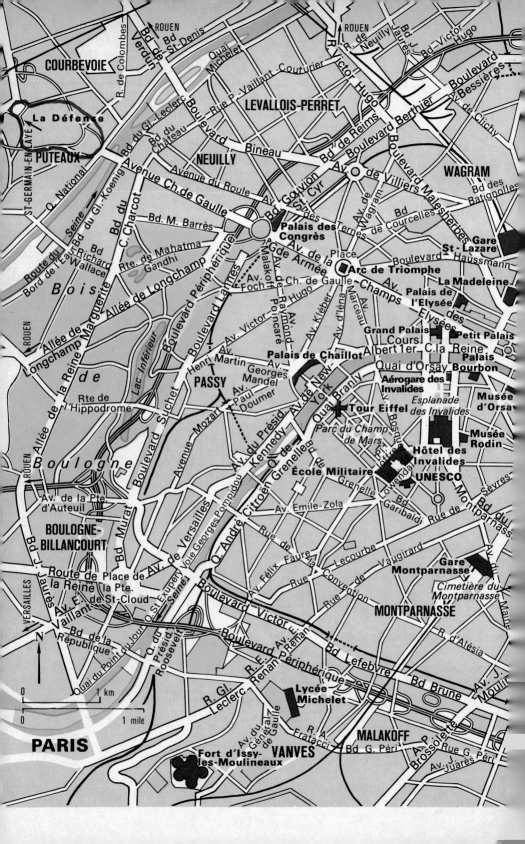

Climate. France enjoys a mainly maritime temperate climate in the northern and western areas (including Paris). To the east and in the interior Massif Central, the régime tends to be more continental, with warmer summers and colder winters. The Mediterranean coastal area is marked by hot, dry summers and mild, showery winters. With the exception of this coast, rainfall is sporadic all year round with most precipitation between January and April and least in August and September. Snow is only rarely a problem in winter city streets, except in high mountain areas.

Paris' climate is in most people's opinion beautiful: its spring is unbeatable, its summer often hot but not scorching, its fall gloriously romantic and gently warm and its winters quite supportable. Broadly, the further south you go the warmer, but beware of high-altitude areas, such as the Auvergne where even if summers are nice and hot, the rest of the year tends to be harsh.

Some average daily temperatures:

Paris		J	F	M	A	M	J	J	A	S	O	N	D
average daily	°F	43	45	54	60	68	73	76	75	70	60	50	44
maximum*	°C	6	7	12	16	20	23	25	24	21	16	10	7
average daily	°F	34	34	39	43	49	55	58	58	53	46	40	36
minimum*	°C	1	1	4	6	10	13	15	14	12	8	5	2

Marseilles													
average daily	°F	50	53	59	64	71	79	84	83	77	68	58	52
maximum*	°C	10	12	15	18	22	26	29	28	25	20	15	11
average daily	°F	35	36	41	46	52	58	63	63	58	51	43	37
minimum*	°C	2	2	5	8	11	15	17	17	15	10	6	3

* Minimum temperatures are measured just before sunrise, maximum temperatures in the afternoon.

Clothing. Except in winter, when you'll need warm outer clothes in virtually all parts of the country—in particular in mountainous regions and in the sometimes damp northeast—mediumweight attire is usually adequate. However, even in the southern summer, when light cotton clothes are all you'll need during the day, a sweater or a jacket comes in handy for an occasional chilly evening. You are likely to need rainwear at any time of the year. Some restaurants require jacket and tie for men.

162

Duty-free allowances

	Cigarettes		Cigars		Tobacco	Liquor	Wine
1)	400	or	100	or	500 g.	1 l. and	2 l.
2)	200	or	50	or	250 g.	1 l. and	2 l.
3)	300	or	75	or	400 g.	1 ½ l. and	5 l.

Perfume: 1), 2) 50 g.; 3) 75 g.
Toilet water: 1) 2) ¼ l.; 3) ³/₈ l.
Gifts: 300 F max. value for merchandise originating outside EEC, and 2,400 F max. value for merchandise originating within EEC.

1) visitors arriving from outside Europe
2) visitors arriving from EEC countries with duty-free items, or from other European countries
3) visitors arriving from EEC countries with non-duty-free items

Hotels and accommodations

Hotels. Hotels throughout France are officially classified from one- to four-star luxury establishments. Room prices, fixed according to amenities, size and the hotel's star rating, must be posted at reception desks and on the inside of each room door. French National Tourist offices abroad have this information on file. Individual city or regional tourist offices supply local hotel lists, and hotel guide books are commercially available. The Accueil de France offices located in tourist officies in the cities will make room reservations for you for a small fee. Major airports and railroad stations have hotel reservation desks. Advance reservations are essential during vacation periods and when trade fairs are on.

Relais et Châteaux. These hotels, covering the whole of France, offer several tempting possibilities, notably in the Loire Valley. All are four-star establishments.

Relais du Silence. A chain of two- to four-star hotels in tranquil settings. Some are genuine, old-time stagecoach inns. Establishments are listed in a free booklet published annually, available from the tourist office.

Logis de France, Auberge de France. Small or quiet hotels, often on the outskirts or outside of towns. *Logis de France* are in the one- and two-

163

star bracket; *auberges de France* are typical inn-type establishments in the country. A *Guide des Logis de France* is produced annually and given out free at national tourist offices abroad.

Gîtes de France; Gîtes ruraux. Officially sponsored, furnished vacation accommodations (houses, apartments or rooms) with standards and prices officially controlled. Rental costs include all charges.

House rental. Local tourist offices *(Syndicat d'Initiative)* can recommend agencies with complete lists of available houses and apartments to let. You should reserve well ahead.

Youth hostels *(Auberge de Jeunesse)*. Your national youth hostel association can give you all the details, or you may contact the Fédération Unie des Auberges de Jeunesse, 27, rue Pajol, 75118 Paris; tel. 42.41.59.00.

Camping. Camping in France is a well-organized business. Campsites are officially graded from one to four stars. There are about 10,000 sites in France, including more than 100 in the Paris area. Free camping is in general not permitted. If you want to camp on private property. you must first get permission from the property owner. During peak seasons you have to make reservations well in advance. For further information about camping consult the special leaflet issued by the French National Tourist Office or contact the Fédération Française de Camping et de Caravaning, 78, rue de Rivoli, 75004 Paris; tel. 42.72.84.08.

French tourist offices abroad

Australia	Kindersley House, 33 Bligh Street, Sydney, NSW 2000; tel. (2) 231-5244
Canada	1981 MacGill College Avenue, Esso Tower, Suite 490, Montreal, Que. H3A 2W9; tel. (514) 288-4264 1 Dundas Street W, Suite 2405, P.O. Box 8, Toronto, Ont. M5G 1Z3; tel. (416) 593-4723
U.K.	178, Piccadilly, London W1V 0AL; tel. (071) 493 6694
U.S.A.	645 N. Michigan Avenue, Suite 630, Chicago, IL 60611; tel. (312) 337-6301 9401 Wilshire Boulevard, Room 840, Beverly Hills, CA 90212; tel. (213) 272-2661 610 Fifth Avenue, New York, NY 10020; tel (212) 757-1125 1 Hallidie Plaza, San Francisco, CA 94102; tel. (415) 986-4174

On the spot

Banks and currency exchange. Most banks open Monday through Friday only. Hours vary from city to city and even from bank to bank. Paris hours are 9 a.m. to 4:30 p.m. In other cities banks tend to open from 9 a.m. to noon and 2 to 4 p.m. on weekdays, and close either on Saturdays (main towns) or Mondays.

Outside of banking hours, money can be changed at a few *bureaux de change,* at international airports and at important rail stations. Most airport currency-exchange bureaus are open from early morning to late evening. Those at train stations close around 8 p.m. as a rule. Some currency-exchange offices, even at airports, close on weekends.

Credit cards and traveler's checks. Leading credit cards are being used in an increasing number of larger and tourist-oriented establishments such as hotels and restaurants. Traveler's checks are also widely accepted, though exchange rates in stores, restaurants, etc., will be less favorable than in a bank or *bureau de change.* Outside the towns, it's preferable to have some ready cash with you. Don't forget to take your passport when going to cash a traveler's check or change money.

Mail and telecommunications. French post offices display a sign with a stylized blue bird and/or the words *La Poste (PTT).* Post offices handle mail, telegrams and telephone calls.

In cities, the main post office is generally open from 8 a.m. to 7 p.m., Monday through Friday, and until noon on Saturdays. In smaller towns the hours are usually from 9 a.m. to noon, and 2 to 5 p.m., Monday through Friday, and 8 a.m. to noon on Saturdays. Paris has a round-the-clock service at 52, rue du Louvre, 75001 Paris. You can also buy stamps at tobacco shops. Mailboxes are yellow.

All local post offices accept domestic and overseas telegrams. You may also dictate a telegram over the telephone.

Within France, all main centers are linked by an automatic telephone network, and direct dialing is possible to many countries.

International and long-distance calls can be made from ordinary phone booths, but if you need assistance in placing the call, go to the post office or ask at your hotel. There are two types of pay phones. One takes a range of coins, the other is card-operated. The *télécarte* system is gradually phasing out coin-operated phones, but the latter can still be found in post offices. Cards are sold at post offices, railroad stations and shops recognizable by a "Télécarte" sign, and are available for 40 or 120 charge units.

For long-distance calls within France, there are no area codes (just

167

dial the eight-digit number of the person you want to call), *except* when. telephoning from Paris or the Paris region to the provinces (dial 16 and wait for the dialing tone, then dial the eight-digit number of the subscriber) and from the provinces to Paris and the Paris region (dial 16 and wait for the dialing tone, then dial 1 followed by the eight-digit number).

To call abroad from France, dial 19 followed, after the change of tone, by the number of the country. The international code numbers are posted in all phone booths and phone books. Have plenty of 1- and 5-franc coins ready. If direct dialing is not available to that country, dial 19 and wait for the tone, then dial 33 followed by the code number of the country in question, to reach the operator (U.S. and Canada 1, and U.K. 44). If you don't know the telephone number of the subscriber, dial 19.33.12, followed by the code number of the country in question.

If you want to make a collect call, ask for *un appel en PCV*. For a person-to-person call, specify *un appel avec préavis pour ...*

For surcharges and low rates, see p. 30.

Some useful telephone numbers:

Information		Telegrams	14
(local Paris)	12	Fire	18
Information		Police & ambulance	17
(rest of France)	16.11.12		

The **Minitel** has invaded most French homes and public buildings. It's used for everything from looking up phone numbers to booking theater tickets to ordering a case of Bordeaux. A little brochure—"Passeport Tourisme Minitel"—with operating instructions in English and a list of useful codes is available from tourist offices. Some of the 7,000 services are in English.

Newspapers. France's leading dailies are *Le Monde, Le Figaro, Le Matin, France Soir* and, in English, the *International Herald Tribune*. A selection of foreign newspapers is generally available at larger newsstands in the main cities on the day of publication. *Pariscope* is the best-known of the weekly information magazines on sale.

Tourist information. Each town of any importance in France has a local tourist office called the *Syndicat d'Initiative*. They are an absolute mine of information on local and regional possibilities with lists and brochures, timetables, suggested excursions, etc. Opening hours vary but the general rule is 8:30 or 9 a.m. to noon and 2 to 6 or 7 p.m. every day except Sunday. Off season, many work greatly reduced hours.

Paris	127, avenue des Champs-Elysées, 75008 Paris; tel. 47.23.61.72. For a selection of the principal weekly events in English, call 47.20.88.98.
Marseilles	4, la Canebière, 13001 Marseille and in railroad station (summer only); tel. 91.54.91.11.
Lyons	Place Bellecour, 69002 Lyon; tel. 78.42.25.75.
Toulouse	Donjon du Capitole, 31000 Toulouse; tel. 61.23.32.00.
Nice	5, avenue Gustave V, 06000 Nice; tel. 93.87.60.60; at airport (parking Ferber); in railroad station.
Strasbourg	Palais des Congrès, avenue Schutzenberger, 67000 Strasbourg; tel. 88.35.03.00; and place Gutenberg, 67000 Strasbourg; tel. 88.32.57.07.
Bordeaux	12 cours du 30 Juillet, 33000 Bordeaux; tel. 56.44.28.41.
Lille	Palais Rihour, 59000 Lille; tel. 20.30.81.00.

Legal holidays

Jan. 1	New Year's Day	**Movable dates:**
May 1	Labor Day	Easter Monday
May 8	Victory Day	Ascension
Jul. 14	Bastille Day	Whit Monday
Aug. 15	Assumption	
Nov. 1	All Saints' Day	
Nov. 11	Armistice Day	
Dec. 25	Christmas Day	

Transportation

Air. Paris is by far the major gateway to France, though a number of international flights operate to Lyons and Nice and to certain other cities.

France's principal domestic airline, Air Inter, and other short-haul carriers fly between Paris and airports in various parts of the country and link some provincial cities directly with each other.

Major airports. Paris: Charles-de-Gaulle-Roissy (16 miles/25 km. northeast of city center) and Orly (10 miles/16 km. south of city center). Both airports have currency-exchange offices, restaurants and duty-free shops. Regular bus service to Paris. Town terminal for Charles-de-Gaulle: Porte Maillot; for Orly: Invalides. Trains from Gare du Nord to

170

Charles-de-Gaulle. From Quai d'Orsay, Saint-Michel or Austerlitz, trains to Orly. **Marseilles:** Provence (17 miles/28 km. from city center). Duty-free shop. Bus service to Gare Saint-Charles. **Lyons:** Satolas (17 miles/27 km. from city center). Duty-free shop. Bus service to Gare de Perrache. **Toulouse:** Blagnac (4 miles/7 km. from city center). Duty-free shop. Bus services to Gare Matabiau. **Nice:** Nice-Côte d'Azur (4 miles/7 km. from Nice). Duty-free shop. Bus service to Nice, another to Cannes. Bus and helicopter services to Monaco. **Strasbourg:** Entzheim (8 miles/12 km. from city center). Duty-free shop. Bus service to Place Kléber, Passage de l'Aubette and Grand Hotel/Place de la Gare. **Bordeaux:** Mérignac (7 miles/11 km. from city center). Duty-free shop. Bus service to Cours du 30 Juillet and Gare St.-Jean. **Lille:** Lesquin (5 miles/8 km. from city center). Duty-free shop. Bus service to Nouvelle Gare Routière.

Rail. The SNCF *(Société Nationale des Chemins de Fer Français),* the national railroad system, operates fast and comfortable trains. Dining cars and sleepers are of good quality. High-speed trains—TGV *(Train à grande vitesse)*—link Paris with other major cities at 150 mph (260 kph). Seat reservation obligatory.

Various categories of tickets, such as *Billet Touristique, Billet de Groupe, Billet de Famille,* that provide reductions, are available for groups, families, etc. Ask for details at the station.

Visitors from abroad can buy a *France Vacances Spécial* pass, valid for specified periods of unlimited travel on first or second class, with reductions on Paris' transportation network and one or two days free car rental (with first class only) depending on type of card. For *Eurailpass,* see p. 33.

Don't forget to validate your ticket, by inserting it in one of the orange machines *(machine à composter)* on the way to the platform. If the ticket isn't clipped and dated, the conductor is entitled to fine you on the train.

Boats, waterways. Car ferries sail to Corsica from Marseilles, Toulon and Nice. Launch services operate between smaller islands like Belle-Ile and Iles d'Hyères and the mainland all year around.

Local public transportation. All major cities have bus services. Paris, Lyons, Marseilles and Lille also operate efficient and speedy *métro* (subway) systems. Reduced-rate booklets *(carnets)* of tickets are available for first or second class. For longer stays in Paris and lots of travel, you can buy an orange identity card *(carte orange)* valid for a week or a month on buses and the subway.

Taxis. You can hail a cab on the street, phone for one or go to a taxi stand. In main cities taxis are metered. You'll pay according to rates posted on the cab window, not necessarily just the price indicated on the meter (for example, extra charges for luggage).

Car rental. International and local car-rental agencies are found at major airports as well as in town centers. See also pp. 30–31.

Driving in France. Drive on the right, pass on the left. Your car must be equipped with a red reflector warning triangle for use in case of breakdown and a set of spare bulbs. You'll also need a blue-zone parking disc, obtainable from police stations and tourist offices. (Rented cars normally come with a parking disc in the glove compartment.) The use of seat belts is compulsory. Children under 10 may not travel in the front. Speed limits are 81 mph (130 kph) on expressways, 68 mph (110 kph) on divided highways, 56 mph (90 kph) on other roads and 28 or 37 mph (45 or 60 kph) in built-up areas. When roads are wet, all limits are reduced by 6 mph (10 kph). Except where otherwise indicated, traffic coming from the right has priority. Blood alcohol limit is a strictly enforced 80 mg./100 ml.

Road conditions are good and expressways (with high tolls) excellent. Main expressways: Paris–Lille–Dunkirk, Paris–Strasbourg, Paris–Lyons–Marseilles–Nice/Lyons–Narbonne. All amenities (restaurants, service stations, etc.) are available, plus orange S.O.S. telephones every two kilometers. Gasoline available is normal (90 octane), super (98 octane), lead-free and diesel (called *gas-oil*).

One of the great charms of driving in France is to use the dense network of smaller roads. Even if signposting generally is adequate it's always wise to carry a set of the excellent and yearly updated maps in 1:200 000 scale. You can count on an average speed of 35 mph.

In blue zones (parking spaces marked with a blue line), parking is free of charge but limited in time. You set the arrival time on the parking disc, which then should be displayed in the windshield.

Some distances: Paris–Calais 185 miles (300 km.), Lyons 290 miles (465 km.) Bordeaux 365 miles (585 km.), Marseilles 485 miles (780 km).

Bicycle rental. Cycling being a highly popular sport in France, it's possible to rent bicycles in most towns. French National Railways (SNCF) operate a cycle-rental service. Bicycles may be rented at one station and returned at another.

Rest rooms. Clean public rest rooms are still not all that common in France. If there is no light-switch, the light will usually go on when you

172

lock the door. If you use the rest room in a café you should order at least a cup of coffee. A saucer with small change on it means that a tip is expected. The women's rest rooms may be marked *Dames,* the men's either *Messieurs* or *Hommes.*

Emergencies. For real emergencies you can get assistance anywhere in France by dialing the number 17 for the police; dial 18 for the fire brigade.

Crime and theft. Paris, Nice, Marseilles and Lyons are cities to be wary in—more so than, for example, Strasbourg and Bordeaux. It's always wise to keep to well-lit streets at night and to watch your wallet. Never leave any belongings in your car parked overnight.

Medical care and health. The standard of medical treatment in France is generally very high. Fees for medical treatment vary widely. Doctors who belong to the French social security system *(médecins conventionnés)* charge the minimum.

Many physicians speak English. Your hotel receptionist can probably recommend an English-speaking doctor or dentist; otherwise ask at the *Syndicat d'Initiative,* or, in an emergency, the police *(gendarmerie).* The American Hospital in Neuilly outside Paris is often preferred by English-speaking people of whatever nationality.

Medicine and pharmaceutical supplies are readily available in all cities. Pharmacies *(pharmacie)* display green crosses. Pharmacists are helpful in dealing with minor ailments and can give medical advice. Duty pharmacies, open after hours as well as on Sundays and holidays, are listed in local newspapers, including "What's On" guides; the addresses are also posted in other pharmacy windows. The Pharmacie des Champs-Elysées, 84, avenue des Champs-Elysées, Paris; tel. 45.62.02.41 is open 24 hours a day. For insurance, see pp. 25–26.

Tap water is safe to drink.

Embassies and consulates. All embassies are in Paris. Consult the "ambassades" or "consulats" entries in the phone book.

Social customs. Don't forget to shake hands when meeting someone or taking your leave. French people always greet very close friends with kisses on both cheeks. Being invited to somebody's home, even after a long acquaintance, is rare, but for such an occasion, a small gift of flowers or chocolates for the hostess will be appreciated.

174

Enjoying France

Food and drink. Eating and drinking is a serious business in France and not just a means of satisfying hunger and thirst. Watch discriminating housewives make their selection of vegetables in the open-air markets; listen to the conversation at the next table as diners choose dishes and the wines to go with them.

A classical French meal consists of apéritif, hors d'oeuvre, fish course, meat course, salad, cheese, dessert and coffee. This exercise takes a good part of the evening. The final touch is a digestif, brandy or liqueur, for a good night's sleep.

You might start with *crudités* (a plate of fresh raw vegetables), *charcuterie* (various kinds of sausage or other cold meats), *jambon* (ham) from Bayonne or Dijon, or *potage* (rich vegetable soup, with a base of leek and potato) or perhaps a *bisque de homard* (a creamy lobster soup).

Fish comes fresh every day, and not just to Paris. Fish delicacies include sole, turbot, trout, *quenelles de brochet* (dumplings of ground pike), and costly lobsters and oysters. Traditionally oysters are not eaten in months without an "r" in the name, that is, avoid them from May to August. Among the fish course sauces, *sauce hollandaise* is made of egg yolks, butter and lemon juice. *Beurre blanc,* literally white butter, is another light and fluffy sauce, while *sauce cardinal* is a rich lobster sauce.

For your main dish, expect your meat to be less well-done than in most countries—extra rare is *bleu*, rare is *saignant,* medium is *à point,* and well-done, *bien cuit* (and frowned upon). Steaks *(entrecôtes* or *tournedos),* of which the best come from Charolais, are often served with a wine sauce *(marchand de vin* or *bordelaise)* or with shallots *(échalotes)* or with *sauce béarnaise,* which gets its distinctive flavor from leaves of fresh tarragon.

General de Gaulle once asked how one could possibly govern a country with 400 different cheeses. Try at least the most famous of them—*Roquefort, Camembert, Brie* and the myriad of goat cheeses *(fromages de chèvre).*

As for dessert, try *tarte Tatin,* made with hot caramelized apples, said to have been invented by mistake by a lady named Tatin who put her pie in the oven upside down. Other favorite old-fashioned desserts are *crème caramel,* and *mousse au chocolat* (chocolate mousse). *Glace* and *sorbet* (ice cream and sherbets), when homemade, *fait maison,* using the best ingredients and the finest fresh fruit and berries, are equally delicious.

Specialties from Lyons include *poulet de Bresse* (farm-raised chicken), incomparable in taste, even if not truffled; and *gras-double lyonnais* (tripe with onions and vinegar). Provence—the home of garlic, olives,

175

tomatoes and fragrant herbs—and the south generally excel in fish, like *loup* (sea bass), fish soup and vegetable preparations; a world-famous specialty is *ratatouille,* a vegetable stew which may be served either hot or cold. From the coast between Marseilles and Toulon comes the celebrated *bouillabaisse* (a Mediterranean fish stew). Burgundy, the wine-growing region, produces the world's greatest beef stew, *boeuf bourguignon,* beef simmered in red wine with mushrooms, small white onions and chunks of bacon. Bordeaux is famous for its *bordelaise* sauce, made with wine, shallots and beef marrow, served with entrecôte steaks. The southwest—Languedoc and Périgord—is the origin for *pâté de foie gras* (goose-liver pâté) and truffles and for all the richness of the goose and duck. The area around Alsace is known for its excellent *quiche lorraine* (a savory pie made of eggs, cream and bacon), *tarte aux oignons* (onion tart) and *choucroute* (sauerkraut).

The modern pace of life and a concern about health and waistline have influenced eating habits in France. *La nouvelle cuisine* features lighter fare, reduced amounts of cream and butter and almost bans flour. Particular emphasis is put on appetizing appearence. But in France there is room for the new style of cooking as well as for the traditional. They prosper side by side and the choice is yours.

The study of French wines is a delectable if—for the beginner—rather daunting pursuit. Follow the general ground rule of red or rosé with meat, and white or rosé with fish and fowl. Don't be afraid to ask the waiter for his advice. Sampling the locally produced wines can be an interesting experience.

Should you want a few basic pointers about the classic wines, the Burgundy reds divide easily into two categories, those that can more safely be drunk relatively young—the supple Côte de Beaune wines of Aloxe-Corton, Pommard and Volnay—and those that need to age a little, the full-bodied Côte de Nuits wines of Vougeot, Gevrey-Chambertin and Chambolle-Musigny. The great Burgundy whites include Meursault and Puligny-Montrachet.

Bordeaux wines have four main regional divisions: Médoc, aromatic, mellow red with a slight edge to it; Graves, a soft easy-to-drink red, both dry and vigorous like the Burgundies; Saint-Emilion, dark strong and full-bodied; and the pale golden Sauternes, sweet and fragrant, the most distinctive of the soft, aromatic whites. The lesser Bordeaux can all be drunk a couple of years old but good ones need five years.

The Loire Valley produces fine dry white wines, such as Vouvray, Muscadet and Sancerre, and robust reds like Bourgueil and Chinon. Perhaps the best known red wine outside Bordeaux and Burgundy is the Châteauneuf-du-Pape, produced in the Rhone Valley and truly magnificent when mature. Other very drinkable regional wines include Côtes du Rhône, Cahors and the Riesling, Traminer and Sylvaner of Alsace.

And for a sparkling finish, the nation's pride and joy, from that little area east of Paris between Reims and Epernay: Champagne, which they describe as *aimable, fin et élégant,* friendly, refined and elegant.

Not to mention the whole array of apéritifs, digestifs, liqueurs and local *alcools blancs* that make other countries pale with envy.

Lunch is served from noon to 2 p.m., dinner 7 to 9 or 10 p.m. (often later in summer).

Entertainment. Paris boasts a plethora of nightclubs, floor-shows and discos, and there's no lack of concerts, plays, ballet and movie theaters. One of the truly great moments of the Paris season is a gala evening at the Opéra. Films are often shown in the original language with French subtitles, especially around the Champs-Elysées and the Latin Quarter. For details consult the weekly entertainment-guides *Pariscope* and *L'Officiel du Spectacle.*

All major cities offer varied music and theater performances. Ballet life in Marseilles has a world reputation. Nightlife in the form of discos also flourishes in the provinces—in particular on the Riviera, where several casinos are located. For admission to these gambling places you will need your passport.

Annual events and festivals. *February:* Nice Carnival. Mimosa Festival in Cannes. Lemon Festival in Menton. *May:* Joan of Arc and National Liberation Day in Orléans. Cannes International Film Festival. Musical May Concerts in Bordeaux. *May–June:* Paris International Tennis Tournament. *June:* Fête Jeanne d'Arc in Chinon. International Festival of Music in Strasbourg. Le Mans 24 hours car race. Paris International Air Show. *June–July:* Tour de France (bicycle race). *July:* Antibes Jazz Festival. International Music and Opera Festival in Aix-en-Provence. Jazz Parade in Nice. Avignon Festival. Celtic Festival in Quimper. *July 14:* Bastille Day celebrated throughout France. *September:* Dijon Wine Festival. *November:* Dijon International Gastronomic Fair.

Taxes, service charges and tipping. Sales tax (in French abbreviated TVA) and a 10–15% service charge will generally be included in your hotel or restaurant bills. Rounding up the overall bill is a gesture of added appreciation to the waiter. Tipping recommendations: hotel porters 5 F per bag, taxi drivers 10–15%, hatcheck attendants 2 F, hairdressers/barbers (if not included) 10–15%, ushers in movie theaters, concert halls and theaters 2–3 F, hotel maids 50–100 F per week.

Sports and recreation. Tennis courts abound, though advance reservation is often necessary. There are golf links with reasonable fees all over France (in the Paris, Cannes, Bordeaux, Lille, Lyons, Strasbourg and Toulouse areas). Hunting and fishing are popular seasonally in all parts of the country. Water-sports facilities are outstanding, with sailing, swimming, windsurfing and snorkeling in all coastal areas. Stables with mounts for rent are found throughout the country. Excellent hiking opportunities to suit all levels. All winter sports are available within striking distance of Nice and Lyons.

Soccer is the most popular spectator sport, followed by rugby and cycling. Paris holds open tennis championships towards the end of May at Roland-Garros. Horse lovers will find notable race courses (including Auteuil and Longchamps) around Paris and along the Riviera. The Tour de France cycle race takes place in June–July and ends with a colorful sprint up the Champs-Elysées.

TV and radio. There are several color TV channels in France. All programs (except for a few late movies) are in French.

BBC programs can be heard on short- or medium-wave radios.

What to buy. Good buys include perfume, silk scarves, antiques, crystal and porcelain, luxury foods such as *foie gras,* wine, liquor and cheese. The fashion capital and other French cities offer a wide range of haute-couture and ready-to-wear apparel for women, but prices are high by international standards. In some cases the sales tax is refunded, see p. 40.

As a rule, large department stores are open between 10 a.m. and 6 p.m. six days a week. Other shops open 9 or 9:30 a.m. and close 6:30 or 7 p.m., Monday through Saturday. Smaller shops outside Paris generally close for two hours for lunch. Food stores are often open on Sunday mornings. Many shops close all or half of Monday. Off season and in winter, most shops tend to close earlier.

World-famous shopping streets include Rue du Faubourg Saint-Honoré and Avenue Montaigne for the masters of *haute couture* and for a change of style the narrow streets on the Left Bank *(Rive Gauche)* between Place Saint-Michel and Place Saint-Germain-des-Prés.

Sightseeing

Paris. The Eiffel Tower★, Paris' best-known symbol, constructed for the World's Fair in 1889. Ile de la Cité, the cradle of the city of Paris, crowned by Notre Dame de Paris★, the nation's parish church with a superb central rose window. Nearby Sainte-Chapelle with its stained-glass windows, built in 1248, a masterpiece in harmony and proportions. The Louvre★, former royal residence, one of the world's largest museums, overflowing with famous paintings, including the *Mona Lisa.* Place de la Concorde, huge and beautiful with Paris' oldest monument, the 3,300-year-old obelisk of Luxor, and nightmarish traffic jams. The bridges crossing the Seine, another Paris attribute, cherished by people in love as well as by *clochards* (down-and-outs). Palais Royal, an arcaded palace with its garden, completed in 1639 for Cardinal Richelieu. Octagonal Place Vendôme with bronze spiral column depicting great battles. Rue du Faubourg Saint-Honoré, elegant shopping street lined with all the glorious names of French Haute Couture; the president's residence in the Elysée Palace at number 55. The Champs-Elysées★, the world's most celebrated avenue, lined with movie theaters, shops and café terraces,

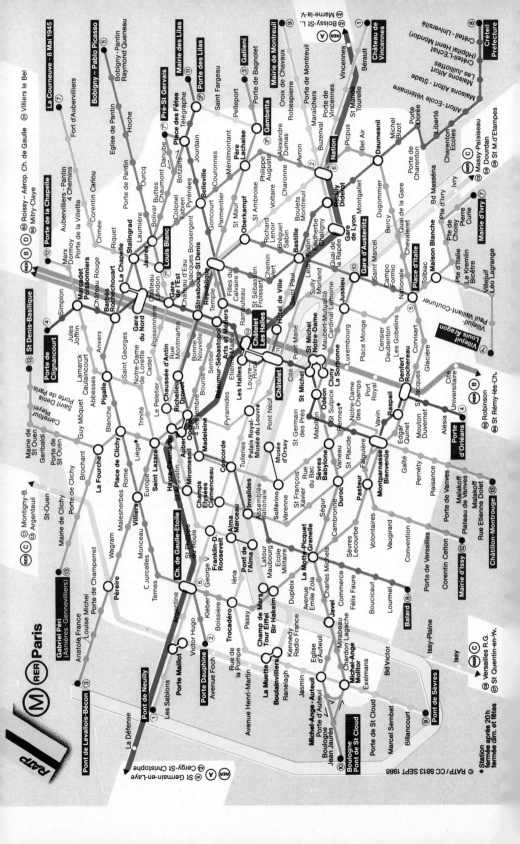

culminating at 19th-century architect Haussmann's creation, Place de l'Etoile, renamed the Place Charles de Gaulle, with Arc de Triomphe; twelve avenues radiating from Napoleon's gigantic triumphal arch with the eternal flame commemorating France's unknown soldier. Bois de Boulogne, where the Parisians take a breather, 2,224 acres (912 ha.) of forests, gardens and sports grounds. Latin Quarter* with busy Boulevard Saint-Michel and Sorbonne, since 1254 citadel of Paris' students. Luxembourg Gardens*, a fairy-tale garden avoiding the rigid geometry of Versailles and with added charm from the statues. Neo-Classic Panthéon, resting place of the nation's military, political and literary heroes. Saint-Germain-des-Prés, home of boutiques, art galleries, bookstores and literary cafés, a charming neighborhood for round-the-clock people-watching. Montmartre with its nightclubs, long famous as the home of real and fake artists and bohemians. Basilica of Sacré-Coeur with its miraculously white façade. Controversial architecture in Beaubourg*, a public library, modern art museum, *cinématheque* and experimental music laboratory combined. Les Halles, with famous market demolished, replaced by Forum des Halles for shopping addicts, but the onion soup still attracts incurable night owls. The Marais* quarter on reclaimed marshland, containing some of Europe's most elegant Renaissance-style houses. Place des Vosges, Paris' oldest monumental square. The Picasso Museum in Hôtel Salé with rich selection from the artist's own production and his personal collection of contemporary works of art. Orsay Museum, recalling France's tremendous creativity from 1848 to 1914 (painting, sculpture, architecture, advertising, publishing, photography and the early days of motion pictures). Orangerie, first-class permanent collections, featuring Monet's *Nymphéas*. Tuileries, French-style formal gardens. La Villette, a striking futuristic complex of cultural and scientific activities.

Ile de France and Champagne. Versailles*, the sumptuous setting for the royal court of the Sun King, Louis XIV; Hall of Mirrors *(Galerie des Glaces)*, Royal Apartments, fountains; Trianons and Le Hameau, Marie Antoinette's little cottage. Malmaison, charming palace with Napoleon's and Josephine's apartments. Rambouillet, the summer residence of the French president. Saint-Denis, early Gothic basilica with medieval and Renaissance tombs of French kings. Sèvres with national ceramic workshops and museum. Fontainebleau, royal palace surrounded by formal gardens and vast forest. Chartres* with one of the world's greatest Gothic cathedrals dominating the flat landscape, known for its gracious stained-glass windows. Senlis, ancient town also with beautiful Gothic cathedral. Chantilly, highlighted by elegant château and park, race

181

course. Reims, in the heart of Champagne country, with superb 13th-century Gothic cathedral, where the kings of France were crowned; champagne factory visits.

Normandy and Channel Coast. Remains of German fortifications and Allied D-Day landings along coast. Rouen boasting a cathedral with dissimilar towers and the tallest spire in France; Place du Vieux Marché, the square where St. Joan of Arc burned at stake. Deauville and Trouville, lively and elegant beach resorts. Bayeux with splendid cathedral and museum displaying the famous tapestry* depicting the Norman invasion of England. Caen with Gothic church and castle. Mont-Saint-Michel*, fairy-tale rock-island with Gothic Abbey and fortress. Ports of Calais and Dunkirk. Boulogne, France's most important fishing port, the old parts of town surrounded by medieval walls. Le Touquet, fashionable seaside resort with extravagant casino. Amiens with Gothic cathedral, the biggest in France, begun about 1220. Lille, industrial and commercial center, with rich art museum, ancient Bourse, a fine example of Flemish architecture.

Brittany. Wild landscapes, rocky coastlines, dramatic tidal waters, beaches. Saint-Malo*, now a fashionable resort, old walled city and ramparts, surrounded on three sides by sea. Fort-la-Latte, sturdy feudal castle beside the sea. Violet-pink rock formations at Côte de Granit Rose. Wild, dramatic Cap Fréhel. Locronan, town of artisans. Small fishing ports or towns like Roscoff, Concarneau, Andierne. Sea food at its best. Pointe du Raz, the westernmost rocky cape of France, awesome panorama of Breton coast. Quimper, site of proud cathedral and medieval Rue Kéréon, lined by half-timbered cantilevered houses leaning out over passers-by. Carnac*, seaside resort near world's greatest concentrations of prehistoric megaliths. Rennes, capital of Brittany, old town with its stately Town Hall. La Baule, stylish sea resort with fine, long beaches. Nantes, one of France's most important ports, with Gothic cathedral and 15th-century ducal castle.

Loire Valley. Angers, site of château with 17 mighty black-and-white layered towers and priceless 14th-century Apocalypse Tapestry; Saint-Maurice Cathedral with pale belfries tower in sharp contrast to black slate roofs. Saumur with 12th-13th-century château on a promontory, high above the town and the River Loire, famous national riding school, equestrian museum. Chinon, famous for château and historic streets, Rue Voltaire, with totally medieval atmosphere; spectacular view. Langeais, feudal castle from 15th century with a massive drawbridge. Azay-le-Rideau*, castle of graceful proportions and white stone,

182

reflected in the green waters of the River Indre. Tours, capital of rich Touraine; towering Saint-Gatien Cathedral with its superb 13th-century stained-glass windows. Nearby Villandry château featuring French Renaissance gardens. Chenonceau* with its unique gallery-bridge over the River Cher; a gift to Diane de Poitiers from her lover Henry II in 1547, taken over by Catherine de' Medici on Henry's death. Amboise, château with Clos-Lucé, now a museum, where Leonardo da Vinci spent his last years. Blois château, a marriage of three architectural styles, with superb Renaissance staircase; home for French kings for several centuries. Massive Chambord* in its 14,000-acre game reserve, built in early 16th century as a hunting lodge for François I; monumental, double-spiraled grand staircase inside, 365 chimneys; impressive sound and light shows. Orléans with house of Joan of Arc and impressive Gothic cathedral. Saint-Benoît with Romanesque 11th-13th-century basilica of historic Benedictine monastery. Germigny-des-Prés, church with 8th-century Carolingian mosaic, the oldest in France. Le Mans, scene of the 24-hour Grand Prix car race. Gien, delightful town, renowned for its chinaworks.

Dordogne and Massif Central. Mountains of Cévennes with Tarn Gorges in the south. Clermont-Ferrand, industrial city, with lava-built cathedral, thermal springs and spectacular view over 60 dead volcanoes from Puy de Dome. Le Puy*, in the heart of dead volcano land, with dramatically situated rock-top church. Vichy, famous spa, World War II seat of French government; Vieux Parc, the fashionable center. Périgord, famed for truffles and caves. Rocamadour*, a town carved out of the cliff side, center of pilgrimage, the 216 steps of L'Escalier des Pèlerins. Les Eyzies-de-Tayac, where the skeletons of prehistoric Cro-Magnon man were found in 1868; prehistoric cave paintings of Lascaux.

Bordeaux and Aquitaine. La Rochelle, the most important fishing port on the Atlantic coast, charming Old Town, beach, ferry to Ile de Ré. Wine country around Bordeaux and Cognac. Bordeaux, capital of Aquitaine, important port with Grand-Théâtre and Saint-André Cathedral; center for the wine trade from wine-growing districts like Saint-Emilion, Pomerol, Médoc, Graves. World-famous wine châteaus*, visits, tastings. Pine forests of the Landes. Sandy beaches down to Spanish border. Saint-Jean-de-Luz, sea resort with wide beach, casino, golf courses. Biarritz*, fashionable turn-of-the-century sea resort.

Languedoc and Pyrenees. Toulouse, capital of Languedoc, with magnificent cathedral, Basilica of Saint-Sernin, and Augustins Museum and its sculptures. Lourdes, pilgrim center with reputation for miracle cures.

Albi with imposing red-bricked Basilica of Sainte-Cecile and Toulouse-Lautrec Museum. Carcassonne★, medieval fortress town with restored ramparts, dual crenellated walls and winding streets, begun in Gallo-Roman times. Mediterranean coast with fine beaches near Narbonne and Perpignan and the charming small town of Sète; the new Riviera.

Alsace and Lorraine. Strasbourg, important commercial and industrial city, seat of the European Parliament; towering, magnificent rose-colored Gothic cathedral★ with astronomical clock; Old Town. Oeuvre Notre-Dame Museum. Colmar★, charming town with old half-timbered houses; Unterlinden Museum, large collection of outstanding medieval religious art and famous altarpiece by Matthias Grünewald. Riquewihr, wine village with old houses, medieval walls. Tastings of Alsace wines. Wine villages like Turckheim and Kaysersberg, with charming half-timbered Alsace-style houses. Nancy, commercial and industrial center; Place Stanislas with harmonious proportions, wrought-iron railings and fountains, Musée Historique Lorrain. Metz with Saint Etienne Cathedral and Gallo-Roman collections.

Burgundy. Wine and gourmet country with medieval and Renaissance masterpieces. Dijon, capital of Burgundy, with Fine Arts Museum, housed in Palais des Ducs de Bourgogne (old palace of the dukes of Burgundy). Vézelay★, hilltop town with ramparts, Romanesque Basilica of Madeleine dominating the valley. Beaune, famed for Hospice de Beaune, Hôtel-Dieu★, built in 1450, now functioning as an old people's home; *Last Judgement,* polyptych by Rogier van der Weyden in the museum; center for winetrade; famous wine auction in November. Great red wines to the north, Chambertin, Musigny. Clos de Vougeot, 16th-century Renaissance château in the middle of vast vineyards★. Most famous whites to the south, Meursault and Montrachet. Tournus with Abbey of Saint-Philibert in Romanesque style. Benedictine Abbey of Cluny, the largest church in the Western world before St. Peter's was built in Rome, but partly demolished in the 18th century. Bourg-en-Bresse with nearby magnificent Church of Brou from 16th century. Lyons, commercial center with roots in prosperous silk industry; world gastronomic reputation; Musée des Tissus (fabric museum). Pérouges, picturesque walled town with unique medieval setting.

The Alps. Chamonix★, ski resort, casino, site of the first Winter Olympic Games 1924; Mer de Glace glacier; view from Aiguille du Midi and Le Brévent over the Alps including Mont Blanc, the highest peak in Europe. Megève, stylish ski resort. Val d'Isère, important new generation Alpine ski resort. Courchevel, for fashionable skiing. Avoriaz with exceptional modern architecture, site of horror film festival. Annecy with picturesque old streets on cleanest lake in France. Evian-les-Bains, summer resort and spa on Lake Geneva; paddlewheel steamer excursions. The monastery of the Grand Chartreuse, originally home of the world-famed liqueur. Aix-les-Bains, spa with roots in Roman times. Chambéry, formerly the home of the dukes of Savoy. Grenoble, important industrial and university city, much revived by the Winter Olympics in 1964. Scenic Route Napoléon. Sisteron, with its fortress on an impressive cliff on the River Rhone, and a hint of Provence.

Provence. Aix-en-Provence with cathedral and Cours Mirabeau, plane tree shaded avenue, and fountains. Arles★ with Roman Arena, scene of Provençal bullfights, and the Christian necropolis Les Alyscamps. The Camargue, beaches, marshlands with flamingos and white horses.

Toulon, important naval port. Marseilles, France's largest port, second largest metropolis with animated central boulevard, La Canebière, and the Old Port; Le Corbusier's "Cité Radieuse", modern architecture; view from Notre-Dame-de-la-Garde. Nîmes with Roman ruins; Roman Arena with bullfights, Maison Carrée, a rectangular temple, dating from Augustus, fine 18th-century park. Pont du Gard, superb Gallo-Roman aqueduct with three levels, constructed in 19 B.C. Avignon, site of the immense Papal Palace *(Palais des Papes)** from the time when the pope lived in Avignon; famous truncated bridge, the "pont d'Avignon", view of illuminated city walls from Villeneuve-les-Avignon. Châteauneuf-du-Pape vineyard. Les Baux*, medieval ghost town in Val d'Enfer, Hell Valley.

Riviera (Côte d'Azur). Côte des Calanques, the limestone coastline between Marseilles and Toulon. Fashionable beaches of Saint-Tropez, Cannes, Juan-les-Pins. Saint-Tropez, port crammed with shiny yachts, cafés, chic boutiques and casual nudity on nearby Tahiti and Pampelonne beaches. Estérel between Saint-Raphaël and La Napoule with reddish porphyry rocks and sheltered coves. Cannes* and La Croisette, gleaming hotels lining the palmlined boulevard; new Palais des Festivals and Palm Beach Casino; glamorous shopping on Rue d'Antibes; spectacular view from the Observatory in Super-Cannes. Mougins, 15th-century fortified hilltop town. Sophia-Antipolis, university campus, research park, with outdoor theater, scene of summer festival. Saint-Paul-de-Vence, a walled feudal city built in 16th century by François I. Just outside, Foundation Maeght* in a grove of dark pines, one of the world's great modern art museums. Grasse, the world's perfume capital and Gorges du Verdon*, a mini Grand Canyon, cutting more than 2,300 feet (700 m.) deep. Biot, another hilltop village, with Fernand Legér Museum. Haut-de-Cagnes, ancient hilltop fortress with narrow cobbled streets. Nice, the most important city on the eastern part of the French Riviera: Promenade des Anglais, legendary Negresco hotel with its Rococo façade, Old Town, Marc Chagall and Matisse museums. Les Corniches between Nice and Menton with Moyenne Corniche offering a contrast of rocky cliffs and the sea with the village of Eze* as highlight. Menton, closest to the Italian border with British turn-of-the-century atmosphere; casino.

Corsica*. Mediterranean island, sandy beaches, high mountains. Underwater sports in north and northwest. Ajaccio, capital, Napoleon's birthplace. Bastia, beautiful old port. Corte, once the island's capital. Bonifacio, medieval fortress town.

Monaco

The other ministates of Europe are tucked away in the mountains, but Monaco, with a population density of Hong Kong proportions, can claim to be a Mediterranean sea power. Yachts of the most glamorous origin and size are parked gunwale to gunwale in the port. The standard of elegance carries on up the hill to the shops, hotels and legendary casino of Monte Carlo. But it's also a cultural capital worth noting, with a national orchestra, a highly reputed opera house, and several serious museums. Much of Monaco's fame and success is due to the ruler, Prince Rainier III and to the charm of the late Princess Grace. Sharing the scenery and mild climate of the French Riviera, Monaco imposes no frontier formalities.

Facts and figures

Population:	27,000
Area:	453 acres (183 ha.)
Capital:	Monaco-Ville (ca. 1,200 inhabitants), which has merged with the harbor district of La Condamine, the district of Monte Carlo and the industrial center of Fontvieille
Language:	French
Religion:	Catholic (ca. 90%)
Time zone:	GMT + 1, EST + 6; DST (Apr.–Sep.)
Currency:	French *franc* (abbr. *F* or *FF*) = 100 *centimes* Coins: 5, 10, 20, 50 centimes; 1, 2, 5, 10 F Bills: 20, 50, 100, 200, 500 F
Electricity:	220 volt, 50 cycle, AC

Planning your trip

Visa requirements. Same as for France.

Vaccination requirements. None (see also p. 25).

Currency restrictions. Same as for France.

Climate. Considered by many to be near-ideal, the region enjoys a mild climate in winter and warm weather in summer. There is generally little continuous rainfall; cloudbursts lasting only an hour or two are the rule.

Some average daily temperatures:

Monte Carlo		J	F	M	A	M	J	J	A	S	O	N	D
average daily maximum*	°F	54	55	57	61	66	73	78	78	74	68	61	56
	°C	12	13	14	16	19	23	26	26	24	20	16	14
average daily minimum*	°F	47	47	50	54	59	66	71	71	67	61	54	49
	°C	8	8	10	12	15	19	22	22	20	16	12	10

* Minimum temperatures are measured just before sunrise, maximum temperatures in the afternoon.

Clothing. Light clothing can be worn from spring through to autumn. Despite the generally mild winters, a topcoat is necessary for occasional cold spells.

Duty-free allowances. Same as for France.

Hotels and accommodations. There are about 20 hotels in the principality that are classified into one-, two-, three-, four-, and four-star deluxe categories. If you are staying during the tourist periods (Christmas–New Year, Easter and July–August) be sure to make reservations.

Tourist information on Monaco

U.K.	Monaco Information Centre, 34 Sackville St., London W1; tel. (071) 437 3660
U.S.A.	Monaco Government Tourist Office, 20 E. 49th St., New York, NY 10017; tel. (212) 759-5227

189

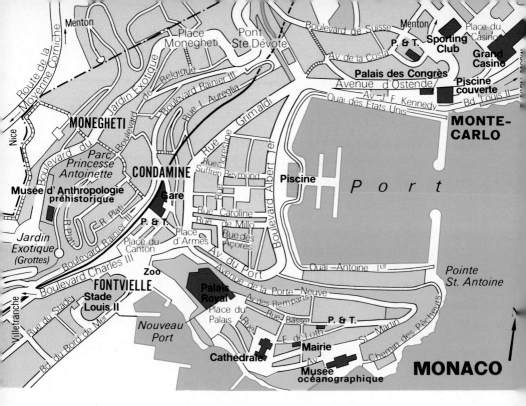

On the spot

Banks and currency exchange. Banking hours are from 9 to 11:30 a.m. and 1:30 to 5 p.m., Monday through Friday. Some banks are also open on Saturday mornings to change currency. Two *bureaux de change* operate every day of the year: Société Monégasque de Change (5 avenue Princesse Alice) and Crédit Foncier de Monaco (1 avenue des Spélugues).

Credit cards and traveler's checks. Main internationally recognized credit cards and traveler's checks are accepted in most establishments.

Mail and telecommunications. Post-office hours are 8 a.m. to 5 p.m., Monday through Friday, and 8 a.m. to noon on Saturdays. The main post office is on Beaumarchais square. You can telephone from the post office between 8 a.m. and midnight seven days a week.

The principality's mail and telecommunications systems are largely integrated with those of France. Postage rates are the same as those in France but Monaco stamps must be used.

Some useful telephone numbers:

Information	12	Fire	18
Operator	10	Hospital	93.25.99.00
Telegrams	140	Police	17
Duty doctor	141		

Newspapers. The principal daily circulated locally is *Nice-Matin* which has a Monaco page in the edition sold in the principality. A wide range of foreign newspapers can be found at newsstands, particularly at the Drugstore, Place du Casino.

Tourist information office

Monte Carlo   Direction du Tourisme et des Congrès, 2a, boulevard des Moulins, Monte Carlo, Monaco; tel. 93.30.87.01/93.50.60.88

Legal holidays

Jan. 1	New Year's Day	**Movable dates:**
Jan. 27	St. Dévote's Day	Easter Monday
May 1	Labor Day	Ascension
Aug. 15	Assumption	Whit Monday
Nov. 1	All Saints' Day	Corpus Christi
Nov. 19	National Day	
Dec. 8	Immaculate Conception	
Dec. 24	Christmas Eve (afternoon)	
Dec. 25	Christmas Day	

Transportation

Air. The principality is served by Nice International Airport (13 miles/22 km. away). Duty-free shop. Access is by bus, leaving from Place d'Armes, La Condamine, about ten times daily. The trip takes one hour and a quarter. A helicopter service operates between the airport and the landing pad west of Monaco Rock. Duration of flight: six minutes.

Rail. The French railroad network serves Monaco, with one station located in the principality. In summer, a special Métrazur service runs half-hourly between Cannes and Menton.

Local public transportation. Buses link various areas of the principality. Fares are paid to the conductor on board. Multi-ride tickets, obtainable from the conductor, must be punched at an automat inside the bus.

Taxis. Monaco has two taxi stands: on allée des Boulingrins (near Place du Casino); tel. 93.50.56.28; and at the train station, avenue Prince Pierre; tel. 93.50.92.27. Taxis are metered, and for trips outside the principality the fare goes up by around 75 percent.

Car rental. Around a dozen agencies rent cars. See also pp. 30–31.

Driving in Monaco. Rules of the road are the same as in France. All cars must carry a red reflector warning triangle for use in case of a breakdown, a fire extinguisher and a spare set of bulbs. Seat belts are recommended but not compulsory. The speed limit is 37 mph (60 kph) throughout the principality. In case of breakdown or accident, dial 17.

Emergencies. In an emergency dial 17 for the police.

Crime and theft. Normal precautions are in order. The principality is known for its low crime rate.

Medical care and health. Medical treatment is excellent, and fees are on a par with those of France. The principality's single hospital, Centre Hospitalier Princesse Grace, is well-equipped. Pharmaceutical supplies are readily available, and some doctors speak English. To find out which pharmacy is open after hours, look for the notice in any pharmacy window. For insurance, see pp. 25–26.
Tap water is safe to drink.

Embassies and consulates. Around 40 consulates are located in the principality. Others responsible for Monaco are in Nice (American and British) or Marseilles (Canadian). All diplomatic representations, including those in Nice and Marseilles, are listed under "Corps consulaire étranger" in a separate section at the end of the yellow pages of the Monaco telephone directory.

Social customs. You should always shake hands when meeting or parting from somebody. In the rare event of an invitation to someone's home, a small gift for the hostess will be appreciated.

Enjoying Monaco

Food and drink. Monaco provides a variety of food including classic French cuisine with certain regional specialties and Italian cooking. Try the *soupe de poisson* (fish soup) or *bouillabaisse* (fish stew). Also from the region comes *pissaladière* (an onion tart with anchovies and black olives) and *tourte de blette* (a Swiss-chard pie). A wide selection of French wines is available, along with imported liquor.

Lunch is served from noon to 2 p.m., dinner 7:30 to 10 p.m., although some restaurants may serve food after 10 p.m.

Entertainment. Plays, concerts, ballet and opera performances are presented regularly. In summer, open-air concerts are held in the court of honor of the Prince's Palace or at the Théâtre du Fort Antoine. Gala evenings enliven the social scene at the Sporting Club, while movies are screened in the club's two movie theaters or (in summer) outdoors. Most movies are dubbed into French, though in summer some English-language films are shown in the original version. The casino dominates Monaco's nightlife, together with about 15 nightclubs.

Annual events and festivals. *January:* Monte Carlo Rally, the final leg of the 2,800-mile (4,500-km.) race. *April:* International tennis championships, sailing regatta. *May:* Monaco Grand Prix. *July:* Concerts by the Orchestre National in the palace courtyard.

Taxes, service charges and tipping. Hotel and restaurant bills are all-inclusive. Tipping recommendations: taxi drivers, barbers and hairdressers 10–15%, railroad porters 5 F per bag.

Sports and recreation. There is a splendid choice of beaches and swimming pools. Sailing, water-skiing, tennis, squash, golf and miniature golf are readily available, and Monaco boasts one of Europe's biggest sports complexes (Stade Louis-II). There are also several saunas and health institutes in Monaco.

Top spectator sports in Monaco are the Monte Carlo Rally and tennis championships, as well as the Grand Prix motor races.

TV and radio. Local services are in French. Radio Monte Carlo also broadcasts religious programs in various languages for Transworld Radio.

What to buy. There is a wide choice of luxury goods in Monaco's large jewelry stores, boutiques and art galleries. Look at the ceramics and glassware, or, at the other end of the price range, buy some of Monaco's delightful postage stamps.

Shops are open from 8 or 9 a.m. to 7 p.m., Monday through Saturday. Most shops close for lunch between noon and 2:30 or 3 p.m., while souvenir shops are open on Sunday mornings.

Sightseeing

Monte Carlo. Casino with gardens, designed by Paris Opéra architect Charles Garnier. Hôtel de Paris next door with Louis XIV's bronze horse, "stroked for luck" by gamblers. National Museum including 2,000-piece doll museum, garden with statues by Rodin, Maillol and Bourdelle.

Monaco Rock. Palais du Prince, home of the Grimaldis and open to the public from June to the middle of October; magnificent 17th-century courtyard with double marble staircase and painted gallery; priceless antiques and exquisite paintings. Old Town with narrow pedestrian streets and joyous atmosphere. Visual history course in L'Historial des Princes de Monaco—a wax museum presenting the Grimaldi family from the earliest to Princess Stéphanie. Louis Bréa triptych in cathedral. Fascinating Oceanographic Museum★ run by underwater explorer Jacques-Yves Cousteau with basement aquarium. Good views★ of the principality from cliff hanging Exotic Gardens. Old jewelry and old bones in the Anthropological Museum.

Some useful expressions in French

good morning/afternoon	bonjour
good evening/night	bonsoir/bonne nuit
good-bye	au revoir
yes/no	oui/non
please/thank you	s'il vous plaît/merci
excuse me	excusez-moi
you're welcome	je vous en prie
where/when/how	où/quand/comment
how long/how far	combien de temps/à quelle distance
yesterday/today/tomorrow	hier/aujourd'hui/demain
day/week/month/year	jour/semaine/mois/année
left/right	gauche/droite
up/down	en haut/en bas
good/bad	bon/mauvais
big/small	grand/petit
cheap/expensive	bon marché/cher
hot/cold	chaud/froid
old/new	vieux/neuf
open/closed	ouvert/fermé
free (vacant)/occupied	libre/occupé
early/late	tôt/tard
easy/difficult	facile/difficile
Does anyone here speak English/German?	Y a-t-il quelqu'un ici qui parle anglais/allemand?
What does this mean?	Que signifie ceci?
I don't understand.	Je ne comprends pas.
Please write it down.	Veuillez me l'écrire.
Do you take credit cards/traveler's checks?	Acceptez-vous les cartes de crédit/les chèques de voyage?
Waiter/Waitress, please!	S'il vous plaît!
Where are the toilets?	Où sont les toilettes?
I'd like…	Je voudrais…
How much is that?	Combien est-ce?
What time is it?	Quelle heure est-il?
Help me please.	Aidez-moi, s'il vous plaît.
Just a minute.	Un moment, s'il vous plaît.

GERMANY

Castles and cathedrals in a romantic treasure-house of European culture.

Long before its cars, cameras and electronic devices conquered world markets, Germany was exporting ideas. Earth-shakers like Martin Luther, Karl Marx and Albert Einstein came from the same intellectual hothouse as Goethe, Heine and Thomas Mann; Bach, Beethoven and Wagner need no translators. The country's cultural life is still rich today; Germany has some of the world's best and most varied museums, and nearly half the world's opera houses.

Germany can trace its prehistory back about half a million years. You can track down the jawbone of Heidelberg Man to the beautiful university town of the same name, or see the skull of Neanderthal Man in Bonn. In the immediate pre-Christian era the country was inhabited by tribes like the Franks, Saxons and Swabians, busy fighting the Romans and each other. The fighting business thrived periodically until World War II, after which the defeated Third Reich was chopped into two Germanys. West Berlin, in the midst of communist East Germany, long remained a brash bastion of Western culture.

But the Germans do nothing with half a heart. Collapse in 1945, unification in 1990—they made a thorough job of both. Visitors can once more compare the Baroque of Dresden and Munich, trace Goethe's life in Frankfurt and Weimar, or hike through the Harz mountains without an electrified fence to stop them. After 45 years of division, a great civilization is whole again.

Boosted by the fall of the Wall, Berlin is more vibrant and forward-looking than ever in its artistic, intellectual and economic activity, a fitting capital for the "new" Germany. It will, however, take some time for the two halves of the city to grow together again. Likewise, the tourist infrastructure in eastern Germany is still in its infancy.

In spite of the reputation for hard work and earnest efficiency, the Germans have a strong romantic streak and relax quite unreservedly at Carnival time. Diversions are as cultural or as lusty as you choose, after which you can restore your strength at a glamorous spa like Baden-Baden or Wiesbaden—but save some Deutschmarks for the elegant shopping.

Facts and figures

Population:	78 million
Area:	137.852 sq. miles (357,039 sq. km.)
Major cities:	**Berlin:** 3.1 million
	Bonn (290,000)
	Hamburg (1.6 million)
	Munich (*München,* 1.3 million)
	Cologne (*Köln,* 965,000)
	Essen (635,000)
	Frankfurt (*Frankfurt am Main,* 615,000)
	Dortmund (580,000)
	Düsseldorf (570,000)
	Stuttgart (555,000)
	Leipzig (552,000)
	Dresden (519,000)
	Hanover (*Hannover,* 515,000)
Language:	German
Religion:	Protestant (61,1%), Catholic (26,1%)
Time zone:	GMT +1, EST+6; DST (Apr.–Sep.)
Currency:	*Deutsche Mark* (abbr. *DM*) = 100 *Pfennig (Pf.)*
	Coins: 1, 2, 5, 10, 50 Pf.; DM 1, 2, 5, 10
	Bills: DM 5, 10, 20, 50, 100, 500, 1,000
Electricity:	220–250 volt, 50 cycle, AC

Planning your trip

Visa requirements. See pp. 29–30.

Vaccination requirements. None (see also p. 25).

Currency restrictions. None.

Climate. Germany's climate is mainly continental with relatively warm summers and cold winters. The northwest has a maritime temperate climate. Precipitation is moderate and distributed quite evenly throughout the year. In winter, city streets and main roads are generally kept clear of snow, but ice can be a menace.

Some average daily temperatures:

Berlin		J	F	M	A	M	J	J	A	S	O	N	D
average daily maximum*	°F	35	37	46	56	66	72	75	74	68	56	45	38
	°C	2	3	8	13	19	22	25	23	20	13	7	3
average daily minimum*	°F	26	26	31	39	47	53	57	56	50	42	36	29
	°C	−3	−3	0	4	8	12	14	13	10	6	2	−1

Frankfurt													
average daily maximum*	°F	38	41	51	60	69	74	77	76	69	58	47	39
	°C	3	5	11	16	21	23	25	24	21	14	8	4
average daily minimum*	°F	29	30	35	42	49	55	58	57	52	44	38	32
	°C	−2	−1	2	6	9	13	14	14	11	7	3	0

Hamburg													
average daily maximum*	°F	36	37	44	55	64	69	73	72	66	55	45	39
	°C	2	3	7	13	18	21	22	22	19	13	7	4
average daily minimum*	°F	28	28	31	38	45	51	55	54	49	43	37	31
	°C	−2	−2	−1	3	7	11	13	12	10	6	3	0

Munich													
average daily maximum*	°F	35	38	48	56	64	70	74	73	67	56	44	36
	°C	1	3	9	14	18	21	23	23	20	13	7	2
average daily minimum*	°F	23	23	30	38	45	51	55	54	48	40	33	26
	°C	−5	−5	−1	3	7	11	13	12	9	4	0	−4

* Minimum temperatures are measured just before sunrise, maximum temperatures in the afternoon.

Clothing. Warm overwear is essential in the cooler months, and an umbrella will prove useful at any time of year. Pack lightweight clothes and a bathing suit in summer, but a sweater, too, for cooler summer evenings and trips in the Alps. At better hotels and restaurants, more formal clothes are expected.

Duty-free allowances

	Cigarettes		Cigars		Tobacco	Liquor		Wine
1)	400	or	100	or	500 g.	1	l. and	2 l.
2)	300	or	75	or	400 g.	1½	l. and	5 l.
3)	200	or	50	or	250 g.	1	l. and	2 l.

Perfume: 1), 3) 50 g.; 2) 75 g.
Toilet water: 1), 3) ¼ l.; 2) ³/₈ l.
Gifts: 1), 3) DM 115 max. value; 2) DM 780 max. value

1) residents of non-European countries
2) residents of European countries, non-duty-free items bought in EEC countries
3) residents of European countries, duty-free items bought in EEC countries; and residents of Europe, goods bought outside EEC countries

Hotels and accommodations

Hotels. Local tourist offices publish lists annually with full details on classifications, amenities and prices of accommodations. The *German Hotel Guide,* distributed free by the German National Tourist Office abroad, also offers a good selection. In addition to hotels, there are inns *(Gasthof)* and boardinghouses. The room price always includes service charges and taxes and generally breakfast. During the summer, weekends and periods with special events, it's advisable to make advance reservations. The Allgemeine Deutsche Zimmerreservierung (ADZ) operates a computer reservation system at: Beethovenstrasse 61, D-6000 Frankfurt am Main; tel. (069) 74 07 67. Major airports and rail stations have hotel reservation services or free telephones connected to the local tourist office.

If you are touring by car and only spending a night or so in any one place, look for *Zimmer frei* ("room to let") signs along the way.

Other types of accommodations are available in castles, mansions and historic hostelries. A booklet on staying in castles, *Gast im Schloss,* can be obtained from tourist offices, local travel agencies or from the association: Gast im Schloss, Vor der Burg 10, D-3526 Trendelburg.

Romantik Hotels is an association of family-run enterprises with charm and atmosphere, offering modern accommodations in historic buildings.

Farmhouse vacations in Germany are described in a booklet called *Ferien auf dem Lande,* obtainable from: Landschriften-Verlag, Kurfürstenstrasse 53, D-5300 Bonn.

In Eastern Germany there are not yet enough hotel rooms to go round. If you intend to visit the east, reserve a room ahead through your travel agent, and stick to your program. The best service here is provided by hotels belonging to the Interhotel chain; the rates at HO and Konsum hotels are more moderate but few rooms are available. It will take some time for the tourist infrastructure here to meet the standards and variety of the west. In some towns, you might be able to stay in private homes; check with the local tourist office.

Youth hostels. Germany's youth hostels are open to holders of membership cards issued by the International Youth Hostels Federation. Cards are available from your national association. For a list of German youth hostels, write to the *Deutsches Jugendherbergswerk* (DJH), Bülowstrasse 26, 4930 Detmold.

There is no age limit except in Bavaria, where you are accepted only if you are under 27.

Camping. Camping is highly developed in Germany. Sites, usually open from May to September, are indicated by the international blue sign with a black tent on a white background. Tourist offices give out a free map-folder with full details on campsites in different regions. The German Camping Club *(Deutscher Camping Club, DCC)* also publishes camping guides: Mandlstrasse 28, D-8000 München 40; tel. (089) 33 40 21.

If you camp off the beaten track, be sure to obtain the permission of the proprietor or the police, and note that camping is not permitted in the rest-areas off the expressways.

German tourist offices abroad

Canada   P.O. Box 417, 2 Fundy, Place Bonaventure, Montreal, Que. H5A 1B8; tel. (514) 878-9885

1290 Bay Street, Toronto, Ont. M5R 2C3; tel. (416) 968-1570

U.K.   61 Conduit Street, London W1R 0EN; tel. (071) 734 2600

U.S.A.   747 Third Avenue, New York, NY 10017; tel. (212) 308-3300

Broadway Plaza, Suite 2230, 444 South Flower Street, Los Angeles, CA 90017; tel. (213) 688-7332

203

On the spot

Banks and currency exchange. Banking hours are generally from 8:30 a.m. to 12:30 or 1 p.m. and 1:30 or 2:30 to 4 p.m., Monday through Friday (often till 5:30 or 6 p.m. on Thursdays).

If you need to change money outside banking hours, the main rail stations in bigger towns have exchange offices *(Wechselstube)* open from early in the morning till late in the evening and on weekends. You can also change your money at hotels and travel agencies, but rates are less favorable.

Credit cards and traveler's checks. Most major hotels and many restaurants and shops accept credit cards and traveler's checks, but Eurocheques are the most popular form of non-cash payment.

Mail and telecommunications. Post offices handle mail, long-distance telephone calls and telegrams, and sometimes have a public telex available, but cables can also be phoned in from hotels or private phones. Opening hours are generally 8 a.m. to 6 p.m., Monday through Friday, and until noon, Saturdays. Late-night and weekend service can be obtained at airports and railroad stations. In most cities, a night telephone and telegraph counter can be found in a central location. Mailboxes are painted yellow with a black post-horn symbol. Stamps can be purchased at yellow vending machines near mailboxes and at some tobacco and stationery shops.

The telephone network in Western Germany is fully automatic and you can dial direct to many foreign countries. Telephone booths, which have yellow frames, bear a sign showing a black receiver in a yellow square (national calls) or a green square (national and international calls). Area code numbers are listed in a special telephone directory. A call to the information number given in the front of the telephone directory will put you in touch with an English-speaking operator who can assist in case of difficulty or emergency. For surcharges and low rates, see p. 30.

Some useful telephone numbers valid in most large towns:

Information (domestic)	1188	Fire/First-aid (nationwide)	112
Information (international)	00118	Police (emergencies)	110
Operator (domestic)	010	Telegrams	1131
Operator (international)	0010		

In Eastern Germany, not all calls can be dialed direct. To place calls through the operator, dial 0114 for Europe, 012 for Western Germany, 181 for all other countries.

Newspapers. Principal dailies are *Die Welt* (Bonn), *Frankfurter Allgemeine* (Frankfurt), *Süddeutsche Zeitung* (Munich) and *Stuttgarter Zeitung* (Stuttgart).

Major British and continental newspapers and magazines are on sale at large railroad stations, airports and newsstands in the city centers and at leading hotels throughout the country, as is the *International Herald Tribune*. The larger cities publish English-language entertainment guides with titles like *This Week in...*

Tourist information. Most towns have a local tourist office, providing free maps, lists, brochures, etc. Many tourist offices offer hotel reservation services.

Bonn	Münsterstrasse 20; tel. (0228) 77 34 66 For information on the Northern Rhineland, contact the Landesverkehrsverband Rheinland, Rheinallee 69, D-5300 Bonn-Bad Godesberg 1; tel. (0228) 36 29 21
Berlin	Europa-Center, 1000 Berlin 30; tel. (030) 262 60 31
Hamburg	Bieberhaus am Hauptbahnhof; tel. (040) 24 87 00
Munich	Main railroad station (Hauptbahnhof), with hotel reservation service: Fremdenverkehrsamt München, Postfach, D-8000 München; tel. (089) 23 91 71/75
Cologne	Am Dom 1 (beside the cathedral); tel. (0221) 221 33 45
Frankfurt	Gutleutstrasse 7–9; tel. (069) 212 36 77
Dortmund	Main railroad station (Hauptbahnhof); tel. (0231) 14 03 41
Düsseldorf	Konrad-Adenauer-Platz; tel. (0211) 35 05 05
Stuttgart	Klett-Passage (underpass to the main rail station); tel. (0711) 222 82 40
Bremen	Bahnhofsplatz; tel. (0421) 36 36 1
Hanover	Ernst-August-Platz 8; tel. (0511) 168 23 19
Nuremberg	Main railroad station (Hauptbahnhof); tel. (0911) 23 36 32; also in Town Hall (Rathaus)

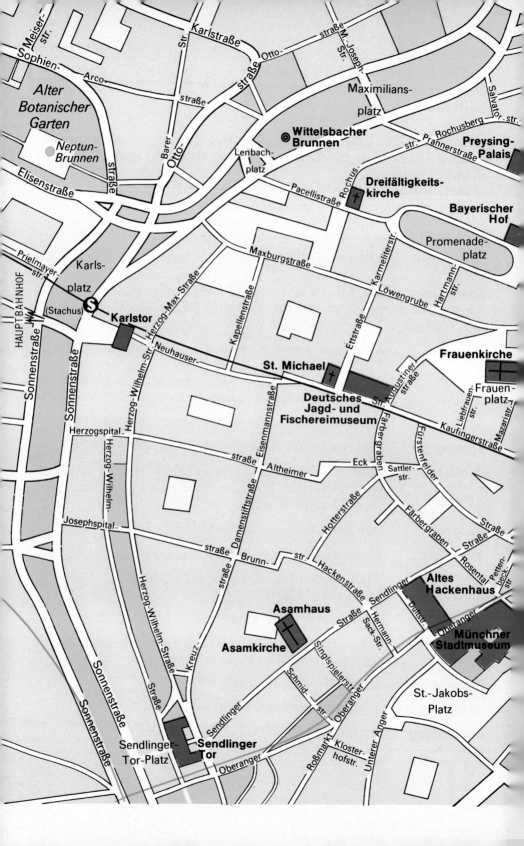

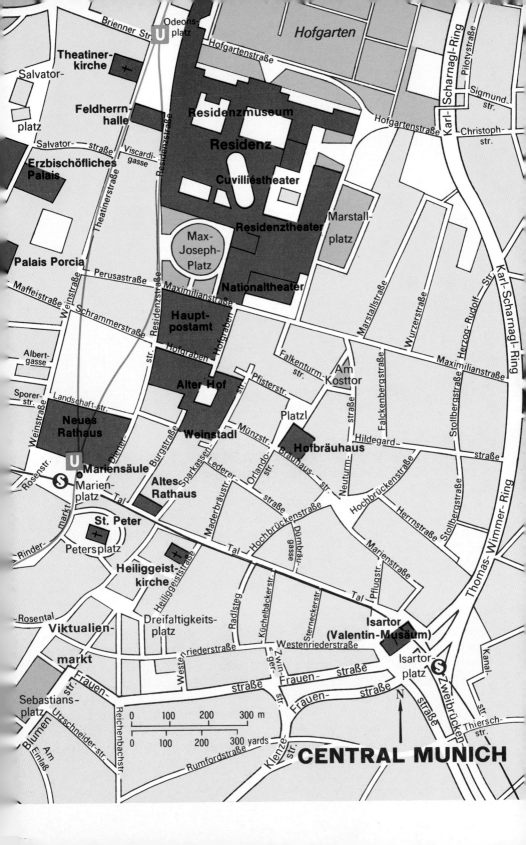

CENTRAL MUNICH

Legal holidays

Jan. 1	New Year's Day	**Movable dates:**
Jan. 6	Epiphany [1], [2]	Good Friday
May 1	Labor Day	Easter Monday
June 17	National Unity Day	Ascension
Aug. 15	Assumption [2], [6]	Whit Monday
Nov. 1	All Saints' Day [1], [2], [4], [5], [6]	Corpus Christi [1], [2], [3], [4], [5], [6]
Dec. 25	Christmas	Day of Prayer
Dec. 26		and Repentance

Notes [1] = Baden-Württemberg; [2] = Bavaria; [3] = Hesse; [4] = North Rhine-Westphalia; [5] = Rhineland-Palatinate; [6] = Saar.

Transportation

Air. Frankfurt is the major gateway to Germany for flights from overseas, with good onward connections. Hamburg, Munich, Cologne, Berlin and other points are linked either directly or with connecting flights to most major cities within Europe.

Early-morning flights provide direct links between many Western German cities, but later in the day a change of plane may be required. Except for long-distance flights such as Munich–Hamburg, many visitors prefer rail travel within the country itself.

Major airports. Cologne-Bonn: Köln-Bonn Airport at Wahn (18 miles/28 km. from Bonn, 12 miles/18 km. from Cologne). Duty-free shop. There are airport bus links to Bonn and Cologne. **Berlin:** Tegel (5 miles/8 km. from city center). Duty-free shop. Regular bus service (No. 9) to city center (Zoo station). Schönefeld (12 miles/19 km. from city center). Regular bus (No. 36) to *S-Bahn* Grünau station. Half-hourly bus link between Schönefeld and Tegel, crossing the city center. **Hamburg:** Fuhlsbüttel (8 miles/12 km. from city center). Duty-free shop. Bus service. **Munich:** Riem (6 miles/10 km. from city center). Duty-free shop. Bus service to main railroad station. **Düsseldorf:** Düsseldorf-Lohausen (7 miles/11 km. from city center). Duty-free shop. Regular rail services from main rail station. **Frankfurt:** Frankfurt (6 miles/10 km. from city center). Duty-free shop. Regular rail service from main railroad station. Also inter-city train connections from the airport via Mainz and Cologne to Dortmund and via Würzburg to Munich. **Stuttgart:** Echterdingen (9 miles/14 km. from city center). Duty-free shop. Bus every 20–30 minutes. **Bremen:** Neuenland (2 miles/3 km. from city center). Duty-free shop. Streetcars to city center. **Nuremberg:** 5 miles/8 km. from city center. Duty-free shop. Frequent bus connections to city center. **Hanover:** Langenhagen (7 miles/11 km. from city center). Duty-free shop. Frequent bus service to city center.

Rail. The Deutsche Bundesbahn (DB) trains are comfortable and fast, as well as punctual. IC are long-distance Inter-City trains and D and FD intermediate- to long-distance trains. Dining service is available on most trains and sleeping-car accommodations are provided on long runs.

Tickets for distances of up to 50 kilometers are valid for two days, those over 50 kilometers, for two months. A number of special reduced-price offers and bargain tickets are available:

DB Tourist Cards for foreign visitors only, through certain travel agencies. Bring along your passport when ordering. The holder can travel for four, nine or 16 consecutive days on the entire network of the Deutsche Bundesbahn.

Tourenkarten, regional rail rover tickets for a given area (such as the central Rhineland) can be bought in Germany. They allow ten days' unlimited travel on regional rail services, with 50 percent reduction on buses; the only requirement is that your rail journey must have covered at least 200 kilometers one way *before* you can obtain it.

DB Junior Passes entitle young people between 12 and 22 and students under 27 to unlimited travel on DB routes of more than 51 km. for one year (also on routes under 51 km. for an additional cost).

A *Germanrail Tourist Card* can be purchased for unlimited first- or second-class travel for a period of four, nine or 16 days. For *Eurailpass*, see p. 33.

Long-distance buses. Rural areas are served by buses of the Federal Railways *(Bundesbahn)* and the Federal Post Office *(Bundespost)*, as well as by local companies. Bus terminals are invariably close to railroad stations, and there you'll find information about routes and fares.

Europabus is an international bus network operated jointly by several European railroad systems through areas of special tourist interest; in Germany, the carrier is the Deutsche Touring-Gesellschaft: Am Römerhof 17, D-6000 Frankfurt am Main; tel. (069) 790 31.

Boats, waterways. Daily scheduled services on the Rhine and Mosel operate from April to the end of October, with the best choice of boats and trips during high season (July–August). The Köln-Düsseldorf line (KD) offers excursions on motorboats, paddle-steamers and hydrofoils. The most popular tour, between Cologne and Mainz, has about 35 stops. Boats are usually well-equipped, with restaurants and sometimes cabins for overnight journeys.

Regular boat services operate also on other rivers, including Main and Elbe, and on lakes like Lake Constance and the Bavarian lakes, Ammersee and Chiemsee.

Local public transportation. Buses and streetcars operate in larger towns. Cities like Bonn, Düsseldorf, Frankfurt and Munich are also served by efficient subway *(U-bahn)* and rapid train *(S-Bahn)* systems. Maps showing the various lines and stations are displayed at every station. The trains usually run from 5 a.m. to 1 a.m. Tickets are sold from vending machines, ticket booths at the bus/streetcar stops or from conductors and/or drivers. Be sure to validate tickets in the canceling machines positioned at platform entrances and in buses and streetcars.

Taxis. In the villages or the big cities taxis abound, either cruising the streets or waiting at stands (usually right beside the rail station). You can also phone for a taxi wherever you are; numbers are listed on a separate page in the front of the phone directories. All cabs have meters; drivers ask for a supplement for luggage carried in the trunk.

Car rental. International and local firms operate, some of which have desks at airports. You can find the addresses of leading firms in the yellow pages of the telephone directory, under "Autovermietung". Chauffeur-driven vehicles are widely available.

The German Federal Railways promote a Rail-and-Road car-rental program. See also pp. 30–31.

Driving in Germany. Seat belts are obligatory, and that includes back-seat passengers if the car is equipped for them. If you don't wear your seat belt, insurance companies reduce compensation in the event of an accident. Traffic police may confiscate the car keys of persons they consider unfit to drive. Drinking and driving is a very serious offence. In Western Germany, the permissible level of alcohol in the blood is 80 mg./100 ml., the equivalent of two glasses of beer; in the east it is 0.

Drive on the right, pass on the left. Traffic in Germany follows the same basic rules that apply in most countries. In the absence of traffic lights or stop or yield signs, vehicles coming from the right have priority at intersections. At traffic circles, approaching cars must give way to traffic already in mid-stream, unless otherwise indicated. Streetcars must be passed on the right and never at a stop (unless there's a traffic island). At dusk, and in case of bad visibility, headlights must be used; driving with parking lights only is forbidden, even in built-up areas. Should police or emergency vehicles need to pass through a traffic jam *(Stau)* on an expressway, cars in the right lane must keep close to the right, and those in the left lane close to the left, thereby opening a passageway down the middle. The police are getting more and more strict, and radar is used both inside and out of town.

Germany has an extensive network of toll-free expressways, still expanding. On these expressways *(Autobahn)* a suggested maximum speed is 81 mph (130 kph), but many drivers habitually exceed 100 mph (160 kph) and will flash their lights if you don't make way quickly. On secondary roads the limit is 62 mph (100 kph) and in cities generally

211

31 mph (50 kph). Germans drive more conservatively on secondary roads and seldom exceed limits in built-up areas. Telephones at frequent intervals on the expressways can be used to summon help from ADAC (automobile association) or from the nearest service station. ADAC patrol cars are often in evidence. Gasoline available is normal (91–92 octane), super (97–99 octane), lead-free (91 octane) and diesel.

Some distances: Frankfurt–Cologne 120 miles (190 km.), Munich 230 miles (370 km.), Hamburg 310 miles (500 km.).

Bicycle rental. Discovering the beauty of the German countryside is a pleasant experience and it's possible to rent a bike in many towns. In some places you can rent one at the railroad station and return it at another station. Rail passengers renting bikes are entitled to a special discount. Ask for details at any station or tourist office.

Tours will be suggested if you wish and itineraries are sometimes indicated on notice boards at the station.

Rest rooms. Public rest rooms are easily found: most museums, all restaurants, bars, cafés, department stores, airports and rail stations provide facilities. If there's an attendant, and hand towels and soap are offered, you should leave a small tip. Always have several 10-Pfennig coins ready in case the door has a coin slot. Rest rooms may be labeled

with symbols of a man or a woman or the initials *W.C.* Otherwise, look for *Herren* (Gentlemen) and *Damen* (Ladies) or a double zero (00) sign.

Emergencies. The emergency numbers below cover the whole country. Others are listed on the first pages of local telephone directories.

Police   110   Fire, first aid, ambulance   112

Police. Germany's police wear green uniforms. You will see them on white motorcycles or in green-and-white cars. Street parking in towns is supervised by policemen and policewomen in dark-blue uniforms. If you are fined, they have the right to ask you to pay on the spot.

Crime and theft. The crime rate is quite low in Germany, though you might feel a bit uneasy walking round the red-light districts in the cities, especially alone at night. Take normal, common-sense precautions— keep an eye on your baggage, watch out for pickpockets in crowded places, and put your wallet in an inside pocket. Leave money and valuables in your hotel safe, not in your car or hotel room, and avoid carrying large sums of money. Always lock your car—you can be fined otherwise. If you are robbed, report the incident to the hotel reception- ist and the nearest police station. The police will provide you with a certificate to present to your insurance company, or to your consulate if your passport has been stolen.

It is a good idea to keep photocopies of the important pages of your passport. If ever it gets lost, embassies will accept photocopies as proof that you do possess a passport, and within a few days they will issue a replacement document. Also keep a list of all your credit card numbers, separate from your cards, and photocopies of your plane tickets.

Medical care and health. In the event of accident or serious illness, call the Red Cross *(Rotes Kreuz)* or the medical emergency service *(Ärztlicher Notdienst)* which will give you doctors' addresses. The telephone number is in the local directory. English is generally spoken by doctors and medical personnel. Pharmacies *(Apotheke)* are open during normal shopping hours. At night and on Sundays and holidays, all pharmacies display the address of the nearest one open. For insurance, see pp. 25–26.

It is perfectly safe to drink the tap water in Germany; only rarely will you see the sign "Kein Trinkwasser" (not drinking water), usually on public squares.

Embassies and consulates. Embassies are listed under "Botschaften" and consulates under "Konsulate" in telephone directories. Get in touch with the consulate of your home country if you're in trouble—for example, if you lose your passport, have problems with the police, or have an accident. The Consul can issue emergency passports, give advice on obtaining money from home, provide a list of lawyers, interpreters and doctors. He cannot pay your bills, lend you money, find you a job or obtain a work permit for you.

Social customs. Germans have great respect for social formalities and take some time to get onto a first-name basis. A lot of hand-shaking takes place on social occasions. If invited to a German home, which is a special privilege, bring some flowers for the hostess. Germans are at their most relaxed in traditional taverns and beer gardens, and the great festivals provide plenty of opportunities for celebrating with local people from all walks of life.

Enjoying Germany

Food and drink. Eating and drinking in Germany is an experience full of conviviality whether you have chosen a *Weinstube,* wine café, in the Rhine or Mosel valley, a Bavarian *Gaststätte,* inn, or a Berlin *Kneipe,* street corner bar or pub.

Breakfast is richer than the traditional continental breakfast and includes cold meats, such as *Schinken* (ham), various salami-like sliced sausages and maybe *Leberwurst* (liver-sausage) in addition to *Käse* (cheese), both hard and soft. Selection of bread is also varied, covering the entire range from white to the dark *Pumpernickel.*

Lunch is usually served from 11:30 a.m. to 2 p.m. and dinner between 6:30 and 8:30. In big cities hot meals are available in the evening until 10 or 10:30. Most Germans prefer to have their main meal at noon and eat lighter fare in the evening—cold meats, cheeses and maybe a salad.

Suppe (soup) is always prominent on German menus. *Tagessuppe* simply means today's soup. *Bohnensuppe* is made of beans and *Linsensuppe* of lentils, often served with pieces of sausage. *Kartoffelsuppe* contains potatoes as the main ingredient but you will also find celery, leeks and parsnips in it. More special is *Leberknödlsuppe* in which spicy dumplings of flour, bread crumbs, beef liver, onions, marjoram and garlic take a swim.

Pork is the cornerstone of German cooking. *Schinken* (ham) comes in many different preparations as does *Wurst* (sausage). It takes a solid appetite to finish the Rheingau specialty *Sulperknochen,* made of the ears, the snout, the tail and the feet, especially as it is served on a bed of

214

Sauerkraut and a puree of peas. It also requires gallons of beer. More refined is *Spanferkel* (a roasted suckling pig from Bavaria).

From the Rhineland come specialties like *Himmel und Erde,* literally heaven and earth, which is a delicious mixture of apples, blood-sausage and leeks. While on the subject of blood-sausage you should know that *Kölsche Kaviar* on a menu in Cologne doesn't mean what you might guess, but blood-sausage with slices of raw onions. Another Rhinelander trick is *Halve Hahn,* which ought to be half a chicken. Instead it turns out to be a rye-bread roll stuffed with hot mustard and Dutch cheese.

Germany offers many fine fish dishes of *Lachs* (salmon) and *Hecht* (pike). A genuine delicacy is *Moselaal in Riesling* (a Mosel eel simmered in Riesling wine).

In and around the deep forests in Germany are the hunting grounds for a wide variety of game—venison, hare, partridge and, with luck, woodcock. *Hunsrücker Rehkeule* is a leg of venison served with red currant sauce and chestnut puree.

The king of vegetables is the potato. *Bratkartoffeln* (sauteed potatoes) might be boring after a while but *Reibekuchen* (potato pancakes) and *Kartoffelsalat* (potato salad) is spiced with different ingredients in different regions, from bacon and onions to fish and green vegetables. *Sauerkraut* is that lovely prepared cabbage in white wine with juniper berries, caraway seeds and cloves, served in Berlin with a puree of peas and pig's knuckle—the city's ultimate delicacy. *Rotkraut* is sweet-and-sour red cabbage, done with apples, raisins and white vinegar.

Desserts are not only linked with the main meals; there is also a *Konditorei,* coffee and pastry shop, on virtually every street corner. Among the favorites is *Schwarzwälder Kirschtorte,* the world-famous cherry cake from the Black Forest. And *Apfelstrudel* (the delicate apple cake) is eaten as often in Munich and Berlin as in Vienna. Dresden is famous for its *Pflaumenkuchen*—plum cake.

The Germans like to say that there is good beer and better beer but no bad beer in Germany. Beer *vom Fass* (on tap) can be had in half-liter glasses in restaurants, but in a Bavarian *Bierkeller* (beer cellar) the standard size is a full-liter tankard called *Masskrug* or simply *Mass*. *Dunkles* means dark, slightly sweet, malt-flavored beer. *Helles* is light and is served cooler.

German wines are worth an entire chapter. *Rotwein* (red wines) are few so the *Weisswein* (white wines) dominate. The Rhine and Mosel valleys produce the most prominent wines. From Rhine come Rüdesheimer, Hattenheimer, Niersteiner, Liebfraumilch and Oppenheimer, just to mention a few. Famous names from Mosel include Bernkasteler, Piesporter and Zeltinger. Non-experts often have difficulties in distinguishing between a Rhine and a Mosel wine. Here is a hint: the Rhine wines come in brown bottles, the ones from Mosel in green. Prime qualities are designated *Spätlese, Auslese, Beerenauslese,* and, for the rarest and most expensive, *Trockenbeerenauslese.* Germany also produces Sekt, a sparkling, champagne-like wine.

Entertainment. Germany is known for its numerous and excellent state-subsidized theaters, operas and concert halls. The opera has a very strong position in Germany with Wagner taking first place. The Hamburg ballet is among the best in the world, as is the Stuttgart ballet. The Berlin Philharmonic Orchestra, under the direction of the late Herbert von Karajan, maintained its reputation as one of the world's greatest orchestras. In summer open-air concerts are held in romantic settings throughout Germany. Several cities, including Wiesbaden, Baden-Baden and Bad Homburg, have casinos. In Bavaria the beer halls still provide the most relaxed night-time entertainment. Reeperbahn, Hamburg's red-light district, is world-famous as a hub of commercial sin. Nightclubs, discos and movie theaters are found in all but the smallest towns. Foreign movies are almost invariably dubbed into German.

Annual events and festivals. *January–Shrove Tuesday:* Fasching (Carnival) in Munich, Cologne, Düsseldorf, Augsburg, Aachen and other places. *February:* Berlin International Film Festival. *May:* Wiesbaden International Music Festival. *July–August:* Münchner Festspiele (Munich Opera Festival). *Late July–late August:* Wagner Festival in Bayreuth. *September:* Oktoberfest, beer festival in Munich. *September–October:* Berliner Festwochen featuring opera, theater, music and art. *October:* Frankfurt Book Fair, with exhibitions from 65 countries.

Taxes, service charges and tipping. Hotel and restaurant bills are all-inclusive. Anything extra for the waiter is optional. Tipping recommendations: porters DM 2 per bag, taxi drivers 10–15%, hatcheck DM 1 and hairdressers and barbers 10%.

Sports and recreation. Public swimming pools are available all over the country. You can do some windsurfing and sailing on the lakes and rivers or along the coast in the North. Tennis courts and golf courses are plentiful. In the winter season skiers are attracted to resorts like Garmisch-Partenkirchen with excellent facilities. Hiking is a major

217

pastime in Germany and mountain climbing in the Alps is a real adventure. Hunting (deer and wild boar) in the Bavarian forests is another possibility if you apply for a license. The lakes and rivers offer good fishing.

Soccer is by far the most popular spectator sport. You also find horse racing and show jumping.

TV and radio. Programming is in German. There are two national TV channels plus one regional channel. Movies are sometimes shown in the original English version. An English-language TV newscast occasionally appears in the late afternoon on the regional channel. On the radio, you can easily pick up the BBC World Service, American Forces Network or the Voice of America anywhere in Germany. Shortwave reception is excellent, especially at night.

What to buy. Good buys are cameras and binoculars, traditional loden clothes (a Bavarian specialty), leather- and sportswear, toys for the children like building sets and model trains, cutlery, linen with modern or traditional designs, chinaware of very good quality, and records, with a selection second perhaps only to the U.S. Mosel and Rhine wines make nice gifts. In some cases, sales tax is refunded (see p. 40).

Fashionable shopping streets include Königsallee, "Kö", in Düsseldorf, Theatinerstrasse and Maximilianstrasse in Munich and of course Kurfürstendamm in Berlin.

Shopping hours are generally from 8:30 a.m. to 6:30 p.m., Monday through Friday, and 8:30 a.m. to 1 p.m. on Saturdays. In some cities stores remain open until 6 p.m. on the first Saturday of each month.

Sightseeing

The North. Westerland, elegant seaside resort on the North Sea island of Sylt; long beaches and casino. Schleswig, an old maritime town, with Gothic cathedral and Prehistoric Museum, displaying in a separate building the 4th-century Nydam ship. Travemünde, seaport, beach resort with casino; ferry connections with Denmark and Sweden. Lübeck*, Hanseatic city, noted for its Holstentor, a fortified twin-towered gate, medieval Town Hall of dark glazed brick and St. Mary's Church *(Marienkirche),* completed in 1330, where the composer Buxtehude was organist. Hamburg on the Elbe River, old Hanseatic town, today Germany's second city and one of Europe's largest ports; Lake Aussenalster bordered by shaded avenues; Alster river boat trip offering view of five church towers and Town Hall campanile; Art Gallery *(Kunsthalle)* housing a fine collection of paintings from Middle Ages to the 20th century, notably 19th-century German Romantics; Renaissance Town Hall with decorative interior hoisted up on 4,000 stilts; panorama from famous tower of Baroque St. Michael's Church *(Michaeliskirche);* nearby, Krameramtswohnungen, quaint old wood and brick houses built in 1670 for poor widows, today converted into galleries and artists' studios; Hagenbeck zoo; notorious nightlife along the red-light Reeperbahn; St. Pauli fish market and boat trip round the bustling port*. Bremen, Germany's oldest seaport; Market Square *(Marktplatz)** with decoratively gabled Town Hall *(Rathaus),* 15th-century statue of Roland and massive St. Peter's Cathedral with lead cellar containing mummies; Focke Museum famed for a superb collection of historical northern artifacts. Medieval town of Celle* with 16th- and 17th-century half-timbered houses. Walsrode, Bird Park housing nearly 1,000 species from all over the world.

Central Germany. Hanover, important economic and industrial center; Kestner Museum displaying a wonderful Egyptian collection; beautiful Herrenhausen Gardens; Town Hall dome for panorama. Goslar, old silver-mining town of timber-fronted houses; Gothic Town Hall with an arcaded gallery opening on to Marktplatz. Hamelin*, town noted for fine old 16th- and 17th-century Weser Renaissance houses, characterized by scrollwork and pinnacles on the gables. The small town of Münden with elaborate Weser Renaissance Town Hall and half-timbered houses. Harz Mountains, attractive vacation area of forests, lakes and streams. Marburg, former great pilgrimage center, famed for Gothic St. Elisabeth's Church erected between 1235 and 1283; castle and Market Square with half-timbered houses; traditional local costumes still worn by country people on market days. Kassel, the home town of the Brothers Grimm; Painting Gallery* in Wilhelmshöhe Castle; Wall Hangings Museum *(Tapetenmuseum)* in Hesse Museum, displaying exceptional wallpapers. The university city of Münster with 13th-century cathedral, Baroque castle and Prinzipalmarkt, historic street lined by Renaissance gabled houses.

The Rhineland. Düsseldorf, business center of industrial Ruhr, fashionable shops along elegant Königsallee, the "Kö"; lively Old Town *(Altstadt)*; North Rhine-Westphalia Art Collection with works by Chagall, Picasso, Paul Klee. Aachen, the town of Charlemagne, with cathedral where German kings were crowned until 1531; magnificent Treasury; Town Hall on the site of Charlemagne's palace. Cologne *(Köln)*, capital of the Rhineland famed for Gothic twin-spired cathedral★ with remarkable stained-glass windows; 12th-century Shrine of the Three Kings in gold behind the High Altar, altarpiece by Stefan Lochner; extensive Old Town; Roman-Germanic Museum★ opposite the cathedral showing the city's Roman origins; Wallraf-Richartz and Ludwig Museum★ displaying old Dutch, Flemish and German paintings and outstanding modern art; Carnival festivities. Bonn, the capital of West Germany from 1949 to 1990, with graceful Town Hall *(Rathaus);* Beethoven's House, where the great composer was born, now museum claiming the largest and most valuable collection of Beethoven memorabilia; Rhineland Museum *(Rheinisches Landesmuseum),* outstanding for its Rhenish painters and the 50,000-year-old Neanderthal Man and Cro-Magnon Couple. Koblenz with strategic position at the confluence of the Mosel and Rhine rivers; Rheinanlagen, an airy river promenade lined with maples and willows; Elector's Palace *(Kurfürstliches Schloss),* a fine example of 18th-century Rhenish-French neo-Classical architecture; Romanesque St. Castor's the town's most important church, notable for monumental Gothic tombs; Deutsches Eck, a gigantic monument erected for Kaiser Wilhelm I in 1897 and now dedicated to German unity; Old Town *(Altstadt)* with splendid Balduin Bridge *(Balduinbrücke)* from 1343; handsome Church of Our Lady *(Liebfrauenkirche),* with some remarkable Renaissance tombstones; Ehrenbreitstein Fortress, reached by a chairlift. For nature lovers, the vast Eifel mountain plateau, the hills of Hunsrück and the forests of the Taunus. Mainz, with Romanesque cathedral *(Dom)* and tombstones honoring archbishops of Mainz; Renaissance fountain *(Marktbrunnen)* from 1526; Gutenberg Printing Museum★. Wiesbaden, international spa with hot springs at the foot of the wooded slopes of Taunus; beautiful Kurpark featuring open-air concerts; Spring Colonnade *(Brunnenkolonnade)* and Kurhaus; casino; Wilhelmstrasse lined with chic boutiques. Bad Homburg, the most famous of Germany's numerous spas, visited by Czar Nicholas II and Edward VII among others; casino opened in 1840.

The Rhine Valley★, a narrow valley of steeply terraced vineyards and pine forests guarded by castles and towering rocks. Inviting town of Boppard, far away from industry and government. St. Goar with castle ruin, Burg Rheinfels, built in 1245. Cat Castle *(Burg Katz)* opposite St. Goar. The castle of Phalzgrafenstein (1327) in the middle of the river. Bacharach, enchanting wine village with flower-decked, half-timbered houses and elegant Gothic ruin of the Wernerkapelle on a slope above

220

town. Mouse Tower *(Mäuseturm)*, the old customs-post out in the river. Rüdesheim★, well-known wine village with national wine museum in Brömserburg castle; Drosselgasse with lively taverns and wine cellars; 15th- and 16th-century Brömserhof, richly decorated with hunting scenes and coats of arms. Germania monument in Niederwald, erected in 1883 to celebrate the unification of Germany. Assmannshausen offering one of the few good red wines of the Rhineland. Lorch with attractive Gothic St. Martin Church. Lorelei, the myth-laden rock of the siren, that inspired Heinrich Heine's celebrated poem. The Reingau wine country; wine tasting in Johannisberg; riverside villages of Geisenheim, Oestrich-Winkel and Eltville, delightful for their timber-framed houses and wine cellars. Monastery of Eberbach★, the best preserved in Germany, whose monks founded the modern German wine industry.

Mosel Valley. Eltz Castle★, a fairy-tale castle built between the 12th and 16th centuries. Cochem, at the foot of its restored turreted castle. Beilstein with its 16th-century timber-framed houses. Bernkastel-Kues, picture-book wine village, famed for its wines and taverns in half-timbered houses on the Römerstrasse; top-heavy Spitzhaus (Pointed House) built in 1583. Trier★, Germany's oldest city, university town and center of the Mosel wine trade; Roman gateway, Porta Nigra, dating from the 2nd century A.D.; lively Hauptmarkt, the heart of Trier; massive and fortress-like cathedral *(Dom)*, with the pulpit from 1572 and All Saints' Altar (1624); 13th-century Gothic Liebfrauenkirche; Landesmuseum with lucid presentation of Roman art and artefacts; huge Imperial Bath *(Kaiserthermen)* dating from the 4th century A.D. Karl Marx House with memorabilia of the auther of *Das Kapital.*

Frankfurt (am Main). Important financial center. Römerberg, pleasant medieval square in the Old City *(Altstadt)*, with graceful fountain statue of Justice from 1543. Römer, one-time City Hall, with distinctive gabled façade, comprising three buildings and containing magnificent Emperor's Hall *(Kaisersaal)*, where the imperial coronation banquets were held from 1562. St. Nicholas' Church in red sandstone with carillon of 40 bells ringing morning, noon and evening. Chapel of Saalhof *(Saalhof-kapelle)* in Historic Museum, the oldest surviving building (1175) in the town center. Cathedral of St. Bartholomew *(Dom)* dating from the 13th to 15th centuries, where German emperors were crowned between 1562 and 1792. Goethe's House★, beautifully restored and furnished authentically, where Germany's greatest poet once lived. Hauptwache in New Town *(Neustadt),* built in 1730, once guardhouse for the municipal police, now a popular café. Old Opera House, restored to is former opulence. Städel Art Institute *(Städelsches Kunstinstitut)*, housing old European masters and an important collection of drawings and engravings. Zoo, renowned for its success in breeding animals in captivity.

The Southwest. Worms, a crossroads of the three spiritual persuasions that have marked Germany's history; Romanesque cathedral; Luther Monument, celebrating Martin Luther's confrontation with the Catholic Church at the Diet of Worms in 1521; the Synagogue from 1034, the oldest stone-built synagogue in Europe. Heidelberg★, university town on the River Neckar with 17th-century atmosphere around Marktplatz; picturesque Old Bridge; castle spanning over 500 years of architecture; Zum Ritter, The Knight's Mansion, fine Renaissance house built in 1592; Philosophers' Path uphill to the Heiligenberg slopes with view of peaceful valley. Schwäbisch Hall, old town with half-timbered houses, beautiful Marktplatz dominated by the stone steps of St. Michael's Church; Baroque Town Hall. Baden-Baden★, luxury spa with casino; white neo-Classical Kurhaus, Roman Baths, beautiful Lichtentaler Allee. Black Forest *(Schwarzwald)*★, wooded mountains with picturesque villages. Stuttgart, automobile city; vineyards on the slopes; aerial view from Television Tower; Solitude Castle, summer residence of the Württemberg court. Ulm, university town, famed for its cathedral with the tallest spire in the world (528 feet/161 m.) and splendid carved choirstalls. Freiburg im Breisgau, with Gothic cathedral in red sandstone and octagonal belfry; pleasant Rathausplatz; Augustine Museum displaying interesting collection of religious art. Splendid view from the Belchen. Lake Constance, famed for its mild climate. Mainau★, island of flowers, a tropical garden. Meersburg, a delightful town with narrow streets and half-timbered houses, two castles; ferry connections to Constance. Lindau, island tourist resort with painted medieval houses.

Munich. Capital of Bavaria. Marienplatz, the heart of the city, with 19th-century neo-Gothic New Town Hall *(Neues Rathaus)* featuring carillon *(Glockenspiel)* and Old Town Hall with stepped gables. 16th-century St. Michael, an Italian Renaissance church with Baroque overtones. Church of Our Lady *(Frauenkirche)*, the symbol of Munich, built in the 15th-century, with 16th-century gold-tipped bulbous domes on twin brick towers. The Palace *(Residenz)* with museum and Treasure Chamber. Palace Theater *(Altes Residenztheater* or *Cuvilliéstheater)*, an exquisite setting for Mozart's works. Old Pinakothek★, one of the world's great art museums displaying all the old European masters. Municipal

Museum *(Münchner Stadtmuseum)* showing the town's development. National Museum of Bavaria *(Bayerisches Nationalmuseum)*, a survey of German cultural history from the Roman era to the 19th century. German Museum *(Deutsches Museum)**, called the biggest scientific and technological collection in the world. Hofbräuhaus, the famous beer hall. Olympic Village, site of 1972 Summer Olympics. Schwabing, university neighborhood, featuring hundreds of restaurants and interesting shopping. Nymphenburg Castle*, the dukes of Wittelsbach's summer refuge, with four 18th-century pavilions in its gardens, notably Amalienburg, a hunting lodge by Cuvilliés.

Bavaria. Schleissheim Castle, noted for formal gardens, State Apartments and glorious staircase. The Bavarian romantic lakes of Chiemsee, with Herrenchiemsee Castle, and Ammersee with boating and fishing opportunities. Dachau, the site of the first Nazi concentration camp; museum. Berchtesgaden, with castle and ruins of Hitler's mountain retreat; salt mines, underground lake. The internationally known winter and summer resort of Garmisch-Partenkirchen*, site of 1936 Winter Olympics, in the Bavarian Alps; cog railroad up to Zugspitze, highest peak in Germany. Popular resort of Oberstdorf. Linderhof, Ludwig's favorite castle in Rococo. Oberammergau, site of the famous Passion Play. Ottobeuren*, ancient Abbey rebuilt in Baroque, with stunning interior, beautifully painted in pink, brown, blue and lilac colors.

The Romantic Route, running from Füssen to Würzburg. White-turreted Neuschwanstein*, a fairy-tale fantasy overlooking the lake and forests, another of King Ludwig's castles, with painted allusions to many of Wagner's operas. Magnificent Wies Church, standing amidst the meadows, the masterpiece of Dominikus Zimmermann, decorated with a sublime ceiling fresco. Augsburg, site of Roman city, 15th-century banking center; gabled houses of the 16th-century Fuggerei quarter; Renaissance Town Hall; Gothic cathedral; Benedictine Abbey. Dinkelsbühl, medieval fortress town. Nördlingen, encircled by ramparts, towers and gateways. Rothenburg-ob-der-Tauber*, delightful medieval town, surrounded by 13th- and 14th-century ramparts; old flower-decked houses, cobbled streets, fountains, Gothic and Renaissance Town Hall with stunning view from belfry; fortified gateway *(Burgtor)* and gardens above Tauber Valley. Würzburg noted for Residence of Prince-Bishops of Schönborn*, 18th-century Baroque palace, with Imperial Hall, decorated by Tiepolo's paintings; vineyards on steep slopes.

Bamberg, old town with beautiful Gothic cathedral, island Town Hall and palace *(Neue Residenz)*. Bayreuth, site of Wagner Festival Theater *(Festspielhaus);* Richard Wagner Museum, devoted to the life and work

of the composer, in Villa Wahnfried, where he lived the last years of his life; Wagner and Liszt tombs; Margrave Opera House built in the middle of the 18th century; castle. Nuremberg *(Nürnberg),* scene of Nazi rallies and postwar trials; Dürer's House; German National Museum*, displaying German art; medieval Emperor's Castle *(Kaiser-burg),* 13th-century Gothic St. Sebald's Church, St Lorenz Church; Schöner Brunnen, 14th-century Gothic fountain. Regensburg, medieval town on the Danube; Gothic cathedral with beautiful stained-glass windows. Passau, a lovely town on a rocky promontory, with well-preserved old buildings, notably near the dominating cathedral and Residenzplatz; excursions to the Bavarian Forest.

Berlin. Kurfürstendamm*. Berlin's preferred promenade, known wide-ly as the Ku'damm, for luxury hotels, shops, nightclubs. Memorial Church *(Kaiser-Wilhelm-Gedächtniskirche),* preserved as a poignant ruin. National Gallery, devoted to 19th and 20th-century art, in a plain,

224

glass-walled building designed by Mies van der Rohe. The imposing Reichstag government building. Tiergarten, a large, beautiful public park with charming lakes. Dahlem museums*, a complex containing Painting Gallery *(Gemäldegalerie)*, displaying 13th–18th-century European paintings, and also ethnographic collections and sculptures. Baroque and Rococo Charlottenburg Castle*, once summer residence for the Prussian royal family; Egyptian Museum, offering a glimpse of three millennia of Egyptian art. Bauhaus-Archiv, documenting Europe's most progressive 20th-century school of architecture. Brandenburg Gate, the supreme symbol of the city, specially restored for unification celebrations. Unter den Linden, the city's grandest avenue. Alexanderplatz, busy hub of East Berlin. Pergamon-Museum* housing works of classical antiquity.

Eastern Germany. Potsdam, for centuries the favorite residence of the Prussian royalty: Sans-Souci Palace*, Frederick the Great's charming Rococo dwelling in terraced gardens; Chinese Pavilion containing a fine collection of porcelain. Brandenburg, cathedral on island, with 13th-century stained glass. Dresden*, charming historic center: Zwinger Palace, Rococo masterpiece; porcelain museum. Meissen, home of Europe's first porcelain manufacture. Weimar, Goethe's home: Ducal Castle, headquarters of Bauhaus. Erfurt, old university town. Eisenach, Bach's birthplace: Wartburg Castle*, dramatically perched on wooded hill. Excursions: Thuringian forest, Harz mountains, lake country of Mecklenburg, bracing Baltic coast: Rügen island, Stralsund, Rostock.

Some useful expressions in German

good morning/afternoon	Guten Tag
good evening/night	Guten Abend/Gute Nacht
good-bye	Auf Wiedersehen
yes/no	ja/nein
please/thank you	bitte/danke
excuse me	Verzeihung
you're welcome	bitte
where/when/how	wo/wann/wie
how long/how far	wie lange/wie weit
yesterday/today/tomorrow	gestern/heute/morgen
day/week/month/year	Tag/Woche/Monat/Jahr
left/right	links/rechts
up/down	oben/unten
good/bad	gut/schlecht
big/small	gross/klein
cheap/expensive	billig/teuer
hot/cold	heiss/kalt
old/new	alt/neu
open/closed	offen/geschlossen
free (vacant)/occupied	frei/besetzt
early/late	früh/spät
easy/difficult	einfach/schwierig
Does anyone here speak English/French?	Spricht hier jemand Englisch/Französisch?
What does this mean?	Was bedeutet dies?
I don't understand.	Ich verstehe nicht.
Please write it down.	Bitte schreiben Sie es.
Do you take credit cards/traveler's checks?	Akzeptieren Sie Kreditkarten/Reiseschecks?
Waiter!/Waitress!	Ober!/Fräulein!
Where are the toilets?	Wo sind die Toiletten?
I'd like...	Ich wünsche...
How much is that?	Wieviel kostet es?
What time is it?	Wie spät ist es?
Help me please.	Helfen Sie mir, bitte.
Just a minute.	Einen Augenblick, bitte.

GREECE

Monuments of a majestic civilization in a sunny land of heartwarming beauty.

The road signs of modern Greece point to the earliest triumphs and conflicts of Western civilization: Athens, Sparta, Marathon, Corinth... Europe's culture was hatched in the sunshine of this heartwarming and beautiful land, still the perfect place to blend intellectual pursuits with total relaxation.

In the home of Zeus and Apollo, legend fades into history. Homer sang of an island called Crete "in the midst of the wine-dark sea"; there, four thousand years ago, the Minoans built sumptuous palaces, feasted, and honored their gods. Athens eventually picked up the torch, and in the 6th century B.C. a general-poet named Solon introduced trial by jury. Democracy (a Greek word, naturally) followed, and thinkers like Socrates, Plato and Aristotle expounded philosophy (another Greek word).

The traveler in contemporary Greece is surrounded by the monuments of a majestic past, starting at the Parthenon, a 2,500-year-old marble miracle. Below the citadel, in the middle of Athens, the rumble of the traffic can't obliterate the timeless sounds of any Greek village: the click of worry-beads and knitting needles, the babble of spirited conversation, *bouzoúki* music.

Aware of their heroic past, the Greeks are a proud people, dignified and sincere. Their hospitality, legendary, is often incredibly generous. Meeting them is easy, since so much of life goes on outdoors—in market places, sidewalk cafés and open-air restaurants. Nobody will mind if you wander into the kitchen to choose your dinner. In a country with a coastline more than nine thousand miles long, the seafood is a good bet. So is the swimming, in some of Europe's clearest waters. Greece's islands, more than 1,400 in all, add up to about one-fifth of the national area. Historic islands like Rhodes and Corfu are geared for sophisticated tourists, while dozens of virtually undiscovered isles offer little more than a hillside of whitewashed houses, a café and a beach. Climb to the hilltop—to the church or monastery or ancient fortress—and survey the surrounding seas. You might find Atlantis.

228

Facts and figures

Population:	9.8 million
Area:	51,000 sq. miles (132,000 sq. km.)
Capital:	Athens (*Athíne*, 885,000/GUA with Piraeus 3.3 million)
Other cities:	Salonica (*Thessaloníki*, 705,000)
	Patras (*Pátre*, 155,000)
	Heraklion (*Iráklion*, 110,000)
	Volos (*Vólos*, 105,000)
	Larissa (*Lárisa*, 100,000)
Language:	Greek
Religion:	Greek Orthodox (97%)
Time zone:	GMT + 2, EST + 7; DST (Apr.–Sep.)
Currency:	*Drachma*
	Coins: 1, 2, 5, 10, 20, 50 drachmas
	Bills: 50, 100, 500, 1,000, 5,000 drachmas
Electricity:	220 volt, 50 cycle, AC

Planning your trip

Visa requirements. See pp. 29–30.

Vaccination requirements. None (see also p. 25).

Currency restrictions. Non-residents may import up to 100,000 drachmas in Greek money and export up to 20,000 drachmas (in denominations no larger than 5,000 drachmas). The import and export of foreign currencies is unlimited, but if more than the equivalent of $ 1,000 is imported it must be declared on arrival.

Climate. In general, the climate is Mediterranean in character, with hot dry summers and mild, rather rainy winters, but inland areas on the mainland are cooler.

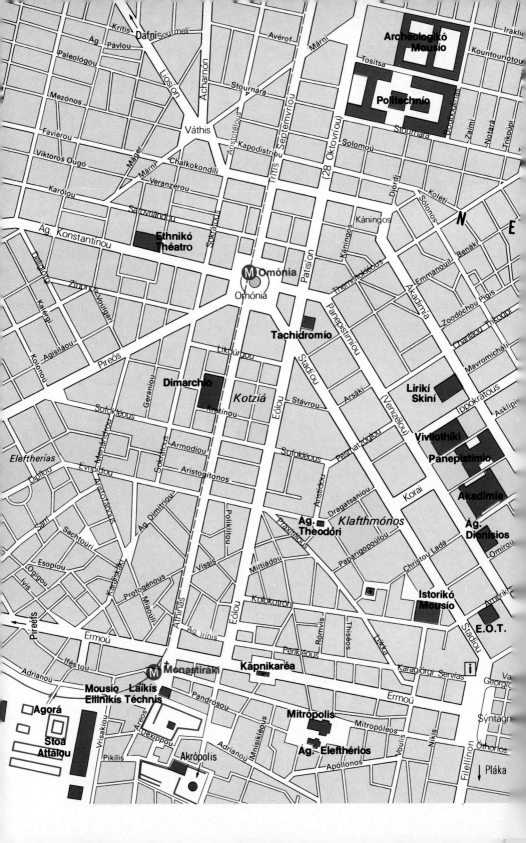

MODERN ATHENS

Ioustinianoú
Poulcherías
Zosimádon
Mesolou
Strófí
Mantáka
Komninón
Voulgaroktónou
Laskáreos
Akríta
Fanariotón
Benáki
Lampárdi
Vatátzi
Ippokrátous
Evgeníkoú
Damaskinoú
Melodoú
Argyroupóleos

Á P O L I S

Ouranoú
Dafnomíli
Nikifórou
Sarantapíchou
Patriárchou Fottoú
Chrissanos
Didótou
Navarínou
Ittis
Doxapatrí
Sína
Thessalías
Solonos
Omírou
Skoufá
Likavittoú
Dimokrítou
Voukourestíou
Anagnostopoúlou
Fokilídou
Stratiotikoú Síndesmou
Akadimía
Pindárou
Iraklitou
Triézotou
Zalokósta
Kanári
Mérlin
Sékeri
Mousío Benáki
Kolonáki
Iródou Attikoú
Vámva
Doúka
Ipsilántou
Karneádou
Loukianoú
Ploutárchou
Glikónos
Spefsíppou
Patriárchou Ioakím
Alopekís
Ploutárchou
Hadou

L i k a v i t t ó s

Ág. Geórgios

N

Aristodímou
Doradistria
Aristíppou
Kleoménous
Dinokrátous
Xenokrátous
Souídias
Marásli
Gennádios Vivliothíki

Maráslio
Gennadíou
Evangelismós

K O L O N Á K I

Vasilíssis Sofías

gnostos tratiótis
Voulí
Ethnikós Kípos
Mouroúzi
Rigíllis
Vizantinó Mousío
Vasilíssis Sofías
Ethnikí Pinakothíki
Vasiléos Konstantínou
Ilíssion
Niríídon

Some average daily temperatures:

Athens		J	F	M	A	M	J	J	A	S	O	N	D
average daily	°F	55	57	60	68	77	86	92	92	84	75	66	58
maximum*	°C	13	14	16	20	25	30	33	33	29	24	19	15
average daily	°F	44	44	46	52	61	68	73	73	67	60	53	47
minimum*	°C	6	7	8	11	16	20	23	23	19	15	12	8
Salonica													
average daily	°F	49	53	58	67	77	85	90	90	82	71	61	53
maximum*	°C	9	12	14	20	25	29	32	32	28	22	16	11
average daily	°F	35	37	41	49	58	65	70	69	63	55	47	39
minimum*	°C	2	3	5	10	14	18	21	21	17	13	9	4

* Minimum temperatures are measured just before sunrise, maximum temperatures
in the afternoon.

Clothing. From mid-May until the end of September, the weather is hot
and dependable enough for visitors to take only light clothing. Cotton is
preferable to synthetics. Pack a sweater or light jacket for the cooler
evenings. Winter can be rather chilly and wet so take a warm coat and
sweaters. You'll need comfortable shoes, with soles that will not slip on
marble steps, when visiting the old sites.

Duty-free allowances

	Cigarettes		Cigars		Tobacco	Liquor		Wine
1)	400	or	100	or	500 g.	see 2) and		3)
2)	300	or	75	or	400 g.	1 ½ l. and		5 l.
3)	200	or	50	or	250 g.	1 l.	or	2 l.

1) residents of non-European countries
2) residents of European countries, non-duty-free items bought in EEC
   countries (alcoholic beverage allowances—also for non-European residents)
3) residents of European countries, duty-free items bought in EEC countries;
   and residents of Europe, goods bought outside EEC countries (alcoholic
   beverage allowances—also for non-European residents)

Hotels and accommodations

Hotels. Hotels ranging from luxury class down to fairly modest establishments are listed in a comprehensive index, giving prices, which can be consulted at Greek National Tourist offices abroad as well as at many travel agencies. It's advisable to reserve in advance if you are traveling in summer. Should you arrive without a reservation, go to the local Greek tourist office or Hotel Information Service, usually at the railroad station (in Athens at the airport and on Sýntagma Square), and consult their list of hotels. The staff will be happy to help you. The local tourist police will also advise on accommodations. In high season you may have to take a room with full or half board.

Villas and bungalows. There are plenty of villas to rent, some of them quite modest, in particular on the islands, but you must make your reservations well in advance.

Private rooms. Homeowners rent rooms to tourists throughout Greece, but mostly on the small islands where people still come to the harbor or the airport and ask visitors in English if they want "room". Usually you will have to share the family bathroom.

Youth hostels. If you're a member of the International Youth Hostels Association you'll be able to stay in a youth hostel in Greece. Otherwise, you can ask for an International Guest Card at the Greek Youth Hostels Headquarters at Dragatsaníou 4 in Athens.

Camping. Camping in Greece is permitted only on organized sites. There are about 20 of them on the Attica mainland, many in the Peloponnese and on islands like Crete and Rhodes. For a full listing of campsites, contact the EOT office on Sýntagma Square in Athens or the Greek National Tourist Office abroad.

Greek tourist offices abroad

Australia 51–57 Pitt Street, Sydney, NSW 2000; tel. (02) 241-1663

Canada 80 Bloor Street West, Suite 1403, Toronto, Ont. M5S 2V1; tel. (416) 968-2220

U.K. 195–7 Regent Street, London W1R 8DR; tel. (071) 734 5997

U.S.A. 645 Fifth Avenue, New York, NY 10022; tel. (212) 421-5777
611 W. Sixth Street, Los Angeles, CA 90017; tel. (213) 626-6696
168 N. Michigan Avenue, Chicago, IL 60601; tel. (312) 782-1084

On the spot

Banks and currency exchange. Banks (*trápeza*) are open from 8 a.m. to 1:30 p.m., Monday through Thursday, and until 2 p.m. on Fridays. Many are also open until 7 or 8 p.m. as currency-exchange offices (*sinállagma*). The Sýntagma branch of the National Bank of Greece in Athens is open continuously from 8 a.m. to 8 p.m. during the week, and from 9 a.m. to 4 p.m. on weekends. Always take your passport along for identification.

Credit cards and traveler's checks. Internationally known credit cards are recognized by large hotels, car rental firms and some shops, but it's better not to rely on them when paying for a meal. Most traveler's checks are readily accepted, provided you have your passport with you.

Mail and telecommunications. Services are generally reliable but rather slow. Post offices (*tachidromío*) are identified by a yellow sign reading ΕΛ.ΤΑ., and are usually open from 8 a.m. to 8 p.m., Monday through Friday. The post office at Sýntagma in Athens is open weekdays from 7:30 a.m. to 8:30 p.m., Saturdays from 7:30 a.m. to 3 p.m. and Sundays from 9 a.m. to 2 p.m. The post office clerk is obliged to check the contents of any registered letters as well as parcels addressed to foreign destinations, so don't seal this kind of mail until it has been "approved". Stamps are sold in machines outside the post office and at newsstands and some souvenir shops, but with a 10 percent surcharge. Most hotels will look after sending the letters for you if you hand them in at the reception desk. Mailboxes are painted yellow.

Major cities have offices of the Greek Telecommunications Organization (O.T.E.) which are open 24 hours a day. Branches may be open only until 10 p.m. or midnight. Greece's telephone system is fairly advanced, but long-distance lines are often busy so it's better to place calls through the international operator.

Telephones in orange phone booths are linked to the international dialing system; these have instructions printed in English. In blue telephone booths you can only make local calls. If you want to send a facsimile message—telefax—the post office's public Intelpost service is available at all main offices. Telegrams and telexes can be sent from the O.T.E. office or from your hotel. For surcharges and low rates, see p. 30. Some useful telephone numbers:

Operator (domestic)	151	Police	100
Operator (international)	162	Tourist police	171
Telegrams		Ambulance	166
(international)	165	Fire	199

Newspapers. Principal dailies in Athens are *Akrópolis, Kathimeriní, To Víma, Eleftherotypía, Eléftheros Kósmos, Ta Néa, To Éthnos, Y Avrianí; Eléftheros Lógos* and *Makedonía* are Salonica papers. Most leading West European newspapers are sold at main newsstands. The *Athens News* and *Greek News* are published in English. *The Athenian* is an English-language monthly.

Tourist information. There are offices of the National Tourist Organization (*Ellinikós Organismós Tourismoú*, E.O.T.) in most towns.

Athens	National Bank, Karagiórgi Servías 2, just off Sýntagma; tel. (01) 3222-545; General Bank building on Sýntagma; tel. 3252-267 (there is also an office at the airport)
Salonica	Platía Aristotélous 8; tel. (031) 222-935
Patras	Iróon Politechníou, Glifáda; tel. (061) 420-305
Heraklion (Crete)	Opposite Archaeological Museum; tel. (081) 228-203/228-225

Legal holidays

Jan. 1	New Year's Day	**Movable dates:**
Jan. 6	Epiphany	1st day of Lent
Mar. 25	Independence Day	Good Friday
May 1	Labor Day	Easter Monday
Aug. 15	Assumption	Ascension
Oct. 28	*Óchi* ("No") Day	
Dec. 25	Christmas Day	
Dec. 26	St. Stephen's Day	

Transportation

Air. Greece's main airport is in Athens, but Salonica, Heraklion, Rhodes and Corfu also have international airports. Domestic flights operate between 30 points on the mainland and the islands.

Major airports. Athens: Hellinikón (7 miles/12 km. from city center). Duty-free shop. There are two terminals: the West Terminal handles only Olympic Airways traffic, foreign and domestic, while the East Terminal serves all international lines. A bus service operates from the East Terminal to the city, and from the West Terminal to the Olympic town-office. **Salonica:** Míkra (10 miles/16 km. from city center). Duty-free shop. There's a frequent bus service into town.

236

Rail. Trains usually have first and second class cars, but cannot be relied upon for punctuality or comfort. It's best to make seat reservations in advance as trains get very crowded. Note that a ticket is valid only for a specific train. The Greek rail system isn't very extensive. There are some fast trains between Athens and Salonica (leaving from the major international station, Stathmós Larísis in Athens), and a good local service to the Peloponnese (from the Peloponnese Station). For *Eurailpass,* see p. 33.

Long-distance buses. Buses provide a fairly good, punctual service to many places not reached by air services.

Boats, waterways. A good alternative to air travel between the mainland and islands is travel by boat. Ask for details at the Greek National Tourist Organization or at the local tourist office on arrival. They have up-to-the-minute details. Always doublecheck departure times, as timetables constantly change. All islands have at least one boat connection a week. The overnight crossing from Piraeus to Heraklion or Chaniá (Crete) and to Rhodes can be recommended. Larger ferries carry cars; advance reservations are absolutely essential in summer months.

Local public transportation. Most large towns have a bus service, while Athens also has a trolleybus and subway system. The subway, connecting the center of Athens with Piraeus, is a fast and good way to go, providing you avoid the rush hours. Keep the ticket until the end of your journey because you'll be asked for it at the exit. You can buy tickets single or in blocks of 10 from a newsstand and cancel them on the trolleybus and subway. If traveling by bus, put the exact fare into a slot machine, if you haven't bought a monthly season ticket, which allows unlimited travel on all three. For moderate distances, it's probably better to walk, as public transportation can get very hot and crowded.

Taxis. Taxis are relatively cheap, except, perhaps, on some of the smaller islands. They are plentiful in the cities and display a taxi sign in either Greek or Latin letters. Although taxi stands exist, you are better off getting the hotel porter to hail a cab or phone for one. Sharing a cab isn't uncommon. Urban taxis are metered, but the meter ticks over twice as quickly if the taxi has to go outside the city. There are some supplements for night rides and extra luggage, for trips from the airport, rail stations, the main bus terminals and the ports. Even if the taxi isn't metered, there are established prices for certain island trips, and it's worth bargaining if you want to rent a taxi for an excursion.

Car rental. Local and international firms have offices in cities and airports. Renting a car is expensive, as is gasoline. Demand is high so it's best to reserve a vehicle in advance. Chauffeur-driven cars are also available. See also pp. 30–31.

Driving in Greece. Drive on the right, pass on the left. Seat belts must be worn, and the car must carry a red reflector warning triangle, a fire extinguisher and a first-aid kit. Blood alcohol limit is 50 mg./100 ml. Sounding a car horn is forbidden, in theory, in town centers, but is allowed and used liberally on winding country roads.

The rules of the road are a little blurred and priority seems to belong to whoever takes it. The toll expressways are well-surfaced, but other roads are not so good, suffering from poor grading, even in cities. Principal expressways link Athens with Salonica as well as with Corinth and Patras. Speed limits are 31 mph (50 kph) in town, 62 mph (100 kph) on expressways and 50 mph (80 kph) on other roads. Parking regulations are fairly strictly enforced. Gasoline available is normal (90 octane), super (98 octane), lead-free and diesel. Breakdown assistance is provided by ELPA, whose patrol network covers all the main highways of the mainland.

Some distances: Athens–Patras 130 miles (210 km.), Larissa 220 miles (355 km.), Salonica 315 miles (510 km.), Evzoni 340 miles (550 km.).

Bicycle rental. Two-wheeled travel is very popular on the islands, but prices vary a great deal. If you're renting for a longer period or for a group you should negotiate a reduction.

Rest rooms. In cities public rest rooms are usually found near the center, in parks and main squares. Leave a small tip if there is an attendant. If you use a café's facilities then order coffee or a drink. In the bigger establishments there are usually two doors marked ΓΥΝΑΙΚΩΝ (ladies) and ΑΝΔΡΩΝ (gentlemen).

Emergencies. In an emergency, dial the following numbers anywhere in Greece:

Police 100 Fire 199

Police. In most of Greece there are two types of police force. The regular police (*chorofílakes*), who can be identified by their gray-green uniforms, deal with the usual police duties, including parking fines. The tourist police (*touristiki astinomía*) are a separate branch whose job it is

to help foreign visitors with any problems. You can identify them by the national flag emblems sewn onto their gray uniforms, which indicate the foreign languages they speak.

Crime and theft. Common sense suggests that if you have anything of particular value, it should be kept in the hotel safe.

Medical care and health. Emergency treatment is free but if you're insured you'll be certain of better medical care in case you are hospitalized. There are English-speaking doctors and dentists.

Pharmacies *(farmakio)* can be identified by a sign with a green, blue or red cross on a white background. Pharmacies take turns in offering a 24-hour service in any main town. The address of the pharmacy on duty is posted on all pharmacy doors. The tourist police will also be able to help you find it. Medical supplies are easily available, but it's advisable to bring any special medication with you. Certain prescription drugs, including tranquilizers and headache preparations, cannot be carried into the country without a prescription or official document. Fines—even jail sentences–have been imposed on the unwary tourist. For insurance, see pp. 25–26.

Tap water is safe to drink.

Embassies and consulates. These are listed (in English) in the blue pages of the telephone directory under "Embassies". Office hours vary so it's better to phone first.

Social customs. Greek hospitality is sincere, generous and sometimes overwhelming. It's good manners to say good morning (*kaliméra*) or good afternoon (*kalispéra*) when entering a shop, and goodbye (*chérete*) when leaving. Shake hands with friends and acquaintances and don't refuse an invitation to someone's house; take flowers or a small gift for the hostess.

Enjoying Greece

Food and drink. Greek cooking is based on seasonal produce. It is simple, colorful, healthy and mouthwateringly good. Rather than eat in your hotel, it's better to venture out to a restaurant or *tavérna*, where the atmosphere tends to be informal and you can choose your food from a counter where it's all displayed, or even go into the kitchen and peer into a few simmering pots before making your choice.

Breakfast, Greek-style, is a few cups of strong black coffee with a cake or some pastry. Foreign tourists usually have instant coffee (known as *nes*) or tea, bread, butter and jam. Cafés can provide eggs, bacon and ham if you need something more substantial.

Lunch is served between 2 and 3:30 p.m. in most restaurants. Because of the heat, it often consists of a cold salad or snack and salad. You'll find the well-known salad made of sweet tomatoes, onions, olives, cucumber and *féta* cheese (white goat's cheese) and doused with olive oil, vinegar and oregano in every restaurant, but there are some other interesting snacks that are good at lunchtime.

Order a *mezé* platter (a sampling platter) to see which appetizers you like best: *dolmádes* (vine leaves stuffed with pine nuts and rice, or meat and rice, served chilled or hot with a tangy lemon sauce), *dzadzíki* (yoghurt, cucumbers and garlic), *taramosaláta* (fish roe with mashed potato, oil and seasonings, served with lemon and bread), *melidzanosaláta* (eggplant purée with oil, garlic and herbs).

There won't be many soups on the menu, but you should try *soúpa avgolémono*—a chicken and lemon soup thickened with egg, and served hot or cold. For a more substantial snack have some *spanakópitta* (spinach pie) or *tiropittákia* (cheese pie). You can get the same thing in bite-sized portions, known as *tirópitta* (cheese-filled pastries) and *pastítsio* (meat-stuffed pastries).

Traditional dishes like charcoal grilled *souvláki* (chunks of meat or fish and onions, green peppers on a skewer) or *souvláki me píta* (grilled meat, vegetables and *dzadzíki* in pitta bread) also make a filling snack.

241

Greece has a fine selection of fish to offer, although these may be quite expensive and are priced according to weight. Fish is usually grilled or fried, and served with olive oil and lemon juice. Choose some *astakós* (clawless spiny lobster), *barboúni* (red mullet), *chtapódi* (octopus), *fagrí* (sea bream), *garídes* (shrimp) or *xifías* (swordfish steaks).

On the meat front, there is an abundance of lamb, veal and pork. *Mousakás* is a traditional dish made from chopped lamb or beef layered through with slices of eggplant, with a cream sauce *au gratin*. Chicken (*kotópoulo*) is usually skewered and grilled with herbs. *Kolokíthia gemistá me rízi ke kimá* is a long way of saying zucchini stuffed with rice and chopped meat. If you're in the hunting area you may be able to try some game (*kinígi*).

To accompany your main dish you may get rice or potatoes. The latter could well be rather limp French fries. On the other hand, any fresh vegetables will be bursting with vitality.

Probably the best dessert is a bowl of fresh fruit, already peeled and cut, including figs and grapes, different types of melon, strawberries, peaches and plums. You can also have *giaoúrti* (creamy yoghurt), with or without *méli* (honey), or even *giaourtokaridómelo* (yoghurt with honey and chopped walnuts). For those with a very sweet tooth there are pastries like *baklavás*, dripping with honey and nuts. Otherwise you can just settle for an ice cream or sherbet.

Before dinner, try an anis-flavored *oúzo,* straight or with chilled water, but you'd better have some appetizers with it. Greek beer is good. There are many wines, of which retsína is probably the best known, a dry white wine with a resin flavor. Some other labels are Demestica, Cambas, Melsina, Santa Helena—all dry whites, with reasonably good dry red counterparts. After dinner, have a glass of Metaxa (Greek brandy) and a tiny cup of strong black coffee *(ellinikó kafé).*

Entertainment. There are nightclubs and discos in Athens and most resorts. Athens also has a casino. If you like *bouzoúki*-music and Greek dancing, head for Pláka in Athens. Movies usually show films in the original language with Greek subtitles. For news of occasional opera performances and concerts, ask at the local tourist office.

Annual events and festivals. *February:* Carnival, all over Greece. *April–October:* Sound and Light spectacles in Athens, Corfu, Rhodes. *May–September:* Athens Greek folkdances. *June–September:* Athens International Festival presenting theater, opera, ballet in the ancient Herodes Atticus open-air theater. *July–August:* Epidaurus Festival featuring ancient drama. *Mid-July–Mid-September:* Athens Wine Festival. *September:* International Fair of Salonica.

Taxes, service charges and tipping. Hotel and restaurant bills are generally all-inclusive, but it's customary to leave the waiter about 5% as a tip. Other tipping recommendations: porters 30 to 50 drachmas per bag, hatcheck 20 drachmas, taxi drivers 10%, barbers/hairdressers 10%.

Sports and recreation. Whether on the mainland or islands the sea dominates leisure time. There is excellent swimming in clear water off the many beaches, although these are rarely very sandy. Snorkeling and skin diving are popular, but strict rules govern the use of diving equipment—check at the local tourist office. Water-skiing has been established in Greece for a long time, but windsurfing is still a relative newcomer. Fishing, boating and yachting are all available.

On dry land there's plenty of climbing and walking. Around Northern Greece you can do some exploring on horseback.

TV and radio. Most hotels, and some bars and restaurants have TV lounges. Many of the programs are well-known TV series in English with Greek subtitles.

The Greek National Radio (ERT) broadcasts the news and weather in English in the morning, afternoon and evening. On short-wave bands, reception of the World Service of the BBC is extremely clear. Voice of America's English programs are also easily picked up (there is a relay station on Rhodes).

What to buy. Good buys include woolen rugs, cushion covers, blankets, sweaters, embroidery, boots, furs, woodcarvings, silver and gold jewelry, leather goods and *féta* cheese.

Shopping hours vary. In Athens they are 8 a.m. to 2:30 p.m. Monday, Wednesday, Saturday, 8 a.m. to 1:30 p.m. and 5 to 8 p.m. Tuesday, Thursday and Friday. Tourist-oriented shops stay open much longer.

244

Sightseeing

Athens. Acropolis*, towering above the city, the most perfect architectural complex of antiquity in Europe, including Parthenon, a miracle of harmony in marble and the Erechtheion with six larger-than-life maidens holding up the roof. Acropolis Museum, with ancient sculptures found on the Acropolis site. Thisíon, Greece's best-preserved Doric temple. The Agora, now in ruins, formerly commercial hub of ancient Athens and birthplace of politics and philosophy. Temple of Olympian Zeus, imposing monument with 15 massives columns still standing. Theater of Dionysus*, where plays of the ancient Greeks were first staged. Odeon of Herodes Atticus from A.D. 161, now the site of plays and concerts during the city's summer festival. Pláka*, the oldest section of Athens, picturesque maze of narrow streets huddled against the northern slope of the Acropolis. The Olympic Stadium, completed in 1896 for the first modern Olympic games, built in white marble as a replica of the ancient Roman stadium. Three Byzantine churches: Ágii Theódori, Kapnikaréa, Agios Elefthérios, all built in traditional Greek Cross plan. Mount Likavittós*, for spectacular panorama of the city. Sýntagma Square, bordered with luxury hotels, expensive cafés and tall glass-and-concrete buildings. Parliament and Presidential Palace, where *évzones* in traditional kilted uniform stand guard. National Archaeological Museum*, spanning every period of Greek history, with more masterpieces of ancient art than any other museum in the world. Benáki Museum, with displays of Greek national costumes and dazzling jewelry, sculpture and frescoes, housed in an elegant 19th-century villa. Piraeus, third largest port in the Mediterranean, harboring local fishing boats as well as luxury yachts and ocean-going vessels.

Around Athens. Delfí (Delphi), with Temple of Apollo*, site of the famous oracle and once the holiest place in all Greece; stadium and theater, built in 200 B.C., set against superb backdrop of cliffs and gorge; Kastalian Spring, gushing from rose-colored rocks, where ancient pilgrims washed and blasphemers met an untimely death; museum, containing an outstanding collection of classical and archaic pieces. Dafní (Daphni), with 11th-century Byzantine monastery celebrated for its splendid multicolored mosaics. Soúnion*, where Poseidon's marble temple commands stunning views over the Aegean.

Peloponnese. Kórinthos (Corinth), site of 6th-century B.C. Temple of Apollo, with magnificent views over the Gulf of Corinth; Corinth Canal *(Isthmós)*, separating Peloponnese from mainland Greece; Agora, market place in Roman times, when Corinth enjoyed a reputation as Greece's "sin city". Akrokórinthos (Acrocorinth), nearby medieval fortress town on site of Aphrodite's temple. Náfplio (Nauplia), well-preserved Venetian town and ideal base for excursions. Epídavros (Epidauros)★, with Greece's best-preserved ancient theater, seating 14,000 spectators. Mikínes (Mycenae)★ with "beehive" tombs and Acropolis, with colossal Lion Gate and 16th-century B.C. graves. Saronic islands, Póros, Spétse (Spetses) and Ídra (Hydra), noted for excellent swimming and water sports. Olimpía (Olympia)★ with the Stadium, site of the Olympic games since time immemorial; Heraion or Temple of Hera at foot of Mount Krónos, built around 600 B.C.; Temple of Zeus, where the sacred flame of the Olympic oracle burnt; museum, with fine sculpture from the site. Mistrás (Mistra)★, medieval Byzantine city with frescoed churches. Fortress-island of Monemvasía, transporting you back to the Middle Ages.

Northern Greece. Thessaloníki (Salonica) with several important Byzantine churches, testimony to Salonica's former status as second city in the Byzantine empire; Archaeological Museum, showing treasures from Neolithic to Byzantine times. Chalkidikí (Halkidiki), thickly-wooded peninsula with miles of breathtaking coastline. Mount Athos *(Ágion Óros)*★, sacred mountain where women are forbidden, inhabited by self-governing monastic community. Thásos, most northerly of Aegean islands, rich in archeological remains. Metéora★, group of isolated monasteries perched dramatically on pinnacles of barren rock. Pélla, ancient capital of Macedonia and important archeological site noted for its mosaics.

Northwestern Greece. Ípiros (Epirus), region of wild and rugged scenery. Pérama★, magnificent stalactite cave. Dodóni, seat of ancient oracle dating back to 2,000 B.C. Párga, unspoiled village, and bay dotted with picturesque islands.

Corfu★. Corfu town with Esplanade, central square where cricket is still played on tree-shaded lawn; Old Town, delightful maze of arched alleys with distinctive Venetian atmosphere; Museum of Asian Art, with remarkable oriental collection; Old Fort, where summer evening sound and light performances are held; Archaeological Museum, featuring two famous sculptures, the Gorgon pediment and the archaic lion, both over 2,500 years old. Paleokastrítsa, coastline of hills and promontories draped in olive, cypress and lemon trees; 16th-century monastery overlooking azure sea. Fine sandy beaches including Mirtiótissa,

Glifáda, St. George's Bay, Sidári. Limpid aquamarine coves and rugged, green mountain slopes on the northeast coast. Paxí (Paxos), tiny island of 300,000 olive trees and spectacular sea caves.

Aegean Islands. Cyclades: Dílos (Delos)*, legendary birthplace of Apollo and rich in archaeological vestiges; Míkonos (Mykonos)*, island of jet-setters and swinging nightlife; Tínos, serenely beautiful center of pilgrimage; Páros, with fine swimming, colorful villages and celebrated Church of 100 Doors; Náxos, with delightful whitewashed port town and early Cycladic tombs; Santoríni*, strangely crescent-shaped island, formed by volcanic eruption 3,500 years ago; important Minoan-era excavation. Dodecanese: Kos*, birthplace of Hippocrates; Kálimnos, barren and mountainous, famous for its sponge-diving; Pátmos, dominated by fortress-monastery of St. John the Divine. Eastern Aegean islands, Sámos, Lésvos (Lesbos) and Chíos, unusually green and mountainous. Thásos, with fascinating antiquities and coastline of coves and beaches. Northern Sporades, archipelago of largely un-spoiled, peaceful islands.

Crete. Iráklion (Heraklion), Venetian walled city with gold-stone castle, 16th-century church *(Agía Ekateríni)* housing six visionary and haunt-ing icons; outstanding Archaeological Museum* containing the world's greatest collection of Minoan art, including Phaistós Disk with its mysterious message. Knossós*, where the reconstructed palace of King Minos evokes the splendor of the ancient court. Phaistós palace ruins, in poetic setting below snow-capped Mount Ídi. Other Minoan palace sites: Káto Zákros and Mália. 13th-century church *(Panagiá Kerá)* in Kritsá, with frescoes considered to be the finest in Crete. Gorge of Samariá *(Farági Samariás)*, with fantastic rock formations. Chaniá and Réthymnon, towns with charming mixture of Turkish and Venetian influences.

Rhodes. Ródos (Rhodes), old town*, stronghold of Knights of St. John in 14th and 15th centuries, with twisting narrow streets leading to Knights' Palace and Hospital; Archaeological Museum, housing ancient treasures, including famous marble statue of Aphrodite and head of Helios; Ippotón, a narrow cobblestoned street; imposing Palace of the Grand Masters; massive outer medieval wall; Turkish quarters, with colorful bazaar and mosques. Temple of Apollo on Monte Smith. Líndos*, commanding spectacular view from ruins of its 4th-century shrine. Kámiros, with sweeping island views and remains of Doric temples and once-flourishing ancient city.

247

Some useful expressions in Greek

good morning/afternoon	kaliméra/kalispéra
good evening/night	kalispéra/kaliníkta
good-bye	chérete
yes/no	ne/óchi
please/thank you	parakaló/efcharistó
excuse me	me sinchoríte
you're welcome	típota
where/when/how	pou/póte/pos
how long/how far	póso keró/póso makriá
yesterday/today/tomorrow	chthes/símera/ávrio
day/week/month/year	iméra/evdomáda/mínas/chrónos
left/right	aristerá/dexiá
up/down	epáno/káto
good/bad	kalós/kakós
big/small	megálos/mikrós
cheap/expensive	fthinós/akrivós
hot/cold	zestós/kríos
old/new	paliós/kenoúrgios
open/closed	aniktós/klistós
free (vacant)/occupied	eléftheros/krasiménos
early/late	eróns/argá
easy/difficult	éfkolos/dískolos
Does anyone here speak English/French/German?	Milái kanis angliká/galliká/germaniká?
What does this mean?	Ti siméni aftó?
I don't understand.	Den katalavéno.
Please write it down.	Parakaló grápste to.
Do you take credit cards/traveler's checks?	Pérnete pistotikés kártes/traveller's checks?
Waiter, please!	Parakaló!
Where are the toilets?	Pou íne i toualéttes?
I'd like...	Tha íthela...
How much is that?	Póso káni aftó?
What time is it?	Ti óra íne?
Help me please.	Voithíste me parakaló.
Just a minute.	Éna leptó.

HUNGARY

Gypsy violins, goulash and joie de vivre in hospitable, dynamic Central Europe

In the Dark Ages, the Huns and Vandals and Avars all came, saw and pillaged what is now Hungary, but that was centuries before the actual Hungarians arrived. The Magyars galloped onto the scene in the 9th century. They're still impressive on horseback, especially on the *puszta,* the Hungarian prairie.

The country, mostly flat, is only half the size of Oklahoma or Missouri, so it's a couple of hundred miles or less from the capital to anywhere. Budapest is ten times the size of Hungary's next biggest town, and a natural focus for the nation's government, economy and culture. Called the Pearl of the Danube, the city sums up the Middle European talent for good taste and good living.

The stately Danube bisects Budapest. On the west bank, hilly old Buda has a monopoly on vantage points, and many of the historic monuments. Across the river, Pest is for strollers, museum-goers and shoppers—see the country folk gawk at the window displays! Anywhere in town, you can break your sightseeing at one of the old-style cafés, where whipped-cream-laden pastries are matched with bracing coffee. The weeping violins don't come on until after dark, along with the goulash and paprika.

Thermal springs all around the country have been exploited since prehistoric times. Budapest itself is a spa, offering every kind of "cure", in luxury health hotels or Turkish baths built by the 16th-century Turkish invaders, and still in use. The Turks left some startling architectural relics around the country, including Europe's northernmost minaret (in Eger).

Recent history has put the country in the vanguard of the new Europe. It was Hungary that tore down the Iron Curtain, signaling the end of the Cold War. The red stars have been toppled from public buildings. No place in Europe is more dynamic.

Facts and figures

Population:	10.45 million
Area:	35,519 sq. miles (93,030 sq. km)
Capital:	Budapest (2.1 million)
Other major cities:	Debrecen (220,000) Miskolc (210,000) Szeged (189,000) Pécs (175,000) Győr (130,000)
Language:	Hungarian
Religion:	Catholic (65%), Protestant (25%), Eastern Orthodox (3%)
Time zone:	GMT + 1, EST + 6; DST (Apr.–Sep.)
Currency:	*Forint* (abbr. *Ft.*) = 100 *fillérs* Coins: 10, 20, 50 fillérs; Ft. 1, 2, 5, 10, 20 Bills: Ft. 10, 20, 50, 100, 500, 1,000
Electricity:	220 volt, 50 cycle, AC

Planning your trip

Visa requirements. See pp. 29–30.

Vaccination requirements. None (see also p. 25).

Currency restrictions. Visitors may be required to report the currencies they're carrying, though there is no limit on the import of foreign funds. As for Hungarian currency, it is forbidden to import or to export more than 500 forints. Note that there is a restriction on the amount of forints that may be converted into hard currency when leaving the country.

Climate. Continental climate: hot summers, cold winters. Rainy season: mainly in early spring and November. Snow can impede road traffic in winter.

251

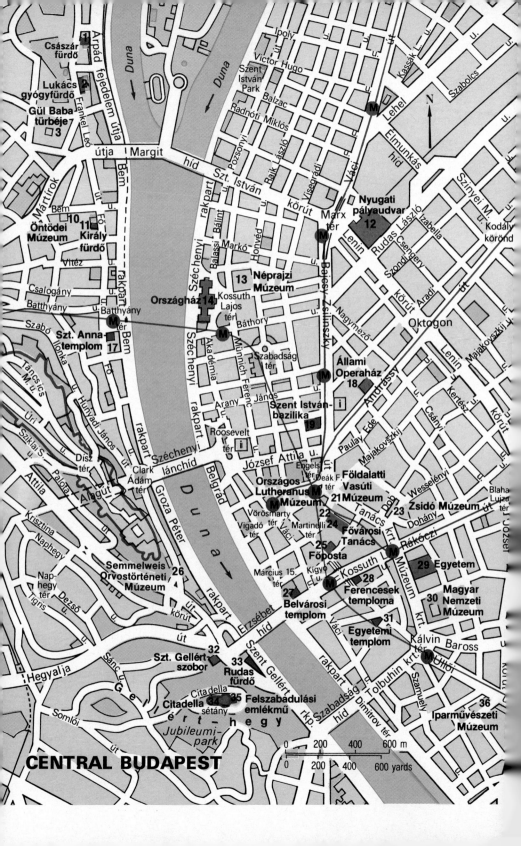

CENTRAL BUDAPEST

1 Császár fürdő
2 Lukács gyógyfürdő
3 Gül Baba türbéje
10 Öntödei Múzeum
11 Király fürdő
13 Néprajzi Múzeum
14 Országház
12 Nyugati pályaudvar
17 Szt. Anna templom
18 Állami Operaház
19 Szent István-bazilika
20 Országos Lutheranus Múzeum
21 Földalatti Vasúti Múzeum
23 Zsidó Múzeum
24 Fővárosi Tanács
25 Főposta
26 Semmelweis Orvostörténeti Múzeum
27 Belvárosi templom
28 Ferencesek temploma
29 Egyetem
30 Magyar Nemzeti Múzeum
31 Egyetemi templom
32 Szt. Gellért szobor
33 Rudas fürdő
34 Citadella
35 Felszabadulási emlékmű
36 Iparművészeti Múzeum

0 200 400 600 m
0 200 400 600 yards

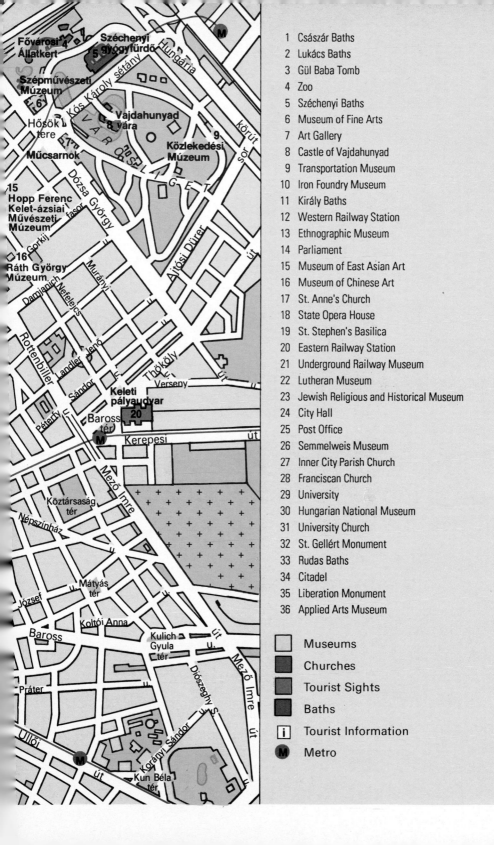

1 Császár Baths
2 Lukács Baths
3 Gül Baba Tomb
4 Zoo
5 Széchenyi Baths
6 Museum of Fine Arts
7 Art Gallery
8 Castle of Vajdahunyad
9 Transportation Museum
10 Iron Foundry Museum
11 Király Baths
12 Western Railway Station
13 Ethnographic Museum
14 Parliament
15 Museum of East Asian Art
16 Museum of Chinese Art
17 St. Anne's Church
18 State Opera House
19 St. Stephen's Basilica
20 Eastern Railway Station
21 Underground Railway Museum
22 Lutheran Museum
23 Jewish Religious and Historical Museum
24 City Hall
25 Post Office
26 Semmelweis Museum
27 Inner City Parish Church
28 Franciscan Church
29 University
30 Hungarian National Museum
31 University Church
32 St. Gellért Monument
33 Rudas Baths
34 Citadel
35 Liberation Monument
36 Applied Arts Museum

- Museums
- Churches
- Tourist Sights
- Baths
- [i] Tourist Information
- M Metro

Some average daily temperatures:

Budapest		J	F	M	A	M	J	J	A	S	O	N	D
average daily maximum*	°F	34	39	50	62	71	78	82	81	74	61	47	39
	°C	1	4	10	17	22	26	28	27	23	16	8	4
average daily minimum*	°F	25	28	35	44	52	58	62	60	53	44	38	30
	°C	–4	–2	2	7	11	15	16	16	12	7	3	–1

Debrecen													
average daily maximum*	°F	33	38	50	62	71	77	81	80	73	61	47	38
	°C	0	3	10	16	22	25	27	27	23	16	9	3
average daily minimum*	°F	21	25	32	41	50	56	59	57	50	41	36	28
	°C	–6	–4	0	5	10	13	15	14	10	5	2	–2

* Minimum temperatures are measured just before sunrise, maximum temperatures in the afternoon.

Clothing. Light clothing in summer; warm clothing (with overcoat) in winter. As for formality, a certain Central European seriousness persists, though there are no definite rules. Evening gowns and dark suits are standard at the Opera House, but jeans are also acceptable. On warm summer days, jackets and ties are abandoned in most areas of life.

Duty-free allowances

Cigarettes	Cigars	Tobacco	Liquor	Wine
250 or	50 or	250 g.	1 l. and	2 l.

Gifts are permitted once a year with a maximum value of Ft. 1,000 per item and a total maximum value of Ft. 5,000 (includes tobacco products up to Ft. 1,000 value in excess of amounts shown in chart above). *Perfume* is permitted in "reasonable quantity".

Hotels and accommodations

Hotels. Hotel rooms are often in short supply so reservations well in advance are advisable. Busiest periods: during international fairs, the summer holiday season and the autumn congress period. Ibusz, the state travel agency, which maintains offices abroad, is preferable for hotel bookings. (Local travel agencies also handle hotel reservations but aren't always reliable). A booking fee is charged. When hotels are full, travel agencies can provide private accommodations.

Hotels are graded by the star system: a five-star hotel is truly luxurious, and a one-star budget hotel has few amenities. Most hotels in the three-to-five star class have their own shopping arcades, tourist agency and airline offices. Rates drop by as much as 30% outside the summer tourist season.

Accommodations in **private homes**—a room with or without breakfast, or a self-contained **apartment**—can be reserved through travel agencies in Budapest and other towns. The rates in Budapest are about the same as those of moderate hotels, but lower in the country.

The equivalent of English "Bed and Breakfast" establishments are found along major roads and in holiday centers. Often the sign *Szoba kiadó* is supplemented by its German equivalent, *Zimmer frei.*

Camping. More than 200 campsites, big and small, are scattered around Hungary, with the biggest concentration on the shores of Lake Balaton. Budapest itself has two large camping grounds. All the sites in the country are graded according to international standards. The top (three-star) establishments have more facilities, a larger area for each family, and tents and cabins for hire. In general, the camping season lasts from May to September, but a few sites open earlier in the year and continue operating into the wintry weather.

Hungarian tourist offices abroad

U.K.	Danube Travel Ltd. General Agent IBUSZ-Hungary, 6, Conduit Street, London W1R 9TG; tel. (071) 493 0263
U.S.A.	IBUSZ Hungarian Travel Ltd., 400 Kalby Street, Suite 1104, Fort Lee, NJ 07024

On the spot

Banks and currency exchange. Banking hours are 9 a.m.–5 p.m., Monday–Friday and 9 a.m.–2 p.m. on Saturdays. Exchange facilities can be found at airports, railroad stations, banks, hotels, travel agencies, some shopping centers and restaurants. Currency-exchange hours are normally 9 a.m.–10 p.m. (closed Saturday afternoons, Sundays and legal holidays). Major hotels, airports and railroad stations will change money virtually round the clock.

Credit cards and traveler's checks. Internationally recognized credit cards and traveler's checks are widely accepted in tourist-oriented establishments.

Mail and telecommunications. Post offices handle mail, telephone, telegraph and telex services, but not international money transfers. Stamps *(bélyeg)* can also be bought at tobacco shops or where postcards are sold. Mailboxes are painted red and usually decorated with a hunting horn.

The main post office in Petöfi Sándor utca in Budapest is open 7 a.m.–8 p.m., Monday–Saturday. An international telex, telefax, telegraph and telephone office at Petöfi Sándor utca, Budapest, is also open 7 a.m.–8 p.m., Monday–Friday, and until 7 p.m. on Saturdays and with limited service on Sunday mornings.

Some useful telephone numbers:

Ambulance	04	Directory inquiries in	
Fire	05	foreign languages	1172-200
Police	07		

Newspapers. Principal dailies: *Népszabadság, Népszava, Magyar Nemzet, Magyar Hirlap, Esti Hirlap*. All the principal foreign newspapers (e.g. *International Herald Tribune, Le Monde, Die Presse*) are available both at hotel newsstands and at kiosks throughout the capital. Local foreign-language newspapers include the bilingual English-German *Daily News/Neueste Nachrichten* (daily except Sunday and Monday) and the daily *Budapester Rundschau*. A free monthly magazine, *Programme in Hungary,* has parallel texts in German, English and French. The journal *New Hungarian Quarterly* (in English) offers profound insights into Hungarian life, culture and politics.

Tourinform. For information by telephone—in English, French, German, Russian or Hungarian—call 426-176 in Budapest, even from abroad. The range of information readily available includes weather

forecasts, bus and railroad schedules, currency rates, plus events of the day.

The Tourinform service operates from 7 a.m. to 9 p.m., Monday through Friday, to 8 p.m. on Saturdays and from 8 a.m. to 1 p.m. on Sundays at 74–76 Rákoczi-ut.

Legal holidays

Jan. 1	New Year's Day	Oct. 23	National Holiday
Mar. 15	National Holiday	Dec. 25	Christmas Day
May 1	Labor Day	Dec. 26	Boxing Day
Aug. 20	St. Stephen's Day	**Movable:**	Easter Monday

Transportation

Air. Budapest Ferihegy is the country's only commercial airport. There are no scheduled domestic flights.

Airport. Ferihegy (10 miles/16 km. from city center). Frequent bus service.

Rail. Hungarian State Railways maintains a dense rail network, with both first- and second-class seating. For express trains, reservations are necessary, either through Ibusz or the railroad station. Rail passes valid for 7 or 10 days of unlimited travel within Hungary are sold.

Long-distance buses. Very efficient, punctual intercity bus services are operated by Mavaut and Volán.

Local public transportation. All Hungarian cities are well provided with efficient and cheap public transportation systems. The most comprehensive of all serves Budapest, where no place is more than 500 meters from a bus, streetcar, trolleybus or subway stop. Maps of all the lines, both surface and underground, are sold at major stations. Transport maps are also available in other major cities, though only Budapest has a subway (metro). Day tickets for unlimited travel can be used interchangeably on all forms of public transportation.

Taxis. Taxis are available in all major towns. Outside of city limits return fare is charged up to the boundary line. You can hail a cab on the street (when the roof sign is lit), phone for one or go to a taxi stand.

Boats. Motor launches ply the Budapest section of the Danube from about 9 a.m. to 8 p.m. daily during the tourist season. Bus tickets are used. Among the principal stations are Gellért tér, Batthyány tér and Petőfi tér, and there are several stops on Margaret Island. Sightseeing excursion boats operate from Vigadó tér, from where boats and hydrofoils leave for Visegrád and Esztergom.

Car rental. Cars can be hired from several agencies, at the airport, at railroad stations, through hotels or tourist offices. Bills must be settled in hard currency.

Driving in Hungary. Roads are adequately maintained. Drive with care: the accident rate is proportionally one of the world's highest. At marked crossings, pedestrians have priority. Speed limits in towns and villages, unless otherwise indicated, 37 mph (60 kph), on country roads 50 mph (80 kph), on two-lane motorways 60 mph (100 kph), on four-lane expressways 70 mph (120 kph).

Use of seat belts is obligatory, and a red reflector warning triangle, a set of spare bulbs and a first-aid kit must be carried. The car must be fitted with rubber mudguards. Blood alcohol limit is a strictly enforced zero. Gasoline available is normal (86 octane), super (92 and 98 octane), lead-free and diesel (with coupons only, which are obtainable at travel agencies and currency-exchange offices).

Along the main roads yellow patrol cars of the Hungarian Automobile Association deal with breakdowns. On the Budapest–Lake Balaton expressway there's an emergency phone callbox every two kilometers. For towing service dial 1260–668 in Budapest.

Some distances: Budapest–Győr 80 miles (125 km.), Szeged 105 miles (170 km.), Pécs 120 miles (190 km.), Debrecen 140 miles (225 km.).

Rest rooms. Public conveniences are found in all Hungarian cities—in train or metro stations, parks and squares, museums and, of course, in hotels, restaurants and cafés. The sign may point to *mosdó* or *W.C.* (pronounced *vay*-tsay), and if pictures don't indicate which room is which, you'll have to remember that *férfi* means "men" and *nói* means "women".

Emergencies. Emergency telephone numbers throughout Hungary:
Ambulance 04—Fire 05—Police 07

Police. Police wear blue-and-gray uniforms. Traffic police and highway patrols dress similarly but with white caps and white leather accessories to make them more visible. Police cars are blue and white. There is no special police unit detailed to deal with tourist questions but the police in general are helpful to foreigners.

Crime and theft. Though violent crime is rare in Hungary, visitors ought to take elementary precautions to protect their property. This means locking car doors and hotel rooms. When you park your car, place valuables out of sight or lock them in the trunk. Don't leave jewelry, money or documents around but use the hotel's safe.

259

Medical care and health. The standard of medical treatment is high. In case of emergency, health authorities will direct foreigners to specialized medical centers. In virtually every hospital some doctors speak foreign languages. Fees are very reasonable, and in emergency cases treatment is usually free. Medicine and pharmaceutical supplies are readily available at low cost. A number of pharmacies are open around the clock on a rotating basis. Their addresses are posted in the windows of all pharmacies. Telephone operators and hotels have details. You can safely drink tap water.

Embassies and consulates. Embassies and consulates are listed in the telephone directory under "Külképviseletek".

Social customs. Invitations to luncheons or dinners in restaurants are customary, though Hungarian hosts usually don't invite their foreign guests to their homes. Hungarians are open and friendly. They are so helpful to foreigners that, if you unfold a map on the street, they may give you directions whether you're lost or not. Because their language is so outlandish, they are genuinely delighted when a foreigner attempts to say a few words in Hungarian.

Enjoying Hungary

Food and drink. Most hotels and restaurants offer a variety of local and international dishes. Eating places in Hungary go under a variety of titles. The word *restaurant* is only used by places targeting foreign clients. An *étterem* serves a wide range of food and drinks. A *vendéglő,* moderately priced, may have rustic decor. A *bisztró* is small and reasonably priced. A *büfé* serves hot and cold snacks. A *csárda* is a country inn.

Gulyásleves (goulash soup) is the Hungarian specialty: chunks of beef, potatoes, onion, tomatoes and peppers with paprika, caraway seeds and garlic. (What is called goulash abroad is a Hungarian meat stew actually named *pörkölt.*) Other dishes worth trying include *ujházy tyúkleves* (chicken broth), *halászlé* (fish soup), *paprikás csirke* (chicken paprika), *töltött káposzta* (stuffed cabbage). Be prepared for heaped servings of meat and fish together with a choice of side dishes and salads—very highly flavored and spiced with the ubiquitous paprika.

Red wines: Egri bikavér, Villányi, Pinot Noir. White wines: Csopaki Rizling, Badacsonyi Kéknyelü, Tokaji. Aperitifs: *barack* (apricot brandy), *cseresznye* (cherry brandy). Better restaurants and bars have imported liquor, though at high prices.

Mealtimes: lunch, noon–2 p.m.; dinner, 7–10 p.m.

Entertainment. Budapest offers many entertainment possibilities, from opera and concerts to movie theaters and discos. They're listed in the monthly *Programme in Hungary,* available free at hotels. Most foreign films are dubbed in Hungarian.

Taxes, service charges and tipping. A sales tax of 25% is included in the price of most goods. A service charge is included in the bill at restaurants but 10% is generally given to the waiter. At top-class hotels 15% service charge is added to the bill. Tip taxi drivers 10%, porters Ft. 30 per bag, barbers/hairdressers 15%.

Sports and recreation. Some hotels have swimming pools and tennis courts; hunting, horse riding and water sports in the Lake Balaton area are also favorite pursuits. Popular spectator sports include soccer, basketball, ice hockey, volleyball, handball and water polo.

TV and radio. Local programming is mainly in Hungarian. Occasionally, on television, there are regional programs in German. Brief news bulletins for foreigners are broadcast, in summer only, on Budapest Radio and on TV; times are listed in the weekly radio-TV guide. Around Budapest, Radio Bridge broadcasts all day in English.

What do buy. Handicrafts, woodcarvings, rugs, books, leather goods, linen, local wines and liquor, Herend chinaware.

Shopping hours: generally 10 a.m.–6 p.m., Monday–Friday (until 7 p.m. on Thursdays). Some shops are open till 2 p.m. on Saturdays.

Sightseeing

Budapest. Buda Castle District, concentrating history and art on a long, narrow plateau overlooking the Danube: Matthias Church★, its lone spire towering over the old town; Fishermen's Bastion★, a 20th-century folly simulating medieval fortifications; Royal Palace★, begun in 13th century, containing Hungarian National Gallery of art. Historic Turkish baths still in use. Óbuda district, notable for ancient Roman remains. Aquincum★, excavations of an ancient Roman town with museum and lapidarium. Margaret Island in the Danube, parks and forests and remains of 13th-century convent and church. Buda, city's commercial center, with best window-shopping in Váci utca★ pedestrian zone; riverside neo-Gothic Houses of Parliament★; Hungarian National Museum containing ancient relics and the Hungarian royal regalia; onion-domed Great Synagogue with Jewish historical collection including 3rd-century gravestone and World War II documents; Art Nouveau palace housing Museum of Applied Arts; Museum of Fine Arts★, from Egyptian mummies to Old Masters to French Impressionists.

262

Danube Bend. Szentendre★, an ancient town upstream from Budapest, a rainbow of Baroque charm; nearby Open Air Village Museum reassembles authentic historic houses. Visegrád, site of fabled 13th-century castle dominating the river. Esztergom★, Hungary's medieval capital, with the country's biggest church, partially restored royal palace and superb art collection in riverside Christian Museum.

Western Hungary. Sopron★, near Austrian frontier, old Roman walled town of fine Gothic and Renaissance houses. Fertöd a hamlet built around the palace★ of the Eszterházy family, where Haydn worked for decades as staff musician. Kőszeg, well preserved historic town with equally pleasing, more modern district outside the walls. Szombathely, with voluminous old Roman remains and 18th-century cathedral. Jak, tiny village boasting Romanesque church★ consecrated in 13th century. Győr, a busy industrial and cultural center with a cathedral begun in the 11th century and fine Baroque churches.

Lake Balaton. Central Europe's largest lake, shallow but rich in minerals, fish and reeds. Tihany★, wooded peninsula with clifftop Abbey Church and views. Badacsony region of vineyards on volcanic hills. Keszthely, site of Balaton Museum and 101-room Festetics Palace★ in its own park.

The South. Pécs★, where Turks held sway for more than a century, leaving elegant Arabic calligraphy in parish church (former mosque); Janus Pannonius museum; ancient Roman vestiges around cathedral square. Mohács, scene of titanic battle won by Turks, commemorated by melancholy memorial park. Kalocsa★, capital of paprika peppers and folk art; 18th-century cathedral and stately Archbishop's Palace.

Great Plains and Puszta. Kecskemét, with Art Nouveau architecture, museum of naïve artists, and thriving apricot brandy industry. Kiskunság National Park★, preserving landscape and way of life of the Hungarian puszta. Szeged, a river port and cultural center, with 12th-century Tower of St. Demetrius, Eclectic-Baroque City Hall and historic churches. Gyula★, a spa town with 14th-century Gothic fortress. Debrecen, Hungary's bulwark of Protestantism, with neoclassical Great Church and Calvinist College. Hortobágy National Park★, puszta wildlife reserve and museums.

Northern Highlands. Eger★, surrounded by vineyards, with elaborate fortress and Europe's northernmost medieval minaret. Baradla Cave, on the Czechoslovakian border, with guided tours for non-spelunkers. Tokaj★, pretty wine-making town. Sárospatak, with giant castle overlooking the Bodrog river, and church founded in 14th century.

263

Some useful expressions in Hungarian

good morning/afternoon	jó reggelt/jó napot
good evening/night	jó estét/jó éjszakát
good-bye	viszontlátásra
yes/no	igen/nem
please/thank you	kérem/köszönöm
excuse me	bocsánat
you're welcome	szivesen
where/when/how	hol/mikor/hogyan
how long/how far	mennyi ideig/milyen messze
yesterday/today/tomorrow	tegnap/ma/holnap
day/week/month/year	nap/hét/hónap/év
left/right	bal/jobb
up/down	fel/le
good/bad	jó/rossz
big/small	nagy/kicsi
cheap/expensive	olcsó/drága
hot/cold	meleg/hideg
old/new	régi/uj
open/closed	nyitva/zárva
free (vacant)/occupied	szabad/foglalt
early/late	korán/késön
easy/difficult	könnyü/nehéz
Does anyone here speak English/French/German?	Beszél itt valaki angolul/franciául/németül?
What does this mean?	Ez mit jelent?
I don't understand.	Nem értem.
Please write it down.	Legyen szives, irja le.
Do you take credit cards/traveller's cheques?	Elfogadnak hitelkártyát/utazócsekket?
Waiter!/Waitress!	Pincér!
Where are the toilets?	Hol van a WC/mosdó?
I'd like…	Szeretnék…
How much is that?	Mennyibe kerül?
What time is it?	Hány óra van?
Help me please.	Legyen szives, segitsen.
Just a minute.	Pillanat.

ICELAND

Grimsey

Ísafjördhur

Siglufjördhur

Húsavík

HÚNAFLÓI

Ólafsfjördhur

Dettifoss

Blönduós

Godhafoss

BREIDAFJÖRDUR

Akureyri

Mývatn

Seydhisfjördhur

Stykkishólmur

Egilsstadhir

Askja ▲

Eskifjördhur

HOFSJÖKULL

Borgarnes

LANGJÖKULL

FAXAFLÓI

VATNAJÖKULL

Akranes

Gullfoss

REYKJAVÍK

Hveragerdhi

Höfn

Keflavík

Grindavík

Hekla ▲

MÝRDALSJÖKULL

Vestmannaeyjar

Vík

*Children of the Vikings cheerily continue
their saga among geysers and glaciers.*

The first settler, according to the saga of Iceland, was a Viking named Ingólfur Arnarson, who landed in A.D. 874. "Saga" is an Icelandic word, as is "geyser"; heroic stories and geological wonders are unquenchable natural resources.

With its glaciers and sputtering volcanoes, Iceland has been called the land of ice and fire, but most of the quarter-million islanders avoid both extremes, living quite comfortably in the attractive towns. Reykjavik, by far the biggest city, gives a warm impression with its modern multistory buildings and cheerfully painted old wooden houses, well-tended gardens, and cultural attractions. The people, of Scandinavian and Celtic origin, are prone to pass the winter evenings at a symphony concert, or reading a book, or playing chess or bridge.

Summer, clearly, is the nicest time to visit Iceland; the air is so unpolluted that suntans are said to develop very quickly. Yet winter is not nearly so harsh as the country's name implies. The Icelanders boast that the average January temperature in Reykjavik is higher than New York's.

The wilderness areas of this island are now reasonably accessible over 5,500 miles of roads and a well-developed network of airline routes. Botanists and birdwatchers can easily pursue bluebells and puffins, fishermen corner whopping trout, and collectors of superlatives can check off Europe's largest glacier, geyser and waterfall. Since the sun scarcely sets for three months at a time, summer golfing goes on until midnight. Swimming in geothermal pools is popular even in winter.

Aside from hot water, most of the comforts of civilization must be imported, so the cost of living is frankly expensive. But you can feast on the local lamb and fish—and dishes as adventurous as sheep's head and shark. If all else fails, the local firewater, called *brennivin,* or, more familiarly, the Black Death, is supposed to transform the frozen north into a tropical paradise.

Facts and figures

Population:	235,000
Area:	39,700 sq. miles (102,830 sq. km.)
Capital:	Reykjavik (86,000/GUA 125,000)
Other towns:	Kópavogur (14,000)
	Akureyri (14,000)
	Hafnarfjörður (12,500)
	Keflavík (6,500)
Language:	Icelandic
Religion:	Protestant (99%)
Time zone:	GMT, EST + 5
Currency:	Icelandic *króna* (abbr. *kr.*) = 100 *aurar*
	Coins: 5, 10, 50 aurar; 1, 5, 10, 50 kr.
	Bills: 100, 500, 1,000, 5,000 kr.
Electricity:	220 volt, 50 cycle, AC

Planning your trip

Visa requirements. See pp. 29–30.

Vaccination requirements. None (see also p. 25).

Currency restrictions. Up to kr. 8,000 may be imported or exported. Any amount of foreign currency may be brought into the country, and up to the same amount taken out again.

Climate. Thanks to the moderating influence of a branch of the Gulf Stream, Iceland enjoys a cool, temperate oceanic climate that is considerably less rigorous than its latitude may lead one to expect. The weather is very changeable; it is almost always windy, with gales sometimes and occasionally hurricanes.

The wettest region is the southwest, and the driest the northeast. In June and July, there is almost perpetual daylight, while the dark period, with only 3–4 hours' light, lasts from mid-November to the end of January. The Northern Lights (Aurora Borealis) begin to appear in autumn.

Some average daily temperatures:

Reykjavik		J	F	M	A	M	J	J	A	S	O	N	D
average daily	°F	35	37	39	43	50	54	57	56	52	45	39	36
maximum	°C	2	3	4	6	10	12	14	14	11	7	4	2
average daily	°F	28	28	30	33	39	45	48	47	43	38	32	29
minimum	°C	-2	-2	-1	1	4	7	9	8	6	3	0	-2

Clothing. Warm outer clothing and well-made shoes are necessary all year round, but in hotels and public buildings, the central heating is usually set at about 68 °F (20 °C) for most of the year. For excursions bring windproof and waterproof clothing. Take a swimsuit, whatever time of year you go, for a dip in the naturally heated pools. Casual dress is popular in Iceland, but at almost all restaurants, men wear jacket and tie.

Duty-free allowances

Cigarettes		Cigars	Tobacco	Liquor	Wine
200	or	250 g. of any other tobacco products		1 l. and	1 l.

Hotels and accommodations

Hotels. Many hotels in the west and east of the country are open only during the summer months, while others are open all year round. They are quite expensive but well-appointed. Slightly cheaper are guest houses in Reykjavik, and farmhouses in the countryside. There are several youth hostels as well. Always make reservations in advance if you are going to Iceland in summer.

Camping. Iceland has more than 60 campsites. If you want to camp elsewhere you first have to get the permission from the property owners.

Icelandic tourist offices abroad

U.K. Icelandair, 73 Grosvenor Street, London W1X 9DD; tel. (071) 499 9971

U.S.A. Iceland Tourist Board, 655 Third Avenue, New York, NY 10017

On the spot

Banks and currency exchange. Banks are generally open from 9:15 a.m. to 4 p.m., Monday through Friday, and on Thursdays from 5 to 6 p.m. as well. They are also open for currency exchange only on Saturdays from 10 a.m. to noon. Outside these hours, money can be changed at hotels, restaurants and souvenir shops, but then only to cover the cost of purchases made.

Credit cards and traveler's checks. Both are accepted at hotels, restaurants and souvenir shops.

Mail and telecommunications. Bad weather sometimes causes delays. The central post office (*Pósthusið*) in Reykjavik is open 8 a.m. to 5 p.m. on Mondays, 9 a.m. to 5 p.m. Tuesday through Friday, and 9 a.m. to noon on Saturdays. The post office in the central bus station is open from 9 a.m. to 7:30 p.m., Monday through Friday, and Saturdays from 8 a.m. to 3 p.m.

Reykjavik's central telephone and telegraph office (*Símstöðin*) is open from 9 a.m. to 7 p.m. on weekdays, and 11 a.m. to 6 p.m. on Sundays. Telephone directories list people by their first names. See also p. 30.

Some useful telephone numbers in the Reykjavik area:

Operator	09	Telegrams (day)	06
Police/Ambulance	11166/11100	(night)	16411

Tourist information

Reykjavik   Iceland Tourist Bureau, Skógarhlið 6,
101 Reykjavik; tel. (01) 25855

Legal holidays

Jan.1	New Year's Day	**Movable dates:**
May 1	Labor Day	Maundy Thursday
		Good Friday
June 17	National Day	Easter Monday
Dec. 24	Christmas Eve	1st day of summer (3rd or
Dec. 25	Christmas	4th Thursday in April)
Dec. 26		Ascension Day
		Whit Monday
Dec. 31	New Year's Eve	Shop and Office Workers'
		Holiday
		(1st Monday in August)

Transportation

Air. All international flights, except the service from the Faroe Islands and the Greenland sightseeing tours, land at Keflavík International Airport. Domestic flights to about a dozen airports connect all the main towns throughout the country. Advance reservations are advised.

Major airport. Reykjavik: Keflavík (30 miles/50 km. from the capital). Duty-free shop serves arriving passengers. Transportation to and from the capital is by bus.

Long-distance buses. There is no rail system, but a network of buses serves all the communities. Schedules are reduced in winter.

Boats, waterways. An infrequent coastal steamer service operates year-round. In addition there are two principal ferry routes: Reykjavik–Akranes and the south coast to the Westmann Islands.

Local transportation. Reykjavik operates an excellent bus service. All routes go via one of the two main transfer points (Laekjargata or Hlemmur). Bus stops are marked SVR, and tickets can be bought from the driver (correct change only), or at the main bus stations (Laekjargata or Hlemmur).

Taxis. There are many about in the towns. They operate from stands, but can also be called for. Fares are displayed on the meter. Tours are also available at flat rates to places of interest. If a cab displays a *laus* sign, then it's free. Fares double at the weekend; waiting charges are high.

Car rental. International and local agencies operate in Reykjavik. Make advance reservations in summer. Anybody planning to drive into the barren hinterland is strongly advised to take a four-wheel drive car fitted with two-way radio. Taxi companies can provide chauffeur-driven cars. See also pp. 30–31.

Driving in Iceland. Drive on the right, pass on the left. The condition of roads varies a great deal; very few, apart from those in and around Reykjavik, are asphalted. Seat belts are compulsory, and the 50 mg./100 ml. alcohol limit is strictly enforced. Speed limits are 31 mph (50 kph) in town, and 44 mph (70 kph) elsewhere, unless a higher limit is posted. Parking in the town is usually metered, and the charge is always the same, but the length of time allowed may vary. Gas stations are rare. If you plan to drive into the interior, take extra blankets, food, warm clothing and gasoline supplies, and listen to local advice on conditions. You may not meet another vehicle for a day or two.

Emergencies. In Reykjavik, in case of an emergency dial 11100 for the ambulance or to report a fire, and 11166 for the police.

Police. Visitors will probably not encounter the police, but most speak English, and they also exercise the right to stop you if your driving is in the least bit suspect.

Crime and theft. The incidence is very low by world standards.

Medical care and health. Health care is excellent and costs are moderate. Hotels and embassies have arrangements with doctors to take care of emergencies. Virtually all medical staff speak English. All drugs and medical supplies can be obtained on a 24-hour basis, but many remedies sold over the counter in other countries require a prescription in Iceland. Pharmacies (*apótek*) are open from 9 a.m. to 6 p.m. on weekdays. Additionally, some are open from 6 p.m. to 10 p.m. during the week and 9 a.m. to 10 p.m. on Saturdays—look for notices in pharmacy windows. For insurance, see pp. 25–26.

Tap water is safe to drink.

Embassies and consulates. These are listed in the telephone directory in their national languages.

Social customs. One of the first things to strike a visitor is the use of first names. Surnames are not used in Iceland except to indicate whose son or daughter the bearer is. For example, Jón Kjartansson would not be addressed as Mr. Kjartansson, but always as Jón, the son of Kjartan. Similarly, Eydís Björnsdóttir will not be known as Mrs. Björnsdóttir, but as Eydís, the daughter of Björn. Married women don't, in general, use their husband's name.

Enjoying Iceland

Food and drink. Not surprisingly, there is a lot of excellent fish and seafood to eat in Iceland. Lobsters, oysters and clams are delicious, and beyond that you could well find yourself eating shark or whale. In the cities, the choice of cuisine is international, ranging from hamburgers and pizzas to vegetarian food. Open sandwiches are a popular lunchtime snack. As in the other Nordic countries, hotels here often put on a sumptuous cold buffet. Icelandic specialties include *svid* (sheep's head) and *hákarl* (shark that has been buried in the sand for a short time). *Sild* (herring) is delicious, particularly in hors d'oeuvres. Iceland's rivers offer trout, alpine char and salmon in abundance.

If you are eating in a hotel, then you can enjoy a wide selection of

271

wines and liquor, but the only available beer is weak. As in other Nordic countries, the sale of alcohol is strictly controlled. Bars do not exist, but you can try some of Iceland's firewater, *brennivin*, in a hotel lounge—but be warned, it is staggeringly strong.

Lunch is served from noon to 2:30 p.m., dinner 7 to 10 p.m.

Entertainment. During the winter months, Icelanders enjoy a variety of entertainment at the theater, opera or concerts. Concerts continue throughout the summer, and there is an English-speaking theater, called Light Nights, with Icelandic entertainment. Foreign movies are shown in their original language. A number of hotels and clubs provide live or disco music for dancing.

Taxes, service charges and tipping. Taxes and service charges are included in hotel and restaurant bills. Tipping is not encouraged, except in response to a special service. The policy applies to taxi drivers, hatcheck attendants, porters and hairdressers. They could even be insulted if offered a tip.

Sports and recreation. Naturally heated swimming pools mean that swimming is a pleasure all year round. The standard of fishing is high, whether in the lakes or rivers—inquire about licenses locally. Skiing is popular in winter, and for insiders, chess remains a favorite. Spectator sports include basketball or handball in winter, while in summer soccer is very popular.

TV and radio. Many foreign programs are shown in their original version on Icelandic television. On Thursdays and in the month of July, there is no television at all. Radio broadcasts are in Icelandic, but the American-manned NATO base at Keflavík can be heard in English on medium wave. Radio Reykjavik Program 1 broadcasts news in English daily in summer.

What to buy. Woolen goods are well-made and attractive, with traditional Icelandic patterns on the sweaters. Ceramics are made from Icelandic clays and lava, and jewelry in gold and silver is often inlaid with opals or moonstones. Books are an Icelandic specialty, often in English and lavishly illustrated, depicting the sagas and history of Iceland. The sales tax will not be refunded on goods bought for exportation.

Stores are open from 9 a.m. to 6 p.m. during the week, and until noon on Saturdays (many are closed on Saturdays in summer). Some shops stay open later on Friday evenings.

Sightseeing

Reykjavik. Laekjartorg Square with statue of first settler, Ingólfur Arnarson. Peaceful Austurvöllur Square with monument to national hero Jón Sigurösson and the city's oldest church, Lutheran Cathedral with font by Danish sculptor Bertel Thorvaldsen. Althing, home of the world's oldest parliament (A.D. 930). National Museum with exhibits highlighting Icelandic history back to the first settlers. Two floors up, National Art Gallery with outstanding collection of contemporary Icelandic art. Nearby Arnamagnaean Institute, within university complex, housing prized saga manuscripts. The Nordic House, a center of cultural relations between the Nordic countries, designed by Finnish architect Alvar Aalto. Turn-of-the-century quaint timber houses on east side of lake. Stately old High School, meeting place of Althing between 1845 and 1881. Reykjavik harbor to the north, and the old fishing harbor to the west, with streets of old houses once owned by ship's captains. Uphill to capital's largest church, Hallgrímskirkja, still unfinished, with marvelous view of city and surroundings. Statue of Leif Eiríksson—"discoverer of America". Naturally heated swimming pool* at Laugardalur sports center. Open-air folk museum* with glimpses of life at the end of last century.

Other sights. Banana farm at hot-spring town of Hveragerði, also grapes, tomatoes, melons and tropical flowers growing in hothouses heated by geothermic water. Extinct Kerið volcano now full of water, and nearby historic Skalholt, seat of Iceland's first bishop. Northern area of hot springs and geysers. Regular performances by Strokkur geyser* reaching 70 feet (20 m.) in the air. Thundering Gullfoss waterfall casting a perpetual rainbow. Original meeting place of Althing at Thingvellir*, lava arena set in dramatic valley. Iceland's loveliest town—Akureyri—with its strange summer lights. Weird and wonderful rock formations in Mývatn Lake area*, with purple-hued sulphur springs and underground hot pools. Midnight sun at Grimsey Island, right on the Arctic Circle. Dettifoss, Europe's biggest waterfall. Breathtaking waterfalls of Goðafoss and Skógafoss*. Glaciers at Vatnajökull and oasis of greenery at Skaftafell National Park. Westmann Islands, hillsides of lava covering former homes on Heimaey Island since 1973 volcanic eruption. Surtsey*, island that came out of the sea during 1963 volcanic activity.

Some useful expressions in Icelandic

good morning/afternoon	góðan dag/gott kvöld
good evening/night	gott kvöld/góða nótt
good-bye	bless
yes/no	já/nei
please/thank you	gjörðu svo vel/takk fyrir
excuse me	fyrirgefðu
you're welcome	verði þér að góðu
where/when/how	hvar/hvenær/hvernig
how long/how far	hvað lengi/hve langt
yesterday/today/tomorrow	í gær/í dag/á morgun
day/week/month/year	dagur/vika/mánuður/ár
left/right	vinstri/hægri
up/down	upp/niður
good/bad	gott/slæmt
big/small	stórt/lítið
cheap/expensive	ódýrt/dýrt
old/new	gamalt/nýtt
open/closed	opið/lokað
free (vacant)/occupied	laust/upptekið
early/late	snemma/seint
easy/difficult	auðvelt/erfitt
Does anyone here speak English/French/German?	Er einhver hér sem talar ensku/frönsku/þýsku?
What does this mean?	Hvað þýðir þetta?
I don't understand.	Ég skil ekki.
Please write it down.	Viltu gjöra svo vel að skrifa þetta niður.
Do you take credit cards/traveler's checks?	Takið þér kredit kort/ferðaávísun?
Waiter!/Waitress!	Þjónn!/þjónustustúlka!
Where are the toilets?	Hvar er snyrtingin?
I'd like…	Mig myndi langa …
How much is that?	Hvað kostar þetta?
What time is it?	Hvað er klukkan?
Help me please.	Viltu hjálpa mér.
Just a minute.	Augnablik.

IRELAND

Wick
Inverness
Aberdeen

ATLANTIC
OCEAN

SCOTLAND
EDINBURGH
Glasgow

NORTH

SEA

Newcastle

Sligo Belfast

Dundalk *I. of*
Man

Galway Athlone Drogheda
Manchester

DUBLIN Liverpool

IRELAND Holyhead

Limerick Birmingham Amsterdam
The Hague

Waterford Wexford **WALES**

Cork **ENGLAND**

Fishguard

Cardiff Ostend

LONDON Brussels

Plymouth Southampton Dover Calais
Boulogne

English Channel

Le Havre

*Even the place-names sound like poetry in
the land of shamrocks and leprechauns.*

The romance of Ireland starts with the terrain of brilliant green pastures and sweeping seascapes. Man has added a wealth of monuments: prehistoric tombs, medieval castles and monasteries, and stately 18th-century city streets and squares. Even the place-names are poetry: Galway, Donegal, Limerick, Tralee.

What keeps the island so green is the rain that falls, on average, at least every other day. A shower is a legitimate excuse for studying that crucial community institution, the old-fashioned pub, where Irish whiskey or creamy stout quench a formidable thirst. No special stimulus is required to animate the convivial, witty Irish. Eloquence has long been an Irish strong point, from Oliver Goldsmith and Richard B. Sheridan to George Bernard Shaw and Sean O'Casey.

One reason the Irish are different from most other Europeans is that the Romans never conquered them. Vikings founded the first towns, and Anglo-Norman forces subdued the people in 1169, relegating the Gaelic language to second place. The island was partitioned after World War I. The Republic of Ireland consists of 26 predominantly Catholic counties, while the six Protestant counties of Northern Ireland are part of the United Kingdom.

Ireland's population density is less than one-fourth that of Britain. This accounts for the uncrowded country roads, on which the almost forgotten pleasures of motoring can still be enjoyed, and the wide-open spaces available for horseback riding, hunting or hiking. Thanks to the temperate climate, year-round golf is played on some 200 courses. Unspoiled lakes and rivers and a 3,000-mile coastline lure fishermen and sailors.

The range of accommodations befits a country of history and tradition—from converted castles to thatched cottages and modest guest houses. Like the shamrocks and leprechauns, Irish hospitality is legendary. Tourists, generously called "visitors", are offered "a hundred thousand welcomes".

Facts and figures

Population:	3.5 million
Area:	27,136 sq. miles (70,282 sq. km.)
Capital:	Dublin *(Baile Atha Cliath,* 425,000/ GUA 1 million)
Other cities:	Cork *(Corcaigh,* 265,000) Limerick *(Luimneach,* 60,000/GUA 100,000) Dun Laoghaire (55,000) Galway *(An Ghaillimh,* 47,000) Waterford *(Port Láirge,* 40,000)
Language:	English; Gaelic, the other national language, is of limited local use, mainly in certain western districts
Religion:	Predominantly Catholic (94%)
Time zone:	GMT, EST + 5; DST (Mar.–Oct.)
Currency:	Irish *punt* or *pound* (symbolized £) = 100 *pence* (abbr. *p*) Coins: 1, 2, 5, 10, 20, 50 p Bills: £1, 5, 10, 20, 50, £100
Electricity:	220 volt, 50 cycle, AC

Planning your trip

Visa requirements. None. *Note:* There is no passport control on traffic between the United Kingdom and the Irish Republic. See also pp. 29–30.

Vaccination requirements. None (see also p. 25).

Currency restrictions: There are no restrictions on the import of local or foreign currencies. Up to 100 Irish pounds may be exported, plus foreign money up to the amount brought in, plus the equivalent of 500 Irish pounds (traveler's checks excluded).

Climate. Thanks to the Gulf Stream, Ireland enjoys a mild, humid climate with few extremes the year round. The weather can be quite changeable, showers often alternating with blue sky several times in a day. May is usually the sunniest month, December the dullest.

Some average daily temperatures:

Dublin		J	F	M	A	M	J	J	A	S	O	N	D
average daily	°F	46	47	51	55	60	65	67	67	63	57	51	47
maximum*	°C	9	9	11	13	16	19	20	20	18	14	11	9
average daily	°F	36	37	39	42	45	51	54	53	50	45	40	38
minimum*	°C	2	3	4	5	7	10	12	12	10	7	4	3

* Minimum temperatures are measured just before sunrise, maximum temperatures in the afternoon.

Clothing. Bring along sweaters and a jacket in summer, adding an overcoat in winter. Rainwear is indispensable all the year round. Matching the easygoing way of life, habits of dress are relatively casual in Ireland. The accent is on comfort in both clothing and footwear. Men are advised to wear a jacket and tie for an evening out.

Duty-free allowances

	Cigarettes		Cigars		Tobacco	Liquor	Wine
1)	400	or	100	or	500 g.	1 l. and	2 l.
2)	300	or	75	or	400 g.	1½ l. and	5 l.
3)	200	or	50	or	250 g.	1 l. and	2 l.

Perfume: 1), 3) 50 g.; 2) 75 g.
Toilet water: 1), 3) ¼ l.; 2) ³/₈ l.
Gifts: 1), 3) £31 max. value; 2) £145 max. value, of which no item may exceed £52 in value

1) residents of countries outside Europe
2) non-duty-free goods bought in EEC countries by European residents
3) goods bought outside EEC countries or duty-free goods bought in EEC countries by European residents

N

Giant's Causeway

North Channel

0 20 40 60 80 km
0 10 20 30 40 50 miles

ATLANTIC

Buncrana
Ballycastle
Coleraine
Limavady
ANTRIM
Londonderry / Derry
Letterkenny
Ballymena
Larne
LIVERPOOL
DONEGAL
LONDONDERRY
Strabane
Lough Neagh
Donegal
TYRONE
Omagh
Dungannon
BELFAST
Killybegs
Ballyshannon
ULSTER
DOWN
Enniskillen
Armagh
Mourne Mountains
Newcastle
Sligo
FERMANAGH
Monaghan
ARMAGH
LEITRIM
MONAGHAN
Newry
Ballina
Carrick-on-Shannon
Cavan
Dundalk
MAYO
SLIGO
Boyle
CAVAN
IRISH SEA
Achill Island
ROSCOMMON
MEATH
LOUTH
Westport
Castlebar
Longford
Kells
Drogheda
Roscommon
LONGFORD
Mullingar
Navan
Clifden
CONNAUGHT
Tuam
WESTMEATH
Trim
Rush
LIVERPOOL, HOLYHEAD
Salthill
Galway
Ballinasloe
Athlone
KILDARE
DUBLIN
GALWAY
OFFALY
Tullamore
DUBLIN
Gort
Birr
LEINSTER
Naas
Bray
Aran Islands
Lisdoonvarna
Portlaoise
Athy
Wicklow
OCEAN
Ennistymon
LAOIS
WICKLOW
Ennis
Nenagh
Carlow
Arklow
Kilkee
Killaloe
TIPPERARY
CARLOW
Gorey
CLARE
Kilkenny
Shannon
Limerick
Thurles
KILKENNY
WEXFORD
Enniscorthy
LIMERICK
Cashel
New Ross
Listowel
Tipperary
Cahir
Wexford
Tralee
Clonmel
Waterford
Rosslare Harbour
Dingle
MUNSTER
WATERFORD
FISHGUARD
Killorglin
Killarney
Mallow
Fermoy
Dungarvan
Tramore
ahirciveen
Kenmare
CORK
Youghal
KERRY
Cork
Cobh
CELTIC SEA
Bandon
Kinsale
SWANSEA
Bantry
Clonakilty
Skibbereen

IRELAND

Hotels and accommodations

Hotels. The Irish Tourist Board inspects and classifies all hotels and issues brochures listing approved establishments with details of rates and facilities. Tariffs are government-controlled. Hotels and motels are officially graded in five categories, from A* (luxury) to C (minimum standard). Guest houses are also listed and graded.

The Tourist Board also has information on families who take in guests, both in town and in the countryside, and thatched cottages for rent.

Youth hostels. The Irish Youth Hostels Association runs about 50 hostels in the Republic. Membership cards issued by national youth hostel associations overseas are required.

Camping. Officially approved campsites in Ireland range from spartan layouts to resort-style parks with tennis courts, mini-golf, shops and nearby beaches. Lists of camping and caravanning parks and their facilities are available from tourist information offices or Irish Caravan Council, 2 Offington Court, Sutton, Dublin 13; tel. (01) 323776.

Irish tourist offices abroad

Australia	MLC Centre, 38th Level, Martin Place, Sydney 2000; tel. (02) 232-7177
Canada	10 King Street East, Toronto, Ont. M5C 1C3; tel. (416) 364-1301
U.K.	150 New Bond Street, London WIY 0AQ; tel. (071) 493 3201 and (071) 629 7292
U.S.A.	757 Third Avenue, New York, NY 10017; tel. (212) 418-0800 and 800-223-6470

On the spot

Banks and currency exchange. Banking hours are 10 a.m. to 12:30 p.m. and 1:30 to 3 p.m., Monday through Friday (until 5 p.m. on Thursdays). Most hotels change money, but the rate is not as favorable. Major post offices, including the General Post Office in Dublin, have a *Bureau de change*.

Credit cards and traveler's checks. Major credit cards are accepted in larger and tourist-oriented establishments, and traveler's checks more widely. Be sure to take along your passport as proof of identity when cashing traveler's checks.

Mail and telecommunications. Post-office hours are 9 a.m. to 5:30 p.m. Monday through Saturday. Dublin's main post office (O'Connell Street) is open until 8 p.m. six days a week (6:30 p.m. on Sundays). Shops that sell postcards sometimes have stamps, too. Mailboxes are painted green.

The traditional telegram has been replaced by the telemessage. Dial 196 and it will be delivered with the next day's mail. The telemessage is accepted at post offices, with similar speed of delivery.

Public telephones are found in post offices, hotels stores and on the street. In the Republic the phone booths, cream-colored with green trim as well as the more modern aluminum and glass booths now increasingly used, are marked in Gaelic. The national telephone network is largely automatic, with direct dialing to many countries. See also p. 30.

Some useful telephone numbers:

Information	190	Operator (international)	114
Operator (general)	10	Telemessage	196
		Police, fire, ambulance	999

Newspapers. Principal dailies are the *Irish Times, Irish Independent* and *Irish Press.* The magazine *In Dublin* contains detailed information about what's on.

The national daily and Sunday newspapers from Britain are sold almost everywhere in Ireland on the morning of publication. Leading news dealers in the major towns also sell a range of other European newspapers. European and American magazines are widely available with the exception of so-called "girlie" magazines, banned in the Republic.

Tourist information. Tourist information offices all over Ireland offer information, advice, and a hotel-reservation service (for a small charge). They usually open from 10 a.m. to 6 p.m., though many local offices operate only in the summer.

Dublin	14 Upper O'Connell Street; tel. (01) 747733
Cork	Tourist House, Grand Parade; tel. (021) 273251

Legal holidays

Jan. 1	New Year's Day	**Movable dates:**
Mar. 17	St. Patrick's Day	Good Friday
Dec. 25	Christmas Day	Easter Monday
Dec. 26	Boxing Day	1st Monday of June
		1st Monday of August
		last Monday of October

Transportation

Air. Both Dublin and Shannon airports handle international and intercontinental traffic; the one at Cork has flights to the U.K. and some countries in Central Europe. Domestic flights link Dublin with Cork and Shannon.

Major airports. Dublin Airport (6 miles/9 km. from city center). Duty-free shop. There is frequent bus service to the city center. **Shannon Airport** (16 miles/26 km. west of Limerick). The duty-free shopping area is unusually vast and varied. Buses between the airport and Limerick operate from about 7 a.m. till midnight.

Rail. Passenger lines in Ireland have been cut back to the main routes, but cross-country services to and from Dublin can be fast and comfortable. The main inter-city routes have air-conditioned, soundproof express trains. There are no sleeping cars in Ireland.

The 8- or 15-day *Rail Rambler* is good for unlimited rail travel, and *Rail-Road Rambler* for rail and inter-city bus travel. They can be purchased at major railroad and bus stations and travel agents throughout the country. For *Eurailpass,* see p. 33.

Dublin has two main stations (Heuston Station and Connolly Station), so be sure to check in advance for the correct terminal.

Long-distance buses. The state-run Bus Eireann operates an extensive network of local, provincial and express bus routes. Almost every town and village in Ireland is covered.

Local public transportation. Buses and suburban trains serve Irish cities. Train tickets must be purchased at stations; on buses the conductor collects fares after you board. On city buses, *An Lar* means "town center".

Taxis. Cabs may be found cruising the streets, but the majority park at designated stands; they can also be ordered by telephone.

Car rental. International and local firms operate, some with airport agencies. See also pp. 30–31.

Driving in Ireland. Drive on the *left,* pass on the right. Caution is advised as the locals have a tendency to disregard lane demarcations. Roads are generally narrow but adequate. Speed limits are 30 mph (48 kph) or 40 mph (64 kph) in towns, 55 mph (88 kph) elsewhere. Use of seat belts is obligatory. Blood alcohol limit is 80 mg./100 ml. The grades of gasoline available are normal (90 octane), super (96–99 octane) and diesel.

In case of breakdown, call (01) 779481 (Automobile Association) or (01) 775141 (Royal Irish Automobile Club) in Dublin for further instructions.

Some distances: Dublin–Cork 160 miles (260 km.), Galway 135 miles (220 km.), Belfast 100 miles (160 km.).

Bicycle rental. Standard models for children and adults, racing bikes and even tandems may be rented from a network of dealers in all areas of the island. Motorbikes and mopeds are not available.

Rest rooms. Rest rooms are relatively abundant in the towns of Ireland. Look for the sign, "Public Toilets". The only hitch is that the gender signs on doors may be printed in Gaelic, not English. *Mna* should not be misconstrued as a misprint for "men"; it's Gaelic for "ladies". *Fir* means "gentlemen".

Emergencies. For police, fire brigade or ambulance, dial 999 from any telephone in Ireland (no coin required). Tell the emergency operator which service you need.

Police. The official name of the civic guard, or police force, of the Irish Republic is the Garda Siochana, less formally known as the Garda (pronounced "gorda"). Except for extraordinary assignments, they are unarmed. There is no special police unit detailed to help tourists.

Crime and theft. Although the incidence of crime is not high, normal precautions should be taken. Beware of pickpockets.

Medical care and health. The standard of medical treatment is excellent, and fees are moderate. Standard remedies and pharmaceutical supplies are readily available during shopping hours; a few pharmacies stay open until 10 p.m. For insurance, see pp. 25–26.

Tap water is safe to drink.

Embassies and consulates. The Dublin telephone directory lists embassies and consulates under "Diplomatic and Consular Missions".

Consular agencies in provincial towns are all listed in part two of the directory under the same heading.

Social customs. The Irish have a talent for conversation, and time to spare, so getting to know them should be no problem. If you're invited to a home for dinner, a gift of flowers or chocolates for the hostess would be appropriate. As for boy-meets-girl opportunities, note that traditions of conservative behavior are maintained more strictly than in some other European countries.

Enjoying Ireland

Food and drink. Ireland is notable for its abundance of fresh meat, fish, butter and eggs. Meals are served in a somewhat baffling variety of establishments—hotels, bars, coffee shops, snack bars, pubs... and even restaurants. "Pub grub" includes meat pies, sandwiches and simple salads. Restaurants range from modest to truly elegant, with prices to match. Keep in mind the "businessman's lunch", a package deal found in many restaurants, usually involving three courses for a fraction of the cost of the evening meal.

A real Irish breakfast starts the day superlatively. You'll feel ready for all manner of exertion after a menu of juice, porridge or cold cereal with milk or cream, fried eggs with bacon and sausages, toast and home-made soda bread, butter, marmalade, tea or coffee. Irish soda bread, white or brown, is made of flour, buttermilk, bicarbonate of soda and salt; it's as delicious as cake.

Irish soups are usually thick and hearty: vegetables, barley and meat stock may be combined with a dab of cream, for instance. Look for potato soup, containing potatoes, onions, carrot and parsley.

Fish is sensationally good, fresh from the Atlantic, the Irish Sea or the island's streams. Among the outstanding Irish delights: fresh salmon (poached or grilled), smoked salmon, sole, trout from sea or stream. Dublin Bay prawns are a worthily famous natural resource, as are Galway oysters.

Meat of the highest quality is the centerpiece of Irish cuisine. The beef is excellent, but there is little veal. Lamb appears as tender chops or roast or as the main ingredient in Irish stew, a filling casserole with potatoes, carrots, onions, parsley and thyme. Irish pork products—bacon, sausages, chops, Limerick ham—are also famous.

285

Vegetables as basic as potatoes and cabbage play a big role in Irish cooking. Mushrooms, which thrive in the cool and humid atmosphere, are Ireland's biggest horticultural export.

A pitcher of tap water is frequently found on the table. However, wine is becoming ever more popular. By an illogical quirk in the law, most restaurants licensed to serve sherry and table wines are forbidden to serve liquor or beer. And in any case, the Irish consider beer a pub pastime, not a dinner companion. The Irish drink nearly 500 million pints of beer a year, mostly a rich creamy dark-brown version, stout, which derives its characteristic taste from roasted barley. The word whiskey comes from the Gaelic *uisce beatha,* "water of life". Irish whiskey, usually made from malt and subject to three distillations, may be drunk as it is or in coffee topped with double cream (Irish coffee). Two Irish liqueurs merit a try: Irish Mist—honey and herbs in a whiskey base—tingles the palate, and Irish Cream Liqueur contains whiskey, chocolate and cream.

Lunch is served from noon to 2 p.m., dinner 7 to 10 p.m.

Entertainment. A distinctly Irish air dominates cabaret nights at hotels and pubs, featuring folk singers, harpists, dancers and storytellers. Discos offer less folkloric entertainment. On the cultural side, Ireland's theatrical tradition persists in Dublin's Abbey Theatre and less celebrated regional houses. Concerts, opera, ballet and movies round out the possibilities. The daily newspapers give full details.

Annual events and festivals. *March:* St. Patrick's Week. *April:* Dublin Arts Festival. *May:* Cork Festival, Killarney Pan-Celtic Week. *June:* Dublin Music Festival. *August:* Dublin Horse Show. *September:* Rose of Tralee Festival, Waterford Light Opera Festival. *October:* Dublin Theater Festival, Cork Film Festival, Wexford Opera Festival. *November:* Dublin Indoor Horse Show.

Taxes, service charges and tipping. Hotel and restaurant bills are generally all-inclusive, though good service may merit an additional gratuity. Other tipping recommendations: taxi drivers 10%, hatcheck 20p, barbers and hairdressers 10%, hotel porters 50p per bag.

Sports and recreation. Water sports include sailing, fishing (sea, game or coarse), boating and swimming. Popular sports ashore are golf, horse riding, hunting and tennis.

Horse and greyhound racing and national games such as Gaelic football and hurling prove favorite spectator sports. Soccer, rugby and even cricket are also widely played.

286

TV and radio. The state-run organization RTE is the largest broadcaster in the Republic, though cable television has greatly expanded viewing possibilities. Most programs are in English, except for a few Irish or bilingual Irish–English broadcasts. RTE operates three radio stations primarily in English, as well as an all-Irish station.

What to buy. Irish craftsmen still produce high quality goods in traditional or imaginative new styles. Elaborately stitched Aran sweaters are so popular that islanders can't keep up with the demand; mainland factories try to fill the gap. Irish lace is still a going concern at convents in Limerick and County Monaghan. Waterford crystal is world renowned. Handwoven Irish tweed comes in a variety of colors and weights. Irish whiskey and smoked salmon are also popular buys.

Shopping hours are 9 or 9:30 a.m. to 5:30 or 6 p.m., Monday through Saturday; often closed one afternoon a week. Smaller shops, particularly groceries and newsstands often open on Sundays, many until 1 p.m.

Sightseeing

Dublin. O'Connell Street, 150-foot-(45-m.-) wide main street, with landmark General Post Office, used as headquarters of 1916 Easter Rising. Trinity College*, founded 1591 by Elizabeth I of England, with Old Library containing the *Book of Kells,* a supreme example of 8th- or 9th-century illustrated manuscript. Merrion Square*, lined with some of Europe's finest Georgian houses; Leinster House, home of the Irish parliament.

National Gallery*, with prized collection of medieval religious art plus Rubens, Rembrandt, Gainsborough and Goya. National Museum*, featuring 8th-century Irish artisans' achievements, notably the delicately worked Tara Brooch and Ardagh Chalice. St. Stephen's Green, one of Europe's biggest city squares, a park containing monuments, flower gardens and a lake. Dublin Castle, originally a medieval castle, later seat of government, prison, courthouse and parliament; magnificent State Apartments, former residence of the British Viceroy, now used to entertain visiting heads of state. Two Protestant cathedrals: Christ Church (begun 1038) with Romanesque, Early English and neo-Gothic architecture and St. Patrick's (consecrated 1192), where satirist Jonathan Swift served as dean. Phoenix Park, three square miles of forests, gardens and playing fields, and the Dublin zoo. Impressive domed Four

287

Courts and majestic 18th-century Custom House, masterpieces of architect James Gandon, both gracing the River Liffey, Dublin's link with the sea.

Daytrips from Dublin. Drogheda, a town straddling the River Boyne near the site of 1690 battle in which James II failed to recapture the crown of England. Monasterboice, ancient monastic settlement with ruins of churches and what was Ireland's tallest round tower. Mellifont Abbey, Ireland's most important early Cistercian monastery. Newgrange*, a massive 4,000-year-old tomb decorated with enigmatic carvings, precisely positioned so that sunshine strikes the central shrine on the shortest day of the year. Castletown House at Celbridge, Paladian-style stately home. The Curragh prairie, home of the Irish Sweeps Derby and the National Stud, where thoroughbreds are pampered. Dun Laoghaire, Ireland's top yachting harbor and Dublin's largest suburb. Sandycove tower, 18th-century fort in which James Joyce once lived. Powerscourt estate, mansion surrounded by an immense formal park. Glendalough*, ruins of an ancient monastic colony, including a graceful thousand-year-old round tower, in a narrow wooded valley.

Southeast Ireland. Enniscorthy, inland port, with folk museum in a restored castle. Wexford, early Viking settlement, with maritime museum housed aboard a former lightship. Rosslare, a popular resort on a six-mile crescent of beach. Waterford, founded by Vikings 18 miles (30 km.) from the sea, where famous glass is produced; the massive circular fortification of Reginald's Tower, survivor of many a siege since 1003; the Mall, elegant Georgian street. Cashel* (County Tipperary), with hilltop cathedral from the 13th century overlooking typically Irish green pastures. Kilkenny, with 13th-century cathedral and castle and contemporary design workshop. Jerpoint Abbey, ancient Cistercian monastery, adorned with remarkable sculptures of medieval knights and churchmen.

The Southwest. Cork, important commercial and cultural center on the River Lee; signposted walking tour of principal monuments, including stately Grand Parade, medieval Red Abbey, lofty St. Finbarre's Cathedral, and Shandon Church with bells that tourists can play. Blarney Castle, where, by kissing the inconveniently placed Blarney Stone, visitors are awarded the gift of the gab. Cobh, big international seaport, with graceful Catholic Cathedral of St. Colman. Youghal, resort with five-mile beach; Sir Walter Raleigh, one-time mayor, lived alongside meticulously restored St. Mary's Collegiate Church. Kinsale,

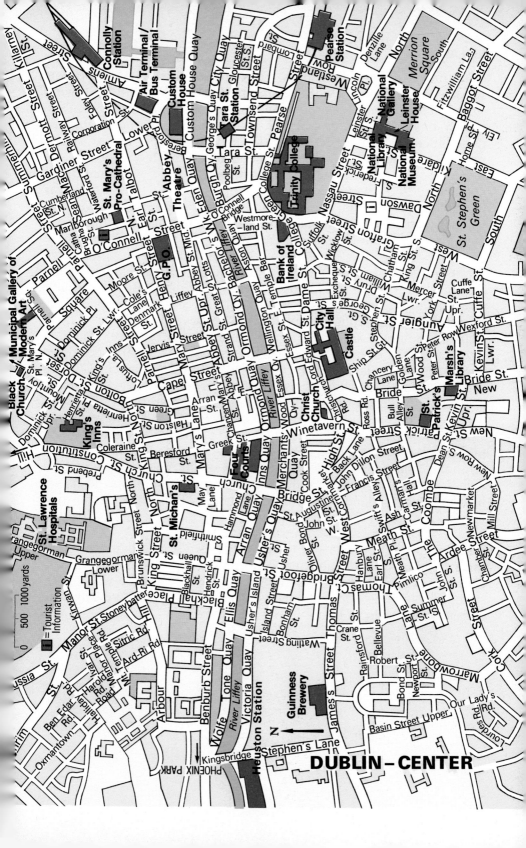

DUBLIN – CENTER

delightful port town backed by steep green hills. Old Head, beyond Kinsale, dramatic cliffs with teeming bird life. Glengarriff*, a town of sumptuous gardens basking in an almost Mediterranean climate on Bantry Bay; boat ride to Garinish Island, a lushly gardened national park. Killarney*, center of lake-district excursions; 15th-century Muckross Abbey, with a cloister surrounded by Gothic, Norman and Romanesque arches. Dingle, in Irish-speaking zone of dramatic cliffs and coves, "most westerly town in Europe". Staigue Fort, 2,500-year-old circular stronghold, one of Ireland's prime archaeological wonders. Ring of Kerry*, a sensational circuit past volcano-like hills and a coast of rugged cliffs and impressive seascapes.

Western Ireland. Limerick, seaport and industrial center; 800-year-old St. Mary's Cathedral and handsome public buildings. Bunratty Castle, near Shannon Airport, with restored 15th-century atmosphere and nearby folk park, replicas of typical old houses. Clonmacnois*, 1,400-year-old monastic settlement in a pastoral setting on River Shannon. The Burren* (County Clare), 200 square miles of bizarre geological phenomena, unusual fauna and flora. Cliffs of Moher*, perched 700 feet (210 m.) above the Atlantic, haunt of seabirds. Galway*, port, resort and cultural center with Lynch's Castle, a restored 15th-century townhouse and a church where Columbus is believed to have prayed. County Mayo: Croagh Patrick, Ireland's "holy mountain", where St. Patrick is said to have spent Lent in A.D. 441; Knock, a place of pilgrimage since a miraculous apparition of the Virgin Mary in 1879; Achill, Ireland's biggest island, with windswept mountains, farms and beaches. Aran Islands, unspoiled outposts of peace and tradition, famous for handmade sweaters.

The Northwest. Sligo, harbor town set between legend-haunted mountains, Ben Bulben and Knocknarea. Strandhill and Rosses Point, beachy resorts. Glencolumbkille (County Donegal), picturesque village, surrounded by prehistoric monuments, where St. Columba's evangelistic career is said to have begun in the 6th century.

ITALY

Under a kindly sun, creativity and la
dolce vita *follow an ancient tradition.*

Since the time of the ancient Romans, Italians have congregated in centers of economic and cultural activity. Nine out of ten Italians choose to live in cities and towns where, under a kindly sun, everyday life takes to the cobbled streets. Haggling at the open market or gossiping *con brio* at the sidewalk café, the Italians make themselves heard over the screeching brakes and outraged horns of the traffic's dilemma, the actors' voices raised as high as their spirits. It's the stuff of grand opera—as Italian as *la dolce vita*.

The Italian boot has left its prints all over Europe and to the far corners of the cosmopolitan Roman empire, which stretched from Britain to Egypt. Roman roads and bridges, still in use, proved a lasting legacy. Less concretely, Roman concepts of law and civil service inspired the West; Christianity, born in the empire, was broadcast by its legions. After Rome's ancient brilliance faded, Italy was shredded into competing provincial powers. It didn't unite into one kingdom until late in the 19th century, becoming a democratic republic after the debacle of World War II.

Creativity has always been an Italian advantage. A single city, Florence, was the home of Boccaccio and Botticelli, Dante and Donatello, Leonardo and Michelangelo. Music may not be an Italian monopoly but opera—devised in Florence in the 16th century—hits the highest notes at La Scala in Milan.

The regional differences underlined in the era of the Renaissance city-states still stand, exaggerating the distance from the Alps to Sicily, from the canals of Venice to the bay of Naples. The industrious north, with its skyscrapers and stylish shops, seems a world away from the siesta-prone south. But everywhere, from the Forum of Rome to the *palazzi* of Florence, the story of Western civilization is spelled out in italics in a setting of beauty and romance.

292

Facts and figures

Population:	57 million
Area:	116,310 sq. miles (301,250 sq. km.)
Capital:	Rome (*Roma* 2.8 million)
Other major cities:	Milan (*Milano*, 1.6 million) Naples (*Napoli*, 1.2 million) Turin (*Torino*, 1.1 million) Genoa (*Genova*, 750,000) Palermo (700,000) Bologna (455,000) Florence (*Firenze*, 455,000) Venice (*Venezia*, 355,000)
Language:	Italian
Religion:	Roman Catholic (99%)
Time zone:	GMT+1, EST+6; DST (Apr.–Sep.)
Currency:	*Lira* (abbr. *L.* or *Lit.*) Coins: L. 5, 10, 20, 50, 100, 200, 500 Bills: L. 1,000, 2,000, 5,000, 10,000, 50,000, 100,000
Electricity:	125/220 volt, 50 cycle, AC

Planning your trip

Visa requirements. See pp. 29–30.

Vaccination requirements. None (see also p. 25).

Currency restrictions. As a foreign tourist, you may import unlimited amounts in local or other currencies, but to take more than L. 1,000,000 or the equivalent of more than L. 5,000,000 in foreign money out again, you must fill in a V2 declaration form at the border when you arrive. All proof of exchange (bank receipts) must be kept for customs purposes.

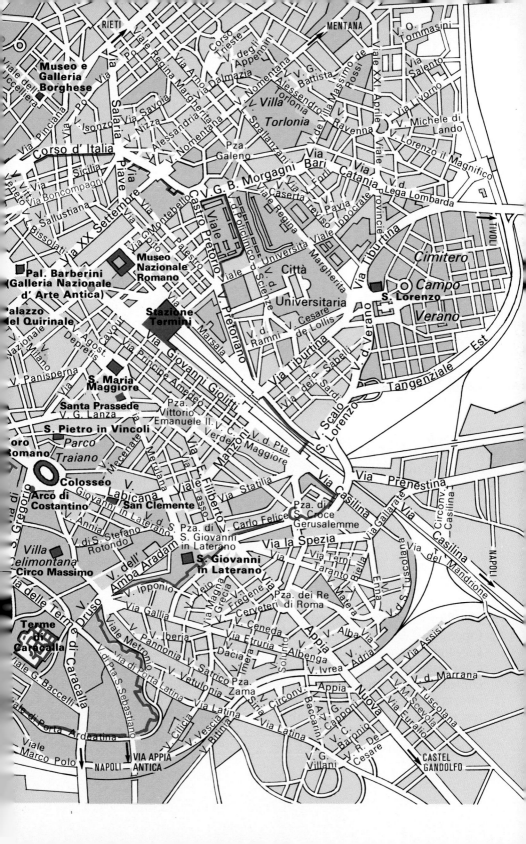

Climate. Inland in the north, the climate tends to the continental, with hot summers and cold winters. The Ligurian coastal strip (Genoa and environs) is famed for its mild winters. Towards the south the weather becomes gradually warmer and more Mediterranean in character. South of Rome, winters are mild and summers hot. Precipitation varies from region to region, but generally rain can be expected between late October and early January, and periodically in early spring.

Fog is often a hazard in Turin and Milan between November and March, and in these areas winter snow occasionally disrupts road traffic.

Some average daily temperatures:

Rome

		J	F	M	A	M	J	J	A	S	O	N	D
average daily maximum*	°F	52	55	59	66	74	82	87	86	79	71	61	55
	°C	11	13	15	19	23	28	30	30	26	22	16	13
average daily minimum*	°F	40	42	45	50	56	63	67	67	62	55	49	44
	°C	5	5	7	10	13	17	20	20	17	13	9	6

Milan

		J	F	M	A	M	J	J	A	S	O	N	D
average daily maximum*	°F	40	46	56	65	74	80	84	82	75	63	51	43
	°C	5	8	13	18	23	27	29	28	27	17	10	6
average daily minimum*	°F	38	35	43	49	57	63	67	66	61	52	43	35
	°C	0	2	6	10	14	17	20	19	16	11	6	2

* Minimum temperatures are measured just before sunrise, maximum temperatures in the afternoon.

Clothing. Bring light- to mediumweight clothing and rainwear if traveling in early spring and autumn. During winter you will need a light topcoat for the south, and a winter overcoat for northern cities. Pack very light summer clothes, preferably cottons, for July and August with a sweater or jacket for the evening, when the temperature drops considerably. Comfortable shoes are indispensable when visiting cities. Shorts and barebacked dresses are frowned upon in churches. Few restaurants insist on a jacket and tie, but in winter, for better restaurants more formal clothing is recommended. In casinos, ties may be required. Italians are very elegant dressers.

Duty-free allowances

	Cigarettes		Cigars		Tobacco	Liquor	Wine
1)	400	or	100	or	500 g.	¾ l. or	2 l.
2)	300	or	75	or	400 g.	1½ l. or	3 l.
3)	200	or	50	or	250 g.	¾ l. or	2 l.

Perfume: 1), 3) 50 g.; 2) 75 g.
Toilet water: 1), 3) ¼ l.; 2) ³⁄₈ l.
Gifts: 1), 3) L. 67,000 max. value; 2) L. 418,000

1) residents of countries outside Europe
2) residents of countries within Europe entering from an EEC country
3) residents of countries within Europe entering from a non-EEC country

Hotels and accommodations

Hotels. Accommodations in Italy range from deluxe hotels to modest inns *(locanda)* and family-style boardinghouses. The government issues an annual list of deluxe, first and second class hotels. You can also rent a villa, apartment or bungalow. Make reservations in advance if traveling in spring, summer or early autumn. Although the local tourist offices aren't generally responsible for arranging accommodations, they should be able to help if you arrive without reservations. Most airports and railroad stations have free hotel-information desks. Breakfast is normally not included in the price of the room. Service charge, tourist tax and sales tax are often included in the room rate, but as much as 20 percent in taxes and service charges may be added to the hotel rates listed. Check when making reservations. Don't forget to take the hotel bill with you when you check out. You may be asked to produce it.

Near Rome, and certainly in Sicily, you may be able to stay overnight in a convent or monastery. Ask for details at the local tourist office.

If you are passing through a big city and need to tidy up, check in at a "day hotel" *(albergo diurno)*. There you will be able to leave your luggage, have a shower, haircut or massage, all at very low prices.

Youth hostels. If you are planning to make extensive use of youth hostels *(ostello della gioventù)* during your stay in Italy, contact your national youth hostel association before departure to obtain an international membership card.

297

Camping. There are about 1,700 campsites in Italy. Offices of the Provincial Tourist Board provide a comprehensive list of campsites, including rates and other details. In Italy you may camp anywhere if you obtain permission either from the owner of the property or from the local authorities. As a rule it's safer to choose a place where there are other campers.

Italian tourist offices abroad

Australia	E.N.I.T., c/o Alitalia, Orient Overseas Building, Suite 202, 32 Bridge Street, Sydney, NSW 2000; tel. (612) 271-308
Canada	1, place Ville-Marie, Suite 1914, Montreal Que. H3B3M9; tel. (514) 849-835
Eire	47, Merrion Square, Dublin 2; tel. (3531) 766397
South Africa	E.N.I.T., London House, 21 Loveday Street, P.O. Box 6507, Johannesburg; tel. 838-3247
U.K.	1 Princes Street, London W1R 8AY; tel. (071) 408 1254
U.S.A.	500 N. Michigan Avenue, Suite 1046, Chicago, IL 60611; tel. (312) 644-0990 630 Fifth Avenue, Suite 1565, New York, NY 10111; tel. (212) 397-5293/4 St. Francis Hotel, 360 Post Street, San Francisco, CA 94108; tel. (415) 392-5266

On the spot

Banks and currency exchange. Banks are generally open between 8:30 a.m. and 1:30 p.m. and between 2:45 and 3:45 p.m., Monday through Friday. Currency-exchange offices (look for the sign *cambio*) in rail stations and at airports usually open from 9 a.m. to 1:30 p.m. and 2:30 to 6 p.m. Many are closed on Saturdays. The rate of exchange is always better at a *cambio* than at a hotel. You may need your passport.

Credit cards and traveler's checks. Most credit cards are accepted at large hotels, restaurants and shops. Traveler's checks are also accepted, sometimes even with a discount, but this may be offset by a poor rate of exchange. It is better to cash them at a bank or *cambio*.

298

Mail and telecommunications. It is probably better not to arrange to receive mail while you are in Italy, as the system works slowly and isn't entirely reliable. The post office (*posta* or *ufficio postale*) handles mail, telegrams and money transfers, and some have public telephones. Opening hours are 8:30 a.m. to 2 p.m. during the week, and until noon on Saturdays. Mailboxes are red. Look for a mailbox marked *altre destinazioni;* the inscription *per la città* means internal city mail only. Stamps can also be bought at tobacco shops.

Older types of public pay phones require tokens *(gettoni)* which you can buy at bars, hotels, post offices and tobacco shops or from a machine next to the booth. Modern ones, with three separate slots, take 100-, 200- and 500-lira coins as well as *gettoni* and telephone credit cards, which are available at the above-mentioned places. You can dial abroad from phone booths, but it's better to make international calls from the main post office. Long-distance lines are often overloaded, so be prepared for a long wait. For surcharges and low rates, see also p. 30.

Some useful telephone numbers:

Information (domestic)	12	International telegrams	185
Operator (for Europe)	15	Emergency	
Operator (for intercontinental calls)	170	(Police)	113

The English-speaking operators of the telephone assistance service provide visitors with information and advice of all kinds. Turn to them with your problems: if they can't help, they'll refer you to someone who will. Dial 116.

Newspapers. Principal dailies are *La Nazione* (Florence), *Il Secolo XIX Nuovo* (Genoa), *Il Corriere della Sera, Il Giornale Nuovo* (Milan), *Il Mattino* (Naples), *Il Messaggero* (Rome), *La Stampa* (Turin), *La Gazzetta* (Venice). Most leading European newspapers are available, as is the Paris-based *International Herald Tribune*.

Tourist information. The complete tourist-office administration is being reorganized—progressively. But each region is looking after itself, so you may find some of the offices listed below closed—or simply "disguised" under a new name. Best simply ask for the "ufficio turistico".

Rome	Via Parigi 11; tel. (06) 461 851
	Termini rail station
	Fiumicino (Leonardo da Vinci) airport

300

Milan	Via Marconi 1; tel. (02) 870 016
Turin	Via Roma 226; tel. (011) 535 181
Florence	Via de' Tornabuoni 15; tel. (055) 216 544
Venice	San Marco, Ascensione 71/c; tel. (041) 522 6356 Piazzale Roma Stazione Santa Lucia
Naples	Via Partenope 10A; tel. (081) 418 988 Palazzo Reale; tel. (081) 418 744
Sicily	Piazza Castelnuovo 35, Palermo; tel. (091) 33 18 61 Punta Raisi airport.

Legal holidays

Jan. 1	New Year's Day	**Movable date:**
Jan. 6	Epiphany	Easter Monday
April 25	Liberation Day	
May 1	Labor Day	
Aug. 15	Assumption	
Nov. 1	All Saints' Day	
Dec. 8	Immaculate Conception	
Dec. 25	Christmas Day	
Dec. 26	St. Stephen's Day	

Transportation

Air. Rome and, to a lesser extent, Milan, are Italy's international gateways, with a number of flights to other provincial airports. The country is linked by a good network of airports for domestic flights.

Major airports. Rome: Leonardo da Vinci (Fiumicino, 18 miles/28 km. from the city center). Duty-free shop. Ciampino (11 miles/17 km. from the city center) handles mainly charter flights. Fiumicino is linked by frequent bus services to the city air terminal at Via Giolitti 36 (Stazione Termini). **Milan:** Forlanini–Linate (5 miles/8 km. from the city center). Duty-free shop. A bus service operates to the central railroad station. Malpensa (29 miles/47 km. from the city center). Duty-free shop. A bus service operates to the central railroad station. **Naples:** Capodichino (4 miles/7 km. from city center). Duty-free shop. Bus service to Piazza Garibaldi (central station). **Turin:** Città di Torino (11 miles/17 km. from city center). Duty-free shop. Bus service coinciding with scheduled flights. **Genoa:** Cristoforo Colombo (5 miles/7 km.: from city center).

301

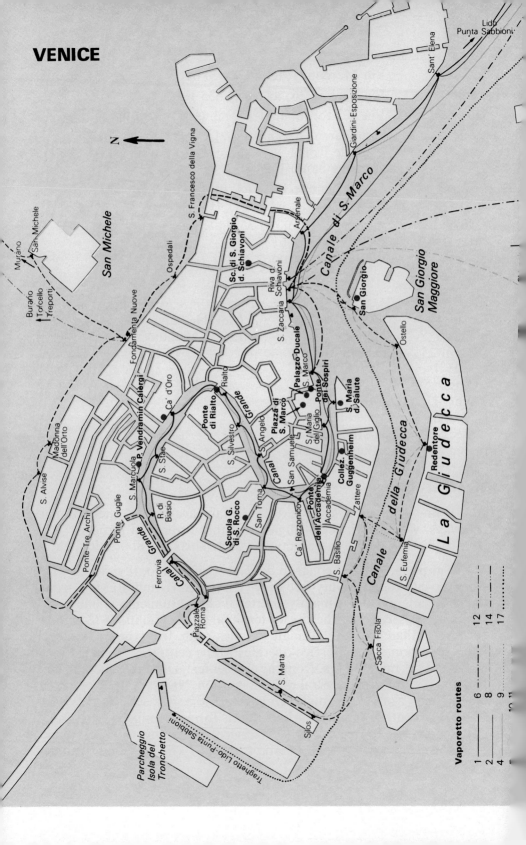

VENICE

N

Lido
Punta Sabbioni
Sant'Elena
Giardini-Esposizione

Canale di S. Marco

San Michele

Murano
Burano
Torcello
Treporti

S. Francesco della Vigna

Ospedali

Fondamenta Nuove

San Michele

S. Alvise

Ponte Tre Archi

Ponte Guglie

Madonna
dell'Orto

Cannaregio

P. Vendramin Calergi

S. Marcuola

R. di
Biasio

Ca' d'Oro

S. Stae

Rialto

Ponte
di Rialto

S. Silvestro

Scuola G.
di S. Rocco

San Tomà

S. Angelo

Canal

Grande

Canal

Grande

Ferrovia

Piazzale
Roma

San Samuele

Ca' Rezzonico

Ponte
dell'Accademia

Accademia

S. Basilio

S. Marta

Sijos

Parcheggio
Isola del
Tronchetto

Traghetto Lido-Punta Sabbioni

Zattere

Sacca Fisola

S. Eufemia

Canale della Giudecca

La Giudecca

Sc. di S. Giorgio
d. Schiavoni

Riva d.
Schiavoni

Arsenale

S. Zaccaria

Palazzo Ducale

S. Marco

Piazza di
S. Marco

Ponte
dei Sospiri

S. Maria
del Giglio

S. Maria
d. Salute

Collez.
Guggenheim

Redentore

San Giorgio

San Giorgio
Maggiore

Ostello

Ostello

Canale di S. Marco

Vaporetto routes

1	
2	
4	
6	- · - · -
8	- - - -
9	
12	
14	
17	·········

Duty-free shop. Bus service to Via Petrarca/Piazza Acquaverde. **Venice:** Marco Polo (8 miles/13 km. from city center). Duty-free shop. *Vaporetto* (boat) service to San Marco or bus service to Piazzale Roma.

Rail. The Italian state-owned railways, *Ferrovie dello Stato* (FS), operate an extensive network all over the country, with train ferries to Sicily. Choose your train carefully as journey times vary a good deal: *Eurocity* (EC)—international express with first and second class; *Intercity* (IC)/ *Rapido*—high-speed super-express, first class only (ticket includes seat reservation, newspaper, refreshments); *Espresso* (EXP)—long-distance train stopping at main stations; *Diretto* (D)—slower than the *Espresso,* it makes a number of local stops; *Locale* (L)—local train which stops at almost every station; *Metropolitana (servizi dedicati)*—connecting service from airports and sea ports to major cities. Express trains often have dining cars.

It is advisable to make a seat reservation (sometimes it's obligatory), but if you don't have one, arrive at the station at least 20 minutes in advance, since the Italian trains are often very crowded.

Non-residents can buy *BTLC* go-as-you-please tickets at reduced prices for unlimited travel on Italian railroads for eight, 15, 21 or 30 days. Ask for details at any travel agency or railroad station. For *Eurailpass,* see p. 33.

Long-distance buses. Inter-city buses are recommended as the best means of public transportation between towns and outlying areas in Sicily since trains may be slow. The principal company, S.A.I.S., has offices in most towns.

Boats, waterways. Ferries run at frequent intervals from Villa San Giovanni and Reggio di Calabria to Messina in Sicily. Hydrofoil crossings between Messina and Reggio take 15 minutes but carry passengers only. The hydrofoil between Naples and Palermo links the two towns in five hours. You can put your car on a ferry at Genoa (a 22-hour trip) or Livorno (18 hours) for Palermo. Ferries run from Civitavecchia north of Rome to Sardinia and it's an easy motorboat or hydrofoil trip out to Capri from Naples or Sorrento.

If you're going by car or if you want a cabin, reserve long boat trips before leaving home, above all in high season (June through September).

Local public transportation. Most cities have a bus or streetcar service, except Venice, where you travel by public passenger boat (*vaporetto*) and water taxi. Rome, Milan and Naples also operate a subway system. The subway is by far the fastest way of traveling in these cities, but the networks are rather restricted. Tickets are sold at a booth at the entrance to the station. Streetcars generally have conductors at the back who sell tickets, and you can usually buy tickets at bars and newsstands.

Taxis. Cabs are yellow. You can hail one in the street, get it at a taxi stand or call for one. Cabs are metered, but check whether the meter is actually running. There's a supplement nights and Sundays as well as for some airport trips. Check with your hotel or the tourist office on the current prices and supplements. Always negotiate the price in advance for airport trips.

Car rental. Major international and local firms have desks at most airports, and offices in larger towns. Chauffeur-driven cars are available. See also pp. 30–31.

Driving in Italy. Your car should carry a red reflector warning triangle for use in case of a breakdown. Drive on the right, pass on the left. The use of seat belts is obligatory.

The speed limit on expressways is 81 mph (130 kph) for cars with engines more powerful than 1,100 cubic centimeters. Less powerful cars cannot exceed 70 mph (110 kph). On other roads the limit is 56 mph (90 kph). These maximum speeds may be revised again. Ask at your automobile association before departure.

The limit in built-up areas is usually 31 mph (50 kph).

At intersections, traffic from the right has priority. Traffic on major roads has right of way over that from side roads, but this is frequently ignored. You pay a toll on expressways, so keep a stock of coins handy, as toll booth attendants don't like having to give change. Emergency phones are located at regular intervals on the expressways. Don't get flustered at the sound of a horn being blown at you, and use your own if you think it will act as a useful warning of your presence. In case of breakdown, dial 116 for service from Automobile Club d'Italia. Gasoline available is normal (86–88 octane), super (98–100 octane), lead-free and diesel. *Note:* Before leaving home, check with your automobile association about the latest regulations concerning gasoline coupons (that give tourists access to cheaper gasoline) in Italy, as they are constantly changing.

Some distances: Rome–Naples 135 miles (215 km.), Florence 175 miles (280 km.), Venice 335 miles (540 km.), Genoa 340 miles (545 km.), Milan 355 miles (575 km.), Palermo 615 miles (990 km.).

Bicycle rental. Renting a bike is becoming increasingly popular, particularly in coastal resorts. Ask at the hotel or tourist office for the address of a rental firm.

Rest rooms. You'll find public rest rooms in most museums and galleries, restaurants, bars, cafés and large stores. If there is an attendant, leave a few coins. Doors are labeled *Donne* or *Signore* for ladies and *Uomini* or *Signori* for gentlemen.

Emergencies. Dial 113 for the police, and 116 for road assistance (Automobile Club d'Italia). All other emergency numbers vary from city to city and are listed in the front pages of telephone directories.

Police. City police handle traffic, parking fines and other routine tasks.

The *carabinieri*—who wear dark blue uniforms with a red stripe down the side of the trousers—deal with theft, more serious crimes, demonstrations and military affairs. The national, or state, police *(polizia di stato)* are distinguished by their dark blue jackets and light blue trousers, and handle other police and administrative matters. Outside of town the Italian traffic police *(polizia stradale)* patrol the highway in motorcycles or Alfa Romeo cars, usually light blue. Speeding fines are often collected on the spot, but ask for a receipt.

Crime and theft. Petty crime is on the increase throughout Italy. By taking a few simple precautions you can reduce the risk. Leave your documents and unneeded cash in the safe at your hotel. Keep money in the form of traveler's checks (with a record of the numbers). Don't carry handbags slung over the roadside shoulder, and don't leave belongings unattended in public places. Never leave anything of value in the car, and if you are robbed, get in touch with the police *(carabinieri)* immediately.

Medical care and health. Most doctors speak only Italian. Get a list of doctors who speak English from the tourist office or your hotel. Pharmacies *(farmacia)* open from 8:30 or 9 a.m. to 1 p.m. and 4 or 4:30 p.m. to 7:30 or 8 p.m., Monday through Friday, and until 1 p.m. on Saturdays. Some pharmacies remain on duty for night and holiday services; others are open 24 hours a day. Details are posted in the windows of other pharmacies and published in the daily newspapers. For insurance, see pp. 25–26.

Tap water is generally drinkable, though those with delicate stomachs may prefer to follow the Italian example and order bottled mineral water.

Embassies and consulates. Embassies are in Rome. Consult the telephone directory listings under "Ambasciate" (embassies) and "Consolati" (consulates).

Social customs. Italians observe certain formal courtesies. On entering or leaving a shop or restaurant always say *buon giorno* (good morning) or *buona sera* (good evening). Handshakes are the rule when meeting people, with a polite *piacere* (it's a pleasure). If invited to someone's home, bring a bottle of wine or flowers. Smoking is prohibited on public transportation, in taxis, movie theaters and theaters.

Enjoying Italy

Food and drink. Sip a glass of vermouth, like Punt e Mes or Cinzano, or try the more bitter taste of Campari with soda while you decide what you're going to eat. At its best an Italian meal can stretch pleasantly over several hours and many courses. At worst it's a swift dish of pasta at the *tavola calda* (literally "hot table") or a pizza from a fast service *pizzeria*.

Starters, known as *antipasto*, can be almost anything: *mozzarella* cheese with tomatoes, basil and olive oil; cold meats like *mortadella* sausage from Bologna, garlic salami from Ferrara, or the excellent *prosciutto di Parma* (Parma ham). In Tuscany you can try *crostini* or *fettunta*, toasted country-bread rubbed with garlic and sprinkled with olive oil. Soups are also on the menu: *minestra di fagioli* (butter bean soup) or *minestrone* (vegetable soup).

As an alternative, or perhaps an addition to the *antipasto*, you can have a dish of *pasta: spaghetti, fettuccine, tagliatelle, penne, cannelloni, ravioli* and *lasagne*, to name but a few. These will be complemented by sauces such as *amatriciana* (tomato, bacon, red peppers and garlic), *bolognese* (minced meat, tomato, herbs), *carbonara* (egg, bacon, cheese, butter, basil), *crema* (cream, Parmesan cheese, butter), *pescatore* (seafood, tomato or white wine, parsley), or *pesto* (basil, oil, pine nuts, cheese, garlic) or just plain *pomodoro* (tomato, garlic, parsley).

After the *pasta* comes the main course: meat, fish or game. *Arista* is roast loin of pork, and *bollito di manzo* or *lesso* is boiled beef served with a piquant sauce. *Pollo* (chicken) comes *alla cacciatora* (with tomatoes and vegetables) or *alla diavola* (charcoal grilled). The tastiest steak you can get is *bistecca alla fiorentina* (a charcoal T-bone steak, grilled). *Vitello* (veal), the Italian national meat, comes in several guises. The region of Emilia-Romagna is known for its pork specialties. In season, try *cinghiale* (boar), in a sweet and sour sauce (*agrodolce*). The Veneto region is famous for its fish dishes. If you can't decide which sort to have, then try a *brodetto di pesce* (Italian bouillabaisse) or a *fritto misto* (mixed

306

fried fish). Sea-food choices include *sogliola* (sole), *calamari* (squid), *scampi* (prawns) and *anguilla* (eel), often served *alla veneziana*, cooked in a lemon, oil and tuna-fish sauce.

Vegetables are often served separately, hot or cold, sometimes with an olive oil and lemon dressing or maybe garlic. Try *fagiolini* or *fagioli all'uccelletto* (boiled green or butter beans sautéed with tomato and sage), or *carciofini fritti* (crisply fried artichokes). *Polenta,* a firm, yellow corn purée, is the omnipresent side dish. *Funghi* (mushrooms) of all shapes and sizes appear on the menu, like *porcini* (giant boletus mushrooms), a great delicacy, served grilled or marinated in oil. *Tartufi bianchi* (white truffle) is a much appreciated specialty from the Piedmont region.

The variety of cheeses is surprising to those who think that Italy produces just *Parmesan*, *Gorgonzola* and *Bel Paese*. *Pecorino* comes from all over Italy in many different shapes and forms, but the one from the part of Tuscany near Florence is a tangy ewe's-milk cheese with a creamy white color. The flavorful *casciotto* also comes from Tuscany.

If you have survived all this, then it's time for dessert. Italian ice cream (*gelato*) is excellent as is the range of fresh fruit. You can overdose on *zuppa inglese*, neither a soup nor English, although it bears a passing resemblance to a very alcoholic "trifle". *Zuccotto* (a chilled, liqueur-soaked sponge and chocolate cake) is also good.

You won't have any difficulty in finding a glass of wine with your meal, since Italy is the biggest producer in the world. Famous red wines include the dark Barolo, Barbera and Barbaresco from Piedmont. The white Soave, which should be drunk young, and the almost cherry-red Valpolicella come from close to Verona. The very best Italian red wines are found in Tuscany—Brolio, Chianti and Brunello di Montalcino, while refreshing white wines such as Frascati, Orvieto and Verdicchio are produced further south.

Finish the meal with a good espresso coffee. If you want coffee with milk, order a *cappuccino*. After-dinner drinks include the potent *grappa,* an eau-de-vie distilled from the residue of grapes.

Don't forget to keep the bill which includes service charges and sales tax, as you might be asked for it outside the restaurant.

Lunch is served from 12:30 to 3:30 p.m., dinner 7:30 p.m. to midnight.

Entertainment. Discos and nightclubs, together with the occasional casino, can be found in most towns and cities. But the real entertainment in Italian cities, such as Milan, Florence, Naples and Venice, centers around opera and concerts. In the summer season you can attend outdoor opera performances in the spectacular setting of the ruined Baths of Caracalla in Rome or in the Arena of Verona. Movies are mostly dubbed into Italian.

The best entertainment in small towns is to be found in the streets when entire Italian clans come out in the evenings and stroll around the main squares, seeing and being seen.

Annual events and festivals. *February:* pre-Lenten carnivals in Venice and Viareggio. *March:* nationwide mid-Lenten festivals. *April:* International Handicrafts Fair in Florence. *Mid-May–June:* Maggio Musicale Fiorentino in Florence, featuring concerts, ballet, opera. Race of the candles, medieval pageant in Gubbio. *June:* Tournament of the Bridge in Pisa. Festival of the Two Worlds in Spoleto. *July:* First Palio of the Contrade, historic pageant and horse race in Siena. Gondola procession in Venice. International Ballet Festival in Nervi. *August:* Second Palio in Siena. Opening of Venice Film Festival. *September:* Historic regatta in Venice. *October:* Festival of Tyrolean brass bands in Merano. *December:* Beginning of opera season at La Scala in Milan, and all over the country.

Taxes, service charges and tipping. Taxes and service charges are generally included in hotel and restaurant bills. Tipping recommendations: hotel porters L. 1,000 per bag, waiters 5–10%, taxi drivers 10–15%, hatcheck L. 300, barbers and hairdressers 15%.

Sports and recreation. The most popular summer sport in Italy seems to be sunbathing with a bit of swimming thrown in. Sailing, windsurfing, scuba diving, snorkeling and tennis are other possibilities. Fishing can be organized as can hunting, although Italy's wildlife has become somewhat depleted over the last few decades. There's not a great deal of golf, but you can get a round, and riding is also possible. Skiing is the natural winter choice in the north in ski resorts like Aosta and Cortina with first-class facilities.

Soccer is by far the most popular spectator sport in Italy; the season runs from September to May.

TV and radio. All TV shows are in Italian. The second radio network puts out news and tourist information in English every morning between 9:30 and 10 a.m., June through September, and the first program broadcasts "Notturno d'Italia" at 10 p.m. with light music interspersed by announcements in English, French and German.

What to buy. In Florence look for: ceramics, straw goods, wooden articles with inlays *(intarsio)*, leather goods such as shoes, bags, suitcases, gloves; also gold filigree work, marble, alabaster. Genoa: gold filigree work. Milan: silks, textiles, alabaster. Naples: corals, cameos. Rome: high fashion, antiques, pottery, woolen goods. Venice: lace, leather goods, Murano glass, silks, masks, musical instruments.

Some fashionable shopping streets include Via Montenapoleone in Milan, Via Condotti, Via Frattina and Via Borgognona in Rome and Via Tornabuoni in Florence.

Stores are generally open between 9 or 9:30 a.m. and noon, then from 3 or 3:30 p.m. to 7:30 p.m. Most shops are closed Monday mornings.

Sightseeing

Rome. Vatican City, sovereign territory of the pope, heart of Catholic world. Colonnaded St. Peter's Square, masterpiece of Rome's leading Baroque sculptor Bernini. St. Peter's Basilica *(Basilica di San Pietro)*★, the largest Catholic church ever built, with sumptuous Baroque interior and soaring dome; Michelangelo's supreme marble *Pietà,* the only work he ever signed. Vatican Museum★, housing many of the world's most famous paintings, with the Sistine Chapel, Michelangelo's masterpiece and private chapel of the popes, where popes are elected. Colosseum★, ancient amphitheater, inaugurated in A.D. 80, once scene of brutal spectacles before some 50,000 spectators. Arch of Constantine, erected in A.D. 315 by the Roman Senate, still nearly intact. Roman Forum *(Foro Romano)*★, relics of the ancient city's religious, political and commercial center, once hub of the mighty Roman empire, including the Arch of Titus and Trajan's Column. Palatine Hill, legendary site of Rome's founding. Capitol Square *(Piazza del Campidoglio)*, built atop the Capitoline Hill, the most sacred site of ancient Rome. Old Appian Way *(Via Appia Antica)*, when opened 312 B.C. the grandest road the world had ever known. Catacombs of St. Callistus★, vast underground Christian cemetery. Baths of Caracalla, for 300 years Rome's finest public baths. Piazza di Spagna★, dominated by the romantic Spanish steps, exceptionally beautiful in springtime when covered with azaleas. White-marble Victor Emmanuel Monument honoring the unification of Italy, with the tomb of the unknown soldier. Contrasting 15th-century Palazzo Venezia, once Mussolini's official residence. Quirinal Palace, the president's residence. Trevi Fountain

(Fontana di Trevi)★, extravagant Baroque monument, where visitors throw coins to guarantee their return to Rome. Via Veneto, Rome's grand thoroughfare, lined with fashionable hotels and cafés. Borghese Gallery★, outstanding collection of Italian masterpieces, displayed in pavilion within beautiful Borghese Park *(Villa Borghese)*. Pantheon with majestic dome, a triumph of architectural harmony, built in 2nd century A.D. on site of ancient temple. Piazza Navona, adorned by Bernini's vivid Fountain of the Four Rivers. Castel Sant'Angelo, built by Hadrian 1,800 years ago as imperial mausoleum, later converted into fortress. Farnese Palace, superb Renaissance palace now housing the French Embassy. Three magnificent patriarchal basilicas: St. Paul's outside the Walls *(San Paolo fuori le Mura)* with strikingly beautiful cloister, St. John Lateran *(San Giovanni in Laterano)*; in edifice facing basilica, the Holy Stairway *(Scala Santa)*, which Jesus, according to tradition, trod in the house of Pontius Pilate. St. Mary Major *(Santa Maria Maggiore)*, built more than 1,500 years ago. St. Peter in Chains *(San Pietro in Vincolo)*, with Michelangelo's great statue of Moses. Il Gesù, mother church of the Jesuits, awash in glittering gold and mosaics. National Museum of Rome, displaying exceptional collections of antique sculptures and paintings. Via Condotti, Rome's most elegant shopping street, with 200-year-old Caffè Greco.

Around Rome. Castelli Romani, charming Alban Hill towns whose vineyards keep Rome supplied with white wine. Castel Gandolfo overlooking Lake Albano, since the 17th century the summer palace of the popes. Hadrian's Villa★ at the town of Tivoli, pleasure palace for Romans during the heyday of the Empire. Villa d'Este in Tivoli itself, Renaissance residence surrounded by fairyland garden with cascades and creeping vineyards. Ostia Antica, ruins of Roman seaport. Etruscan tombs in Cerveteri.

Northern Italy. Turin, capital of Piedmont, commercial and automobile center on River Po, with beautiful squares and impressive avenues; Royal Palace *(Palazzo Reale)* with sumptuously decorated State Apartments; Madama Palace featuring Museum of Ancient Art; rich Egyptian Museum; white marble cathedral containing the Holy Shroud, in which Jesus is said to have been wrapped; interesting Automobile Museum. Popular summer and winter resorts including Aosta, Cervinia and Courmayeur. Milan, dynamic metropolis famed for La Scala Opera Theater, where the operas of Rossini, Bellini and Verdi were first performed and Toscanini conducted; Gothic Cathedral *(Duomo)*★, marvel of white marble adorned with spires and statues; glass-vaulted

Galleria Vittorio Emanuele, a shopping arcade and meeting place, with restaurants and cafés; Brera Palace and Gallery *(Pinacoteca)*, with fine collection of paintings featuring North Italian masters; 15th-century Sforza Castel *(Castello Sforzesco)*, former residence of the despotic dukes of Milan, now museum; Poldi-Pezzoli Museum, a sumptuous private palace enriched by paintings, Gobelin tapestries and silver; Biblioteca Ambrosiana, a library and art gallery containing 600,000 books; Church of Santa Maria delle Grazie, containing Leonardo da Vinci's *Last Supper*. Lake Maggiore★, with famed Borromean Islands and stunning Alpine scenery. Stresa, beautiful lake resort amidst orange trees and vineyards. Lake Como, bordered by picturesque villas, ports and castles. Lake Garda, deep blue and fjord-like. Bergamo★, with lovely Old Town; Piazza Vecchia surrounded by Renaissance and medieval houses; ornate Colleoni Chapel with façade of inlaid marble and Romanesque Church of Santa Maria Maggiore. Verona★, historic town of marble villas and piazzas, scene of Romeo and Juliet's ill-fated romance; Roman amphitheater, used for open-air opera; Romanesque Church of San Zeno Maggiore. Dolomites, rugged limestone massif rich in flora and fauna. Winter resort of Cortina d'Ampezzo, site of 1956 Winter Olympics. Merano, old spa recalling the days of the Habsburgs, famed for its table grapes. Bolzano, lively commercial center with towering cathedral.

Adriatic. Trieste, Adriatic seaport with Castello, begun by the Venetians in 1470; excellent collection of antique arms; Cathedral of San Giusto with beautiful Gothic rose-window. Treviso, lovely old town of winding streets and houses decorated with porticoes and frescoes; Gothic red-brick Church of San Nicolò. Padua *(Pádova)* with imposing 13th-century Basilica of Sant'Antonio crowned by eight Byzantine cupolas; bronze sculptures of Donatello at the main altar; Scrovegni Chapel★ from 1305 featuring a series of frescoes by Giotto, recounting the lives of Mary and Jesus. Venetian villas★, stately homes built between 15th and 18th centuries along the Brenta Canal between Padua and Venice. Ferrara, noted for its Castello Estense, a moated medieval castle. Bologna, old university town and gastronomic capital as well as city of magnificent churches and Renaissance palaces; enormous Basilica of San Petronio with fine Gothic brickwork façade, never finished; Pinacoteca Nazionale, national picture gallery concentrating on the Bolognese school; imposing bronze statue of Neptune by Giovanni da Bologna in Piazza del Nettuno. Ravenna★, former capital of the Byzantine Empire of the West, famed for 6th-century Basilica of San Vitale and Basilica of Sant'Apollinare in Classe containing the finest

313

mosaics in Europe. The Marches, region of delightful coastal resorts and picturesque hill towns. Cosmopolitan Rimini, for generations leading summer resort of the Adriatic, noted for white sandy beaches. San Marino, world's smallest and oldest Republic perched on the slopes of Monte Titano. Urbino, Renaissance town dominated by elegant Ducal Palace*; Raphael's birthplace. Ancona, important seaport, featuring Romanesque cathedral and Trajan's Arch, erected in A.D. 115.

Venice. Grand Canal*, serving as the main street of Venice and lined with some 200 palaces built between 12th and 18th centuries. St. Mark's Square* and 900-year-old St. Mark's Basilica, with interior covered in stunning mosaics and displaying bronze horses of Constantinople and Pala d'Oro, screen covered with jewels. View from atop the Campanile. Doges' Palace *(Palazzo Ducale)**, Gothic edifice of pink-and-white marble, with magnificent apartments and Baroque Bridge of Sighs *(Ponte dei Sospiri)*. Rialto Bridge, lined with a double 400-year-old row of shops. Accademia Museum*, housing masterpieces of Venetian art, including painters like Bellini, Giorgione, Titian, Tintoretto and Veronese. Scuola Grande di San Rocco, containing 56 canvases by Tintoretto. Guggenheim collection of modern art. San Giorgio Maggiore church, Palladio's masterpiece of harmony on island of the same name. Other memorable churches: Santa Maria della Salute, Santa Maria Gloriosa dei Frari and delightful 15th-century Santa Maria dei Miracoli. Lido, fashionable resort across the Venetian lagoon. Burano, unspoiled little island in the Venetian lagoon.

Italian Riviera. Dramatic cliffs, panoramic drives. Long sandy beach of Alassio. San Remo*, glittering cosmopolitan resort. Genoa, Italy's chief seaport; Via Garibaldi and Via Balbi, grand thoroughfares lined with sumptuous palaces and villas; Palazzo Balbi Durazzo, with elegant Hall of Mirrors and art collection; Piazza San Matteo, medieval square with handsome mansions built by illustrious Doria family; Palazzo Bianco displaying Ligurian, Flemish and Dutch collections; Cathedral of San Lorenzo, a harmonious blend of styles; Old Town, a maze of lanes and steps. Camogli, ancient seaport with idyllic harbor. Yachting and jet set life at Rapallo and Portofino*, celebrated resort of the rich and famous. Cinque Terre, five isolated villages nestling among steep rocks. Carrara with famous marble quarries.

Tuscany. Pisa, with Leaning Tower *(Campanile)** and superb 11th-century marble cathedral *(Duomo)*. Several medieval towns, including San Gimignano, picturesque walled hill town with 15 stone towers.

Prato and Lucca, centers of Italian art. Siena*, Italy's best-preserved medieval city with splendid Gothic marble-covered cathedral dominating town; Piazza del Campo, where the exciting Palio horse race takes place; the Pinacoteca, an important art gallery, exhibiting the finest artists of the Siennese school. Roman ruins in Fiesole. Arezzo, Etruscan and medieval town and birthplace of Petrarch, with 14th-century Church of San Francesco; Jousting in September in Piazza Grande.

Florence. Duomo*, lofty marble-fronted cathedral in green, white and pink, with mighty cupola and graceful free-standing bell tower *(campanile)* and baptistery featuring famous bronze doors. Palazzo Vecchio*, with elaborate courtyard and lavishly decorated apartments. The Uffizi Gallery*, housing one of the richest collections of paintings in the world, covering the cream of Italian and European art from the 13th to the 18th century. Museum of St. Mark, where Fra Angelico lived as a monk and containing his finest paintings and frescoes. Galleria dell'Accademia, boasting some of Michelangelo's major sculptures, including the original *David*. Museo Archeologico, with ancient Egyptian and Etruscan collections in former grand-ducal palace. Santa Maria Novella, monastic church with admirable frescoes by Ghirlandaio. Bargello palace and museum, with fine collection of sculpture including Donatello's bronze *David*. Loggia della Signoria with Cellini's *Perseus* in bronze. Green-and-white Church of San Miniato, remarkable example of Florentine-style Romanesque architecture; panoramic view over the city from Piazzale Michelangelo. Ponte Vecchio, dating back to 1345, with boutiques overhanging the Arno river. Palazzo Pitti, sumptuous Renaissance palace comprising museums and galleries plus ornate Italian gardens. Santa Maria del Carmine, unpretentious church, sheltering some of the most momentous frescoes ever painted.

Central Italy. Abruzzi, highest massif of the Apennine range, national park of harsh natural beauty. Assisi*, birthplace of St. Francis, whose life is depicted in Giotto's famous cycle of frescoes in the 13th-century basilica; tomb of St. Francis. Hilltop town of Perugia with 13th-century Town Hall, Gothic cathedral and Collegio del Cambio, decorated with frescoes by Perugino.

Southern Italy. Naples, colorful port on beautiful bay; National Archaeological Museum, housing Greco-Roman treasures, especially from Pompeii and Herculaneum; Royal Palace, featuring sumptuously decorated halls and apartments; Santa Lucia district, offering animated street life; Spacca, crowded and bustling heart of old city; world-famous San Carlo Opera House; Catacombs of San Gennaro, dating back to the 2nd century. Carthusian Monastery of St. Martin *(Certosa di San Martino)*, commanding superb views over Bay of Naples. Vesuvius, active volcano with unforgettable panorama from crater. Pompeii*, town preserved by volcanic lava since eruption of Vesuvius in A.D. 79, telling the story of everyday provincial Roman life. The excavated site of the town of Herculaneum, buried by the same eruption, smaller and less famous, but fascinating. Sorrento peninsula, with deep gorges and Amalfi Drive*, hairpin bends along a breathtakingly rugged coast. Idyllic resorts like Amalfi, Ravello and Positano, perched on the steep hillside. Capri*, island of spectacular beauty honeycombed with caverns including the famed Blue Grotto; Villa Jovis, the hilltop vacation palace of the Roman Emperor Tiberius; Axel Munthe's Villa of San Michele. Ischia, vine-growing island with hot springs and tropical vegetation. Paestum*, ancient Greek colony with Temple of Neptune, perfect example of Doric architecture. Sardinia, island of wild rugged scenery and coast riddled with grottoes; Maddalena archipelago, 14 islands and islets of unspoiled natural beauty; Alghero, for skin diving at Porto Conte and Capo Caccia. Apulia Coast, Italy's heel, noted for attractive beaches and marinas, punctuated by ports of Taranto, Brindisi and Bari. Gargano promontory, quaint harbors, white beaches, grottoes and islands.

Sicily. Palermo, capital of Sicily, old city with three pretty squares— Quattro Canti, Piazza Pretoria and Piazza Bellini; La Martorana church, studded with Byzantine mosaics; Palace of the Normans *(Palazzo dei Normanni)*, with magnificent Palatine chapel decorated in Arab-Norman style; San Giovanni degli Eremiti with its pink domes. Monreale*, hill town whose Benedictine Abbey boasts finely sculpted cloisters and Norman church decorated with dazzling mosaics. Cefalù, noted for its twin-towered cathedral with golden façade. Taormina, picturesque town perched overlooking the sea with well-preserved Greek theater. Mount Etna*, largest active volcano in Europe. Syracuse (Siracusa), ancient ruins of Greek city once the rival of Athens, with Greek theater, Paradise Quarry, important Archaeological Museum and Roman amphitheater. Agrigento*, with Valley of the Temples, graceful complex of Greek ruins in impressive coastal setting. Segesta, where beautifully preserved temple stands alone among sun-scorched mountains. Aeolian Islands: Vulcano, with sulphur mud baths, hot springs and breathtaking views from vocano crater; Lipari*, island of black volcanic rock and delightful fishing villages; Stromboli, with spectacularly awesome active volcano.

Some useful expressions in Italian

good morning/afternoon	buongiorno
good evening/night	buona sera/buona notte
good-bye	arrivederci
yes/no	si/no
please/thank you	per piacere/grazie
excuse me	mi scusi
you're welcome	prego
where/when/how	dove/quando/come
how long/how far	quanto tempo/quanto dista
yesterday/today/tomorrow	ieri/oggi/domani
day/week/month/year	giorno/settimana/mese/anno
left/right	sinistra/destra
up/down	su/giù
good/bad	buono/cattivo
big/small	grande/piccolo
cheap/expensive	buon mercato/caro
hot/cold	caldo/freddo
old/new	vecchio/nuovo
open/closed	aperto/chiuso
free (vacant)/occupied	libero/occupato
early/late	presto/tardi
easy/difficult	facile/difficile
Does anyone here speak English/French/German?	C'è qualcuno che parla inglese/francese/tedesco?
What does this mean?	Cosa significa?
I don't understand.	Non capisco.
Please write it down.	Lo scriva, per favore.
Do you take credit cards/traveler's checks?	Accetta carta di credito/traveller's cheques?
Waiter!/Waitress!	Cameriere!/Cameriera!
Where are the toilets?	Dove sono i gabinetti?
I'd like…	Vorrei…
How much is that?	Quant'è?
What time is it?	Che ore sono?
Help me please.	Per favore, mi aiuti.
Just a minute.	Un attimo.

MALTA

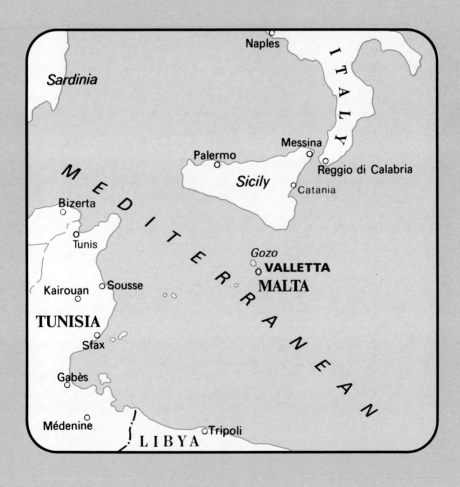

Naples

Sardinia

ITALY

Messina

Palermo

Reggio di Calabria

Sicily

Catania

M E D I T E R R A N E A N

Bizerta

Tunis

Gozo

VALLETTA

MALTA

Kairouan

Sousse

TUNISIA

Sfax

Gabès

Médenine

Tripoli

L I B Y A

Besieged over centuries, honey-colored ramparts and castles proud above the sea.

Thanks to its strategic position at the crossroads of the Mediterranean, Malta has been fought over since the Punic Wars. For four months in 1565, Suleiman the Magnificent besieged the island, the base of the Knights of St. John, but finally gave up and sailed away. In World War II the Germans and Italians repeated the punishment, and again Malta endured. Invaders aside, though, foreigners who come to the sunny archipelago find the proud Maltese altogether helpful and welcoming.

Of all the influences shaping the unique Maltese culture, one of the earliest and strongest was religion. Christianity arrived most authoritatively when St. Paul himself was shipwrecked here, around A.D. 60. Paul converted the Roman governor, Publius, and made him the first Bishop of Malta. To this day religious issues are taken seriously. Churches and wayside chapels crop up all over the countryside, and saints' days and other important religious occasions are celebrated with parades, band concerts and fireworks as well as special masses.

Three inhabited islands and two rocky islets comprise the Republic of Malta. The largest island, Malta itself, has 86 miles of coastline, including sandy beaches and rocky stretches. The historic walled cities are rich in sightseeing potential, with honey-colored stone ramparts and castles, narrow streets and venerable churches. Gozo is an even more relaxed island, greener, with the most striking archaeological site in the archipelago, the giant Ġgantija Temples, nearly 5,000 years old. The third isle, little Comino, is strictly for escapism.

With the North African desert just across the sea, summer breezes can be torrid. All the more reason to join the islanders somewhere shady for a long, leisurely meal—perhaps today's swordfish, tuna or red mullet—with some of the unpretentious local wine.

320

Facts and figures

Population:	370,000
Area:	122 sq. miles (316 sq. km.)
Capital:	Valletta (14,000)
Other city:	Sliema (20,000)
Languages:	Maltese and English
Religion:	Roman Catholic (98%)
Time zone:	GMT + 1, EST + 6; DST (Apr.–Sep.)
Currency:	*Malta Lira* (abbr. *Lm*) or *Pound* = 100 *cents* (¢), the cent = 10 *mils (m)*
	Coins: 2, 3, 5 mils; 1, 2, 5, 10, 25, 50 cents; Lm 1
	Bills: Lm 2, 5, 10, 20
Electricity:	240 volt, 50 cycle, AC

Planning your trip

Visa requirements. See pp. 29–30.

Vaccination requirements. None (see also p. 25).

Currency restrictions. Visitors may bring in any amount of foreign currency (providing it's declared upon arrival), and up to Lm 50. Not more than Lm 25 may be taken out of the country, plus any unspent foreign currency of the sum declared upon arrival.

Climate. Some average daily temperatures:

Valletta		J	F	M	A	M	J	J	A	S	O	N	D
average daily	°F	58	59	61	65	71	79	84	85	81	75	67	61
maximum*	°C	14	15	16	18	22	26	29	29	27	24	20	16
average daily	°F	50	51	52	56	61	67	72	73	71	66	60	54
minimum*	°C	10	10	11	13	16	19	22	23	22	19	16	12

* Minimum temperatures are measured just before sunrise, maximum temperatures in the afternoon.

The islands enjoy a temperate to warm climate. Rain can occur between late October and early March.

Clothing. Summer can be very hot, so bring along plenty of light cottons. A word of warning for sun-worshippers: topless sunbathing is strictly prohibited. Warmer clothes and rainwear are advisable in winter. Catholic religious sentiment is strong, and people visiting churches, especially women, are expected to be suitably clad. In the evening, certain luxury hotels and the casino require jacket and tie for men.

Duty-free allowances

Cigarettes	Cigars	Tobacco	Liquor	Wine
200 or	250 g. of other tobacco products*		¾ l. and	¾ l.
* of which nor more than 50 g. in loose tobacco				

Hotels and accommodations

Hotels. Hotels are rated according to comfort and amenities by the Hotels and Catering Establishments Board. The categories range from de luxe (five star) downward. It is imperative to reserve well in advance for the popular summer season or even early autumn.

Villas and apartments. A wide range of housekeeping facilities are available. The National Tourist Organization brochure gives details.

Youth hostels and camping. There are several youth hostels in Malta and one in Gozo. For information, contact the Valletta Youth Hostels Association: 17, Tal-Borġ Street, Paola; tel. 229361
There are no official campsites and camping independently is not allowed.

Maltese tourist offices abroad

Eire Honorary Consul for Malta, 1, Upper Fitzwilliam Street, Dublin 2; tel. (01) 760333

U.K. Malta National Tourist Office, Suite 207, College House, Wright's Lane, Kensington; tel. (071) 938 2668, telex 266083 BCC G

U.S.A. Maltese Consulate, 249 East 35th Street, New York, NY 10016; tel. (212) 725-2345/8

Embassy of Malta, 2017 Connecticut Avenue N.W., Washington D.C. 20008; tel. (202) 462-3611/2

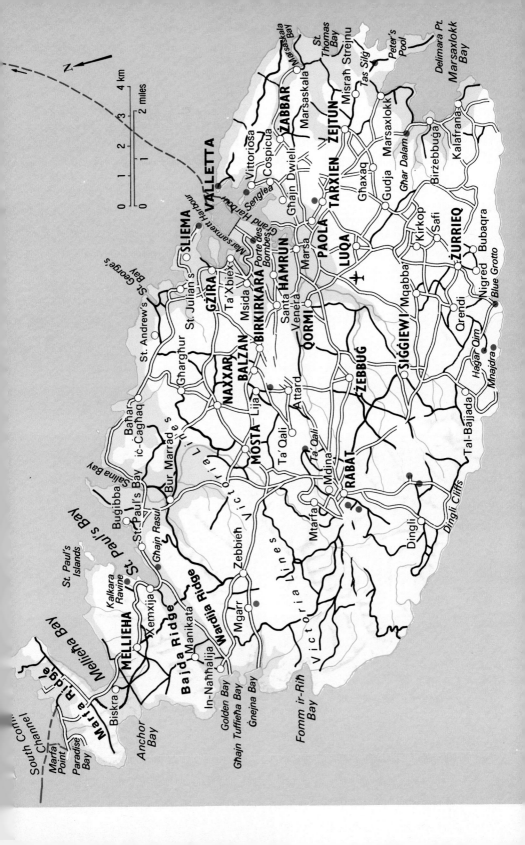

On the spot

Banks and currency exchange. In summer, banking hours are 8 a.m. to 12 noon, Monday through Friday, and 8 to 11:30 a.m. on Saturdays. In winter, banks open and close half an hour later. Certain banks make foreign-exchange transactions after normal hours. At Luqa Airport, a 24-hour currency-exchange service operates. On Saturdays, banks usually limit foreign exchange to the value of Lm 100 per customer.

Credit cards and traveler's checks. Credit cards are widely accepted by better shops, hotels and restaurants in the bigger towns. Many hotels give unfavorable rates for traveler's checks, so it's usually better to go to a bank. Traveler's checks are rarely accepted in shops.

Mail and telecommunications. The main post office (Auberge d'Italie, Merchants Street, Valletta) is open 7:45 a.m. to 6 p.m., Monday through

Saturday (8 a.m. to 6 p.m. in winter). Branches are open from 7:30 a.m. to 12:45 p.m., Monday through Saturday all year round. Luqa Airport post office is open 7 a.m. to 7 p.m. Stamps may also be bought at most hotels and at some tobacco shops.

Telegrams, telexes and faxes can be sent from the main telegraph office in St. George's Road, St. Julian's (open 24 hours a day), the branch office in South Street in Valletta or the Luqa Airport post office.

Overseas calls can be dialed directly to European countries and the U.S. For other countries, dial 994 (894 from Gozo) to get the overseas telephone exchange. If you're calling long distance from Gozo, dial 8 first. Telephone booths are painted blue. Information in the telephone directory is in Maltese and English. See also p. 30.

Newspapers. Maltese dailies include *L'Orizzont* and *Il-Hajja*. There is one English-language daily published in Malta, *The Times,* and three weeklies—the *Sunday Chronicle* and *The Democrat* (Saturday) and *The Sunday Times.* All the British dailies are widely available. A *What's On* guide published every two weeks covers tourist needs.

Tourist information. The Air Malta information desk at the airport advises about hotels and gives other tourist information. Other offices:

Valletta Tourist Information Office, 1, City Gate Arcade; tel. 227747

Gozo Mġarr harbor; tel. 553343

Legal holidays

Jan. 1	New Year's Day	Sep. 8	Our Lady of Victories
Feb. 10	St. Paul's Shipwreck	Sept. 21	Independence Day
Mar. 19	St. Joseph	Dec. 8	Immaculate Conception
Mar. 31	National Day		
May 1	May Day	Dec. 13	Republic Day
June 21	St. Peter and St. Paul	Dec. 25	Christmas Day
Aug. 15	Assumption Day	**Movable:**	Good Friday

Transportation

Air. The Maltese islands are served by Luqa Airport (4 miles/6 km. from Valletta). Bus service to Valletta. There is a small duty-free shop at

325

the airport. Summer travelers are advised to check in early, as flights are often overbooked.

Boats, waterways. The only way to get to Gozo is by boat. Services between Malta and Gozo are frequent, but bad weather may interrupt service. A daily ferry leaves from Pietà, outside Valletta, and takes 1 hour 15 minutes to reach Gozo. Ferry services from Ċirkewwa in northwest Malta run several times a day and the trip takes 20 minutes.

Buses. Malta and Gozo operate a frequent, cheap bus service. The driver takes your fare. In Valletta, the main terminal is by the Triton Fountain, just outside the City Gate.

Taxis. These are clearly marked "taxi" and have red license plates. All taxis have meters. There are plenty of taxis at the airport, as well as at the main hotels, in tourist centers and at the ferry docks.

Horse-drawn cabs. The Maltese horse-drawn cab—the *karrozzin*—was introduced in the 1850s and remains a favorite means of tourist transportation in Valletta, Mdina and Sliema. Be sure to negotiate the price in advance; it takes an hour or so to cover the main sights of the above towns.

Car rental. In addition to the usual international companies, various local firms do business in Malta; some have desks at the airport. In peak tourist periods advance reservations are advisable. See also pp. 30–31.

Driving in Malta. Malta is one of the few European countries where you drive on the *left* and pass on the right. In traffic circles, yield right-of-way to cars already in transit. Seat belts are not compulsory. Your car has to carry a red reflector warning triangle for emergencies. It's illegal to drive under the influence of alcohol. Only two kinds of gasoline are available: super (98–100 octane) and diesel.

Country roads are often very poor, and even main roads can be in a bad state of repair. There are no toll roads. Speed limits are 25 mph (40 kph) in built-up areas, and 34 mph (55 kph) on the main roads. Beware of the rather reckless style of Maltese driving. Parking can be difficult in Valletta during the day.

Bicycle rental. The tourist organization has addresses of bike rental firms.

Rest rooms. There are few public rest rooms and only in the larger towns; the signs designating "ladies" or "gentlemen" are very subtle—sometimes you have to ask. If there is an attendant, it's appropriate to leave a few cents.

326

Emergencies. In an emergency phone:

| Ambulance | 996 | Police | 224001/2 (Malta) |
| Fire | 999 | | 556011 (Gozo) |

Police. Most towns have a police station, clearly marked. Some stations are not manned around the clock. Police officers dress in khaki uniforms in summer, black uniforms in winter, with visored hats.

Crime and theft. Malta is still relatively crime-free compared with the rest of the world, but car thefts, in particular, are on the increase. It's a good policy to take the usual precautions. Any loss or theft should be reported immediatedly to the nearest police station and, in the event it happened at the hotel, to the hotel management.

Medical care and health. Medical and pharmaceutical supplies are readily available at all pharmacies. One pharmacy remains open after hours in every locality; the addresses appear in the local weekend newspapers.

Don't eat unwashed fresh fruit and vegetables. Tap water is safe for drinking.

The government operates a modern medical center, and there are also two privately run hospitals. All Maltese doctors speak English and Italian. For insurance, see pp. 25–26.

Embassies and consulates. Look under "Embassies" and "Consulates" in the Yellow Pages.

Social customs. The Maltese have a strict Catholic upbringing. They are usually very polite, even formal, on a one-to-one basis, but they also have the casual Mediterranean "mañana" approach to life.

Enjoying Malta

Food and drink. Nowadays more and more restaurants serve local specialties, using the best of local ingredients—juicy red tomatoes, gleaming onions, crisp green peppers and the freshest of fish. The British and Italian have left their culinary legacies too—you'll find pasta and pizza as well as fish and chips.

327

Soup is served with most meals, the most popular being *minestra,* a vegetable hot-pot similar to Italian *minestrone,* but even more hearty and filling. Alternatively, you can often find Italian-style *antipasti,* which might include slices of local pepper sausages, Parma ham *(prosciutto)* and melon, marinated vegetables and shrimp cocktail. All kinds of pasta are popular with the Maltese. Specialties include *ravjul,* a tasty version of ricotta-stuffed ravioli, and the true Maltese dish, *timpana,* flaky pastry filled with macaroni, minced meat, onions, tomato puree, eggplant, eggs and cheese.

Fish in Malta is cooked simply, and the true flavor and freshness speaks for itself. Try the local *lampuka,* a firm-fleshed white fish special to Malta, in season from late August to December. It's often baked in a pie with vegetables and olives *(torta tal-lampuki),* or in a casserole with wine and herbs. Other fish to look for are *dentici* (dentex), *pixxispad* (swordfish), *tunnagg* (tuna), and *ćerna* (grouper). Any fish *alla Maltese* comes with a tomato and green pepper sauce.

Island meat specialties rarely appear on restaurant menus, though you might find "Maltese-style" beef or lamb, prepared in a casserole with potatoes and onions, as it is in Maltese homes. Another typical dish is *braġoli,* thin slices of steak stuffed with minced meat, bacon, eggs and breadcrumbs. *Fenek* means rabbit, a favorite fried, casseroled with wine and garlic, or in a delicious pie *(torta tal-fenek)* with pork, peas, tomatoes and spice. Country-raised chicken is a treat, especially when it's roasted *alla diavola* or *diable,* grilled with shallots, mustard and breadcrumbs.

After such a gastronomic onslaught, a perfect finish is fresh fruit: juicy plums, peaches, figs, pomegranates and grapes are all grown locally. But there's also Italian-style ice cream and *gateaux,* rich cakes often made with almonds and ricotta cheese. And each festival has its own special dessert. The most decadent is *prinjolata,* eaten at carnival time, a luscious combination of sponge fingers, butter cream and almonds decorated with chocolate and cherries. The most popular local cheese is *ġbejna,* made from sheep's milk. The best *ġbejna* comes from Gozo.

Maltese wines are cheap. Reds, best drunk slightly chilled, include Marsovin, Lachryma Vitis, La Valette (considered the best) and Farmers. Local white wines are refreshing, but sometimes too sweet unless you spend a few cents extra for a "Special Reserve". Most potent are the Ġgantija wines (red and white) produced on Gozo. Many types of beer are sold, and the local beer, Farson's Ċisk is good, and inexpensive. Coffee, tea and all kinds of soft drinks are readily available.

Lunch is served between noon and 2:30 p.m., dinner 7 to 10 p.m.

Entertainment. There are several lively discos, especially in Sliema and St. Julian's, although most close down at midnight. However, the casino, at St. George's Bay, stays open into the small hours. Concerts and ballet performances take place at the Manoel Theatre in Valletta, except during the hottest summer months. There are several movie theaters in Valletta and Sliema. Most films are shown in English.

Annual events and festivals. Every parish celebrates its patron saint's feast with three days of colorful festivities leading up to a religious procession with street bands and fireworks. *March:* National Day, with parades and fireworks in Valletta and Vittoriosa. *Springtime:* Carnival in Valletta, Victoria and elsewhere. *June:* Imnarja Folk Festival at Buskett Gardens, Rabat. *September:* Regatta at Senglea, Mellieħa, Naxxar and Xagħra (Gozo). *December:* Republic Day, with fireworks in Vittoriosa.

Taxes, service charges and tipping. A service charge is sometimes included in restaurants and hotels, but in any case it is customary to leave a small tip on top. Tipping recommendations: porters 10 cents per bag, waiters 5–10%, taxi drivers 10%, hairdressers 10–15%, hatcheck 10 cents, hotel maid 50 cents a week.

Sports and recreation. Surrounded by warm, clear water, Malta is perfect for scuba diving, water skiing, sailing, windsurfing and fishing. Or if you just want to have a swim, there's a choice of sandy beaches (particularly in north and northwest Malta) and delightful rock-bathing sites.

As for inland sports, the Marsa sports club near Valletta offers just about everything, including tennis, golf, squash, riding and cricket. If you prefer to watch, there's soccer at the stadium in Ġzira (from October to June), and water polo is played all over Malta.

TV and radio. Xandir Malta, the local TV channel, transmits about five hours of programs in Maltese and English each evening, including both British and American features. An English newscast is a daily feature. The BBC World Service and Voice of America are easily picked up. Malta broadcasts radio programs in English between 8 a.m. and 8 p.m. daily.

What to buy. Look for delicate filigreed silver, brightly colored Mdina glass, ceramics, cotton goods, sturdy woolen knits, woven gloves and lace. Ta'Qali, just outside Mdina, is a crafts village that welcomes visitors. There is also a crafts center opposite the cathedral in St. John's Square in Valletta with a permanent display of local crafts and souvenirs.

Shops are generally open from 9 a.m. to 7 p.m., but most take a one-to three-hour lunch break.

Sightseeing

Valletta. National Museum of Archaeology, showing artefacts from all Malta's prehistoric periods. St. John's Co-Cathedral★ with sumptuous Baroque interior and Caravaggio's masterpiece *The Beheading of St. John.* Grand Master's Palace, headquarters of the Knights of St. John for more than two centuries and now the seat of the House of Representatives, featuring grand state rooms and Knights' armory. National Museum of Fine Arts, housing paintings from various schools plus works of the 20th-century Maltese sculptor Antonio Sciortino. Upper Barracca Gardens★ with impressive view of the Grand Harbour. Manoel Theatre, built in 1731 and one of the oldest theaters in Europe

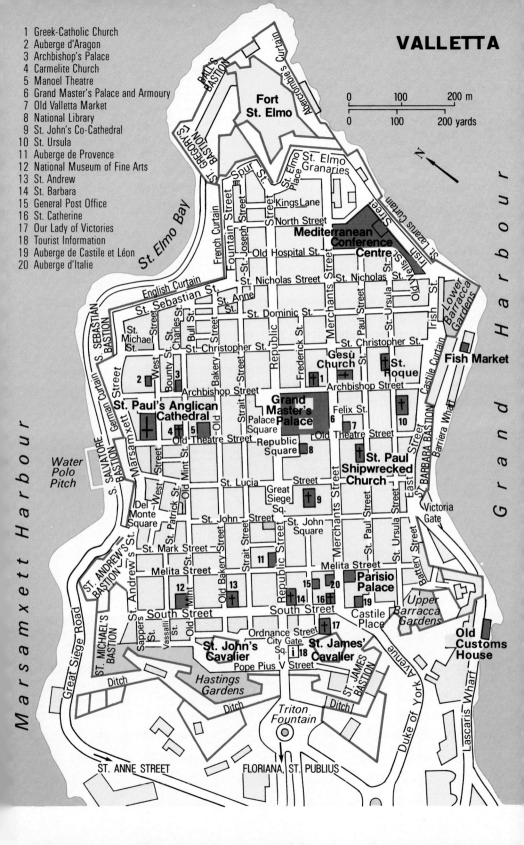

VALLETTA

1 Greek-Catholic Church
2 Auberge d'Aragon
3 Archbishop's Palace
4 Carmelite Church
5 Manoel Theatre
6 Grand Master's Palace and Armoury
7 Old Valletta Market
8 National Library
9 St. John's Co-Cathedral
10 St. Ursula
11 Auberge de Provence
12 National Museum of Fine Arts
13 St. Andrew
14 St. Barbara
15 General Post Office
16 St. Catherine
17 Our Lady of Victories
18 Tourist Information
19 Auberge de Castile et Léon
20 Auberge d'Italie

0   100   200 m
0   100   200 yards

Marsamxett Harbour

Grand Harbour

St. Elmo Bay

Fort St. Elmo

St. Elmo Granaries

Mediterranean Conference Centre

Lower Barracca Gardens

Fish Market

Water Polo Pitch

Grand Master's Palace

Gesù Church

St. Roque

St. Paul's Anglican Cathedral

St. Paul Shipwrecked Church

Victoria Gate

Del Monte Square

Great Siege Sq.

St. John Square

Parisio Palace

Upper Barracca Gardens

Old Customs House

St. John's Cavalier

City Gate Sq.

St. James' Cavalier

Castile Place

Hastings Gardens

Triton Fountain

Ditch

Ditch

Ditch

ST. ANNE STREET

FLORIANA, ST. PUBLIUS

Pope Pius V Street

Ordnance Street

South Street

Melita Street

St. Mark Street

St. John Street

St. Lucia

Republic Square

Palace Square

Archbishop Street

Republic Street

Merchants Street

Frederick Street

St. Christopher St.

St. Dominic St.

St. Nicholas Street

Old Hospital St.

North Street

Kings Lane

English Curtain

St. Sebastian St.

St. Anne St.

Bull St.

Bakery Street

Old Theatre Street

Felix St.

St. Paul Street

St. Ursula Street

East Street

Battery Street

Strait Street

Old Bakery Street

Old Mint Street

West Street

St. Patrick St.

St. Charles St.

Bounty St.

St. Michael St.

Marsamxett Street

German Curtain Street

S. SALVATORE BASTION

S. SEBASTIAN BASTION

ST. ANDREW'S BASTION

ST. MICHAEL'S BASTION

Great Siege Road

Sappers St.

Vassalli St.

St. Old Mint

St. John's St.

Duke of York Avenue

St. James Street

ST. JAMES BASTION

Lascaris Wharf

Barriera Wharf

S. BARBARA BASTION

Castile Curtain

Irish Street

St. Nicholas

St. Lazarus Curtain

St. Pio Street

St. Nells St.

St. Elmo Place

St. Elmo Street

Spur St.

Fountain Street

French Curtain

St. Joseph Street

BALL'S BASTION

GREGORY'S BASTION

BAKERY BASTION

Abercrombie

Curtain

still in continuous use. Mediterranean Conference Centre, originally the hospital of the Order of St. John. Several Baroque churches, notably that of St. Paul Shipwrecked with an outstanding statue of St. Paul and Our Lady of Victories, the oldest church in Valletta.

Around Valletta. St. Julian's Bay*, quaint old fishing village. Sliema, modern resort and yacht marina. Tarxien temples ruins* featuring magnificent bas-relief carvings, remains of three prehistoric temples. Hypogeum, underground labyrinth of 3000–1800 B.C. excavated on three levels.

Inland Malta. Mdina*, old capital of Malta and typical medieval town with Baroque cathedral and rich Cathedral Museum. Rabat, site of early Christian catacombs and Grotto of St. Paul, where the apostle is said to have lived during his three-month stay on the island. Mosta, famed for the parish church of St. Mary's*, boasting one of the largest unsupported domes in Europe, visible from all over the island.

Southeast Malta. Blue Grotto*, limestone caves, where crystal-clear waters mirror multicolored rock formations. Għar Dalam, prehistoric cave with fossilized bones embedded in the rock. Hagar Qim* and Mnajdra, megalithic temple complexes on majestic site overlooking the sea. Marsaxlokk and Marsaskala, colorful fishing villages.

Northwest Malta. Numerous bays for swimming and water sports, including Qawra, St. George's Bay and Golden Bay. Skorba, important prehistoric site with remains of farmers' huts and two megalithic temples. St. Paul's Bay, traditional site of St. Paul's shipwreck in A.D. 60. Melliha, known for its sandy bay and superb view of Comino and Gozo; 18th-century church and medieval chapel, now a site of pilgrimage.

Gozo. Victoria, with Old Town, picturesque narrow alleyways and simple old houses; It-Tokk, shady central square, edged with small shops; citadel and ramparts, surrounding Gozo's magnificent cathedral* with mosaic tombs. Ġgantija temples, two impressive prehistoric temples, aptly named "The Giant's Tower", erected on the Xaghra plateau. The Inland Sea, natural bathing pool with dramatic overhanging cliffs. Unspoiled picturesque villages: Xlendi*, pastel houses tucked away at the end of a narrow bay surrounded by two high rocky promontories. Sannat, a lace-making center. Gharb, village of pretty pastel houses, many with beautifully carved balconies.

NETHERLANDS

History, art and vitality amid the flowers
in the land behind the dunes and dikes.

The home of Erasmus and William the Silent is the original low profile country, flat as the North Sea. Millions of Netherlanders live below sea level on reclaimed land protected by two thousand miles of dunes and dikes. With Dutch stubbornness the struggle against the sea, begun by thousands of pumping windmills, goes on with the latest innovations in hydraulic engineering.

The North Sea led the Dutch to their Golden Age, when the East India Company raised the flag from Japan and Java to South Africa and the Caribbean. As the empire's riches flowed back to Amsterdam, patrician 17th-century mansions were built, and patrons of the arts discovered the local talent—Rembrandt, Frans Hals and Vermeer. Their masterpieces mostly hang out in Amsterdam's vast Rijksmuseum, a superpower of the museum world.

In this compact nation everything is easy to reach on the intensive networks of expressways and railroads. Within a couple of days you can ply the canals, sniff the tulip fields and check out the beaches. You can tour the world's busiest port, all-modern Rotterdam, and soak up the stately atmosphere of The Hague, the seat of government. Amsterdam itself is strong on history, art and vitality; this live-and-let-live city has survived many a trend. The smaller towns are bastions of charm: Delft, where you can watch artists painting the blue porcelain; Gouda, with its 15th-century Town Hall and Thursday cheese market; and the medieval university town of Leiden.

The food is hearty and sometimes overwhelmingly abundant. The most popular Dutch treat, oddly, came the long way around, from Indonesia: *Rijsttafel*, a spicy cornucopia of dozens of dishes, is yet another welcome legacy of the old empire. The Indonesian connection also explains the special aroma of Dutch cigarillos and full-sized cigars. Other traditional shopping attractions run to pewter, silver and diamonds.

Facts and figures

Population:	14 million
Area:	15,770 sq. miles (41,582 sq. km.)
Capital:	Amsterdam (675,000/GUA 995,000)
Other major cities:	The Hague (*Den Haag* or *'s-Gravenhage*, seat of government, 445,000/GUA 670,000) Rotterdam (555,000/GUA 1 million) Utrecht (230,000/GUA 500,000) Eindhoven (195,000/GUA 375,000) Groningen (170,000/GUA 210,000) Haarlem (150,000/GUA 220,000)
Language:	Dutch
Religion:	Catholic (38%), Protestant (31%), Jewish (4%)
Time zone:	GMT + 1, EST + 6; DST (Apr.–Sep.)
Currency:	*Gulden* (abbr. *f, fl* or *gld.*) = 100 *cents* (*c*) Coins: 5, 10, 25 cents; *f* 1, 2½, 5 Bills: *f* 5, 10, 25, 50, 100, 250, 1,000
Electricity:	220 volt, 50 cycle, AC

Planning your trip

Visa requirements. See pp. 29–30.

Vaccination requirements. None (see also p. 25).

Currency restrictions. The Dutch impose no limits on importation or exportation of money.

Climate. Holland's maritime temperate climate is unpredictable. Summer days can be either rainy and chilly or warm and dry. Spring and fall are characterized by cooler, equally unstable weather, and the wind can be piercing. In winter, ice-cold weather rarely prevails for more than a few days at a time and it snows only occasionally.

335

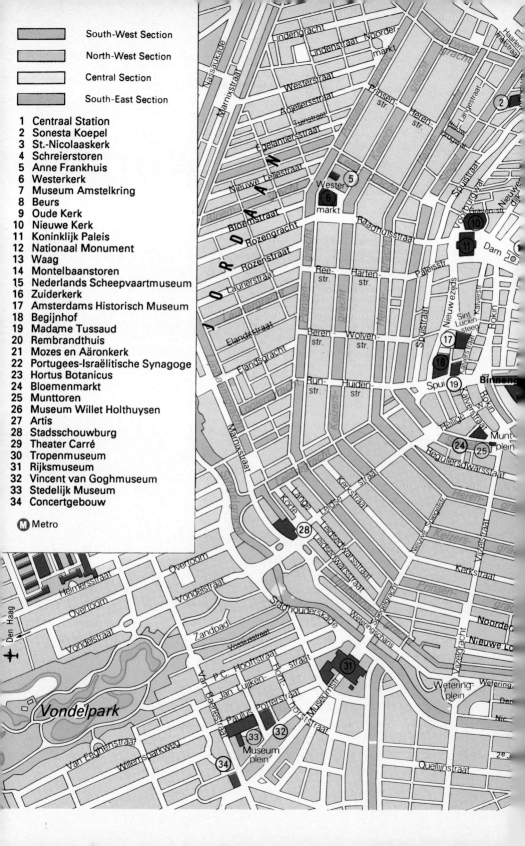

Legend

- South-West Section
- North-West Section
- Central Section
- South-East Section

1 Centraal Station
2 Sonesta Koepel
3 St.-Nicolaaskerk
4 Schreierstoren
5 Anne Frankhuis
6 Westerkerk
7 Museum Amstelkring
8 Beurs
9 Oude Kerk
10 Nieuwe Kerk
11 Koninklijk Paleis
12 Nationaal Monument
13 Waag
14 Montelbaanstoren
15 Nederlands Scheepvaartmuseum
16 Zuiderkerk
17 Amsterdams Historisch Museum
18 Begijnhof
19 Madame Tussaud
20 Rembrandthuis
21 Mozes en Aäronkerk
22 Portugees-Israëlitische Synagoge
23 Hortus Botanicus
24 Bloemenmarkt
25 Munttoren
26 Museum Willet Holthuysen
27 Artis
28 Stadsschouwburg
29 Theater Carré
30 Tropenmuseum
31 Rijksmuseum
32 Vincent van Goghmuseum
33 Stedelijk Museum
34 Concertgebouw

Ⓜ Metro

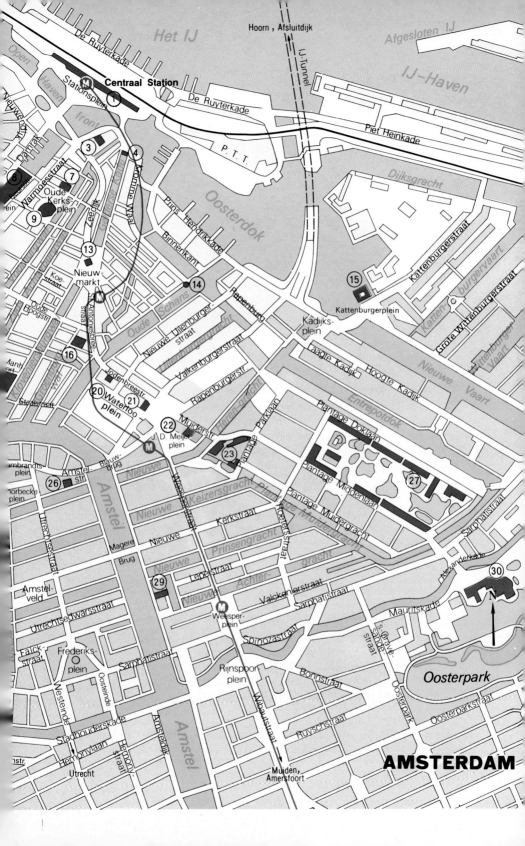

AMSTERDAM

Some average daily temperatures:

De Bilt (near Utrecht)		J	F	M	A	M	J	J	A	S	O	N	D
average daily maximum*	°F	40	42	49	56	64	70	72	71	67	57	48	42
	°C	4	5	10	13	18	21	22	22	19	14	9	5
average daily minimum*	°F	31	31	34	40	46	51	55	55	50	44	38	33
	°C	-1	-1	1	4	8	11	13	13	10	7	3	1

Vlissingen (Flushing)

		J	F	M	A	M	J	J	A	S	O	N	D
average daily maximum*	°F	41	41	47	53	61	66	69	70	66	57	49	43
	°C	5	5	9	12	16	19	21	21	19	14	9	6
average daily minimum*	°F	34	33	37	42	48	54	57	58	55	48	41	36
	°C	1	1	3	5	9	12	14	14	13	9	5	2

* Minimum temperatures are measured just before sunrise, maximum temperatures in the afternoon.

Clothing. Even in summer, evenings can be chilly or it may cloud up suddenly during the day, so you may need a sweater or wrap. Spring and fall can be warm, but often very windy, so be prepared. The only sensible way to dress in the often windy winter is to bundle up warmly. Always pack an umbrella or raincoat. In the evening, at the better restaurants and hotels, men are required to wear a jacket (though not necessarily a tie).

Duty-free allowances

	Cigarettes		Cigars		Tobacco	Liquor		Wine
1)	400	or	100	or	500 g.	1 l.	and	2 l.
2)	200	or	50	or	250 g.	1 l.	and	2 l.
3)	300	or	75	or	400 g.	1½ l.	and	5 l.

Perfume: 1), 2) 50 g.; 3) 75 g.
Toilet water: 1), 2) ¼ l.; 3) ³/₈ l.
Gifts: 1), 2) ƒ 125 max. value; 3) ƒ 890 max. value

1) residents of countries outside Europe
2) residents of Europe with goods bought outside EEC or duty-free inside EEC
3) residents of Europe, with goods bought inside EEC not duty-free

Hotels and accommodations

Hotels. Dutch tourist-information offices will give you a hotel list which incorporates both a quality assessment and a rating system. Breakfast is usually included in all but luxury-class and many first-class hotels. Advance reservations are advised, especially in summer and during exhibition periods.

Hotel-reservation services at Schiphol and Zestienhoven airports and at larger rail stations can help with last-minute hotel problems. In Amsterdam, the VVV tourist-information office opposite the Central Station runs a reservation service.

Boardinghouses are cheaper than a moderate hotel, but cannot be reserved through the Dutch tourist-information office.

Motels are beginning to spring up all over the country. They are well-equipped and comfortable, but can cost almost as much as a good hotel.

Youth hostels. The addresses and prices of cheap accommodations—including youth hostels—are given in the above-mentioned hotel list. Otherwise, you can call Nederlandse Jeugdherbergcentrale, Prof. Tulpplein 4, Amsterdam, tel. 551 31 55.

Camping. The Netherlands is well provided with campsites, which are usually clean and have full facilities. Advance reservations are recommended.

Dutch tourist offices abroad

Australia	6th floor, 5 Elizabeth Street, Sydney, NSW 2000; tel. (02) 276-921
Canada	25 Adelaide Street East, Suite 710, Toronto, Ont. M5C 1Y2; tel. (416) 363-1577
U.K.	25–28 Buckingham Gate, London SW1E 6LD; tel. (071) 630 0451
U.S.A.	355 Lexington Avenue, New York, NY 10017; tel. (212) 370-7367 255 North Michigan Avenue, Suite 326, Chicago, IL 60601; tel. (312) 819-0300 90 New Montgomery Street, Suite 305, San Francisco, CA 94105; tel. (415) 543-6772

On the spot

Banks and currency exchange. Banks are open Monday through Friday, 9 a.m. to 4 p.m. In the cities they also stay open from 4:30 p.m. to 7 p.m. on Thursdays. Outside banking hours, currency can be changed at Amsterdam's Central Station and Schiphol Airport. Most major hotels will cash traveler's checks, as will travel agencies.

Credit cards and traveler's checks. Major credit cards are accepted by most large hotels and restaurants and some stores. Traveler's checks are widely accepted with passport identification.

Mail and telecommunications. There are post offices *(postkantoor)* in every district. Opening hours are usually Monday through Friday, 9 a.m. to 5 p.m. Main post offices have slightly longer hours and some open also on Saturday mornings. The main post offices in Amsterdam are at Oosterdokskade and Singel, in The Hague at Prinsestraat, and in Rotterdam at Coolsingel and Delftesplein. Stamps can be bought from newsstands and souvenir shops, Dutch mailboxes are red, and are mounted on walls at eye level.

The Dutch telephone system is automated, and you can dial direct to almost anywhere in Europe, the U.S.A., Canada and South Africa. Public coin telephones take 25-cent, 1- and 2½-gulden pieces. When calling long distance, dial the code, wait for a second tone and then dial the rest of the number. There's a 24-hour telegram and telephone service in Amsterdam at Telehouse, Raadhuisstraat 46–50, behind Dam Square, and in Rotterdam at Coolsingel post office (the Meent entrance). For surcharges and low rates, see p. 30.

Some useful telephone numbers:

Information		Operator	
(domestic)	008	(outside Europe)	0016
Information		Telegrams	009
(international)	06-0418		
Operator			
(domestic			
and Europe)	0010		

Emergency telephone numbers for fire, accidents and police vary from place to place. Local emergency numbers are printed on the back cover of the telephone directory.

Newspapers. The principal Dutch newspapers are *NRC/Handelsblad, De Volkskrant, De Telegraaf* and *Het Parool*. Major British and continental dailies are available at larger newsstands, which also carry the Paris-edited *International Herald Tribune* and a local English-language monthly, *Holland Herald*.

Tourist information. In most Dutch towns, tourist affairs are handled by an organization known simply by its initials VVV (pronounced vay-vay-vay). Blue signs with the triple-V emblem will guide you to the tourist office from the edge of town. The VVV offices can help with hotel rooms, tickets, travel advice and more.

Amsterdam   VVV, Stationsplein 10 (opposite the Central Station); tel. (020) 26 64 44

Rotterdam   Stadhuisplein 19; tel. (010) 414 14 00

The Hague   Groot Hertoginnelaan 41; tel. (070) 354 62 00

Legal holidays

Jan. 1	New Year's Day	**Movable dates:**
Apr. 30	Queen's Birthday	Good Friday
Dec. 25	Christmas Day	Easter Monday
Dec. 26	St. Stephen's Day	Ascension
		Whit Monday

Transportation

Air. Amsterdam's Schiphol Airport is the major gateway to the Netherlands. The smaller airports of Rotterdam, Eindhoven and Maastricht have some international flights within Europe.

Domestic flights serve six airports around the country: Schiphol, Rotterdam's Zestienhoven, Groningen's Eelde, Eindhoven's Welschap, Enschede's Twente and Maastricht's Beek.

Major airports. Amsterdam: Schiphol (9 miles/15 km. southwest of city center). Extensive duty-free shops. Regular rail service to Central Station with direct connections to towns throughout Holland. Also frequent train service from the airport to Amsterdam RAI (congress center). **Rotterdam:** Zestienhoven (4 miles/6 km. north of city center). Duty-free shop. Bus service to Central Station. Regular rail service to Amsterdam Airport.

Rail. Trains are punctual and comfortable with first and second class compartments, but sometimes very crowded. Dining cars with beverages and sandwiches are found only on express trains. The *Holland Rail Pass,* obtainable at any railroad station in Holland, entitles the holder to three days' unlimited train travel within a period of 15 days. There is also a *Benelux Tourrail* ticket, giving 16 days' unlimited travel within Belgium, Luxembourg and the Netherlands. This flat-rate ticket must be bought in a Benelux country. Ask for details at a local travel agency or rail station. For *Eurailpass,* see p. 33.

Local public transportation. Buses and streetcars serve most cities. Amsterdam and Rotterdam also have subway systems. In Amsterdam, enter buses and streetcars at the front, buy your ticket from the driver and then cancel it in the yellow stamping machine. At the municipal transportation board's ticket office (*kaartverkoop*) outside Central Station in Amsterdam, you can buy one-, two- or three-day go-as-you-please tickets.

Taxis. Cabs do not generally cruise the streets. Go to a taxi stand or call for one (look under "Taxi " in the telephone directory). Taxis have a taxi sign on the roof.

Car rental. International and local firms operate, some with offices at the major airports as well as in town centers. They are listed in the Yellow pages under "Autoverhuur". See also pp. 30–31.

Driving in the Netherlands. Drive on the right, pass on the left. Generally traffic coming from the right has priority. Streetcars have priority. Beware of cyclists, particularly when turning right. Expressways, connecting all main cities, are well-maintained. Yellow emergency phones are located along principal expressways. Otherwise in case of breakdown, call ANWB Wegenwacht (in Amsterdam 06-0888, in Rotterdam 01890-5433, in the Hague 63 69 68). Speed limits are 19 mph (30 kph) or 31 mph (50 kph) in town, 62 mph (100 kph) or 75 mph (120 kph) on expressways and generally 50 mph (80 kph) on other roads. The only tolls are at the Maastunnel and on some bridges near Rotterdam. Seat belts must be worn, and blood alcohol limit is strictly enforced at 50 mg./100 ml. All cars must carry a red reflector warning triangle for use in case of breakdown. Gasoline available is lead-free (95 and 98 octane), super and diesel.

Some distances: Amsterdam-The Hague 31 mile (50 km.), Rotterdam 43 miles (70 km.), Groningen 125 miles (200 km.).

Bicycle rental. It's possible to rent bicycles for getting about town or for longer jaunts around the countryside. There are specialist shops in the towns, and bicycles can also be rented at many railroad stations around the country. The cyclist is so much a part of Dutch life that all recently built roads include a cycle path.

Rest rooms. There are few public rest rooms, but in the cities the numerous café-bars are designated as public places, so you may use their facilities; it's probably a good idea to have a beer or a coffee, too. Department stores have clean rest rooms, usually with an attendant on duty. Be sure to put a coin in the saucer. Ladies are *Dames* and Gentlemen are *Heren.*

Emergencies. Telephone numbers for the various emergency services differ from city to city. Look in the telephone directory or on the back cover; otherwise ask hotel staff or a taxi driver for help; language is unlikely to be a problem.

Police. In cities the police patrol on foot and in white Volkswagens. City police are dressed in navy blue, with peaked caps. Police stations are recognizable by a prominent *POLITIE* sign.

Crime and theft. Watch out for pickpockets in the main cities. Be particularly careful in the red-light districts and anywhere away from the main entertainment areas. Try to keep as little as possible in the car, as car theft is on the increase.

Medical care and health. Treatment is excellent but rather expensive. English is widely spoken in medical circles. Medicine and pharmaceutical supplies are readily available. Pharmacies *(apotheek)* are identified by the word APOTHEEK, and the addresses of duty pharmacies are posted in the windows of other pharmacies. For insurance, see pp. 25–26.

Tap water is safe to drink.

Embassies and consulates. Most countries have a consulate in Amsterdam, while the embassies often are in The Hague. Look under "Ambassade" and "Consulaat" in the Yellow pages.

Social customs. Dutch people are very open and are quite likely to invite visitors to their homes. A bunch of flowers or a souvenir from your own country would be appreciated. Despite the apparently easygoing attitude, they are quite formal at heart and a handshake on meeting and parting is a must.

Enjoying the Netherlands

Food and drink. Eating and drinking in Holland is a very pleasant affair, and enough time has to be set aside to do justice to the enormous portions provided. However, authentic Dutch food is no longer so easy to find. Traditionally it is real winter-warming nourishment like *erwtensoep* (a thick pea soup) or *groentensoep*, a clear consommé with the addition of a garden full of vegetables, vermicelli and tiny meatballs. If you're about on 3 October, you'll find most people starting a meal with bread and salted herring, followed by *hutspot* (a great pot of potatoes, carrots and onions) with *klapstuk*, stewed lean beef.

Herrings of all descriptions, "green" (caught in the first three weeks of the season) or otherwise, ought to be tasted. Try them filleted on toast, or whole from a street vendor. There is no shortage of seafood, but price could be a factor when it comes to lobster or oysters. You find good fresh *zalm* (salmon), *heilbot* (halibut), *tarbot* (turbot), *kabeljauw* (cod) and *mosselen* (mussels). *Gerookte paling* (smoked eel) is a Dutch specialty that you shouldn't miss.

344

While meat is good without being exceptional, the vegetables are first-class. Ask for artichokes (*artisjokken*) in season, and the usual peas (*erwtjes*), beans (*bonen*), spinach (*spinazie*) and carrots (*worteltjes*).

For something a little more exotic, go to one of the many Indonesian restaurants. *Rijsttafel* has come to be known as Holland's national dish. Start off by putting a mound of rice in the center of your soup bowl, and then surround it with small portions of side dishes such as *babi ketjap* (pork in soya sauce), *daging bronkos* (roast meat in coconut-milk sauce), *sambal goreng kering* (spicy pimento and fish paste), *oblo-oblo* (mixed soya beans) and many others. If a dish contains the word *sambal*, watch out; it will be very hot and plain rice is the only thing to follow it with. If you feel you can't manage the whole *rijsttafel*, try a smaller and cheaper dish called a *nasi goreng*, or, more usually, a *mini-rijsttafel*.

The Dutch don't go in for desserts in a big way, but they have a good range of ice creams, fruit with cream, Dutch apple-tart or *flensjes*, thin pancakes. For something different try *gember met slagroom*—lumps of fresh ginger with lots of cream.

Snacks are a national pastime and, as more sandwich bars spring up, the fillings become more imaginative. Also served are pancakes (*pannekoeken*) filled with apple rings, ginger, currants, bacon or cheese, and, if you have a sweet tooth, reach for the molasses (*stroop*) as the Dutch do.

You won't find any cheese on the dinner menu, for the Dutch like to eat it at breakfast (together with ham, an egg, jam, coffee, tea, or chocolate) or lunch (same as breakfast but with a warm side dish). The favorites are *Gouda, Edam* and *Leidsekaas* (Leiden cheese).

The Dutch drink a lot of coffee, but on another level the favorite drink is beer. It's a light *pils* type of beer, always kept cold, and stronger than British or American beer. Wine is rather expensive since it's imported. After the meal there is a wide choice of Dutch liqueurs, from Curaçao and Triple Sec to locally brewed gins (*jenevers*) for almost any occasion. *Oude* is the traditional tipple and is downed undiluted.

Entertainment. There's no problem in finding somewhere to go in the evening if you're in Amsterdam, Rotterdam or The Hague. Amsterdam takes the lead with numerous daring nightclubs and discos. It's worth trying to get a ticket to hear the Concertgebouw Orchestra itself at the Concertgebouw in Amsterdam. In ballet the avant-garde Nederlands Danstheater and the classic Dutch National Ballet have worldwide reputation. Traditional and modern music come out into the open-air during the summer months in the many parks and squares. Most movies are shown in the original language with Dutch subtitles.

Annual events and festivals. *March:* Arts Week in Amsterdam offering opera, ballet, theater (including English-speaking companies). *Late March–mid-May:* Keukenhof National Flower Show at Lisse. *June:* Festival of Holland with concerts, opera, ballet in Amsterdam, The Hague, Scheveningen, Rotterdam. *June–September:* Cheese market on Fridays at Alkmaar. *July–August:* Kinderdijk windmill days. *September:* Aalsmeer-Amsterdam flower procession. *October:* Delft Antique Fair.

Taxes, service charges and tipping. Sales tax (in Dutch abbreviated BTW) and service charges are usually included in the hotel and restaurant bill. It's customary to round off taxi fares and leave a few coins for the waiter in restaurants. Other tipping recommendations: hotel porters *f* 2 per bag, hatcheck and theater usher *f* 1. Hairdressers and barbers are not tipped.

Sports and recreation. If it has anything to do with water, you can probably do it in Holland. Water sports of all sorts are popular. Indeed, the demand for boats and yachts is so great in high summer that it's practically impossible to rent a vessel at short notice.

It's rarely cold enough in winter for the canals to freeze over, but you can skate on indoor or outdoor rinks or watch a big race. The Dutch are high among the world-champion speed skaters.

Cycling is a favorite sport and a great way of seeing some of the countryside. Watch a game of soccer and see one of Europe's top teams in action.

TV and radio. Radio and TV programming is in Dutch, but BBC domestic broadcasts from England can also be picked up. All English-language movies are shown on Dutch television in the original version with subtitles. Amsterdam has cable television, which enables programs to be seen from neighboring countries.

What to buy. If you've saved a little money for a diamond, Amsterdam is the place to buy it. Notices all over town invite you to come and look around exhibitions and diamond workshops. Silver is also quality-controlled in Holland and pewter has a long tradition. Antiques, Delft pottery or Makkum pottery, more delicate in color and design, are excellent purchases. The world-famous cigars and Dutch gin, flowers and plants make good presents but check on import regulations for returning home. Or you might buy a pair of Dutch clogs, a typical souvenir from the land of wooden shoes.

Most shops are open from 9 a.m. to 5:30 or 6 p.m., Monday through Saturday (though many don't open on Mondays until 1 p.m.).

Sightseeing

Amsterdam. City set around four main canals* : Singel with Amsterdam's narrowest house; Herengracht, good address in golden age, number 502 official residence of burgomaster (lord mayor of Amsterdam); Keizersgracht, number 123, house of the six heads; Prinsengracht, 17th-century warehouses, now transformed into apartments. Leidseplein, busy square, with Stadsschouwburg, the municipal theater. American Hotel with Jugenstil restaurant (Mata Hari's wedding reception, 1894). Vondel Park, 120 acres (48 ha.) of lawns, lakes and flowers. Palace-like Rijksmuseum* at Museumplein, housing priceless art collection including Rembrandt's *Night Watch*. Anachronistic Vincent van Gogh Museum* and Stedelijk (Municipal) Museum with modern art. Colorful 200-yard-long floating flower market along Singel canal, overlooked by musical Mint Tower *(Munttoren)*. Peaceful Beguine court *(Begijnhof)** on Spui, quadrangle bordered by perfect 17th- and 18th-century almshouses, two small churches and 15th-century wood house. Newly restored Amsterdam Historical Museum covering the city's history from 1275 to 1945. Bustling Dam Square dominated by Royal Palace *(Koninklijk Paleis)* and late-Gothic New Church *(Nieuwe Kerk)* with miniature steeple. West Church *(Westerkerk)* boasting Amsterdam's tallest tower and multicolored shining replica of Maximilian I's crown and orb on top; incomparable view of the city from the tower. Anne Frank House, where the young Jewish girl wrote her now famous diary hiding for two years from the occupying power. Jordaan area between west bank of the Prinsengracht and the Lijnbaansgracht, sought after area for artists, boutiques and restaurants, bohemian atmosphere. Round Lutheran Church with high copper dome, now banqueting hall and conference center. Central Station on Damrak boulevard, built on three artificial islands and 8,687 wooden piles. Controversial building of the Stock Exchange *(Beurs)* with ultra-modern design of 1903. Old Church *(Oude Kerk)* consecrated around 1300, squeezed between student hostels and sex shops on edge of red-light district. Museum Amstelkring, one of Amsterdam's 60 once-clandestine Catholic churches, still in original condition. Netherlands' Maritime Museum with panoramic view of harbor. Montelbaanstoren—city's best-proportioned tower. Weigh House now Jewish historical museum. South Church *(Zuiderkerk)* admired by Wren and Rembrandt. Rembrandt's House *(Rembrandthuis)* at Jodenbreestraat, where Holland's greatest painter lived for 20 years. Portuguese synagogue said to be patterned on

347

plan of King Solomon's temple. Moses and Aaron Church, liveliest in Amsterdam. Blue Bridge *(Blauwbrug)* for fine river view and skinny bridge *(Magere Brug)*, single-file traffic only.

North Holland Province. Broek in Waterland, peaceful village, narrow streets and wooden houses. Marken, Calvinist village, former island, now linked by causeway, severe local costume and strict adherence to Sunday restrictions. Volendam tourist-conscious village with picturesque harbor. Edam, the famous village of cheese, remarkably unspoiled with 17th-century village center and large cobbled bridge connecting two main streets, informal museum at captain's house. Hoorn, point of departure for several early explorers. Enkhuizen, thriving small port with 16th-century watchtower—good view of IJsselmeer⋆. Alkmaar, weekly Friday cheese market in summer. Zaanse Schans, picturesque windmill village. Makkum, home of potteries. Haarlem with massive 15th-century St. Bavo's Church and one of Europe's finest organs, Renaissance meat market *(Vleeshal)*, Frans Hals Museum. South towards Lisse, acres of tulips. Keukenhof⋆, a showpiece flower garden for two months from end of March. Hilversum, garden suburb of Amsterdam, headquarters of Dutch TV and radio services.

The Hague, officially 's-Gravenhage, but known as Den Haag. Holland's diplomatic city, seat of government, home of international court. Inner and Outer Courts *(Binnenhof⋆* and *Buitenhof)* with courtyards and palaces, some walls dating back to 13th century. Magnificent Gothic Knights' Hall *(Ridderzaal)* in Binnenhof. Mauritshuis⋆ with excellent art collection. Lange Voorhout, elegant tree-lined avenue with stately 16th- and 17th-century houses. Seaside scenes of Scheveningen at Panorama Mesdag. Peace Palace *(Vredespalais)*, seat of the International Court of Justice. Municipal Museum with Mondriaan collection. Miniature city of Madurodam, featuring some 150 of Holland's most famous buildings.

Famous seaside resort of Scheveningen, with its spa hotel and casino.

Rotterdam. Largest port⋆ in the world, totally re-built after Second World War except for Town Hall, central post office, stock exchange and statue of Erasmus on Coolsingel. View of city from Euromast (600 feet/180 m.). Boymans-Van Beuningen Museum⋆ displaying old masters as well as modern collections. Imposing De Doelen complex with theater, concert hall and congress center. Lijnbaan, traffic-free shopping zone. Wholesale building, tunnel under Maas. Blijdorp Zoo, where animals are allowed maximum freedom. Delfshaven, from where the Pilgrim Fathers sailed in 1630; restored Pilgrim Fathers' Church, Sack Carriers' House, Crane House.

South Holland Province. Schiedam, formerly the greatest gin-producing city in Europe; fine collection of miniature bottles at Melchers Company. Vlaardingen, important cod and herring fishing center, boat sails on top of church tower. Delft★, home of picturesque blue and white pottery of the same name; charming market place and medieval houses, Baroque Town Hall *(Raadhuis)*, and 14th-century New Church *(Nieuwekerk)*, burial place of William the Silent, founder of the Netherlands; Oude Delft canal, Old Church with beautiful tower and leaning spire, and Prinsenhof; collection of old Delft tiles and pottery in Huis Lambert van Meerten Museum. Leiden★, Rembrandt's birthplace, and leading Dutch university town; Lakenhal, former guildhall of cloth merchants, with exhibition of early weaving techniques; splendid Renaissance façade on Town Hall, unusual covered Cornmarket bridge, Windmill Museum; Burcht, 12th-century artificial fortified hillock, fine almshouses, 14th-century St. Pancras' Church. Katwijk aan Zee, popular seaside resort with Roman lighthouse. Alphen aan de Rijn with Avifauna International Bird Park and 400 different species. Boskoop, Waddinxseen, plants, shrubs and trees in different shapes. Gouda, weekly cheese market, clay-pipe factory, St. John's Church *(Sint Janskerk)* with magnificent stained-glass windows. Oudewater, rope-making village famous for providing certificates that the bearer is not a witch; bells of 15th-century Town Hall cast from ships' cannons. Dordrecht featuring Great Church with gleaming white interior and organs with 10-second echo.

Utrecht Province. Utrecht, fourth largest Dutch city with twice yearly industrial fairs. Recently reconstructed wharves and cellars along main canals. Dom★, oldest Gothic church in Holland with superb view from tower; lovely Bruntenhof almshouses for old ladies and Bartholomew Guesthouse for old men, Gobelin tapestries.

Gelderland Province. Dutch Rhine area. Arnhem, best-known for battlefields and parks; 75-acre (44-ha.) Netherlands open-air museum★. Castle Rosemdael, headquarters of International Castles Institute. Hoge Veluwe National Park with St. Hubert's hunting lodge and Kröller-Müller Museum★ displaying van Gogh collection. Zuidelijk Veluwezoom National Park and magnificent views from Posbank and Zijpenborg. Nijmegen, former residence of Charlemagne at Falcon's Court *(Valkhof)*, remaining 16-sided chapel. Groesbeek, beautiful spot with re-creation of life of Jesus in park. Tiel, heart of orchard land

349

(cherries, apples, pears). Zaltbommel, where Faust claimed to have signed contract with the devil.

Overijssel Province. Widely varying scenery, off the tourist route. Deventer, with municipal museum collection of costumes and furniture, large library of 16th-century books. Flevehof, 350-acre (150-ha.) farm with demonstrations and exhibitions relating to farming. Giethoorn★, village with no streets, only canals. New towns springing up on reclaimed land in West Overijssel, new pattern of building with straight roads and canals.

Zeeland Province. String of islands rapidly becoming a tourist attraction for water sports. Delta Expo★ explaining massive Delta Project to protect land by series of barriers after 1953 flooding. Walcheren, popular for its beaches and woodland. Middelburg, Cooper's Gatehouse, Blue Gateway, Cow Gate, fish market, Town Hall. Veere, Napoleon's

stronghold for the sick and wounded in 1811. Flushing (Vlissingen), the only large Dutch port directly on sea. Goes, underwater sports, nearby castle and hunting seat of tragic Jacobin of Holland. Zierikzee, one of Holland's best-preserved towns, incomplete cathedral tower; Town Hall with wooden steeple and statue of Neptune.

North Brabant Province. A landscape of windmills along River Dommel. 's-Hertogenbosch, birthplace of Hieronymus Bosch, with late-Gothic cathedral *(St.-Janskathedraal)*. Tilburg, woolen mills. Oisterwijk, nature reserves, bird sanctuary, monkey park. Baarle-Nassau-Baarle-Hertog, city on Dutch-Belgian border, split personality. Overloon, with largest war museum in the Netherlands.

Limburg Province. Region strongly influenced by Latin strain, Appian Way passed through Maastricht and Heerlen. Tegelen, passion play acted by local people. Maastricht, mixture of German, Dutch and Belgian customs and currency; impressive Church of St. Servaas *(St.-Servaaskerk)*★; Stokstraat, pleasant pedestrian street of beautiful 17th- and 18th-century houses; annual carnival. Tunneled hill of St.-Pietersberg. Valkenburg, known as the Dutch alps, grotto of Valkenburg with chapel, Roman galleries, sculpture and murals.

Drenthe Province. More than 200 miles of cycle paths, green fields, lakes and picturesque villages; peaceful province with few large towns. Assen, provincial capital, motorcycle grand prix. Region of large boulders *(hunebedden)* found in groups, relics left by prehistoric dwellers at Borger, Rolde, Anlo, Emmen, Sleen, Vries and Havelte.

Groningen Province. Groningen, architecturally distinguished city with many museums and St. Martin's Church noted for its tower. Leek, national carriage museum. Uithuizen, delightfully restored 15th-century castle.

Friesland Province. Inhabitants keeping to themselves, speaking a separate language. Dairy province of Holland with famous black and white cattle. Harlingen, large sea port with ferries to Vlieland and Terschelling. Franeker, small town with 18th-century planetarium and Renaissance Town Hall. Leeuwarden, capital of Friesland, with Fries Museum. Wieuwerd, mummies in crypt of church. Bolsward, home of national dairy school. Bakkeveen, Een, defense works of 1593 used by Peter Stuyvesant as examples for construction of New Amsterdam (New York).

351

Some useful expressions in Dutch

good morning/afternoon	Goedemorgen/goedemiddag
good evening/night	Goedenavond/goedenacht
good-bye	Dag
yes/no	ja/nee
please/thank you	alstublieft/dank u
excuse me	pardon
you're welcome	tot uw dienst
where/when/how	waar/wanneer/hoe
how long/how far	hoelang/hoever
yesterday/today/tomorrow	gisteren/vandaag/morgen
day/week/month/year	dag/week/maand/jaar
left/right	links/rechts
up/down	boven/beneden
good/bad	goed/slecht
big/small	groot/klein
cheap/expensive	goedkoop/duur
hot/cold	warm/koud
old/new	oud/niew
open/closed	open/dicht
free (vacant)/occupied	vrij/bezet
early/late	vroeg/laat
easy/difficult	gemakkelijk/moeilijk
Does anyone here speak English/French/German?	Spreekt er hier iemand Engels/Frans/Duits?
What does this mean?	Wat betekent dit?
I don't understand.	Ik begrijp het niet.
Please write it down.	Wilt u het opschrijven, alstublieft.
Do you take credit cards/ traveler's checks	Accepteert u credit cards/ reischeques?
Waiter!/Waitress!	Ober!/Juffrouw!
Where are the toilets?	Waar zijn de toiletten?
I'd like…	Ik wil graag…
How much is that?	Hoeveel kost het?
What time is it?	Hoe laat is het?
Help me please.	Help mij, alstublieft.
Just a minute.	Een ogenblik, alstublieft.

NORWAY

At the top of Scandinavia, romantic fjords
and glaciers glisten in the midnight sun.

In a world that seems to be bursting at the seams, Norway offers endless elbowroom in an inspiring setting. Take a deep breath of old-fashioned, pure air and appreciate the difference.

The Norsemen, who used to pillage and plant their outposts in Scotland, Ireland, Iceland, Greenland and beyond, eventually settled down to fish and farm at home and, latterly, get rich on offshore oil. The tall, blond descendants of the Vikings are still intrepid. They may have given up exploring, but they do risk life and limb on the ski jump.

At the top of Europe, Norway is more than a thousand miles long, yet as narrow as four miles across in a pinch. The coastline, honeycombed with inlets, coves and fjords, measures perhaps 13,000 miles. About half the country stretches north of the Arctic Circle into the land of the midnight sun, where summer brings a couple of months of continuous daylight. The fishing port of Hammerfest claims to be the world's northernmost town—latitude 70°39'48".

Most of the towns are close to the sea and, like the robust Norwegians who live in them, unsophisticated and unostentatious. Oslo, a capital of less than half a million inhabitants, is one of the world's largest cities—in area. On Oslo's own fjord are enshrined three Viking ships, miraculously preserved for more than a thousand years, as well as the flagship of the explorers Nansen and Amundsen, and the Kon-Tiki raft of Thor Heyerdahl.

The only other sizable towns, Bergen and Trondheim, have more than their quota of historic charm. Although Norwegian nightlife suffers from provinciality and an early-to-rise tradition, the food warmly celebrates the great outdoors: elk, reindeer, ptarmigan, salmon and shrimps... if you don't overdo the bountiful breakfast buffet.

Most travelers come to Norway to see its romantic fjords, which penetrate up to a hundred miles inland. Luxury liners come from afar to glide between the sheer cliff walls; or you can simply join the locals on the deck of a fjord ferry.

354

Facts and figures

Population:	4 million
Area:	125,000 sq. miles (324,000 sq. km.)
Capital:	Oslo (450,000/GUA 695,000)
Other cities:	Bergen (205,000) Trondheim (135,000) Stavanger (95,000) Kristiansand (60,000) Drammen (50,000)
Language:	Norwegian
Religion:	Protestant (94%)
Time zone:	GMT + 1, EST + 6; DST (Apr.–Sep.)
Currency:	Norwegian *krone* (abbr. *kr.*) = 100 *øre* Coins: 10, 50 øre; kr. 1, 5, 10 Bills: kr. 50, 100, 500, 1,000
Electricity:	220 volt, 50 cycle, AC

Planning your trip

Visa requirements. See pp. 29–30.

Vaccination requirements. None (see also p. 25).

Currency restrictions. There is no restriction on the amount of currency you can import. On leaving the country, you may take out 5,000 kroner and foreign currency up to the amount imported.

Climate. Considering its latitude, most of Norway enjoys a mild climate, thanks to prevailing southwest winds and the moderating influence of the Gulf Stream. While some rain falls in spring and fall, most precipitation in Oslo is from winter snowfalls. Bergen is noted as a rainy city.

HOLMENKOLLEN, SKIMUSEET, TRYVANNSTÅRNET

NRK

gate/gata	= street
kai/kaia	= quay
kirke/kirken	= church
plass/plassen	= square
torg (torv)/torget	= market place
vei/veien	= road
museum/museet	= museum

T = tunnelbanestasjon
= Subway station

Vigelands-
anlegget

Frogner-
parken

Vigeland-
museet

Sørkedalsveien

Slemdalsveien

Suhms

Analveien

Gydas vei

Gardeveien

H. Hårfagres gate

Kirkeveien

Jacob Aalls gate

Sorgenfrigata

Schultz gate

Industrigata

Vibes gate

Bogstadveien

Major-
stua

Essendrops
gate

Middelthuns

Amaldus
Nielsens
plass Professor

Dahls gate

Eilert Sundts gate

Holtegata

Briskebyveien

Oscars gate

Camilla Colletts vei

Slotts-
parken

Kirkeveien

Jonsrudveien

Askeveien

Thunes vei

Madserud allé

Halvdan Svartes gate

Kristinelundvn

Drammensveien

Bygdøy allé

Sjølystveien

Dronning Blancas vei

Nobels gate

Thomas Heftyes gate

Frognerveien

Nordraaks gate

Tidemands gate

Eckersbergs gate

Odins gate

Løvenskiolds gate

Gyldenløves gate

Niels Juels gate

Skovveien

Frognerveien

Bygdøy allé

Elisenbergveien

Sophus Lies gt.

Frederik Stangs gt.

Thomas Heftyes gate

Gabels gate

Niels Juels gate

Kruses gate

Thomas Thorsens gate

Colbjørn
sens gate

Slottet
Dronning-
parken

Drammensveien

Parkveien

Løkke
veien

Huitfelds
gate

B Y G D Ø Y

Frognerkilen

Museumsveien

Bygdøyveien

Dronninghavn-
veien

Mellbyedalen

Huk aveny

Norsk
Folkemuseum

Vikingskipshuset

Fredriksborgveien

Konsul
Schjelderups vei

P. Mallings vei

Admiral
Børresens vei

Bygdøynesveien

Langviksbukten

Kon-Tiki-
museet

Frammuseet

Norsk
Sjøfartsmuseum

Svoldergata

Munkedams-
veien

Filipstadveien

Munkedams-
veien

Drammensveien

Frognerstranda

Drammensveien

FORNEBU LUFTHAVN,
HENIE-ONSTAD KUNSTSENTER

O s l o f j

Kavringen

| 0 | 300 | 600 | 900 m |
| 0 | 300 | 600 | 900 yards |

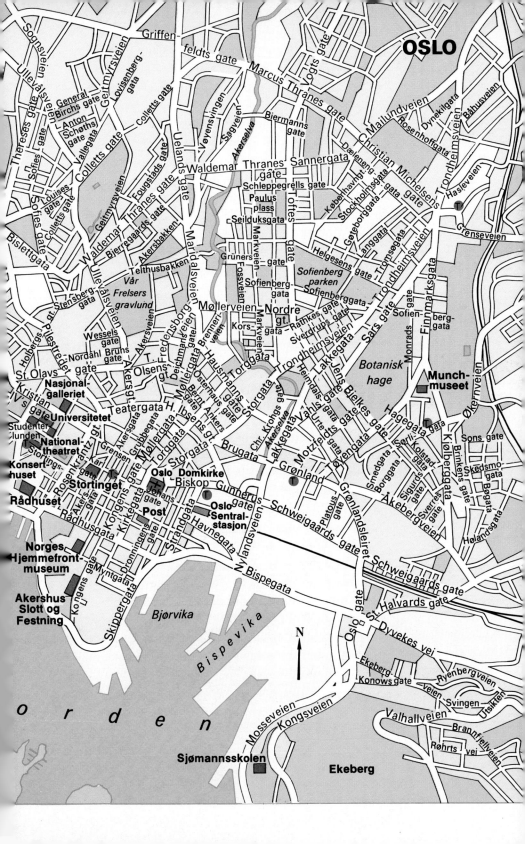

Some average daily temperatures:

Oslo		J	F	M	A	M	J	J	A	S	O	N	D
average daily maximum*	°F	28	30	39	50	61	68	72	70	60	48	38	32
	°C	-2	-1	4	10	16	20	22	21	16	9	3	0
average daily minimum*	°F	19	19	25	34	43	50	55	53	46	38	31	25
	°C	-7	-7	-4	1	6	10	13	12	8	3	-1	-4
Bergen													
average daily maximum*	°F	38	38	43	49	58	61	66	65	59	52	46	41
	°C	3	3	6	9	14	16	19	19	15	11	8	5
average daily minimum*	°F	31	30	33	37	44	49	54	54	49	43	38	34
	°C	-1	-1	0	3	7	10	12	12	10	6	3	1

* Minimum temperatures are measured just before sunrise, maximum temperatures in the afternoon.

Clothing. It's a good idea to dress in layers in summer, shedding or adding pieces according to the altitude and the weather. A raincoat can be useful, too. Remember that nights are cool in Norway, even in summer. You'll need heavy clothing in winter, and good, waterproof, non-slip footwear. Except for outings to concerts, better restaurants and nightclubs, Norwegians don't dress up.

Duty-free allowances

	Cigarettes		Cigars		Tobacco	Liquor	Wine
1)	400	or	500 g.	or	500 g.	1 l. and	1 l.
2)	200	or	250 g.	or	250 g.	1 l. and	1 l.

Perfume: 1) 50 g.; 2) small quantity
Toilet water: 1) ½ l.; 2) small quantity
Gifts: 1) up to kr. 3,500; 2) up to kr. 1,200

1) residents of countries outside Europe
2) residents of Europe

Hotels and accommodations

Hotels. Tourist office brochures list hotels and boardinghouses, with full details of their facilities and liquor licensing regulations. Some of these lists also give rates. Hotels always include service charges; usually breakfast as well.

Oslo and Bergen hotels are often fully booked, so it's advisable to make reservations in advance. However, if you arrive in Oslo without a reservation, try the Tourist Information Center at the City Hall (*Rådhuset*). In Bergen, the Tourist Information Office at Torgalmenningen can help you find a room, but it is open only during regular office hours.

Youth hostels. The majority of hostels (*vandrerhjem*) require a membership card. If you aren't a member of the youth hostel association, you can obtain a guest card from the Norwegian Youth Hostels Association. No age limit is imposed.

Camping. Campsites in Norway provide clean, comfortable, though spartan, accommodations amid beautiful scenery. They are classified by one, two or three stars according to amenities. Though most campers live in tents, cabins have become increasingly popular, and rates are reasonable. The season is normally from mid-May or early June till the end of August.

Norwegian tourist offices abroad

U.K.	Norwegian Tourist Board, Charles House, 5–11, Lower Regent Street, London SW1Y 4LR; tel. (071) 839 2650
U.S.A.	Scandinavian National Tourist Offices, 655 Third Avenue, 18th floor, New York, NY 10017; tel. (212) 949-2333

On the spot

Banks and currency exchange. Most of the year banks open from 8:15 a.m. to 3:30 p.m., Monday through Friday, (until 5 or 6 p.m. on Thursdays). Between June 1 and August 31 they close half an hour earlier.

Oslo Airport: 7 a.m.–10 p.m. daily, 7 a.m.–7 p.m. on Saturdays. Oslo Central Railway Station: 8 a.m.–7 p.m., Monday–Saturday, 12 noon–6 p.m. on Sundays. In summer 7 a.m.–11 p.m. daily.

359

Most large hotels will change foreign currency, but at less favorable rates.

Credit cards and traveler's checks. Major international credit cards are honored in most large hotels and restaurants and in many department stores and tourist shops. Traveler's checks are easy to cash almost everywhere provided you have proper identification.

Mail and telecommunications. Usual post-office hours are 8 a.m.–5:30 p.m. (till 4:30 p.m. in summer), Monday–Friday, and 9 a.m.–1 p.m. on Saturdays. Oslo's General Post Office, Dronningens gt. 15, opens from 8 a.m. to 8 p.m., Monday through Friday, until 3 p.m. on Saturdays. Stamps can also be bought at tobacco shops, newsstands and hotels. Mailboxes are painted red.

Direct-dialing facilities are available to more than 40 other countries from most towns in Norway. Telegrams can be sent from private telephones and from public phones.

Conveniently located in city centers, telegraph offices (*telegrafkontor*) handle long-distance telephone calls, telex messages and telegrams. See also p. 30.

Some useful telephone numbers:

Operator (international)	0115	Ambulance	
Information (domestic and		Oslo/Bergen	003
other Scandinavian)	0180	Fire	
Information		Oslo/Bergen	001
(international)	0181	Police	
Telegrams	0138	Oslo/Bergen	002

Newspapers. Principal dailies are *Aftenposten, Dagbladet, Verdens Gang* and *Bergens Tidende.* There is usually an excellent assortment of foreign-language newspapers and magazines at centrally located newsstands, as well as at large hotels, airports and railroad and bus stations. *What's on in Oslo,* a monthly pamphlet, and *Bergen This Week* are distributed free at hotels.

Tourist information. Tourist information offices throughout the country are identified by an "i".

Oslo   City Hall (enter from the harbor side); tel. (02) 42 71 70

Bergen   Torgalmenningen; tel. (05) 32 14 80

Legal holidays

Jan. 1	New Year's Day	**Movable dates:**
May 1	Labor Day	Maundy Thursday
May 17	Constitution Day	Good Friday
Dec. 25/26	Christmas	Easter Monday
		Ascension Day
		Whit Monday

Transportation

Air. Oslo is Norway's major gateway, though Bergen and Stavanger also handle some international flights. For getting around Norway—in view of the long distances involved and, in certain cases, difficult road conditions—tourists often prefer to fly. Of the country's 50 airfields, 20 are served by scheduled flights.

Major airports. Oslo: Fornebu Airport (5.5 miles/9 km. from city center). Duty-free shop. There is regular bus service from the airport to the city center from about 8 a.m. to 10 p.m. Gardermoen Airport (30 miles/50 km. from city center) handles mostly charter flights. Duty-free shop. Bus meets flights. **Bergen:** Flesland Airport (12 miles/20 km. from city center). Duty-free shop. Buses meet flights.

Rail. Trains of the Norwegian State Railways (NSB) run on schedule. Oslo Central Station is the main terminal. There is direct service to Sweden and to the continent via Copenhagen; the main domestic destinations are Stavanger, Bergen and Trondheim, with connections to Bodø. Some long-distance trains have cars especially equipped for parents traveling with babies and for people in wheelchairs. Seat reservations should be made, especially on express trains, such as the Oslo–Bergen run *(Bergensbanen)*. Ask at any travel agency or railroad station about special group, family and weekday (Monday–Friday) excursion tickets. The *Nordic Tourist Ticket* is good for 21 days of unlimited rail travel in Norway, Denmark, Finland and Sweden. For *Eurailpass,* see p. 33.

Boats, waterways. Comfortable steamers link coastal towns from Bergen to the far north. Traveling by road in western Norway involves numerous fjord crossings by ferryboat—there's usually no other way to go. The frequency of ferry services depends on the season. In rural areas, local hotels will always be able to tell you exact ferry times, or consult the schedule published by the Norway Travel Association, available at most tourist offices. At the height of the summer tourist season, try to reserve a place for your car in advance or you may find yourself spending hours in line before getting on. Fares vary according to size and weight of the vehicle.

Local public transportation. Depending on the town, a traveler has the choice of getting around by bus, streetcar, elevated train, ferry, and, in Oslo, subway. Bus and streetcar fares are paid on board either to the driver or a conductor.

The *Oslo Card (Oslo-kortet)* offers visitors unlimited access to museums, sights and public transportation, as well as reductions on car rental, sightseeing tours and hotel rates. Similar in appearance to a credit card, the pass is valid for one, two or three days. Hotels, stores and the Tourist Office sell them.

Taxis. The best place to find a taxi is at one of the many taxi stands around town, or you can phone for a cab. Hailing a taxi is permitted, but drivers are not allowed to pick up passengers within 100 meters (110 yards) of a taxi stand. There's a 15 percent surcharge after 8 p.m.

Car rental. International and local companies have offices in all the major towns. Agencies are listed in the classified telephone directory under "Bilutleie". Chauffeur-driven cars are also available. See also pp. 30–31.

Driving in Norway. The use of seat belts is obligatory, and that includes back-seat passengers if the car is so equipped. A red reflector warning triangle must be carried for use in case of accident or breakdown. Dipped (low-beam) headlights must be *switched on,* even in broad daylight. Gasoline available is normal (93 octane), lead-free (91 octane), super (98 octane) and diesel.

Drive on the right, pass on the left. Traffic entering from the right has priority unless otherwise indicated. Roads are generally good though narrow outside urban centers. Many secondary roads are unsurfaced. In winter, certain mountain roads can be dangerous, and some are closed. Toll-free expressways make up part of the highway system between Hamar–Oslo–Moss–Gothenburg (Sweden) and Oslo–Drammen. Speed limits are 19–31 mph (30–50 kph) in town, 50 mph (80 kph) on major roads and 56 mph (90 kph) on expressways. Fines for drinking and driving are prohibitive. Police checks are frequent in the evening and at night and, if the slightest suspicion of drink is involved, a breath test is immediately given: with more than 50 mg./100 ml. alcohol in the blood, a driver faces a stiff fine, suspension of driving privileges for at least six months, and possible imprisonment for 21 days. Don't count on

362

any indulgence for foreigners, there won't be any. The same goes for speeding. In case of breakdown, call (02) 42 94 00 in Oslo (NAF Alarm Center, open day and night) for further instructions.

Some distances: Oslo–Bergen 300 miles (495 km.), Trondheim 340 miles (545 km.), Stavanger 365 miles (585 km.).

Bicycle rental. Considering its terrain, Norway is not an ideal country for a bicycle vacation. However, the intrepid cyclist will get the opportunity to admire some truly marvelous scenery. Bikes can be rented at major campsites and some countryside hotels and local tourist offices.

Rest rooms. Public rest rooms are located at railroad stations, in department stores and in some squares and parks. They're generally designated by symbols, but may also be marked *Toaletter, WC, Damer/Herrer* or *D/H* (for women/men).

Emergencies (Oslo and Bergen)

Ambulance   003
Fire   001
Police   002

Police. Policemen wear black uniforms. They patrol on foot, on motorcycles or in white cars marked "Politi". The police are very helpful and courteous in the normal course of events, but they're absolutely inflexible when it comes to driving offenses.

Crime and theft. Both Oslo and Bergen, as cities elsewhere, have seen an increase in crime. Cars—and replacement parts—are astronomically expensive, so they are the most likely objects of theft. Make sure valuables are locked up.

Medical care and health. Medical services in Norway are excellent though expensive. English is spoken by most doctors and many nurses. Most medicine is available only with a doctor's prescription. The addresses of pharmacies *(apotek)* open after hours are listed in newspapers and posted in the windows of all other pharmacies. For insurance, see pp. 25–26.

Tap water is more than drinkable—it even tastes good.

Embassies and consulates. Embassies are listed in the business section of telephone directories under "Ambassader og legasjoner"; consulates under "Konsulater".

Social customs. Norwegians do not make a fuss of visitors, nor are they likely to open a conversation with a stranger; he will normally have to make the first move. But if he does, he will soon feel the warmth of the welcome wherever he goes.

It is common to shake hands upon meeting, even if introductions have already been made. Social conventions are generally informal, and titles, apart from Mr., Mrs. and Miss (followed by the surname), are never used. Christian names are very quickly adopted among the post-war generation. If invited home, a small gift of flowers or chocolates for the hostess is appreciated. At more informal meetings a bottle of wine provides a popular gift. The ritual—and, among Norwegians, essential—"takk for maten" (thank you for the food), addressed to the hostess at the end of a meal, expresses your appreciation of everything, including her invitation. In an informal setting it's perfectly acceptable (for women, too) to roll one's own cigarettes.

Enjoying Norway

Food and drink. Some of the best food in Norway comes fresh from the sea, which is only natural in one of the world's leading fishing nations. You can dine on lobster or salmon or pick up a picnic lunch of shrimp and herring.

Breakfast is usually served between 8 and 10 a.m., lunch between 11 a.m. and 1 p.m., but sandwiches and snacks are available in a variety of eating places from mid-morning. Dinner at hotels and big restaurants may start about 7 p.m., much earlier in smaller establishments.

Smørbrød means bread and butter, which is quite an understatement when you consider Scandinavia's reputation for elaborate open sandwiches. Almost anything may turn up on one of these appetizing *smørbrød:* roast beef, ham, shrimp, fried cod roe with bacon, hamburger steak with fried onions, mayonnaise and herring salads, and so on. Cheese is also eaten on open sandwiches. Try one of the brown cheeses made of goat's milk *(geitost).*

Another Scandinavian specialty is the luncheon or supper buffet. The Swedish name, *smörgåsbord,* is better known than its Norwegian equivalent, *koldtbord* (literally, cold table). Some restaurants and mountain hotels specialize in this bountiful self-service banquet.

The most "national" food of all is what Norwegians call *spekemat,* cured food: be sure to try cured ham *(spekeskinke),* sausage *(spekepølse),* leg of mutton *(fenalår)* and mutton sausage *(fårepølse),* which all have a long tradition in the country.

Among the tastiest, but most expensive fish are salmon *(laks)*, trout *(ørret)* and sea trout *(sjøørret)*. Boiled cod, often served with its liver *(kokt torsk med lever)*, is a great delicacy, as is halibut *(hellefisk)*. Whale steak *(hvalbiff)*, is tender and steak-like, with no hint of the sea in its flavor. An exquisite treat as a starter is *gravlaks,* cured salmon.

Among the meat dishes, *fårikål,* a stew of lamb or mutton and cabbage, is a national tradition. Meat balls *(kjøttkaker)* are as popular as they are filling. And *lapskaus* is a tasty stew of chopped meat, potatoes, onion and other vegetables. Game and fowl are important variations on the menu, as mundane as roast chicken, as unfamiliar as woodcock *(rugde),* elk *(elg),* ptarmigan *(rype)* and roast reindeer *(reinsdyrstek),* thinly sliced.

Desserts usually turn out to be cakes or whipped cream confections. Typical examples include *tilslørte bondepiker,* literally, "veiled farmgirls"—layers of stewed apples, cookie crumbs, sugar and whipped cream, and *bløtkake,* "soft cake"—a sponge cake filled with fruit and whipped cream. Norwegians go berserk over berries. The supreme delicacy in this realm is *multer med krem,* arctic cloudberries with cream.

Norwegians often drink plain tap water with their meals. Alcoholic beverages of any sort are subject to stringent regulations. Liquor is served at most major hotels and restaurants, but only from 3 to 11 p.m. or midnight and never on Sunday or holy days; the prices are discouraging, too. Beer and wine are more widely available, Sundays included. Local beers meet international standards. *Pils* is the generic term for lager, *export* is stronger. *Akevitt,* aquavit, the local firewater, is derived from potatoes or barley. Served ice-cold in tiny glasses with meals, it is usually washed down with beer.

Entertainment. For a city of its size, Oslo provides a varied nightlife, with nightclubs, discos, bars and pubs of all sorts. Outside the capital, possibilities are few. Rich cultural opportunities exist in both Oslo and Bergen, including ballet, theater, concerts (many outdoors in summer) and opera (in Oslo only). In June and July, English-language plays are also staged in Oslo. The latest foreign movies are shown, always in their original language with Norwegian subtitles.

Annual events and festivals. Check with the local tourist offices so you don't miss out on any special celebrations. Norway's main events are: *March:* Holmenkollen ski-jumping championship (Oslo), *May 17:* Constitution Day, with parades in all the towns, *May–June:* Bergen International Festival (two weeks), *June 23:* Midsummer Eve, with bonfires and folklore everywhere, *July 29:* St. Olav Festival or Olsok at

365

Stiklestad, *August:* Molde Jazz Festival and Stavanger Sea Fishing Competition.

Taxes, service charges and tipping. Sales tax and service charges are included in hotel and restaurant bills. Tipping recommendations: hotel porters kr. 5 per bag; waiters, no tip expected; taxi drivers, round off the sum (unless extra service is rendered, then 10%); hatcheck, charge posted.

Sports and recreation. Visitors can go hiking, skiing, swimming, sailing, fishing, riding or camping according to the season. Soccer matches and regattas are popular with spectators in summer, and in winter, ski jumping, cross-country skiing, speed skating, ice hockey, bandy (a game similar to hockey) and curling draw crowds.

TV and radio. Virtually all programming is in Norwegian, but TV movies and imported shows are in the original language.

What to buy. Norway's cost of living rules out any bargain shopping. Visitors can, however, avoid paying the sales tax (see p. 40).

Here are some items to look for: hand-knitted or machine-made sweaters in typical Norwegian patterns, painted wooden figurines, miniature Viking ships, pewter mugs, reindeer skins, sealskin slippers, sporting goods, hunting knives, woven goods.

Shopping hours vary enormously. In Oslo, shops normally open from 9 or 10 a.m. to 5 or 7 p.m., Monday through Friday, until 1, 2 or 4 p.m. on Saturdays; closed on Sundays and legal holidays. Centrally situated kiosks selling newspapers, tobacco, fruit, sweets, and so on, may stay open till 11 p.m.

Sightseeing

Oslo. Akershus Castle and Fortress (founded 1300) with dungeons, secret passages, royal halls and museums. Red-brick Town Hall *(Rådhuset)*, decorated with modern narrative murals. Karl Johan's Street, the city's main thoroughfare, running from the Central Station to the Royal Palace, lined with stores, cafés and public gardens. Vigeland Sculpture Park*, one sculptor's view of human life. National Gallery, displaying a cross-section of European art. Munch Museum*, containing the life work of Edvard Munch, Norway's greatest painter (1863–1944). Bygdøy peninsula with five outstanding museums: Viking Ship Museum*, enshrining three authentic Viking ships; Norwegian Folk Museum* with more than 150 old buildings moved here from various parts of the country; Kon-Tiki Museum, commemorating the voyages of the daring Norwegian ethnographer Thor Heyerdahl; Fram Museum, built around the veteran polar exploration ship of Fridtjov Nansen and Roald Amundsen; Maritime Museum *(Norsk Sjøfartsmuseum)*. Magnificent panorama of fjord from Holmenkollen Ski Jump.

The South Coast. The Norwegian "Riviera", a series of charming seafaring towns, beaches and coves dotted with holiday cottages—a favorite vacation region. Among the towns: Tønsberg, at the mouth of the Oslo Fjord, Norway's oldest municipality (A.D. 871); ruins of a Viking castle. Sandefjord, home of the Norwegian whaling fleet. Grimstad, picturesque houses and a pretty archipelago. Kristiansand, important gateway town; 11th-century church and 17th-century fortress. Stavanger, fish-canning capital and oil city, a base for North Sea oil-drilling operations; late 11th-century Anglo-Norman cathedral.

The Bergen Railway (Oslo–Bergen). 292 miles (470 km.), 200 tunnels, 17 miles (28 km.) of snowsheds; dramatic scenery with wild forests, primitive lakes, snow-covered mountain peaks; winter-sports resorts, like Geilo.

Bergen*. Bergenhus Fortress, containing the step-gabled 700-year-old Håkon's Hall. St. Mary's Church, built in the 12th century and decorated with medieval works of art. The Wharf *(Bryggen)*, domain of the Hanseatic merchants from the 14th century till the Reformation. The Hanseatic Museum, a collection of ship models from Viking times to the supertanker era. Old Bergen, an outdoor museum of 18th- and 19th-century houses. Grieg Hall, Bergen's glamorous concert hall, site of the annual international festival of music, ballet and drama. 12th-century

Fantoft Stave Church, typical Norwegian timber church. Troldhaugen, home of composer Edvard Grieg (1843–1907). Fløybanen, a funicular from the center of town to Mount Fløyen with panoramic view.

The Western Fjords★. Hardanger Fjord east of Bergen, 100 miles (160 km.) long; forested hillsides and orchards. Sogne Fjord, Norway's longest fjord (110 miles/176 km.), a striking world of glaciers, waterfalls, cliff-faces striped like layer cake, coves and narrow inlets; Borgund stavkirke★ near Lærdal, Norway's best preserved medieval wooden church. Nordfjord, craggy hills, pretty meadows, turquoise waters. Geiranger Fjord★, the paragon of fjords—white-dusted mountains, green terraces, frothing white waterfalls, and the town of Ålesund, the country's biggest fishing port. Romsdal's Fjord, with the view of 87 mountain peaks covered in snow, and cheerful Molde, the "Town of Roses".

The Oslo–Trondheim Route. A medieval pilgrims' route connecting the capital to Nidaros Cathedral in Trondheim. North of Oslo, along Mjøsa, Norway's biggest lake with the world's oldest paddle steamer (built 1856) still in operation. Lillehammer, a resort town with an important and interesting open-air museum. Further north through the mighty valley of Gudbrandsdalen, the Dovre mountains, the fairy-tale home of trolls, and of Henrik Ibsen's troll giant, Dovregubben (The Mountain King). Also along this route, a view of many of the country's highest mountains.

Trondheim. Norway's medieval ecclesiastical and cultural center, with Gothic Nidaros Cathedral★ (12th–13th centuries). Stiftsgården, the royal residence, a Rococo mansion, one of the largest wooden buildings in Europe. Ringve Manor, housing a fascinating museum of musical history.

Northern Norway. Bodø, a busy town totally reconstructed after World War II bombing; famous modern cathedral; excursions to nearby Lofoten archipelago★, inhabited by fishermen and millions of sea birds. Harstad, an important fishing and military town on an island, known for its 13th-century fortress church. Tromsø, home of the world's northernmost university; Tromsø Museum specializing in arctic phenomena and Lapp folklore. Hammerfest, Norway's northernmost town, a fishing and fish-processing center. North Cape★, an imposing cliff 1,007 feet (307 m.) above the sea. Kirkenes, a busy iron-mining port on the Soviet border.

Some useful expressions in Norwegian

good morning/afternoon	god morgen/dag
good evening/night	god kveld/natt
good-bye	adjø
yes/no	ja/nei
please/thank you	vennligst/takk
excuse me	unnskyld
you're welcome	ingen årsak
where/when/how	hvor/når/hvordan
how long/how far	hvor lenge/hvor langt
yesterday/today/tomorrow	i går/i dag/i morgen
day/week/month/year	dag/uke/måned/år
left/right	venstre/høyre
up/down	opp/ned
good/bad	god/dårlig
big/small	stor/liten
cheap/expensive	billig/dyr
hot/cold	varm/kald
old/new	gammel/ny
open/closed	åpen/lukket
free (vacant)/occupied	ledig/opptatt
early/late	tidlig/sent
easy/difficult	lett/vanskelig
Does anyone here speak English/French/German?	Er det noen her som snakker engelsk/fransk/tysk?
What does this mean?	Hva betyr dette?
I don't understand.	Jeg forstår ikke.
Please write it down.	Vennligst skriv det ned.
Do you take credit cards/traveler's checks?	Tar De imot kredittkort/reisesjekker?
Waiter!/Waitress!	Kelner!/Frøken!
Where are the toilets?	Hvor er toalettet?
I'd like...	Jeg vil gjerne ha...
How much is that?	Hvor mye koster det?
What time is it?	Hvor mange er klokken?
Help me please.	Hjelp meg, er De snill.
Just a minute.	Et øyeblikk.

POLAND

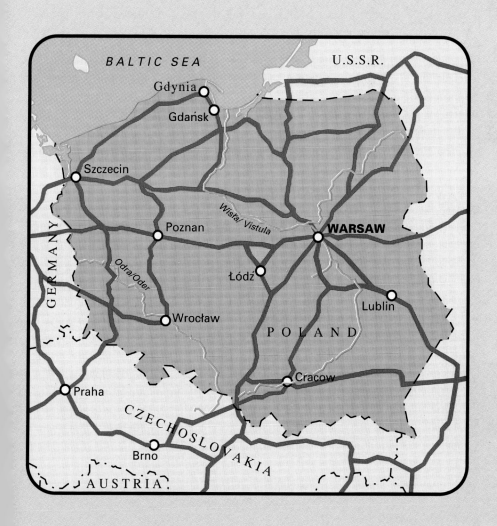

Often invaded but never vanquished, the Poles rebuilt from the rubble, preserving a great cultural heritage.

The Poles—nearly all 38 million of them—go to church more than almost any other Europeans. Even under communist rule, the country was notable for the fervor of its Catholicism. When a Pole became Pope in 1978, it was the first time since the 16th century that a non-Italian got the job. And John Paul II is easier to pronounce than Cardinal Wojtyla of Cracow.

The Cathedral of Cracow, one of the country's treasured landmarks, escaped destruction in World War II, as did the nearby Castle and central Europe's second-oldest university. In Warsaw, though, almost no historical building was spared, so the people gamely rebuilt the Old Town from the rubble. Memories of the war are never far away in Poland, where six million people were wiped out during the German occupation.

Poland is about the size of Italy or New Mexico, and nearly all of it is as flat as the northern European plain. A happy exception is the unspoiled Polish part of the Carpathians, where there are national parks and ski resorts. There is plenty of snow in winter at all altitudes; the country is bitterly cold in winter, rarely more than cool in summer, when the Poles go sunbathing on the beaches of the Baltic.

Poland has given the world a wealth of cultural heroes: the Renaissance astronomer Copernicus; musicians like Chopin, Paderewski (a statesman, too) and Artur Rubenstein; three Nobel prizes in Literature (Sienkiewicz, Reymont and Milosz); and the film director Andrzej Wajda. Like Ireland, Poland has produced armies of emigrés over the years, so a hefty proportion of today's tourists come in search of their roots.

An unavoidable skyscraper dominates the center of Warsaw. The Palace of Culture, a Stalinesque "gift of the Soviet People", is reckoned to stand equidistant between Moscow and Brussels (1,122 kilometers either way, the signs say). Since the development of post-communist democracy in Poland, Brussels seems nearer.

Facts and figures

Population:	37 million
Area:	120,725 sq. miles (312,677 sq. km.)
Capital:	Warsaw (*Warszawa,* 1.6 million)
Other major cities:	Łódź (845,000)
	Cracow (*Kraków,* 725,000)
	Wrocław (625,000)
	Poznań (565,000)
	Gdańsk (460,000)
Language:	Polish
Religion:	Catholic (85%)
Time zone:	GMT + 1, EST + 6; DST (Apr.–Sep.)
Currency:	*Złoty* (abbr. *zł*) = 100 *groszy*.
	Coins: 1, 2, 5, 10, 20 zł.
	Bills: 10, 20, 50, 100, 200, 500, 1,000, 5,000, 10,000, 20,000, 50,000, 100,000, 200,000, 500,000 zł.
Electricity:	220 volt, 50 cycle, AC

Planning your trip

Visa requirements. See pp. 29–30.

Vaccination requirements. None (see also p. 25).

Currency restrictions. No złotys may be imported or exported. Import and export (up to the amount brought in) of foreign currencies is unlimited. A currency declaration form must be completed on arrival and presented again on departure. Western visitors who have not prepaid their stay in Poland are required to purchase (through Orbis, the national travel organization) currency-exchange vouchers for about $15 per day.

Climate. Poland's climate is continental, with warm summers and cold winters. Moderate rainfall is well distributed throughout the year.

Some average daily temperatures:

Warsaw		J	F	M	A	M	J	J	A	S	O	N	D
average daily maximum*	°F	32	32	42	53	67	73	75	73	66	55	42	35
	°C	0	0	6	12	20	23	24	23	19	13	6	2
average daily minimum*	°F	22	21	28	37	48	54	58	56	49	41	33	28
	°C	–6	–6	–2	3	9	12	15	14	10	5	1	–3
Cracow													
average daily maximum*	°F	32	34	45	55	67	72	76	73	66	56	44	37
	°C	0	1	7	13	20	22	24	23	19	14	6	3
average daily minimum*	°F	22	22	30	38	48	54	58	56	49	42	33	28
	°C	–5	–5	–1	3	9	12	15	14	10	5	1	–2

* Minimum temperatures are measured just before sunrise, maximum temperatures in the afternoon.

Clothing. Light- to medium-weight clothing is adequate in summer. In winter, a heavy coat and a warm hat are advisable as well as stout shoes or boots to combat street snow and slush. Rainwear will come in handy at any time of year. On the whole, Poles don't attach much importance to dress, and casual attire is generally worn.

Duty-free allowances

Cigarettes	Cigars	Tobacco	Liquor	Wine
250 or	50 or	250 g.	1 l. and	1 l.
Gifts: Up to a value of $200.				

Hotels and accommodations

Hotels. Unless your Polish host is taking care of hotel accommodations for you, hotel bookings are best made through your home travel agency at the same time as you apply for your visa. Reserve well ahead, especially in summer. Hotel receptionists are liable to tell the casual caller that they're filled up even when they do, in fact, have vacant rooms.

Polish tourist offices abroad

U.K.   POLORBIS Travel, 82 Mortimer Street,
London W1N 7DE; tel. (071) 637 4971

U.S.A.   ORBIS, 342 Madison Avenue, New York,
N.Y. 10173; tel. (212) 867-5011

On the spot

Banks and currency exchange. Banks are open 8 a.m.–noon, Monday–Friday; also open one Saturday a month.

Currency can also be changed at major hotels at convenient hours, at the Orbis office, 8 a.m.–4 p.m., Monday–Friday, and at Warsaw airport. Syrena, the Warsaw tourist organization, and the national bank also change money, but at the bank you'll have to contend with crowds. Beware of money changers on the street; currency offences are severely punished.

Credit cards and traveler's checks. Both are accepted at major hotels, airlines, restaurants and some stores, e.g. Cepelia souvenir shops and Pewex hard-currency shops.

Mail and telecommunications. All services are generally reliable, though mail may sometimes be delayed.

Post-office hours are 8 a.m.–8 p.m., Monday–Saturday, and until 9 p.m. for telephone service. The main post office (ul. Świetokrzyska 31–33) and the branch in the central railroad station are open 24 hours a day.

Long-distance telephone, telegraph and telex services are available at major hotels and large post offices. Telex facilities are offered by some post offices and also at hotels where, however, due to lack of staff, telex messages are often not transmitted after 6 p.m. Be prepared for long delays in placing calls outside Europe. The Polish telephone network is to a large extent automated.

Useful telephone numbers:

Ambulance	999	International calls	901
Fire	998	Operator (general)	900
Information	913	Police	997

Newspapers. The principal dailies are *Trybuna Ludu* and *Zycie Warszawy* (German editions are produced twice weekly). Periodicals of interest to visitors are *Poland*, an illustrated monthly published in English, French, German, Spanish and Swedish, and *Polish Perspectives*, produced monthly in English, French and German.

Tourist information

Warsaw: Orbis, 16 ul. Bracka, 00-028 Warsaw; tel. 26 02 71; tourist information center: Plac Zamkowy 1/13; tel. 27 00 00.

Legal holidays

Jan. 1	New Year's Day	Nov. 11	National Day
May 1	Labor Day	Dec. 25	Christmas Day
May 3	Day of the Third of May Constitution	Dec. 26	St. Stephen's Day
		Movable:	Easter Monday
Aug. 15	Assumption		Corpus Christi
Nov. 1	All Saints' Day		

Transportation

Air. Warsaw is Poland's gateway airport, with good access by direct flights or connections from most parts of the world. Poland's national airline operates frequent flights to all major cities.

Major airports. Warsaw. Okecie airport (6 miles/10 km. from city center). Duty-free shop. Airport and city buses. **Cracow.** Balice airport (10 miles/18 km. from city center). Bus service.

Rail. Trains are often the only convenient means of travel. Express trains (not always punctual) operate to important centers. For comfort, travel first-class. Rates are very moderate. Full dining service is available on some trains while others sell only snacks such as sausages or *bigos* (cabbage and pork).

Local public transportation. All major cities have bus and streetcar networks. Tickets must be bought in advance from *ruch* stands found at most shops and elsewhere throughout the town. Punch your ticket at a machine inside the vehicle.

Taxis. Taxis are inexpensive and recommended in preference to public service vehicles. Tip about 10%.

Car rental. To be sure of having a vehicle at your disposal, it is advisable to reserve a car when you organize your trip. There is often little or no choice of model. On the spot, rental charges must be paid in hard currency. Chauffeur-driven cars are usually available.

Driving in Poland. An international driver's license is required. Always carry this and your passport with you as police sometimes carry out spot checks. Drivers of cars rented in Poland can buy gasoline for złotys, but if your vehicle has non-Polish registration plates you must pay with special coupons (available for hard currency at border points, hotels and tourist offices inside and outside Poland). These coupons are often cheaper when bought at Polish tourist offices abroad. Gasoline available is normal (78 octane), super (94 octane) and diesel. Some gas stations offer 98 octane and lead-free gasoline.

Speed limits: in town, 37 mph (60 kph) except where otherwise indicated; outside town, 56 mph (90 kph) on the open road, 68 mph (110 kph) on the expressway. Seat belts are obligatory, and a red reflector warning triangle must be carried. Blood alcohol limit is a strictly enforced zero, and police are entitled to take you for an immediate blood test. They also levy on-the-spot fines for speeding and similar infringements.

On a traffic circle, priority is from the right. Surfaces are adequate on arterial routes; secondary roads tend to be rather narrow. Night driving can be hazardous due to badly lit farm carts.

Call the Polski Zwiazek Motorowy (PZM) in case of breakdown; in Warsaw the number is 954, elsewhere often 981. A full list of numbers is obtainable from any PZM office.

Some distances: Warsaw–Cracow 180 miles (290 km.), Poznań 185 miles (300 km.), Gdańsk 210 miles (340 km.).

Crime and theft. Normal precautions are in order. Beware of illegal currency transactions, which could cause problems.

Medical care and health. The standard of medical treatment is good in large towns but otherwise rather poor. Costs are moderate by Western standards. Special provision is made for foreigners to receive paid medical aid at Polish health-service units. First-aid is free, as is all medical service for those visiting Poland at the invitation of Polish institutions. Visitors from some countries receive free medical treatment under inter-governmental agreements. Anyone suffering from a specific complaint requiring special drugs should bring plentiful supplies of them as often only basic medicine is available. Some doctors speak basic German or English. Every pharmacy displays addresses of duty pharmacies open after hours.

Tap water is generally safe to drink in major cities and resorts, though often rather tasteless.

Embassies and consulates. Hotels keep listings of diplomatic representations.

Social customs. Consumption of hard liquor is widespread in Poland. Many Poles look askance at teetotallers, but they respect the excuse that you have to drive afterwards or that your doctor forbids it. Poles also like to down a few vodkas with hors-d'œuvre before lunch or dinner. A common toast is *na zdrowie* ("to your health"), although you won't normally be saying it much before 1 p.m.—alcohol is not served or sold before this time in Poland. It's customary to observe name days rather than birthdays.

Enjoying Poland

Food and drink. Restaurants serve Western European and typical Polish dishes. Some specialities are *kotlet schabowy* (pork chop), *golonka* (pork knuckle with horseradish sauce), *bigos* (sauerkraut with smoked pork).

The national drinks are vodka and beer. Wines are mostly Bulgarian and Hungarian (such as Debroei, white, and Egri Bikaver, red), though Spanish and Yugoslavian imports are sometimes found. Foreign beer, wine and liquor are available in major hotels.

Lunch is served from 3 to 5 p.m., dinner from 8 to 10 p.m. Traditionally Poles eat one big meal at around 4 p.m.

Entertainment. Theaters abound in every town. There are opera houses in Warsaw, Poznań, Katowice, Gdańsk and Cracow. Concerts and ballets are also part of the cultural life. Quite a number of movie theaters show foreign films in their original language. Folk festivals take

place in various towns during the year. There are several nightclubs as well as jazz clubs or cafés and restaurants with live jazz.

Taxes, service charges and tipping. Hotel and restaurant charges are usually all-inclusive. Though tipping is officially discouraged, gratuities, given discreetly, are welcomed. Some recommendations: taxi drivers 10%; hairdressers and barbers 10%; porters 200–500 zł per piece; hat-check 50 zł or the equivalent in dollars—foreign currency is appreciated much more.

Sports and recreation. Swimming, tennis, sailing and, in season, skiing are easily available, as is hunting.

Favorite spectator sports are soccer in spring and autumn; cycling and athletics in summer; basketball, skiing and boxing mainly in winter; and horse-racing most of the year except winter.

TV and radio. Programming is in Polish only, but several times a day you can watch CNN's Headline News in English.

What to buy. Amber, jewelry, cut glass, embroidery, leather, rugs, carved wooden ornaments, silver- and metal-ware are good buys. Cepelia shops specialize in handicraft and folkloric articles; credit cards, hard currency and złotys are accepted. A chain of Desa shops sells works of art. (Antiques are usually not for export.) Articles in any quantity bought in hard currency or złotys at Pewex shops (liquor, cigarettes, cosmetics, watches, jewelry and Polish-made crystal) can be exported dutyfree. You can take out gifts to a value of $200 beyond this amount.

Shopping hours: 9/10/11 a.m.–7/8 p.m., Monday–Saturday.

Sightseeing

Warsaw. 15th-century Old Town*, rebuilt after World War II devastation: Old Market Square with restored architectural ensemble, Gothic St. John's Cathedral, begun in 13th century and rebuilt after the war, city Historical Museum documenting wartime destruction, 17th-century King Sigismund III column, reconstituted Royal Castle, pre-war residence of Poland's president; Barbican town walls, remains of medieval fortifications; Łazienki Park, beautifully landscaped park

380

of palaces and monuments. Wilanów Park featuring restored Baroque palace, now part of National Museum. Palace of Culture, Warsaw's tallest building, Stalinist landmark from 1950s.

Southern Poland. Cracow *(Kraków)**, medieval capital on the Vistula, almost unscathed in World War II: Main Market Square, one of Europe's biggest medieval squares, with great Renaissance Cloth Hall, containing shops and Gallery of Polish Painting; St. Mary's Church, founded 1222, with glorious Gothic altar; Jagiellonian University's Collegium Maius (late 15th century); Wawel Castle, Poland's most majestic castle with 14th-century Cathedral where Polish kings were crowned and buried. Excursion to Oświęcim (Auschwitz), Nazi extermination camp in which four million died, and Martyrdom Museum. Częstochowa, home of Jasna Góra monastery and Black Madonna, Poland's most sacred icon. Tatra Mountains, sanctuary of eagles, chamois and bears, and the ski resort town of Zakopane.

Northern Poland. Gdańsk, shipbuilding center and birthplace of Solidarity movement, with medieval Main Town: 14th-century Town Hall; late Gothic Church of the Holy Virgin, Poland's largest church; modern Monument to Shipyard Workers outside Gdańsk shipyards. Gdynia, a Baltic port, fishing harbor, naval base and industrial city. Szczecin, Poland's biggest port, destroyed in 1945, with restored 15th-century Town Hall and Pomeranian Castle, damaged and rebuilt several times over the centuries.

Some useful expressions in Polish

good morning/afternoon	dzień dobry
good evening/night	dobry wieczór/dobranoc
good-bye	do widzenia
yes/no	tak/nie
please/thank you	proszę/dziękuję
excuse me	przepraszam
you're welcome	witam
where/when/how	gdzie/kiedy/jak
how long/how far	jak długo/jak daleko
yesterday/today/tomorrow	wczoraj/dzisiaj/jutro
day/week/month	dzień/tydzień/miesiąc
left/right	lewo/prawo
up/down	góra/dół
good/bad	dobry/zły
big/small	duży/mały
cheap/expensive	tani/drogi
hot/cold	gorące/zimne
old/new	stary/nowy
open/closed	otwarty/zamknięty
free (vacant)/occupied	wolny/zajęty
early/late	wczesny/późny
easy/difficult	łatwy/trudny
Does anyone here speak English/French/German?	Czy ktoś mówi po angielsku, francusku, niemiecku?
What does this mean?	Co to znaczy?
I don't understand.	Nie rozumiem.
Please write it down.	Proszę to napisać.
Do you take credit cards/traveller's cheques?	Czy przyjmujecie karty kredytowe/czeki podróżne?
Waiter!/Waitress!	Kelner!/Kelnerka!
Where are the toilets?	Gdzie są toalety?
I'd like…	Chciałbym…
How much is that?	Ile płacę?
What time is it?	Która godzina?
Help me please.	Proszę mi pomóc.
Just a minute.	Chwileczkę.

PORTUGAL

*Dignified and kindly, the heirs of a great
empire find harmony in a song of longing.*

In the 16th century the world's farthest-flung empire belonged to
Portugal. Life was grand in this small country during the Golden Age,
when the caravels brought back fabled riches from colonies in South
America, Africa and Asia. Many of the imperial relics remain, but the
Portuguese couldn't be more modest and unassuming, facing the
realities of today's world with quiet dignity.

Clinging to southwesternmost Europe, Portugal descends from
mountains to vineyards and almond groves and down to the baked
beaches of the Algarve, where the Atlantic feels more like the
Mediterranean. The towns delight with pretty details: red tile roofs,
mosaic sidewalks and flower-potted balconies. In Lisbon, few of the
capital's Golden Age castles and palaces are left, for in 1755 the city
suffered an earthquake counted among history's all time worst calami-
ties. But in the narrow, hilly streets that survived, the atmosphere hasn't
changed. The music of the fado—Portugal's sad song of longing—still
echoes into the night. Nostalgia also haunts the resort of Estoril, the
classic choice of deposed kings for their sunny exile.

The Romans, who colonized the country in the 3rd century B.C.,
started the business—and pleasure—of Portuguese wine. Port and
Madeira wines are only part of the story, which continues happily with
the local red, white and rosé, and a titillating young variety called *vinho
verde*, "green wine". The North African Moors, who occupied Portugal
for four centuries, left their mark in ways you will see—blinding white
villages, the decorative tiles called *azulejos*, filigreed jewelry... and the
dark, intense eyes of so many of the people.

Portugal and its only neighbor, Spain, have much in common but the
difference in mood is profound. Portuguese festivals are less exuberant,
the influence of tourism more restrained, and in Portuguese bullfights,
the bull leaves the ring on its own four feet.

384

Facts and figures

Population:	10 million
Area:	35,550 sq. miles (92,082 sq. km.)
Capital:	Lisbon *(Lisboa,* 830,000/GUA 2 million)
Other cities:	Oporto *(Porto,* 330,000/GUA 1.5 million) Coimbra (55,000) Barreiro (55,000) Vila Nova de Gaia (50,000) Setúbal (50,000)
Language:	Portuguese
Religion:	Roman Catholic (98%)
Time zone:	GMT, EST + 5; DST (Apr.–Sep.)
Currency:	*Escudo* (abbr. *esc.*; symbolized $) = 100 *centavos.* The $ sign normally replaces the decimal point in prices (e.g. 100$50 means 100 escudos 50 centavos) Coins: 50 centavos; 1, 2½, 5, 10, 20, 25, 50 esc. Bills: 100, 500, 1,000, 5,000 esc.
Electricity:	220 or 110 volt, 50 cycle, AC

Planning your trip

Visa requirements. See pp. 29–30.

Vaccination requirements. None (see also p. 25).

Currency restrictions. Visitors can bring any amount of local or foreign currency into Portugal, but sums exceeding the equivalent of 1,000,000 escudos in foreign currency must be declared on arrival. No more than 100,000 escudos in local money may be exported per person per trip. Non-residents may take out foreign currencies up to the amount imported and declared.

Climate. Most of Portugal enjoys a temperate Atlantic climate influenced by the Mediterranean. Winter is when most rain falls; the summers are in general dry. In the southern Algarve the climate is semi-tropical.

385

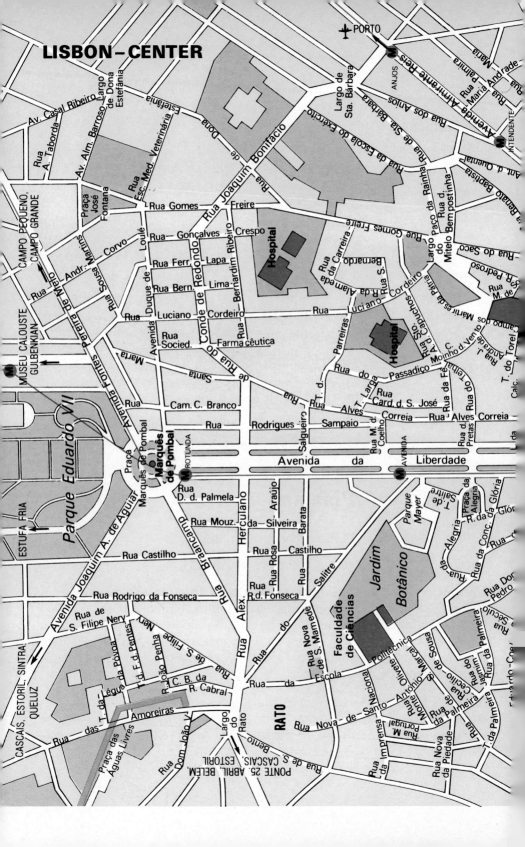

IGREJA DA MADRE DE DEUS,
MUSEU DA CIDADE

Museu Militar

Santa Engracia

ALFAMA

São Vicente de Fora

Castelo de São Jorge

Casa dos Bicos

Santo Antonio da Sé

Bolsa

Estação Fluvial

CAÇILHAS

Medicina Legal

Monumento dos Restauradores

Teatro Nacional D. Maria II

Palácio Foz

Estação do Rossio

São Roque

Ruinas do Convento do Carmo

Praça Rossio (Dom Pedro IV)

BAIXA

Museu de Arte Contemporânea

CHIADO

BAIRRO ALTO

Paços do Conceicho

Praça do Comércio

Rio Tejo

N

PONTE 25 ABRIL, BELÉM,
ALGES, CASCAIS, ESTORIL.

Estação Cais do Sodré

Some average daily temperatures:

Lisbon		J	F	M	A	M	J	J	A	S	O	N	D
average daily maximum*	°F	57	59	63	67	71	77	81	82	79	72	63	58
	°C	14	15	17	20	21	25	27	28	26	22	17	15
average daily minimum*	°F	46	47	50	53	55	60	63	63	62	58	52	47
	°C	8	8	10	12	13	15	17	17	17	14	11	9

Faro (Algarve)													
average daily maximum*	°F	60	61	64	67	71	77	83	83	78	72	66	61
	°C	15	16	18	20	22	25	28	28	26	22	19	16
average daily minimum*	°F	48	49	52	55	58	64	67	68	65	60	55	50
	°C	9	10	11	13	14	18	20	20	19	16	13	10

* Minimum temperatures are measured just before sunrise, maximum temperatures in the afternoon.

Clothing. Light cotton clothes are sufficient in summer, but bring along a light wrap or jacket for the cooler, windy evenings. In winter something warmer will be necessary. As for formality, Lisbon has changed drastically. Now virtually no establishment requires a tie. The Estoril Casino recommends that men wear jackets in the evenings.

Duty-free allowances

	Cigarettes		Cigars		Tobacco	Liquor	Wine
1)	300	or	75	or	400 g	1½ l and	5 l
2)	200	or	50	or	250 g	1 l and	2 l

1) from EEC countries
2) from other countries

Perfume: 1) 75 g.; 2) 50 g.
Toilet water: 1) 0.375 l.; 2) 0.25 l.
Gifts: 1) 52,000 esc. max. value (7,000 esc. if bought duty free);
2) 7,000 esc. max. value.

Hotels and accommodations

Hotels. Except for the family-run *hotéis rurais,* hotels in Portugal are graded from 2-star to 5-star deluxe. Continental breakfast is included in the cost of a room. Between July and September advance reservations is essential.

Inns and boardinghouses. Inns *(estalagem)* are usually smaller and simpler than hotels of the same category, as are boardinghouses which are classified with one to three stars. They both have lower rates than hotels.

Pousadas. These are state-run establishments in scenic castles, palaces, convents and other historical sites. Special attention is given to local food and wine, as well as to the architecture and handicrafts of the region. Ask for the detailed list of *pousadas* at any tourist office.

Youth hostels. Young tourists can stay in dormitories at very low rates if they're members of a national or international youth hostel association. Membership of the Portuguese Youth Hostel Association is open to "juniors" (aged 14 to 21), and "seniors" (22 to 40).

Camping. Portugal has about 70 campsites, mostly near beaches or historic monuments. Several are in the Lisbon area. Facilities range from the most simple to quite elaborate. The tourist office has an excellent brochure with details of Portuguese campsites. Camping on beaches or anywhere outside a recognized site is illegal.

Portuguese tourist offices abroad

Canada	Suite 704, Canada Square, 2200 Young Street, Toronto, Ont. M4S 2C6; tel. (416) 485-9004
	1801 McGill College Avenue, Montreal, Que. H3A 2N4; tel. (514) 282-1264
U.K.	New Bond Street House, 1–5 New Bond Street, London W1Y 0DB; tel. (071) 493 3873
U.S.A.	548 Fifth Avenue, New York, NY 10036; tel. (212) 354-4403
	Suite 3001, 969 Michigan Avenue, Chicago, IL 60611; tel. (312) 266-9898
	Suite 616, 3640 Wilshire Boulevard, Los Angeles, CA 90010; tel. (213) 580-6459

On the spot

Banks and currency exchange. Banking hours are from 8:30 to 11:45 a.m., and 1 to 2:30 or 2:45 p.m., Monday through Friday. In large towns one bank usually stays open after hours and on Saturdays during the tourist season. In Lisbon, currency can be changed outside of banking hours at the airport, at the Santa Apolónia railroad station and at one bank in Praça dos Restauradores. Curiously, certain foreign currencies are difficult to convert in Portugal. Check with your bank before leaving. Hotels will also change money, but usually at a less favorable rate.

Credit cards and traveler's checks. Internationally recognized credit cards and most traveler's checks are accepted in large hotels, restaurants and shops, and other tourist-oriented enterprises, such as major garages and car-rental agencies. Be sure to take along your passport when cashing traveler's checks.

Mail and telecommunications. Main post offices, identified by the letters CTT *(Correios, Telégrafos e Telefones)*, are open from 8:30 or 9 a.m. to 6 or 6:30 p.m., Monday through Friday and also operate on Saturday mornings till noon. Lisbon's main post office at Praça dos Restauradores 58 is open from 8 a.m. to midnight daily. At the height of the tourist season, mail might take a little longer to get through. Stamps can also be bought at many tobacco shops and at souvenir stands. They usually display a "Correios" sign. Mailboxes follow the English pillar box design and are painted bright red, too.

Automatic coin phones can be found in bars and restaurants, as well as on street corners. You can dial most of the world direct or make international calls through the clerk at any post office or at your hotel. For international direct dialing, use 00 for calls within Europe and 097 for the rest of the world (e. g. U.K. 0044, U.S.A. 0971) followed by the area code (without the initial "0") and subscriber's number.

Information	16	Operator	
Operator		(European calls)	099
(general)	12	Operator (intercontinental	
Operator		calls)	098
(long-distance		Telegrams	10
calls, domestic)	09/19	Police, fire, ambulance	115

Newspapers. Principal dailies in Lisbon are *Diário de Notícias* and *A Capital*, in Oporto *Jornal de Notícias*. Europe's leading newspapers, including the *International Herald Tribune* and most British dailies, are sold in many hotels and newsstands. Also available is a publication called the *Anglo-Portuguese News*, with information about current events. Down in the Algarve you will find the monthly *Algarve Magazine*, published in English.

Tourist information. There are tourist information offices in most average-size towns, identified by a "T" (for *turismo*).

391

Lisbon	Posto de Turismo da Câmara Municipal de Lisboa, Av. António Augusto de Aguiar, 86, 1000-Lisboa; tel. 36 36 24
Oporto	Praça do Município; tel. (029) 327 40

Legal holidays

Jan. 1	New Year's Day	**Movable dates:**
April 25	Liberty Day	Carnival
May 1	Labor Day	Good Friday
June 10	National Day	Corpus Christi
Aug. 15	Assumption	
Oct. 5	Republic Day	
Nov. 1	All Saint's Day	
Dec. 1	Independence Day	
Dec. 8	Immaculate Conception	
Dec. 25	Christmas Day	

Transportation

Air. Lisbon is Portugal's major gateway, while Faro and Oporto handle a limited number of flights. Domestic flights link Lisbon with Faro, Oporto, Funchal in Madeira and Santa Maria in the Azores. A few flights a week operate to Bragança and Chaves; advance reservation is advised.

Major airports. Lisbon: Portela (5 miles/8 km. from city center). Duty-free shop. Frequent bus service to Santa Apolónia and Rossio railroad stations. **Oporto:** Pedras Rubras (12 miles/18 km. from city center). Public transportation is available.

Rail. Trains are comfortable but not always punctual. Some of the inter-city trains have dining cars, while others may have snack bars. Lisbon has four main stations: Santa Apolónia station for northern Portugal and abroad; Cais do Sodré for the western suburbs, Estoril and Cascais; Rossio station for Sintra and the west; and Sul e Sueste with its ferryboats that cross the Tagus to meet trains from as far south as the Algarve. In major stations, first- and second-class tickets are sold at separate windows. For *Eurailpass*, see p. 33.

Long-distance buses. The state-run Rodoviaria Nacional and some private firms run express buses linking Lisbon with most major centers

392

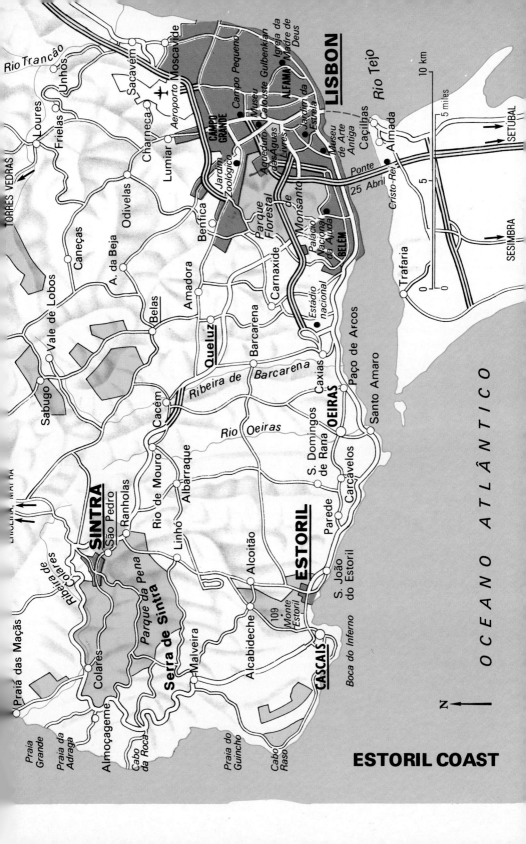

ESTORIL COAST

and with Algarve resorts. Some buses have air conditioning. Travel agencies can provide timetables, information and reservations.

Local public transportation. Buses, streetcars or trolleybuses operate in most cities. In Lisbon there is a limited subway system, called the Metropolitano, with stations mainly in the residential areas. Tickets for the subway are bought at the ticket office; on other forms of transportation you usually pay the conductor.

Taxis. Cabs are black with green roofs. In Lisbon they display a prominent *taxi* sign, while in rural areas they display an "A" (for *aluguer*–for rent). Taxis don't normally cruise for business but wait for customers at specific taxi stands. In the cities, taxis have meters and it is worthwhile checking that they are running. In the countryside there are no meters, but a chart with standard fares based on mileage should be displayed.

Car rental. International and local car-rental agencies operate in Lisbon and other major tourist areas. Chauffeur-driven vehicles are often available. See also pp. 30–31.

Driving in Portugal. Seat belts are obligatory, and your car must carry a red reflector warning triangle. Blood alcohol limit is 50 mg./100 ml. Gasoline available is normal (85 octane), super (96 octane) and diesel. The road conditions vary from good expressways to poor rural roads. Speed limits are 37 mph (60 kph) in built-up areas, 75 mph (120 kph) on expressways, and 68 mph (110 kph) on other roads. A toll is charged on the Lisbon–Oporto expressway, currently under construction. Watch out for rustic obstructions, and the somewhat moody style of Portuguese driving. Parking time is unlimited unless otherwise indicated. In case of breakdown, call 77 54 75 (Automóvel Clube de Portugal), where English-speaking personnel are generally on duty.

Some distances: Lisbon–Setúbal 25 miles (40 km.), Coimbra 125 miles (215 km.), Oporto 205 miles (330 km.).

Bicycle rental. Local tourist information offices will give you the address of a rental firm. Avoid riding during the hottest hours of the day.

Rest rooms. The most likely place to find rest rooms is in hotels and restaurants. In Lisbon you will also find public conveniences in most subway stations. "Ladies" is *Senhoras* and "Gentlemen" is *Homens*.

Emergencies. Dial 115 anywhere in Portugal in an emergency.

Police. In resorts and towns with tourist traffic, look for police wearing armbands marked "CD" (*Corpo Distrital*–local corps). They are assigned to help tourists and normally speak one or more foreign languages. On highways, traffic is controlled by the Guarda Nacional Republicana (GNR) in white cars or on motorcycles.

Crime and theft. Keep your valuables in the hotel safe and do not leave tempting objects visible in your car. Park your car in well-lit or guarded areas, and keep a firm grip on handbags and totebags when out walking. Pickpockets are on the increase in the cities and tourist areas. The problem is particularly acute in the subway in Lisbon and in main city squares.

Medical care and health. Any local tourist office has a list of doctors and dentists who speak English. Pharmacies *(farmácias)* are open during normal business hours, and after hours there is one open in each neighborhood. The address will be posted in the windows of other pharmacies and in the local newspaper. For insurance, see pp. 25–26.

Tap water is safe to drink in Lisbon. Elsewhere those with delicate stomachs may prefer to buy bottled mineral water.

Embassies and consulates. Look under "Embaixadas" and "Consulados" in the telephone directory.

Social customs. There is a great deal of hand-shaking in Portugal, and if you get to know any Portuguese well, prepare for the *abraço* (embrace) between men, a great hugging and slapping on the back, and for women, kisses on both cheeks. If you are invited to someone's home for a meal or a drink, it's an offer you can't refuse without offending.

Enjoying Portugal

Food and drink. Try freshly caught sardines, still salty from the sea, swiftly grilled and washed down with a glass of local red wine. It could well tempt you into trying one of the 365 different ways of preparing cod (according to legend and the average Portuguese housewife). But don't get the idea that there's no meat in Portugal; there's plenty, with some interesting and unusual combinations.

As if to prepare you for the solid-sized portions to come, breakfast is usually quite a small and simple meal. It's mostly coffee, toast or rolls, butter and jam, although an English or American breakfast will be provided if requested.

Lunch is served between noon and 3 p.m., dinner between 7:30 and 9:30 p.m.

Start with a soup like *caldo verde*, a thick potato and cabbage mixture; it often has some sausage thrown in, too. Or *sopa à Portuguesa*, which is similar but with added beans, broccoli, carrots and turnips, and anything else that the cook has at hand. *Canja de galinha* is a chicken and rice soup, while *sopa de cozido* is a rich meat broth with cabbage and perhaps macaroni. The latter is often followed by *cozido*—or everything that was boiled up to make the soup.

For the main course try an Algarve specialty, *amêijoas na cataplana*, which is steamed clams with sausages, ham, white wine, tomato, onion and herbs. Or taste the national dish of Portugal—*bacalhau* (dried salted cod). One of the many cod variations is *bacalhau à Gomes de Sá*, chunks of cod baked together with parsley, potatoes, onions and olives, after which the whole dish is garnished with grated hard-boiled egg. Once you've exhausted the cod possibilities why not try some *atum* (tuna) or *espadarte* (swordfish steaks).

Alternatively, there is the meat menu. *Bife na frigideira* is a beefsteak, fried and served in a wine sauce. *Espetata mista* (chunks of beef, lamb and pork on a spit) harks back to the cuisine of the one-time rulers of Portugal, the Moors, while *feijoada* makes a filling meal with its pigs' feet and sausage, white beans and cabbage.

Frango or *galinha* (chicken) is served in a variety of ways: fried, barbecued, stewed in wine or roasted. Some restaurants specialize in game: *codorniz* (quail), *perdiz* (partridge), *lebre* (hare), and even *javali* (wild boar).

If you have a sweet tooth then you'll enjoy the different desserts produced by almost every town—mostly from figs, almonds and eggs. For a traditional pudding try *pudim flan* (caramel custard) and *arroz doce* (rice pudding with a dash of cinnamon). If you want to let caution fly to the winds, have the *pudim Molotov*, an amazing concoction of fluffy eggwhite mousse immersed in caramel sauce.

The richest and most expensive cheese in Portugal is *Serra da Estrela*. This is a cured ewe's-milk cheese from the country's highest mountain range. *Flamengo* is rather like Gouda in taste and *queijo fresco* is a soft white cheese often served as an appetizer even before you've looked at the menu.

There are virtually no mistakes to be made when asking for wine in Portugal; it is usually very good, and sometimes remarkable. Simply ask for *tinto* (red) or *branco* (white), or *vinho verde* (green wine), a thoroughly delightful young white wine with a sparkle. A similar red version exists, confusingly called *vinho verde tinto*. Do not leave without tasting some of the ports and Madeiras that Portugal is famous for, in their pre- and post-prandial versions.

To round off your meal, order a *bica*, a tiny strong black coffee or have a *galão* (coffee with milk) in a tall glass. And there is *chá* (tea) at any time of the day.

Entertainment. Try to see the colorful pageant of the bullfight. In Portugal, children over the age of six are admitted. Although the matador demonstrates his domination of the bull, the animal leaves the arena alive. Other diversions range from elegant casinos, in particular the one in Estoril, to fishermen's bars on the coast. In between is a variety of nightclubs, discos, *fado*-clubs and restaurants.

In Lisbon you'll be able to see some fine ballet and opera at São Carlos Opera House, as well as symphony concerts and recitals. Check at the tourist office to see what's coming up. Most foreign movies are shown in their original language with Portuguese subtitles.

Annual events and festivals. These are too numerous to list, but almost every town has an annual saint's feast which is celebrated with processions, fireworks and even dancing in the streets. Check with the local tourist office when you arrive. *May 12–13:* First Annual Pilgrimage to Fatima. *June 13:* Feast of St. Anthony in Lisbon. *July:* Colete Encarnado in Vila Franca de Xira, with running bulls. *July–August:* Estoril Concerts. *September:* Senhora da Nazare Folk Pilgrimage with processions, dancing, bullfights.

Taxes, service charges and tipping. Hotel and restaurant bills are generally all-inclusive. Waiters are sometimes given an additional 10% if service has been very good. Other tipping recommendations: hotel porters 50–100 esc., taxi drivers 10%, hatcheck 25 esc., hairdressers and barbers 10%.

Sports and recreation. With such a long coastline, Portugal is naturally well-served for water sports. The water (except close to Lisbon) is very clear, making it perfect for swimming, snorkeling and scuba diving. Windsurfing has caught on in the last few years, and of course there's plenty of sailing and fishing.

Back on dry land, Portugal is strong on golf, with some particularly good courses in the Algarve and two major 18-hole courses in the Lisbon area. Horse riding is another popular sport, whether you are on the horse or watching the races. Soccer enjoys the fanatical support that most European countries give it.

397

TV and radio. Two government-operated television channels serve Portugal; foreign feature movies are usually shown in the original version with subtitles. The government also operates four radio channels. Program Two is almost all classical music, while Program Four is uninterrupted pop. At certain times of the day you can also pick up Voice of America, BBC World Service and Radio Canada International.

What to buy. Try all the shopping venues, from the elegant shops in Lisbon, to the small boutiques in coastal resorts. In Lisbon, the most important shopping area is the Baixa district. And if you can't find what you're looking for there, go out to the country markets.

Look for *azulejos,* hand-painted glazed tiles, and articles made from cork; brass, bronze and copper in the form of candlesticks, scales, pots and bowls; dolls beautifully dressed in authentic Portuguese costumes;

embroidery from Madeira; jewelry including fine filigree work. Other good buys are knitwear, leather goods and ceramics and Madeira or port wines.

The stores are open 9 a.m. to 1 p.m. and 3 to 7 p.m., Monday through Friday, and on Saturday morning from 9 a.m. to 1 p.m. New shopping complexes usually operate from 10 a.m. to midnight, often on Sundays as well.

Sightseeing

Lisbon. Praça do Comércio, extravagant plaza with pink arcades in Baixa area. Rossio, Lisbon's main square, former venue for bullfights and witch-burning. Praça dos Restauradores commemorating overthrow of Spanish rule in 1640. Elegant Avenida da Liberdade with palm trees and pavement mosaics. Exotic Estufa Fria (cold greenhouse) in Edward VII park with plants from Africa, Asia and South America. St. George's Castle *(Castelo de São Jorge)** dating back to the Moors, for finest panorama of city and splendid park with resident peacocks and flamingos. Church of St. Vincent Beyond the Walls *(São Vicente de Fora)* with blue-and-white glazed tiles depicting French life and leisure in 18th century, also tombs of royal Bragança family. Grandiose marble Church of Santa Engrácia with dome reminiscent of Washington's Capitol. Impressive, though tucked away, medieval cathedral *(Sé)** with 13th-century cloister. Alfama*, oldest part of Lisbon, little changed since the Middle Ages, a cobbled labyrinth of narrow streets, steps and alleys, like Beco do Carneiro, wide enough for one and a half pedestrians, and Rua de São Pedro, Alfama's main shopping street, lined with vegetable and fish shops. Bairro Alto, hilly section of Lisbon with old houses, *fado*-nightclubs and X-rated entertainment. Church of St. Rock *(Igreja de São Roque)* undistinguished façade but most lavishly decorated chapels in Lisbon. Next door Museum of Sacred Art containing collection of precious reliquaries, jewelry and vestments. Ruins of Carmelite Church *(Igreja do Carmo),* destroyed by 1755 earthquake. Elevador de Santa Justa, mass transit elevator, designed by Gustave Eiffel and inaugurated 1901. Belém, western district of Lisbon with monuments and museums. Lisbon's greatest religious monument, the Mosteiro dos Jerónimos*, famed for intricate stonework and richly sculptured cloister, a masterpiece in Manueline art, with tombs of explorer Vasco da Gama, and poet Luís de Camões; also houses

399

National Museum of Archaeology and Ethnology. Naval Museum (*Museu da Marinha*) with scores of model sailing ships. The modern Monument to the Discoveries (*Padrão dos Descobrimentos*) with Prince Henry the Navigator standing on the prow, followed by statues of the men he motivated. Portuguese folk art and customs presented region by region in the Popular Art Museum. Belém Tower (*Torre de Belém*)* in waterfront park, with finely carved details in Manueline style. Ponte 25 de Abril, longest European suspension bridge offering excellent view. Just across the River Tagus, statue of Christ the King (over 90 feet/27 m.) and breathtaking panorama of Lisbon. Aqueduct of Aguas Livres, 11-mile (18-km.)-long, going through Lisbon's biggest park, Monsanto. Calouste Gulbenkian Museum* with brilliant collection ranging from modern French paintings to Egyptian sculptures. National Museum of Ancient Art featuring masterpieces like *The Adoration of St. Vincent* and *The Temptation of St. Anthony* (Bosch). Convento da Madre de Deus* containing one of Lisbon's most memorable churches with an overpowering rich interior and in adjoining convent building the Tile Museum (*Museu do Azulejo*) with about 12,000 decorated tiles.

Central Portugal. Aveiro, a fishing town, surrounded by watery area and crossed with networks of canals that are spanned by tiny bridges; history of town told in blue-and-white tiles at railroad station; main square with pink-, blue- and pistachio-colored houses, and 16th-century blue-tiled church. Southwards along coast, miles of sandy beaches and small towns frequented by vacationing Portuguese. Coimbra*, spiritual capital of Portugal in natural amphitheater setting on the right bank of the Mondego, with old university founded in 1290; rich library magnificently decorated in gilded wood; austere cathedral; paintings and sculptures at Machado de Castro Museum; beautiful parks and steep, narrow alleyways. Leiria, castle on a volcanic hill, outstanding example of medieval military architecture, and splendid view of the old town from battlements. Fátima, place of pilgrimage on the 13th of every month with thousands of pilgrims visiting the shrine, going to the square in front of the neo-Classical Basilica of Our Lady of Fátima, and tiny Chapel of the Apparitions where three children saw the Virgin Mary in 1917. Batalha*, magnificent Gothic monastery ranking with best in France and Germany, beautiful stained-glass windows and royal cloister with successful mixture of Gothic and Manueline styles. Nazaré*, charming fishing village and seaside resort, packed with tourists in summer, attracted by beaches, whitewashed houses and fishermen's picturesque costumes and women's skirts with seven petticoats. Miles of beach visible from Sítio; cliff at north end of Nazaré.

400

Alcobaça, 12th-century monastery with largest church in Portugal; in the transept the tombs of ill-starred King Pedro and his beloved, Inêz de Castro; attractive pottery made locally. Tomar, town dominated by Convent of Christ, built over five centuries; remarkable series of seven cloisters; Manueline window. Santarém, built on a hill, once the royal residence, with narrow streets, neat pantiled and tile-fronted houses, well-known for bullfights in June. Obidos, one of Europe's finest medieval cities; narrow streets, tiny white houses, small squares, occasional carved window and unusual doorways; main street leading to city dominated by castle, now a *pousada*. Mafra, impressive monastery and palace, built to rival Escorial Palace near Madrid; beautifully proportioned church with walls of pink, gray and white marble. Sintra*, summer home for Portuguese kings for centuries, known for its palaces and exotic vegetation; Pena Palace built in 19th century—pastiche of architectural styles; panoramic view from the terraces. Estoril, fashionable resort, beaches, palm avenues, Victorian houses, flower garden and casino. Cascais*, fishing port and popular resort. Queluz*, noted for its 18th-century royal palace with lavishly decorated throne room and formal gardens. Evora, charming town, surrounded by medieval walls, with old houses carrying coats of arms over doorways, narrow cobbled streets, arches; cathedral *(Sé)* and Roman temple dedicated to Diana.

Northern Portugal. A green and hilly landscape threaded through with rivers, and dotted with fortresses. Oporto *(Porto)**, important trading port, country's second largest and possibly oldest city; cathedral *(Sé)* with Chapel of the Holy Sacrament (fine altar); St. Francis Church *(Igreja São Francisco)* with rich Baroque interior; around 80 wine stores for the harvest from slopes of Upper Douro; three technically interesting bridges including railroad bridge designed by Gustave Eiffel. Braga, severe cathedral with several remarkable carvings, well-endowed cathedral treasury; King's Chapel *(Capela dos Reis)* and St. Gerard's Chapel. Nearby shrine of Bom Jesus do Monte with Chapel of Miracles in heart of wooded parkland. Guimarães, referred to as "the cradle of Portugal" and first capital of the country; castle with defensive tower, worthwhile view from ramparts; Alberto Sampaio Museum, Church of St. Francis of Assisi with carved altar decorated with 18th-century tiles *(azulejos)*. Minho region, stretching from Oporto to Spanish border in the north, meeting place for Christian armies before setting out to recapture Portugal from the Moors. Folklore festivals, colorful costumes and small whitewashed villages. Extensive view of the region from Monte de Faro.

401

The Algarve. A beach for every taste on the Atlantic Ocean, but with a definite Mediterranean feel. Olhão*, fishing port with strong North African influence; flat-topped houses with terraces or belvederes. Welcoming countryside with olive groves and vineyards surrounding town of Tavira*; seven-arch Roman bridge across River Gilão; Town Hall with medieval arcades; Church of St. Mary of the Castle, national monument built on ruins of a mosque soon after Portugal's reconquest in 13th century. Beaches reaching maximum size at Monte Gordo with its busy nightlife and gambling facilities. Castro Marim*, fortress town with view of Spain; nature reserve to protect marshland birds. Vila Real de Santo António, with rigid 18th-century town plan. Faro, provincial capital with relaxed atmosphere and good shopping, former fishing and commercial port until area silted into tidal flat; Maritime Museum; 16th-century Convent of Our Lady of the Assumption *(Convento de Nossa Senhora da Assunção),* now an archaeological museum with beautiful cloister, the biggest chimney in the Algarve, and 2,000-year-old mosaic; Regional Ethnographic Museum containing simulated village street, with life-like dummies and authentically furnished rooms; Carmelite Church *(Igreja do Carmo)* with Capela dos Ossos (chapel of bones). Estoi, 18th-century palace and ruins of Milreu, country home of eminent Roman figure, with temple to water gods. São Brás de Alportel, with *pousada* overlooking town, surrounded by almond, carob and olive trees. Loulé, prosperous market town with medieval castle walls and parish church with distinguished Gothic interior; mock Moorish architecture housing market for fish, fruit and handicrafts; town becomes lively center during spring at Carnival time. Quarteira, booming resort town with room for both tourists and fishing boats. Traveling west, coastline begins to show unusual rock formations, with remarkable rocks at Olhos de Agua. Clifftop beach resort of Albufeira, continuous open-air market reaching its peak on Sundays. Silves*, white town set on a hillside reaching up to a castle at the top. Caldas de Monchique, spa town. Monchique, handicrafts center. Foia, highest point in the Algarve. Armação de Pêra, with beach spanning several miles. Carvoeiro, dramatic cliffs with houses perched on top. Geological wonder of Algar Seco in east. Portimão*, big professional fishing port and Largo 1° de Dezembro park with benches of blue-and-white tiles. Lagos*, Roman town made important as trading port by Moors; Church of St. Anthony with exquisite carved wood altar in Chapel of St. Anthony; unusual relics in Regional Museum of Lagos. Ponta da Piedade, unforgettable sea-cliff ensemble outside Lagos. Sagres and the Cape St. Vincent*, most westerly point of Europe, bleak cliffs, lighthouse.

Some useful expressions in Portuguese

good morning/afternoon	bom dia/boa tarde
good evening/night	boa noite
good-bye	adeus
yes/no	sim/não
please/thank you	faz favor/obrigado
excuse me	perdão
you're welcome	de nada
where/when/how	onde/quando/como
how long/how far	quanto tempo/a que distância
yesterday/today/tomorrow	ontem/hoje/amanhã
day/week/month/year	dia/semana/mês/ano
left/right	esquerdo/direito
up/down	em cima/em baixo
good/bad	bom/mau
big/small	grande/pequeno
cheap/expensive	barato/caro
hot/cold	quente/frio
old/new	velho/novo
open/closed	aberto/fechado
free (vacant)/occupied	livre/ocupado
early/late	cedo/tarde
easy/difficult	fácil/difícil
Does anyone here speak English/French/German?	Alguém fala inglês/francês/alemão?
What does this mean?	Que quer dizer isto?
I don't understand.	Não compreendo.
Please write it down.	Escreva-mo, por favor.
Do you take credit cards/traveler's checks?	Aceita cartas de crédito/cheques de viagem?
Waiter!/Waitress!	Faz favor!
Where are the toilets?	Onde estão os toiletes?
I'd like...	Queria...
How much is that?	Quanto custa isto?
What time is it?	Que horas são?
Help me please.	Ajude-me, por favor.
Just a minute.	Um momento.

404

ROMANIA

After the great dictator, a Latin outpost
among the Slavs counts its blessings.

Romania's fame as "The Breadbasket of Europe" obscures the rich variety of this country, whose name and Latin language reflect its origins as an outpost of the Roman empire. If the fields, orchards and vineyards of the plains are prodigal with grain, fruits and wine, the forested mountains, rising to nearly 10,000 feet (3,000 m.) in the Southern Carpathians, are laced with hiking trails and ski runs; the ethnic Hungarian and German villages in the rolling hills and meadows of Transylvania preserve the costumes and customs of a bygone age, and the watery maze of the vast Danube River Delta contains one of the world's greatest concentrations of birdlife.

The Danube rolls for a thousand kilometers in Romania, rushing through narrow, steep-walled canyons and meandering past villages and castles on its way to the Black Sea. You can see a cross-section of the whole country in comfort aboard a Danube cruise ship. Romania's coast became a sort of Socialist Miami Beach under the dictator Ceauşescu. The personality cult was ousted in 1990. The regime's neglect of rural areas had the effect of leaving intact landscapes of great beauty and villages of an antique charm.

All those names ending in "-u" are a leftover from the Roman ending "-us". If you know a little French or Italian, you'll be surprised at how many Romanian words will be recognizable. The Roman rule ended in the 2nd century A.D. but there are ruins to be seen, along with an unusual mix of monuments, from Turkish minarets to the medieval streets of old Braşov, and from the Orthodox monasteries of Bukovina, beautifully decorated with frescoes on the outside walls, to sleekly modern Brancusi sculpture.

There are several castles pointed out as "Count Dracula's" despite the fact that Dracula was the invention of a 19th-century British novelist. Stranger than fiction was Vlad the Impaler, a 15th-century tyrant who had 20,000 enemies executed, some skewered on sharp stakes. 20th century Romanian gypsies, transported to Hitler's concentration camps, fared little better. But you'll still find gypsy caravans on country roads and violinists playing Enesco's Romanian Rhapsodies.

406

Facts and figures

Population:	23.4 million
Area:	91,699 sq. miles (237,500 sq. km.)
Capital:	Bucharest (*Bucureşti,* 2.2 million)
Other major cities:	Braşov (335,000)
	Constanţa (305,000)
	Timişoara (300,000)
	Cluj-Napoca (300,000)
	Iaşi (280,000)
	Galaţi (280,000)
	Craiova (255,000)
Language:	Romanian
Religion:	Romanian Orthodox (88%), Roman Catholic, Protestant and other minorities
Time zone:	GMT + 2, EST + 7; DST (Apr.–Sep.)
Currency:	*Leu* (plural: *lei*) = 100 *bani*
	Coins: 5, 10, 15, 25 bani; 1, 3, 5 lei
	Bills: 10, 25, 50, 100 lei
Electricity:	220 volt, 50 cycle, AC

Planning your trip

Visa requirements. See pp. 29–30.

Vaccination requirements. None (see also p. 25).

Currency restrictions. No local currency may be taken into or out of the country. Foreign bills and other means of payment may be imported and exported. Accommodations in most hotels must be paid in foreign currency.

407

Climate. Romania has a generally temperate continental climate, though the Black Sea coast is milder. Summers have moderate rainfall. In the Transylvanian Alps winters are often severe, with heavy snow.

Some average daily temperatures:

Bucharest		J	F	M	A	M	J	J	A	S	O	N	D
average daily	°F	34	38	50	64	74	81	86	85	78	65	49	39
maximum*	°C	1	4	10	18	23	27	30	30	25	18	10	4
average daily	°F	19	23	30	41	51	57	60	59	52	43	35	26
minimum*	°C	−7	−5	−1	5	10	14	16	15	11	6	2	−3
Constanţa													
average daily	°F	37	40	46	56	66	75	81	80	73	63	51	43
maximum*	°C	3	4	8	13	19	24	27	27	23	17	11	6
average daily	°F	25	28	33	42	52	60	64	63	57	49	40	31
minimum*	°C	−4	−3	1	6	11	16	18	17	14	9	4	−1

* Minimum temperatures are measured just before sunrise, maximum temperatures in the afternoon.

Clothing. Light clothing is adequate in summer, with a raincoat for surprise showers. Something warmer is called for in spring and fall, and the mid-winter cold should not be underestimated.

Duty-free allowances

Cigarettes	Cigars	Tobacco	Liquor	Wine
200 or	250 g. of other tobacco products		1 l. and	4 l.
Perfume: A reasonable quantity for personal use.				

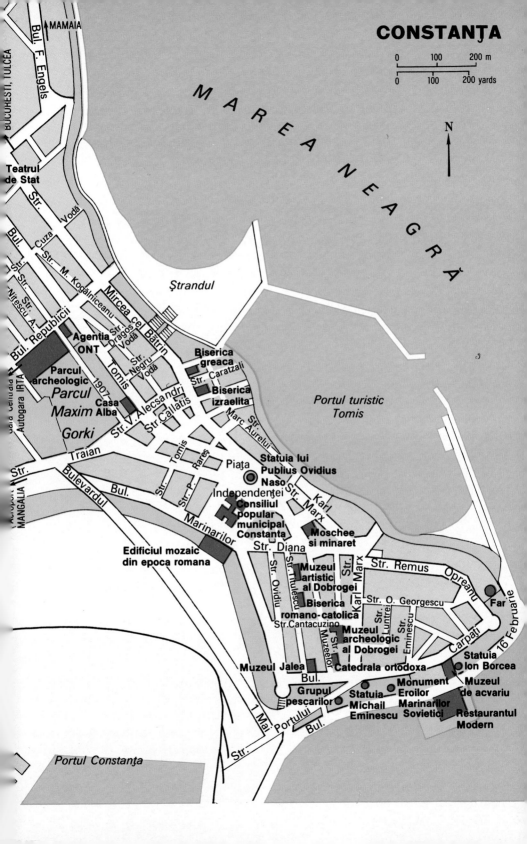

CONSTANŢA

0   100   200 m
0   100   200 yards

N

MAMAIA

Bul. F. Engels

BUCUREŞTI, TULCEA

Teatrul
de Stat

Str.

Voda

Bul.

Cuza

Str.

Str. M. Kogălniceanu

Str.

Mircea cel Bătrîn

Niţescu A.

Autogara IRTA

Gara Callatia

Republicii

Agenţia
ONT

Parcul
archeologic

Parcul

Maxim

Gorki

Casa
Alba

1907

Str. V. Alecsandri

Tomis

Str.
Dragos
Vodă

Str.
Negru
Vodă

Str. Callatis

Ştrandul

M A R E A   N E A G R Ă

Biserica
greaca

Str. Caratzali

Biserica
izraelita

Marc Aurelui

Str.

Portul turistic
Tomis

Traian

Bulevardul

Str.

MANGALIA

Bul.

Tomis

Str.

Rareş

Str. P.

Str.

Piaţa

Statuia lui
Publius Ovidius
Naso

Independenţei

Str. Karl Marx

Consiliul
popular
municipal
Constanţa

Moschee
si minaret

Marinarilor

Str. Diana

Str. Ovidiu

Str. Titulescu

Str. Karl Marx

Str. Remus

Opreanu

Far

Edificiul mozaic
din epoca romana

Muzeul
artistic
al Dobrogei

Biserica
romano-catolica

Str.Cantacuzino

Str. O. Georgescu

Str. Luntrei

Str. Eminescu

Muzeul
archeologic
al Dobrogei

Str. Muzeelor

Carpaţi

Statuia 16 Februarie

Statuia
Ion Borcea

Muzeul Jalea

Bul.

Catedrala ortodoxa

Muzeul
de acvariu

Grupul
pescarilor

Statuia
Michail
Eminescu

Monument
Eroilor
Marinarilor
Sovietici

Restaurantul
Modern

Str.

1 Mai

Str. Portului

Bul.

Portul Constanţa

Hotels and accommodations

Hotels. Accommodations should be reserved well in advance, especially in summer, at Black Sea resorts and during trade fairs in Bucharest.

Hotel reservation services are available at airports and main railroad stations. They are also available at O.N.T. (National Tourist Agency) offices abroad. Hotel rooms paid in advance from abroad can be cheaper than locally reserved rooms.

Romanian tourist offices abroad

U.K.   Romanian National Tourist Office,
                17 Nottingham Street, London W1M 3RD;
                tel. (071) 224 3692

U.S.A.   Romanian National Tourist Office,
                573 Third Avenue, New York, N.Y. 10016;
                tel. (212) 697-6971

On the spot

Banks and currency exchange. Banking hours are 8:30 a.m.–1 p.m., Monday–Friday.

Outside of banking hours, money can be changed at currency-exchange offices at airports, railroad stations, large hotels and all border crossing points.

Credit cards and traveler's checks. Major international credit cards and traveler's checks are accepted at large hotels, restaurants and shops of the Ministry of Tourism.

Mail and telecommunications. Telecommunications services are reliable for both domestic and international use but international telephone lines are often hard to get.

A 24-hour telephone service operates at Bucharest central post office (37 Calea Victoriei), the North Railway Station and airports. A late-night telex facility (until 11 p.m.) is available at the telex office located at 2 Covaci St., Bucharest. Night telegram service (8 p.m.– 7 a.m.) is provided at an office located at 10 Matei Millo St., Bucharest.

Some useful numbers:

Emergency	061	Taxi	053
Fire	081	Telegrams	057
International call	071	Time	058
Pharmacies	065	Weather/cultural	
Police	055	events	051
Romanian automobile club (Bucharest)	027		

Newspapers. Principal dailies are *Adevărul* and *România Liberă.* Foreign newspapers (mainly British, French, German and Russian) and magazines are available in large hotels. Some foreign-language periodicals are published locally.

Tourist information

Bucharest 7 Magheru Blvd.; tel. 14-51-60

Legal Holidays

Jan. 1, 2	New Year	Aug. 23, 24	Romanian
May 1, 2	Labor Days		National Days

Transportation

Air. Bucharest has the nation's principal international airport, while Arad and Constanţa maintain some foreign air services. A dozen domestic airports, served by frequent Tarom flights, link Romania's main centers.

Major airport. Otopeni (12 miles/19 km. from city center). Duty-free shop. Hourly airport bus service, urban bus service.

Rail. A dense railroad network offers frequent *rapid* (express), *accellerat* (fast) and *personal* (local) services, all with first- and second-class compartments. Some trains are modern, heated and clean. Dining and sleeping cars are available on some routes.

Long-distance buses. Though not very comfortable, punctual buses provide service to most parts of the country.

Local public transportation. All larger towns have bus, trolleybus or streetcar networks which tend to be crowded and not always punctual.

411

Tickets are purchased at tobacco shops, at stands near bus stops or from a conductor on board.

Taxis. Cabs are available in major towns (tel. 053).

Car rental. Cars can be rented from the Carpati National Tourist Office at moderate rates.

Driving in Romania. A red reflector warning triangle is required for use in case of breakdown. Seat belts are not compulsory. The alcohol limit is a strictly enforced zero. Fuel (gas) coupons are available (in foreign currency only) at the border, at Romanian travel agencies, at major hotels and at offices of the Automobil Clubul Roman (ACR). Gasoline for sale is super (95–97 octane) and diesel.

Road conditions are fair on main roads but tend to be poor on secondary ones. Night driving outside cities is not recommended. Speed limit in towns is 37 mph (60 kph), and outside towns 50–62.5 mph (80–100 kph) depending on the type of car.

For emergency road assistance, telephone 027 or 18-02-73 in the Bucharest area, or 12345 in the rest of the country.

Some distances: Bucharest–Braşov 110 miles (175 km.), Constanţa 165 miles (265 km.), Timişoara 335 miles (570 km.).

Crime and theft. Normal precautions are in order.

Medical care and health. The public health system has excellent doctors but few supplies. Fees are moderate. Many doctors speak at least one foreign language. A clinic often visited by foreigners in Bucharest is the Geriatrics Clinic—which, despite its name, provides all-round care. Pharmaceutical supplies for most needs might not be readily available, and you are advised to bring with you anything you need. For after-hours pharmacies, dial 065 in Bucharest or the telephone information service in the provinces. Tap water is safe to drink in most cities.

Embassies and consulates. Embassies and consulates are listed under part VI of the telephone directory ("Telephone numbers of public organizations").

Social customs. Any opportunity to accept or offer hospitality should be taken. If invited to a Romanian home, don't forget flowers for the hostess. Hand-kissing is still customary among Romanians when a man meets a woman.

Enjoying Romania

Food and drink. Most large hotels and restaurants offer a variety of international and local dishes. Some local specialties: *mămăligă cu brînza* (cornmeal porridge with salted white cheese), *sarmale* (meatballs with sauerkraut), *mititei* (meatballs grilled with garlic, pepper and paprika), *pui cu mujdei* (roast chicken with garlic sauce).

Romania produces some very good wines, some of which are exported. Names to look for: *Murfatlar* (red or white), *Segarcea* (red) and *Cotnari* or *Tîrnava* (white). *Tzuica* is a popular plum brandy. Western brand-name drinks are served in deluxe and first-class hotels.

Lunch is served from noon to 2 p.m., dinner from 7 to 11 p.m.

Entertainment. Many movie theaters show foreign films in their original language. Nightclubs, dance clubs and bars with Western music are available. Major towns stage plays and opera.

Taxes, service charges and tipping. A service charge is included in hotel and restaurant bills but small gratuities are expected (higher in the capital than in the provinces). Some tipping recommendations: waiters 5–10%, porters 5 lei per piece, taxi drivers 5–10 (less for short distances), hatcheck 5 lei, hairdressers/barbers 10–15%.

Sports and recreation. Water sports, mountaineering, skiing and tennis. Spectator sports include soccer, handball, volleyball and tennis.

TV and radio. Radio and TV programming draws on Romanian and foreign sources. Foreign films are telecast in their original language.

What to buy. Handicrafts, carpets, textiles, food and drink are favorite purchases. Ceramics are produced in a variety of regional styles (Maramureş, Suceava and Argeş). The Maramureş area is also noted for its woollen rugs, and the Argeş region for a particular style of embroidered blouses. In Bucharest, special "dollar shops" offer a range of traditional products. Romanian wines, brandy and *tzuica* (plum brandy) can be obtained at bargain prices in all grocery stores. Antiques may not be exported.

Shopping hours: generally 8 a.m.–noon and 3–7 p.m., Monday–Saturday. Large stores stay open an hour later during the week and also work until noon on Sundays.

Export regulations are under review and should be checked before purchases are made.

413

Sightseeing

Bucharest. Grandiose buildings of the communist era lining extravagantly landscaped boulevards. 17th-century Patriarchal Church, rebuilt in modern times. Triumphal Arch in ancient Roman style commemorating World War I. Romanian Atheneum, neo-classic opera house from late 19th century. Art museum, endowed with a varied collection of Old Masters and lesser-known Romanian artists. 18th-century St. Stavropoleos church. History Museum*, with exhibits ranging from Stone Age and artifacts to late 20th-century political documents. Village Museum*, Romania in a nutshell, comprising hundreds of reconstitued folkloric buildings from all parts of the country. Excursion to Mogosoaia, colonnaded 17th-century palace in a lovely garden.

Provincial towns. Braşov: Black Church*, 14th-century Gothic church with immense organ and collection of oriental rugs; 15th-century town hall, containing local history museum; Transylvanian color of old town's cobbled streets; cable car to Mount Timpa for panorama over Braşov. Summer and winter sports complex of Poiana-Braşov. Excursion to medieval hilltop Bran Castle, recalling the Dracula saga. Sibiu: town fortifications from middle ages; 15th-century Old Town Hall tower; Brukenthal Museum, specializing in peasant art and culture. Cluj: St. Michael's church, begun in 14th century, with 17th-century additions; Museum of Art, Romanian and international, in distinguished Baroque Banffy Palace; Franciscan monastery, 15th-century Gothic; Botanical garden, biggest in Romania, with 10,000 species from all over the world.

Moldavian monasteries. Suceava: remains of churches, castles and fortifications from the town's golden age as medieval capital of Moldavia (and base for monasteries tour). Arbore, early 16th-century church with remarkable frescoes on outer and inner walls. Sucevita*, walls and towers guarding 16th-century monastery with a plethora of brightly colored internal and external frescoes. Moldoviţa, within impressive ramparts, a monastery filled with medieval art. Voroneţ*, a UNESCO-protected monument built in 15th century and covered with exquisite murals. Humor, a small monastery with starlingly colored, monumentally designed frescoes.

414

Black Sea coast. Constanţa, founded by ancient Greeks, Romania's principal seaport, center of beach resort zone, with huge mosaic tile floor from ancient Roman days, also Greek and Roman relics in Museum of National History and Archaeology, and Archaeological Park. Mamaia, highly developed seaside resort; smaller resorts reach south from Constanţa to the Bulgarian border.

The Danube Delta. The Danube ends its course in the middle of the Danube Delta, 2,850 km from its point of departure. Essentially a very large, (relatively) unpolluted swamp, the triangular delta★ harbors a fantastic flora and fauna, with some rare spieces of wild birds, including 70-odd species unique to the area. At Tulcea★, the river Danube divides, the northern branch, 120 km long, forming the frontier with the U.S.S.R., before reaching the Black Sea. Danube Museum with fantastic aquarium. The middle branch, 72 km long, leads to the port of Salina★ on the Black Sea, the official mouth of the Danube, originally a small fishing village that has now acquired a dockyard and is gradually becoming a resort. The southernmost branch zigzags to Sfîntu Gheorghe, a small fishing village from which Romania's black caviar mostly comes. Large pelican colony.

Northwestern Romania. Villages★ and wooden churches in little visited region of Maramureş near Baia Mare, especially Şurdesti, Deseşti and Sat-Şugatag.

Some useful expressions in Romanian

good morning/afternoon	buna dimineaţa/ziua
good evening/night	buna seara/noapte bună
good-bye	la revedere
yes/no	da/nu
please/thank you	vă rog/mulţumesc
excuse me	scuzaţi-mă
you're welcome	pentru puţin
where/when/how	unde/cînd/cum
how long/how far	cît durează/este departe
yesterday/today/tomorrow	ieri/azi/mîine
day/week/month/year	zi/săptămînă/lună/an
left/right	stînga/dreapta
up/down	sus/jos
good/bad	bun/rău
big/small	mare/mic
cheap/expensive	ieftin/scump
hot/cold	cald/rece
old/new	vechi/nou
open/closed	închis/deschis
free (vacant)/occupied	liber/ocupat
early/late	devreme/tîrziu
easy/difficult	uşor/dificil
Does anyone here speak English/French/German?	Vorbeşte cineva aici engleza/franceza/germana?
What does this mean?	Ce înseamnă aceasta?
I don't understand.	Nu înţeleg.
Please write it down.	Vă rog scrieţi.
Do you take credit cards/traveller's cheques?	Acceptaţi cărţi de credit/cecuri de voiaj?
Waiter!/Waitress!	Chelner!/chelneriţă!
Where are the toilets?	Unde este toaleta?
I'd like…	Aşi dori…
How much is that?	Cît costă?
What time is it?	Cît este ora?
Help me please.	Vă rog să mă ajutaţi.
Just a minute.	Un minut.

SPAIN
and ANDORRA

The timeless fascination of a thousand hilltop castles, bullfights and flamenco.

Millions of package tourists, smitten by the good life along the beach-lined Costas, miss the best of eternal Spain–Gothic cathedrals, gardened monasteries and whitewashed villages. Castles in Spain are really there, perched on thousands of hilltops; the enterprising traveler can sleep in one, at no more than the cost of a hotel.

Sprawling from the Atlantic to the Mediterranean, with vacation islands in both seas, Spain is Western Europe's second-largest country. Its scenery lacks nothing: lush hills and skiable mountains, orange groves and rice fields, and, of course, every kind of beach under the sun. There are activities for all tastes, from sailing (Columbus started here) to donkey treks (so did Sancho Panza).

The bullfight, a ritual drama rather than a sport, shows the florid, fatalistic face of Spain. The other inevitable manifestation of Spanish-ness, the fiery flamenco, provides a song and dance show that pours from the soul. Nightlife goes on very late, for Spaniards are Europe's night people. They don't sit down to dinner until 10 or 11 p.m., not quite starved after an hour or two nibbling on *tapas* and sipping sherry. The table wines meet high standards without a lot of mumbo-jumbo.

Spain's regional diversity, reinforced after the advent of democracy in the 1970s, adds to the country's timeless fascination. The Basques, with their bagpipes and inscrutable, outlandish language, breathe new life into their ancient culture. So do the dynamic Catalans of the east coast, and the dark-eyed Andalusians of the south, and other elements of the polyglot population radiating from the central plain, home of the proud Castilians.

Spain's artistic heritage is also decentralized, from the 12th-century cathedral of Santiago de Compostela to Gaudí's fantastic 20th-century "sandcastle cathedral" in Barcelona to the Moorish palaces of Andalusia, and in the middle of the country, in Madrid, the precious Prado Museum, home of El Greco, Velázquez and Goya.

Facts and figures

Population:	38.2 million
Area:	195,000 sq. miles (505,000 sq. km.)
Capital:	Madrid (3.2 million)
Other major cities:	Barcelona (1.8 million) Valencia (750,000) Seville (*Sevilla,* 655,000) Zaragoza (590,000) Málaga (505,000) Bilbao (435,000)
Language:	Spanish; Catalan and Basque are crucial languages in the Barcelona–Tarragona and Bilbao–Santander areas, respectively
Religion:	Roman Catholic (99.9%)
Time zone:	GMT + 1, EST + 6; DST (Apr.–Sep.)
Currency:	Spanish *peseta* (abbr. *pta.*) Coins: 1, 5, 10, 25, 50, 100, 200, 500 ptas. Bills: 1,000, 2,000, 5,000, 10,000 ptas.
Electricity:	125 or 220 volt (voltage varies, ask at your hotel), 50 cycle, AC

Planning your trip

Visa requirements. See pp. 29–30.

Vaccination requirements. None (see also p. 25).

Currency restrictions. Tourists may bring an unlimited amount of Spanish or foreign currency into the country. Departing, though, you

419

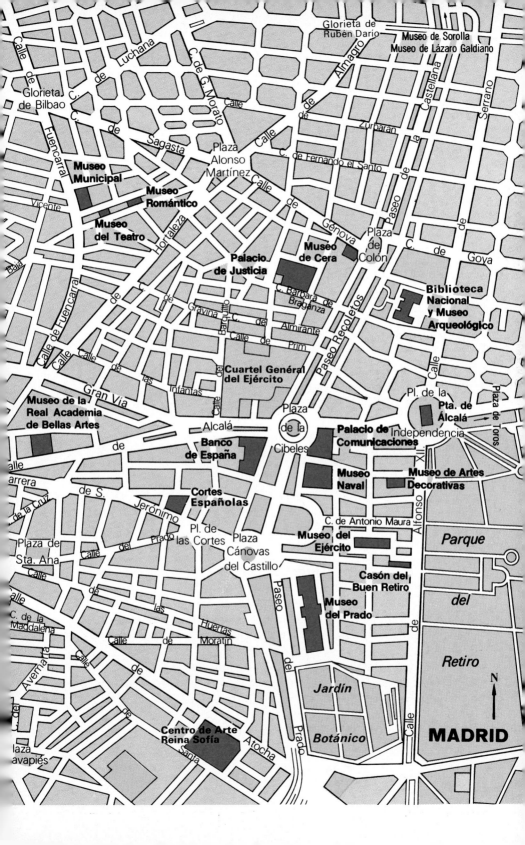

Calle de Luchana

C. de G. Morato

Glorieta de Rubén Darío

Museo de Sorolla
Museo de Lázaro Galdiano

Glorieta de Bilbao

Almagro

Castellana

Serrano

C.

C. de

Sagasta

Zurbarán

Plaza Alonso Martínez

C. de Fernando el Santo

Museo Municipal

Museo Romántico

Museo del Teatro

Fuencarral

Vicente

Baja

Hortaleza

Paseo de la

Genova

Plaza de Colón

Museo de Cera

C. de Goya

Palacio de Justicia

C. Barbara de Braganza

Biblioteca Nacional y Museo Arqueológico

Calle de Fuencarral

Gravina

C. de

Almirante

Prim

Barquillo

Cuartel Genéral del Ejército

Paseo Recoletos

Gran Vía

de las Infantas

Museo de la Real Academia de Bellas Artes

Pl. de la

Pta. de Alcalá

Plaza de Toros

Alcalá

de S.

Plaza de la Cibeles

Banco de España

Palacio de Comunicaciones

Independencia

Cortes Españolas

Jeronimo

Museo Naval

Museo de Artes Decorativas

Alfonso

arrera

de la Cruz

Pl. de las Cortes

del Prado

Plaza Cánovas del Castillo

C. de Antonio Maura

Museo del Ejército

Plaza de Sta. Ana

Parque

Calle

C. de la Maddalena

Huertas

Moratín

Cason del Buen Retiro

Museo del Prado

Calle

de las

XII

del

Avemaria

Calle

de

Jardín

Retiro

N

laza avapiés

Centro de Arte Reina Sofía

Santa

Atocha

Prado

Botánico

MADRID

must declare any amount beyond 100,000 pesetas and the equivalent of 500,000 pesetas in foreign currency. Thus if you plan to carry large sums in and out again it's wise to declare your currency on arrival as well as on departure.

Climate. In the north and northwest the climate is moderate with well-distributed rainfall. The south and southeast coastal plains are Mediterranean—hot and dry in summer, mild and rainy in winter. Most inland areas have a continental climate—hot in summer, cold in winter, with generally light rainfall.

Some average daily temperatures:

Madrid		J	F	M	A	M	J	J	A	S	O	N	D
average daily	°F	47	52	59	65	70	80	87	85	77	65	55	48
maximum*	°C	9	11	15	18	21	27	31	30	25	19	13	9
average daily	°F	35	36	41	45	50	58	63	63	57	49	42	36
minimum*	°C	2	2	5	7	10	15	17	17	14	10	5	2
Barcelona													
average daily	°F	55	57	60	65	71	78	82	82	77	69	62	56
maximum*	°C	13	14	16	18	21	25	28	28	25	21	16	13
average daily	°F	43	45	48	52	57	65	69	69	66	58	51	46
minimum*	°C	6	7	9	11	14	18	21	21	19	15	11	8

* Minimum temperatures are measured just before sunrise, maximum temperatures in the afternoon.

Clothing. Weather is variable in spring and autumn, so it's best to have a sweater or light overcoat handy. By day between July and early September, dress in light, preferably cotton clothes; you'll rarely need a wrap, but have one handy in the evenings. During winter an overcoat is usually necessary. Inland in Madrid, winters can be uncomfortably cold, not only because of the temperature but also on account of the mountain winds which carry the chill to your bones. Pack warm clothes. When visiting churches women no longer have to cover their heads, but decent dress is certainly expected. Some restaurants require ties for men, and jackets are suggested for the opera.

422

Duty-free allowances

	Cigarettes		Cigars		Tobacco	Liquor	Wine
1)	300	or	75	or	400 g.	1½ l. and	5 l.
2)	200	or	50	or	250 g.	1 l. and	2 l.

Perfume: 1) 75 g.; 2) 50 g. *Toilet water:* 1) ⅜ l.; 2) ¼ l.
Gifts: 1) 48,675 ptas. max. value provided bought inside EEC non-duty free;
2) 6,255 ptas. max. value.

1) entering from an EEC country
2) entering from another country

Hotels and accommodations

Hotels. Accommodations range from luxury hotels to modest boarding-houses *(pensión)*. Spanish hotel prices are no longer government-controlled. A hotel guide *(Guía de Hoteles)* may be consulted at tourist offices and major hotels. It's advisable to make reservations well in advance in summer as many hotels are entirely booked by tour operators. The overwhelming majority of tourists who arrive in the islands, Majorca, Ibiza or the Canary Islands, have reserved and paid for their accommodations in advance through package tour operators abroad. Tourists arriving without reservations at the height of the summer season may be hard pressed to find adequate lodging. In Madrid hotel-reservation desks are found at Barajas Airport and at Chamartín and Atocha rail stations.

When taking a room you will be asked to sign a form that specifies the hotel category, room number and price; breakfast is rarely included. If you're asked to leave your passport, you can insist that any formalities be completed on the spot or within half-an-hour—without leaving the passport overnight.

Apart from hotels, look for accommodations in village inns *(fonda)*, family hotels, usually without restaurants *(hostal; hotel-residencia)*, or state-run inns *(parador)*. The *parador* is often located in old or historic restored buildings in beautiful settings, usually in isolated or touristically less developed areas of Spain. Advance reservations are essential.

Youth hostels. To be able to stay overnight in a Spanish youth hostel *(albergue de juventud)* you must present a youth-hostel membership card. For addresses and other information, contact the Oficina Central de Albergues Juveniles: Calle José Ortega y Gasset 74, 28006 Madrid.

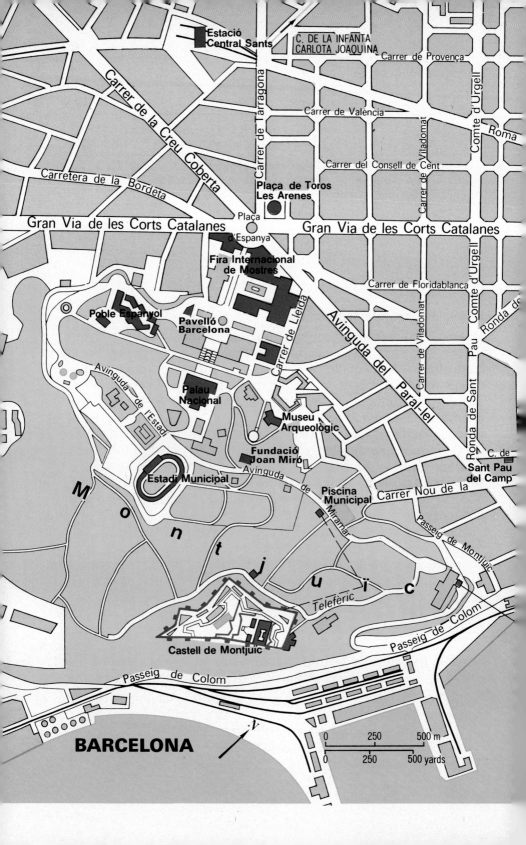

Estació
Central Sants

C. DE LA INFANTA
CARLOTA JOAQUINA

Carrer de Provença

Carrer de la Creu Coberta

Carrer de Tarragona

Carrer de València

Comte d'Urgell

Roma

Carrer del Consell de Cent

Carrer de Viladomat

Carretera de la Bordeta

Plaça de Toros
Les Arenes

Plaça

Gran Via de les Corts Catalanes

Gran Via de les Corts Catalanes

d'Espanya

Fira Internacional
de Mostres

Carrer de Floridablanca

Comte d'Urgell

Poble Espanyol

Pavelló
Barcelona

Carrer de Lleida

Avinguda del Paral·lel

Carrer de Viladomat

Ronda de Sant Pau

Ronda de

Palau
Nacional

Museu
Arqueològic

C. de
Sant Pau
del Camp

Fundació
Joan Miró

Avinguda de l'Estadi

Avinguda

Estadi Municipal

de

Piscina
Municipal

Carrer Nou de la

M

o

n

Miramar

Passeig de Montjuïc

t

j

u

ï

c

Teleféric

Passeig de Colom

Castell de Montjuïc

Passeig de Colom

N

250   500 m

BARCELONA

0   250   500 yards

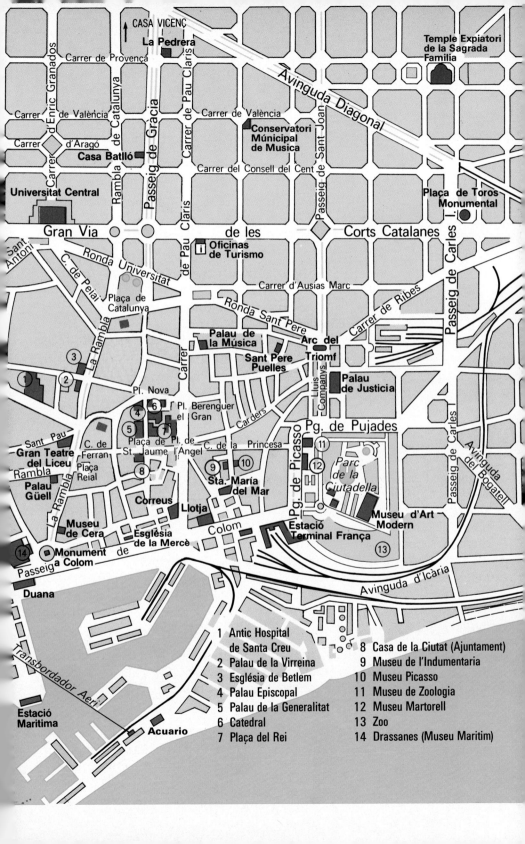

CASA VICENÇ
La Pedrera
Carrer de Provença
Temple Expiatori
de la Sagrada
Familia
Avinguda Diagonal
Carrer de València
Carrer de València
Conservatori
Múnicipal
de Musica
Carrer d'Aragó
Casa Batlló
Carrer del Consell del Cent
Plaça de Toros
Monumental
Universitat Central
Gran Via   de les   Corts Catalanes
Sant Antoni
Ronda Universitat
Oficines
de Turisme
C. de Pelai
Plaça de Catalunya
Carrer d'Ausias Marc
Ronda Sant Pere
Carrer de Ribes
③
①
②
Palau de
la Música
Arc del
Triomf
Sant Pere
Puelles
Palau
de Justicia
Pl. Nova
Pl. Berenguer
el Gran
Carders
Pg. de Pujades
⑥
④
⑦
Parc
de la
Ciutadella
Sant Pau
Gran Teatre
del Liceu
⑤
C. de
Ferran
Plaça de
St. Jaume
Pl. de
l'Angel
C. de la Princesa
⑪
Rambla
Plaça
Reial
⑧
⑨
⑩
⑫
Palau
Güell
Correus
Sta. María
del Mar
Llotja
Museu d'Art
Modern
Museu
de Cera
Església
de la Mercè
Colom
Estació
Terminal França
⑬
⑭
Monument
a Colom
Passeig   de
Avinguda d'Icaria
Duana
Transbordador Aeri
1 Antic Hospital
   de Santa Creu
2 Palau de la Virreina
3 Església de Betlem
4 Palau Episcopal
5 Palau de la Generalitat
6 Catedral
7 Plaça del Rei

8 Casa de la Ciutat (Ajuntament)
9 Museu de l'Indumentaria
10 Museu Picasso
11 Museu de Zoologia
12 Museu Martorell
13 Zoo
14 Drassanes (Museu Maritim)

Estació
Maritima
Acuario

Camping. There are more officially approved campsites along the Mediterranean coast than elsewhere in Spain. Facilities vary according to the classification, but most have electricity and running water. Some have shops, small playgrounds for children, restaurants, swimming pools and even launderettes. For a complete list of campsites, consult any Spanish National Tourist Office.

Spanish tourist offices abroad

Canada	60 Bloor Street West, Suite 201, Toronto, Ont M5W 3B8; tel. (416) 961-3131
U.K.	57–58 St. James's Street, London SW1 A1LD; tel. (071) 499 1169
U.S.A.	845 N. Michigan Avenue, Chicago, IL 60611; tel. (312) 944-0216
	4800 The Galleria, 5085 Westheimer Road, Houston, TX 77056; tel. (713) 840-7411
	8383 Wilshire Boulevard, Suite 960, Beverly Hills, Los Angeles, CA 90211; tel. (213) 658-7188/93
	665 Fifth Avenue, New York, NY 10022; tel. (212) 759-8822

On the spot

Banks and currency exchange. Banks are open from 9 a.m. to 2 p.m. on weekdays, although some banks stay open until 4:30 p.m. Monday through Thursday. On Saturdays (October–April), they are open until 1 p.m. There are variations, though, and a few have money-changing facilities open till late at night. Outside banking hours money can be exchanged at currency-exchange offices *(cambio)*, airports, rail stations, major hotels, and other establishments displaying the *cambio* sign. Banks and *cambios* offer a slightly better rate for traveler's checks than cash. Always take your passport with you when you want to change money.

Credit cards and traveler's checks. All internationally recognized cards are accepted by hotels, restaurants and stores in Spain. Traveler's checks are widely accepted in tourist areas, but you can get a better exchange rate at a bank or *cambio*.

Mail and telecommunications. Post offices *(correos)* deal with mail and telegrams only. Post offices are open from 9 a.m. to 1 or 2 p.m., and from

426

4 or 5 p.m. to 6 or 7 p.m., Monday through Friday. They are also open Saturday mornings. Madrid's cathedral-like main post office is located on Plaza de la Cibeles, Barcelona's on Plaza Antonio López. Mailboxes are yellow and red. If you see a mailbox marked *extranjero,* it's for foreign-destination mail. Stamps can also be bought at tobacco shops.

Main post offices in major centers are open 24 hours a day, but only for telex and telegrams. You can also send telegrams by phone.

Telephone offices, identified by a blue and white sign, are almost always separate from post offices. The domestic telephone network is almost completely automatic and direct dialing is available to many countries. Street telephone booths are springing up everywhere. Public phones take 5-, 25-, and 100-peseta coins. Line up the coins on the ledge provided, and the machine helps itself. Hold on to the leading coin when you hang up as the machine sometimes takes a last swallow. For surcharges and low rates, see p. 30.

Some useful telephone numbers:

Information		Telegrams	222 2020
(domestic)	009	Police	091
International service		Ambulance	409 5530
(Europe)	008	24-hour pharmacies	098
International service			
(outside Europe)	089		

Newspapers. Spain's leading newspapers are, in Madrid, *El País, ABC* and *Diario 16;* in Barcelona, *La Vanguardia* and *El Correo Catalán;* in Bilbao, *Gaceta del Norte* and *El Correo Español.* Local English-language publications include the daily *Iberian Sun,* the weekly *Guidepost, the Costa Blanca News,* and the monthly magazine *Lookout.* Foreign newspapers and magazines are usually available late on the day of publication at large newsstands.

Tourist information. There are tourist offices (*oficinas de turismo*) in all major cities and leading resorts. Most offices have an English-speaking member of staff.

Madrid	Torre de Madrid (Plaza de España); tel. 541 23 25; Barajas Airport; Chamartín railroad station; Plaza Mayor, 3; Calle Duque de Medinaceli, 2
Barcelona	Plaça de Sant Jaume (in the City Hall); tel. 302 42 00
Bilbao	Alameda de Mazarredo; tel. 424 48 19
Palma de Mallorca	Avinguda Rei Jaume III, 10; tel. 71 22 16/72 40 90

| Málaga | Marqués de Larios, 5; tel. 21 34 45 |
| Marbella | Avenida Miguel Cano, 3; tel. 77 46 93/77 14 42 |

Legal holidays

Jan. 1	New Year's Day	**Movable dates:**
Jan. 6	Epiphany	Maundy Thursday
May 1	Labor Day	Good Friday
July 25	St. James's Day	Immaculate Conception
Aug. 15	Assumption	(normally December 8)
Oct. 12	Discovery of	Corpus Christi
	America Day	
	(Columbus Day)	
Nov. 1	All Saint's Day	
Dec. 6	Constitution Day	
Dec. 25	Christmas Day	

Transportation

Air. Madrid is the main gateway to Spain, though international flights also come in to Barcelona, Bilbao, Palma de Mallorca and other cities. All major cities are linked by frequent domestic air services.

Major airports. Madrid: Barajas (8 miles/12 km. from city center). Duty-free shop. There is an airport bus service, and an hourly shuttle flight links Madrid and Barcelona. **Barcelona:** Muntadas (7 miles/11 km. from city center). Duty-free shop. There is a regular train service to the city center, and a shuttle operates between Madrid and Barcelona. **Málaga:** Aeropuerto Internacional (5 miles/8 km. from city center). Duty-free shop. There are bus services every 30 minutes to Málaga, Torremolinos and other coastal resorts. **Majorca:** Son San Juan. Duty-free shop. A bus service operates to Palma rail station. **Bilbao:** Sondica (9 miles/15 km. from city center). Bus service.

Rail. While local trains are very slow, stopping at almost every station, long-distance services, especially the *Talgo* and *Ter* trains, are fast and reasonably punctual. Some trains are air-conditioned. First-class cars are comfortable, second-class adequate. Seat reservations are recommended and often required. Tickets may be bought at travel agencies as well as at rail stations. The *Cheque-tren* card gives a 15 percent reduction on train tickets, including supplements and sleeping accommodations. For *Eurailpass,* see p. 33.

Long-distance buses. For trips between resorts and cities, there are many private bus companies that run a fairly good service. These buses are cheaper than trains. Information on schedules and fares can be obtained from tourist information offices or from the central bus station in larger towns.

Local public transportation. Most cities have bus services. Madrid and Barcelona also have subway systems, but these are very crowded and become oven-hot in summer.

Taxis. Cabs are recognized by the letters SP (for *servicio público*) on the front and rear bumpers. In major cities they have meters. Cabs are found at stands or can be hailed on the street. If unoccupied, they display a green light in the top right front corner, and a *libre* (free) sign. Additional charges are legitimately made at night and on holidays, for picking up at airports and rail stations, etc. All taxis carry lists of charges in several languages. These lists have been approved by the authorities. If you feel you've been overcharged, you can always ask the driver to show you the list. In the country, where there are no meters, it's usual to agree on the approximate price before you leave. If you take a longer trip—for example between two villages—you will be charged the round trip fare whether you return in the taxi or not.

Car rental. International and local car-rental firms operate throughout Spain. Chauffeur-driven cars are available. See also pp. 30–31.

Driving in Spain. The car should carry a red warning reflector triangle and a spare set of bulbs. Seat belts are compulsory outside the city. Drive on the right, pass on the left. Traffic from the right has priority, and you must use indicators when passing. Spaniards often use the horn, too. Speed limits are 75 mph (120 kph) on expressways, 62 mph (100 kph) or 56 mph (90 kph) on other roads and 36 mph (60 kph) in towns and built-up areas. Gasoline available is normal (92 octane), super (97 octane), lead-free (95 octane) and diesel. Blood alcohol limit is 80 mg./100 ml.

Spain's expanding expressway network is excellent but rather expensive tolls are charged. Secondary roads can be bumpy. The main danger of driving in Spain comes from impatience, especially on busy roads. Spanish truck drivers will often wave you on (by hand signal or by flashing their right directional signal) if it's clear ahead. The most common offenses include passing without flashing the directional indicator lights before *and after,* traveling too close to the car ahead and driving with a burned-out head- or tail-light. Use one of the strategically positioned emergency telephones to call for help in cases of breakdowns. Otherwise phone the Guardia Civil.

Some distances: Madrid–Zaragoza 200 miles (320 km.), Valencia 215 miles (350 km.), Málaga 340 miles (545 km.), Barcelona 385 miles (620 km.).

Bicycle rental. In a few resorts it's possible to rent a two-wheeled vehicle. You may have to leave a deposit.

Rest rooms. Public rest rooms are found in most large towns, but rarely in villages. However, most bars and restaurants have rest rooms. If you drop into a bar specifically to use the facilities, it's considered polite to buy a cup of coffee or a glass of wine as well. *Aseos, servicios, W.C., water* and *retretes* are some ot the most commonly found expressions for rest rooms. New, French-style toilets have been introduced on street corners in Madrid.

Emergencies. In case of an emergency, first try the hotel receptionist, otherwise dial the police emergency number—091.

Police. There are three police forces in Spain. The best-known are the *Guardia Civil* (civil guard), who wear olive-green uniforms. The motorcycle branch of this force is Spain's traffic police. If you are stopped for an offense, the fine must be paid immediately. Most towns also have a *Policía Municipal* (municipal police) whose officers wear blue and gray uniforms. The third force is the *Cuerpo Nacional de Policía,* a national anti-crime unit, recognized by their blue uniforms. All three forces are armed.

Crime and theft. Spain's crime rate has increased dramatically over the last few years, in particular in cities and larger resorts. Muggings and petty theft are all too common these days, so it's only sensible to take certain precautions. Take care of wallets and purses in crowded places like markets and bullfight arenas. Put all valuables in the hotel safe—it's better not to wear jewelry. Secure traveler's checks, credit cards and reserves of cash in a money belt. Don't leave anything of value, such as a camera, on view in the car, even when you are in it. Enterprising thieves have been known to smash the window with a rock and make off while the car was waiting at the traffic lights. Don't offer resistance should you be attacked.

Medical care and health. Health care in the resort areas and in the major cities is good. Most of the major resort towns have private clinics; the cities and rural areas are served by municipal or provincial hospitals. For minor ailments go to the local first-aid post *(ambulatorio/dispensario)*. Pharmacies *(farmacias)* are open during normal business hours.

431

After hours, at least one per town is open all night, called *farmacia de guardia*. The address is posted in the window of all other pharmacies. For insurance, see pp. 25–26.

Tap water is usually safe to drink but those with a delicate stomach may prefer to drink bottled mineral water and it's best to drink this during drought periods.

Embassies and consulates. Embassies and consulates are listed in the normal telephone directory or in the yellow pages under "Embajadas" and "Consulados", respectively.

Social customs. Politeness and simple courtesies still matter in Spain. Shaking hands when you meet and part company is customary, at every encounter. If you don't, it is considered impolite. Always begin any conversation, whether with a friend, shop girl, taxi driver, policeman or telephone operator, with *buenos días* (good morning) or *buenas tardes* (good afternoon). Always say *adiós* (goodbye) or, at night, *buenas noches* when leaving. *Por favor* (please) should precede all requests. *Adiós* means also, familiarly, "hello". Spaniards have no appreciation for haste, and consider it bad form when anyone pushes them. An invitation to someone's home is rather unusual, but if you should get one, then send a bunch of flowers to the hostess the following day.

Enjoying Spain

Food and drink. The old Spanish institution of giving a free *tapa* with a drink is sadly dying out; instead these are more usually sold. A *tapa*, literally a lid, is a bite-sized morsel served on a saucer. It can be almost anything: meat balls, olives, fried fish, vegetable salad, grilled mushrooms in garlic sauce or seafood.

Spaniards tend not to spend much time on breakfast, and it's usually a *café con leche* (half coffee, half hot milk) and a sweet pastry. In the Balearic Islands and Catalonia in general, this might be *ensaimades* (a large fluffy roll dusted with sugar). Throughout Spain *churros* (fritters) also dusted with sugar are ideal for dunking in your coffee or chocolate.

Lunch tends to be eaten between 1 and 3 p.m., but it can go on until 4 or 4:30 p.m. Dinner is usually served between 8 and 10 p.m. or even later.

There are some splendid soups to start the meal with, such as *gazpacho* (tangy chilled soup of tomatoes, green peppers and cucumber)

432

or *ajo blanco* (cold garlic soup made with Málaga almonds and raisins)—both come from the hot south.

For the main course a traditional lunchtime dish is *paella*. It's usually made to order and takes about half an hour. It is based on seafood and either chicken, pork or rabbit, served on saffron rice with green peppers, peas and any other vegetable that the cook has at hand.

A very tasty Catalan dish is *zarzuela,* up to 12 different types of seafood topped with a brandy and wine sauce. From Majorca comes *lechona* (roast suckling pig), while Ibiza offers a hearty meat and potato stew, with saffron, garlic, cinnamon and cloves, called *sofrit pagés*.

A good standby all over the country is *tortilla española*. This is less of an omelet than an egg and potato pie that can be eaten hot or cold. *Tumbet* is a mixture of aubergine, peppers, potatoes and tomatoes fried in olive oil, while *garbanzos* (chick peas) can be cooked with parsley, oil and garlic.

Wherever you go the fish will be fresh and very good. It is normally grilled and served plain with a salad and some potatoes, or it could be accompanied by a sauce such as *romesco* from Tarragona, which seems to be based largely on almonds and red peppers. Look for *lenguado* (sole), *mero* (sea bass), *salmonetes* (Mediterranean red mullet), *calamares* (squid), *gambas* (prawns) and *langosta* (spiny lobster).

Dessert can be fresh fruit or one of the many custards and flans that Spain produces; try a *crema catalana* (a creamy custard topped with a crisp caramel glaze). Otherwise just press your nose against the window of a pastry shop and point out the one you want.

The most famous Spanish wine is sherry from Jerez de la Frontera, which is fortified with the addition of brandy. As an aperitif, try *fino* (pale, dry sherry). An *oloroso* (dark gold sherry with fuller body) goes well after dinner.

When the average Spaniard sits down to a meal, he simply orders *vino*, and it means red wine to the average waiter. Often served chilled, this house wine can go with fish or meat, or anything. For better-class wines, try those from Rioja. A bottle of Rioja Reserva or Gran Reserva is a serious competitor to a good-quality Bordeaux, and Vega Sicilia is one of the most rare and expensive red wines in the world.

Make sure you try some *sangría* during your vacation. It's made of red wine, brandy, lemonade and diced fruit. It's very refreshing but packs quite a punch. An unusual soft drink is *horchata de chufa* made from a fruity wrinkled nut that has a taste similar to that of almonds.

Entertainment. Concerts, opera, theater and the *zarzuela* (Spanish form of light operetta) flourish in major cities. Famous opera and ballet companies appear at Barcelona's opera house, Gran Teatre del Liceu, said to be one of the finest theaters in the world when it opened in 1857. There are discos and casinos in all resorts as well as in the cities. Try to see a bullfight in Madrid, the world's bullfighting capital. Flamenco shows with singing and dancing are an attraction in large cities. Regional folk dancing festivals are frequent all over the country. Foreign movies are generally dubbed into Spanish.

Annual events and festivals. *March:* Valencia Fallas (carnival). *April:* Seville Fair. Jerez Horse Show. *May:* Córdoba Flamenco Competition. *June:* St. John's and St. Peter's Day festivals in Alicante, Barcelona, Segovia. Granada International Festival of Music and Dance. *July:* Pamplona bull running. *August:* Málaga Fair. *September:* Jerez Grape Harvest Festival, with bullfights, flamenco, parades and wine tastings. San Sebastián Basque Festivals. Córdoba Autumn Fair.

Taxes, service charges and tipping. Service charges are generally included in hotel and restaurant prices. Porters at airports have a set, posted rate per bag. Tipping recommendations: porters at hotels a minimum 50 ptas. per bag, waiters 5%, hatcheck 25–50 ptas. per person, barbers and hairdressers 5%, taxi drivers 5%.

Sports and recreation. There are many excellent golf courses in Spain. Tennis courts are plentiful near all cities. There is an abundance of water sports all the way along the coastline, and good freshwater and deep-sea fishing are available. Skiing in the Catalonian Pyrenees is good.

Spain's top spectator sport is soccer followed by bullfighting. The bullfight season extends through spring, summer and autumn. Other sports include horse racing in Madrid, greyhound racing in Madrid and Barcelona, and pelota, *jai alai,* in the Basque country.

TV and radio. Radio and TV broadcasts are in Spanish. Both BBC and the Voice of America can be heard on short-wave radios.

What to buy. Look for Toledo gold, leather goods (suede and leather coats, shoes and handbags), local porcelain and ceramics, mat and basket work, rugs, ponchos and knitted shawls, mantillas from Seville, fans, and bullfighter posters and hats. Sherry and Cuban cigars are other popular buys. In some cases, sales tax is refunded (see p. 40).

Most shops are open between 9:30 a.m. and 1:30 p.m., and from 4 or 5 p.m. to 8 p.m.; department stores tend to be open nonstop between 10 a.m. and 8 p.m.

Calle de Serrano is Madrid's most fashionable shopping street. In Barcelona, the most elegant shops are along Paseo de Gracia.

Sightseeing

Madrid. Puerta del Sol, New Year's meeting place, from where all radial highways of Spain are measured. 17th-century Plaza Mayor*, heart of city, broad arcades surrounding cobbled rectangle. Ornate, delicate Casa de Cisneros. Town Hall *(Ayuntamiento)* with towers and slate spires, characteristic of the 17th-century official buildings all around Madrid. Formidable 18th-century Basilica of St. Francis of Assisi, dome larger than that of St. Paul's in London. Famous fountain of Greek fertility goddess at Plaza de la Cibeles. Museum of

436

Royal Academy rubbing shoulders with high finance on Calle de Alcalá and displaying works of Goya, Velázquez, Murillo and Rubens. National Museum at Convent of Descalzas Reales* containing outstanding paintings by Titian and Brueghel the Elder, theatrical grand stairway and 17th-century tapestries based on original Rubens drawings. Prado Museum*, the world's greatest collection of Spanish paintings but also other masterpieces. Royal Palace *(Palacio Real)** overlooking Manzanares Valley with lavishly decorated state apartments and private apartments, notably the Throne Room with red velvet and mirrors on the walls and ceiling painting by Tiepolo; Carriage Museum. Plaza de España, with Cervantes Monument, honoring the author and his immortal creations, Don Quixote and Sancho Panza. Ancient jewelry at Lázaro Galdiano Museum*. Prado annex at Calle de Felipe IV with Picasso's *Guernica*. Museum of Contemporary Art with works by Picasso, Dalí and Miró. Archaeological Museum emphasizing the art of the ancient inhabitants of Spain. El Retiro Park, until little over a century ago a royal reserve, today the place to take a family outing. Rastro, vast Sunday flea market.

Castile. Toledo*, hilltop town crammed with tradition, grandeur and art and famed for glorious cathedral with prominent Gothic spire, stained glass, polychrome retable and walnut wood choir stalls, wrought iron, sculpture and painting; Alcázar, an old fortress, stronghold of pro-Franco forces during Spanish Civil War; Hospital of the Holy Cross, museum with wide selection of El Greco's works; Bridge of Alcántara, 9th- and 12th-century elements; Parish Church of Santo Tomé with stately tower in mudéjar style, containing El Greco's painting *Burial of the Count of Orgaz;* 14th-century El Greco House, built by Samuel Levi, next to intricately decorated Synogogue of the Dormition *(La Sinagoga del Tránsito)*; superb cloister at San Juan de los Reyes combining Gothic and Renaissance styles. The village of Illescas noted for five El Grecos in Convent of the Virgin of Charity. Segovia*, with a Roman aqueduct, a work of art and a triumph of engineering, still in use; Alcázar, Segovia's incomparable royal castle with an unimpeded view of the plateau; elegant Gothic cathedral adorned with fine stained-glass windows and two flamboyant organs; 12th-century Romanesque St. Martin's Church; 12-sided Vera Cruz Church, dating from early 13th century. Avila*, city protected by 11th-century walls; cathedral with fine stained-glass windows accentuating the grace of the interior; Romanesque St. Vincent Basilica; Royal Monastery of St. Thomas with Dominican-run Museum of Oriental Art; Convent of the Incarnation outside the city wall, where St. Theresa spent some 30 years. El Escorial*,

437

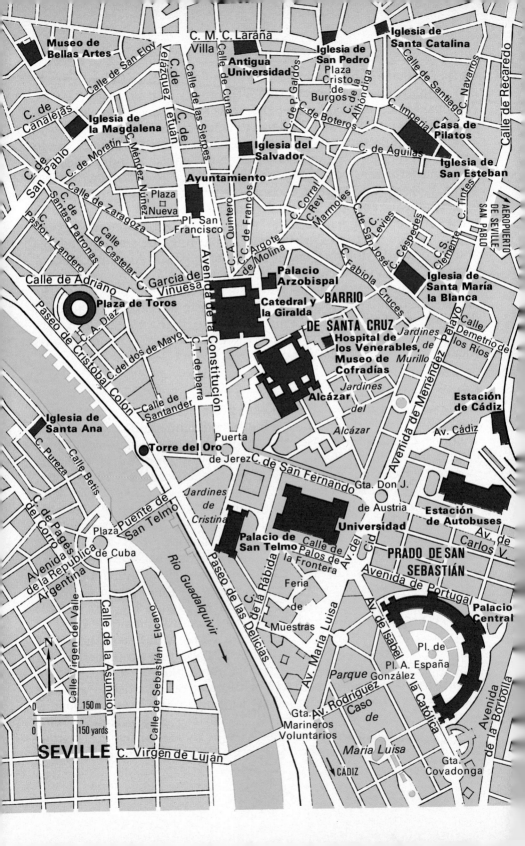

Museo de Bellas Artes

C. M. C. Laraña
Villa

Iglesia de Santa Catalina

Iglesia de San Pedro

Antigua Universidad

Plaza Cristo de Burgos

C. de Santiago

Calle de San Eloy

Calle de Canalejas

C. de Velázquez

Calle de Cuna

C. de P. Galdós

C. de Alhóndiga

C. Navarros

Calle de Recaredo

C. de Canalejas

Iglesia de la Magdalena

Calle de Velázquez

Calle de Tetuan

C. de las Sierpes

C. de Boteros

C. Imperial

Casa de Pilatos

C. de San Pablo

C. de Moratín

Iglesia del Salvador

C. de Águilas

Iglesia de San Esteban

C. Méndez Núñez

Calle de Zaragoza

Ayuntamiento

C. Corral

C. Rey

C. de Tintes

AEROPUERTO DE SEVILLE SAN PABLO

Calle de San Pablo

C. de Santas Patronas

Plaza Nueva

Marmoles

C. de San Levíes

C. S. Clemente

Calle de Recaredo

Pastor y Landero

Calle de Zaragoza

Pl. San Francisco

C. A. Quintero

C. de Francos

C. C. Argote de Molina

C. de San José

Céspedes

C. S. Clemente

Calle de Adriano

C. García de Vinuesa

Palacio Arzobispal

C. Fabiola

Cruces

Iglesia de Santa María la Blanca

Plaza de Toros

C. A. Díaz

Catedral y la Giralda

BARRIO DE SANTA CRUZ

Jardines de los Ríos

Calle Demetrio de

Paseo de Cristóbal Colón

C. del dos de Mayo

C. T. de Ibarra

Hospital de los Venerables, Museo de Cofradías

Jardines de Murillo

Avenida de Menéndez Pelayo

Calle de Santander

Alcázar

Jardines del

Estación de Cádiz

Iglesia de Santa Ana

Puerta de Jerez

Alcázar

Av. Cádiz

C. Pureza

Calle Betis

Torre del Oro

C. de San Fernando

Gta. Don J.

C. de Pagés del Corro

Jardines de Cristina

Puente de San Telmo

Palacio de San Telmo

de Austria

Estación de Autobuses

Avenida de la República Argentina

Plaza de Cuba

Río Guadalquivir

Paseo de las Delicias

Calle de Palos de la Frontera

Universidad

PRADO DE SAN SEBASTIÁN

Av. de Carlos V.

Calle Virgen del Valle

Calle de la Asunción

Calle de Sebastián Elcano

C. de la Rábida

Feria

Av. María Luisa

Av. del Cid

Avenida de Portugal

Palacio Central

N

de

Av. de Isabel la Católica

Pl. de

150 m

Muestras

Parque

Pl. A. España

González

150 yards

Gta. Av. Rodríguez

Caso de

Avenida de la Borbolla

SEVILLE

C. Virgen de Luján

Gta. Marineros Voluntarios

María Luisa

Gta. Covadonga

↓CÁDIZ

somber complex built on extravagant scale, more than a palace—a royal city with church, monastery, museum, mausoleum, living quarters. Valle de los Caídos with Church of the Valley of the Fallen, a spectacular monument to the dead of the Spanish Civil War; the massive church hewn out of the side of the mountain, topped by high stone cross. Aranjuez*, vacation retreat for Spanish monarchs since Ferdinand and Isabella, with parks and 18th-century Royal Palace reminiscent of Versailles. Chinchón, home of liqueurs and garlic, an old-fashioned village with cargo-carrying donkeys, bullfights held in main square. Cuenca, old town of tall, narrow houses in magnificent setting. Burgos, noted for the third largest cathedral in Spain in exuberant Spanish style. León, a dynamic modern part and an ancient city, site of a Gothic cathedral with unique stained-glass windows and medieval basilica. Salamanca*, university town of narrow streets and many fine squares like Schools square *(Patio de Las Escuelas)* and Plaza Mayor; New Cathedral *(Catedral nueva)*.

Andalusia. Málaga, founded more than 3,000 years ago; Alcazaba, Moorish fortress and palace; unfinished 16th-century cathedral; tremendous variety of tropical and subtropical plants in Paseo del Parque.

Costa del Sol. Flamboyant and swinging resorts—Torremolinos; Fuengirola with old Moorish Castle of Sohail*; Marbella, jet-set capital with magnificent port and popular Plaza de los Naranjos, bordered by open-air cafés and 15th-century Town Hall; Estepona*, one of the prettiest villages along the coast, with futuristic bullring doubling as an open-air theater. Resorts interspersed with relatively undeveloped coastal villages, particularly east of Málaga. Nerja, town built on a cliff edge with Balcony of Europe*—view for eight miles along coast. Gigantic caves in nearby Maro, rock paintings. Cerro Gordo, lookout point. Almuñecar, beaches, old quarter, Moorish castle. Almería, tranquil town, Moorish castle Alcazaba, cathedral-cum-fortress, 15th-century St. Peter's Church.

Inland. Churriana, Hemingway's home while he was writing *A Movable Feast*. Mijas*, popular village with many foreigners. Benalmádena, offering museum with collection of pre-Columbian art. Vélez-Málaga, practically untouched by tourism, with Moorish castle and Church of Our Lady of the Incarnation. Competa, famous for sweet wine. Frigiliana*, outstanding example of Moorish architecture. Ronda*, split down the middle by a gorge, sitting right on the edge of a high cliff, well-preserved old quarter, La Ciudad, Moorish in character; birthplace of modern bullfight at El Mercadillo; Palace of the Moorish King *(Casa del Rey Moro)*, Moorish Baths, Palace of Mondragón; view from New

439

Bridge. Nearby Pileta Cave with 2,000-year-old drawings. Seville*, the
capital of Andalusia; Barrio de Santa Cruz, ancient Jewish quarter, a
maze of white houses and narrow streets; 15th-century cathedral with
cross made of gold brought back by Columbus; breathtaking view from
elegant Giralda Tower; lovely Court of the Orange Trees; the most
beautiful of all the bullrings in Spain; Tower of Gold *(Torre del
Oro)* built by the Moors and nearby castle, Alcázar. Jerez de la
Frontera, famed for its sherry, guided tours through the cellars; La
Colegiata, largest church in the city, Moorish castle. Córdoba, once a
bastion of Islam containing 300 mosques; 8th-century Grand Mosque

440

*(La Mezquita)**, featuring 850 columns, some taken from Roman temples and Christian churches; Fine Arts museum, Roman bridge, former Royal Castle *(Alcázar Real)*, old Jewish quarter. Granada, famed for its fantastic Moorish palace, Alhambra*, with stunningly beautiful patios and fountains, like Court of the Myrtles, Court of the Lions, Hall of Secrets, Hall of the Two Sisters, Hall of the Ambassadors; Alcazaba, guarding the palace and Generalife serving as a summer residence; Sacromonte, the gypsy quarter; cathedral and Royal Chapel, containing the graves of Ferdinand and Isabella.

Levant (Costa Blanca). Largely mountainous with lush green plains in foreground and thriving coastline. Valencia with narrow streets of Old Town, cathedral, 15th-century Gothic Palacio de la Generalidad. Alicante, with Town Hall *(Ayuntamiento)* distinguished by beautiful Baroque façade; Iglesia de Santa María dating from the 14th-century; Barrio de Santa Cruz, remains of old town. Nearby Castillo de Santa Bárbara above city, Castillo de San Fernando on opposite side. Candelabrum Cave *(Cuevas de Canalobre)*—stalagmites, stalactites, splendid acoustics. Villena, notable castle, Bronze Age treasure displayed in Town Hall. Villajoyosa, picturesque, relatively unspoiled village, annual reenactment of 1538 defeat of Algerian pirate Zala Arráez. Benidorm, cosmopolitan resort, small old town. Guadalest, 1,200-year-old eagle's nest fortress. Jávea, proclaimed by World Health Organization as "environmentally nearly perfect". Gandía with impressive Palacio de los Duques, palace of the dukes of Gandía. Játiva, town of fountains and huge plane trees; Collegiate Church, old hospital with ornate façade, well-presented Municipal Museum with 11th-century Moorish basin. Near Callosa, El Algar waterfalls.

South of Alicante. Elche* with thousands of date palms introduced in 300 B.C., Priest's Grove *(Hort del Cura)*, Calahorra Tower, once part of the wall that surrounded Elche; annual mystery play at Church of St. Mary. Orihuela, old university town, Gothic cathedral with Velázquez *Temptation of St. Thomas Aquinas*. Murcia, famous for its market gardens; Cathedral of St. Mary offering splendid western façade; Salzillo Museum. Mar Menor, shallow salt-water lagoon separated from sea by two strips of land called La Manga. Cartagena with Castillo de la Concepción dating back to Roman times, surrounded by Parque de las Torres; Archaeological Museum noted for its Roman mining tools.

Barcelona. Gothic Quarter *(Barri Gòtic* in Catalan)*, a walk through 15 centuries of history; the short, narrow street of Gate of the Angel

441

(Portal de l'Angel), the intimate and appealing patio of the 11th-century Archdeacon's House, St. Eulalia's Cathedral, built between 1298 and 1448, historic Plaça del Rei (King's Square), a splendid medieval ensemble, where Columbus is said to have been received by royalty on return from New World. La Rambla*—promenade from Plaça de Catalunya to the port, full of life and charm. Church of St. Paul-in-the-Fields *(Sant Pau del Camp)* with thousand-year-old stone carvings. Plaça Reial, Barcelona's most perfectly formed square. Church of the Sagrada Familia*, the controversial architect Antoni Gaudí's unfinished "sandcastle cathedral". Nearby Montjuïc, modest mountain with many museums: Museum of Art of Catalonia, one of the world's greatest collections of medieval art. Spanish Village *(Poble Espanyol)*, a five-acre exhibition of Spanish art and architecture. Near the waterfront, Drassanes, medieval shipyards and Columbus Monument. Carrer de Montcada, street of mansions and palaces. Picasso Museum*, located in three 13th-century palaces in Carrer de Montcada.

Costa Dorada. Sitges*, resort of natural beauty and liveliness; Cau Ferrat Museum, containing a moving El Greco portrait. Casa Papiol, recreation of 18th-century life, in town of Vilanove i la Geltrú. Outside Comarruga, Arch of Berà, tall monument from the 2nd century A.D. Tarragona with archaeological promenade, ancient city wall tour *(Passeig Arqueològic)*; Balcony of the Mediterranean with unbeatable view of the sea; cathedral. Salou, cosmopolitan resort with fine beaches. Cathedral of Tortosa, a classic example of Catalan Gothic.

Inland. Monserrat*: 12th-century polychrome wood image, La Moreneta, the little brown Madonna, in Benedictine monastery, inspiring choir singing. Poblet, church with tombs of the kings of Aragon. Santes Creus, monastery founded in the 12th century, preserved as museum. Vilafranca del Penedés, wine museum.

Costa Brava. Miles of sandy beaches, coves, tourist resorts and very occasional undiscovered villages. Cadaqués, picturesque, welcoming village of dazzling white houses. Roses, outstanding beaches, glorious sunsets. Castelló d'Empúries, magnificent church, cobbled streets. Peralada, home of sparkling wine *cava*. Figueras, theater-museum of Salvador Dalí. Sant Pere Pescador, fishing village with boats but no sea. L'Escala, ruins of Ampurias, formerly an island. L'Estartit, booming tourist town. Ullastret, discovery of the 4th–5th century Iberian city. S'Agaró, exclusive resort with 11th-century Porta Ferrada. Tossa de Mar, attractive resort, favored by painters and writers. Vila

Vella, 12th-century walls guarding town. Lively Lloret de Mar. Blanes, active fishing fleet and resort. Girona*, beautiful old quarter with cathedral, St. Felix's church, Arab baths, Sant Pere de Galligans. Banyoles, town with a lake, nearby Porqueres, two-house hamlet with exquisite church. Besalú, medieval village, restored fortified bridge. Ripoll, monastery with resplendent arched doorway and cloister.

Navarra and Aragon. Pamplona, famous for its July festival featuring spectacular bull running and bullfights; Gothic cathedral and elegant cloisters. Zaragoza, university town with fine cathedral (the *Seo)* and outstanding Tapestry Museum.

Cantabrian coast. Altamira*, prehistoric cave paintings. Laredo, old town of narrow streets, popular summer resort. Santander, sophisticated resort with attractive seashore promenade. Santillana del Mar, well-preserved medieval village. Collegiate Church. San Sebastián*, beautiful setting, vast beaches, gastronomic capital. Marvelous panorama from nearby Mount Igueldo. Bilbao, the third largest port in Spain. Picos de Europa, beautiful mountain range (8,688 feet/2,648 m.).

Galicia. Reminiscent of Wales and Brittany, bagpipes played. Santiago de Compostela*, city of pilgrimage, cathedral from 11th to 13th centuries, accessible from all four sides, outstanding Baroque façade, university, old quarter.

Balearic islands. **Majorca**: Palma de Mallorca*, famous Gothic cathedral, ancient Almudaina Palace, long white beaches, active nightlife, Almudaina Arch, Arab baths, Palacio Vivot, Convent of St. Francis, Bellver castle, Spanish village—outdoor museum. Capocorp Vell, Bronze Age settlement. Cala Figuera, "Venice of Majorca". Porto Cristo, Caves of the Dragon, Caves of the Hooks. Pollensa, 365 steps of Calvario to tiny church. Lluch, local place of pilgrimage. Banyalbufar, fertile terraces, nearby Tower of the Souls.
  Minorca. Island of peace and tranquility. North Minorca, lush undulating farmland. South Minorca, rock-strewn wilderness.
  Ibiza. Ibiza Town*, La Marina district, Old Town—walled city with seven-bulwark defenses, archaeological museums—Carthaginian treasures. Sant Antoni Abad, fortress church, resort. Santa Eulalia del Riu, old white church. Jesús, Gothic church with triptych. **Formentera:** relatively unspoiled island. Sant Francesc Xavier, prominent fortress church. Es Caló, tiny Roman harbor, view from mirador above town. Ca Na Costa, prehistoric stone circle, nearby salt pans, Las Salinas.

Andorra

For more than seven centuries the mountain fastness of Andorra has been jointly ruled from France and Spain. The principality still pays a token feudal tithe to its protectors, the President of France and a Spanish bishop of local Urgel. French francs and Spanish pesetas are legal tender, but in the duty-free shops that account for much of Andorra's fame, almost any currency is accepted. The official language is Catalan, a derivative of Latin. Neutral Andorra has no army, but the police force is mobilized to deal with the serious traffic problem—yes, it's hard to believe, there is one. So intertwined are the two cultures, French and Spanish, so many the recognizable elements from one or the other side of the frontier, that a visitor can be forgiven for wondering on occasions which country he or she is in. But even if much is "borrowed", this unique toy-like ministate has fought long and hard for its independence—you'll see why when you look out over the grandiose, spectacular scenery in which it is set.

Facts and figures

Population:	40,000
Area:	175 sq. miles (453 sq. km.)
Capital:	Andorra la Vella (13,500)
Language:	Catalan
Religion:	Catholic
Time zone:	GMT + 1, EST + 6; DST (Apr.–Sep.)
Currency:	French *franc* (see France) and Spanish *peseta* (see Spain)
Electricity:	125 or 220 volt, 50 cycle AC.

Planning your trip

Visa requirements: No requirements exist other than those of France or Spain, whichever must be transited to reach Andorra. See pp. 29–30.

Vaccination requirements. None (see also p. 25).

Currency restrictions. None.

Climate. Winters are cold but rather dry and sunny. The summer months are warm but the nights can get quite cold.

Some average daily temperatures:

Les Escaldes		J	F	M	A	M	J	J	A	S	O	N	D
average daily maximum*	°F	43	45	54	58	62	73	79	76	71	60	51	42
	°C	6	7	12	14	17	23	26	24	22	16	10	6
average daily minimum*	°F	30	30	35	39	43	39	54	53	49	42	35	31
	°C	-1	-1	2	4	6	10	12	12	10	6	2	-1

* Minimum temperatures are measured just before sunrise, maximum temperatures in the afternoon.

Duty-free allowances. Andorra is duty-free. No regulations apply other than those of France or Spain, whichever must be transited to reach Andorra.

Hotels and accommodations. There are over 230 hotels and inns for summer visitors, many of which stay open throughout the year. Make reservations well in advance for the summer months.
 Andorra has several campsites.

Andorra tourist offices abroad

U.K.	Andorra Official Information Office, 63 Wesover Road, London, SW18 2RF
U.S.A.	Andorran National Tourist Board, P.O. Box 69617, Hollywood, CA 90069

On the spot

Credit cards and traveler's checks. Both are widely accepted.

Tourist information

Andorra la Vella	National Tourist Office, Carrer Anna Maria Janer 5

446

Transportation

Air. Andorra has no airport, fly to Toulouse or Perpignan (France), or Barcelona (Spain). There are regular bus services from Barcelona and Toulouse to Andorra.

Local public transportation. The main villages in Andorra are linked by *microbus* services, but there is no fixed schedule.

Driving in Andorra. The speed limit in built-up areas is 25 mph (40 kph), and on other roads 43 mph (70 kph). In some villages the speed limit is 12 mph (20 kph). Remember that it's difficult to find parking spaces.

Emergencies. For the police, dial 21222; for ambulance and fire services, dial 20020.

Embassies and consulates. None.

Enjoying Andorra

Annual events and festivals. Local holidays: *July:* Canillo, Les Escaldes, Sant Julià de Lória. *August:* Andorra la Vella, Encamp, La Massana. *September:* Meritxell, Ordino.

Taxes, service charges and tipping. Hotels and restaurants usually add 10–15% service charges. If service is not included, add 10%.

Sports and recreation. Trout fishing and chamois hunting are popular; get permits from the tourist office. During the winter there is skiing.

What to buy. Everything is duty-free and often cheaper than in the country of origin.

Sightseeing

Andorra la Vella. 16th-century House of the Valleys *(Casa dels Valls)*, the parliament and court buildings, with nation's archives in a strong chest with six locks. Romanesque church with gilded altars in central square. Chapel of Santa Coloma outside capital—round tower, 12th-century wall paintings and horseshoe chancel arch. Outside the villages and tourist areas, wild untamed countryside.

447

Some useful expressions in Spanish

good morning/afternoon	buenos días/buenas tardes
good evening/night	buenas tardes/buenas noches
good-bye	adiós
yes/no	sí/no
please/thank you	por favor/gracias
excuse me	perdone
you're welcome	de nada
where/when/how	dónde/cuándo/cómo
how long/how far	cuánto tiempo/ a qué distancia
yesterday/today/tomorrow	ayer/hoy/mañana
day/week/month/year	día/semana/mes/año
left/right	izquierda/derecha
up/down	arriba/abajo
good/bad	bueno/malo
big/small	grande/pequeño
cheap/expensive	barato/caro
hot/cold	caliente/frío
old/new	viejo/nuevo
open/closed	abierto/cerrado
free (vacant)/occupied	libre/ocupado
early/late	temprano/tarde
easy/difficult	fácil/difícil
Does anyone here speak English/French/German?	¿Hay alguien aquí que hable inglés/francés/alemán?
What does this mean?	¿Qué quiere decir esto?
I don't understand.	No comprendo.
Please write it down.	Escríbamelo, por favor.
Do you take credit cards/traveler's checks?	¿Acepta usted tarjetas de crédito/cheques de viaje?
Waiter!/Waitress!	¡Camarero!/¡Camarera!
Where are the toilets?	¿Dónde están los servicios?
I'd like…	Quisiera…
How much is that?	¿Cuánto cuesta esto?
What time is it?	¿Qué hora es?
Help me please.	Ayúdeme, por favor.
Just a minute.	Un momento.

SWEDEN

Bigger than California, a land of forests, 100,000 lakes and a cosmopolitan capital.

More than a thousand years ago, Vikings from Sweden ravaged the towns of Russia before proceeding to pillage Constantinople. There followed a rousing history of wars against most of the countries closer at hand. Then, early in the 19th century, Sweden gave up belligerence and stayed neutral as two world wars swirled around it. Peace has proved to be a crucial natural resource—along with iron, timber and brain power—in the development of Sweden's enviable 20th-century prosperity. The neat, slumless cities advertise the very model of a modern welfare state.

Stockholm, challenging Copenhagen as the most cosmopolitan of Scandinavian capitals, exploits a lovely waterfront setting, with a distinguished historic district and a sparkling new central area. On one of the 14 linked islands that make up the city, the world's first outdoor museum, Skansen, shows all you need to know about Swedish culture in a single outing.

Sweden's second city, Gothenburg, knows how to relax among its parks, gardens, canals and boulevards, even if it is an important industrial and trading center. For romantic atmosphere, the top attraction is found on the Baltic island of Gotland, the medieval walled city of Visby.

Sweden's scenic variety includes vast forests, meadows, sandy beaches, nearly 100,000 lakes, and fjords—perfect if, like the late Swedish actress Greta Garbo, you want to be alone. The nights are long in winter, and the weather so cold that ice skaters take to the Baltic bays. But summer is the reward, when the sun scarcely sets at all, and the city dwellers fan out into the countryside to pick berries and mushrooms.

Swedish design, a fusion of form and function, excels in glassware, ceramics, tableware, furniture and textiles. Another specialty is *smörgåsbord,* a feast so formidable that the word itself has been absorbed into foreign languages. The Swedes are too polite to count how many times you return to the groaning board.

Facts and figures

Population:	8.3 million
Area:	173,665 sq. miles (449,793 sq. km.)
Capital:	Stockholm (650,000/GUA 1.5 million)
Other major cities:	Gothenburg *(Göteborg,* 425,000/GUA 700,000) Malmö (230,000/GUA 470,000) Uppsala (150,000) Norrköping (120,000) Västerås (120,000)
Language:	Swedish
Religion:	Protestant (98%)
Time zone:	GMT + 1, EST + 6; DST (Apr.–Sep.)
Currency:	Swedish *krona* (abbr. *kr)* = 100 *öre* Coins: 10, 50 öre; 1, 5 kr Bills: 10, 50, 100, 500, 1,000, 10,000 kr
Electricity:	220 volt, 50 cycle, AC

Planning your trip

Visa requirements. See pp. 29–30.

Vaccination requirements. None (see also p. 25).

Currency restrictions. There is no restriction on the amount of foreign or local currency non-residents can bring into or take out of the country (provided it is declared upon entry).

Climate. Except in the far north, Sweden has a moderately continental climate. Thanks to the warm currents of the Gulf Stream, the country's west coast enjoys a milder maritime weather. Rain falls mostly in March, April and July. May, early June and September are usually the best months, with sunny clear days. Beyond the Arctic Circle the midnight sun shines from mid-May to mid-July, but even farther south the days are long and it never gets really dark during this period. In winter, days are short and temperatures often plunge far below freezing. Snow and ice call for caution when walking in winter city streets.

451

Some average daily temperatures:

Stockholm		J	F	M	A	M	J	J	A	S	O	N	D
average daily maximum*	°F	30	30	37	47	58	67	71	68	60	49	40	35
	°C	-1	-1	3	8	14	19	22	20	15	9	5	2
average daily minimum*	°F	23	22	26	34	43	51	57	56	49	41	34	29
	°C	-5	-5	-4	1	6	11	14	13	9	5	1	-2

Gothenburg													
average daily maximum*	°F	34	34	39	49	60	66	70	68	61	51	43	38
	°C	1	1	4	9	16	19	21	20	16	11	6	4
average daily minimum*	°F	26	25	29	37	45	53	57	56	50	43	37	32
	°C	-3	-4	-2	3	7	12	14	13	10	6	3	0

* Minimum temperatures are measured just before sunrise, maximum temperatures in the afternoon.

Clothing. The weather can be ideal in the summer, pleasantly warm and with low humidity, and light- and mediumweight clothing is adequate. But the weather is never 100 percent predictable, so an umbrella is useful no matter what time of the year you're visiting Sweden. Summer evenings are often a bit cooler, requiring a sweater or jacket. In spring and fall you need a light overcoat and of course winter calls for boots, gloves and a warm coat. It's fashionable again to dress up, particularly in Stockholm and major cities, to go to the theater, opera and chic restaurants.

Duty-free allowances

	Cigarettes		Cigars		Tobacco	Liquor	Wine
1)	400	or	100	or	500 g.	1 l. and	1 l.
2)	200	or	50	or	250 g.	1 l. and	1 l.

Perfume: A reasonable quantity
Gifts: 600 kr max. value

1) residents of countries outside Europe
2) residents of Europe

Hotels and accommodations

Hotels. Hotels in Sweden have a well-deserved reputation for cleanliness, regardless of category, and are efficiently run. It may be difficult to find accommodations, especially in Stockholm, without advance reservations. Before leaving home, get a copy of the annual brochure published by the Swedish Tourist Board entitled *Hotels in Sweden,* which gives details of amenities and prices. Ask for it at the nearest Swedish tourist office or at your travel agency.

At the same time inquire about the Hotel Check system for cut-rate prices at some 250 Swedish hotels. This is especially useful if you plan to see part of the country outside of Stockholm. You can book your first night in Sweden before you leave home, then make reservations (free) for the following nights through the reception desk of each hotel. Children up to 12 stay free if they share their parents' bed. The Hotel Checks, valid from mid-June to September 1, can only be purchased outside Sweden.

If you arrive in Stockholm without a reservation, Hotellcentralen, run by the tourist office, can find you a hotel, boardinghouse or youth hostel. There's a desk at Arlanda Airport and one at the Central Railway Station; tel. 24 08 80. During the high season staff are on duty every day until late at night; in low season they keep business hours.

Motels. Motels are found along the main highways all over Sweden. Most of them are relatively new and offer swimming pool, sauna, restaurant and cafeteria.

Holiday cottages. There are thousands of vacation cottages for rent nationwide. You can choose between the typical red wooden cottage, perhaps in a forest glade by a lake, or a specially built chalet in one of Sweden's many vacation villages.

Youth hostels. Many of the youth hostels *(vandrarhem)* in Sweden are located in the southern and central part of the country. They provide inexpensive, adequate lodging to people of all ages. Many have special family rooms. If you're a member of an organization affiliated with the International Youth Hostel Federation, your card is valid in Sweden. For more information on Swedish hostels contact: Svenska Turist-föreningen (Swedish Touring Club), Drottninggatan 31–33, Stockholm; tel. (08) 790 31 00.

Camping. Sweden has more than 500 campsites that are officially approved. For a complete list of sites get a copy of "Campingboken", published by the Swedish Tourist Board, available at any Swedish bookshop.

Swedish tourist offices abroad

U.K. Swedish National Tourist Office, 29–31 Oxford Street, 5th floor, London W1R 1RE; tel. (071) 437 5816

U.S.A. Scandinavian National Tourist Offices, 655 Third Avenue, 18th floor, New York, NY 10017; tel. (212) 949-2333

Scandinavian Tourist Board, Denmark–Sweden, 150 North Michigan Avenue, Suite 2110, Chicago, IL 60601; tel. (312) 726-1120

Scandinavian Tourist Board, Denmark–Sweden, 8929 Wilshire Boulevard, Suite 300, Beverly Hills, CA 90211; tel. (213) 657-4808

On the spot

Banks and currency exchange. Banks are open 9:30 a.m. to 3 p.m., Monday through Friday (some open again in the afternoon one day a week from 4 to 5:30). The bank at Arlanda Airport operates daily from 7 a.m. to 10 p.m., and the exchange bureau at the Central Railway Station in Stockholm from 8 a.m. to 9 p.m. Foreign currency can also be changed at larger hotels and department stores, but the rate is less advantageous.

Credit cards and traveler's checks. Most international credit cards are welcome almost everywhere—shops and restaurants usually display signs indicating the ones they accept. Traveler's checks are best cashed in banks and exchange bureaus.

Mail and telecommunications. Swedish post offices, indicated by a yellow sign with a blue postal horn, handle only mail. Post offices are open from 9 a.m. to 6 p.m., Monday through Friday, from 10 a.m. to 1 p.m. on Saturdays. The post office in Klarabergsviadukten 63 in Stockholm is open 9:30 a.m. to 7 p.m., Monday through Friday. Stamps can be bought either at the post office or at tobacco shops, newsstands, department stores and hotels. Mailboxes are yellow.

All phones have fully automatic dial systems and are conveniently located in glass-enclosed sidewalk booths and in "Tele" offices. Dialing instructions are posted in Swedish and English. Direct dialing is available to most cities in the U.S. and Europe. Public phone and telegraph offices (marked "Tele") offer telex as well as fax, telegram and telephone services. The main office in Stockholm is located at Skeppsbron 2. You can also dictate a telegram over the phone. For surcharges and low rates, see p. 30.

Some useful telephone numbers:

Operator (information		Telegrams	0021
for all services,		Emergency	90 000
nationwide)	001		
Overseas information	0019		

Newspapers. The country's principal newspapers are *Svenska Dagbladet, Dagens Nyheter* and *Expressen* (Stockholm) and *Göteborgs Posten* (Gothenburg). Major European papers, including the *International Herald Tribune,* are available at leading newsstands and railroad stations. *Stockholm This Week* is distributed free at hotels.

Tourist information. There are more than 300 non-profit tourist offices in Sweden. They have a good selection of brochures and maps of their regions, and can provide you with information on sightseeing, excursions, restaurants, hotels, camping, sports, etc. In Sweden, tourist offices are indicated by a white "i" on a green background.

Stockholm	Stockholm Information Service, Sweden House, Hamngatan 27, near Kungsträdgården; tel. (08) 789 20 00 (789 24 28/29 on weekends). Tourist information in English (Stockholm) 22 18 40
Gothenburg	Kungsportsplatsen 2; tel (031) 10 07 50
Malmö	Hamngatan 1; tel. (040) 34 12 70

Legal holidays

Jan. 1	New Year's Day	**Movable dates:**
Jan. 6	Epiphany	Good Friday
May 1	Labor Day	Easter Monday
Dec. 25	Christmas Day	Ascension
Dec. 26	St. Stephen's Day	Whit Monday
		Midsummer Day (Sat. between June 20 and 26)
		All Saints' Day (Sat. between Oct. 31 and Nov. 6)

Transportation

Air. Stockholm is Sweden's principal gateway, though international flights also operate on a smaller scale through Gothenburg, Malmö and Norrköping. An efficient airline network links about 20 domestic airports around the country.

Major airports. Stockholm: Arlanda (26 miles/41 km. from city center). Duty-free shop. Bus service to city terminal near the railroad station; limousine service. **Gothenburg:** Landvetter (15 miles/24 km. from city center). Duty-free shop. Bus service to Central Station. **Malmö:** Sturup (19 miles/31 km. from the city center). Duty-free shop. Bus service to Central Station; regular hydrofoil and bus as well as hovercraft services also operate to Copenhagen Airport in Denmark.

Rail. The Swedish State Railways *(Statens Järnvägar* or *SJ)* operate an extensive network of rail lines, with more than 90 percent of the traffic carried by electric trains. Trains leave Stockholm for most big cities every hour or two. Swedish trains are clean and comfortable, and are constantly being modernized. They have 1st- and 2nd-class cars, either open or divided into compartments. On longer journeys, couchettes and sleeping cars are available. The new InterCity trains even have telephones. Seat reservations are often compulsory, especially on express trains. Tickets can be purchased and reservations made at travel agencies and at central stations.

Within Sweden visitors can take advantage of various rail bargains. *Nordic Tourist Ticket* allows unlimited travel within Sweden, Denmark, Finland and Norway for 21 days (and a discount on boats to Finland and the island of Åland). For *Eurailpass,* see p. 33.

Long-distance buses. Traveling by bus is an inexpensive though time-consuming way of seeing the country. Although there are private companies, Swedish Railways operates a low-priced, efficient bus system connecting towns, cities and outlying areas. Tickets can be purchased in any railroad station. Advance reservations can be made.

Boats, waterways. White steamers ply the waters of Lake Mälaren and serve the islands of the archipelago in the Baltic. There are also boat connections to the islands of Öland and Gotland. You can travel by boat between Gothenburg and Stockholm on the idyllic Göta Canal.

Local public transportation. All major cities provide public bus transportation. Gothenburg also has streetcars. In Stockholm a very efficient and modern subway, commuter train and bus system makes it easy to get around the city and its suburbs from about 5 a.m. to 2 a.m. Subway stations are indicated by a blue "T". Special one- and three-day tourist tickets and multi-unit cards are sold in the Pressbyrån kiosks. Some buses have a machine inside for validating tickets bought beforehand.

The Stockholm Card offers visitors the chance to see the city at a fair price. It provides free entry to about 50 museums, castles and other sights and free public transportation, including sightseeing tours by bus and boat. The pass is valid from one to four days. It is sold at Sweden House, Central Station and several other places.

Taxis. Cabs can be ordered by telephone or picked up at taxi stands. Theoretically you can flag them down anywhere in Stockholm but it seldom works. When a taxi is available, the vacant sign *(Ledig* in Swedish) is lighted. Cabs are difficult to find during rush hours and on rainy days. It's possible to reserve one in advance.

Car rental. Major international car rental agencies are widely represented in Stockholm and other cities and towns and at airports. You'll find addresses in the business telephone directory under "Biluthyrning". See also pp. 30–31.

Driving in Sweden. Drive on the right, pass on the left. Traffic on the main roads (and very often in the main city streets) has the right-of-way. At traffic circles, cars already in the circuit have priority, but in other situations traffic from the right has the right-of-way.

Most Swedish roads are good, though only a small proportion are expressways. Many secondary roads are unsurfaced. Watch out for elk wandering on the road, especially at sunrise and sunset and in wooded areas.

The driver, as well as passengers in the front and back (if the car is so equipped) seats, are required to use seat belts and the car must carry a red reflector warning triangle available for emergencies. All vehicles (including motorcycles) must have low-beam headlights switched on at all times, even in broad daylight. Routine spot checks to inspect driver's licenses and the condition of vehicles are common in Sweden. Police also check to see if drivers have been drinking, which is a very serious offense in Sweden. You can be fined or even sent to jail if the level of alcohol in your blood exceeds 20 mg./100 ml. On principal expressways the speed limits are 70 mph (110 kph), on other roads outside built-up areas 56 mph (90 kph) or 44 mph (70 kph) and in towns 31 mph (50 kph). There's no shortage of gas stations, most of which are self-service. A lot of

459

stations have automatic pumps, open at night. They work with 10- and 100-kronor bills. Gasoline available is normal (93 octane), super (96–98 octane), lead-free and diesel. In case of a breakdown, phone Larmtjänst for emergency assistance, tel. (08) 24 10 00.

Some distances: Stockholm–Uppsala 43 miles (70 km.), Norrköping 145 miles (170 km.), Gothenburg 290 miles (465 km.), Malmö 305 miles (655 km.).

Bicycle rental. Cycling is very popular in Sweden and bikes can be rented at railroad stations, sports shops and other outlets. The local tourist office can give you information about organized bicycle tours.

Rest rooms. Public facilities are located in subway stations (Stockholm), department stores and in some of the bigger squares and parks. They are often labeled with symbols, or marked *WC, Damer/Herrar* or *D/H* (women/men). Some require coins.

Emergencies. The general emergency telephone number in Sweden is 90 000. This number covers the police and fire departments, ambulance and medical services. It can be dialed free (no coins needed) from any telephone. English is usually understood.

Police. Swedish police cars are marked "Polis". Members of the force are courteous and helpful to tourists, and all of them speak some English, so don't hesitate to ask for assistance. The police wear blue-green overall uniforms when they patrol on the roads. "Meter maids" on parking-meter patrols do a thorough job of ticketing all offenders.

Crime and theft. In Stockholm, as in other big cities in Sweden and elsewhere, crime is on the increase. Take commonsense precautions: check your valuables in the hotel safe. It's wise to avoid certain parts of Stockholm—parks like Humlegården or subway stations—late at night.

Medical care and health. The standard of medical treatment is high. Doctors and most nurses speak English. Medical and pharmaceutical supplies are readily available. Pharmacies *(apotek)* stock all prescriptions and over-the-counter remedies like cough medicine and aspirin. In all the major cities, at least one pharmacy remains open seven days a week and at night. The address can be obtained from your hotel or by calling 90 140. For insurance, see pp. 25–26.

Water from the tap is perfectly safe to drink.

Embassies and consulates. Embassies and consulates are listed in the telephone directory under the name of the country (in Swedish).

Social customs. Usually you shake hands when meeting someone or taking your leave. If you're invited to a Swedish home, bring the hostess some flowers, chocolates or a bottle of wine. Swedes still observe certain formalities at dinner. It's customary to lift your glass and say *skål* before drinking and the guest of honor should always make a short speech of thanks for the meal. But customs are changing in Sweden, partly perhaps because of the now wide-spread habit of using the familiar form *du* instead of the more formal *ni* and titles, so you'll be on first-name terms right away.

Enjoying Sweden

Food and drink. The full-size *smörgåsbord* remains Sweden's most famous culinary attraction, even if a stripped-down version, the *sillbord* or herring buffet, is almost as common today.

The *smörgåsbord* (or groaning board, if you will), can consist of as many as 100 different dishes. Don't overload your plate—you can go back to the table as many times as you wish.

Most important is the order of courses. Start off by sampling the innumerable herring dishes, with boiled potatoes and bread including *knäckebröd* (crisp rye bread) and butter. Then you move on to other types of seafood, like different preparations of *lax* (salmon), such as *rökt lax* (smoked), *inkokt lax* (boiled and served cold), *gravad lax* (pickled in dill with a mustard sauce). Other delicacies are *rökt ål* (smoked eel), *räkor* (shrimps) and *västkustsallad* (seafood salad). Next come the egg dishes, salads and cold meats sometimes featuring *rökt renstek* (smoked

462

reindeer), that delicacy of northern Sweden. The small warm dishes now loom on the horizon—such as meat balls, fried sausages and omelets —and finally the cheese tray. Look for *västerbottenost, herrgårdsost* and *sveciaost*—typical hard, well-aged cheeses—before tackling the fruit basket.

Curiously, the *smörgåsbord* may be hard to find, except on Sunday afternoons and during the Christmas season. In Stockholm the elegant Operakällaren (Opera Restaurant) offers a daily luncheon *smörgåsbord*, reputed to be the best in the world.

Breakfast usually consists of a cup of coffee or tea with rolls, butter and jam and sometimes cheese. More substantial breakfast buffets with eggs, ham, fruit stews, etc. are normally included in the price of your hotel room.

Lunch is served around noon, and dinner from 6 p.m. At lunchtime on weekdays most restaurants offer a very reasonably priced *dagens rätt* (daily special), usually a traditional Swedish dish. Among these you might try *Janssons frestelse* (Janssons's Temptation, a delicious casserole of potatoes, sprats, onion and cream), *kåldolmar* (stuffed cabbage rolls), *pytt i panna* (finely cut meat, onion and potato hash), *kalops* (beef stew with bay leaves), *dillkött* (lamb or veal in dill sauce), *köttbullar* (the famous Swedish meatballs), *bruna bönor* (baked brown beans in molasses sauce), *strömmingsflundror* (fried boned herring) and on Thursday, join the Swedes in eating *ärter med fläsk* (yellow pea soup with pork), followed by *pannkakor med sylt* (pancakes with jam).

Weekday dining in first-class restaurants in big cities is not exactly cheap. However, on Saturdays and Sundays many restaurants offer dinner for the whole family *(familjemiddag)*, with set menus at good prices.

Among the seasonal events, a delightful custom in August is the *kräftor* (crayfish) party. The usually proper Swedes abandon all rules of table etiquette to attack heaps of the small lobster-like creatures gleaming bright red in the light of the paper lanterns strung over the table. *Kryddost* (cheese spiced with caraway) and buttered toast and fresh berries, such as *hallon* (raspberries), *hjortron* (cloudberries) or *smultron* (wild strawberries) complete the traditional menu. Another late summer specialty is *surströmming* (salted and fermented Baltic herring). The smell, to put it mildly, is staggering, but there are Swedes, particularly those from the northern part of the country, who consider it a great delicacy. The star of November dinner events is *stekt gås* (roast goose). You begin the meal with a highly spiced *svartsoppa* (blood soup) and finish with *spettekaka* (a lacelike pyramid cake baked on a spit).

463

The Swedes are inordinately fond of *kaffe* (coffee), which they consume in great quantities at all times of the day and night. Adults and children alike drink a lot of milk with their meals. Yoghurt and other kinds of fermented milk are equally popular. On another plane, the Swedish national drink is aquavit, also called *snaps,* distilled from potatoes or grain and flavored with various herbs and spices. It should be ice-cold and served in small glasses, taken straight in a grand gulp or two. You can wash it down with beer or mineral water. Other Swedish alcoholic specialties include *glögg* (a hot, spiced wine) drunk during the Christmas season, and *punsch* (a light liqueur), usually served well chilled after dinner with coffee or hot with the traditional Thursday dinner of yellow pea soup and pancakes. Exposure to continental life styles in combination with the heavy taxes on hard liquor has promoted a recent change of tastes in favor of wine.

Entertainment. Stockholm is rich in cultural opportunities. The Royal Opera offers first-rate opera and ballet. In the summer the scene shifts to the unique Drottningholm Court Theater. Main venue for classical music is the Stockholm Concert Hall and in the summer you can enjoy concerts in public parks and courtyards of landmark buildings throughout the Stockholm area. Outside the capital, cities like Gothenburg and Malmö stage top-notch concerts, opera, ballet and theater.

In the bigger cities many nightclubs, discos and dance restaurants stay open until the early hours of the morning. All foreign movies are shown in the original language with Swedish subtitles.

Annual events and festivals. Throughout the year in all parts of the country festivals brighten up the calender. *March:* Vasa Ski Race, from Sälen to Mora. *April 30:* Walpurgis Night, with huge bonfires, especially exuberant celebration in university towns like Uppsala and Lund. *June 6:* The Swedish National Day. *June:* Midsummer Eve, dances around decorated maypoles. *July:* Folklore festivals in Dalarna. International tennis tournament in Båstad. Swedish Derby, horse race at Jägersro, Malmö. *December 13:* St. Lucia Day throughout the country.

Taxes, service charges and tipping. Service charges are included in hotel and restaurant bills. Gratuities for waiters and others in the tourist-related industries are purely optional. In a few areas, however, the habit is slightly more ingrained. Tipping recommendations: taxi drivers 8–10%, hatcheck, charges posted or 4–5 kr.

Sports and recreation. Sweden offers an immense richness of unspoiled countryside and endless woods, lakes and islands—all freely accessible

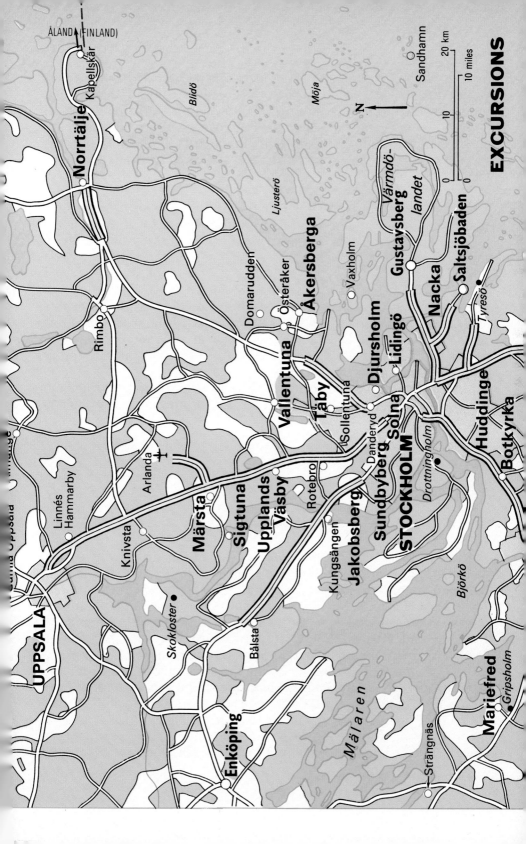

EXCURSIONS

ÅLAND (FINLAND)

Kapellskär

Norrtälje

Bidö

Sandhamn

20 km

Möja

10 miles

N

Ljusterö

10

Värmdö-landet

Gustavsberg

Domarudden

Österåker

Åkersberga

Vaxholm

Saltsjöbaden

Tyresö

Rimbo

Nacka

Djursholm

Lidingö

Vallentuna

Täby

Solna

Sollentuna

Danderyd

Sundbyberg

STOCKHOLM

Linnés Hammarby

Rotebro

Drottningholm

Huddinge

Arlanda

Botkyrka

Knivsta

Märsta

Sigtuna

Upplands Väsby

Jakobsberg

Kungsängen

UPPSALA

Björkö

Skokloster

Bålsta

Mälaren

Enköping

Mariefred

Gripsholm

Strängnäs

for everybody according to the unique, ancient *allemansrätten,* literally "every man's right". Consequently, the possibilities for hiking, cycling, sailing, swimming, fishing and cross-country skiing are virtually without bounds. Tennis courts can be rented almost anywhere and there are about 200 golf courses throughout the country. The most popular spectator sports are soccer and ice hockey, followed by tennis and horse racing.

TV and radio. All broadcasting is in Swedish, except for programs for Finnish and other immigrants. Movies and shows on TV are aired in the original language, often English. News in English is broadcast in summer.

What to buy. Look for glassware (Sweden's most famous design product), ceramics and stainless flatware—practical as well as attractive—silver and jewelry, coats, jackets and skirts in suede and furs. Brightly painted wooden Dala horses, Swedish clogs and candles in all shapes and colors make nice souvenirs. In some cases the sales tax is refunded, see p. 40.

Most shops and department stores open from 9:30 or 10 a.m. to 6 p.m., Monday through Friday, until 1 p.m. on Saturdays (later in winter).

Sightseeing

Stockholm. Old Town *(Gamla stan)*★, heart of the historic city center; medieval step-gabled buildings and cobbled lanes like Österlånggatan, Köpmangatan, Mårten Trotzigs gränd, the narrowest street in Stockholm. Royal Palace *(Kungliga slottet)* with 600 rooms, until recently the largest inhabited castle in the world; apartments with magnificent Baroque and Rococo interiors; Royal Armory; the changing of the guard. Stockholm Cathedral *(Storkyrkan)* from the 13th century, Sweden's coronation church, containing the striking 15th-century sculpture of *St. George and the Dragon.* Great Square *(Stortorget),* lined with fine old buildings; the Baroque palace housing the Stock Exchange, where the Swedish Academy meets to elect the Nobel Prize winners in literature. Riddarholmen Church with distinctive cast-iron spire, burial place of Swedish kings for 400 years. Classical 17th-century House of

Nobility *(Riddarhuset)*, considered by many to be Stockholm's most beautiful building. The Royal Warship Wasa*, capsized on its maiden voyage in 1628, now housed in the Vasa Museum. Graceful City Hall *(Stadshuset)** right on Lake Mälaren, setting for the Nobel Prize festivities; Golden Hall decorated with mosaics; glass-domed Blue Hall; fabulous view from the tower with three gilded crowns. Djurgården, unspoiled island, former royal hunting park, just next to the city center, perfect for jogging and picnicking with woodland trails and restaurants. Skansen*, the world's first open-air museum; 150 historic buildings from various parts of Sweden; zoo. Millesgården*, the beautifully situated home of the 20th-century Swedish sculptor Carl Milles. Museum of National Antiquities *(Historiska museet),* containing rich collections from the Stone Age to medieval times: the Vendel treasure of the 6th to 9th centuries. Castle-like Nordic Museum, showing many aspects of Swedish life in all layers of the society. National Art Gallery *(Nationalmuseum),* displaying old Russian icons and Dutch 17th-century, French 18th-century and Swedish 19th-century paintings. Museum of Far Eastern Antiquities *(Östasiatiska museet),* featuring magnificent collection of ancient Chinese art including priceless objects donated to the museum by the late King Gustaf Adolf VI, a distinguished archaeologist. Splendid panorama over Stockholm and the Baltic from Fjällgatan and from the Kaknäs Tower.

Stockholm Archipelago*. More than 20,000 islands, many accessible by white steamers; swimming and boating opportunities. 16th-century Vaxholm Fortress. Sandhamn, center for sailing and boating.

Around Lake Mälaren. Drottningholm Palace, the present royal residence, and its unique 18th-century Court Theater, preserved in original form, and charming Rococo Chinese Pavilion. Gripsholm Castle*, built by Gustav Vasa in the 16th century; Europe's largest collection of historical portraits. Skokloster Castle, Baroque palace with 20,000 rare books and manuscripts; arms collection; motor museum. Idyllic little Sigtuna, probably the oldest town in Sweden, and Mariefred, with yellow and red-frame houses.

Skåne. Sweden's southernmost province, a region of rich farmland and more than 200 castles, like 15th-century Glimmingehus and Bosjökloster, containing vaulted medieval halls decorated with Gobelin tapestries. Long, white sandy beaches. Medieval town of Ystad with half-timbered houses. Malmö, Sweden's third city, opposite Copenhagen; Malmöhus Castle, housing Municipal Museum. Helsingborg and

467

its immense 14th-century brick tower of Kärnan offering panoramic view over the strait of Öresund with Hamlet's Elsinore on the Danish side. University town of Lund, founded in 1020, with Romanesque cathedral* featuring a 14th-century astronomical clock; open-air Museum of Cultural History. Trinity Church, one of northern Europe's largest Renaissance churches, in Kristianstad. Magnificent view of Kattegat from 16th-century lighthouse, the highest in Europe, at Kullen. Båstad, fashionable summer resort, site of international tennis tournament.

Småland. Heart of the glass-making industry, home to the factories of Orrefors, Kosta, Boda. Typical red wooden houses embedded between forests and lakes. Kalmar, site of a 16th-century Renaissance castle.

Baltic Islands. Europe's longest bridge* linking the mainland and 85-mile-(135 km.-) long Öland, where more than 400 typical windmills still stand; Viking colony ruins at Eketorp; royal summer residence at Solliden; ruins of Borgholm Castle. Gotland in the middle of the Baltic; medieval Visby*, encircled by a 44-tower city wall covered by roses; curious rock formations *(raukar)*; 100 churches from Hanseatic times; excellent recreation region, bicycling, boating, surfing; turning point for yearly Baltic Race.

West Coast. Long sandy beaches at Tylösand. Gothenburg, Sweden's second largest city and important North Sea port; 18th-century buildings from the days of the East Indian colonial trade; Gustav Adolfs Torg, lined by the Exchange and the Town Hall; Götaplatsen square with ensemble of contemporary yellow-brick buildings, including Museum of Art, surrounding a giant sculpture Poseidon by Milles; Liseberg, Sweden's most famous amusement park; Feskekörka in the harbor, covered fishmarket looking like a church. Bohuslän, with an archipelago of barren rocks stretching to the Norwegian border, including towns like Kungälv with mighty ruins of Bohus Fortress and Marstrand, elegant summer resort on a small island with 17th-century fortress; charming fishing village of Smögen and attractive seaside resort of Lysekil; rock carvings from the Bronze Age at Tanumshede.

Around the Great Lakes. Vänern and Vättern, among the largest lakes in Europe, "just the holes left when some prehistoric giant put Gotland and Öland in the Baltic". The 350-mile (560-km.) waterway Gothenburg–Vänern–Vättern–Stockholm held together by the 65-lock, 55-mile-(90-km.-) long Göta Canal* served by passenger steamers.

468

Mårbacka, the home of Selma Lagerlöf, one of Sweden's most famous authors, and Rottneros Manor, a sculpture park displaying works of prominent Scandinavian artists, in Värmland. On the shores of Lake Vänern, the superb Läckö Castle and on Lake Vättern the sleepy town of Vadstena noted for its lace making; huge Vasa castle and medieval church and cloisters of St. Birgitta, founder of Birgittine order. Scenic lakeside drive from Jönköping to charming little town of Gränna, famous for its candy. Linköping, university town with impressive Gothic cathedral; Old Linköping (*Gamla Linköping*), a reconstruction of the town with original 17th- to 20th-century timber buildings having survived fire and wars.

Dalarna★. Sweden's folklore region; colorful Midsummer celebration around Lake Siljan. Churchboats in Rättvik and Leksand, popular lakeside resorts. Stora Kopparberg Company, called the world's oldest business, with charters from 1288. Coppermine in Falun (*Falu gruva*) open to visitors. Provincial town of Mora with 600-year-old timber buildings, home of the Swedish painter Anders Zorn; Zorns Gammelgård outdoor museum; 55-mile (90-km.) Vasa Ski Race.

North of Stockholm. Uppsala with university founded 1477; twin-spired cathedral★, seat of the archbishop of Sweden; characteristic purple red castle dominating the city; Carolina Rediviva, university library, housing, notably, 6th-century Codex Argenteus (Gothic Silver Bible). Gävle, Sundsvall, Umeå, Luleå, but a few of the cities along the 600 mile (1,000 km.) stretch of the Baltic to the very north. More than a dozen magnificent rivers (*älvar*). The Tännforsen waterfalls in a nature reserve and Storforsen, Sweden's biggest waterfall, dropping 810 feet (252 m.) over a stretch of 3 miles. In parallel with the shore but far inland, the wilderness railroad (*Inlandsbanan*). Åre, popular winter and summer resort, with Sweden's best downhill skiing facilities.

The Arctic Circle. Jokkmokk, capital of Lapland, just north of the Arctic Circle; Lapp church and museum housing fine collection of Lapp art. Abisko, popular resort by Lake Torneträsk. Kiruna, mining town of the great north; iron ore mines; remarkable Town Hall. Midnight sun in summer, all day darkness in winter. Kebnekaise, Sweden's highest mountain (6,946 feet/2,117 m.). Numerous nature reserves of immense beauty including National Parks of Abisko and Sarek★. Hiking trails, like the Royal Trail (*Kungsleden*), canoeing and fishing challenges. Riksgränsen on the Norwegian border, scene of night skiing by the light of the midnight sun.

Some useful expressions in Swedish

good morning/afternoon	god morgon/dag
good evening/night	god kväll/natt
good-bye	adjö
yes/no	ja/nej
please/thank you	var så god/tack
excuse me	ursäkta mig
you're welcome	ingen orsak
where/when/how	var/när/hur
how long/how far	hur länge/hur långt
yesterday/today/tomorrow	igår/idag/i morgon
day/week/month/year	dag/vecka/månad/år
left/right	vänster/höger
up/down	uppe/nere
good/bad	bra/dålig
big/small	stor/liten
cheap/expensive	billig/dyr
hot/cold	varm/kall
old/new	gammal/ny
open/closed	öppen/stängd
free (vacant)/occupied	ledig/upptagen
early/late	tidig/sen
easy/difficult	enkel/svår
Does anyone here speak English/French/German?	Finns det någon här som talar engelska/franska/tyska?
What does this mean?	Vad betyder det här?
I don't understand.	Jag förstår inte.
Please write it down.	Skulle ni kunna skriva det?
Do you take credit cards/traveler's checks?	Kan jag betala med kreditkort/resecheckar?
Waiter!/Waitress!	Vaktmästarn!/Fröken!
Where are the toilets?	Var är toaletten?
I'd like...	Jag skulle vilja ha...
How much is that?	Hur mycket kostar det?
What time is it?	Hur mycket är klockan?
Help me please.	Var snäll och hjälp mig.
Just a minute.	Ett ögonblick.

SWITZERLAND
and LIECHTENSTEIN

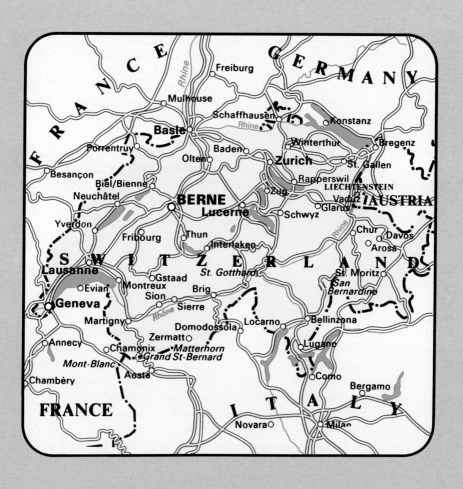

Cowbells, ski runs and chalets in the pretty, prosperous homeland of tourism.

The summit of Switzerland, in the awesome Alps, juts nearly three miles into the sky. From there it's all downhill to the outdoor cafés along Lake Maggiore, at a negligible 635 feet (194 m.) above sea level. Between the high and the low points, from the skiing to the swimming, you could lose your heart to the pine-covered hillsides, green valleys and trim, flower-decked towns.

Switzerland has always been the ideal place to unwind in the fresh air, the bucolic calm undisturbed but for the clang of cowbells and the occasional yodel. The homeland of tourism knows how to look after its visitors; you'll soon understand why the world's best hotelkeepers are Swiss or Swiss-trained.

Small as it is, Switzerland is divided into four linguistic regions. The majority speak a form of German, but English is fluently available wherever the tourists roam. A fine network of highways and rail lines, supplemented by funiculars and lake steamers, makes every place accessible. Clean, efficient buses and streetcars ease travel within the cities, all of them small by European standards. Historic towns like Basle, Lucerne, cosmopolitan Geneva and the cozy capital, Berne, are all splendidly set alongside rivers or lakes. Zurich has one of each.

Mountain resorts like St. Moritz, Davos, Zermatt and Gstaad enjoy worldwide reputations as glittering as their *après-ski* social life. But nearly 200 lesser-known communities cater to equally demanding skiers, and, in summer, hikers, golfers and plain nature lovers.

Political stability, neutrality and hard work have made this decentralized democracy one of the world's most prosperous countries. It's hardly the place for bargain-basement shopping, but you can't beat the quality, whether it's watches, chocolate or cheese. As for the food and wine, they fit the Swiss character: honest, wholesome, unsophisticated.

472

Facts and figures

Population:	6.4 million
Area:	15,940 sq. miles (41,290 sq. km.)
Capital:	Berne *(Bern,* 145,000/GUA 285,000)
Other major cities:	Zurich *(Zürich,* 365,000/GUA 710,000) Basle *(Basel,* 180,000/GUA 365,000) Geneva *(Genève,* 160,000/GUA 335,000) Lausanne (130,000/GUA 225,000)
Languages:	German (65%), French (18%), Italian (10%) and Romansh (1%)
Religion:	Catholic (48%), Protestant (44%)
Time zone:	GMT + 1, EST + 6; DST (Apr.–Sep.)
Currency:	Swiss *franc* (in German: *Franken,* in French: *franc),* (abbr. *Fr.*) = 100 *centimes* (in German: *Rappen,* in French: *centimes).* Coins: 5, 10, 20, 50 centimes; Fr. 1, 2, 5 Bills: Fr. 10, 20, 50, 100, 500, 1,000
Electricity:	220 volt, 50 cycle, AC

Planning your trip

Visa requirements. See pp. 29–30.

Vaccination requirements. None (see also p. 25).

Currency restrictions. There is no restriction on the import or export of either Swiss or foreign currencies.

Climate. Switzerland has a moderately continental climate. Temperatures can vary within a few miles, a few hundred feet of altitude, or a few hours of the day. Precipitation is well distributed throughout the year. The *föhn* is a warm wind from the south, the *bise* the cold north wind from Central Europe. Limited areas in the canton of Ticino and along the Lake of Geneva enjoy milder weather.

473

Some average daily temperatures:

Zurich		J	F	M	A	M	J	J	A	S	O	N	D
average daily maximum*	°F	36	41	51	59	67	73	76	75	69	57	45	37
	°C	2	5	10	15	19	23	25	24	20	14	7	3
average daily minimum*	°F	26	28	34	40	47	53	56	56	51	43	35	29
	°C	-3	-2	1	4	8	12	14	13	11	6	2	-2
Geneva													
average daily maximum*	°F	38	42	51	59	66	73	77	76	69	58	47	40
	°C	4	6	10	15	19	23	25	24	21	14	8	4
average daily minimum*	°F	29	30	36	42	49	55	58	58	53	44	37	31
	°C	-2	-1	2	5	9	13	15	14	12	7	3	0

* Minimum temperatures are measured just before sunrise, maximum temperatures in the afternoon.

Clothing. In summer light- to mediumweight clothing is adequate, but bring a warm jacket or sweater just in case, or if a trip to the mountains is planned. In winter a warm overcoat is necessary and if you're in the mountains, snow boots. You might need a raincoat or umbrella at any time. In a smart restaurant you may feel out of step without jacket and tie, but generally speaking casual clothing is appropriate.

Duty-free allowances

	Cigarettes		Cigars		Tobacco	Liquor	Wine
1)	400	or	100	or	500 g.	1 l. and	2 l.
2)	200	or	50	or	250 g.	1 l. and	2 l.
Gifts (including perfume): up to Fr. 100 max. value							
1) residents of countries outside Europe; 2) residents of Europe							

Hotels and accommodations

Hotels. Hotels of all categories are listed in the *Swiss Hotel Guide* issued annually by the Swiss Hotel Association. You can find the publication at

Swiss National Tourist offices abroad as well as at many travel agencies. In Switzerland local tourist offices will supply you with last-minute details and offer suggestions for all types of accommodations from luxury hotels to modest, family-run establishments.

Hotels of all classifications in Switzerland are very clean and provide all the essentials. Rates include taxes, service charges and continental breakfast. A *hôtel garni* provides bed but not board, permitting you to eat out more adventurously.

Private rooms. Local tourist offices maintain lists of rooms to let in private homes—the Swiss equivalent of bed-and-breakfast establishments. Or take your chances and stop at a house with a "Zimmer" or "Chambres à louer" sign outside. Most such accommodations are in German-speaking Switzerland.

Chalets and apartments. For family vacations, particularly in mountain resorts, furnished apartments and chalets may be rented through agencies abroad or on the spot.

Youth hostels *(Jugendherberge/auberge de jeunesse)*. There is no maximum age, though members 25 and under have priority. Advance reservations are recommended in summer and in popular winter sports regions. In the cities certain hostels are closed in winter. For addresses and regulations, write to Schweizerischer Bund für Jugendherbergen, Postfach, 3000 Berne 26; tel. (031) 24 55 01.

Camping. Several hundred campsites, some high in the Alps, are approved by the Swiss Camping and Caravan Association. For a list of sites, facilities and rates, write to Schweizerischer Camping- und Caravanning-Verband (SCCV), Habsburgerstrasse 35, 6000 Lucerne 4.

Camping on private property or outside a recognized campsite requires special permission.

Swiss tourist offices abroad

Canada	154 University Avenue, Toronto, Ont. M5H 3Y9; tel. (416) 971-9734
South Africa	Agency with Swissair. Swiss House, 86 Main Street, P.O. Box 3866, Johannesburg; tel. (011) 836-9941
U.K.	Swiss Centre, 1 New Coventry Street, London W1V 8EE; tel. (071) 734 1921
U.S.A.	608 Fifth Avenue, New York, NY 10020; tel. (212) 757-5944 260 Stockton Street, San Francisco, CA 94108; tel. (415) 362-2260

On the spot

Banks and currency exchange. Most banks are open weekdays from 8:30 a.m. to 12:30 p.m. and again from 1:30 to 4:30, 5 or 5:30. Main offices generally remain open during the lunch hour. One day a week, branches keep slightly later hours, till 6 or 6:30 p.m., the day varying from town to town. In Zurich the big banking day is Monday. Currency-exchange offices at airports and the larger rail stations do business from around 6:30 a.m. to 9 p.m. (sometimes even later) every day of the week. A money-changing machine at Zurich airport takes bills in four currencies—French, German, Italian and English (£10 and £20).

Credit cards and traveler's checks. Smaller businesses don't like to deal with credit cards, but they're widely accepted in major establishments. You'll find the signs prominently displayed at the entrance. The well-known, international traveler's checks are generally accepted everywhere, but the banks will give you a better rate of exchange than shops, hotels and restaurants. You must show your passport when cashing one.

Mail and telecommunications. Post offices display a distinctive sign bearing the letters PTT *(Post, Telegraf, Telefon)*. In addition to normal postal business, they handle telephone calls, telegrams and much of the population's bill-paying. Most post offices are open from around 7:30 a.m. to 6 or 6:30 p.m. with a break for lunch, and on Saturday mornings from 7:30 to 11 a.m. In bigger towns the main post office does not close at midday, and a window may be open until 10 p.m. or even later, and at weekends, for express or special delivery mail.

After hours you can buy stamps from vending machines outside post offices and some train stations, as well as in souvenir shops and at hotel receptions desks. Mailboxes are yellow.

The telephone network is automated and efficient, and street corner coin telephones are kept clean and in good working order. Phone booths post instructions in four languages (including English). International calls can be made from public phone booths. For overseas calls, many phones have a 5-franc slot and a slot for a credit card (*taxcard*—sold at post offices). You can also make such calls from a post office, where payment is made at the window afterwards (ask for a phone). For surcharges and low rates, see p. 30.

Main post offices accept telegrams, telex and fax messages from 7:30 a.m. to 10 p.m. You can also send a telegram by telephone from your hotel. The charge will be added to your bill.

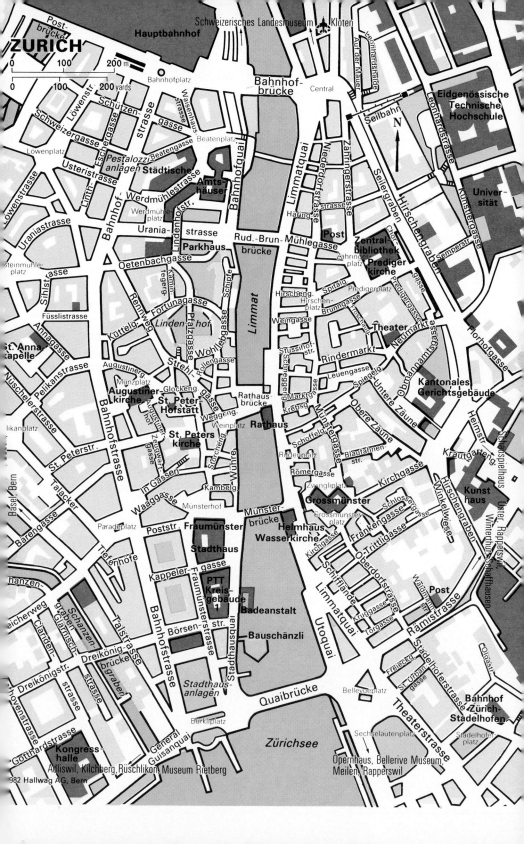

Some useful telephone numbers, valid in most areas:

Information (domestic)	111	Telegrams	110
Information (international)	191	Police (emergencies)	117
		Fire	118
Operator (international calls)	114		

Newspapers. Leading dailies are *Basler Zeitung* (Basle), *Der Bund* and *Berner Zeitung* (Berne), *Journal de Genève, Tribune de Genève* and *La Suisse* in Geneva, and *Neue Zürcher Zeitung* and *Tages-Anzeiger* in Zurich. Newspapers from many European countries can be found at major newsstands, with the best selection and earliest delivery at main railroad stations and airports. The British dailies and the *International Herald Tribune* (edited in Paris, printed in Zurich) are widely available, along with magazines of all kinds.

Tourist information. Almost every Swiss town or resort has its own autonomous tourist office well-stocked with free brochures and booklets, local hotel lists and other information about the town itself and often other parts of the country as well.

Zurich	Bahnhofplatz 15 (Main Railroad Station); tel. (01) 211 40 00
Basle	Blumenrain 2; tel. (061) 25 50 50
Berne	Central Railroad Station; tel. (031) 22 76 76
Lucerne	Frankenstrasse 1; tel. (041) 51 71 71
Geneva	Central Railroad Station (Gare Cornavin); tel. (022) 738 52 00
Lausanne	Avenue de Rhodanie 2; tel. (021) 617 73 21
Lugano	Riva Albertolli; tel. (091) 21 46 64

Legal holidays

Jan. 1	New Year's Day	**Movable dates:**
Dec. 25	Christmas Day	Good Friday*
Dec. 26	St. Stephen's Day*	Easter Monday*
		Ascension
*celebrated in most cantons		Whit Monday*

On August 1, the Swiss National Day, some banks and shops are closed in the afternoon; the whole day in some places.

The calendar of holidays varies from canton to canton. The most important local additions to the preceding list are: Basle—May 1; Berne—January 2; Geneva—first Thursday of September, December 31; Zurich—January 2, May 1.

Transportation

Air. Switzerland's three major international airports are, in order of importance, Zurich-Kloten, Geneva-Cointrin and Basle/Mulhouse. The Swiss national airline provides frequent flights between these airports. Small airports serve Berne and Lugano.

If you're departing from Zurich, Geneva or Basle on a scheduled or charter flight, you can register baggage all the way to your final destination from many Swiss railroad and postal bus stations. The service is called *Fly Luggage.* You may be required to check in your baggage, for which a small charge is made, up to 24 hours in advance. You must show your air ticket. When arriving in Switzerland, you can register bags at the *Welcome-Luggage* counter at the airport, who will forward them to the railroad station of your choice.

Major airports. Zurich: Kloten (8 miles/12 km. from city center). Duty-free shop. Frequent train service links Zurich Airport (there is a station in the airport itself) to the city's main rail station, a 10-minute trip. Direct trains to and from the airport also serve many other Swiss cities. **Geneva:** Cointrin (3 miles/5 km. from city center). Duty-free shop. Frequent train service to the city's main rail station, a 6-minute trip. Direct trains to and from the airport also serve many other Swiss cities. **Basle:** Basle/Mulhouse (7 miles/12 km. from city center). Duty-free shop. Regular airport bus service to rail station.

Rail. Swiss trains are fast, clean, comfortable and very punctual. Trains run at least hourly between all major centers.

You can criss-cross the whole country with a *Swiss Pass,* valid for four, eight or 15 days or 1 month of unlimited travel on the federal rail network (16,000 km.), plus scores of private railroad companies, nine boat lines, 120 postal bus routes and on local buses and streetcars in 24 cities. Good for discounts on mountain railroads, aerial cableways, etc., the card offers convenience and significant savings for travelers resident outside Switzerland. Apply for the card at travel agencies or Swiss tourist offices abroad, and at major railroad stations in Switzerland. You must show your passport. For *Eurailpass,* see p. 33.

Apart from the Swiss Pass, reductions are available in the form of excursion tickets and circular tickets. The *Skipass* is good for rail travel to certain resorts plus unlimited use of ski lifts.

479

Postal buses. Wherever the trains don't go, the bright yellow postal buses do. They carry mail and passengers—the local population and sightseers —over mountain roads to the smallest of hamlets. Advance seat reservations are made free of charge.

Boats, waterways. Sizable passenger boats, often with restaurants, ply all the big lakes. In some cases you can make the return trip by train. Local tourist offices have maps and timetables and can give advice. Remember that the Eurailpass is valid for travel by boat.

Local public transportation. Swiss cities have efficient public transportation networks (buses, trolleybuses, streetcars). In Zurich you can also get around rapidly by the brand-new S-Bahn system. Before boarding the bus, buy a ticket from a vending machine, or—if there is none—from the driver. Hold on to it in case an inspector makes a spot check at some point during your trip.

Tourists intending to make intensive use of buses or streetcars can save money by purchasing a one-day ticket for 24 hours of unlimited travel on a town's public transportation network, or a multiple-trip ticket. These tickets can be bought from machines or—sometimes— newsstands and tobacco shops.

Taxis. You might try hailing a taxi on the street, but a better bet is a taxi stand at a major hotel or the railroad station; or you can telephone for a cab. Taxis are metered and there can be set prices for extras such as baggage. The tip is generally included in the fare.

Car rental. International and local agencies operate throughout Switzerland, some with airport offices. You can rent a car at many railroad stations. Chauffeur-driven cars are also available. See also pp. 30–31.

Driving in Switzerland. A red reflector warning triangle must be carried for use in case of breakdown. If you normally wear glasses when driving, you are required to have a second pair with you. Blood alcohol limit is 80 mg./100 ml. Speed limits are generally 31 mph (50 kph) in towns, 75 mph (120 kph) on expressways and 50 mph (80 kph) on other roads unless otherwise indicated. The use of seat belts is compulsory.

Drive on the right, pass on the left. In general roads are good and well maintained. Expressways link most big towns. Motorists who use them must purchase a sticker (valid for the current year) to be displayed on the windshield, or risk a heavy fine. Expressways are provided with emergency telephones at regular intervals. On difficult stretches of mountain roads, priority is given to postal buses—otherwise to the ascending vehicle. Sounding your horn is recommended on blind corners of mountain roads. In winter you may be required to use snow chains on Alpine passes. These can be obtained at filling stations along the way. Several passes are closed for varying periods between November and June. Snow is rarely a problem in city streets. In case of breakdown, call 140 for the Touring-Club Suisse (TCS). Gasoline available is lead-free (91 and 95 octane), super (98 octane) and diesel. Most cities have parking meters and blue zones, where parking is limited to 1 hour. In red zones you can park for up to 15 hours. Parking discs are available free of charge at gas stations and banks.

Some distances: Zurich–Basle 53 miles (85 km.), Berne 75 miles (120 km.), Lugano 135 miles (220 km.), Geneva 170 miles (275 km.).

Bicycle rental. You can rent a bicycle at the railroad station in most sizable towns in Switzerland and return it to any other station at no extra charge. At smaller stations it's advisable to reserve a bike in advance. Tourist offices distribute leaflets describing special cycle routes.

Rest rooms. Throughout Switzerland you'll find clean public rest rooms at convenient locations. Rest rooms are marked by conventional symbols for men and women, or the expressions *Toiletten/toilettes/gabinetti* or *WC*. Otherwise, depending on the region, women should look for the signs *Damen* or *Frauen* in German, *dames* in French or *signore* or *donne* in Italian, and men for *Herren* or *Männer* in German, *messieurs* in French, *signori* or *uomini* in Italian.

Emergencies

Police	117	Fire	118

For other emergency numbers dial the information service—111—or check the pages in the front of any telephone directory, where information is given in English.

Police. Switzerland has no uniformed federal police. Law and order is the responsability of the individual cantons and communities, and thus the uniforms vary greatly from place to place. Police are armed, efficient and courteous.

Crime and theft. Muggings and crimes of violence are rare in Switzerland. You can come and go, day and night, in peace. But burglars, pickpockets and associated operatives can strike in any country, so it's always wise to lock your car and put your valuables in the hotel safe. Skis can easily disappear from car roof racks and the entrances to après-ski spots. In these cases, the culprits are not usually Swiss skiers —they have their own equipment.

Medical care and health. Most major resorts have clinics, and all cities are served by modern, well-equipped hospitals. The standard of treatment is high, especially when it comes to ski-related injuries. All hospitals and clinics are accustomed to dealing with foreigners, and English is often spoken. Medicine and pharmaceutical supplies are readily available. All pharmacies display the addresses of those on duty after hours. Any pharmacist can recommend and supply remedies for minor ailments and advise you where to find a doctor if you need one. For insurance, see pp. 25–26.

Tap water is drinkable.

Embassies and consulates. Listings for embassies and consulates are found in telephone directories under "Ambassades" and "Consulats" or "Konsulate".

Social customs. If the Swiss tend to be a little reserved, the scene is more relaxed in the resorts. In social as well as business situations, punctuality is considered most important. If you should be invited to a Swiss home for dinner, don't forget flowers or sweets for the hostess. Entering and leaving small shops or offices, be sure to say hello, goodbye, please and thank you; the Swiss are very polite.

Enjoying Switzerland

Food and drink. There's more to Swiss cuisine than *fondue*. But, like that inspired cheese concoction, most dishes tend to be very filling. The portions are huge, and many restaurants serve second helpings as big as the first, on a clean plate. Just hold on to your knife and fork.

More than a meal, cheese *fondue* is a social occasion. The celebrants gather around a bubbling cauldron containing a mixture of cheeses melted with white wine and a dash of *Kirschwasser,* a brandy distilled from cherries. Special long forks are used to dip chunks of bread in the melted cheese. When *raclette* is served, half a big wheel of cheese is brought close to a heating element—or more authentically, the flame of a wood fire. As it begins to melt, the cook scrapes off a portion—crispy rind and all—onto your plate. Eaten with boiled potatoes (peel them yourself), pickled onions and gherkins. For a lighter cheesy snack, try a hot cheese tart, *Käsewähe* or *ramequin,* or a *Käseschnitte* or *croûte de fromage,* an open-face melted cheese sandwich.

On the subject of the world-famous Swiss cheeses, *Emmentaler* is the mild cheese with holes known in some other countries as "Swiss cheese". *Appenzeller* tastes tangier; *Gruyère (Greyerzer* in German), usually more salty, has a nutty flavor. *Sbrinz* resembles Parmesan. *Vacherin,* an unctuous, runny cheese, is available only in winter. Hard, round and pungent, *Tête de moine* does indeed look like the head of a bald monk. There is a variety of bread to go with the cheeses. *Pain de seigle,* a rich dark rye bread, is particularly good when it comes studded with walnuts.

Long, cold winters inspire an enormous variety of appetizing soups. Among them: *Basler Mehlsuppe* (Basle flour soup), eaten in the wee hours during the city's carnival, and *Brotsuppe* (bread soup), a favorite of Lucerne.

Omble chevalier (char) is maybe the most delicate and flavorful of all freshwater fish. Otherwise look for *truite* or *Forelle* (lake trout). Simple preparations are the best: the fish just poached and served with

483

hollandaise sauce. *Perche* or *Egli* (perch) is usually filleted, fried and served with half a lemon and tartar sauce.

Zurich's nationally esteemed specialty is *Geschnetzeltes Kalbfleisch,* diced veal in a rich cream sauce, known in the French-speaking part of the country as *émincé de veau.* Another dish linked to a specific region is *Bernerplatte* (Bernese board) laden with a variety of meats, sausage, sauerkraut or dried French beans and potatoes. A specialty of the Grisons, *Bündnerfleisch* (paper-thin slices of air-dried beef) is a favorite snack or starter.

Served during the September-to-February hunting season, venison, deer, wild boar and hare dishes are much appreciated. *Selle de chevreuil* or *Rehrücken* (saddle of venison) is roasted and served with red cabbage and a cream sauce.

Don't leave Switzerland without trying *Rösti,* potatoes fried with onion. Another companion to meat, especially game dishes, is *Spätzli,* tiny, noodle-like dumplings.

Swiss fruit tarts are eaten as dessert as well as snacks. *Tarte au vin cuit* or *raisiné* is made from apples which are cooked for hours to produce a dark brown tasty curd. *Zuger Kirschtorte* is an enticing *Kirsch* brandy cake from Zug. *Rüeblitorte* features carrots with eggs, almonds, cinnamon and brandy.

In a bar or restaurant wine is ordered by the bottle or half bottle, or by the carafe in multiples of one deciliter (one-tenth of a liter). Many Swiss wines are named after the grape used. In some establishments you can ask for the wine of a specific region. A list is always displayed in cafés and bars. Note that the Swiss normally drink white wine with fondue, raclette and other cheese preparations.

The Valais, Vaud and Geneva are the biggest wine-producing regions in Switzerland. Most common and best by far are white wines—the fruity Fendant and the slightly stronger Johannisberg. Swiss white wines have a distinctive, slightly acid taste, often faintly fizzy with a flinty quality. As for the reds, try the full-flavored Dôle or Pinot Noir.

While the wine of German-speaking Switzerland has less renown, you may want to try some of the light, dry reds (Hallauer, Maienfelder, Klevner, Stammheimer).

Swiss coffee is generally weaker than French or Italian brews but stronger than American coffee. In Switzerland espresso goes by the Italian name, *ristretto.*

Lunch is served from noon to 2 p.m., dinner 7 to 9 p.m. (sometimes earlier in the German-speaking region).

Entertainment. Classical music holds a strong position in Switzerland's cultural life, reflected in a host of concert events in all major cities and

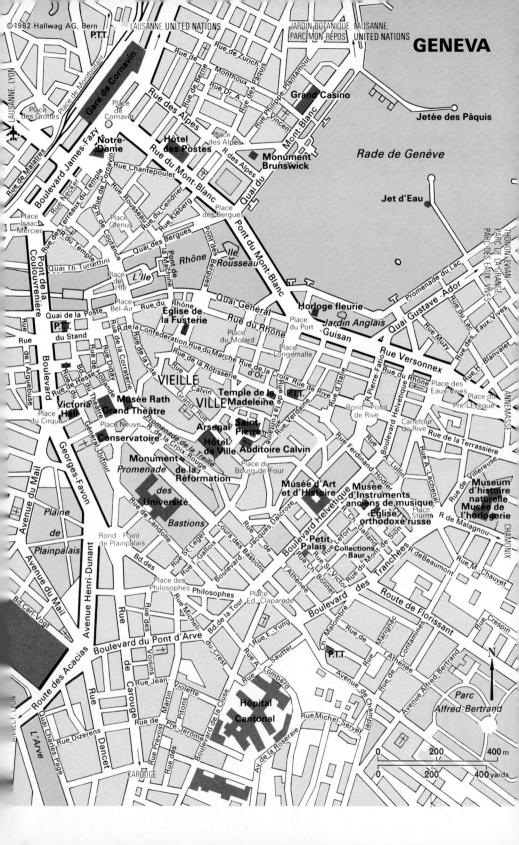

© 1982 Hallwag AG, Bern

GENEVA

P.T.T.

LAUSANNE, UNITED NATIONS

LAUSANNE, LYON

JARDIN BOTANIQUE, LAUSANNE,
PARC MON-RÉPOS, UNITED NATIONS

Rue de Zurich

Rue de

Monthoux

Rue de Berne

Rue Dr.-A.

Rue Philippe-Plantamour

Rue Vincent-

Grand Casino

Jetée des Pâquis

Gare de Cornavin

Rue des Alpes

Place de Cornavin

Place des Grottes

Rue du Mont-Blanc

Place des Alpes

Mont-Blanc

Rade de Genève

Notre-Dame

Hôtel des Postes

R des Alpes

Quai du

Monument Brunswick

Jet d'Eau

Boulevard James-Fazy

Rue Necker

Rue du Temple

Rue de Cornavin

Rue Chantepoulet

Rue Rousseau

Rue du Cendrier

Place des Alpes

Rue de Malatrex

R. des Terreaux-du-Temple

Rue Kléberg

Place des Bergues

Promenade du Lac

Place Isaac-Mercier

Rue du Temple

Place Grenus

Rue de Courance

Quai des Bergues

Pont des Bergues

Ile Rousseau

Pont du Mont-Blanc

Quai Gustave-Ador

Rue des Eaux-Vives

Rue du Lac

Rue Muzy

Rue H. Blanvalet

PARC DE LA GRANGE
PARC DES EAUX-VIVES

THONON, ÉVIAN

Pont de la Coulouvrenière

Quai Th. Turrettini

Pont de la Machine

Rhône

Place de l'Ile

L'Ile

Pont de la Machine

Quai de la Poste

Place Bel-Air

Rue du Rhône

Quai Général-Guisan

Horloge fleurie

Place du Port

Jardin Anglais

Rue de Hesse

P.T.T.

Rue du Stand

Rue de la Corraterie

Rue de la Confédération

Rue du Rhône

Eglise de la Fusterie

Rue du Marché

Place du Molard

Rue de la Croix-d'Or

Rue de Rive

Rue d'Italie

Rue Versonnex

Place Longemalle

Rue du Rhône

Place des Eaux-Vives

Place du Pré-L'Evêque

Rue de Rive

R. Pierre-Fatio

Carrefour de Rive

Rue de la Terrassière

ANNEMASSE

Rue Pierre-Fatio

Rue de l'Athénée

Boulevard Georges-Favon

Rue du Diday

Rue Général-Dufour

Bd. du Théâtre

Victoria Hall

Place du Cirque

Musée Rath
Grand Théâtre

Place Neuve

Conservatoire

Rue de la Cité

Rue de la Rôtisserie

Calvin

Grand-Rue

Temple de la Madeleine

P.T.T.

Rue Verdaine

VIEILLE VILLE

Arsenal

Saint-Pierre

Hôtel de Ville

Auditoire Calvin

Rue Ferdinand-Hodler

Boulevard Helvétique

Rue A.-Lullin

Promenade de la Treille

Promenade de la Croix-Rouge

Monument de la Réformation

Promenade des Bastions

Rue de la Croix-Rouge

Place du Bourg-de-Four

Musée d'Art et d'Histoire

Musée d'Instruments anciens de musique

Eglise orthodoxe russe

Museum d'histoire naturelle

Musée de l'horlogerie

Université

Rue de Candolle

Rue St.-Léger

Bastions

Cours des Bastions

Rue Jacques-Dalcroze

Boulevard Helvétique

Petit Palais

Collections Baur

Place Sturm

Rue de Malagnou

R. de Beaumont

CHAMONIX

Georges-Favon

Avenue du Mail

Plaine de Plainpalais

Rond-Point de Plainpalais

Bd des

Rue de la Tour

Rue Gallox

Boulevard des Bastions

Place des Philosophes

Philosophes

Place Ed.-Claparède

Rue Le Fort

Rue St.-Victor

Rue Michel-Servet

Rue du Mont-de-Sion

Rue St.-Léger

Boulevard des Tranchées

Route de Florissant

Rue de Villereuse

Rue M.-Chauvet

Avenue Henri-Dunant

Rue du Crest

Bd. de la Tour

Rue Michel-Chauvet

Rue E.-Yung

Rue A.-Lombard

Rue Sautter

P.T.T.

Avenue de Champel

Rue des Contamines

Rue Marignac

Rue de Malombré

Ch. Malombré

Avenue Alfred-Bertrand

Rue Crespin

N

Boulevard du Pont d'Arve

Rue de Carouge

Rue des Voisins

Rue Jean-Violette

Rue Martin

Rue des Pitons

Rue Prévost

Rue Pré-Jérôme

Bourg de Four

Av. de la Roseraie

Hôpital Cantonal

Rue Michel-Servet

Parc Alfred-Bertrand

Route des Acacias

Quai Charles-Page

Bd Carl-Vogt

L'Arve

Rue Dizerens

Rue Dancet

CAROUGE

0 200 400 m

0 200 400 yards

also smaller towns. Local chamber groups and symphony orchestras, like the renowned Orchestre de la Suisse Romande, often appear. Opera featuring guest stars and local talent alike is an important part of the scene in Zurich, Geneva, Basle and Berne. Basle and Lausanne have an international reputation for ballet. The nightclubs will hardly remind you of Paris, but the discos are lively. In resort and metropolitan areas some movie theaters show films in the original language with subtitles in French and German. Otherwise the soundtrack is dubbed into the language of the region.

Annual events and festivals. The Swiss Tourist Office publishes a booklet entitled *Events in Switzerland,* listing everything from jazz concerts to alpine herdsmen's festivals. Some events from a typical year's calendar: *January:* Horse racing on snow in St. Moritz and Arosa. *February:* International ballet competition for young dancers, Prix de Lausanne. *February–March:* Carnival processions in Basle, Lucerne and lesser-known Fasnacht centers. *March:* Engadine cross-country ski marathon. International Motor Show in Geneva. *April–May: Landsgemeinde* (plebiscite) in Appenzell and some other cantons. *June:* Zurich's International June Festival featuring concerts, opera, theater and art exhibitions. *July:* Montreux Jazz Festival. Nyon Folk Music Festival. *August:* National Day celebrations. Music festivals in Lucerne and Gstaad. Locarno International Film Festival. Fête de Genève with fireworks and parades. *September:* Music festivals in Montreux and Vevey. *September–October:* Vintage festivals in vineyard regions. *November:* Onion market, of medieval traditions, in Berne.

Taxes, service charges and tipping. In Swiss hotels and restaurants the service charges are included and tipping has in principle been phased out, but if the service has been especially good, an extra coin or two is appropriate and appreciated. As for taxis, in many cities like Geneva and Zurich the tip is included in the fare, as indicated by a sign inside the cab, otherwise a 10–15% tip is appropriate.

Sports and recreation. Facilities are plentiful for swimming (lakes and outdoor swimming pools), cycling, boating, tennis and squash. The legendary Swiss countryside, never more than a few minutes away from any city, offers unparalleled hiking and climbing opportunities. Nearly 200 Swiss towns and villages are geared for downhill skiing. In most areas the season runs from late November to early April. Cross-country skiing has grown in popularity in recent years.

Popular spectator sports are Alpine ski racing, soccer, tennis and bicycle racing.

TV and radio. Swiss TV and radio have German-, French- and Italian-language channels. In many hotel rooms, closed-circuit radios relay news in English at certain hours, as well as the English programs of Swiss Radio International, the short wave service based in Berne.

What to buy. Favorite purchases are watches of all the famous makes, gold and silver jewelry, fabrics, chocolate, cheese, Swiss army knives, wooden toys, high fashion shoes or sturdy hiking boots, cuckoo clocks, embroidery like table cloths or blouses with the stitching of St. Gall. Fashionable shopping streets are Bahnhofstrasse in Zurich and Rue du Rhône in Geneva. Switzerland has no sales tax.

Stores are open from 8 or 9 a.m. to 6:30 or 7 p.m., Monday through Friday, and until 4, 5 or 5:30 p.m. on Saturdays. Stores, large and small, have a half-day closing, perhaps Monday morning or Wednesday or Thursday afternoon. Neighborhood shops often close at lunchtime.

Sightseeing

Zurich. Economic powerhouse with 2,000 years of tradition. One inhabitant in 200 is a Swiss franc millionaire. ETH, the polytechnic institute, one of the world's great universities, connected to bustling downtown life by shaky cable car, the Polybahn. River Limmat lined with guild houses like Zunfthaus zur Meise, Zurich's finest Baroque building, built for the wine merchants in 1757 and the older Zunfthaus zur Waag, headquarters of the linen weavers and hatmakers from 1637. Narrow old-world streets in Old Town*. Numerous churches including St. Peter's Church with one of Europe's largest clock faces, 30 feet (10 m.) in diameter, on 13th-century tower. Grossmünster from 1100–1250, the cathedral, where Zwingli preached the Reformation from 1519; its twin towers make it the city's most distinctive landmark. Wasserkirche, late-Gothic church built right on the Limmat. Fraumünster on the west river bank, a 13th-century church with Chagall stained-glass windows from 1970 in Romanesque choir. The streetcar-and-pedestrians-only Bahnhofstrasse, one of Europe's most elegant shopping streets. Richly ornamented Town Hall *(Rathaus)*. Fine Arts Museum *(Kunsthaus)*, with emphasis on 19th- and 20th-century European works. Swiss National Museum *(Schweizerisches Landesmuseum)**, displaying Swiss culture, art and history. Good view of the Limmat from historic Lindenhof.

Northeast Switzerland. Schaffhausen with old town center of 16th- to 18th-century houses, embellished with frescoes, statues and richly carved oriels. Stein am Rhein*, a beautiful little town, with market square and main street lined by frescoed, half-timbered houses. The Rhine Falls *(Rheinfall),* Europe's biggest waterfall. St. Gall* with Baroque cathedral and magnificent Abbey Library *(Stiftsbibliothek)* housing 100,000 volumes and ancient manuscripts. The small town of Appenzell with attractive square, site of traditional *Landsgemeinde* in April.

Basle. The country's second biggest city and most important port on the Rhine, situated at the junction of France, Germany and Switzerland. Center for chemical and pharmaceutical industry. Old Town rising steeply from the river. 12th-century cathedral *(Münster)* in red sandstone. Late-Gothic Town Hall *(Rathaus)* facing the market place *(Marktplatz).* 14th-century Spalentor, western gateway to the city, surmounted by a clock tower. Fine Arts Museum *(Kunstmuseum)**, one of Europe's major museums, covering works from Holbein to Monet, Picasso, Chagall and the Swiss sculptor Jean Tinguely. Zoo* focusing on breeding threatened species.

Berne. Federal capital of Switzerland. A bear on the coat-of-arms, live bears in the Bear Pit *(Bärengraben)* since the 15th century. Old Town with fountains and extraordinary clock tower, Zytgloggeturm. Old arcaded streets* lined with shops—Spitalgasse, Marktgasse and Kramgasse. Justice Fountain in Gerechtigkeitsgasse. Gothic Town Hall *(Rathaus)* in its own little square. Late-Gothic cathedral *(Münster)* with 15th-century stained-glass windows and magnificent Renaissance choir stalls. Guided tours of Federal Parliament Building *(Bundeshaus).* Paul Klee collection in Fine Arts Museum *(Kunstmuseum).* Natural History Museum known for excellent presentations. View over old Berne from the Kirchenfeld bridge.

Bernese Oberland*. Lakes of Thun and Brienz. Panoramic view from Niesen at 7,749 feet (2,362 m.) above Spiez. Interlaken with Victorian hotels and dazzling view of the Eiger, Mönch and Jungfrau Alpine peaks. Waterfalls of Trümmelbach. Revolving mountaintop restaurant atop Schilthorn, at 9,744 feet (2,970 m.). Tourist towns of Grindelwald and Wengen linked by railroad that extends to Jungfraujoch* at 11,401 feet (3,454 m.). Superb skiing including the Lauberhorn downhill run. Further away the high Alpine passes of Grimsel, Furka and Susten with endless hairpin turns and glorious panoramas. Gstaad, fashionable resort combining scenery and social life.

489

Central Switzerland. Lucerne*, with early 14th-century covered bridge *(Kapellbrücke)*, featuring some 100 gable paintings; octagonal Water Tower; twin-towered Jesuit Church, one of the most beautiful Baroque buildings in Switzerland; impressive early 17th-century Town Hall *(Rathaus)*; famous lion monument *(Löwendenkmal);* Swiss Transport Museum *(Verkehrshaus der Schweiz)**, Europe's largest and most modern of its kind.

Richard Wagner Museum at Tribschen. Excursions to the mountains of Pilatus and Rigi. Lake of Lucerne *(Vierwaldstättersee)**, with pastoral shores where the Swiss confederation was formed on August 1, 1291. Twin-towered Benedictine Abbey* with gold and white interior, dominating the small town of Einsiedeln.

Geneva. Rivaling Zurich as the internationally renowned city of Switzerland. The site of international organizations like the Red Cross and the World Health Organization. World-famous water jet *(Jet d'Eau)*, reaching 40 stories over Lake of Geneva. Lakeside promenades and lovely parks. View of the lake and Mont Blanc, Europe's tallest mountain in the distance, from elegant Quai du Mont Blanc. The English Garden *(Jardin Anglais)*, best known for its clock of flowers. Cobbled streets and historic mansions in the Old Town*, with charming Place du Bourg-de-Four and St. Peter's Cathedral, where Calvin preached for more than 20 years. Reformation Monument, with sculptural group portraying Reformation leaders like Calvin and John Knox. Watch Museum *(Musée de l'Horlogerie et de l'Emaillerie)* housing a rich collection of clocks, watches and enamelwork. Museum of Art and History, including a prized altarpiece of 1444. United Nations Palace, the European headquarters of the U.N. Adjacent town of Carouge founded in the late 18th century by the King of Sardinia; Mediterranean charm and colorful open-air markets.

Lake of Geneva (Lac Léman)*. Lausanne with Switzerland's finest Gothic building, the cathedral from 1175–1232; Roman excavations; bustling harbor and tourist site of Ouchy on the lake; beautiful lakeside promenade; headquarters of the International Olympic Committee; center of the best wine districts of Switzerland. Excursions to the village of St. Sulpice with Romanesque church, to the west, or along the panoramic Route des Vignobles* through vineyards and charming villages to Montreux, a full-time tourist resort, to the east. Chillon Castle* on the shoreline, a feudal fortress with turrets and towers, famed through Byron's *The Prisoner of Chillon*. Cog wheel railroad to Rochers-de-Naye at 6,699 feet (2,042 m.) with panoramic view over the lake, the mountains and the vineyards.

West Switzerland. The Jura, an unspoiled region of pine forests, verdant pastures and rugged cliffs. Romainmôtier, charming village with church built in the 10th and 11th centuries noted for early Christian pulpit from the 7th century. Lakeside town of Neuchâtel with picturesque Old Town and fine Museum of Art and History. The small town of Payerne claiming Switzerland's greatest Romanesque church★, all that survives of a flourishing Benedictine Abbey. Fribourg, a bilingual, Catholic city of churches, seminaries and religious bookshops in a dramatic setting. Gruyères★, fortified medieval town situated on top of its own hill.

Valais★. The twin hills in the old town of Sion with ruins of a 13th-century episcopal castle and a formidable fortress-church. Summer and winter resorts of Verbier, Crans-Montana, Saas-Fee. Enchanting car-less village of Zermatt★ with the famous 4000s—the dozen Alpine peaks reaching over 4,000 meters or 13,000 feet, including the Matterhorn. Excursion by railroad to Gornergrat at 10,272 feet (3,131 m.) with unforgettable view over Mount Rosa and the Dufour peak at 15,203 feet (4,634 m.) and its glaciers. Narrow-gauge train ride from Zermatt to St. Moritz, the Glacier Express★, over 291 bridges and through 91 tunnels.

The Grisons. Unspoiled and sparsely populated mountain region including the summer and winter resorts of Laax and Flims. Even more remote Engadine★ with sturdy stone village houses embellished by characteristic *sgraffito* decoration. Famous Alpine resorts of Davos, Klosters and St. Moritz. Not only skiing but also sailing, golf and hiking in the summer season.

Ticino. Part of Switzerland south of the Alps; the best of two worlds, Italian language, charm, music and food and Swiss efficiency and cleanliness. Locarno in subtropical foliage on Lake Maggiore, with Piazza Grande serving as the site of Locarno's annual International Film Festival. Nearby sunny and sophisticated resort of Ascona. Boat excursions to Isles of Brissago. Lugano with generous microclimate giving early spring. 17th-century Villa Favorita★, a fabulous private art collection (due to move to Madrid). Funicular excursion to Monte Brè for fresh air and clear view over lake and hills.

For some useful expressions in French, see p. 196.
For some useful expressions in German, see p. 226.
For some useful expressions in Italian, see p. 318.

491

Liechtenstein

The Alpine principality of Liechtenstein, which disbanded its army more than a century ago, enjoys peaceful prosperity, snuggled between two neutral republics, Switzerland and Austria. Liechtenstein offers the tourist the expected delights of a fairy-tale enclave: castles, vineyards, steep forests and winning villages...plus interesting tax laws and postage stamps. Liechtenstein has such close relations with Switzerland that the Swiss franc is the official currency and there are no border controls. The capital, Vaduz, has an exceptional cultural attraction in the National Art Gallery, containing masterpieces owned by the reigning prince, who lives in the castle up the hill.

Facts and figures

Population:	26,500
Area:	62 sq. miles (160 sq. km.)
Capital:	Vaduz (5,000)
Language:	German
Religion:	Catholic (86%), Protestant (9%)
Time zone:	GMT + 1, EST + 6, DST (Apr.–Sep.)
Currency:	Swiss franc (*Franken,* abbr. *Fr*) = 100 *Rappen*
Electricity:	220 volt, 50 cycle, AC

Planning your trip

Visa requirements. See pp. 29–30.

Vaccination requirements. None (see p. 25).

Currrency restrictions. None.

Climate. Liechtenstein enjoys a continental climate with warm summers and cold winters. Precipitation is spread more or less evenly throughout the year, with a slight peak in March–April.

Clothing. Lightweight clothing is generally adequate in summer, with something warmer for evenings. Wrap up for cold and snowy winters.

Duty-free allowances

	Cigarettes		Cigars		Tobacco	Liquor		Wine
1)	400	or	100	or	500 g.	1 l.	and	2 l.
2)	200	or	50	or	250 g.	1 l.	and	2 l.

Gifts (including perfume): up to Fr. 100 max. value

1) residents of countries outside Europe
2) residents of Europe

Hotels and accommodations. A list of hotels is available from the tourist office, which also has a reservation office.

Liechtenstein tourist offices abroad. The principality is represented by the Swiss National Tourist Office (see Switzerland).

On the spot

Banks and currency exchange. Banks are open from 8 a.m. to noon, and 2 to 4:30 p.m., Monday through Friday. There are no after-hours exchange offices but larger hotels will change the more familiar foreign currencies into Swiss francs.

Credit cards and traveler's checks. Both are widely accepted.

Mail and telecommunications. The principality produces its own postage stamps, but the mail and telecommunications systems are largely integrated with those of neighboring Switzerland. Post offices are open from 7:30 a.m. to noon, and 1:30 to 6:30 p.m., Monday through Friday, and 7:30 to 11 a.m. on Saturdays.

Some useful telephone numbers:

Information (local and Switzerland)	111	Telegrams	110
		Fire	118
Information (international)	191	Police (emergencies)	117
Operator	114		

Legal holidays

Jan. 1	New Year's Day	**Movable dates:**
Jan. 6	Epiphany	Good Friday
Feb. 2	Candlemas Day	Easter Monday
Mar. 19	St. Joseph's Day	Ascension
Mar. 25	Annunciation	Whit Monday
May 1	Labor Day	Corpus Christi
Aug. 15	Assumption	
Nov. 1	All Saints' Day	
Dec. 8	Immaculate Conception	
Dec. 25	Christmas	
Dec. 26	St. Stephen's Day	

Newspapers. The principality's two dailies are *Liechtensteiner Volksblatt* and *Liechtensteiner Vaterland.* Leading West European newspapers, the *International Herald Tribune* and some American magazines are available at larger newsstands.

Tourist information

Vaduz   Engländerhaus, Städtle 37, 9490 Vaduz; tel. 2 14 43

Transportation

Air. Liechtenstein has no commercial airport. Visitors usually fly to Zurich, Switzerland, and then continue by train and bus or rented car.

Rail. International expresses stop in Sargans or Buchs (Switzerland), where taxis and buses are available to destinations within Liechtenstein.

Local public transportation. The principality is served by an efficient postal bus network. Tickets can be bought at post offices or directly from the driver.

Taxis. Cabs can be hailed on the street or ordered by phone.

Car rental. International and local rental agencies operate in Liechtenstein. See also pp. 30–31.

Driving in Liechtenstein. The car must carry a red reflector warning triangle. If you wear glasses you must have a spare pair in the car. Seat belts must be worn. The blood alcohol limit is 80 mg./100 ml. Gasoline available is lead-free (91 and 95 octane), super (98 octane) and diesel. Speed limits are well signposted. In case of breakdown, telephone 140. Use of horn is recommended on winding mountain roads but not elsewhere.

Emergencies. The emergency police number is 117.

Crime and theft. Normal precautions are in order.

Medical care and health. Health care is excellent but expensive. Many doctors speak English. If hospitalization is required, patients are sent to neighboring Swiss hospitals. Medical and pharmaceutical supplies are readily available. Of the two pharmacies in Vaduz, one always stays on duty after hours. For insurance, see pp. 25–26.
Tap water is safe to drink.

Social customs. Handshakes on meeting and departure are the rule.

Enjoying Liechtenstein

Food and drink. Liechtenstein cooking is strongly influenced by its Swiss neighbor; dishes are usually given their German names. You may come across *Bündnerfleisch* (wafer-thin slices of dried beef), *Egli* (perch), *Felchen* (white fish), *Forelle* (trout), *Geschnetzeltes Kalbfleisch* (sliced veal in a cream sauce), *Leberspiesschen* (skewered liver) and *Rösti* (hashed-brown potatoes).

Local or Swiss wines and beers are worth trying. Imported drinks are considerably more expensive than traditional aperitifs like *blanc-cassis* (white wine with blackcurrant liqueur) or *pastis* (aniseed liquor).

Lunch is served from noon to 2 p.m., dinner 7:30 to 10 p.m.

Entertainment. Concerts are held regularly. Foreign movies are often shown in their original language. A few discos operate.

Taxes, service charges and tipping. Hotel and restaurant bills are all-inclusive. Tipping recommendations: porters Fr 1 per bag, waiter 5% (optional), taxi drivers 10–15%, hatcheck Fr 1.

Sports and recreation. Mountain climbing, skiing, hiking, swimming, tennis and horse riding are all available to visitors.

TV and radio. While Liechtenstein has no radio or TV of its own, reception of Swiss, Austrian and German programs is good.

What to buy. Watches, cameras, jewelry, pottery–but compare prices. Shops are open from 8 a.m. to noon and from 1:30 to 6:30 p.m., Monday through Saturday.

Sightseeing

Vaduz. Hillside castle. National Art Gallery *(Liechtensteinische Staatliche Kunstsammlung)* with pieces from ruling prince's collection: Brueghel, Rubens, Van Dyck and Hals. Gallery also houses philatelic museum *(Postmuseum)*. National Museum *(Landesmuseum)* in former inn, the "Stag"–also former seat of government. Seven principal wines and local champagne from surrounding vineyards. Charming villages scattered through hills and orchards. Malbun, summer and winter spa.

For some useful expressions in German, see p. 226.

UNITED KINGDOM

*A culture familiar yet foreign amid the
scenery that inspired poets and artists.*

Tradition grips the visitor—flamboyantly at the Changing of the Guard,
reverently in a medieval cathedral, even soberly beside the fireplace in a
timbered country pub. You know what to expect from movies, books
and school, but surprises hide behind every comfortable stereotype. The
culture you thought familiar turns out to be as foreign as warm beer and
boxy black taxis driving on the left. To understand it you'll first have to
learn the babble of baffling accents—jerky cockney, the lilt of the Welsh,
the trill of the Scots.

The United Kingdom packs in a population of more than 56 million.
But since most Britons live in cities, the countryside is abandoned to
natural beauty, even within sight of the big towns. The scenery has
always inspired poets, artists and camera-slung tourists.

Most tours start in London, an immense, low-rise city overstocked
with historic and cultural monuments as rich as the empire it com-
manded. After a day flitting from the Tower of London to St. Paul's
Cathedral to the Houses of Parliament to Buckingham Palace, you may
risk dozing off at the opera. The remainder of England enjoys a
gratifying variety of sights: charming Cotswold villages, the white cliffs
of Dover, the crystal lakes of Cumbria, and Shakespeare's Stratford.
North of the border in Scotland, bagpipes really skirl amidst the
romantic moors and lochs. In Wales, land of legend and song,
battlements glower over the sea and narrow-gauge trains still puff past.
The fourth element of the U.K., Northern Ireland, offers the open road
through glens to sweeping beaches.

When it comes to the weather, the general rule in Britain is
moderation, but anything can happen at short notice. If you're caught
short without a raincoat or umbrella, this is the right place to buy one.
For all kinds of shopping, from Harrods to Petticoat Lane, from
boutique to bazar, Britain is hard to resist.

500

Facts and figures

Population:	56 million
Area:	94,226 sq. miles (244,046 sq. km.)
Capital:	London (2 million, Greater London 6.7 million)
Other major cities:	Birmingham (1 million) Glasgow (760,000) Leeds (705,000) Sheffield (535,000) Liverpool (510,000) Manchester (450,000) Edinburgh (420,000) Bristol (390,000) Belfast (360,000/GUA 550,000) Cardiff (275,000) Aberdeen (190,000)
Language:	English; Welsh and Gaelic, of certain local importance in parts of Wales and Scotland, will not affect the non-resident
Religion:	Protestant, Anglican (55%), Roman Catholic (10%)
Time zone:	GMT, EST + 5; DST (Mar.–Oct.)
Currency:	*Pound sterling* (symbolized £) = 100 *pence* (abbr. *p*) Coins: 1, 2, 5, 10, 20, 50p; £1, 2 Bills: £5, 10, 20, 50
Electricity:	240 volt, 50 cycle, AC

Planning your trip

Visa requirements. See pp. 29–30.

Vaccination requirements. None (see p. 25).

Currency restrictions. None.

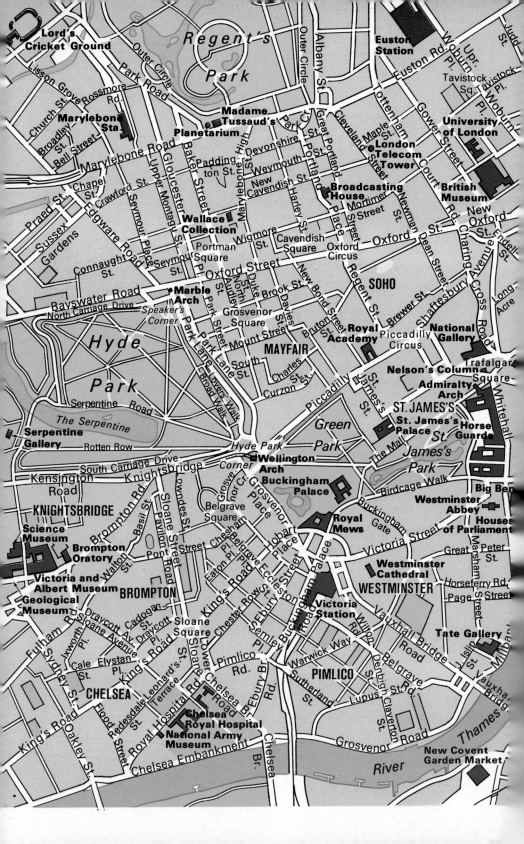

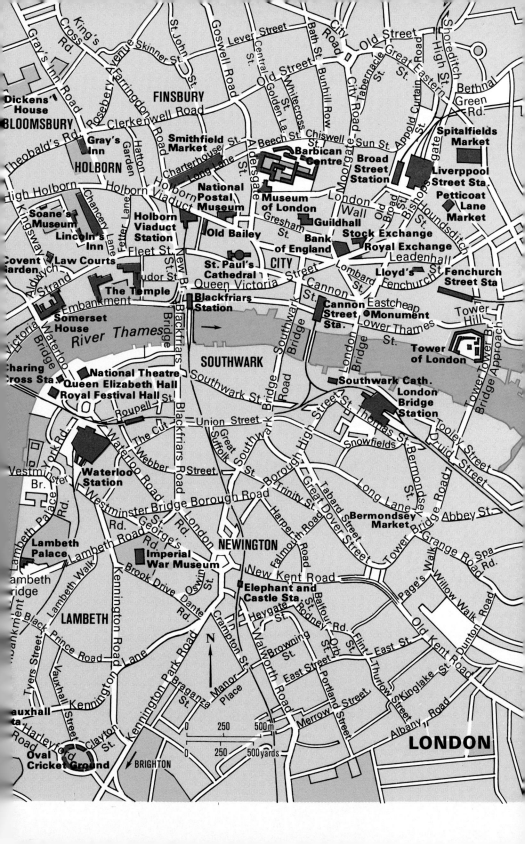

Climate. The United Kingdom enjoys a temperate maritime climate with few prolonged periods of extreme weather. Rain can be expected at any time of the year. Though snow can lie for considerable periods in Scottish areas, it rarely affects city streets for more than a few hours. In the south, snowfall is generally lighter. Fog can be a driving hazard in winter.

In recent years, England has in summer and in fall experienced long dry spells that even reached near-catastrophic proportions. It has also had summers where rain barely let up at all. Alas, it's very hard to count on anything. The key word is "unpredictable".

Some average daily temperatures:

London		J	F	M	A	M	J	J	A	S	O	N	D
average daily maximum*	°F	43	44	50	56	62	69	71	71	65	58	50	45
	°C	6	7	10	13	17	20	22	21	19	14	10	7
average daily minimum*	°F	36	36	38	42	47	53	56	56	52	46	42	38
	°C	2	2	3	6	8	12	14	13	11	8	5	4
Edinburgh													
average daily maximum*	°F	42	43	46	51	56	62	65	64	60	54	48	44
	°C	6	6	8	11	14	17	18	18	16	12	9	7
average daily minimum*	°F	34	34	36	39	43	49	52	52	49	44	39	36
	°C	1	1	2	4	6	9	11	11	9	7	4	2

* Minimum temperatures are measured just before sunrise, maximum temperatures in the afternoon.

Clothing. Mediumweight clothes are generally adequate in summer, with a warm jacket for cool spells. Warm clothes are advisable in winter including a warm overcoat, hat and gloves. An umbrella or rainwear is essential. In winter the humidity and wind may make you feel colder than the thermometer shows. Even indoors you'll need to wrap up; the English, great believers in fresh air and drafts, do not overheat their homes.

Rare are the occasions when men are required to wear ties; only a handful of conservative restaurants retain restrictions on attire. You can go to the theater in blue jeans or evening dress.

Duty-free allowances

	Cigarettes		Cigars		Tobacco	Liquor	Wine
1)	400	or	100	or	500 g.	1 l. and	2 l.
2)	300	or	75	or	400 g.	1½ l. and	5 l.
3)	200	or	50	or	250 g.	1 l. and	2 l.

Perfume: 1), 3) 50 g.; 2) 75 g.
Toilet water: 1), 3) ¼ l.; 2) ³/₈ l.
Gifts: 1), 3) £28; 2) £207

1) residents outside Europe
2) residents of Europe, non-duty-free goods bought in an EEC country
3) residents of Europe, duty-free goods bought in an EEC country or goods obtained outside the EEC

Hotels and accommodations

The U.K. offers a variety of accommodations at all price levels. Official guides covering all types of accommodations are published by the British Tourist Authority. Hotels are classified by the English Tourist Board, from a simple listing for modest "bed and breakfast" establishments, to five "crowns" and, best of all, five "gold crowns". This ensures that an establishment meets the standards laid down by the Tourist Board. The cost of breakfast is normally included in the room charge. It's wise to make reservations well in advance, in particular during the peak tourist season. Tourist information centers at most airports and in most towns can make last-minute reservations for you either locally or "Book-a-Bed-Ahead".

Hotels. There are plenty of large, modern hotels situated throughout the U.K., as well as small family hotels, and in country areas many splendid mansions and even castles are now comfortable hotels.

Inns and boardinghouses. Britain has hundreds of country inns, as much as several centuries old, but with modern amenities and about six to 20 bedrooms. Boardinghouses (Guest houses) are much cheaper than hotels and offer clean and adequate accommodations (usually about six rooms) but without all the facilities of a large hotel. Breakfast is always included.

505

Bed and Breakfast. Many families have one or two rooms to rent in their own homes. Full English breakfast is always included in the price of the room. Just look for the sign as you travel around. You don't have to make reservations in advance and it's usually inexpensive.

Simple, comfortable accommodations are also available at farmhouses. Ask for the British Tourist Authority's special pamphlet *Stay on a Farm: Where to Stay in England.*

Motels. These are usually found alongside main roads and expressways.

Youth hostels. The U.K. has an excellent network of 260 youth hostels which are good and inexpensive. Most accept advance reservations. International membership is available from: YHA Services, 14 Southampton Street, London WC2E 7HY and a temporary membership pass can be bought at any youth hostel.

Camping. Camping is a popular pastime in the United Kingdom. Most sites open only from March or April to September or October, though a few remain open year-round. For complete lists of campsites and services, consult the British Tourist Authority brochure *Camping and Caravan Parks in Britain,* or write to: Camping & Caravanning Club Ltd., 11, Lower Grosvenor Place, London SW1V OEY; tel. (01) 828 1012.

British tourist offices abroad

Australia and New Zealand	Associated Midland House, 171 Clarence Street, Sydney, NSW 2000; tel. (612) 29-8627
Canada	Suite 600, 94 Cumberland Street, Toronto, Ont. M5R 3N3; tel. (416) 925-6326
Eire	123 Lower Baggot Street, Dublin 2; tel. (01) 614-188
South Africa	7th Floor, JBS Building, 107 Commissioner Street, Johannesburg 2001; tel. (011) 296-770
U.S.A.	3rd Floor, 40 West 57th Street, New York, NY 10019; tel. (212) 581-4700
	John Hancock Center (Suite 3320), 875 North Michigan Avenue, Chicago, IL 60611; tel. (312) 787-0490
	2580 Cumberland Parkway, Suite 470, Atlanta, GA 30339; tel. (404) 432-9635
	Cedar Maple Plaza, 2305 Cedar Springs Road, Dallas, TX 75201; tel. (214) 720-4040
	World Trade Center, Suite 450, 350 Figueroa St.; Los Angeles, CA 90017; tel. (213) 628-3525

On the spot

Banks and currency exchange. Banking hours are 9:30 a.m. to 3:30 p.m., Monday through Friday. Banks in Scotland and Northern Ireland close for an hour at lunchtime. Some branches are open Saturday mornings. Outside normal banking hours money can be changed at currency-exchange offices in main cities and ports, and in many large hotels, travel agents and big department stores. They are indicated, rather exotically, by a sign in French—*bureau de change.*

Credit cards and traveler's checks. Internationally recognized credit cards are accepted in hotels, restaurants and stores, which display symbols of the cards they accept on their doors or windows. Traveler's checks, on the other hand, may be refused in some stores and restaurants, mostly due to unfamiliarity with foreign exchange procedures. It's best to change them in a bank or currency-exchange office. Take your passport as proof of identity when cashing traveler's checks. On the whole it's not a good idea to offer foreign currency as payment. Except in a handful of large stores, the exchange rate you receive will be noticeably to your disadvantage and many establishments will refuse all but British money.

Mail and telecommunications. These services are generally reliable. During the height of the tourist season, however, mail might take a little longer to get through. Many post offices in towns are open from 9 a.m. to 5:30 or 6 p.m., Monday through Friday, 9 a.m. to 12:30 p.m. on Saturday. Smaller branches work shorter hours and may be part of a village general store. In London, the office in William IV Street, near Trafalgar Square, is open until 8 p.m. Stamps can also be purchased from "Postal Centre" stamp dispensers at large stores and major tourist attractions. They are now also sold in a variety of other shops with a red sign "stamps". In Scotland you may be given Scottish stamps, but they are valid throughout the U.K. A two-tier mail system is in operation for domestic destinations with first-class mail delivered the following day, and second-class mail generally a day later. Mailboxes are painted red.

Overseas telegrams may be sent from any telephone. Dial 190 or 193. Telemessages have replaced domestic telegrams.

British Telecom has coin-operated payphones sited throughout the U.K, by the roadside and in public places such as railroad stations and shopping centers. Additionally, you may use payphones in pubs, restaurants, hotels and other places open to the public. International

507

calls can be dialed direct from most U.K. telephones, but there may be delays in summer. The older type of red-painted phone booths take only 10p coins. In city centers, mainline rail stations, airports and central London subway stations, new blue payphones (which take all U.K. coins except 1p) and cardphones are in operation. For the latter, small plastic phonecards are used and these come in 40, 100 and 200 units—on sale at post offices, newsstands and shops displaying the green and white sign "Phonecards sold here". For surcharges and low rates, see p. 30.

Some useful telephone numbers:

Operator (general, nationwide)	100	Directory information	192
Operator (Australia, Canada, U.S.A.)	107	Emergency (police, fire, ambulance, nationwide)	999

Newspapers. Principal quality British dailies are *The Times, The Financial Times, The Daily Telegraph, The Guardian* and *The Scotsman. The Observer, The Sunday Times* and *The Sunday Telegraph* appear on Sundays. Principal newspapers from other Western European countries, including the Paris-edited *International Herald Tribune,* are sold at many hotels and newsstands.

Tourist information. The U.K. has over 700 tourist information centers found in most average-sized towns and also at most airports and ports. A directory of tourist information centers is available free of charge.

London   London Tourist Board and Convention Bureau, 26 Grosvenor Gardens, London SW1W ODU; tel. (071) 730 3488

Birmingham   2 City Arcade; tel. (021) 643 2514

Bristol	Colston House, Colston Street; tel. (0272) 20767
Manchester	Town Hall Extension, Lloyd Street; tel. (061) 234 3157/8
Edinburgh	Waverley Market, Princes Street; tel. (031) 577 2727
Glasgow	35–39 St. Vincent Place; tel. (041) 227 4880
Aberdeen	St. Nicholas House, Broad Street; tel. (0224) 632727
Cardiff	3 Castle Street; tel. (0222) 27281
Belfast	52 High Street; tel. (0232) 246609

Legal holidays

	England and Wales	*Scotland*
New Year's Day	Jan. 1	Jan. 1 and 2
St. David's Day	Mar. 1 (Wales only)	
May Day	1st Mon. in May	1st Mon. in May
Spring Bank Holiday	last Mon. in May	last Mon. in May
Summer Bank Holiday	last Mon. in Aug.	1st Mon. in Aug.
Christmas Day	Dec. 25	Dec. 25
Boxing Day	Dec. 26	Dec. 26
Movable dates:	Good Friday/ Easter Monday	Good Friday

Northern Ireland observes the same legal holidays as England, with the addition of St. Patrick's Day (mid-March) and Battle of the Boyne Day (mid-July).

Transportation

Air. London (Heathrow and Gatwick) is the U.K.'s major gateway, while Prestwick handles Scotland's inter-continental air traffic. More than 20 British airports serve destinations abroad and there are nearly 60 domestic airports.

Major airports. London: Heathrow (15 miles/24 km. west of city center). The Piccadilly subway line to Heathrow provides a fast, inexpensive connection with all parts of London. The journey takes approximately 45 minutes. Airbuses from the airport to the city center and Victoria Station (bus A1) and Euston Station (A2) run about every 15 minutes

510

during the day. Gatwick (25 miles/40 km. south of city center). A railroad links Gatwick with Victoria Station and there is an express train service every 15 minutes (journey time 30 minutes). Facilities at both airports include duty-free shops. **Prestwick** (Scotland) (28 miles/45 km. from Glasgow). Duty-free shop. Public bus, train and taxi service to Glasgow (journey time about one hour). **Birmingham:** Eldon (8 miles/ 13 km. from city center). Duty-free shop. There is an airport bus service and a train service to the city center. **Manchester:** Ringway (12 miles/ 20 km. from city center). Duty-free shop. Half-hourly airport bus service to the city center.

Rail. The train is generally recommended for inter-city trips within the U.K. Where a return to London the same day is required for journeys to Scotland or Northern Ireland, travelers often opt for air travel. Trains are comfortable and reasonably punctual, with first- and second-class compartments. The InterCity 125 (125 mph/200 kph) train service on many of the main routes has greatly reduced journey times.

Apart from normal one-day round-trip reductions available on most services and a bewildering array of special offers and passes, the *Britrail Pass* offers savings for those traveling frequently by train. This ticket must be bought before arrival in Britain and covers unlimited travel for different periods in the U.K.

London has six main stations: King's Cross/St.Pancras for the Northeast and Edinburgh; Euston for the Northwest and Glasgow; Paddington for the West and Wales; Victoria for the South; Waterloo for the Southeast; and Liverpool Street for East Anglia. They are all connected by subway.

Long-distance buses. Buses serve over 3,000 destinations in the U.K. National Express buses are a quick, comfortable and economical way of traveling around the country. The Rapide service, with movie shows and hostess-served refreshments, offers non-stop journeys from London to over 100 towns and cities. *Britexpress Cards* can be purchased before you arrive in Britain.

Local public transportation. In London, there's a reliable subway (Underground). Tickets are dispensed by automatic ticket machines or, if you don't have change, at the ticket office. Liverpool and Glasgow also have subways. Bus services operate in all areas. Bus fares are paid either to the driver on entry or inside the bus to a conductor. Have small change ready. The "Visitor Travelcard", valid for unlimited travel on both subway and all London Transport buses and British trains in Greater London, is sold for periods of one, three, four or seven days.

511

Taxis. In London and the main cities these are stubby black cabs. Substantial luggage goes beside the driver (at an extra fee). Though city streets often seem full of taxis, it can be hard to find a free one at rush hours. Generally, all you do in London is hail a cab on the street when its yellow "For Hire" sign is lit. They also congregate at taxi stands. In the country, taxis often have no meters, but a board with standard fares based on mileage should be displayed. In London privately run cabs, known as minicabs, can be ordered by phone and are listed under *Minicabs* in the yellow pages. They are useful for late-night or exceptionally long trips. A more modern vehicle, the Metrocab, is taking to the streets. Even roomier than its predecessor, it carries up to five passengers.

Car rental. International and local car rental firms operate in London and throughout the U.K. with offices at most points of entry. They are listed in the yellow pages under "Car Hire". Chauffeur-driven vehicles are generally available. See also pp. 30–31.

Driving in the United Kingdom. The driver and front-seat passenger must use seat belts; fines for not attaching them are very high. Cars are driven on the *left* in the U.K. Those unused to this system should pay special attention at crossroads and traffic circles. Road traffic signs are similar to those used in the rest of Europe.

Road conditions are generally good but can be congested in many urban areas particularly during rush hour. Speed limits are 30 mph (48 kph) or 40 mph (64 kph) in towns and cities (unless otherwise marked), 70 mph (112 kph) on expressways and 60 mph (96 kph) on other roads. Blood alcohol limit is a strictly enforced 80 mg./100 ml. Gasoline available is 2-star normal (92 octane), 3-star normal (94 octane), 4-star super (98 octane) and diesel. A growing number of garages carry unleaded gasoline.

Pedestrians have absolute priority at striped ("zebra") crossings. A tollfree expressway network covers most main routes. Emergency phones are provided at regular intervals along expressways; follow arrows marked on posts at the side of the road.

Some distances: London–Birmingham 110 miles (175 km.), Manchester 200 miles (320 km.), Edinburgh 400 miles (640 km.).

Bicycle rental. Local tourist information centers will give you the address of a local rental firm. Bicycles can be taken on trains at no extra charge.

Rest rooms. The U.K. is quite well supplied with public rest rooms in rail stations, parks and museums etc., as well as in hotels and restaurants; most are free. Look for signs at city street corners pointing the way to Public Conveniences, Toilets, WC (for "water closet"), or Lavatories.

Emergencies. Dial 999 anywhere in the U.K. in an emergency (no coin needed) for police, fire brigade or an ambulance.

Police. Police in the U.K. are unarmed and are most helpful to tourists. All wear uniforms similar to the ones made famous by London's "bobbies". Policemen in patrol cars wear peaked caps and those on foot wear the traditional helmets. A police officer should be addressed as "Constable".

Crime and theft. Guard against pickpockets and petty thieves. Wherever crowds gather—for example at markets, in buses and in stores—close watch should be kept on wallets and purses. Cars should always be locked when parked, and all visible belongings removed. Hotels advise their guests to lock up valuables in the hotel safe.

Violence is, unfortunately, prevalent at soccer matches.

Medical care and health. Pharmacies (chemists) are open during normal business hours; out of hours one is open in each neighborhood. The address will be posted in the windows of other pharmacies and in the local newspaper. A doctors' prescription is required for some items. The standard of medical treatment is high. The National Health Service is free for anyone in need of urgent attention. For insurance, see pp. 25–26.

Tap water is safe to drink.

Embassies and consulates. These are listed alphabetically in the telephone directory under the name of the country or its derivative, e.g. United States of America.

Social customs. The reserved, controlled façade of the average Briton generally conceals an easygoing, good-hearted nature.

People want to be helpful but their traditional reserve often prevents them from taking the first step. Don't hesitate to ask directions; it often breaks the ice.

You may be addressed as Sir or Madam by a waiter or clerk in a store or even a policeman, but you should never return the compliment; it might be construed as sarcasm. Find out a person's name and use the formal address—"Mr. Smith" or "Mrs. Jones". No first names unless specifically requested. If you don't know a person's name, start the conversation with "Excuse me".

Among young people, attitudes are much more relaxed. Making friends—in pubs or stores or even on the street—is no problem; you'll be on first-name terms right away.

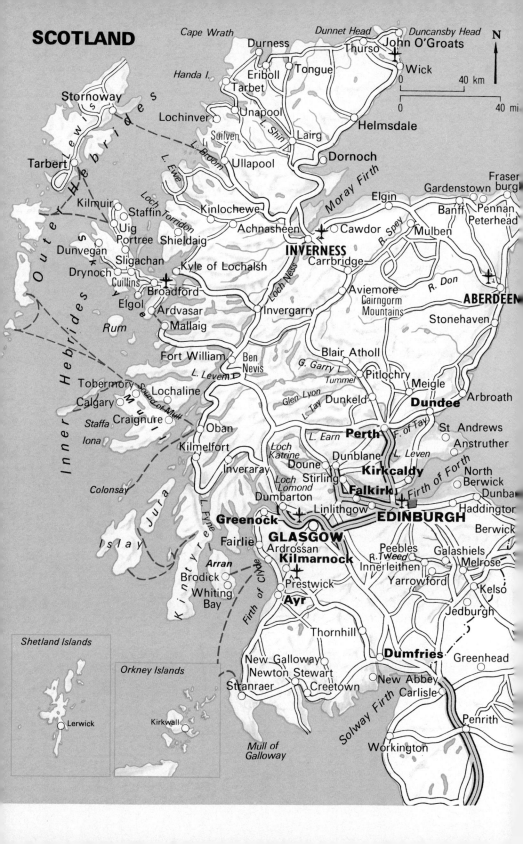

Enjoying the United Kingdom

Food and drink. The raw materials of British cooking are generally of excellent quality. There is an enormous variety of restaurants, from the grand to the cheap and cheerful. Each region has its own traditional specialties—you'll be surprised how menus change as you travel around. Look for "Taste of England" and "Taste of Scotland" signs.

The traditional English breakfast will keep you going until teatime. It usually consists of a choice of dishes: fruit juice, cereal with milk (or oatmeal porridge in Scotland), eggs (poached, boiled, scrambled or fried), bacon, sausages, kidneys, tomatoes or perhaps kippers (a kind of smoked herring) or Finnan Haddock ("Haddie") in Scotland. This is followed by toast with butter and marmalade, and tea or coffee. Continental breakfasts are also available.

After a hearty breakfast you'll only need a light lunch (normally served between noon and 3 p.m.). Light lunches are the rule in Britain (except for Sunday lunch), especially in the pubs, which offer excellent value for money. Britain is renowned throughout the world for its pubs. With the liberalization of licensing hours, many pubs remain open all day, from 11 a.m. to 11 p.m. Sunday hours are shorter, from noon to 3 p.m. and from 7 to 10:30 p.m. Children under 14 are not permitted in pubs, except where a special room has been set aside; alcohol is served to adults aged 18 or over. Typical bar snacks served at lunch times might include: Ploughman's lunch, cheddar cheese, bread, salad and pickle relish; Toad-in-the-Hole, sausages baked in batter; Shepherd's Pie, a casserole of minced lamb or beef, onions and carrots, topped with oven-browned mashed potatoes; Cornish Pasty, a pastry turnover filled with meat, potatoes and onion; pork pies. Not all pubs serve food in the evening or on Sunday.

Beer in the U.K. is a subject of national pride. It's served by the pint and half-pint. Standard English beer is bitter, a caramel colored, naturally carbonated brew; other beers include mild, darker and sweeter than bitter; draught Guinness, stout, barley wine, not a wine at all but a strong dark ale; brown ale; and lager, resembling American beer but never served ice-cold.

Afternoon tea is a long and honored tradition and is served between 3 p.m. and 5 p.m. It can be simple—strong tea (served with milk) and cookies, or a cream tea of scones (like American biscuits) with cream (clotted cream being the best) and strawberry jelly. A normal tea might consist of a pot of Indian tea with lemon or milk; small sandwiches of cucumber, cress, tomato, ham or cheese; scones or crumpets (muffins)

515

served with whipped cream and jelly; followed by tarts, fruit cakes and cookies, such as Dundee Cake, oatcakes and shortbread. High Tea is even more substantial (taking the place of dinner in the North) and is served between 4:30 and 6:30 p.m. It includes the normal selection of cookies or cakes plus one hot dish, perhaps fish and chips, or ham and eggs.

Dinner tends to be the main meal of the day and is served from 7:30 to 10:30 p.m. (earlier in country areas). Start with a soup like oxtail, Scotch broth (a thick mutton, barley and vegetable soup) or cock-a-leekie, a chicken and leek soup; or potted shrimps, small buttered shrimps in a jar; a pâté of smoked fish or game; smoked mackerel or smoked salmon.

For the main course try a traditional British dish such as: roast beef and Yorkshire pudding; roast lamb, often served with rosemary or a mint sauce; gammon (a cut of ham), boiled or fried; steak and kidney pie or pudding; Lancashire hot-pot, a tasty meat and vegetable dish. Game is popular in season—pheasant, grouse, wild duck. In Scotland try Haggis, a dish of minced meat and oatmeal cooked in a sheep's bladder; and stovies, sliced potatoes and onions stewed together. Another regional dish is Irish Stew, layers of potato, onion slices and lamb. Main courses are served with cooked vegetables such as peas, beans, carrots, cauliflower, cabbage or Brussels sprouts, and potatoes which can be baked, roast or French fried ("chips"). A number of restaurants specialize in high-quality fresh fish and shellfish—oysters, mussels, prawns, salmon, trout, Dover sole.

If you have a sweet tooth you'll have a wonderful time in the U.K. Britain's array of desserts is wide, but disastrous for the line! It can be cake (gâteau), cheesecake, or pudding, a flour-thickened fruit dessert, baked or steamed to make it rise and set, or trifle, a blend of sponge cake smothered in sherry, fruit, custard or cream; fruit fool, a light cream dessert whipped up from seasonal fruit like gooseberry; syllabub, wine, lemon juice and whipped cream; or fruit tarts and pies, served with cream or custard.

The king of British cheeses is Stilton, a strong blue-veined cheese (traditionally eaten with a glass of port) and there are numerous other regional cheeses. Choose from Cheddar, Cheshire, Wensleydale, Double Gloucester and Lancashire from England; Caerphilly from Wales, or Caboc, Hramsa and Orkney from Scotland, as well as many specialty cheeses. Cheese is usually eaten with crackers and with oatcakes in Scotland. It is often had after dessert.

A number of restaurants offer Tourist and Set Menus where you can get standardized set meals.

516

Britain also has an impressive range of foreign restaurants of a generally high standard in its cosmopolitan cities—Indian, Chinese, Italian, Greek, American and French are well represented. Vegetarians are also well-served.

Wine is produced in a number of small vineyards in Southern England. It's very pleasant but the price tends to be quite high compared to imported wines since it is produced in limited quantities. Most restaurants offer a varied selection of imported wines (more limited in Scotland). Mead, made from honey, is available in several places. Cider, made from apples, is found in the South of England. In Scotland the locally made whisky, with its worldwide reputation, is distilled using pure mountain water with its peat aroma. Most Scotch is now blended and there are over 2,000 brands. Irish whiskey also has its faithful fans.

Entertainment. London is the nation's undisputed entertainment capital with something to suit every taste. London's theater is unsurpassed in the world and extremely varied, from a West End show to the National Theatre and Royal Shakespeare Company. You'll be able to see some fine ballet and opera at the Royal Opera House in Covent Garden and at the Coliseum (home of the English National Opera), as well as good concerts and recitals at the South Bank Cultural Centre, Royal Albert Hall and the Barbican Centre. The variety of nightclubs, discos and restaurants is enormous.

Throughout the U.K. most towns and cities offer something in the way of nightlife as well as cultural activities—movie theaters and theaters and often nightclubs and discos as well as folk and jazz clubs. It's best to check at the tourist information center to see what's coming up.

In Scotland and Northern Ireland *Ceilidhs* or folk nights are held frequently featuring dancing, pipers, fiddlers and other local or touring entertainers.

Annual events and festivals. These are too numerous to list, so check with the tourist information center when you arrive. Among the most famous fixtures: *February:* Cruft's Dog Show. *May:* Chelsea Flower Show. *June:* Trooping the Colour, celebrating the Queen's birthday. Wimbledon Lawn Tennis Championship. Royal Ascot Race Meeting. *June–August:* Glyndebourne Opera Season. *July:* International Eisteddfod in Wales with over 200 choirs and dance groups. British Open Golf Championship. *July–September:* Sir Henry Wood Promenade Concerts at London's Royal Albert Hall. *August:* Edinburgh Festival. *September:* Highland gathering in Braemar, Scotland.

Taxes, service charges and tipping. Hotel and restaurant bills generally include taxes and service charges, but it's advisable to ask. If service is not included, leave waiters 10–15%. Tipping recommendations: hotel porters, minimum 50p per bag, taxi drivers 10–15%, hatcheck 20p, barbers and hairdressers 15%, plus 5% to the assistant.

Sports and recreation. Most cities have excellent parks, London being particularly fortunate. Public swimming pools are available all over the country and there are sailing and windsurfing centers around the coast. There are good golf courses throughout the U.K., especially in Scotland which has some of the best and most famous golf courses in the world. Clubs allow non-members to play during the week and many municipal courses are open to all (including the celebrated St. Andrews, near Edinburgh). Fishing is good and very popular, again in Scotland, with fly fishing for salmon and trout, coarse fishing for perch and pike, or sea angling and perhaps even shark fishing. You'll be able to use the squash and tennis courts as well as athletics facilities operated by many towns. You can rent boats on canals and rivers or punts at Oxford and Cambridge and a few other places. Pony trekking and horseback riding are popular, in particular in Scotland and Wales, and also hunting.

The British are inveterate soccer fans (the season runs from August to April) and rugby fans (winter). The slow and languid game of cricket can be watched throughout Britain in the summer—look for a typical English match on a village green on Sundays or watch a Test Match (professional) in London, Leeds or Manchester. Horse events are very popular all over, either racing or polo, or point-to-point, and also other forms of racing—motor and greyhound.

TV and radio. Two BBC television channels and several commercial, independent television networks are on the air, some of them round the clock. On radio, five BBC stations provide news, music and feature shows for all tastes: radio 1 pop and rock music, radio 2 light entertainment, radio 3 mostly classical music, radio 4 current affairs, arts and drama; the BBC World Service provides excellent international coverage. BBC local radio stations and commercial stations are useful for local news and events.

What to buy. Particularly good buys are: classic cashmere, lambswool and Fairisle knitwear, suits and fabrics, tweeds (Harris tweed and tartans from Scotland), silks and cottons, and sheepskin products; tablecloths and tea towels in Irish linen; English bone china, lead crystal and glassware.

518

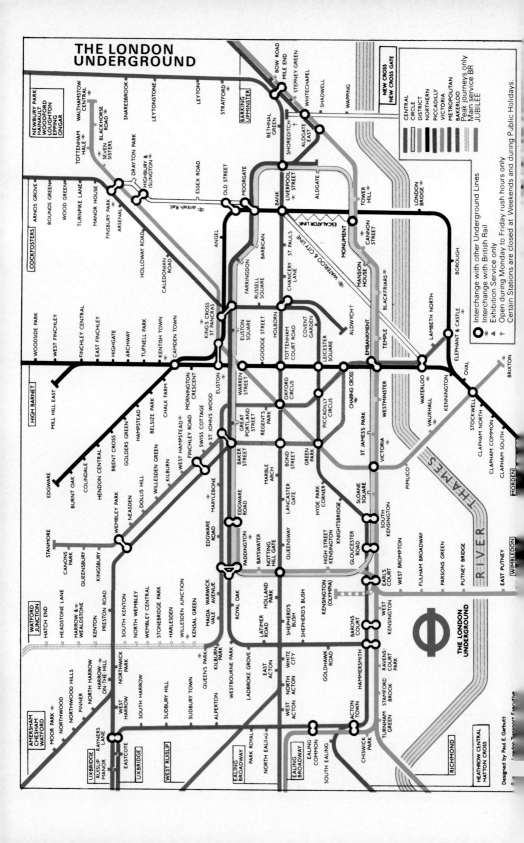

THE LONDON UNDERGROUND

THE LONDON UNDERGROUND

Designed by Paul E. Garbutt

London Transport Executive

Interchange with other Underground Lines
Interchange with British Rail
▲▲ Exhibition Service only
† Open during Monday to Friday rush hours only
Certain Stations are closed at Weekends and during Public Holidays.

CENTRAL
CIRCLE
DISTRICT
NORTHERN
PICCADILLY
VICTORIA
METROPOLITAN
BAKERLOO
Peak journeys only
Main service BR
JUBILEE

NEW CROSS
NEW CROSS GATE

Craft workshops where skilled craftsmen use traditional materials and techniques are spread throughout the U.K. Look for handmade jewelry and knitwear, wooden toys and furniture, hand-tooled leather products, woven tweeds and fabrics, pottery, ceramics and stoneware, candles, natural cosmetics and paintings by local artists.

Food products include: cheese (Stilton, Cheddar—often sold whole), sweets (treacle toffee, humbugs, fudge or handmade chocolates), shortbread and cookies, marmalades and chutneys, jellies and honey, smoked salmon and kippers; tea (English breakfast, Ceylon, Earl Grey) cider, mead and fine malt whiskies from Scotland and Ireland.

Shopping hours are generally 9 a.m. to 5:30 or 6 p.m., Monday through Saturday. In country towns smaller shops close for an hour at lunchtime and at 1 p.m. on one day (Wednesday or Thursday). Many cities have a "late" night once a week when shops stay open until about 8 p.m.

In some cases, the sales tax is refunded (see p. 40).

Famous shopping streets in London are Oxford Street, Bond Street and Regent Street. Markets you find at Portobello Road, Camden Passage and Covent Garden.

Sightseeing

London. Buckingham Palace, the home of Queen Elizabeth II. Changing of the Guard, at Buckingham Palace and Whitehall. St. James's Palace, the royal residence from 1698 to 1837. Kensington Palace, the official home of the Prince and Princess of Wales. Houses of Parliament (Palace of Westminster)*with neo-Gothic spires and Big Ben, the world-famous bell. Trafalgar Square with Nelson's Column and fountains, a vast gathering place for tourists and pigeons. Westminster Abbey*, begun in 11th century, where kings are crowned and poets buried, and Westminster Cathedral (Roman Catholic). Museums: British Museum* with the Elgin Marbles, Egyptian Collection, prints, drawings and maps; Natural History Museum; Geological Museum; Science Museum; Victoria and Albert Museum* for fine and applied arts; Museum of London depicting London life from prehistoric times. Art Galleries: National Gallery* where the principal schools of European painting are represented; National Portrait Gallery; Tate Gallery with English painting from the 16th century, also modern art. Madame Tussaud's, the ever-popular waxworks. No. 10 Downing Street, the office and residence of British prime ministers. Banqueting House, with magnificent ceiling paintings by Rubens. Covent Garden, the former fruit and vegetable

521

market, a delightful 17th-century square by Inigo Jones, now a pleasant shopping arcade and home of the Royal Opera House, Transport and Theatre museums. Monumental modern Barbican Centre for Arts and Conferences, housing multiple halls, theaters, movie theaters and art gallery. St. Paul's Cathedral*, the masterpiece of Sir Christopher Wren (1710), containing the tombs of Nelson and the Duke of Wellington. The Guildhall, the City of London's beautiful City Hall constructed in the 15th century and the Mansion House, a Renaissance-style palace, official residence of London's Lord Mayor, featuring the magnificent Egyptian Hall. Tower Bridge, one of the City's most famous landmarks with its two towers. Inns of Court—The Temple, Lincoln's Inn and Gray's Inn. The Tower of London*, originally built in the 11th century as a royal residence, now home of the Crown Jewels, defended by the Beefeaters. Parks and gardens: elegant St. James's Park, Green Park, huge Hyde Park with Speakers' Corner and Kensington Gardens, Regent's Park and London Zoo, one of the world's greatest, the Royal Botanical Gardens at Kew. Oxford Street, London's busiest shopping street, lined with huge department stores and smaller fashion stores and boutiques. Piccadilly Circus with fountain presided over by a statue of Eros, a principal symbol of London. Regent Street*, a wonder of architectural harmony and stately grandeur. Old Bond Street glittering with fashionable stores, art galleries and fine antique shops.

Daytrips from London. Greenwich and the National Maritime Museum, the Observatory, the home of Greenwich Mean Time and the *Cutty Sark*. Windsor Castle, dating from the 11th century, a royal residence since the reign of Henry I, including State Apartments and Queen Mary's doll's house, the Great Park (4,800 acres) and Windsor Safari Park. Red-bricked Hampton Court*, Henry VIII's palace, built in the 16th century by Cardinal Wolsey with State Apartments and beautiful gardens including the Maze. St. Albans with remains of Roman Verulamium, museum, St. Albans Abbey. Sheffield Park Gardens and Bluebell Steam Railway. Jacobean stately home of Hatfield House and 18th-century Woburn Abbey.

The West Country. Land's End, the most westerly point of England, Minack Theatre perched on the cliffs and St. Michael's Mount. The impressive ruins of Tintagel Castle, famous for its association with Arthurian legend. The vacation centers of Newquay, with rolling surf, and Torbay, the "Devon Riviera". St. Ives*, artists' haven, a picturesque cluster of gaily colored stone cottages. Exeter with its magnificent cathedral, medieval buildings in Cathedral Close and Maritime Museum. Torquay, fashionable beach resort. Plymouth, seaport from which the Pilgrim Fathers sailed in the *Mayflower* in 1620. The Moors—wild Bodmin Moor and "Jamaica Inn"; the open wilderness of Dartmoor and its thatched villages; the moorland and heathland of Exmoor, "Lorna Doone" country. Popular vacation resorts and sailing centers of Salcombe and Dartmouth in the South Hams, claiming United Kingdom's mildest climate. The Mendip Hills, dramatic Cheddar Gorge and famous caves at Cheddar and Wookey. Bath*, surely the most complete and best-preserved Georgian city in Britain and famous since Roman times for its warm mineral springs—Roman Baths and Pump Room, and the American Museum at Claverton. Bristol, a thriving historic city with historic steamship *Great Britain,* and Avon Gorge and suspension bridge.

Southern England. Chalk hills of Salisbury Plain and the hauntingly imposing Bronze Age site of Stonehenge* (megaliths and dolmens). Salisbury*, a pleasant country town with one of the most magnificent of England's cathedrals, and Wilton House. Stourhead House and Gardens, and Longleat House, a great Elizabethan mansion and lion park. The white horses and hill figures carved out of chalk hills, and the wild heathlands of Thomas Hardy country. Lulworth Cove and Durdle Door, spectacular cliff formations. New Forest, once a royal hunting preserve for William the Conqueror, now famous for its tranquility and wild ponies, and the Montagu Motor Museum at Beaulieu. Broadlands at Romsey, the graceful home of the Mountbattens. Winchester, capital of Saxon England, dominated by its huge Norman cathedral. Portsmouth, an ancient and thriving sea port, and home of *HMS Victory,* Lord Nelson's flagship at the Battle of Trafalgar (1805), and Charles Dickens's house.

Southeast England. Canterbury, ancient city with over 2,000 years of history, cathedral dating from A.D. 597 with superb medieval stained glass. Channel port of Dover; white cliffs. Elegant seaside resorts—Brighton*, made famous in the 18th century by the Prince Regent, Royal Pavilion, Palace Pier and the "Lanes" for antiques; Eastbourne, with a 3-mile seafront and fine parks and gardens. Seven Sisters, seven dramatic chalk cliffs near Beachy Head. The South Downs and the North Downs, rolling chalk hills. Chartwell, former home of wartime premier and statesman, Sir Winston Churchill. Penshurst Place, an 800-year-old semi-fortified house. Petworth House and medieval town. Fishbourne Roman Palace, site of largest Roman palace discovered in England. Rye and Romney Marsh, and the secret landing places of 18th-century smugglers. Leeds Castle, near Maidstone, home of Catherine of Aragon, Henry VIII's first wife.

Heart of England and South Midlands. Oxford*, lovely old stone university town, of towers, colleges and steeples, architectural and intellectual treasure house; Ashmolean Museum, strong on archaeological remains and European paintings; the 15th-century Bodleian Library, one of the world's oldest and finest; New College, one of the university's most venerable college complexes of the 30-odd, still functioning as over the centuries; Christ Church College, founded in 1525, with Tom Tower of Christ Church, an Oxford university landmark, built by Wren 1681 and the cathedral. Magdalen College, founded in 1458, with Gothic clock tower, deer in park, idyllic riverside. Blenheim Palace*, a palatial Baroque-style mansion built in 1720 by Vanbrugh and home of Duke of Marlborough (Churchill family). Beechwoods of the Chilterns, and Milton's Cottage at Chalfont St. Giles where poet John Milton lived. Uffington and the Vale of the White Horse. Stratford-upon-Avon*, birthplace of William Shakespeare with fine 15th- and 16th-century timber-framed houses and numerous Shakespearian associations—Anne Hathaway's Cottage, Royal Shakespeare Theatre, Hall's Croft, a charming authentic Elizabethan house. Charlecote Park and Ragley Hall. 14th-century Warwick Castle, a stately Elizabethan mansion with State Apartments, surrounded by a vast deer park. Sulgrave Manor, near Northampton, the ancestral home of the Washington family. Belvoir Castle, home of the Duke of Rutland. The Cotswold Hills with sheltered, honey-colored villages and many lovely churches and manor houses built between the 15th and 17th centuries by rich wool merchants. Cirencester, site of the largest Roman town in Britain. Cheltenham, with a wealth of Regency houses and elegant squares and crescents. Ross-on-Wye and the Wye Valley. Gloucester with its cathedral, and Berkeley Castle where Edward II was murdered in 1327. The cathedral cities of Worcester, on the river Severn, and Hereford, by the river Wye. Malvern, a spa town set in the 9-mile (15-km.) range of the Malvern Hills.

East Anglia. Glorious Cambridge*, university city, with colleges dating from 1284 — King's College Chapel, Fitzwilliam Museum, punting on the river Cam past the "Backs". Norwich, beautiful cathedral city with castle, Sainsbury Centre for Visual Arts, and cobbled Elm Hill. Norfolk Broads, an open expanse of water with daily tours by boat. Newmarket, headquarters of British horse racing. Sandringham House and Gardens, a 7,000-acre (2,870-ha.) estate owned by the Royal Family. Ely with a magnificent cathedral. Southwold, an elegant small seaside town, and Aldeburgh, with its world-famous music festival held annually. Burghley House, one of England's greatest Elizabethan houses.

Elegant Jacobean Audley End House, near Saffron Walden. The picturesque Essex villages. East Bergholt and Dedham Vale, John Constable country. The Suffolk wool town of Lavenham. Spalding, the center of "Tulip-land", and Springfields Show Gardens.

The North Midlands. Ludlow and its massive red-sandstone castle, built in the 11th century to repel Welsh raiders. Iron Bridge Gorge and Coalbrookdale, birthplace of the Industrial Revolution. The great pleasure-park of Alton Towers. The "Potteries" of Staffordshire and the famous china factories. Lincoln with its medieval cathedral. Chatsworth House, one of the great stately homes, built 1707 and with world-renowned collections. The lovely limestone valleys (dales) of Derbyshire—Dove Dale, Monsal Dale, and the Peak District—Castleton and Blue John Caverns, the spa town of Buxton.

The Lake District and the Northwest. Chester, a Roman city with remaining amphitheater and walls encircling the town, galleried streets "The Rows". Liverpool, a historic port on the river Mersey and home of "The Beatles"—Mersey Ferry, Walker Art Gallery. Blackpool, the North's famous fun resort with miles of sandy beaches, 518-foot (158-m.)-high Blackpool Tower, "Golden Mile". Kendal, a peaceful country town, gateway to Lakeland, and Levens Hall, a large Elizabethan mansion. Lake District★, some of the world's most beautiful lakes and mountains—16 lakes from the largest Windermere (10 miles/ 17 km. long) to Brothers Water (less than half a mile/800 m. long) and 4 peaks—Scafell Pike (England's highest peak 3,210 feet/979 m.), Great Gable, Pillar and Helvellyn. Windermere, a popular center with steam railroad and lake cruises. Ullswater, with lake cruises. Keswick, among the Cumbrian Fells. Dove Cottage, Grasmere, home of the poet Wordsworth. Penrith, Appleby and the Eden Valley. Long Meg and her Daughters, a ring of standing stones.

Yorkshire. York★, a fine medieval city with four gates and city walls, timber-framed houses in The Shambles and Stonegate, majestic York Minster, Castle Museum, Jorvik Viking Centre and the National Railway Museum. Castle Howard, an 18th-century mansion nearby. Harrogate, a 19th-century spa town, known as the "floral resort" because of its parks and gardens—visit the Stray, Royal Pump Room and Royal Bath Assembly Rooms. Ripon and its cathedral, 13th-century Wakeman's House and excellent market, and the gardens of Studley Royal Park and Newby Hall. Haworth and the Parsonage home of the 19th-century Brontë family of novelists, and the Worth Valley Steam Railway. Conisbrough Castle, built around 1185 and the oldest surviving circular keep in England. Elizabethan Burton Agnes Hall. James Herriot Country and the Yorkshire Dales with their waterfalls —Aysgarth and Hardraw, and villages, the romantic old ruin of Bolton Castle in Wensleydale, where Mary Queen of Scots was imprisoned, and Bolton Abbey in Wharfedale. The attractive town of Richmond with an 11th-century castle and colorful market. The North York Moors and Steam Railway. Evocative Rievaulx Abbey*, founded 1131, one of the earliest Cistercian buildings in England and the ruins of Fountains Abbey, founded 1132 by Benedictine monks. Harewood House, designed by John Carr and Robert Adam and its gardens laid out by "Capability" Brown. The popular seaside resort of Scarborough and the fishing port of Whitby, once home of Captain James Cook, and with a magnificent ruined abbey.

The Northeast. The market town of Barnard Castle, Bowes Museum*, and Raby Castle with its ancient deer park. Durham with its superb cathedral and Norman castle towering over the steep banks of the river Wear, university and Gulbenkian Museum of Oriental Art. Teesdale and the waterfalls of High Force (70 feet/21 m.) and Cauldron Snout (200 feet/61 m.). Hadrians Wall, the most spectacular relic of Roman Britain, 73 miles (117 km.) long. Housesteads Roman Fort and Museum, Vindolanda Roman excavations, Chesters Fort and museum. The Northumberland coast and its castles: dramatic Bamburgh, gaunt craggy Dunstanburgh and impressive Alnwick. Holy Island (Lindisfarne) with a Priory, 16th-century castle and Mead factory. Cragside House at Rothbury, the first house in Britain to be lit by electricity, with lovely grounds. Kielder Water, the largest man-made lake in Britain and Kielder Forest, part of the Border Forest Park.

Scotland

Edinburgh. Edinburgh Castle dating from the 7th century, with St. Margaret's Chapel, Mons Meg Cannon, Great Hall, Royal Apartments and Crown Room, housing the oldest royal regalia in Europe. The Royal Mile* leading to the royal palace of Holyroodhouse. Camera Obscura on Castle Hill. Statuette of Greyfriars Bobby. St. Giles, the High Kirk (church) of Scotland. The shops of Princes Street, Princes Street Gardens with floral clock and Scott monument. National Gallery of Scotland. Royal Botanic Gardens.

Daytrips from Edinburgh. The fine Adam mansion of Hopetoun House, near South Queensferry. Linlithgow Palace. Dirleton Castle and Gardens. Roslin and Tantallon castles. The vacation district of East Lothian. Abbotsford, the home of Sir Walter Scott for 20 years. The golf courses of Fife. Forth road and rail bridges. Peebles and the Tweed Valley. Border abbeys of Melrose, Dryburgh, Kelso and Jedburgh.

The Southwest and Lowlands. Glasgow with lively cultural scene: Art Gallery and Museum; The Burrell Art Collection★; University collections; fine Gothic cathedral; Botanic Gardens; Camphill Museum; Museum of Transport. Robert Burns Country of Dumfries and Galloway including his birthplace at Alloway, and Museum at Dumfries. The John Adam Mansion, Culzean Castle. Moffat and the Grey Mares Tail waterfall. The Isle of Arran, "Scotland in miniature" with mountains, lowlands, streams, glens and lochs—Brodick Castle, Goat Fell, King's Caves. The Isles of Bute, Islay and Jura.

Central Scotland. Stirling and its proud Renaissance castle, Auld Brig across the river Forth and the battlefield of Bannockburn. Dunblane Cathedral, one of the finest Gothic churches in Scotland. Callander, and the lochs and glens of the Trossachs. Loch Lomond, the largest loch (23 miles/37 km. long) and Ben Lomond. Inveraray Castle★, the headquarters of the Campbell clan since the 15th century. The small, ancient city of Perth, once the capital of Scotland, and Scone Palace, a 19th-century castellated mansion and the coronation place of Scottish kings until 1651. Dundee and 14th-century Glamis Castle, the ancestral home of the Earl of Strathmore, father of the Queen Mother.

The Northeast. Aberdeen, Scotland's third city and its harbor and fish market★; Marischal College, one of the largest granite buildings in the world, King's College, St. Machar's Cathedral, Provost Skene's House and Hazlehead Park. The Dee Valley, from Aberdeen to the Cairngorms. Balmoral Castle, a private residence of the Queen. Castles at Craigievar and Slains. Braemar, world-famous for its annual Royal Highland Gathering. Pitmedden Gardens.

The Highlands. Inverness, capital of the Highlands at the eastern end of Loch Ness. Glencoe, Scotland's wildest glen and the lochs of North Argyll. Oban, the center of Gaelic culture, and Fort William, a touring center with Ben Nevis, Britain's highest mountain (4,406 feet/1,322 m.) towering above. The popular vacation resort of Pitlochry, its Festival

Theatre, and the fairy-tale fortress of Blair Castle. Mallaig, at the western end of "the road to the isles". Culloden Moor and Cawdor Castle*. The Moray coast, the beautiful Spey Valley and the "Whisky Trail". The modern vacation center of Aviemore and the lofty crags of the Cairngorms. Glenmore Forest Park and the Highland Wildlife Park at Kincraig. Dramatic Loch Torridon. Subtropical Inverewe Gardens overlooking Loch Ewe. Eileen Donan castle at Dornie. Scenery on coast above the little fishing port of Ullapool.

The Islands. The Inner Hebrides—much-loved Skye* with the rugged Cuillins and Quiraing highlands and Dunvegan Castle. Mull with mountains, peaceful moorland glens and sandy beaches. Iona where St. Columba's Abbey was established in A.D. 563. Staffa Island with the dramatic Fingal's Cave. The Outer Hebrides—Lewis and Harris. The Orkneys and the Shetlands.

Wales

Cardiff. Cardiff Castle dating from 1093 on the site of a Roman fort. The National Museum of Wales* with art, Welsh archaeology and industrial exhibits. Llandaff Cathedral. Welsh Folk Museum (St. Fagan's).

Daytrips from Cardiff. Brecon Beacons, Brecon and the Dan-y-Ogof Caves. Abergavenny and its castle. The Black Mountains*. The Wye Valley, Tintern Abbey, and Chepstow and Monmouth castles. The port of Swansea, second largest city in Wales, and the Gower with fishing villages and sandy beaches. Llandaff Castle.

South Wales. The rugged Pembrokeshire Coast and the resorts of St. David's and Tenby. Carmarthen and Pendine, 5 miles of sandy beach. Coracle fishermen on the rivers Teifi and Tywi. Laugharne, the home of poet and playwright Dylan Thomas. Caerphilly Castle.

Mid Wales. Cardigan Bay, Aberystwyth, and Devil's Bridge over the river Mynach. The Vale of Rheidol narrow-gauge railroad. Radnor Forest. The popular spa of Llandrindod Wells. The market town of Llanidloes. Berwyn Mountains. The Severn Valley* along the English Border, and Offa's Dyke. Castles at Powis, near Welshpool, and Montgomery.

North Wales. Mount Snowdon (3,560 feet/1,086 m.) and the Snowdonia National Park* with craggy peaks and high passes (Llanberis, Nant Francon and Nantgwynant) and the Snowdon Railway. Castles at Caernarvon*, Penrhyn, Denbigh, Conway and Harlech. The narrow-gauge Festiniog, Talyllyn, and Llanberis Lake railroads. The Festiniog slate quarries. Wild scenery of the Vale of Llangollen.

Northern Ireland

Belfast. Ulster Museum with Irish and British painting, archaeological and industrial exhibits. The Botanic Gardens. City Hall. Stormont Castle. Cone Hill.

Daytrips from Belfast. The Glens of Antrim. The famous Giant's Causeway, basalt columns forming "stepping stones" out to sea. The Lakes of Fermanagh. The Mourne Mountains. Ulster Folk and Transport Museum with old farmhouses, mills and a church. Mount Stewart Gardens. Carrickfergus Castle.

U.S.S.R.

SWEDEN

FINLAND

Helsinki

Viborg
Выборг

LENINGRAD
ЛЕНИНГРАД

Gulf of Finland

Stockholm

Tallin
Таллин

Novgorod
Новгород

Yaroslavl
Ярославль

Baltic Sea

Riga
Рига

Kalinin
Калинин

Volga
Волга

Smolensk
Смоленск

MOSKVA
МОСКВА

Minsk
Минск

U. S. S. R.

Wisła

C C C P

Orel
Орел

Warsaw

Brest
Брест

Kursk
Курск

POLAND

Kiev
Киев

Kharkov
Харьков

Kraków

Lvov
Львов

Dnepr
Днепр

From Ivan the Terrible to Perestroika, the Russian drama is rich in superlatives.

The Soviet Union is the world's largest country, spanning 11 time zones and sprawling from the frozen taiga down to semitropical beaches. The next superlative is the people. They represent more than a hundred racial groups from blue-eyed northerners to swarthy southerners to slight orientals. Amazingly, they can all communicate—in Russian, anyway, and ever more in English, too.

Linking Europe and Asia, steppe and desert, the U.S.S.R. is a startling mixture of skyscrapers and *izba* huts, of onion-domed churches and minaretted mosques. Shostakovich shares the stage with the music of the balalaika, *Swan Lake* with cossack dances.

Even in topographical relief it's a country of extremes, from the Soviet summit, Communist Peak (altitude 24,590 feet or 7,495 meters), to the Turan Plain in Central Asia, where depressions go as deep as 433 feet (132 meters) *below* sea level. It's impossible to exaggerate the dramatic climate. In the far-northern town of Verkhoyansk, temperatures have been recorded from a sweltering 98° F (36.7° C) all the way down to an end-of-the-world superfreeze: minus 94° F (minus 70° C).

With so much terrain to cover, it's hard to see more than a few of the highspots: the Moscow of Ivan the Terrible and Josef Stalin; the Leningrad of Peter the Great and Pushkin; Kiev, "mother of Russian cities"; Georgia, the home of hospitality; and the wide open spaces of Siberia, the eternal land of the future.

After 70 years of communism, collectivization and Five-Year Plans, after giving the world words like *bolshevik, kolkhoz* and *sputnik*, a new Russian term was heard: *perestroika*. With *glasnost* (openness), the future—and even the past—could be freely discussed. And a new generation of tourists rushed to a giant nation in flux to see its marvels and find out how it might all work out.

532

Facts and figures

Population:	286 million
Area:	8,649,489 sq. miles (22,402,200 sq. km.)
Capital:	Moscow (*Moskva,* 8.8 million)
Other major cities:	Leningrad (5 million) Kiev (2.3 million) Tashkent (1.9 million) Baku (1.6 million) Kharkov (1.4 million)
Languages:	Russian and local national languages
Religion:	Authorities recognize Russian Orthodox, Catholic, Lutheran, Baptist and other denominations as well as Judaism, Islam and Buddhism.
Time zone (Moscow):	GMT + 3, EST + 8 (the Soviet Union has 11 time zones); DST (Apr.–Sept.)
Currency:	*Rouble* (abbr. *p*) = 100 *kopeks* Coins: 1, 2, 3, 5, 10, 15, 20, 50 kopeks; 1 rouble Bills: 1, 3, 5, 10, 25, 50, 100 roubles
Electricity:	Mostly 220 volt, 50 cycle, AC, but in older buildings sometimes 127 volt, 50 cycle, AC.

Planning your trip

Visa requirements. See pp. 29–30.

Vaccination requirements. None (see also p. 25).

Currency restrictions. All foreign currency must be declared on entry and exit. No Soviet currency may be taken into or out of the country.

Climate. The climate of the Soviet Union shows wide variations, but in general is continental with warm to hot summers and sometimes fiercely cold winters. A small part of the southern Crimea and western Georgia enjoys a mild Mediterranean climate.

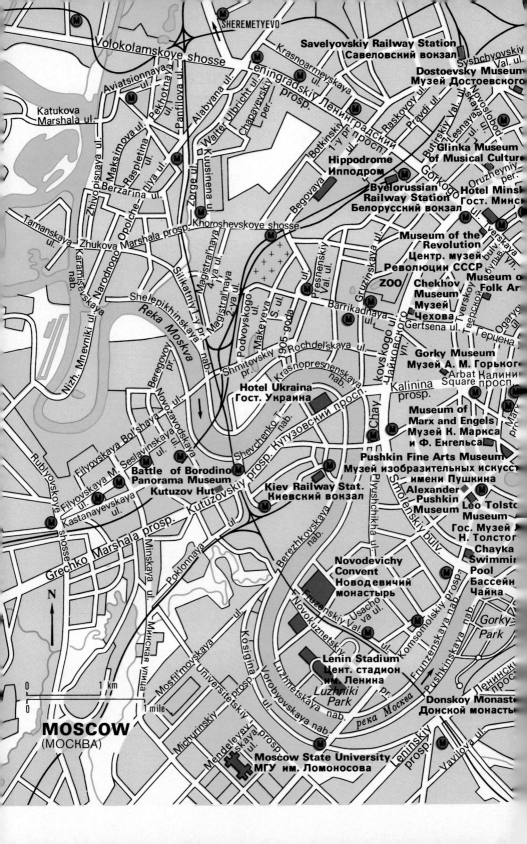

SHEREMETYEVO

Volokolamskoye shosse

Savelyovskiy Railway Station
Савеловский вокзал

Syschyovskiy
Val. ul.

Dostoevsky Museum
Музей Достоевского

Krasnoarmeyskaya ul.

Aviatsionnaya ul.

Pekhotnaya ul.

Panfilova ul.

Alabyana ul.

Leningradskaya ul.

L per.

Chapayevskiy per.

Botkinskiy 1-y pr.

Leningradskiy prosp. Ленинградский просп.

Raskovoy ul.

Pravdi ul.

Butirskiy Val. ul.

Lesnaya ul.

Novoslobod- ul.

Novoslobod-skaya ul.

Glinka Museum
of Musical Culture

Oruzheyniy per.

Katukova
Marshala ul.

Maksimova ul.

Raspletina ul.

Zhivo pisnaya ul.

Berzarina ul.

Kuusinena ul.

Zorge ul.

Begovaya ul.

Gorkogo ul.

Hippodrome
Ипподром

Byelorussian
Railway Station
Белорусский вокзал

Hotel Minsk
Гост. Минск

Tamanskaya ul.

Zhukova Marshala prosp.

Opolche niya ul.

Narodnogo

Khoroshevskoye shosse

Tverskoy bulv. ul.

Museum of the
Revolution
Центр. музей
Революции СССР

Tverskaya ul.

Nizh. Mnevniki ul.

Silikatniy 1-y pr.

Magistral'naya 4-ya ul.

Magistral'naya 2-ya ul.

Presnenskiy Val. ul.

Gruzinskaya ul.

ZOO

Chekhov
Museum
Музей
Чехова

Museum of
Folk Art

Shelepikhinskaya nab.

Reka Moskva

Beregovoy pr.

Shmitovskiy pr.

Podvoyskogo Makeyeva S. ul.

905-goda ul.

Barrikadnaya

Gertsena ul.

Chaykovskogo ul.

Ogaryova ul.

Герцена ul.

Gorky Museum
Музей А. М. Горького

Novozavodskaya ul.

Rochdel'skaya ul.

Krasnopresnenskaya nab.

Kalinina prosp.

Arbat Калини
Square просп.

Hotel Ukraina
Гост. Украина

Chay

Kalinina prosp.

Museum of
Marx and Engels
Музей К. Маркса
и Ф. Енгельса

Shevchenko T. nab.

Kutuzovskiy prosp. Кутузовский просп.

Plyushchikha ul.

Smolenskiy bulv.

Pushkin Fine Arts Museum
Музей изобразительных искусст
имени Пушкина

Filyovskaya Bol'shaya ul.

Seslavinskaya ul.

Kastanayevskaya ul.

Kievskiy Railway Stat.
Киевский вокзал

Alexander
Pushkin
Museum

Leo Tolsto
Museum
Гос. Музей
Н. Толстог

Rublyovskoye shosse

Filyovskaya M. ul.

Battle of Borodino
Panorama Museum
Kutuzov Hut

Berezhkovskaya nab.

Plyushchikha ul.

Chayka
Swimmin
Pool
Бассейн
Чайка

Grechko Marshala prosp.

Minskaya ul.

Poklonnaya ul.

Kosigina ul.

Fruzenskiy Val.

Novokuznetskiy

Usacho va ul.

Novodevichy
Convent
Новодевичий
монастырь

Komsomolskiy prosp.

Frunzenskaya nab.

Pushkinskaya nab.

Gorky
Park

Ленинск

N

Mosfil'movskaya ul.

Universitetskiy prosp.

Vorobyovskaya nab.

Luzhnetskaya nab.

Luzhnetskaya nab.

Lenin Stadium
Цент. стадион
им. Ленина

Luzhniki
Park

река Москва

Leninskiy prosp.

Donskoy Monast
Донской монасты

0   1 km

0   1 mile

MOSCOW
(МОСКВА)

Michurinskiy prosp.

Mendeleyev skaya ul.

Minskaya улица

Moscow State University
МГУ им. Ломоносова

Vavilova ul.

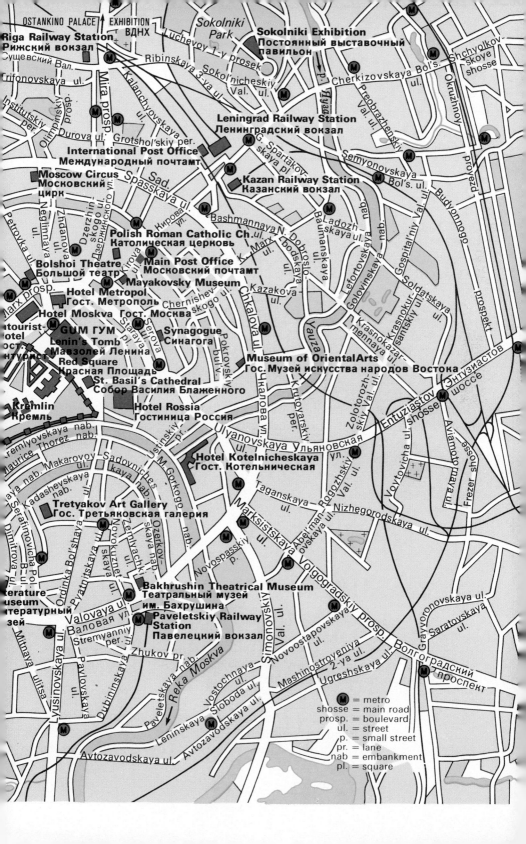

Some average daily temperatures:

Moscow		J	F	M	A	M	J	J	A	S	O	N	D
average daily maximum*	°F	15	22	32	50	66	70	73	72	61	48	35	24
	°C	–9	–6	0	10	19	21	23	22	16	9	2	–5
average daily minimum*	°F	3	8	18	34	46	51	55	53	45	37	26	15
	°C	–16	–14	–8	1	8	11	13	12	7	3	–3	–10
Leningrad													
average daily maximum*	°F	19	22	32	46	59	68	70	69	60	48	35	26
	°C	–7	–5	0	8	15	20	21	20	15	9	2	–3
average daily minimum*	°F	3	8	18	34	46	51	55	53	45	37	26	15
	°C	–13	–12	–8	0	6	11	13	13	9	4	–2	–8

* Minimum temperatures are measured just before sunrise, maximum temperatures in the afternoon.

Clothing. In summer, medium-weight clothes are adequate, but during the rest of the year do not underestimate your needs. Especially in winter, wrap up well, from head to toe, in very warm clothing and sturdy overshoes.

Duty-free allowances

Cigarettes	Cigars	Tobacco	Liquor	Wine
250 or	250 g. of other tobacco products		1 l. and	2 l.

Perfume: A "reasonable quantity" for personal use.
Gifts: Up to an amount of 30 roubles.

Note that photographs and printed matter which might be directed against the U.S.S.R. are prohibited. Any articles of value should be declared upon entry to facilitate their re-export. Loss of arrival customs

536

declaration forms and incomplete listing of valuables can result in confiscation of the property in question.

Hotels and accommodations

Hotels. The U.S.S.R. issues visas only after hotel reservations have been confirmed. All accommodations must be paid for in advance. Make reservations through a travel agency that cooperates with Intourist (the state travel agency) or Sovincentr (an agency operating hotels geared to the businessman). While you're free to request the hotel of your choice, the final arrangements rest with Intourist or Sovincentr who let you know the decision on arrival at the airport.

Youth hostels. While there are no youth hostels per se in the U.S.S.R., Sputnik, the Soviet youth travel association, organizes group tours for students with accommodations included in the package arrangement. Unless the Sputnik holiday is planned in advance, students have to take ordinary tourist accommodations.

Camping. During the brief summer season—June to August and, in some areas, part of September—authorized campsites are operated near many Soviet cities. Campers may park a car and pitch a tent for a fixed rate that includes amenities, from showers to cooking facilities, plus a guided tour of nearby attractions. At some campsites, bungalows are available.

Arrangements must be made in advance through travel agents outside the U.S.S.R.

U.S.S.R. tourist offices abroad

U.K.	Intourist, 219 Marsh Wall, Isle of Dogs, London E14 9F; tel. (071) 538 3202
U.S.A.	Intourist, 630 Fifth Avenue, New York, N.Y. 10020; tel. (212) 757-3884

On the spot

Banks and currency exchange. Banking hours are 9 a.m.–1 p.m., Monday through Friday. Currency may only be exchanged at currency-exchange offices in hotels and airports, or the state bank. Visitors must be able to account for money exchanged. A special Tourist Exchange Rate provides roubles at a generous rate, approaching the black market value. However, hard currency or credit cards are required for many

537

purchases. Hotel and airport currency-exchange offices are often open outside normal hours.

Credit cards and traveler's checks. Major credit cards are accepted by most Intourist shops and hotels, but otherwise few Soviet establishments recognize them. Foreign-currency shops also accept most traveler's checks as do exchange offices.

Mail and telecommunications. Postal and telecommunications services are moderately reliable but subject to thorough surveillance. The post office handles postal, telegraph and telephone services. Major hotels have their own branches of the post office. In Moscow the main post office (open 8 a.m.–10 p.m.) is situated at 26 Kirov Street; and in Leningrad in Soyuz Svyazi Street.

A local call from public telephone booths on the street costs 2 kopeks (2×1 or 1×2) but a 10-kopek piece will also do the trick. Long-distance calls may be made from hotel rooms or, in Moscow, by going to the Central Telephone and Telegraph Office at 7 Gorky Street (open 24 hours a day). International calls are best placed through the hotel service desk, and if you are in a position to do so, well in advance. If not, arm yourself with patience; a four-hour wait is perfectly usual. Some hotels have international phones, enabling you to dial direct to any part of the world. It's not possible to reverse the charges for calls from the U.S.S.R. Telex messages can also be handled by hotels and telephone offices. Fax machines are rare.

Some useful numbers:

Ambulance	03	Police	02
Fire	01	Time	100

Newspapers. Principal Moscow dailies are *Pravda* and *Izvestia*. Foreign, mainly Western Communist, newspapers can be found on city newsstands. Certain non-communist newspapers are available at special kiosks. They include the *International Herald Tribune,* the *Times* and *Guardian,* and the U.S. newsmagazines, *Time* and *Newsweek*.

The weekly tabloid, *Moscow News,* formerly a vehicle for propaganda pieces and boring official texts, has been transformed into a lively exponent of *glasnost*. More conventional Soviet magazines aimed at a foreign audience are also available.

Tourist information. Contact the nearest Intourist office (located in hotels and at airports). For general inquiries, tel. 203-69-62 in Moscow.

538

Legal holidays

Jan. 1	New Year's Day	May 9	Victory Day
Mar. 8	International	Oct. 7	Constitution Day
	Women's Day	Nov. 7, 8	Anniversary of the
May 1, 2	Labor Days		Oct. Revolution

Transportation

Air. Direct, often non-stop, flights operate into Moscow and to a lesser extent Leningrad from all parts of the world. Domestic flights link Moscow with hundreds of points throughout this vast country, from major cities to Siberian settlements. Air travel can definitely be recommended in the Soviet Union, though visitors should not expect the same degree of personal attention accorded to air travelers in other parts of the world.

Major airports. Moscow: Sheremetyevo (18 miles/30 km. from city center). Beryozka and duty-free shops. Bus service to city terminal on Leningrad Boulevard. Vnukovo (18 miles/30 km. from city center), domestic. Domodevodo (25 miles/40 km. from city center), domestic. **Leningrad:** Pulkovo (11 miles/17 km. from city center). Beryozka (tourist) shop. Airport bus service about every 15 minutes. **Kiev:** Borispol (24 miles/38 km. from city center). Beryozka shop. Rail and bus service to city center.

Rail. Trains are punctual and comfortable and can be recommended for travel between major cities if time is not too much of an object. A single class of seating is available, though sleeping cars offer *standard* (equivalent to second class) and *soft* (like first class) categories. Don't be surprised if the berth arrangements mix up the sexes among perfect strangers. Long-distance trains include dining cars. The best way to get the feel of Siberia is to take the Trans-Siberian Railroad.

Local public transportation. Cheap streetcar, bus and trolleybus services are available in principal cities. Moscow and Leningrad have extensive, efficient subway systems.

Taxis. You can hail a cab on the street, pick one up at one of the many taxi stands in main cities, or have someone phone for one (Moscow, tel. 927-00-00; Leningrad, tel. 311-52-15). Reserve two hours in advance.

Piskarevsky Cemetery
Пискаревское
мемориальное
кладбище

in eniupsimaS
Metallistov pr.
Sverdlovskaya nab.
Polustrovskiy pr.
Zhukova ul.
ul. Komsomola
B. Sampsonievskiy
Arsenal'naya ul.
Finland Station
Финляндский
вокзал
Lenin Monument
Памятник
В. И. Ленину

Нева
Neva

Malookhtinskiy prosp.
Neva

Voinova ul.
Shpalernaya nab
Shchedrina ul.
Tverskaya ul.
Orlovskaya ul
Smol'niy prosp.
Novgorodskaya ul.
Moisevenko ul.
Suvorovskiy prosp.

Hotel October
Гост. Октябрьская
Moscow Station
Московский вокзал
Nevskiy prospekt

Metallistov pr.
OPRa ul.
Polustrovskiy pr.
Polustrovskiy pr.
Litovskaya ul.
Chugunna ya ul.
Lesnoy prospekt
Лесной пр.
Лесной пр.
Карла Маркса пр.
Karl Marx prospekt
Karl Marx prospekt
Fokina nab.
Fokina nab.
Aurora
Аврора
Peter's Cottage
Музей-домик
Петра I.
Vyborgskaya nab.
Viborgskaya nab.
Большая Нева
Большая Нева
Bol'shaya Neva

**Peter and Paul
Cathedral and Fortress**
Петропавловский
собор и крепость

Chaykovskogo ul.
Robespierre nab.
Voinova ul.
Litejny prosp.
Literaturniy
Saltikova ul.
Kutuzova nab.

Liteyniy prospekt
Vosstaniya

Parad-
naya ul.

Lenin Museum
Музей Ленина
Pushkin House
Квартира-музей А. С. Пушкина
Pushkin Sq.

Russian Museum
Русский музей
Hotel Europa
Гост. Европейская
**Cathedral of Our Lady
of Kazan**
Казанский
собор
Hotel Astoria
Гост. Астория

Ligovskiy prospekt
Ligovskiy prospekt

Sadovaya
T.A.

Петроград-
skaya nab.
Petrograd-
skaya nab.
Aptekarskaya nab.

Planetarium
Планетарий
Artillery Museum
Музей артиллерии

professora Popova ul.
Lva Tolstogo ul.

Kirovskiy prospekt
Кировский проспект
Bol'shoy prosp.
Большой проспект

Winter Palace
Зимний
дворец
Hermitage
(Эрмитаж)
Palace Sq.
Дворцовая
пл.
Nevskiy

St. Isaac's Cathedral
Исаакиевский собор

Мойки
Moyki nab.

Bol'shaya
Nevka
Bol'shoy
Nevka nab.
Kamennoostrovskiy prosp.
Professora Popova ul.
Karpovki reki nab.
Levashovskiy prosp.
Pionyerskaya ul.
Bol'shaya ul.
Chkalovskiy prosp.
Zhdanovki reki nab.
Krasnogo kursanta ul.

Kirov Theatre
Театр им. Кирова

Dekabristov
Dekabrista
reki nab.
Bol'shaya Neva

Kronverkskiy prosp.
Makarova nab.
Malaya Neva
Малая Нева

Naval Museum
Военно-морской
музей

Dimitri Mendeleev Museum
Музей Менделеева
Admiralty
Адмиралтейство
Peter the Great Monument
Памятник Петра I.

Srednyaya
Nevka
Bol'shaya
Nevka nab.
Martinova nab.
Krestovskiy prospekt
Morskoy prospekt
Dinamo prosp.
Ryukhina ul.
Kemskaya ul.
Derptatskaya ul.
Lazareva
admirala Nevka
Zelenina ul.
Malaya Nevka
Malaya Neva

Нева
Neva
400 m
400 yards
200
200

Linii 8
9-ya Linii
6 17-ya Linii
Sredniy prospekt
Maliy prospekt
Bol'shoy prospekt
Ural'skaya ul.
Zheleznovod ul.
KIMa prosp.
Smolenki reki nab.
Detskaya ul.
Nal'chnaya ul.
22-23
26-ya Linii
27-ya
Sredniy prospekt
Bol'shoy prospekt
Kosaya Linija
Kosaya

Z

LENINGRAD
(ЛЕНИНГРАД)

Car rental. Cars may be rented through Intourist or Europcar, and reservations should preferably be made at the same time you apply for your visa and other arrangements. Foreigners must pay in hard currency or with a major credit card. In practical terms, a rental car can only be used for getting around the specific city you are visiting, not for traveling long distances. The advance paperwork involved in moving about the country by car rules out any spontaneity.

Driving in the Soviet Union. An international drivers' license or national license preferably with a Russian translation is required to drive in the U.S.S.R. The speed limit in all cities and town is 38 mph (60 kph) and 56 mph (90 kph) outside towns—except where signs permitting higher speeds are displayed. Use of seat belts is obligatory, and a red reflector warning triangle, a fire-extinguisher and a first-aid kit must be carried. Blood alcohol limit is a strictly enforced zero.

Horns may not be sounded in residential areas except to prevent an accident. In urban driving after dark, only parking lights are used. A left turn or U-turn can usually only be made when specifically allowed, mostly as indicated by an arrow signal on the main traffic lights. Yield to official limousines driving in special outside lanes. Beware of undisciplined city traffic as well as poor street lighting and vehicle illumination at night. Road surfaces are often rather poor by Western standards. Gasoline is bought with coupons supplied by Intourist. It is generally available in normal (70–93 octane), super (95–98 octane), lead-free (76–95 octane) and diesel, but high-grade and diesel fuel is sometimes difficult to find. On the open road it's advisable to fill up when you see a gas station, as they are few and far between.

Traffic in cities is controlled by armed officers of the militia (police) on foot, in observation towers, patrolling on motorcycles and in radio cars. You can recognize a traffic policeman by his gray uniform and white baton. For minor infractions, fines are sometimes levied on the spot and receipts given. Highways are patrolled by state traffic police on motorcycles and in yellow cars with broad blue stripes.

Rest rooms. Sign language ought to direct you to a couple of doors marked M and Ж. M is the men's room which is easy to remember. Public conveniences may also be advertised by the familiar letters, WC.

A lot of Russian plumbing is old-fashioned and clanking but operative.

Emergencies. It's hard to imagine an emergency beyond the competence of Intourist or your hotel staff. Turn to your embassy or consulate in case of difficulties.

542

However, here are some vital telephone numbers:

Fire	01
Police	02
Ambulance	03

Police. The only policemen you're likely to see are traffic patrolmen. In summer these armed officers wear gray uniforms and carry white billy clubs. In winter they bundle up in blue overcoats and fur hats.

Crime and theft. Be careful not to get involved with blackmarketeers or illegal currency-dealers. This could lead to serious consequences.

Normal precautions are in order to guard against petty crime such as pickpocketing, though, happily, thefts from hotel rooms are virtually unknown in the U.S.S.R. Don't tempt fate by leaving valuables lying around or wallets jutting from hip pockets in crowded places. Beyond pickpocketing and burglaries, the incidence of violent crime has greatly increased. Another new peril: passengers' baggage stolen at Moscow's international airport.

Medical care and health. In general, medical care in the U.S.S.R. suffers from lack of sophisticated equipment and medicines. Bring along your own supply of basic medicines. Even adhesive tape and absorbent cotton can be unobtainable.

If you should fall ill, tell your Intourist guide or the hotel service desk. A doctor will visit you in your hotel, or you may be taken to a special clinic for tourists. Medicine is charged to the tourist-patient but the care is free of charge.

Drugstores are usually open from 8 a.m. to 8 or 9 p.m. Several pharmacies operate around the clock; Intourist can give you the addresses.

Dysentery or diarrhoea is sometimes a problem in the southern areas of the country.

Tap water is safe to drink in Moscow, but elsewhere bottled water is recommended.

Embassies and consulates. Embassies and consulates are not listed in the telephone directory. Ask Intourist or consult *Information Moscow*.

Social customs. Never drop anything, not even an old movie ticket, on the street—it's both offensive to Russian tidiness and illegal. Don't call your Soviet interlocutor "comrade" unless you are a member of the Communist party.

Enjoying the U.S.S.R.

Food and drink. Most hotels and restaurants offer a variety of international and local dishes and have standard menus printed in four languages. Some specialities are *borsht* (beet and cabbage soup with chunks of boiled meat), *solianka* (cabbage soup), *pelmeni* (meat dumpling), *blini* (Russian pancakes with sweet, savory or caviar fillings), *okroshka* (a chilled summertime soup made of cucumber, onion and hardboiled eggs), *kasha* (a type of porridge), *pirozhki* (small pies), *shashlik* (skewered and grilled mutton and onions served with a hot sauce), *beef Stroganov* (beef tenderloin in a sauce of sour cream, onions and mushrooms), *kotleti po-kiyevski* (chicken Kiev; boned chicken breasts filled with melted butter) and, of course, caviar.

Soviet table wines are well regarded but erratically distributed. Many sunny regions produce quite drinkable wines, but the biggest reputation probably belongs to Georgian reds and whites; if you can't decipher the incredible Georgian alphabet look for the Russian transliteration. In practice, the waiter will tell you whether there's any choice at all. Vodka is drunk straight. Russian beer and tea can be recommended. Mineral water holds an honored place on Soviet tables. If you can get it, *Narzan* fizzes tastily. *Borzhomi,* more commonly available, is so good for you that its heavy mineral taste may put you off.

If you are not eating at your hotel, it is necessary to reserve a table; ask the service bureau at your hotel to do it for you.

Lunch is served from 11 a.m. to 3 p.m., dinner 6 to 10 p.m.

Entertainment. In all the big cities there's a full program of concerts, plays, opera and ballet almost every night. Intourist has the inside track on tickets, though at short notice you might have to settle for second or third choice. There are many movie theaters, showing mainly Russian films. The rare western film is usually dubbed into Russian.

Taxes, service charges and tipping. In hotels and restaurants, all charges are included. Though officially discouraged (and occasionally refused), a gratuity for good service, given discreetly, is appreciated (5 to 10% for taxi drivers, waiters, hairdressers and barbers, 50 kopeks for porters and lavatory attendants).

Sports and recreation. Visitors can arrange horse-riding or tennis through Intourist. There's a bowling alley in Moscow's Gorky park. A giant well-heated open-air swimming pool operates year-round close to Moscow's Kremlin.

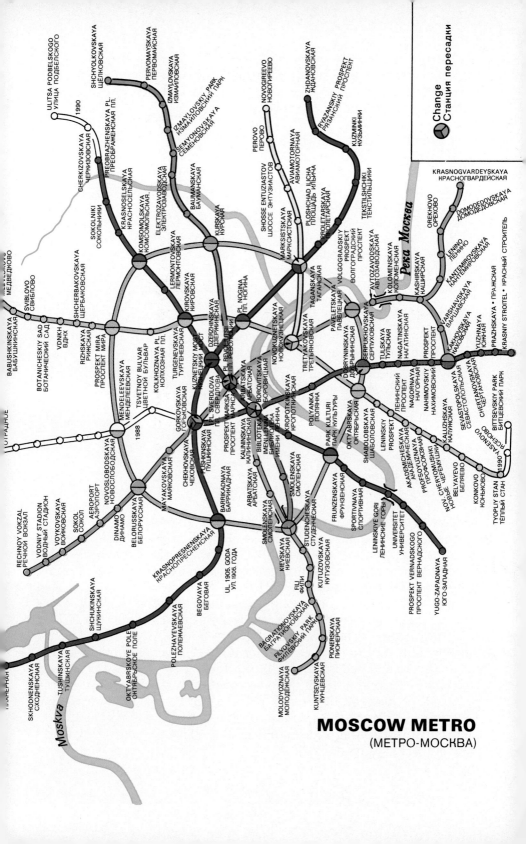

MOSCOW METRO
(МЕТРО-МОСКВА)

Spectator sports: In winter, ice hockey is the most popular spectator sport, and during the rest of the year, soccer. Basketball is also a favorite as well as a variety of other sports.

TV and radio. All radio and TV programming is in Russian or minority Soviet languages. Soviet television transmits programs on four channels. The language problem may prove insurmountable, except for international sporting events which are always popular. All programs are telecast in color.

Two official radio networks broadcast to the farthest reaches of the U.S.S.R.: Moscow Radio and the less solemn Radio Mayak.

If you crave news from the outer world in a language you can comprehend, the BBC and Voice of America, among other foreign stations, may be picked up at certain times of the day.

What to buy. Good buys include caviar, vodka, amber, traditional painted wooden handicraft items, lacquered boxes with fine miniature paintings, matryoshka dolls, Bukhara and other Central Asian carpets, furs, phonograph records. All can be purchased for hard currency in Beryozka shops for foreigners (most of these items are hard to find in ordinary shops). Shopping hours vary considerably. Most stores are open 10 a.m.–6 p.m., with major ones operating longer hours (often 8 a.m.–9 p.m.), Monday through Saturday.

Sightseeing

Moscow. The Kremlin*, a walled city of churches, palaces and art treasures, as well as the seat of government. Among splendid Kremlin churches: 16th-century Cathedral of St. Michael the Archangel; gold-domed Cathedral of the Annunciation; Cathedral of the Assumption, where tsars were crowned. Outside the wall, cobbled vastness of Red Square*, for parades or strolling; St. Basil's Cathedral*, fabulous eight-domed folly; Lenin's Tomb, besieged by queues of pilgrims; GUM department store, bizarre Victorian giant. Gorky Street, city's liveliest thoroughfare. Bolshoi Theater, sumptuous 19th-century opera house. Arbat Square and pedestrian mall for offbeat shopping. Moscow State University, 32-storey Stalinesque tower overlooking the city, Gorky Park, for a look at the locals pursuing fresh air and recreation. Tretyakov Gallery*, treasure-house of old Russian icons and 19th-century realist paintings. Pushkin Fine Arts Museum*, covering world art from Babylon to Picasso.

546

Daytrips from Moscow. Arkhangelskoye, princely palace and park. Abramtsevo, estate where Gogol and Turgenev were guests. 14th-century town of Klin, where Tchaikovsky lived. Borodino, site of Napoleon's defeat in 1812.

The Golden Ring. Historic towns of Old Muscovy, northeast of Moscow. Zagorsk*, often-besieged Russian Orthodox monastery-fortress full of ancient Russian art, where Peter the Great once took refuge. Pereslavl-Zalessky, ancient cathedral town with three monasteries. Rostov Veliky (the Great)*, walled town of onion-domed churches on a peaceful lake. Yaroslavl*, founded in 1010, with ancient monasteries and churches galore. Kostroma, old trading station on the wide Volga, with fine 17th-century architecture. Suzdal*, religious capital of early Russia, with five monasteries and countless historic churches. Vladimir, 12th-century cathedral decorated with frescoes by Andrei Rublev.

Leningrad. Aristocratic, elegant Palace Square, dominated by monument to tsar Alexander. 18th-century Winter Palace*, where Russia's last six tsars lived, now the home of Russia's greatest museum, the Hermitage*, with two million items from prehistoric artefacts to 20th-century Western European classics. St. Isaac's Cathedral, inspired by St. Peter's of Rome, built by hundreds of thousands of workmen. Nevsky Prospekt, Leningrad's Broadway since the time of Peter the Great. Peter and Paul Fortress*, citadel on the Neva, featuring Dutch-style 18th-century cathedral. Russian Museum*, Russian art from the 10th century onward.

Excursions from Leningrad. Petrodvorets*, dazzlingly restored palace complex from which Peter the Great surveyed the Baltic. Pushkin*, a town containing two imperial palaces. Pavlovsk, summer palace Catherine the Great gave her son Paul, in a vast formal park. Novgorod*, fortified town founded in the 9th century, with its own kremlin, cathedral, and noteworthy churches and monasteries.

Baltic republics. Estonia: Tallinn*, capital and port city with charmingly preserved old town, varied towers in town wall, 13th- and 14th-century churches and town hall. Latvia: Riga*, river port founded in 1201, featuring a castle, churches and other buildings from Hanseatic League days. Lithuania: Vilnius*, with ruins of Gediminas Castle overlooking well-restored old town, Gothic and Baroque churches and an onion-domed synagogue, recalling the city's role as one of Europe's main centers of Jewish culture before World War II.

Ukraine. Kiev*, 1,500-year-old capital city of parks along the Dnieper, noted for Russo-Byzantine St. Sophia's Cathedral, an 11th-century architectural wonder inspired by its namesake in Constantinople and well filled with art treasures; also Baroque Church of St. Andrew on a hilltop in Old Kiev; Monastery of the Caves (Pecherskaya Lavra) with churches, museums, monuments and catacombs. Lvov, western Ukrainian center of commerce and culture with a tormented history, indicated by buildings in many foreign as well as local styles. Kharkov, big regional capital with early Soviet-style monumental buildings and blue-domed 17th-century Pokrovsky cathedral and hilltop Uspensky Cathedral with bell tower honoring 1812 victory over Napoleon.

Black Sea and Crimea. Odessa, lively port city founded in late 18th century, besieged in World War II; Potemkin Steps, scene of classic film sequence by Eisenstein; Catacombs, kilometers of caves used as hiding place for revolutionaries and wartime partisans; Archaeology Museum, stocked with antiquities from Scythian and Kievan Rus cultures; Concert Hall, formerly Stock Exchange, with stately Gothic features. Kherson, deepwater port upstream on the Dnieper, with fortress founded according to Catherine the Great's defensive strategy, 18th-century Church of the Saviour. Sevastopol, major Black Sea port, besieged in World War II, Museum of the Black Sea Fleet (founded 1869), Sevastopol Panorama housing huge circular painting of 1855 battle. Yalta, lovely setting and mild climate, Russia's original resort, now center for sanatoria: Livadia, Palace, site of historic 1945 summit meeting of Stalin, Roosevelt and Churchill; suburban botanical garden. Sochi, sprawling subtropical resort of sanatoria and hotels between Caucasus mountains and the beach; harbor, seaside promenade, botanical garden. Sukhumi, subtropical resort settled by ancient Greeks and Romans, historic defensive installations. Batumi, near the Turkish border, popular resort despite rain-forest climate, parks, beaches, museums.

Central Asia. Tashkent, fourth biggest city in U.S.S.R. and capital of Uzbekistan, completely rebuilt as model of modern Soviet metropolis from ruins of 1966 earthquake, though small sample of old town architecture remains. Samarkand*, astride ancient trade routes, conquered by Alexander the Great and Genghis Khan, now an industrial and cultural city preserving fabled monuments: medieval mosques and tombs (including Tamerlane's burial place) and 15th-century Ulugbek observatory. Bukhara*, traditional oasis crowded with exotic historic monuments: the Ark fortress, mosques, minarets, mausoleums, theological schools, inns and bazaars.

Some useful expressions in Russian

good morning/afternoon	dobroye utro/dobriy dyen'
good evening/night	dobriy vyechyer/spokoynoy nochi
good-bye	dosvidaniya
yes/no	da/nyet
please/thank you	pozhalusta/spasibo
excuse me	izvinitye
you're welcome	pozhalusta
where/when/how	gdye/kogda/kak
how long/how far	skol'ko/kak dalyeko
yesterday/today/tomorrow	vchyera/sevodnya/zavtra
day/week/month/year	den/nyedyelya/myesyats/god
left/right	lyeviy/praviy
up/down	vvyerkh/vniz
good/bad	khoroshiy/plokhoy
big/small	bol'shoy/malyen'kiy
cheap/expensive	dyeshoviy/dorogoy
hot/cold	goryachiy/kholodniy
old/new	stariy/noviy
open/closed	otkritiy/zakritiy
free (vacant)/occupied	svobodniy/zanyatiy
easy/difficult	lyogkiy/trudniy
Does anyone here speak English/French/German?	Zdyes' kto-nibud' govorit po-angliyski/po-frantsuzski/po-nyemyetski?
What does this mean?	Chto eto znachit?
I don't understand.	Ya nye ponimayu.
Please write it down.	Pozhalusta, napishitye.
Do you take credit cards/traveller's cheques?	Vi byeryote Kryeditniye Kartochki/dorozhniye chyecki?
Waiter!/Waitress!	Ofitsiant!/Ofitsiantka!
Where are the toilets?	Gdye tualyety?
I'd like…	Ya khotyel bi…
How much is that?	Skol'ko eto stoit?
What time is it?	Kotoriy chas?
Help me please.	Pomogitye mnye, pozhalusta.
Just a minute.	Syechas.

YUGOSLAVIA

*A multinational Balkan buffer state with palaces
at the sparkling seaside and on a mountaintop.*

It's been a buffer between east and west since prehistoric times, yet the country called Yugoslavia is an invention of the 20th century. And the present boundaries weren't drawn until after World War II.

Scarcely bigger than Britain, Yugoslavia is a curious compound of four principal nationalities plus a couple of dozen minority groups. They communicate in three main languages and a number of minority tongues. To make it all even more exotic, two different alphabets are in use, the familiar Latin letters and the Greek-based Cyrillic variant.

For tourists the country's most appealing physical feature is the shallow, transparent Adriatic Sea. Taking into account a thousand or so islands and islets, the length of the Yugoslavian coastline, much of it beachy, can be computed at some 1,300 miles (around 2,000 kilometers). Among the most popular coastal towns are Dubrovnik, so beautiful it's been called a poem in stone, and Split, where the Roman Emperor Diocletian built his palace. Inland, the countryside runs from the world-class ski slopes of the Julian Alps to the moody beauty of Lake Ohrid on the Albanian border. Belgrade, the national capital, is strong on museums, and Cetinje, onetime capital of the mountain kingdom of Montenegro, basks in an irresistibly quaint time warp.

All over Yugoslavia the past comes up and startles the present: one of Rome's biggest amphitheaters still in use in Pula, masses of medieval monasteries... and on to Saravejo and the spot where an assassin ignited World War I. Even the lovely Lipizzaner horses of Slovenia can trace their history back to the 16th century. The teeming local markets, too, seem unchanged; the carpets are hand-woven as always; and a bit of old-fashioned haggling might prove useful.

Facts and figures

Population:	22.8 million
Area:	98,766 sq. miles (255,804 sq. km.)
Capital:	Belgrade (*Beograd,* 1.4 million)
Other major cities:	Zagreb (1.2 million) Skopje (505,000) Sarajevo (450,000) Ljubljana (305,000) Novi Sad (260,000) Split (235,000)
Languages:	Serbo-Croatian; both Latin (in the northwest) and Cyrillic (in the southeast) alphabets are used. Regional languages include Slovenian, Macedonian and Albanian.
Religion:	Eastern Orthodox (42%), Catholic (32%), Islam (10%)
Time zone:	GMT + 1, EST + 6; DST (Apr.–Sep.)
Currency:	Yugoslavian *dinar* (abbr. *din.*) = 100 *paras* Coins: 10, 20, 50 paras, 1, 2, 5 din. Bills: 50, 100, 200, 500 din.
Electricity:	220 volt, 50 cycle, AC

Planning your trip

Visa requirements. Entry visas may be issued at the Yugoslav border. See pp. 29–30.

Vaccination requirements. None (see also p. 25).

Currency restrictions. While you may bring unlimited sums of foreign currency into Yugoslavia, you may not carry more than 1,200 din. (in all denominations except 500 din.) across the border in either direction.

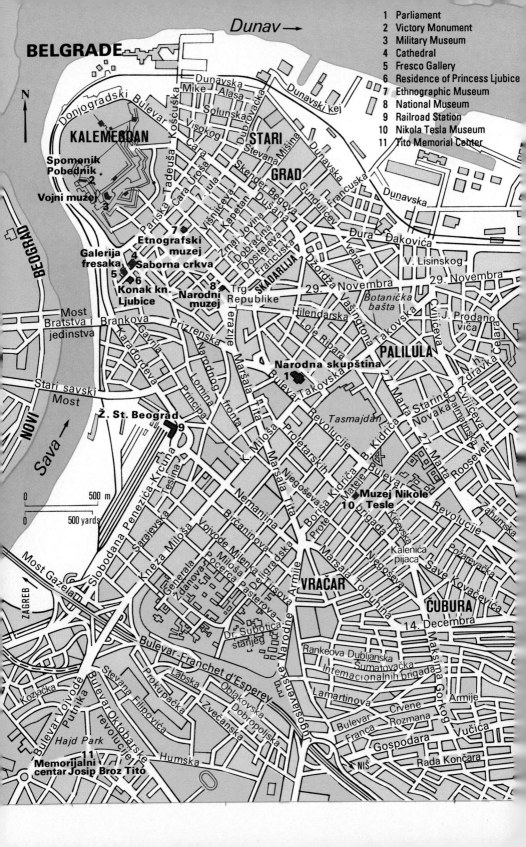

Climate. Yugoslavia's climate ranges from Mediterranean on the Adriatic coast through moderate temperate in most inland areas to alpine in the mountains. The rainiest months are April and November.

Some average daily temperatures:

Belgrade		J	F	M	A	M	J	J	A	S	O	N	D
average daily	°F	37	42	52	64	73	79	83	83	76	64	51	42
maximum*	°C	3	5	11	18	23	26	28	28	24	18	11	5
average daily	°F	26	29	36	45	54	59	62	62	56	47	39	32
minimum*	°C	-3	-2	2	7	12	15	17	17	13	8	4	0
Dubrovnik													
average daily	°F	53	55	58	63	70	78	83	82	77	69	62	56
maximum*	°C	2	5	10	15	20	24	27	26	22	15	8	4
average daily	°F	25	25	32	40	48	54	57	57	51	43	36	30
minimum*	°C	-4	-4	0	4	9	12	14	14	11	6	2	-1

* Minimum temperatures are measured just before sunrise, maximum temperatures in the afternoon.

Clothing. Warm clothing is necessary for winter, with light clothing adequate for summer. Formality in dress is confined to sophisticated nightclubs and casinos. Elsewhere it's all very egalitarian. Rare is the restaurant where anyone is fussy about what clothes are worn, even though the waiters may dress ever so formally.

Duty-free allowances

Cigarettes	Cigars	Tobacco	Liquor	Wine
200 or	50 or	250 g.	1 l. and	1 l.

Hotels and accommodations

Hotels. Most travel agents can supply a hotel list showing facilities and rates. Reserve well in advance during the summer season.

Hotels in Yugoslavia are officially graded in five categories. "L" means de luxe and from there the ratings descend from A to D; breakfast is only included in half and full-board arrangements. Daily rates are normally lower for long stays and considerably reduced off-season. A tourist tax is charged in addition.

Motels *(motel)* are situated along a main highway or on the edge of town. Most offer facilities similar to a B-class hotel. Car-repair services and fuel may be available.

Boardinghouses *(pansion)*. Comfortable but with fewer facilities than a hotel. Officially these establishments are graded in three catergories, I to III.

Tourist Villages *(turističko naselje)*. A self-contained resort. May consist of bungalows or low-rise hotel facilities built around a central core of restaurants, shops and public rooms.

Apartments and Villas *(stan; vila)*. Popular with tourists who prefer a self-catering holiday, but it may be difficult to make arrangements on short notice. Write in advance to the tourist office in the resort of your choice.

Rooms *(soba)*. In some of the popular resorts, rooms for tourists in private homes outnumber hotel rooms. They're closely supervised and graded (from I to III) according to the degree of comfort provided. Accommodations, sometimes including meals, can be arranged through the local tourist office. Landladies canvassing near ferry and bus terminals sometimes descend on arriving tourists.

Youth and student hostels *(omkadinski dom; studentski dom)*. You can obtain a list of Yugoslav hostels and their facilities from your own national youth-hostels association. There's no age limit, but priority is given to visitors under 27.

Camping. Yugoslavia has plenty of facilities for campers, particularly along the Adriatic coast and its islands. Many sites occupy privileged situations of natural beauty. In addition to electrical and sanitary installations and shops, amenities may include restaurants, garages and entertainment. Some sites also have bungalows and chalets. Rates depend on the setting and the extent of services provided. Like boardinghouses, campsites are rated class I, II or III.

Camping is permitted only at official sites. Elsewhere, permission must be obtained from the local authorities. Simply pulling up for the night at the side of the road is quite illegal.

A free booklet listing campsites throughout Yugoslavia, complete with charts of facilities and prices, is published each year by the Automobile Association of Yugoslavia (AMSJ). The booklet is available at tourist offices or direct from AMSJ (address: Ruzveltova 18, 11000 Beograd, Yugoslavia).

Yugoslav tourist offices abroad

U.K.	Yugoslav National Tourist Office, 143 Regent Street, London W1; tel. (071) 757 2801
U.S.A.	Yugoslav National Tourist Office, 630 Fifth Avenue, New York, N.Y. 10020; tel. (212) 757-2801/2

On the spot

Banks and currency exchange. Banking hours are generally 8 a.m.–noon and 1–7 p.m., though some banks close much earlier (around noon), Monday–Friday, and 8 a.m.–noon on Saturdays. Outside these hours hotels and some currency-exchange offices can change money. Try to assess how much dinar cash you will need, and remember to keep currency-exchange receipts if you intend to reconvert money. Money transfers can be a time-consuming process.

Credit cards and traveler's checks. Internationally recognized credit cards are accepted, as are most traveler's checks.

Mail and telecommunications. Services are generally reliable. Most post offices are open 7 a.m.–8 p.m. without a break, though some operate on a reduced schedule. Some main post offices: Belgrade: Takovska 6 (open 7 a.m.–10 p.m. daily for telephone and telegraph services, with telex facilities round the clock); Ljubljana: Cigaletova 15; Zagreb: Jurisiceva 13 or Branimirova 4.

Mail boxes in Yugoslavia, square and painted yellow, are normally affixed to walls. Post offices are marked by yellow PTT signs.

Most public places have coin- or token-operated telephones for local calls. An increasing number of pay phones can be used for long-distance, too. Tokens *(žetone)* are available from post offices and

557

tobacco shops. For calls abroad it's best to go to the local post office. From most localities in Yugoslavia you can dial direct to western Europe.

Some useful numbers:

Ambulance	94	Directory information	988
Fire	93	Police	92
General information	9812	Telegrams	96

Newspapers. Principal dailies: *Borba, Politika, Politika Ekspress, Večernje novosti* (Belgrade); *Vjesnik, Večernji list* (Zagreb); *Oslobodjenje* (Sarajevo), *Delo* (Ljubljana), *Nova Makedonija* (Skopje), *Rilindja, Jedinstvo* (Priština), *Dnevnik* (Novi Sad), *Probjeda* (Titograd). Newspapers from France, Great Britain, Italy, the United States and Germany are on sale in major cities. *Yugoslav Tourist News* is published monthly in English, French and German.

Tourist information

Belgrade   Pedestrian underpass at Terazije Street, next to the Albania Building, 11000 Belgrade; tel. 635-343/ 635-622.

Zagreb   Zrimjevac 14, 41000 Zagreb; tel. (041) 441-880, telex 21622.

Ljubljana   Titova 11, 61000 Ljubljana; tel. 215-412, telex 31693.

Legal holidays

Jan. 1, 2	New Year	July 4	Veteran's Day
May 1, 2	Labor Days	Nov. 29, 30	Republic Days

Regional holidays: July 7 (Belgrade), July 22 (Ljubljana), July 27 (Zagreb), Oct. 11, Aug. 2 (Skopje), July 27 (Sarajevo), July 3 (Titograd).

Transportation

Air. Belgrade is the major gateway to Yugoslavia, though international flights operate to certain other cities (Zagreb, Ljubljana, Split).

Domestic airlines serve 16 Yugoslav airports. Air-taxi service is available.

Major airports. Belgrade. Surčin (13 miles/20 km. from city center). Duty-free shop. Regular bus service to city center. **Zagreb** (11 miles/ 17 km. from city center). Duty-free shop. Regular bus service to city

center. **Ljubljana.** Brnik (22 miles/35 km. from city center). Duty-free shop. Bus service keyed to arrivals and departures.

Rail. The country's rail services include punctual, fast links between main cities. The rail network has shrunk in recent years, but the surviving lines have been improved. Trains often include dining and sleeping cars. In season trains tend to be crowded and slow; it's wise to reserve seats and sleeping accommodations in advance. You save about one-fourth in second class.

The most appealing train journey for tourists is the route linking Belgrade with the Montenegrin coast at Bar, famous for its engineering marvels and spectacular scenery.

Local public transportation. Major centers have buses and streetcars, all efficiently run, but often overcrowded. During rush hours (6–8 a.m., 2–4 p.m.), city traffic slows down. Bus fares are paid either to the conductor on board or to the driver. Bus-ticket offices and newsstands sell tickets cheaper than on the vehicle.

Taxis. Cabs are available at stands in all towns. City taxis have meters; in smaller towns, agree on a price in advance. Tipping is optional (round off the fare).

Car rental. A number of firms operate, some with airport offices. Chauffeur-driven vehicles are also available.

Driving in Yugoslavia. Speed limits are 38 mph (60 kph) in towns, 75 mph (120 kph) on expressways, 62 mph (100 kph) on other main roads and 50 mph (80 kph) on secondary roads. Seat belts must be worn. Motorists are required to have in their vehicle a spare set of bulbs, a first-aid kit and a red reflector warning triangle for use in case of breakdown. Blood alcohol limit is 50 mg/100 ml.

Most major highways are asphalt- or concrete-surfaced, though minor roads are often insufficiently maintained. Main routes are: Ljubljana–Zagreb–Belgrade–Niš–Skopje, and the Adriatic coast road. Tolls are charged on some stretches of expressway. In case of breakdown, phone 987 in most areas for the Automobile Association of Yugoslavia *(Auto-Moto Savez Jusoglavije, AMSJ).*

Fuel coupons. These coupons can be bought at travel agencies, at automobile clubs in the country of departure, at the Yugoslav frontier or from an authorized exchange dealer in Yugoslavia, and mean a slight reduction on the price of gasoline. Unused coupons are refunded at the border when leaving the country or at the place where they were bought.

Ask your automobile association about the latest regulations, as they are constantly changing. Gasoline available is normal (86 octane), super (98 octane), lead-free (in big cities) and diesel.

Note that it is prohibited to enter Yugoslavia with a spare can of gasoline in the car.

Rest rooms. Much of Yugoslavia preserves reminders of the centuries of Turkish rule, among them the seatless squat toilets you'll find in public conveniences and country restaurants and cafés. But hotels and restaurants serving foreigners normally have western-style facilities.

The pertinent doors are usually marked by symbols—often a silhouetted high-heeled shoe for women and a flat shoe for men—rather than words (*muški* for men and *ženski* for women). In public toilets cubicle doors almost never have locks or latches. The cleaning lady may look in at any time. Be sure to tip her on your way out of her domain.

Emergencies. In most cities the standard number to telephone in an emergency is 94. Note that you need a coin to dial this or any other number from a pay phone.

Police. The national police, wearing blue uniforms (white in summer), maintain public order and control traffic. Each officer's identity is revealed by his service number, clearly engraved on his belt buckle. Police cars, blue and white, are marked *Milicija* or one of the local linguistic variations.

Crime and theft. Violent crime is rare in Yugoslavia, but pickpockets and sneak thieves know no frontiers. In resort areas thefts pick up in the tourist season, so it's prudent to store valuables in the safe deposit box in your hotel. Lock your car and, if you're camping, close your tent well.

Medical care and health. Charges for medical services in Yugoslavia are very reasonable, and standards are satisfactory. Citizens of the following Western countries are entitled to virtually free medical care: Austria, Belgium, Luxemburg, Netherlands, U.K. and Germany. Medicine and pharmaceutical supplies are readily available, though not necessarily the same brands you're used to. The addresses of pharmacies on duty after hours are published in the daily newspapers. Tap water is generally safe to drink, though to be on the safe side you would be advised to order bottled water.

An *apoteka* supplies over-the-counter non-prescription remedies as well as medicines made up according to a prescription. A *drogerija* sells a great range of toilet articles, cosmetics, and sometimes films.

Embassies and consulates. Embassies are listed in the telephone directory under "Ambassade" and consulates under "Konzulaí".

Social customs. Handshaking, seemingly at every opportunity, is a must when greeting almost anybody. If a Yugoslav offers you a drink it's just about obligatory to accept. If you're not in the mood for brandy, say yes to coffee. You aren't expected to stand the next round; the hospitality can be returned at a later date.

Enjoying Yugoslavia

Food and drink. National dishes include: *pršut* (smoked or air-dried ham), *ćevapčići* (spiced, ground meat grilled), *ražnjići* (pieces of pork or veal on the spit, grilled), mixed grill, *sarma* (ground meat and rice in cabbage or grape leaves), stuffed peppers, *duveč* (vegetable and meat stew), *musaka* (baked eggplants with ground meat), *bosanski lonac* (vegetables, especially cabbage, and meat stew), *studel* (pastry with nuts and sultanas). Along the coast, fish restaurants most commonly serve mackerel and sardines, with bass, dentex or bream as more distinguished fare. Lobster and crab, though delicious, are rather expensive. Various white cheeses are produced from cow's and sheep's milk. *Kajmak* (cream from boiled milk) is also made.

Restoran means restaurant, but you'll encounter other names: a *gosliona* is a village inn. A *kafana* is a pastry-and-snack coffee shop. *Ekspres restoran* means an inexpensive self-service restaurant. And a *bife* is a snackbar.

Yugoslavia produces some excellent wines and spirits. The best known red wines are: *Župsko, Prokupac, Tikveško, Vranac, Viški plavac*. Whites include: *Smederevka, Risling, Žilavka, Traminac, Silvanac, Graševina*, and *Otonel*. *Šljivovica vinjak* (brandy), *travarica, lozovača* and *maraskino* are some of the Yugoslav liqueurs and aperitifs worth sampling. Imported alcoholic beverages are readily available.

Mealtimes: lunch, noon–3 p.m.; dinner, 7–10 p.m.

563

Entertainment. Theaters, opera, ballet, movie theaters, concerts, folk shows, nightclubs and discos exist variously in larger cities and resorts. Historic coastal towns like Dubrovnik, Pula, Split and Zadar stage plays and concerts in the setting of great monuments. Some large hotels operate casinos. Foreign films are shown in their original language.

Taxes, service charges and tipping. Hotel bills are all-inclusive. Though restaurant bills feature a 10% service charge, it is usual to tip the waiter 5–10%. Other tipping recommendations: hotel porters about U.S.$0.50 per bag, barbers and hairdressers 10% hatcheck $0.25, for taxi drivers, round off the fare.

Sports and recreation. Extensive facilities are available for swimming and various water sports along the Adriatic. Hunting expeditions may be arranged in various parts of the country.

Favorite spectator sports are soccer, basketball, handball, water polo, boxing and, in season, skiing and ice hockey.

TV and radio. Programs are broadcast in all the official languages of the country, according to region. Foreign films are not dubbed.

If you have a short-wave set you can tune in to the BBC and Voice of America.

What to buy. Good buys include hand-made embroidery, lace, leather goods, woodcarvings, wool, hand-made carpets, filigree jewelry, ceramics, national costumes, textiles, tapestry, clothes, woolens, alcoholic drinks, chocolates and other confectionery. Art lovers have a chance to buy paintings by accomplished Yugoslav artists at the numerous exhibitions held in large towns. Prices are normally lower than for similar quality in other European countries. Shopping hours: 8 a.m.–8 p.m. Monday–Friday (some shops close between noon and 4 p.m.); Saturdays until 3 p.m.

Annual events and festivals. *April:* Yugoslavian song festival in Sarajevo. *May:* Spring festival of pop, folk and jazz music in Belgrade. Operatic evenings in Skopje. *June:* Wedding festival in Ljubljana. *July:* Folk festival in Zagreb. *July–August:* Festival of drama, dance and music in Dubrovnik. Opera, ballet and symphony festival in Opatija. Summer gala in Split. *October:* Classical music festival in Belgrade.

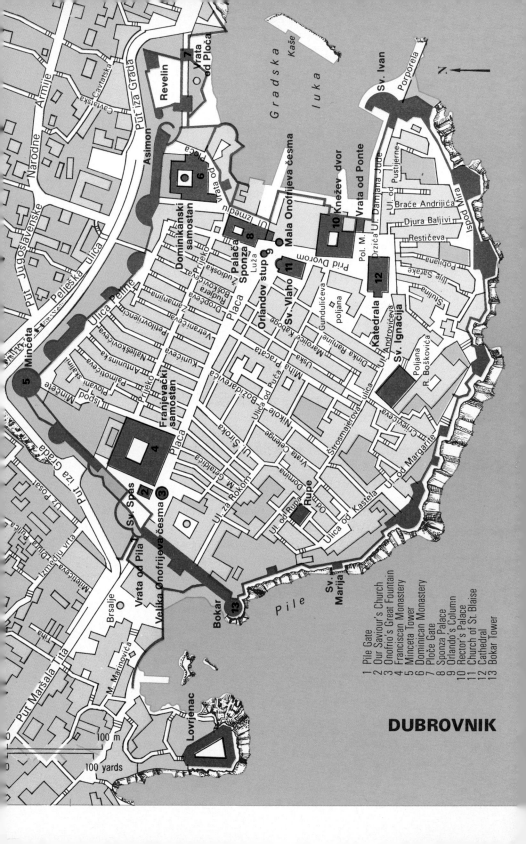

DUBROVNIK

1 Pile Gate
2 Our Saviour's Church
3 Onofrio's Great Fountain
4 Franciscan Monastery
5 Minčeta Tower
6 Dominican Monastery
7 Ploče Gate
8 Sponza Palace
9 Orlando's Column
10 Rector's Palace
11 Church of St. Blaise
12 Cathedral
13 Bokar Tower

Sightseeing

Northern Adriatic. Koper, Venetian relics in a busy modern port. Portorož, elegant beach resort. Piran*, onetime buccaneers' hideout with medieval fortifications. Poreč, popular resort surrounding perfectly preserved historic center with Basilica of Bishop Euphrasius, splendid Early Christian church. Rovinj, charming port town. Pula*, 2,500-year-old city with impressive Roman amphitheater, center of beach resort region.

Adriatic islands. Rab, with mostly Mediterranean landscape, beaches and Romanesque churches. Hvar*, sunny, lush and quiet hideaway island with tidy main town. Korčula*, legendary birthplace of Marco Polo, with elegant Renaissance palaces.

Dalmatia. Zadar, much-bombed port with 9th-century circular church of St. Donatus, 12th-century St. Anastasia Cathedral with Romanesque façade and two rose windows. Šibenik, thousand-year-old town with glorious St. James's Cathedral, noted for frieze of 74 portraits. Trogir, conserving Venetian cultural monuments notably St. Lawrence Cathedral with outstanding Romanesque portal. Split*, Dalmatia's fastest-growing city and a busy seaport, where Roman Emperor Diocletian built his retirement palace, a walled town in itself. Dubrovnik*, elegant walled city, once a republic, full of worthy architectural monuments and entrancing atmosphere.

Montenegro. Bay of Kotor*, vast fjord-like bay with its own miniclimate and spectacular scenery. Kotor*, walled town dramatically sited between mountains and sea. Budva*, inhabited since the Bronze Age, resembling a scaled-down Dubrovnik. Sveti Stefan, much-photographed little island of beauty with medieval village now a luxury hotel. Ulcinj, colorful oriental-style atmosphere and an enormous beach stretching to the Albanian border. Cetinje*, mountaintop capital of a 15th-century kingdom, an evocative focus of nostalgia. Lake Skadar*, big, moody lake shared by Yugoslavia and Albania. Tara Gorge*, called Europe's deepest, narrowest river valley, popular raft expeditions.

Northern Yugoslavia. Ljubljana, dynamic capital of Slovenia, combining skyscrapers and Baroque monuments. Postojna Cave*, karst caverns visited by million. Škocjan Caves*, less publicized but no less dramatic underground complex. Lipica*, home of the handsome white Lipizzaner horses, who perform for tourists. Lake Bled*, dizzyingly scenic lake with a fairy-tale island in the middle. Zagreb★, capital of Croatia, a heavyweight cultural center with 13th-century cathedral and other noteworthy churches as well as Mimara Museum, one of the world's major private art collections.

Continental Yugoslavia. Belgrade★, one of Europe's oldest cities: Kalemegdan Fortress, first built by ancient Celts, with Roman wall and medieval fortifications; and the definitive museums of Serbian art and history. Novi Sad, capital of Vojvodina, dignified Danube port beneath imposing Petrovaradin Castle. Plitvice Lakes★, cascading series of linked lakes of extraordinary beauty. Sarajevo★, exotic capital of Bosnia-Hercegovina, with skyscrapers and historic minarets and swarming bazaar; also Young Bosnia Museum recalling assassination of Austrian Archduke here in 1914, touching off World War I. Mostar★, a town of mosques and churches and a landmark 16th-century Turkish bridge across the River Neretva. Medjugorje, late 20th-century shrine in the karst wilderness now besieged by pilgrims.

The South. Field of Kosovo *(Kosovo Polje),* site of climatic 1389 battle in which Turks wiped out Serbs. Priština, capital of Kosovo, with 15th-century Imperial Mosque. Peć, longtime seat of Serbian Orthodox Church. Dečani Monastery, near Albanian border, with largest collection of medieval Serbian art. Skopje, Macedonian metropolis, rebuilt after catastrophic 1963 earthquake. Ohrid★, delightful hillside town with admired medieval churches and remains of 10th-century fortress, on Lake Ohrid★, remarkable for beauty, translucency and rare fish.

Some useful expressions in Serbo-Croatian

good morning/afternoon	dobro jutro/dobar dan
good evening/night	dobro veče/laku noć
good-bye	zbogom
yes/no	da/ne
please/thank you	molim/hvala
excuse me	izvinite
you're welcome	molim
where/when/how	gde/kad/kako
how long/how far	koliko dugo/koliko daleko
yesterday/today/tomorrow	jučer/danas/sutra
day/week/month/year	dan/nedelja/mesec/godina
left/right	levo/desno
up/down	gore/dole
good/bad	dobro/loše
big/small	veliko/malo
cheap/expensive	jeftino/skupo
hot/cold	vruće/hladno
old/new	staro/novo
open/closed	otvoreno/zatvoreno
free (vacant)/occupied	slobodno/zauzeto
early/late	rano/kasno
easy/difficult	lako/teško
Does anyone here speak English/French/German?	Govori li neko ovde engleski/francuski/nemački?
What does this mean?	Šta ovo znači?
I don't understand.	Ne razumem.
Please write it down.	Molim Vas napišite mi to.
Do you take credit cards/traveller's cheques?	Da li primate kreditne karte/putne čekove?
Waiter!/Waitress!	Konobar!/Konobarica!
Where are the toilets?	Gde su toaleti?
I'd like…	Želeo bih…
How much is that?	Koliko staje?
What time is it?	Koliko je sati?
Help me please.	Pomozite mi, molim Vas.
Just a minute.	Samo trenutak.

568

For your reference

All countries of continental Europe use the metric system throughout.

Temperature

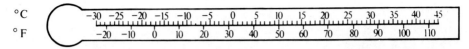

To convert centigrade into Fahrenheit, multiply centigrade by 1.8 and add 32.
To convert Fahrenheit into centigrade, subtract 32 from Fahrenheit and divide by 1.8.

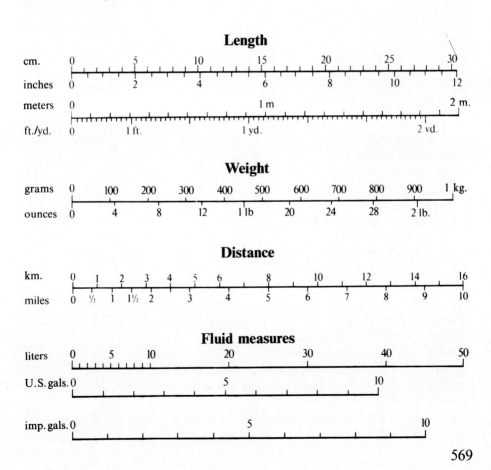

Length

Weight

Distance

Fluid measures

To convert:	multiply by:
acres into hectares	0.40
centimeters into inches	0.39
centimeters into feet	0.033
feet into meters	0.31
gallons, British (imperial) into liters	4.55
gallons, U.S. into liters	3.79
gallons, British into gallons, U.S.	1.20
gallons, U.S. into gallons, British	0.83
grams into ounces	0.035
grams into pounds	0.0022
hectares into acres	2.47
inches into centimeters	2.54
inches into millimeters	25.4
kilograms into pounds	2.20
kilometers into miles	0.62
liters into gallons, British	0.22
liters into gallons, U.S.	0.26
liters into pints, British	1.76
liters into pints, U.S.	2.11
liters into quarts, British	0.88
liters into quarts, U.S.	1.06
meters into feet	3.28
meters into miles	0.0006
meters into yards	1.09
miles into kilometers	1.61
millimeters into inches	0.039
ounces into grams	28.3
pints, British into liters	0.57
pints, U.S. into liters	0.47
pints, British into pints, U.S.	1.20
pints, U.S. into pints, British	0.83
pounds into kilograms	0.45
quarts, British into liters	1.14
quarts, U.S. into liters	0.95
quarts, British into quarts, U.S.	1.20
quarts, U.S. into quarts, British	0.83
square feet into square meters	0.093
square kilometers into square miles	0.39
square meters into square feet	10.8
square miles into square kilometers	2.59
yards into meters	0.91

Clothing sizes

In Europe, sizes vary somewhat from country to country, so these charts must be taken as an approximate guide.

Women

Dresses, skirts, coats

Junior sizes						Misses sizes					
U.S.A.	7	9	11	13	15	8/30	10/32	12/34	14/36	16/38	18/40
Europe	36	38	40	42	44	38	40	42	44	46	48

Blouses, sweaters

U.S.A.	10	12	14	16	18	20
Europe	38	40	42	44	46	48

Shoes

U.S.A.	4½	5	5½	6	6½	7	7½	8	8½	9	9½	10
Europe	35½	36	36½	37	37½	38	38½	39	39½	40	40½	41

Men

Suits

U.S.A.	34	36	38	40	42	44	46	48
Europe	44	46	48	50	52	54	56	58

Shirts

U.S.A.	14	14½	15	15½	16	16½	17	17½	18
Europe	36	37	38	39	40/41	42	43	44	45

Shoes

U.S.A.	6½	7	8	9	10	10½	11	12	13
Europe	39	40	41	42	43	44	45	46	47

International direct dialing (telephone)

The international direct dialing (IDD) network is not yet fully inter-locking—not all the countries listed on p. 573 can be dialed direct from any other country mentioned. Furthermore, within any one country some exchanges may not yet be hooked up to the system.

Though the access codes given below are valid for most destinations, exceptions may exist.

Procedure: First dial the international access code of the country you are in, then the foreign-country code, followed by the area code[1] and the subscriber's number. Example: if you are in Great Britain and wish to call Geneva, Switzerland, 712 34 56, dial 010 + 41 + 22 + 712 34 56

International telephone access codes

Austria	050	Netherlands	09
Belgium	00	New Zealand	00
Bulgaria	00	Norway	095
Czechoslovakia	90	Poland	80
Denmark	009	Portugal	07
Finland	990	South Africa	091
France	19	Spain	07
Germany (East)	06	Sweden	009
Germany (West)	00	Switzerland	00
Greece	00	Turkey	99
Hungary	00	United Kingdom	010
Ireland	010	United States of	
Italy	00	America	011
Luxembourg	00	Yugoslavia	99
Monaco	19		

---

[1] In many countries, area codes include an initial digit or digits which, while necessary for calls made within that country, must be dropped when phoning from abroad. Some countries do not have area codes.

Principal telephone country codes

Algeria	213	Liechtenstein[1])	4175
Argentina	54	Luxembourg	352
Australia	61	Malta	356
Austria	43	Mexico	52
Belgium	32	Monaco[2])	3393
Brazil	55	Morocco	212
Bulgaria	359	Netherlands	31
Canada	1	New Zealand	64
Chile	56	Norway	47
Colombia	57	Philippines	63
Czechoslovakia	42	Poland	48
Denmark	45	Portugal	351
Finland	358	Romania	40
France	33	Saudi Arabia	966
Germany (Eastern)	37	Singapore	65
(Western)	49	South Africa	27
Gibraltar	350	South Korea	82
Greece	30	Spain	34
Hong Kong	852	Sri Lanka	94
Hungary	36	Sweden	46
Iceland	354	Switzerland	41
India	91	Taiwan	886
Iran	98	Tanzania	255
Iraq	964	Thailand	66
Ireland	353	Tunisia	216
Israel	972	Turkey	90
Italy	39	United Kingdom	44
Japan	81	U.S.A.	1
Kuweit	965	U.S.S.R.	7
Lebanon	961	Venezuela	58
		Yugoslavia	38

[1]) integrated with Swiss national telephone network
[2]) integrated with French national telephone network

Baggage codes for principal European airports:

AMS	Amsterdam	FRA	Frankfurt	NAP	Naples
ANR	Antwerp	GLA	Glasgow	NCE	Nice
ARN	Stockholm	GOA	Genoa	NUE	Nuremberg
BCN	Barcelona	GOT	Gothenburg	OPO	Oporto
BEG	Belgrade	GVA	Geneva	ORY	Paris Orly
BFS	Belfast	HAJ	Hanover	OSL	Oslo
BGO	Bergen	HAM	Hamburg	PMO	Palermo
BHX	Birmingham	HEL	Helsinki	PRG	Prague
BOD	Bordeaux	KEF	Keflavík	RTM	Rotterdam
BRN	Berne	LGW	London	SKG	Salonica
BRU	Brussels		Gatwick	SNN	Shannon
BUD	Budapest	LHR	London	SOF	Sofia
BSL	Basle		Heathrow	STR	Stuttgart
BUH	Bucharest	LIS	Lisbon	SVO	Moscow
CDG	Paris Charles-	LUX	Luxembourg	SXB	Strasbourg
	de-Gaulle	LYS	Lyons	TRN	Turin
CGN	Cologne	MAD	Madrid	TXL	Berlin Tegel
CPH	Copenhagen	MAN	Manchester	VCE	Venice
DUB	Dublin	MLA	Valletta	VIE	Vienna
DUS	Düsseldorf	MRS	Marseilles	WAW	Warsaw
EDI	Edinburgh	MUC	Munich	ZRH	Zurich
FCO	Rome	MXP	Milan		
	L. da Vinci		Malpensa		

Average **flying times** between some major cities:

	Athens	C'hagen	Frankfurt	London	Madrid	New York	Paris	Rome
Athens		3¾	3¼	4	4¼	11	3¼	2
C'hagen	3¾		1½	1¾	3¼	8½	1¾	3¼
Frankfurt	3	1¼		1½	2¾	9	1¼	1¾
London	3¾	1¾	1½		2	7¼	1	2½
Madrid	4	3	2¾	2		8	1¾	2¼
New York	9	7½	8¾	6½	7		6½	8
Paris	3	1¾	1¼	1	1¾	7¼		2
Rome	1¾	3¼	2	2¼	2¼	9	2	

International **motor vehicle codes** in Europe:

A	Austria	GBZ	Gibraltar
AL	Albania	GR	Greece
AND	Andorra	H	Hungary
B	Belgium	I	Italy
BG	Bulgaria	IRL	Ireland
CC	Consular Corps	IS	Iceland
CD	Diplomatic Corps	L	Luxembourg
CH	Switzerland	M	Malta
CS	Czechoslovakia	MC	Monaco
D	Germany	N	Norway
DK	Denmark	NL	Netherlands
E	Spain	P	Portugal
F	France	PL	Poland
FL	Liechtenstein	R	Romania
GB	Great Britain and	RSM	San Marino
	Northern Ireland	S	Sweden
GBA	Alderney	SF	Finland
GBG	Guernsey	SU	U.S.S.R.
GBJ	Jersey	TR	Turkey
GBM	Isle of Man	V	Vatican City
		YU	Yugoslavia

Average direct **road distances** in miles between some major cities:

	Athens	C'hagen	Frankfurt	London	Madrid	Paris	Rome	Vienna
Athens		1,800	1,550	2,000	2,400	1,800	1,500	1,100
C'hagen	1,800		500	800	1,550	750	1,250	650
Frankfurt	1,550	500		500	1,100	350	800	450
London	2,000	800	500		1,050	300	1,100	950
Madrid	2,400	1,550	1,100	1,050		750	1,350	1,500
Paris	1,800	750	350	300	750		850	700
Rome	1,500	1,250	800	1,100	1,350	850		700
Vienna	1,100	650	450	950	1,500	700	700	

Some European road signs

No vehicles

No entry

No passing

Oncoming traffic
has priority

Maximum
speed limit

No parking

Caution

Intersection

Dangerous
curve

Road narrows

Intersection
with secondary
road

Two-way traffic

Dangerous hill

Uneven road

Falling rocks

Yield right
of way

Main road

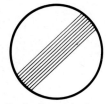

End of restriction

One-way traffic

Traffic goes
this way

Traffic
circle

Bicycles only

Pedestrians
only

577

EUROPE
Road Atlas

1991/92
Ausgabe — Edition — Issue — Edizione

EUROPA   EUROPE

Autobahn mit Anschlussstelle Motorway with interchange		Autoroute avec échangeur Autostrada con svincolo
Autobahn im Bau mit Eröffnungsdatum Motorway under construction with opening date	1991 1992	Autoroute en construction avec date de mise en service Autostrada in construzione con data d'apertura
Autostrasse (international, regional) Dual carriageway (international, regional)		Route rapide à chaussées séparées (internationale, régionale) Superstrada a carreggiate separate (internazionale/regionale)
Grosse internationale Durchgangsstrasse Major international throughroute		Route de grand transit internationale Strada di gran transito internazionale
Sonstige internationale Fernverkehrsstrasse Other International throughroute		Autre route de transit internationale Altra strada di transito internazionale
Interregionale Verbindungsstrasse Interregional throughroute		Route de transit interrégionale Strada di transito interregionale
Regionale Verbindungsstrasse Regional connectin road		Route de liaison régionale Strada di collegamento regionale
Strassen im Bau Roads under construction		Routes en construction Strade in construzione
Entfernungen in km Roads under construction	40 10 12 28 10 28 12 40	Distances en km Strade in construzione
Europastrasse European road	E5	Route européenne Strada europea
Pass, Berg mit Höhenangabe (m) Pass, summit with altitude (m)	1528 2967	Col, sommet avec altitude (m) Valico, vetta con altitudine (m)
Autoverlad per Eisenbahn Car transport by rail		Transport des autos pàr voie ferrée Trasporto automobili per ferrovia
Autoverlad per Fähre Car transport by ferry		Transport des autos par bac Trasporto automobili su chiatta
Internationaler Flughafen International airport	✈	Aéroport international Aeroporto internazionale
Grenzübergang Osteuropa Border crossing Eastern Europe	⊖	Passage de la frontière Europe de l'Est Valico di confine Europa orientale
Staatsgrenze National boundary		Frontière d'Etat Confine di Stato

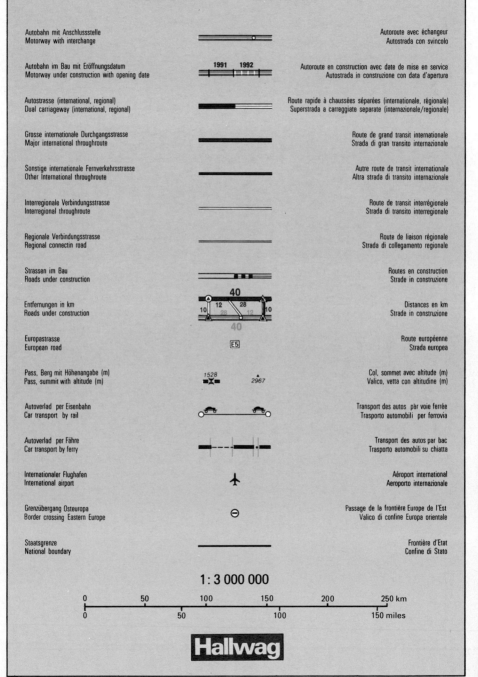

1: 3 000 000

0	50	100	150	200	250 km
0		50		100	150 miles

Hallwag

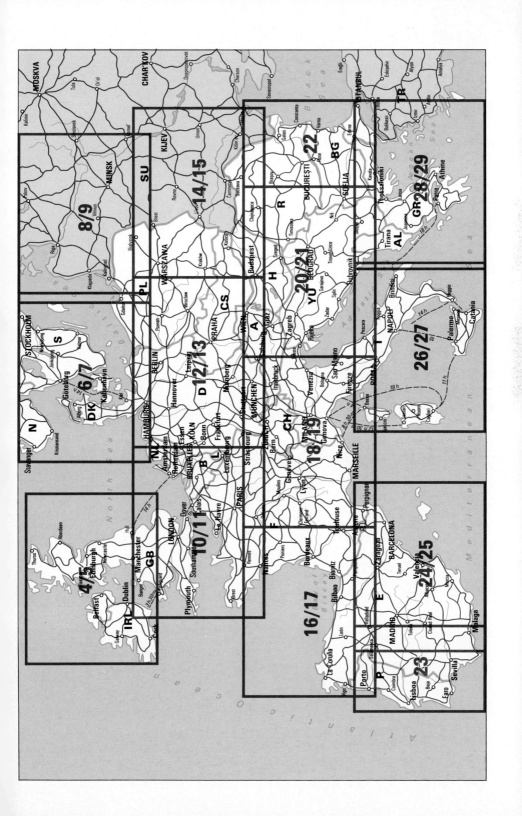

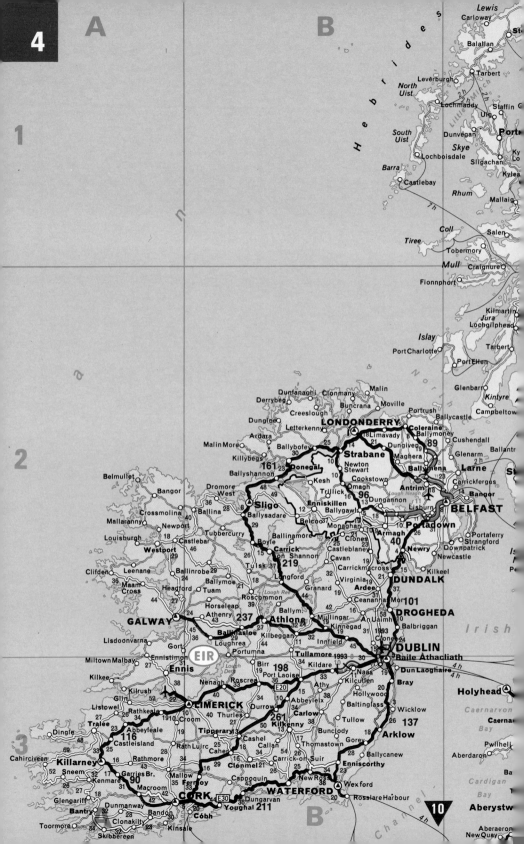

Durness · St. Margaret's Hope
Bettyhill · Scrabster · Dunnet · John o'Groats
Scourie · Laxford Br · Tongue · Melvich · THURSO
Kyleskus · Altnaharra · Forsinard · Watten · Wick
Inchnadamph · Overscaig · Kinbrace · 16 · Latheron
Ullapool · Lairg · 156 · Helmsdale
Rosehall · 5 · 11 · Brora
Bonar Br. · 22 · Golspie
Braemore L. · 20 · Tain · Invergordon
Garve · 23 · Dingwall · Elgin · Buckie · Cullen
Beauly · Nairn · Forres · Fochabers · Banff · Fraserburgh
INVERNESS · Keith · 26 · 18
Drumnadrochit · Dava · E15 · Huntly · Turriff · Peterhead
Carrbridge · Grantown-o-S. · 106 · Mintlaw · Ellon
Fort Augustus · Aviemore · Lumsden · Inverurie · Kintore
Kingussie · 117 · Tomintoul · Alford
Newtonmore · Crathie · Ballater · Banchory · ABERDEEN
Dalwhinnie · Braemar · Balmoral
Fort William · Blair Atholl · Spital of Glenshee · Laurencekirk · Stonehaven
Kinlochleven · Rannoch St. · Pitlochry · Brechin · Bervie
Tyndrum · Aberfeldy · 13 · Blairgowr. · Forfar · Montrose
Killin · Dunkeld · Coupar · 87 · Arbroath
Lochearnhead · Angus · DUNDEE
Crianl. · Callander · PERTH · Cupar · Newport-on-T.
Aberfoyle · Dunblane · Kinross · St. Andrews
Stirling · Dunfermline · Elie
Dumbarton · Falkirk · KIRKCALDY · Firth of Forth
GLASGOW · Whitburn · Inverkeithing · Leith · North Berwick
Hamilton · E5 · 46 · Lanark · EDINBURGH · Dunbar
Kilmarnock · Peebles · Lauder · Eyemouth
Douglas · Biggar · Ayton
Cumnock · Abington · Galashiels · Berwick upon Tweed
Sanquhar · 95 · Selkirk · Kelso · Belford
Thornhill · Moffat · Jedburgh · Wooler
New · 91 · Hawick · 161 · Alnwick
Galloway · Lockerbie · Langholm · Otterburn
Newton Stewart · Dumfries · GB · Morpeth
Castle Douglas · Gretna Green · Longtown · Blyth
Whithorn · Brampton · Bellingham · Tynemouth
CARLISLE · Hexham · Sth. Shields
Workington · Cockermouth · Alston · NEWCASTLE upon Tyne · SUNDERLAND
Whitehaven · Keswick · Penrith · Durham · Seaham
Gosforth · Ambleside · Appleby · Brough · West Hartlepool
Broughton · Windermere · Shap · Stockton · TEESSIDE
Barrow · Kendal · Scotch Corner · Darlington · WHITBY
E5 · Kirkby Lonsdale · Leyburn · Northallerton
Lancaster · 20 · Settle · Ripon · Thirsk · Pickering · Scarborough
Fleetwood · Garstang · Skipton · Boroughbr. · Filey
BLACKPOOL · Clitheroe · Harrogate · 77 · Malton · Bridlington
Preston · Burnley · Bradford · YORK · Gt. Driffield
Southport · Blackburn · Halifax · LEEDS · Beverley
Bolton · Huddersfd · Wakefd · Selby · HULL
LIVERPOOL · Wigan · MANCHESTER · Goole · Withernsea
Birkenhead · Warringtn · Stockport · Barnsley · Scunthorpe · New Holland
Chester · E20 · Doncaster · Grimsby
Mold · SHEFFIELD · Cleethorpes
Wrexham · Macclesfd · Buxton · East Retford · Market Rasen · Louth
Corwen · Oswestry · 147 · Tarporley · Matlock · Chesterfield · Lincoln · Mablethorpe
Whitchurch · Ashbourne · 61 · Newark · Skegness
Mallwyd · Stoke on Trent · Partney
Shrewsbury · Derby · NOTTINGHAM · Sleaford · The Wash
Welshpool · Stafford · Burton · Grantham · Boston · Wells
Newtown · Cannock · Ashby · Sutterton · New Hunstanton · Fakenham
Wolverhampton · Sutton · LEICESTER · 11 · Spalding · King's Lynn · East Dereham · Cromer
BIRMINGHAM · Wisbech · North Walsham
Kiddermister · Market Harborough · Stamford · Peterborough

Moray Firth

Aberdeen — Lerwick 14 h

Orkney Islands
Pomona (Mainland)
Stromness · KIRKWALL
St. Margaret's Hope
Scrabster · Dunnet · John o'Groats
Melvich · THURSO

Newcastle — Bergen 22–25 h

N o r

Distances in GB in Miles
1M = 1,6 km

Sunne Munkfors Hällefors Löa Ramnäs Enköping Sigtuna Märsta 17 Össeby-Garn E4
Arvika Brunsberg Filipstad Grythyttan Lindesberg Karmansbo Västerås Bålsta E18 Sundbyberg Lidingö
Vannacka Molkom Köping Fellingsbro Arboga Strängnäs Mariefred STOCKHOLM
342 Fagerås Forshaga Storfors Nora ÖREBRO Eskilstuna 188 Södertälje Dalarö Västerhaninge
Årjäng Malsjö Karlskoga E18 49 Kumla Malmköping E3 25 Nynäshamn
Sillerud Nysäter KARLSTAD Kristinehamn Hallsberg Ås Flen Vingåker Katrineholm Gnesta Aspa Trosa
Bengtsfors Säffle Grums Laxå E3 Pålsboda Hjortkvarn 167 E4
Bäckefors ÅMÅL Gullspång Askersund Simonstorp Stigtomta Kila Nyköping
Kömpannebro Mariestad Medevi Finspång Åby NORRKÖPING
Mellerud Töreboda Borensberg Söderköping Gotska Sandön
Lidköping Karlsborg Motala Linköping Gusum 12 h
VÄNERSBORG Sötene Vadstena Skänninge Mjölby Valdemarsvik 10 h
SKARA 309 Skövde Tibro Hjo Ödeshög 174 Boxholm Åtvidaberg Edsbruk Kappelshamn Fårösund Holmu
Grästorp Jung Falköping Tidaholm Gränna Kisa Överum Gamleby Lummelunda Lärbro Slite
Vara L.Edet Vårgårda Mörlanda Mullsjö Tranås Österbymo S.Vi Blackstad Västervik Visby 40 Roma Kräklingbo
Lödöse Alingsås Fristad Bottna-ryd HUSKVARNA JÖNKÖPING Eksjö Vimmerby Solstadsström 5 h Klintehamn Ljugarn Ekethem
BORÅS 159 Stigamo Nässjö Marianelund 260 Hultsfred Hemse
Mölndal Bollebygd N.Unnaryd Vaggeryd Sävsjö Vetlanda Målilla Böda Källa Burgsvik Gotland Sundre
Skene Kinna Svenljunga Skillingaryd Adelfors Berga Oskarshamn Högsby Uggletorp
Veddige Gislaved Vrigstad Lammhult Grönskåra Mönsterås Borgholm
Köinge Smålandsstenar 244 S 279 Alvesta Lenhovda Ålem
Falkenberg E6 Torup Hyltebruk Ljungby Växjö Hovmantorp Rockneby Nybro Färjestaden Öland
231 Oskarström Känna Vislanda Lessebo Emmaboda Kalmar
Halmstad Vrå Älmhult Härlunda Tingsryd Vissefjärda E66 Mörbylånga
Båstad Traryd Almundsryd Bergkvara Degerhamn Grönhögen
Ängelholm Laholm Markaryd E4 Osby Lönsboda Olofström Bredåkra Lyckeby
Höganäs Astorp Orkelljunga Broby Ronneby Karlshamn Karlskrona
Helsingør HÄLSINGBORG Häsleholm Kristianstad Sölvesborg
Landskrona Höör 295 Åhus
Lund Hörby Olseröd
Brösarp Sjöbo Tomelilla Simrishamn
MALMÖ Skurup Borrby Bornholm (Dan.) Sandvig Allinge
Skanör Vellinge Ystad Hasle Svaneke
Køge Falsterbo Trelleborg Rønne Åkirkeby Neksø
St.Heddinge 148 Praestø Stege Møn Travemünde – Kalmar 24 h Travemünde – Helsinki 23 – 38 h
Falster Travemünde – Gdansk 20 h Władysławowo
Gedser Rügen Sassnitz Łeba Puck
Bergen Göhren Oderbucht Ustka Lębork GDYNIA Sopo
Stralsund 138 SŁUPSK E28 Mianowice Kartuzy Sopot GDAŃ
Ribnitz-Damgarten Greifswald Wolgast Koszalin Sławno Suchorze Kościerzyna Starogard Tczew
ROSTOCK Grimmen Kamień Pom. Kołobrzeg Trzebiatów Karlino Białogard Bytów Miastko Bobolice Zblewo Gniew
Laage Jarmen Demmin Świnoujście Wolin E65 Świdwin Biały Bór 206 Skórcz Czersk Nowe
Teterow Anklam Płoty Nowogard Łobez Połczyn Zdrój Czaplinek Chojnice Tuchola Świecie
E55 Malchin Ueckermünde 285 Neubrandenburg Goleniów 13 Szczecinek Człuchów Sępólno Chełmno

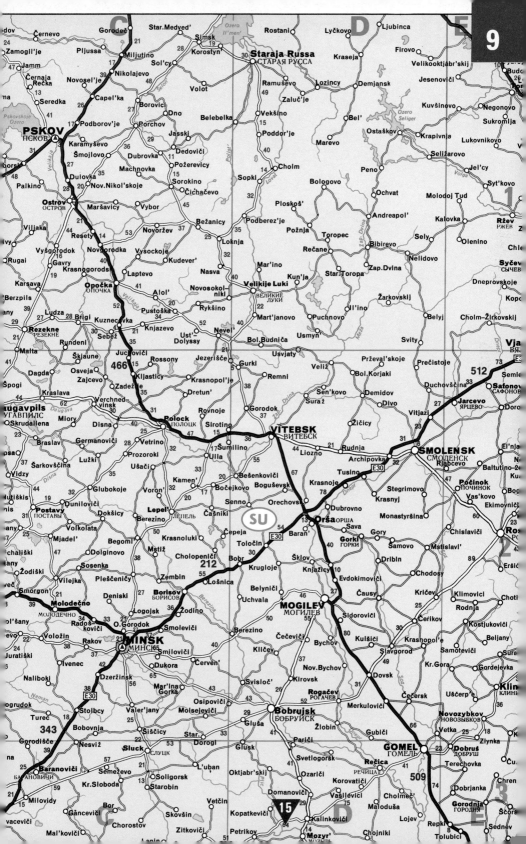

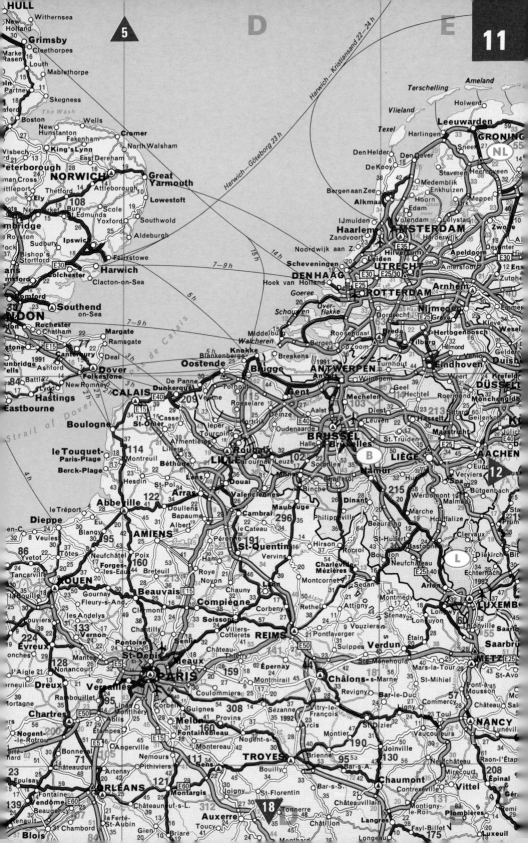

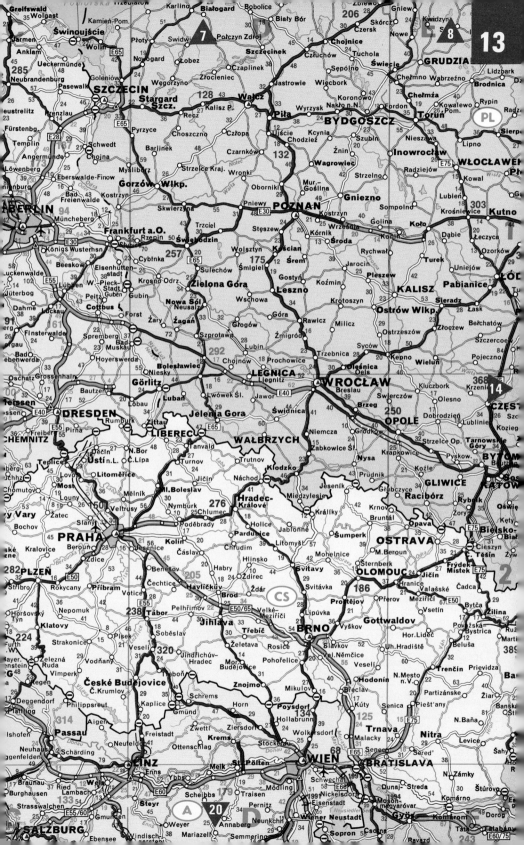

Corse

Rogliano

l'Ile-Rousse

Calvi

Bastia
20

Golfo de St-Florent

Calacuccia
50 26
Cervione

Evisa
Corte
31

Vizzavona
24

52
Ghisoni

AJACCIO
Zicavo
31

Zonza

41
Sartène
27 Porto Vecchio

Bonifacio
Porto Torres

Toulon - Porto Torres 9-11 h

Genova 11-13 h

Bocche de Bonifacio

S.Teresa
Palau
18 7

I.Asinara

Golfo dell'Asinara

Castel Sardo
Templo
31 15
Olbia

Porto Torres
19
41

Sassari
96
42 Martis
24 Monti
57

35
Oschiri
57
Tanaunella

Alghero
34
Ozieri
Buddusò
Siniscola

Thiesi
62
23
49
36

Sardegna
Bosa
23
57 Nuoro
Drosei

Suni
16
Macomer
257
Dorgali
21

Cúglieri
18
68
79
48

42
Sorgono
Fonni
Baunei

Oristano
33
69
Tortoli
16

28
25
Seui
Lanusei
53

Terralba
Uras
46
Tertenia
36

21
24 Mandas
40

Guspini
Sanluri
15
Senorbi

52
23
20

Villacidro
Muravera

Iglesias
25
Monastir
21
64

Siliqua
31
Quartu Sant'Elena

30 Carbonia
CAGLIARI

S.Giovanni
Pula

S.Antioco
11

Teulada

Golfo di Cagliari

Elba

Cecina

S.Vincenzo
Massa Marítt.
28
19

Plombino
Roccastrada

Portoferraio
Follonica
14

2 h
19

Grosseto 330
Orvieto

E80
S.Lorenzo
26

336 33
Montefiascone

Orbetello
Albinia
40

Montalto
19

Civitavecchia
Tarquinia

72

Fiumicino

Lido di Ostia

Anzio

PERUGIA
298

Assisi

287
269

Foligno

Todi
Spol

Terni

Narni

Fara

Monterosi

Bracciano
Tivoli

ROMA

Saba

Mare   Tirreno

Olbia - Civitavecchia 7 h

12 h

Olbia - Livorno 8 h

13 h

Cagliari - Genova 19 h

15 h

Genova - Palermo 23 h

Cagliari - Palermo 13 h

Genova - Tunis 24 h

Trapani

I.Égadi
Salem

Marsala
31
21

Mazara
15

24 h

24 h

Tunis - Palermo 10 h

Tunis-Nap

Pantelleria - Trapani 6 h

Bizerte

Sedjenane
Mateur
37

ANNABA
(Bône)
Tabarka

la Calle
Djebel Abiod
Protville

la Marsa

Kélibia

TUNIS

Golfe de Tunis

Silaqua

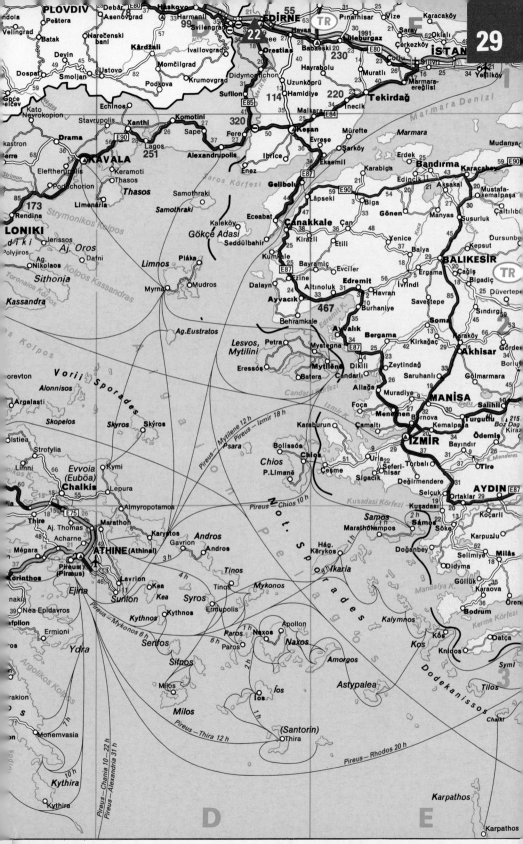